70 YEARS

OF

AMERICAN CAPTIVITY

THE POLITY OF GOD, THE BIRTH OF A NATION
AND THE BETRAYAL OF GOVERNMENT

CHRIS MEIER

Tellwell Talent
www.tellwell.ca

ISBN
978-1-77302-112-6 (Hardcover)
978-1-77302-114-0 (Paperback)
978-1-77302-113-3 (eBook)

Table of Contents

Dedication

To Jesus, the Author and Finisher of my faith, Amen and Amen.

To the folks at Christ-Centered Ministries, thank you. You know who you are. To the folks at Faith Bible Church, Pastors Jerry and Connie Sherstad, (Ret.) and to the folks at The River, Pastors Wayne and Lisa Morrison, you are the Headwaters of the Nation. Stay strong in His Love. To my husband, as always, the backbone of the family. This book, or frankly any thing else I do, would be impossible without you. To friends; believers and unbelievers who have been faithful in speaking truth to lies, thank you.

To a generation young, and those not yet born: You have been lied to and I am sorry. Whilst we were asleep, those who desired to hold our nation captive to an ideology foreign to our shores, crept into your schools, places of higher learning, courts, government, media as well as other social constructs. They carried out a plot to undermine and infiltrate your thinking to the point of putting you to sleep as well. The ultimate goal is to hold you hostage and then take you captive. This book is my attempt in obeying the Highest voice I know. That's the voice who speaks to open deaf ears. He sets beacons to clear blinded eyes to prevent what had been a great nation from self-destruction.

Preface

In the late 1980s, I read about 21 civilizations which had crossed the pages of history. None had been conquered initially from standing armies without. All had started their decline from within. That fact was not always obvious on the surface pages of history. After some digging, the moral degradation which had taken place from within their borders became apparent. Then the economic decline started. That always took time so no one noticed the fall had already begun. Once bereft of moral and financial security the standing armies had a very easy job.

In an effort to include all, I give a fair warning in two of the four sections of this book. Section One is geared more toward the religious, providing Scriptural texts in support of our covenant, while reviewing why the early settlers and colonies might have had a different biblical outlook from our modern doctrine. Section Two is geared more toward the unbeliever. Among other facts, I mention a book many quote in support of a secular tradition of governmental documents. Sections Three and Four should help all of us understand our need for covenant, now more than ever.

I do not follow an exacting method of linear time in writing this book. Instead my goal is to allow you, the reader, have a similar experience with the history as our ancestors might have had in living it. This is not necessarily easy to do and may not be realized until after you are done reading the book. I made that attempt because quite often we can have preconceived ideas because of our knowledge of history. This sometimes leads to bias. In order for us to understand an earlier colonial mindset, some explanation of biblical covenant and broken covenant needs to take place. Section One will help in that effort. My goal was to infuse us with a flavor of covenantal/religious understanding within history; before, during and after I put forth actual documentation.

Secondly, this is not a book shaking a proverbial finger at any particular group. In fact, I will prove emphatically when believer and unbeliever alike remain in covenant we never, ever fall into captivity. This is the dynamics of the "secular" covenant. I hesitate to call it that because from the history it was a non-sectarian, non-denominational covenant. We will review this in more detail. Nevertheless, there is a different dynamic here in America instilled and embedded into our governing compact through exact wording, as well as tradition. That dynamic is the religious covenant believing Americans have to their God. Believers must maintain that covenant as well. This was the secret of our early colonial ancestors: They maintained their biblical covenant responsibilities. As a result, all of us Americans have profited from the religious who founded our nation. The modern church has lost the skills in maintaining this sacred national trust. It is we, who have benefited from those early Americans who have dropped the ball, to use a modern phrase.

So why prove that? Why write a book or series of books? For some odd reason— and this is where the atheist as well as the agnostic should be afraid— there is a diabolical plan afoot to strip all citizens of our rights. I am not on some conservative political witch hunt, trying to pit one side against the other. No, folks; this is plain and simple proof: Written biblically for the religious. It is written scientifically and as factually as possible for the atheist and/or agnostic. I am not a conspiracy theorist. In fact, I always thought such things nonsense, until I started doing this research. I was flabbergasted once I realized there is such a conspiracy.

I don't think those who started the "plan" did so to strip America of her moral compass. I don't think they planned on ripping her financial blessings away or destroying her government by the people and for the people. Yet over the last 100 years, this insidious plan has done exactly that. I think those starting merrily down the road toward the demise of America thought they were doing a good thing. Many still spout how morally good their brand of ideas are for all involved. From science, history and Scripture, if we don't come back into agreement; the religious, nonreligious and atheist alike, all have the potential to be sent into captivity.

Captivity, you say? What kind of captivity could keep this large and robust nation bound? Read on. Will it look like standing armies? I don't know. Will it look like bombs exploding? Not sure. Will it lock the religious in prisons? Most definitely. Will it remove and replace all those who work hard for their financial rewards from those rewards? Most assuredly. Will it taint scientific research and silence the enlightened? Already has, but it will get much worse. We all need to sound the alarm, shake the sleeping and expose the short sheet to the innocent to avoid the bed of deception.

What I am about to share has been a discovery for me of one of the best con jobs in history. The thing about a great con is you don't realize it until it's too late. By that time the crook or crooks have moved on to their next mark, leaving not a trace to either indict them or, in some cases, even find them. Fortunately for those of us who love truth, there is more than enough evidence to prove what has gone on. That is not in question. What is the question? Will we have eyes to see and ears to hear?

SEVENTY YEARS
(FOR THE RELIGIOUS)

Chapter One

70 YEARS

Sitting at my desk to collect my thoughts before work, my gaze fell on an adding machine tape with the number "seventy" on it. Keeping no such tape in the office, I was a bit curious. "Where on earth did that come from? I know I didn't make it." Immediately I sensed the presence of the Lord, compelling me to drop my curiosity and turn my attention toward Him. As soon as I did, within an instant I knew what He was saying. For the non-religious who decided to read this section, I will have to explain to you what the biblically religious may already know about that number. The Bible has very specific patterns which carry through from the Old Testament to the New Testament. One of its patterns is numbers. Seven is always the number for spiritual/divine completion or perfected-ness (on the seventh day God rested; see Genesis 2:2 & 3). Ten is always a symbol for the responsibility of human function, even governmental functions of some type: Ten toes and fingers, Ten Commandments, ten plagues on Egypt's ruling demonic forces. So seven multiplied by ten is divine completion or judgment on some ruling human governmental function, type or force.

While we are on the subject of captivity or "judgment," let me say right from the start I am not suggesting God is judging America, or anyone else, for that matter. Captivity is not caused by God. Captivity takes place because of things we humans do, or don't do. For the religiously minded, let me make a point of Scripture from the New Testament. Jesus died once and for all time for mankind's sin. God is not, at this time judging us by sending us into some kind of captivity. Our time now is for sharing Christ's death and the salvation made available by God because of His sacrifice. It is a time to release the miraculous working power of Jesus into a planet of humans who inflicted their own disease. God loves mankind, sending His own Son to die for our sin as individuals, thereby redeeming whole nations.

The Bible does talk about a time at the end of the ages where two types of judgment will take place. I am not writing about those events here. What I am writing about is a warning from a loving God who wants us to continue to enjoy our religious, political and financial freedom in this country; freedoms which are being eroded at an alarming pace. God is not removing our freedoms from us. It is unfortunate, but we as Americans are doing that, quite frankly, without His help. This is the captivity I speak of.

As a note to the atheist and non-Christian, let me say specifically to you I am not saying God is judging you with any 70-year period of captivity. If He did, He would have to apologize to all humanity since Christ died. Let me make that point from the Bible. It was Peter's writings, recorded in the New Testament which says specifically: "For the time is come that judgment must begin at the house of God: and if it first begin at us, what shall the end be of them that obey not the gospel of God" (1 Peter 4:17)?[1] Peter lets the saints know it is because they no longer carouse and party with the sinners of the world they are experiencing the persecution. The sinners are not, at that time, attacking God but attacking other humans.

The understanding in the Greek is twofold. One, if God's judgment begins with God's people, and they are barely saved, what will become of the sinner? Two, "at the house of God," can be translated "from the house of God." In other words, we must see the church or saint judged first and since we are not seeing that now, then it is not time for the unbelieving to be judged.

There is also another sense here which can be viewed as controversial within some circles, but I think can be applied in light of the beginning of Peter's discussion in chapter 4. It is clear Peter is talking to a body of people who are not being attacked for doing ungodly or criminal behavior, but for following God. That attack is in violation of the brotherhood of mankind seen from Genesis (Cain and Abel) and its covenant, mankind to mankind. So the church, as the plaintiff in petitioning God, can begin to speak with the word of God and command realignment (hence judgment beginning from the house of God). I believe all three aspects of translation are seen here especially in light of other passages in the New Testament of the church being light and salt and a hindering force to satan (Matthew 5:14; Matthew 5:13; 2 Thessalonians 2:3-8). In secular or non-sectarian terms, the covenant of mankind to mankind can be religious. Even when it is not, we can still function with covenantal attitude.

Getting back to the word I experienced of "70 years;" it came to me before May 2011. I remember this because I hadn't seen one of my relatives in ten or eleven years. The family was coming to stay with us in May and I was trying to get the house in order. I follow biblical patterns when I receive what I believe to be a word from Jesus, which is "At the mouth of two or three witnesses a thing would be confirmed." (See Deuteronomy 17:6; 19:15; Matthew 18:16; 2 Corinthians 13:1; 1 Timothy 5:19; Hebrews 10:28.) I knew if this were, in fact, a word from God, He would confirm it. He did confirm it in no uncertain terms.

Thinking I knew biblically where we had gone wrong as a nation, I didn't really know what else to do with the word. I had this sinking feeling which caused me to pray. It finally dawned on me I needed to bring the word to the attention of the folks at the meeting house (otherwise called church for those of you who may not attend). I felt we needed to pray collectively for greater understanding as well as God's mercy on us as a nation. As time went on we began to repent for our nation, as well as offer up prayer for specific issues the Lord revealed.

My relatives came and went and moved on with life. So did we. At the beginning of 2012 an unforeseeable event took place which caused me to call our former pastor. What I did not know is before the end of 2011, the Lord had told him to call me. He had lost my number, and as happens with all of us, life kind of takes over. If it had not been for this event, I probably would not have called him. He agreed to help me and asked me to come and preach four services. I said I would have to go back to the Lord and ask His thoughts on the subject. As I went to prayer to ask God what He wanted said over four services, quite clearly He said, "You already have the word." My heart sank because immediately I knew which word He meant. I also knew that word had the potential to upset many folks. The reality is I have experienced sharing the word of the Lord with many people and therefore have upset many people.

As I'm standing before the Lord, I remember thinking something like, "Besides which, that word is not long enough for four services. What could I possibly say in four services with, 'Oh, yes folks, we are going into CAPTIVITY! Let's load up the traveling vans!' " I'm thinking this privately, knowing full well the Lord hears all. And as has happened to me in the past— God only knows why He still talks to me— He says, quite clearly, and still, like a Father correcting an errant child, "Do the research." Silent He went, and I'm standing there thinking, "Research? What research? We all know what's been done. Research? Oh, well, I've got to get started, if nothing else than to prove to myself I've done what I could."

Some of you might be thinking, "Exactly when is this going to happen?" Well, that's a very good question for which I do not have an exact answer. I will tell you after the Lord gave me an okay to go and preach, I had a very interesting spiritual encounter which left me with more questions along those lines than answers. But I will share what I think the Lord was trying to convey to me. First, I have no idea when this will start. Maybe it has already. Secondly, I did get the implicit sensing if the folks where I preached would also go to prayer, or if I was able to get this word out to more people, we could either forestall it by 35 years, totally reverse the situation or experience the worst option of 70 years.

I have had another word of great healing revivals as well as great spiritual awakenings with signs and wonders following. I sense the timing for those events before, possibly during, and after this "70-year" time period as well. Some might question why this would be. I have learned something about these type of conditional words. The Lord wants to give as many as possible time to repent and turn a very bad situation around. After all, we are doing this. God is not doing this to us. He has given us freedom to choose, but freedom does carry responsibility as well as consequences. We are the only ones who can turn things around.

Frankly, only God knows exactly what people will do. So those answers are in His Council, not mine. Within the pages of the Bible we can see where God tells a prophet a word, but then not tell them the outcome. The prophet Jonah, swallowed by a whale ("great fish") comes to mind immediately. Jonah did have some sensing of what might happen (see Jonah 4:1-3). Obviously, he didn't know exactly what was going to take place. He is told to preach repentance to Israel's mortal enemies, the Assyrians. These are the people who stacked their captives' heads high enough to make building structures.[2] When Jonah decided a cruise was a better life experience, God sent "the fish" to bring his wayward prophet back onshore to preach. As a result, Jonah's success probably saved thousands and thousands of Assyrians and Jews.

Most religious folks know the story of Abraham and God telling him to sacrifice his only son. At the very last minute, with his hand on the hilt ready to take the boy's life, the Lord tells him to stay his hand. Then God makes this very odd statement: "Now I know that you fear God, because you did not withhold your son, your only son, from me" (Genesis 22:12b, NET Bible®). Didn't God know before? Of course He did. But Abraham did not and God was dealing with a nation of people housed inside of Isaac. He was also showing mankind a perfect human example of Divine sacrifice in sending His own Son. Yet God's dealings with nations and individuals and prophets summed up and connected inside of those nations is not something we humans have pat little answers for. We do not see down thousands of years of timeline to know outcomes and consequences; only God knows. So I am sorry to say I do not know exactly how all of this will play out.

What started as research into biblical periods of captivity quickly turned into research concerning covenant and its breaking. I then became shocked to find a deep, and many centuries long understanding of religious covenant connected to secular or non-sectarian covenant, which was connected to our three governing documents. For the religious, and all others brave enough to wade into these waters, I will share the pattern I took in order to research this book.

First I looked at captivity periods of time in the Bible, both Old and New Testaments. Most folks do not realize Jesus lived during Israel's Roman captivity. By quite a few estimates, 70 percent of the planet's population during the time Rome ruled were slaves. Here is hope for billions on the planet: Jesus procured salvation's freedom while the nation He lived in was in captivity! Even though the New Testament was written during captivity, it was the Jewish prophet Malachi who prophesied this captivity period some 400 years before it took place. Here is where I saw a pattern of God speaking to His people over and over again. He would send a messenger who would say something like, "You've broken Covenant. Come back in line and I will heal you." This pattern was repeated constantly. We will be looking at the Babylonian captivity period of time for the nation of Israel, and specifically, the tribe of Judah from 586 BC to 516 BC. After that we will look at modern-day research to see if there is a similar pattern.

The Old Testament Babylonian captivity books are Esther (the Jewish Babylonian queen from which the holiday of Purim is celebrated); portions of Jeremiah (the prophet thrown into the pits); Daniel (remember him from the Lion's den?); Nehemiah, Ezra, Haggai (Jewish leaders who rebuilt after the captivity); some of the Psalms (Scripture set to song) and Zechariah (another post-captivity leader). They cover different aspects of God speaking to the people concerning the captivity as well as what these different saints went through while experiencing it for themselves. So each book has a different 'flavor.' But each one keeps the same theme of breaking covenant and/or being delivered from captivity, with the steps taken for deliverance. The whole book of Malachi is dedicated to God's indictment of Israel as a nation and why captivity (again) will be inevitable.

So some Scripture would be in order for the religious amongst us. Isaiah 5:13:

"Therefore my people are gone into captivity because they have no knowledge: and their honourable men are famished, and their multitude dried up with thirst."

Men of honor are folks with leadership qualities in government, both religious and civic as well as heads of families. Being famished in the Scriptures always speaks of economic thirst as well as moral fortitude with spiritual abundance and insight. It not only speaks to the intangible, but it speaks to the obvious aspect of physical hunger and lack.

Proverbs 29:16-19: "When the wicked are multiplied, transgression increaseth: but the righteous shall see their fall. Correct thy son, and he shall give thee rest; yea, he shall give delight unto thy soul. Where there is no vision, the people perish: but he that keepeth the law, happy is he. A servant will not be corrected by words: for though he understand he will not answer."

The significance of this passage cannot be underestimated. We have all experienced this. In this passage a servant is considered someone you are not close with. For people who respect you, or you are close with, you can speak into their lives and correct them or give them warning. For those who listen, a vision can be given of hope and future. The Bible gives warnings and lays down a relationship in the Old and New Testament of *Covenant*. When we live by our relationship with Jesus, we are told we are no longer servants or bond-slaves, but now sons. So we no longer need experience captivity. Why? We understand the correction because we understand we have broken relationship or broken *Covenant*.

Our colonial forebears, as well as Bible believers from centuries past, would have known covenant was how God relates to mankind. They would have been able to call up at least one Scripture from memory to support it. Our modern culture has lost that ability. So one last Scripture would be in order from Daniel 9:1, 2: "In the first year of Darius the son of Ahasuerus, of the seed of the Medes, which was made king over the realm of the Chaldeans; In the first year of his reign, I Daniel understood by books the number of the years, whereof the word of the Lord came to Jeremiah the prophet, that he would accomplish seventy years in the desolations of Jerusalem."

Not a single one of us people of the Book (Bible), both Jews and Christians, can ignore the one single fact of Covenant. From my youth I can remember the old timers calling the Old and New Testaments the Old Covenant and New Covenant. It's been decades since I've heard anyone refer to them that way. But my Jewish friends have told me it's not the "Old Covenant" to them; it's the *ONLY* covenant for them. Yet the pattern is still the same for both of us people of The One Book. Every time God wants to work in the affairs of men, He works within the framework of a covenant. An agreement is made between mankind and Himself. The word *agreement* is somewhat of a misnomer. Whenever God says something, it can technically be referred to as covenantal. But for those not involved in a seminary class, let me explain that *covenant* originates with God and ends with God. The word agreement would assume co-equal affirmation. We are not equal with God. When He extends His hand in fellowship and makes requirements of us within that relationship, as humans we have the right to refuse His covenant and refuse a relationship with Him. We also have the right to accept His covenant and all the blessings can then flow to us. But what we can never do is negotiate or change the terms.

There are two kinds of covenants in the Bible: Conditional and Unconditional. A conditional covenant depends upon man obeying. An unconditional covenant depends upon God only. There is also a huge difference under the New Covenant and that would be the relationship of love as a result of Jesus' sacrifice. The New Testament tells us it is the kindness (some translations, goodness) of God leading us to repentance (Romans 2:4). So God shows up to see whom He can show favor to. We either accept this relationship or we ignore the thought as bunk: A late night of pizza producing strange dreams or some other idea or flight of childhood fantasy. We become blind to the realization God is reaching out to us. This modern idea of the God of the Bible with a big club or stick ready to punish every word or thought, is not a true representation of the awesome Being we see within its pages.

There is also a different aspect in the meaning of the Greek and Hebrew words seen in our understanding of covenant. The New Testament phraseology brings in the thought of covenant but should really be seen as describing a Last Will and Testament. Throughout this book, many different aspects of covenant will be examined; but for now, let's just make it simple. For those who accept God's invitation, we then come under the awesome experience of covenant as a result of our relationship of love with the Creator of the Universe.

In times past, children would have all known the stories associated with each covenant: Adam and Eve with the upright, walking and talking "serpent." Noah's great boat and menagerie collection. Abraham's wanderings and Moses' wave-producing deliverance. David's slaying of Goliath and Jesus' garden prayer. As they became adults, each story from childhood would have been examined and understood in light of the last covenant's promise concerning Israel's rebirth in her land. Young Christian children, turned young adults would understand these stories in the light of Christ's sacrifice and their benefit from that act of love. Each of these biblical Covenants are different. There are eight covenants in the Bible. Some theologians subscribe to some and not others and use different terminology to describe some. Nevertheless, I will lay out, in loose terms, what the eight are:

1. Edenic: Governing the life of mankind in Eden (Genesis 1:28-30; 2:25-17).
2. Adamic: Made with Adam and Eve before their expulsion; governing the life of mankind outside of Eden (Genesis 3:14-19).
3. Noahic: Governing God's dealings with mankind concerning the destructive flood of the earth (Genesis 8:20-9:17).
4. Abrahamic: Governing God's dealings with Abraham's descendants (Genesis 12:1-3).
5. Mosaic: Governing Israel's life with God on the face of the earth—primarily in the first five books of the Bible, also known as the Torah or Pentateuch.
6. Davidic: Governing God's promise to keep a descendant on David's throne (2 Samuel 7:8-19).
7. New Covenant: Governing mankind's resurrection and eternal life with Father, Son and Holy Spirit as well as life here on Earth before physical death. It is based on God's promise to accept Jesus Christ's sacrifice as payment for an individual's sin. See the whole

New Testament, as well as Old Testament prophecies concerning Messiah.

8. The post-Palestinian Covenant (Deuteronomy 30:1-10): Governing Israel's return to the land after she is dispersed (v 1) and after the return of Messiah (the first time, see v 3). This Covenant is conditional upon the repentance of scattered Israel (see v 10). Many scholars simply see this as a continuation of the Mosaic Covenant.

As you have noticed in our list of eight, covenant extends to governance. It governs how we behave with God (religiously) and each other (sometimes secularly). There are several covenantal understandings between mankind in groups, individuals and/also with the God of the Bible. He is either the direct overseer of the parties in covenant and/or benefits from them. Though it could accurately be argued the whole of mankind benefits from them as well. Three I would like to highlight are:

✦ The Covenant of the Priesthood: In that one individual agrees to mediate in whatever area between God and man to effectuate God's purposes on earth. In this covenant mankind benefits because of hearing, seeing and experiencing God's word and purposes revealed in a real experiential dimension on earth.

✦ The Covenant of Marriage: In that one man and one woman covenant to biologically reproduce or otherwise care for children within that relationship. Within the context of that covenant mankind benefits in a stable, healthy and sociologically reproductive next generation.

✦ The Covenant of Sacrifice and Worship: In that one individual gives back to God in sacrifice (time, service, money, praise, prayer or fasting). Within the context of that covenant mankind benefits because God's blessings are spread across a geographic area, even to the ends of the earth.

The reason I will include these three is because the God of the Bible does and the evidence (for my non-religious friends) totally supports it. These three are included in every captivity period as a reason why they are going into captivity. This includes the overall breach of covenant. During the Babylonian captivity, the breaking of these three are included, as well as other areas of broken covenant. In Malachi they are outlined by name. Prophesied almost 400 years before the Roman captivity, a whole chapter is devoted to the effects of refusing to worship God in tithing. A tithe is ten percent of one's income. It is one example of our Covenant of Faithful Sacrifice and Worship.

I will prove to all of us when we break Covenant, we lose a healthy and beneficial civic government. When we break the Covenant of the Priesthood, we lose a superior civic educational system, and a healthy military. We lose something far greater: Religion, and specifically the people of the Book (the Bible) in the public square. These bring the ideas and philosophy which has governed an overwhelming amount of beneficial breakthroughs.[3] Over time, they become lost to the public in general; thus an archeological dig, of sorts, must be done to find them. We even lose a free and unbiased press or media. When we break our Covenant of Marriage we lose a civil and moral society, which is so important to raising a healthy generation of great thinkers. We lose healthy-minded children; stable, both emotionally and spiritually. It seems odd to some, but there are real benefits to a child's wellbeing when they have an image of both mom and dad while growing up.

Lastly, when we break our Covenant of Sacrifice (worship) we lose a healthy civic economy, as well as the land which has been given to us. These affect not only the religious, but atheists as well as agnostics. I don't need the Bible to prove this. But because our society has all kinds of folks living in it, I will use science as well as hard, cold facts to prove this. Future books will discuss the three aspects of human covenant in more detail. This book will prove spiritual covenant, secular (non-sectarian) covenant, federal covenant, and prove broken covenant, while sharing steps to bring us back to national health.

ENDNOTES

1 Even though I use the KJV, see an excellent discussion from the translators of the Greek and the Hebrew, which is what Peter is quoting from here: NET Bible® copyright©1996-2006

by Biblical Studies Press, L.L.C." <http://netbible.com><https://bible.org> All rights reserved. See also Proverbs 11:31

2   Belibtreu, Erika; Editor, H.S. (2002;2002) "Assyrian Record of Torture and Death," Biblical Archeological Society BAR 17:01 (Jan/Feb 1991) Accessed 2/23/16 <http://faculty.uml.edu/ethan_Spanier/Teaching/documents/CP6.0AssyrianTorture.pdf> (see 5 in pdf)

3   There is no argument American innovation has been advantageous for the rest of the world. Quite often though, we forget about Israel, the other covenant people of the Book. A recent video documentary concerning the amazing innovations the nation of Israel has blessed the world with can be seen at this © <http://www.cbn.com/special/made-in-israel> accessed 2/28/16. They research 5 areas: agriculture, water, medicine, environmental (clean & green) and technology.

Chapter Two

COVENANT AND THE KINGDOM

For our forebears who founded this country, understanding covenant would have been like drinking water. Once taught, one cannot forget the lesson. The understanding the settlers had of biblical covenant is not what we understand well today. For them it was life itself: necessary, paramount and unchangeable. Most commonly today, many have a mixed understanding of Law (Mosaic Law from the Old Testament) and grace (New Testament), which forms their knowledge of biblical covenant. Quite a few Christians today understand covenant because they understand what it means to live after the Law (Mosaic) has been fulfilled by the sacrificial death of Christ.

Not well understood by unbelievers is church history regarding the loss of her spiritual and biblical knowledge. This was because of a mandate removing the Bible from private reading. As this knowledge was restored from the time of the Reformation to the Renaissance, doctrinal knowledge connected to spiritual application was also restored. This is why there are differences in some understanding between Bible-believing Christians of today and those of generations gone by. It was as if a whole race of people had to rediscover their roots all over again. During this time period the biblical understanding of *Covenant* was rediscovered.

Early settlers brought that understanding with them from America's gestation to her birth.

Christians living over 400 years ago would have understood they could not fulfill The Law (Mosaic) even if they tried. That was why Christ came. But they would have mixed The Law (torah) with a system in works of righteousness, somewhat ignoring the Apostle Paul's warning a mixture cannot take place. They remind me a bit of progressives today when they try to mix socialism with capitalism and pretend the outcome works (by the way, it does not).

The founders understood the principle that without the shedding of blood there is no remission for sin (Hebrews 9:22). But they ignored some of the supernatural actions of the Holy Spirit who lives on the inside of Christians. It is this aspect of covenant-keeping God conveys. This aspect keeps Christians living holy. This and many related doctrines took time to be restored to the point they are today. Early settlers received God's joyfulness in life and prosperity easily. They would have seen the hand of the Lord in bountiful harvests, prosperous economic ventures, even a tranquil home life. But in maintaining the relationship of covenant, it was easier to develop a "works" mentality in which you were doomed if you stepped out of line and forgot God forgives sin (1 John 1:9). This may very well be where misconceptions about God as punisher comes from.

One can easily ask the question, "Why should God forgive us?" Well, He keeps the Covenant. It is part of who He is as well as part of His Kingdom principles. I am not saying Christ did away with The Law (Old Testament). On the contrary, the New Testament makes it clear He fulfilled all of The Law's requirements for those who ask Him to. Nor did I say the Ten Commandments were ever abolished. I've heard more than one preacher state they are not the Ten Suggestions! Following the Ten Commandments was never abolished by the disciples. Rather, we are told to live after the Spirit, not The Law. We are also told to be followers of Christ and to partake of Him. Because I live after or through the indwelling Holy Spirit, it is now near impossible for me to break the Ten Commandments. I don't live by them or follow them. I live by the

Holy Spirit. The Holy Spirit on the inside of me would **never** break the Ten Commandments.

Because I am a partaker with Christ, I don't desire to break The Law (Ten Commandments). While I no longer follow The Law, my life takes on a pattern similar to it simply because I follow and live by the Holy Spirit. Keeping the Ten Commandments becomes a byproduct of living according to the Holy Spirit. Early Americans easily understood God forgave sin once repentance was made. But they had already followed down a slippery slope in mixing Law and grace. Some of that had to do with the fact America was a wild continent and to keep people behaving in good order, many a preacher took a hard line, thus mixing biblical doctrines of law and grace.

When we mix Law and grace, we will fail at both. Jesus spoke concerning the things pertaining to The Law in Matthew 5. Chapter 5 takes Christianity into a whole new realm when it comes to being model citizens of God's Kingdom and what our attitude toward sin and spiritual events should be. The Law made provision for sin and healing by animal and material sacrifices offered by the Jewish priesthood (Mosaic Law). When they sinned they offered an animal or bird in payment for their redemption and/or healing. For atheists, this makes no sense. While this is due to non-belief, it may also be due in part to living during a time period in which another has already paid the price for our sin and healing. Christ's sacrifice abolished all other sacrifice needed to redeem sinners.

We are a priesthood now following after the Holy Spirit and His directions laid out in the New Testament by the apostles. Jesus changed the Jewish priesthood forever. Because Christ ascended, the Holy Spirit is now on earth and living inside of us, helping us understand things. He reveals when I have grieved Him and I don't want to do that. One might ask then why Christians aren't perfect today or why they weren't perfect back then either. It's simply because we don't always obey or follow the Holy Spirit. Sometimes we try to "pay" for our sin by doing some good deed. The payment has already been made. In order to avoid sin, we pray, worship and read our Bibles. This allows the Holy Spirit to renew our minds and speak with us concerning attitudes and actions we must change personally. Sometimes we become lazy in reading and studying the Bible and following correct doctrine.

Paul said as much when he said, ". . . In the last days perilous times shall come. For men shall be lovers of their own selves, covetous, boasters, proud, blasphemers, disobedient to parents, unthankful, unholy. . ." (See also 2 Timothy 3:1-9; 2 Peter 1:16-3:15). The New Testament tells us to renew our minds (Romans 12:2) and to take on the mind of Christ (Philippians 2:5-9). The preceding verse says: "Let this mind be in you, which was also in Christ Jesus." That word *let* is the Greek word *phroneo*. It means mind, but it means to *allow* or to *let* the mind be in you. You can resist if you desire. But when the Holy Spirit leads you, you want Jesus' mind to be in you.

The Apostle Paul goes to great lengths in the epistle to the Romans on our need to follow after life in the Spirit and no longer having the need to follow The Law or Commandment. Why is this important? Covenant is governance. Our covenant as Bible believers is spiritual with secular outreach because it governs us physically. It is a covenant which governs in a spiritual realm simultaneously. Because America has a secular and/or non-sectarian covenant attached to a people with a religious or spiritual covenant, there can be mental missteps when Americans view their governing documents. Many of the early laws in our colonies were also seen within biblical principles. We will look at some of that documentation in Section Three.

There is another understanding concerning covenant the ancestors would have known without any confusion. Once a covenant is requested of the Lord and He is brought into the equation, He does not leave, even if other parties no longer request Him. I'm not trying to insult our Jewish American brethren, but by way of example, let's look at Israel. How often have her people decided they were not going to follow the Lord— yet with only a tiny minority left of those who wanted to keep Covenant— the Lord showed up and brought the nation back from the precipice? That pattern of a tiny minority was used by the Lord to bring them back into a majority of Covenant-believing people. As humans, we have a "to-heck-with-you" attitude. When we turn our backs on someone, that's it; they are forgotten. This is not true for the Creator of the Universe. He "shall neither slumber nor sleep" Psalm 121:4 ". . . one day is with the Lord as a thousand years, and a thousand years, as one day" (2 Peter 3:8; see also Psalm 90:4). Time for Yahveh (YAH, Yahweh, G-d) is not like time for us. We don't always get what we deserve, thankfully. Unfortunately, though, we don't always see the effects of our broken covenant choices immediately.

The pattern we see biblically is God will do whatever He can to make it plain we have broken Covenant. First, the respective blessings disappear. These include good government, superior education, free speech of free ideas (especially biblical) in the public square; an excellent military; a moral and clean society with stable families. The last blessing to disappear is a healthy economy, even the blessings of healthy land and agriculture. This does not happen because God took them away. This happens because they are a byproduct of the Covenant. Breaking Covenant breaks fidelity in these areas. It is our own action which causes this. In the hope we will notice impending doom, the Lord allows the results of our actions to harvest their crop. The remedy can be quick, especially for Christians who can repent, invite God back into the equation to do what is necessary to remedy the breach. In fact, all can repent and see the turn-around. Yet, as mentioned before, this realization may take time. When it does, one generation may not see the immediate danger. It is hard for many to understand that breaking covenant in specific areas produces specific results. This happened frequently to Israel.

Quite often we forget the importance of our Covenantal relationship with the God of the Universe. According to the New Testament we are a Kingdom. We are a totally new creation under the New Covenant. We are to function according to His kingdom principles. Jesus talks about the kingdom in the gospels roughly 124 times. We get into the kingdom by accepting the Covenant through Christ. We accept the sacrifice Jesus made. God ratifies our decision to come in agreement with Him, and gives us what the Bible calls an 'earnest' or deposit of our inheritance by baptizing us in the Holy Spirit with the evidence of speaking in other tongues. It is through covenantal understanding we govern the events which take place in His kingdom. He gives us the ability to speak

His word, according to His will, and see changes take place around us. Conversely, we totally forget judgment BEGINS at the house of God (see 1 Peter 4:17). In other words, if we mess up, things around us can go haywire. When we leave our Covenant, this is precisely why the secular government goes kaput. As Christians, we are a new creation of human never before seen on the planet. It is He who gave us the ability to speak His word and see awesome things happen for those around us.

The nonreligious among you will say, "This is crazy talk." It is exactly this *talk* which got Jesus killed, and all the apostles and early church imprisoned, persecuted and murdered. It is exactly why Christianity is the number one persecuted religion on the planet. Of course, number two, right behind us are the Jews. This kingdom is not an earthly kingdom. Jesus made that clear. But He also made it clear as Covenant citizens of this supernatural kingdom, we have the full right to exercise Godly authority in it. Not according to our fleshly lusts or ideas, but according to what His will is for the earth. It is our responsibility to care for the earth as He laid out in the Old Testament Covenant. Those commands were not abolished by the New Testament. It is our responsibility under the New Testament to share the Gospel story with unbelievers and God makes the promise signs and wonders will follow the preaching of His word (see Mark 16:17-18).

Some of the early settlers would have disagreed with the signs and wonders part of this equation. Unknown to many today, is the fact that doctrinal disagreements, even some relating to issues like these, were the reasons why some states were formed. Believers such as Roger Williams, who formed Rhode Island, would have welcomed what was then considered a less orthodox approach to sharing the Gospel. As the apostles of old functioned in signs and wonders, those involved in witchcraft would watch this experience (see Acts 8). Seeing similar results, they assumed the methods were the same, when they were not. For this and many reasons, we have a history in accusing people of witchcraft because the method can, sometimes, look similar. Thus new states would be formed in an effort to live their lives according to what they felt were the best biblical approaches to creating a healthy environment. In this way they avoided the accusation of witchcraft.

Believers today know it will take all of us people of the "Book" (Bible) doing our part, to see the health of our planet and its occupants return. Then, as now, believers know earthly government or the government of nations are supposed to function in conjunction with— not have a wall of separation from— the kingdom of God. As Americans, we know, almost by osmosis, that our members "are the government" to effectuate an atmosphere in which we can all fulfill our best potential. The reason for this state of being is because of the biblical doctrines we see evident today. These echo much, and in some cases, ALL of the doctrines of the early settlers. Many of those doctrines were echoed in early law, which found secular applications. I will show you documentary proof of this as we view our next sections.

These early peoples also gave us another understanding in how to change our government when necessary. Our understanding today as Christians is that we, as Covenant citizens of the kingdom, have the full right to exercise Godly authority by speaking God's word to situations which flow contrary to His word. We invite God to enter into them to affect the changes He wants to see so everything functions according to His kingdom design. (Thus the accusation of witchcraft in years gone by.) If a covenant was made, and is now being broken, we have the full right and authority to invite God to heal the breach of our respective covenant partners. In this way healing takes place for people and nations. The Puritans would have done this by laws, rules and regulations. They would have agreed on the matter in church, prayed, sought God's will and then voted to change laws. In this way, two sides to government would have been reproduced, echoing the Old Testament priestly line seen by Aaron, and the governing side carried out by his brother, Moses.

Let me share with you the Scriptures which could have been used from both the Old as well as the New Testaments. You already know the Scriptures in Matthew 6: 9-13; Luke 11:2-4: *"OUR FATHER WHICH ART IN HEAVEN, HALLOWED BE THY NAME"*.......First, Father is not here on earth. Where is he? He is in heaven. Not only does this define what Father we are talking about but exactly where He is. *"THY KINGDOM COME, THY WILL BE DONE— IN EARTH AS IT IS IN HEAVEN"*.......Second, we affirm our worshipful Covenant of faith in Him by announcing that He and His name are holy. Then we make a proclamation and a request, both at the same time, by stating we invite His Kingdom, and that It Is Come and we invite His will to be done— as well as proclaim it is already done— both on earth and heaven. *"GIVE US THIS DAY, OUR DAILY BREAD"*......No citizen of the Kingdom can survive without sustenance, again reiterating our Covenant of faithful worship in His sustaining our very lives. *"AND FORGIVE US OUR DEBTS, AS WE FORGIVE OUR DEBTORS."*.........Next we affirm our desire to keep Covenant and remain in His Kingdom by asking for our sins (trespasses or debts) to be forgiven. This encourages us to forgive those who have also sinned, especially against us. A lack of forgiveness affects us as citizens in the Kingdom by blocking the flow of our Covenantal benefits. *"AND LEAD US NOT INTO TEMPTATION, BUT DELIVER US FROM EVIL:"*.........Temptation can potentially put us in a realm which is not of our Covenant Kingdom citizenship and can also potentially put us in need of deliverance from the same intruder from that realm. *"FOR THINE IS THE KINGDOM, AND THE POWER, AND THE GLORY, FOR EVER, AMEN"*......The last sentence affirms our Covenant of worship and the lasting nature of His Kingdom, with an Amen or So Be It.

I know so many Christians think this is some cute little prayer we teach our children. But Jesus talked about the kingdom of heaven from Chapter 4 of Matthew until Chapter 18. He was constantly talking about the kingdom of heaven or His Father's kingdom. When they ask Him how the kingdom works in prayer, He tells them and then gives them what we call the Lord's prayer. To make this point, let me ask my Christian friends some questions. How did you get into the kingdom? Romans 10:9 & 10 told you. You believed in your heart, and you confessed with your mouth God raised Jesus from the dead. Well, it's no different when you need healing or finances or anything else needed in the kingdom. We read the promise (covenant) in the Bible, we believe it in our heart, then we speak it with our mouth, in faith, receiving what we need. Now, we may have to follow that up with other actions recommended by the Scriptures, like paying our tithes, or praying, but you get the picture.

When things go awry in our lives and in the lives of those around us, Jesus told us to invite God Almighty in miracle-working power to bring His kingdom as it is in heaven to earth. This is not hocus-pocus. God doesn't *have* to do anything we say. But He does respond and honor His word spoken in faith through our Covenant. These are supernatural laws which do not obey our human desires. They are not subject to mankind's mindset and worldview. When we understand the Bible, we understand spiritual laws. We used to be a supernatural body. In many circles we still are. But so many today forget the supernatural power which keeps us healthy and alive because so many church leaders got distracted by money and power and stopped preaching the Bible.

Am I against money and the Scriptural principles which apply to it? No, certainly not. But money is not our source for the church. I don't mind big buildings if we are feeding and/or taking care of lots of people. But if we are a small congregation, having a big building with big debts and asking for more money to fulfill our lusts instead of feeding the poor and/or making many disciples is not going to cut it with Jesus. Sorry, but there it is. We have left our Covenant relationship and our civic government is now bankrupt of the health and wholeness the earliest founders of the 1600s and 1700s gave it because of their Covenant with the same God. All of them may not have signed on to the "signs and wonders" but they wholeheartedly received the miraculous when it came to prosperity. From meager church buildings with folks in near starvation circumstances to the star-studded events sometimes called worship services, it can easily be argued the wonder of the mega-church is the success of the Scriptures which gave them foundational birth.

You might ask, "Why would a government be in disarray just because the faithful of all stripes ignore it?" Because they are the other half of the equation. Not all people receive the same spiritual gifts in a covenant with the Creator. We may all be created equal to access Him, but we are not all given the same gifts and talents. When the faithful are removed from the covenant agreement they started, and a new generation of faithful fail to take their place, the very prosperity and healthy government which is an outcome of covenant relationship is lost. In fact, everyone involved in a covenant with the faithful who are in a covenant with the God of the Bible prosper, even a whole nation.

Let's look at this from the Old Testament (before Christ) in 2 Chronicles 7:14:

> "If my people, which are called by my name, shall humble themselves, and pray, and seek my face, and turn from their wicked ways; then will I hear from heaven, and will forgive their sin, and will heal their land."

Christians love to quote this verse, but forget the reason why it was written. In 2 Chronicles 6, Solomon reminds God about the covenant God had with his father, David. (We reviewed the Davidic Covenant earlier.) In verse 17, Solomon asks God to ratify that Covenant, which included the command of God to David to build Him a house or temple. God told David his son would build the house while David only assembled the material. God would keep one of David's descendants on the throne for eternity.

When Solomon is done praying (2 Chronicles 7:1), God ratifies or verifies that Covenant by showing up with fire on the animal sacrifices laying on the altar. So much so that 2 Chronicles 7:2, says the priests could not enter into the house because the glory of the Lord had filled it. Why weren't the priests allowed in? Because that covenant was between God and David. David was not present and God Himself was the verifier of it at that point. The Covenant extends to all Israel and even us today (the other people of the Book). Even the strangers and aliens among them benefited. We have to get that in our heads. The unbelievers were blessed because of the believer's covenant. That Covenant is now unconditional.

They are still under the Old Covenant so animals must be sacrificed. God shows up in response to Solomon's prayer and it is extended out to the people as they see the glory of God and the fire of God. They then praise, worship (vv 3-9) and keep all the covenantal commands necessary under the Old Testament. It is when they are finished with those requirements (vv 10 & 11) God then speaks to Solomon. Verse 13 alludes to the effects breaking Covenant has on the land, atmosphere and natural earth around them. Verse 14 promises recovery. Verse 13 is captivity and Verse 14 is restoration by restoring Covenant relationship. It's all about Covenant. For us in the New Testament that means it's all about a relationship with Jesus.

Two covenants, the Abrahamic Covenant and the Davidic Covenant unconditionally apply to New Testament believers. The New Covenant becomes unconditional only when we accept Christ's sacrifice and live in a love relationship with Him. In Abraham's case, he assembles the sacrifices, but is unable to walk between the cut pieces, as is required in his day to be a party to the agreement. He is unable because he is, quite literally, knocked out by the glory of God. The Bible tells us it is God in glory who walks between the pieces. So Abraham does nothing but accept God's promise and assemble the pieces. David has passed on by the time his Covenant is ratified by God. All David did was accept God's promise and assemble the building material to build the temple. This leaves his son, Solomon, to dedicate the temple. Over a thousand years after Abraham, as Solomon dedicates this temple, the priests in the temple have a very similar experience as Abraham had before them: They are unable to perform their duties because God in glory has shown up with such power.

Under the New Covenant all we do is present ourselves a living sacrifice (Romans 12:1-3) and accept Christ's offer or promise of redemption. Once we do this, it is Jesus' sacrifice which takes over. Ephesians 2:8 & 9 tells us it is by grace we are saved; it is a gift. There is nothing we could do with our own works to receive this gift. All we have to do is be willing to accept it. Under the New Covenant, the covenants of both David and Abraham also pass on to us. Galatians tells us we are the spiritual seed of Abraham by faith. David's Covenant also extends to us as a result of Jesus now sitting on the throne of David; Jesus, by human birth, being one of David's descendants (Matthew 1:1-17 and Luke 2:4; 3:23-28). Like Abraham and the priests of old, many who have attended modern-day revivals still experience this "phenomenon" of God in glory as He comes among them to effectuate His plan and will in their lives.

In the same portion of Galatians we are told, under the New Covenant, there is neither male nor female, bond nor slave, Jew nor Gentile, but all are equal co-heirs to the blessings of Abraham and his Covenant with God. So often some churches misrepresent the responsibilities of male and female, rich and poor, Jew and Gentile. Clearly Paul says all are able to function in everything God has for the heirs of salvation. So much confusion and pain could be avoided if we would represent the heirs of salvation in an accurate way as opposed to the bondage some would display as a caricature of the Bible. Treating women as inferiors is one more holdover in a lack of understanding the Bible.

Another one has to do with "acting" holy. Without the indwelling Holy Spirit, it is impossible to live in a love relationship with Jesus. People who act holy are probably just acting. I honestly cannot take credit for the change which took place in my life after I accepted Jesus. The Holy Spirit gave me a new outlook and a new spirit (quickened my dormant spirit) or inner man when I accepted Christ. My only responsibility in this is to obey Him. In other words 'present myself a living sacrifice,' (Romans 12:1) and do what He tells me to. Now, sometimes that's easy and sometimes it's not. But the more I obey, the easier it gets— usually. It's like being in any other relationship only way more intense. The more I experience the benefits the more I want to stay in the relationship, and the Holy Spirit is constantly helping me! It's like plugging an electric cord into a socket. When you do, electricity is a byproduct of that action. When you accept Christ, living by faith and love in Christ is a byproduct of that relationship, and a byproduct of that relationship is a maintained Covenant with all its blessings intact.

These can be some of the differences in our present day understanding of covenant from those early colonists. Some of those differences are also why it is important not to automatically transfer our present-day Christian religions with those from the past. Other differences have to do with some of the more complex puzzles known to Bible students. As we shall soon see, one of these mysteries evolved two different trains of thought which had a direct impact upon our understanding of inalienable rights. A portion of Scripture from Philippians 2:12 & 13, can sum it up for us. It says, "Wherefore, my beloved, as ye have always obeyed, not as in my presence only, but now much more in my absence, work out your own salvation with fear and trembling. For it is God which worketh in you both to will and to do of his good pleasure."

Which one is it? Is it you working out your salvation or is it God? It's both. The non-religious among us would say something can't be both at the same time. Well, in the case of Elohim, the Creator of the Universe, that is exactly what it is. Is Jesus 100 percent God? My Christian friends would say absolutely yes. Is Jesus 100 percent man? My Christian friends would again say yes. Of course, this is what has knocked most folks out of the Christian ballpark for centuries. The same reality applies to the Trinity. When Christians study the Old as well as the New Testaments, we see Father, Son and Holy Spirit as three distinct personalities, yet we see One True God. Many the world over have rolled their eyes and said this is totally impossible. Frankly, I would find it totally impossible to serve or have a relationship with a God who did not challenge my thinking. It would be impossible for me to believe in a God who existed in a totally neat little box I put Him in, so my little brain could understand all there is to know about Him. Let's face it, a Being who created the entire universe should make us think outside the box of what that Being is.

There are several of these 'moments' or 'mysteries' in the Bible. They are defined as two equally true facts which must be taken together in the same degree. You cannot lift one side of the equation over the other or you fall into error. BUT when you do take both sides of the equation equally, you go against the law of human reasoning. In point of fact, quantum physics on what I would call cosmic steroids can do a reasonable job by explaining some of these concepts. Unfortunately, discussing these 'moments' or concepts has caused wars among people for centuries. It is a sad fact, but unfortunately, a true one. Thankfully enough, Christians realized going to war over this stuff was pretty dumb.[1]

These mysteries formed Calvin's doctrines from one point of view and Arminius' doctrines from another. Both these trains of thought had a considerable influence in early colonial thinking. So as covenant citizens we are going to have disagreements we can agree to disagree with. The early founders did, yet they were still able to form a covenant which governed, not just well, but laid the foundation for later compacts. These and other doctrinal differences are what formed the various denominations who made up early America and forged the bedrock of religious freedoms in this country. Also unknown to many today, is the impact biblical doctrinal differences made to our secular or non-sectarian American covenant (more on that later).

One concern people have when reading any subject concerning biblical Covenant and God is some ulterior motive in order to subjugate people in some way, shape or form. I realize so many false practices and doctrines have tried, over many centuries, to use our proper and Godly relationship in Covenant to hoodwink and/or restrain God's people in one form or another. The latest attempt, on a worldwide stage is socialism or progressivism, as it is called in this country. I discuss this in detail in the section "Broken Covenant." But when I speak or refer to God's Covenant with His people, first and foremost I refer to God and His people. I am not bringing anyone else into the Covenant relationship.

Secondly, when a Covenant does relate God's people to another, I refer only to those relationships which are meant to fulfill a Godly purpose. Once the parties feel that is no longer the case, no one should feel obligated or compelled to remain in a situation which is unhealthy or any situation they no longer feel the need to be in. Obviously, this can encompass so many situations that naming one would potentially omit another. We must also realize when God ratifies a Covenant with blessings abounding and we disregard or break it, our actions have consequences. Those consequences often speak for themselves.

Lastly, I should mention those involved in what might be called Christianity, but do not follow the Bible. Many Christian-type religions tinker with the Bible's doctrines in an effort to eliminate or solve the conundrum presented to us humans concerning much of what God says (see the last endnote). In modern times, many just walk away from the issue, ignoring the Bible and/or Christianity as "the problem." But now, much the same as in the early history of our country, there is another group who has decided we Bible believers have gotten it all wrong and there is another explanation other than the one the Bible presents. In doing so they change some aspect of the Bible in order to fit whatever doctrine they have devised.

My mention of them here is not to judge, but to ask the question, "Are they included in the secular/non-sectarian compact-covenant?" My answer is, "Of course, they are." They were included in it when some of them helped to write our three-part compacting documents. Belief in a God is not necessary to be a part of our non-sectarian covenant. Like atheists and folks from other religions, this does not exclude them from the blessings of the Covenant extended to a nation whose people as a majority have covenanted with the God described in the Bible. We shall read about this shortly.

In making a covenant with the people who believe in the God of the Bible, they may not make an agreement to believe or follow the God Bible believers do, but they do make a secular covenant with the various people of God. We will look at some of these distinctions in more detail later. This is an aspect of secular covenant or political covenant. We will review that history, as well as some of the founders and framers of our American compacting documents who believed in various and different ways.

ENDNOTES

1   There are 10 of these "moments," truths or conceptual events in the Bible. Some Bible schools try to teach them under the principle of hypostasis. For me, that doesn't quite explain these events in a complete manner. It takes me six months to teach this course. I will also review some basics in quantum physics with a view to many of the principles of cold fusion, that can help some people in realizing the awesomeness of who God is. Eventually the truth dawns on folks. But some folks love to argue simply because one must still surrender to Godly revelation and there are people who will not subscribe to that. For me that is not a problem. Each one of us can decide to believe or not to believe. One of the best books out there explaining these mysteries is by Kenneth Boa, titled "God, I Don't Understand." © 1975, 2007, published by Victor Books. It is still available on Amazon. I accessed copies in August of 2012 and then again in 2015. I mention these truths not because their discussion is central to this book; it is not. But many different folks will read this book and many have varying levels of theological training. I was shocked to watch the

44th President of the United States, before he became so, speak to 'The Call To Renewal Conference' (June 28, 2006). He made statements which made it obvious he understood little or nothing about the Bible, and seemingly less about our founding fathers' faith. Unfortunately, he is not alone. That is why I have written this note. The Bible states clearly faith comes by hearing, and hearing by the word of God (Romans 10:17). So if you are not hearing and/or studying God's word, no faith and no understanding of biblical foundations will be evidenced. Since Bible literacy in our generation has dropped to near nothing, many people don't seem to understand some of the basic and foundational doctrines of the Scriptures. They then make assumptions that are inaccurate as well. Many who have faith as a mustard seed listen to someone like a politician or movie star make a statement which challenges their faith, when, if they had some good foundational doctrine added to their faith, would be able to spot the lie quickly instead of struggle in a challenge which never needed to take place. Jesus talked about this phenomena in the gospels when He was speaking concerning the word (Matthew 13). You have to read and study and receive God's truth through revelation (Joshua 1:8; 1 Corinthians 2:14). Many folks study with their minds (soul) but their spirit is not active and thus God's truth is truncated and/or corrupted. Some don't spend the time it takes and their roots are also affected. This is why the Holy Spirit was given to us to lead and guide us into all truth (John 16:13).

Chapter Three

CAPTIVITY

Now here in America we've been born free. We may not know what captivity looks like. So let's look at captivity from the 70 years Israel went through it. Remember the Scripture reference of Daniel 9:1, 2, from Chapter Two?

"In the first year of Darius the son of Ahasuerus, of the seed of the Medes, which was made king over the realm of the Chaldeans; In the first year of his reign I Daniel understood by books the number of the years, whereof the word of the Lord came to Jeremiah the prophet, that he would accomplish seventy years in the desolations of Jerusalem."

Daniel 9:3-6: "And I set my face unto the Lord God, to seek by prayer and supplications, with fasting, and sackcloth, and ashes: And I prayed unto the Lord my God, and made my confession, and said, O Lord, the great and dreadful God, keeping the covenant and mercy to them that love him, and to them that keep his commandments; We have sinned, and have committed iniquity, and have done wickedly, and have rebelled, even by departing from thy *precepts* and from thy *judgments*: Neither have we hearkened unto thy servants the *prophets*, which spake in thy name to our *kings*, our *princes*, and our *fathers*, and to *all the people* of the land."

I've italicized some words. That word *precept* is quite interesting. It is the word mitzvah, like a bar or bat mitzvah. It's a command or law or ordinance. Jewish folks use it as a meaning for the Covenant, as in Mosaic. Mitzvah means to covenant or ordain. In English it gave meaning to the word **constitute**. So young thirteen year olds are ordained or brought into the adult side of following the Law by a celebration. They now enter to become a part of the Covenant people. It comes from another Hebrew word which means to constitute, as in constitution. It means to set in order by constituting or charging, usually by sending with a messenger. The word *judgment* means law, as in governing authority as well as lower-level leaders and leaders within families. Remember the pattern we talked about where God sends a prophet or messenger and says, "You've broken my covenant?" This is the verse where we see these named leaders of society refusing to listen to the warning.

What's the result? Daniel 9:7, 8: "O Lord, righteousness belongeth unto thee, but unto us *confusion of faces,* as at this day; to the *men of Judah,* and to the inhabitants of Jerusalem, and unto all Israel, that are near, and that are far off, through all the countries whither thou hast driven them, because of their trespass that they have trespassed against thee. O Lord, to us belongeth *confusion of face, to our kings, to our princes, and to our fathers,* because we have sinned against thee."

This is spiritual as well as physical judgment. Why? First, it is not isolated to one location in Israel but everywhere Jews were found. Secondly, let's look at the words I have italicized. The phrase, *confusion of face(s)* literally means shame or disappointment of feelings, ideas, stature and refers to the part of the head which turns (thus the reference to face because it turns with the head). The idea of, "which way do I go?"— and then you see someone turn their head one way and then the other way. Who has this problem? Government. The phrase, *men of Judah* refers to the ruling kingly line. The word *fathers* would refer to the local leaders and leaders within families. And we wonder why the Congress and U.S. government can't figure out what to do to fix problems? The answer is stated here in Daniel as to what the problem is: "because we have sinned against thee." Have you ever wondered why some people have solutions to problems and others, their *solutions* have only made the problem worse? I have come to the conclusion this portion of Scripture is key. It has nothing to do with intelligence, but to a willingness to accomplish whatever we do according to biblical revelation.

These covenantal agencies are like gravity. Once spoken into existence by God, they govern outcomes. It becomes a spiritual law. Everyone thinks all we need are all democrats (socialists) or all republicans to solve what's wrong. As long as we continue to ignore the spiritual atmosphere of covenant, we will continue to experience difficulty.

The Lord never wants us to experience catastrophe. God is a good God. God does not cause suffering, neither does He cause evil on the planet. As humans in charge of the planet, we do that all by ourselves. If we refuse His hand reached out to us over and over again, He lets us go our stubborn ways. When He does so, the enemy of our souls rushes in to do to us what our actions have allowed. When I have preached this I take two little dolls as an illustration. One is a little girl doll and the other is usually some monster I can find in the toy store. I cover my hand over the little girl doll, representing that as the covering of a loving God over His creation. Then the little girl doll decides to move out from under the hand covering her. The monster grabs her.

I also quickly explain the fact evil does have two varieties, if you will. In other words, why do bad things happen to good people? One evil is of the natural type. For example, God created the atmosphere and creation on the planet to be beneficial and healthy to all involved. We were supposed to live forever. Our bodies regenerated because of the atmosphere/water and lack of what the Bible terms sin. Animals did not kill other animals to eat and neither did we. When Adam sinned that changed. This type of evil is what we would call natural. The second is the evil of the human variety: Our own actions cause pain, suffering and hideous evil.

Can bad things still possibly happen when we are under the hand of God's covering? Yes. Why? I don't think I have ever seen an instance where a human did not cause an act, and unfortunately someone else who did nothing wrong, experiences the pain and suffering instead. This encompasses cancer and other sicknesses as well. "Cancer, you say? Now wait a minute, preacher, you're going too far." Do you know they are discovering more and more cancers, not all, but more and more have to do with a virus which was already in our bodies from some outside source? We were not created to mutate our cells. Today we have developed vaccines to prevent some cancers based on inoculating folks against the human papilloma virus. That's just one which we have a vaccine for. There are others in research. Our toxic environment is based on human or moral evil. We try to ignore the toxins in our food; toxins in plastics and body and bath products. But someone in some lab somewhere knew of the dangers and was either ignored when they sounded the alarm, or they ignored what they knew would eventually become a problem. Children, in the womb and outside of it, with no sin of their own, get sick from this stuff (see the next endnote).

Does God cause children to become sick? No. Thankfully, we do have an answer in word and prayer to be set free and healed. Does everyone get healed? No. Why not? Remember what I said before about Jesus being 100 percent God and 100 percent man and both truths must be taken equally at the same value; you cannot lift one up over the other? It is the same here (see the previous endnote). God is totally Divine and Sovereign yet we are responsible as humans. Both concepts must be treated equally or you will fall into error. Just because we as humans are not personally responsible for an error, but that error can have dire consequences— even generations later— does not make God any less sovereign. I was watching a documentary where they proved the possibility RNA can be altered because of something your forebears experienced.[1] They used the condition of a famine causing diabetes or affecting cardiovascular health in the grandchildren. Let's ask the theological question of how was the famine caused? Famines can be caused by manmade issues, but quite often they are as a result of natural evil.

Sometimes we have the attitude Jesus addressed in Luke 13:1-4, where he asks the disciples if they think the Galileans Pilate killed were more evil or worse sinners than anyone else (moral evil); or if the men whom the tower of Siloam fell on were worse sinners (natural evil). In both cases He said no; the real problem was our own salvation issues. I realize this theological stuff is not always easy to receive. Oversimplifying it here doesn't help. But there are good reasons for why we study the Scriptures: All this is academic until it happens to you. While having the academic knowledge doesn't always help when you have to go through catastrophe or heartache in life, it can soften the blow and eventually give you the comfort to turn back to or get even closer with God. In my experience when we take that path, the healing process is quicker and more complete.

Jesus does not want us to go into captivity. My dialogue here is not to judge folks or even correct them. Believe what you will. My method here is to help us understand the spiritual forces at work when we ignore what is a secular/non-sectarian covenant between parties, yet birthed and still operational as a spiritual covenant stamped and approved by the Highest of Authorities.

Contrary to popular theories, my question here is not whether the Constitution is a Christian document or whether the Federal government was started with ecclesiastical hierarchy. Oddly enough, while the Constitution was written by a supermajority of Christ followers, and we see evidence of biblical theories of government inherent in it, it was not written as a Christian document. After all, we see evidence of Greek, Roman and English theories of government in it as well, but it is not Greek, Roman or English. We also see no evidence of a cabinet position controlled by an ecclesiastical authority.

My question is did we start as a covenantal people, covenanting with the God of the Bible, in which a covenant agreement stayed in full force and effect, even throughout the early Federal government straight through to today? Were there those who believed we were given our land just as Israel was given her land by the same God? Are people still in this country today who covenant with that same God? We see by ignoring to follow their Covenant with God, Israel's actions sent her into captivity and that captivity was a Jewish government which no longer functioned. Did Israel violate the covenant of the priesthood? Have we? Did Israel violate the marriage covenant? Have we? Did Israel violate her covenant of worship? Have we? Those last six questions will be answered by separate books. But for now, let's take a quick history lesson to see if we were ever a covenant people.

ENDNOTES

1   <http://www.nrcresearchpress.com/doi/abs/10.1139/y09-006> site © 2014
        Canadian Science Publishing. <http:www.nature.com/news/starvation-in-pregnant-
        mice-marks-offspring-dna-1.15534> site © 2015 Nature Publishing Group, a division
        of Macmillan Publishers Limited. <http://www.medicinenet.com/script/main/art.
        asp?articlekey=52069><http://www.nrdc.org/health/kids/ocar/chap7.asp><http://
        www.emedicinehealth.com/environmental_illness-health/page3_em.htm> accessed
        3/17/16.

SOME GROUND RULES
(FOR DISSENTERS)

Section Two

SOME GROUND RULES

I know there are many who will probably not like this, but the America we know today actually started as a church relocation program. I will prove it to you, and I will also tell you there are those who disagree, citing various differences in what is considered "foundational." They also refuse to acknowledge any legal connection of biblical foundations within the Puritan ranks. I firmly disagree. Our history, laws, our practices and even frameworks within our documents for government come through many avenues; one of them is biblical. These folks were actually persecuted missionaries, relocating to a new area of the world. Of course we also have the testimony of those who lived some 300 to 500 years ago.

In doing this research I found so many instances of personal stories of prayer, faith, personal faith and practices which showed everyday heroes and heroes of faith. Unfortunately, I will not be able to tell all of those stories. We have a more immediate issue as a nation to deal with. That will compel me to view history from a slightly different overview. To look at that history, I will share many heroes of America. Sadly, I will have to skip over countless heroes and their stories which formed and had an effect in our land.

Before you get too upset that I've ignored your favorite parts of American history and, adding insult to injury, I'm too darn religious, let me make this statement: The religious do not always "know" God. There really is no nice way to say that. We misrepresent Him all the time. We may know a lot about Him, but never really come to an intimate relationship with Him. You may say, "Well, he doesn't exist." Well, here is my take on that: When astronomers look into the skies through a telescope they realize a black hole exists by the enormous effect it has on objects around it. When they want to find extrasolar planets they also use indirect methods like radial velocity and transits. These methods look for a drop in the brightness planets cause when passing in front of their parent star, or the wobble effect on that star. Ultimately, having Hubble and other missioned spacecraft has told them more than anything we could hope to have known from observation here on earth. Just because you can't see something does not mean it does not exist. The Bible has always been like Hubble or any other tool helping astronomers to actually see the object they are searching for.

I won't argue with you that there is no God. Opinions are like brains, we all have one. You might argue I am not using mine because I believe there is a God and I might argue that your opinion is equally invalid. What we should never do is rip apart the very fabric of what has made this country work, in an effort to try a new experiment we know has failed in other countries, killed millions and imprisoned twice that many. All in an effort to squash religious thinkers, change moral values and create a place like we have now where children really are not safe to walk home from school alone.

I was a latchkey kid in the New York City metro area. I walked twenty city blocks each day. While I had to have some skill in spotting trouble my 'rurally-schooled' counterparts may not have had, my mom never feared for my life. My, how forty years of secularism, socialism and welfare have changed us! I have never seen or heard any modern official— secular, Christian or Jewish— suggest atheists should be arrested, demoted or not hired because they do not believe there is a God. Right now in the U.S., Canada, Britain, Germany and Sweden, I have read the testimony and seen the evidence of folks arrested for their religious beliefs, denied jobs and denied to speak on a newscast because of their belief in God. People are even being denied access because of scientific evidence some socialist or progressive disagrees with because they feel it is not politically correct.[1]

If you can acknowledge that quantum physics has explained how two things can be in one place at the same time or how principles of cold fusion have shown how two things can actually be one thing, you can acknowledge those same principles written in the Bible (thousands of years ago), which explain the nature of that same God. But if you still don't believe, I have no problem with someone believing there is no God. When I see people have civilized and informed discussions with one another on this topic, it restores some sense in me that we are still human. What harms all of us is when you have people shouting or behaving rudely, or using profanity. One especially nasty, recent instance I witnessed was an individual who had a joyful expression because finally these Christians are going to be persecuted as they should be!

Almost all of these situations which I experienced personally were done to prove whoever was talking in favor of God's existence is wrong, horrible for talking about it publicly, and they are some other unprintable words. The way I read the Bible, even God Almighty Himself gives every human being the right to believe He doesn't exist. If your feet felt a rumble in the ground and your ears heard the blow of a whistle and you knew you were standing on train tracks, most thinking people would see the need to walk off the tracks. My point is just because we can only see the evidence and pattern being set up for captivity, doesn't mean we should rule out the fact it can happen again, even if you ignore my experience, both past and present of hearing from God.

An annoyance for some folks is with people who say they hear from God. Believe me, I try with everything in me to keep these experiences to myself. I really am one of those typical New Yorkers: Didn't see it, didn't hear it and DON'T BOTHER ME! Having an experience with the Creator of the Universe is kind of like living through the fun side of careening down the slope of a snow-covered mountain. Once the "ride" stops, you pick your head up out of the snow, seeing the sunlight, you're overjoyed to realize you have no broken bones. That's when you can't wait to tell your friends all about it. I've learned personally to keep my mouth shut. But then there is this BIG God who tells you to share the experience with someone.

I realize over the centuries people who read the Bible have been like five-year olds with a Desert Eagle. Even handling the thing has been dangerous to those standing by watching. Never mind if they actually get a shot off. Revelation is a continuing entity for humans when we're talking about the God of the Bible. Nobody gets it immediately. In fact, centuries can go by with people not 'getting it.' The Jewish people have understood this all too well. Unfortunately, Christians have come to that dinner table a little late. The history of persecution from all sides, but especially in the name of God, makes a favorite argument for unbelief. It also seems to be an excuse recently for unbelievers to promote religious racism, even though the New Testament never, ever gives anyone the "right" to kill someone for their religious belief or non-belief.

My question is, "If God does not exist why does the Bible carry the power it does?" You would say because people give it power. I wish that were true. For those who actually speak God's word forth with His blessing, it has power all on its own. Unfortunately, people still mishandle it today. Because it is God's word it is used inappropriately, blamed unnecessarily and trashed constantly. Yet it remains for those who thoughtfully, carefully and humbly decide to open it up. Still the best seller of all time.

If God does not exist you never have to worry about me, or anything written in this book or written in the Bible from ever coming to pass. Christians and Jews always have to worry about persecution and worse from those who do not believe. Remember Greece, Rome, the Spanish Inquisition, French Revolution, the Holocaust, Christians/Jews in Muslim nations and in socialist/communist nations? Atheists have fared no better in some of those instances either. Most recently, the FBI reports 60.9 percent of religious hate-crimes in America are against Jews.[2] All of this takes place while we have seen so very much of the Bible coming to pass. This has gone on for centuries.

To be fair to the religious, one must separate out those folks who say they are Christian or Jewish but have no idea of what the Bible commands concerning adherence to that inalienable right. Sadly, the new statistics are quite shocking about those who claim they are Christians concerning their Bible reading: Only 19 percent say they read their Bibles daily.[3] Quite a few folks say they are a designated religion simply because their family is, but have no idea you cannot be a Christian simply because you are birthed into a family of Christians. Others sit in a church or synagogue but have never picked up a Bible to read for themselves. This seems to be less of a problem for Jews.

I will make you a promise. I will never write anything I do not believe is true, even though you may disagree with it. I will also not knowingly try to disrespect you. I come from an area of the country taking no one seriously as a big deal, except God. The political correctness that has ruined our country masquerades as respect. What it actually does is silence us from discussing the important and critical needs of a nation sending itself into captivity. The solutions offered at the end of this book are similar to solutions our founders "found." If political correctness handcuffs us from revealing history and a path toward solutions, we will indeed "find" captivity.

I need to explain the method I used for researching this book. My "gold standard" was to use original documents. If I was not able to view the documents myself, I relied on those who possessed them or had actually seen them. If I did find information from several websites, I used it only if I was able to find the information confirmed from original information. So if you happen to be one of those folks who just know I am totally wrong for not mentioning one of your favorite quotes or facts, it may very well be because it has no original-fact status. I tried to make notes in the text or endnotes when I came across that situation.

If information was such common knowledge, as some of the history of the founding of our country is, or as other history or information is, I made no note. I will also say I am not perfect and do not claim to be superior as a researcher, or as a spokesperson for God. Actually, I feel as if someone would have to be full of pride to claim such perfection. While I cannot deny God's voice, I cannot deny my fallibility. I easily make mistakes. If you find one, please know I have done everything in my power to make sure there are none. But alas, not being perfect, I'm sure someone will find something. This is why I tried to stick with original documented sources.

My adherence to original documentation was also because I came to the conclusion so many sources of academia just quoted each other rather than going directly to original documents. There was also a problem from religious sites and books which quoted each other, but obviously did not view original documents any better than academia. The effect from this, in my opinion has left us, as Americans, lacking in truth. I also use broad strokes in painting early colonial history. I do the same with modern history. My purpose there is not to deceive. My purpose is to limit what lent itself to covenantal practice. In that sense and for that time period the practice or history was common knowledge and can be easily obtained on many different sites, including university-based sites or commonly used encyclopedias.

I also used direct quotes from many early books of history where public domain permissions allowed me. Frequently early books had easy access to original documents. If I found no documentary error, I would use them to show how a topic governing covenant-keeping by Christians, or the practice or belief by people of yesteryear was viewed. On occasion this was important to show there are those who still view a topic in the same way today and/or expose a revision of history. I also attempted to show how opinions and practices have changed; for example, drinking alcohol or tobacco use. The preaching of yesteryear did not abhor the use of either as it does today, just its overuse.

You should also understand the history documented by this book was based on covenant and religious covenant in particular. So there may very well be secular events connected to a historical event which I may not mention. That's because my focus is on finding covenant. I am not omitting secular events to misrepresent our history. Instead my goal was to focus on a covenantal aspect of history. Quite often I have read how someone will totally secularize an event which showed no dichotomy in helping affirm a religious practice simply because there were secular and/or non-sectarian reasons for doing the practice. Sometimes there will be an argument those practicing Christianity were not particularly religious because they did not attend church or they were, in some cases, scoundrels. Being a scoundrel or not going to church or having secular reasons for doing a thing or not doing a thing does not show proof of belief or non-belief in God. It also does not negate a desire to help people read their Bibles or some other religious practice of covenant-keeping.

For example, the Continental Congress made a resolution to discuss ordering Bibles. They did not do so and no Bibles were ever ordered. I have read many misquote what took place to show government was financially supporting the reading of the Bible, and I have read others using this to prove Congress was against doing so to stop religion in government. Neither conclusion is supportable. You can see the full treatment of this in a future chapter. Quotes used by founders were used to show an understanding of covenant-keeping. Or said in another way, an understanding of how believers would view things or function because they believed in keeping covenant with God. That same understanding or function could also be applied to a non-believer or used secularly.

There also seems to be a need to explain things which were known and understood by Americans 50 or 60 years ago. For example, American Christians have always had a view it is their God-given right to free speech in the public square and in the government to expose ideology contrary to the Bible or morality (in some cases that might also include on the job). Yet today people are being denied acceptance into university programs because they are Christians. Professors are being fired if they prove misfeasance and/or criticize some aspect of global-warming research. Books are being banned from school libraries if they show some aspect of Christianity, specifically if an author is Christian or a publisher publishes Christian books.[4] I expose this prejudice to show you cannot raise "free-thinkers" if you refuse to allow them to view other ideas.

Likewise, science needs differences of opinion in research to unveil what is good or faulty research. The media needs to report the news and not pick and choose how they treat different people's belief systems to make a decision as to whether they will report news they may not like. The very reason why we have lost the life-saving example of covenant among us is because of this tendency in the last 40 years to omit anything "religious" from public view. Supposedly this is done in an effort to avoid offense; but in doing so, we are denying our history as well. A people ignorant of their history make easy fodder for capture simply because they are ignorant of how their ancestors overcame similar destructive forces (not all destructive forces are physical).

I have seen a tendency in young atheists to think they must fight and sue for their rights. This is a shame. It is now something Christians must do as well. Atheists believe their rights have been violated if they have to come in contact within the public square with religious artifacts they do not agree with. Christians have always believed that rights— all of our rights to think and believe— are given us by Our Creator. These rights cannot be given by government and they cannot be taken away by the government. Atheists have those exact same rights. Christians believe humans are given rights by God to believe as they choose to. We all breathe the same air, so the public square is and must be open to "ideas," even the symbolism of those ideas. Two generations ago, understanding inalienable rights made legal action unnecessary.

Let's take the theory behind all the legal action to its zenith with some examples. Turbaned men, veil-covered women, yarmulke wearing, Star of David and cross donning people shouldn't be allowed to work in public buildings while wearing these outward displays of religion. Countering the argument goes something like this: "Well, these folks are paying for their attire on their own bodies." Let's take these personal examples to public examples. Monuments depicting history are targeted for lawsuit because someone doesn't like the history or the fact they are displayed in public venues. Much like the folks working in public buildings, the monuments depicting moments in history or law are paid for by private entities. The counter argument goes something like this: "Allowing the monuments supports one certain religion." Let's take this argument personally: Only certain groups of people benefit from abortion, welfare, medicare, medicaid, sex-change operations— you get the picture. Why should these specialized people have access to government benefit? If we refuse to allow monuments to our history displayed on public land because they tell a national history connection to "a certain religion," then we single out one group of covenant people.

Recent cases are telling us where this is going. A church erected a huge cross on its property. There is a lawsuit surrounding this event.[5] Whatever the case's merits or lack of them, intimidation is the outcome. We are really one screw loose from communism. You can tell the premise is false for some of these suits, because now we have systemized prejudice against Christianity and Judaism. As you will read on, cross-wearing at work is being targeted, along with Christmas celebrations depicting the real reason for the season (Christ). These are being expelled from public spots. Respect for religious belief and those espousing non-belief seems to be in short supply.

In suing to silence people and separate them from their inalienable rights, which also separates them from their savings— or their "stuff"— we forget God-believers of all stripes and Christians in particular make up an overwhelming majority of the population. They serve your food, volunteer in the military, serve in hospitals, fire departments, police departments, etc. Persecuting them violates the secular/non-sectarian covenant and by doing so, forces them as well to violate their individual sacred covenant. This creates an atmosphere of hate and bullying. Secondly, by taking their "stuff" as a symbol says clearly, "We don't need you, we need your stuff." The reality is you don't need their stuff, but you do need them. When the wolves hit the threshold of the door— and they are frighteningly close— you will need the reality of a secular covenant with the God-believing in ways you cannot imagine.

The way some people treat the religious history of this country, one would think we were talking about exposing children before the age of 24 to sexual content or other pornographic practices. Unlike the pornographic lobby, this is not an attempt to hide "free thinking" in debauchery. Some have the erroneous idea Christianity is trying to be "taught" to children if we teach the true history of the nation, thereby harming them in some way. They equate this to their children viewing pornography. When I review the Covenant of Marriage in a future book, I will prove when you expose children before the age of 24-25 to pornographic content, you create behavior which has the potential to harm society. This is totally different from teaching accurate history. It is impossible to teach the full and correct history of this nation without the understanding of why the settlers came here and why they chose the forms of government they followed. That means children are going to hear the words *Christian* and *covenant*. These are not dirty words. Truth in history is critical for our children to learn.

Likewise, the public square should and must be open to all ideas which can be proven beneficial. I can prove these are biblical ideas and belief systems— and more importantly, they are foundational for the beginning of this country— and they are quite beneficial to the country. I was taught many of the foundational truths of this nation in public school. I learned about Puritan Christianity. This made no contribution toward my decision for Christ. Personal relationship in friends and family are far more important for that kind of decision making. So there should be no fear in teaching the truth of America's foundational roots. Our children are in far more danger from the modern secular culture based on Hollywood values depicting quick gratification through power, money, sex, drugs and alcohol. Arrogance and pride ruin more societies of people than a cross, a Bible or a statue. This is the final outcome of a people when our non-sectarian covenant and sacred covenants are trashed and ignored.

I also draw biblical truth and conclusions from some practices and events which took place. Sometimes other authors or historians agreed. If I could find such agreement I noted it in a endnote. Otherwise, because my field is in biblical studies, I made no note. You can assume it is my opinion, based upon my field of study that I write. The other field I have certificates is within a field of paralegal work, so I can read legal opinions. I make endnotes of legal opinions as necessary. Like so many other individuals the world over, I have studied and taken courses in quite a few other fields, mainly because a line of work took me there (medical, spiritual counseling, agricultural, animal husbandry, musical, among others). I am not degreed or certified in any of those studies, so I will most definitely note a sourced opinion. If, for some reason there is no endnote, you can assume it is my opinion and/or it was such common knowledge, I felt it unnecessary.

The goal of this book is not to prove every single last person coming to our shores was a Christian, or all our documents were deeply religious, or they conform to some modern idea of religiosity. That would include the ideas atheists have concerning religion or the ideas modern believers hold. I don't intend to prove the founders of the 1770s through the 1790s were deeply religious men. Some were, others were not. Instead, my purpose is to see if evidence exists that our founding religious forebears made a covenant with God and that covenant also extended to the unbeliever or the non-religious. I then looked for evidence to see if covenant found some form in our initial Federal documents. Do Federal documents covenant among "the people," and do "the people" believe or covenant with God?

This means I may highlight a religious element which showed covenant from our history or documents when there are secular and non-sectarian elements there as well. If I am silent about those elements, it is not because I am trying to make everything about "religion." For example, many reading this may not know our Federal documents have a principle inherent in them that "The People" are The Sovereign.[6] When our Federal documents were in their formation, the idea was prevalent and well rehearsed, that the people replaced the sovereign king; in our case, King George. Popular sovereignty, what we view the Federal documents embodying, is something we understand today, but without a king. So the king was in covenant with the people. Many original charters covenanted an understanding of God by mentioning some aspect of religious endeavor. But our original charters were primarily entered into for economic and secular reasons. In most cases, I will try to enunciate a dual religious and secular approach, but in some cases I may highlight the covenantal aspect of a religious nature more succinctly.

In our modern times, we understand popular sovereignty as the people in charge and in covenant with one another, the state they live in and the Federal government. Unfortunately, there has been a subtle shift among a younger generation in which the Federal government is like a king. This is one detail of evidence in a broken covenant. If you read the first chapter you will see my premise that the benefit of keeping the covenant is a functioning government.

Likewise, you will not read any defense for our modern sense of covenant-keeping. The parameters for deciding whether or not a covenant is still in place are really not up to me or you. I say that because we, as the people, are able to change secular aspects of our Federal covenant. It is not our decision as to whether or not a covenant in which God was invoked to oversee is still in full force and effect. For example, from Israel's history of covenant all I need to show is ONE single, solitary Christian, Jew or dissenter left in the country who still keeps covenant— at any one given time— for God to honor the Covenant. Abraham asked for ten righteous for Sodom to be spared. Why do I mention Israel? Because it is the same God. He updated believers in Christ to the New Testament. Where the New Testament has not updated the Old, the Old would apply (concerning the religious covenant). Those believers are covenant-holders with atheists and other dissenters to our non-sectarian/secular American covenant.

This is what the Puritans did when they settled the land. Although, as we shall see, the Puritans were not always correct in their theology as to whether the Old or New Testaments were applicable. Nevertheless, it is the same physical land and the same spiritual, and in some cases, physical descendants. The reason why we can apply it to spiritual aspects is because the New Testament says we are the seed of Abraham by faith (Galatians 3:26-29). Atheists and agnostics must also understand God does not disavow the Covenant just because they walk away from it. Once they enter into a covenant with believers and believers enter in to Covenant with God, it is sealed. I wondered if that might not be the psychological reason—I understand the other reasons—so many unbelievers attempt to shut Christians up and out of the public square. It's an effort to remove all signs of Judaism and Christianity from this nation. If that can be done, some feel they are then justified to ignore the Covenant and its after effects. Yet this will not nullify those consequences of Covenant-breaking.

This removal of religious tradition is almost complete in our legal system and our schools. Let me ask a question. If we were talking about Buddhists in Tibet, Hindus in India or the Inuit of Canada, and we told them their "myth" and the founding of their various habitat was not what the documentation, history or what their ancestors said and passed down to them was, wouldn't we call this rude and racist against that religion and culture? I have witnessed exchanges which have mocked and belittled, to the point of hatred, anyone who gave proof for the religious aspects of the founding of our nation as well as the documents that produced. The arguments have shown how little we understand of the founding era and frankly what substandard education is going on in a good portion of our colleges. A myth is a story which cannot be proven. This is hardly the case with the religion foundational to the traditions and practices of America.

When Joshua was leading the second generation of Israelites to the Jordan, they set up stones as a memorial of the Covenant. They then circumcised themselves again because a new generation had been born who had not so consecrated themselves to the Covenant. I thought about that and realized why so many are kept busy in court trying to remove religious symbols is because so many different generations of Christians and Jews have set up memorials to remind themselves, their children and God about our Covenant. This is the significance of the memorials. Thus the real need by others to remove them. In ISIS controlled areas of the world, they destroy any monument which does not support their worldview.

I wonder what would happen to these groups or individuals if they headed overseas to Saudi Arabia or some other Islamic region and tried to remove some reference to Islam from their graveyards and their national memorials. I think we all know the answer to that. Unfortunately, Joshua neglected to raise up a leader, and generation of leaders after him. While memorials can be set, if you neglect to teach the next generation the truth, they will lack the spiritual, legal and economic skills necessary to maintain a nation of covenant-keepers. In our unique American tradition that means the spiritual, legal and economic tools necessary to maintain liberty and freedom in those three areas.

Do you want to know why Christians and Jews don't go through a huge, slice-your-throat-and-storm-the-streets through demonstrations, rioting and plundering when you insult them and the God of the Bible? Because they don't have to defend Him. He does a pretty good job defending Himself. If unbelievers are so sensitive in their non-belief that a cross or menorah dedicated generations ago offends, then I would submit it is possible some are having a hard time reconciling the defense of their philosophy with the evidence seen concerning the existence of God.

Because Christians and Jews don't seem to protest violently, they can make an easy target for groups to remove and destroy monuments through the guise of "freedom of religion." Historically the pretense for attacking our First Amendment started early. It has taken time, but the methodology has become perfected. We will review some of the history concerning this in a future chapter. One evidence for our lack in understanding covenant are the attacks. In days gone by, the understanding and attitude of covenant prevented one group of Americans from attacking others. We were brothers and sisters as Americans. Now, the easiest marks make for prolific bullseyes of abuse. It is amazing to watch the bullying going on against anyone who would stand up for their First Amendment and Second Amendment rights. Under any unbiased view, it would be quite easy to spot these attacks as a targeted campaign to undermine our form of government.

If our captivity is in our decline, standing armies or some other loss of freedom through socialism (progressivism), sharia law or some other philosophy or our own addictions— as much as I do not want that to happen— those circumstances all by themselves are proof of captivity for any generation reading back through the pages of history. Facts and history should not be ignored to view our Covenant. Covenant should be viewed as a defense technology which keeps the country safe. One group may not like another's freedom of religion or right to bear arms, but when you erode one inalienable right, you erode all inalienable rights. That's the beauty of our specialized covenant in this country. Unfortunately, that is its Achilles' heel. It matters very little the methods used, whether lawsuits, social media or ignoring the law concerning an individual's inalienable right; a successful attack on one inalienable right is a successful attack on all inalienable rights.

In days gone by the assault was waged under our freedom of speech laws. A healthy argument ensued from all sides and uncovered the blitz for what it was: A sham argument to become a protected entity, thus weakening all inalienable rights. Since that method produced no success, it became obvious freedom of speech needed to be silenced another way, and our educational system needed to be controlled. The only way to do that is illegal. The enemies of freedom found no hope to control the population. The population needed to be dumbed down for the bombardment to be successful. Then a doctrine foreign to our laws needed to be infused, without notice, and without a fuss. Let's see . . . money has always bought populations in the past. Can money do it again? The answer, of course, is yes; but then there are those pesky freedom of religion types that find their inalienable right to practice religion as a sacred trust. They are constantly teaching people money is only a tool, and they must take the long view to prosperity, not quick gratification. We've got to take them out first. And that my friends is how the plans have been birthed. America is too great of an economic prize for her people to be left free and in liberty, not beholden through money, health or psychology to the captivity and angst of Eurasian monarchy (socialism), Oriental anxiety and Middle Eastern tyranny.

I will prove this as you read. But for now, let's take for example, the book, "The Godless Constitution." I got my copy and was looking forward to a lively debate based on the title. I went to the footnote section to review what I thought had to be hundreds of privately held and/or university archived documents. Well, imagine my shock when I discovered there were none! I went to the front cover and saw another odd title, "A Moral Defense of the Secular State." As I read on I soon discovered these authors had no intention of proving their initial claim.

The second claim (to be moral) gave me no basis for their morality. You can be your own sense of morality or you can be someone else's. There is no standard unless you use Karl Marx, who some claim as the father of the modern secular state. The only 'code,' if you will, would be the Socialist (Communist) Manifesto. I enunciate that in the last section, so I won't do that here. You can use Greek or Roman secular definitions or you can use various secularisms. You can even go back to the Hammurabi Code. Those authors also try to hook their definition of secularism with the understanding of separation of church and state. That would be a fine premise if they actually followed through as to why the theory developed and the reality of the book it came from. But alas, to acknowledge one of arguably only a handful of the oldest legal and social texts in the world (the Bible) as a source would, frankly, disprove their theory.

No matter how hard you try, if you actually review the hard-copy documentation, you cannot make America a state founded on secularism. Yet, at the same time, within the same parameters, you cannot make us a nation exclusively founded as a strict theocracy. There were early theocracies within early state territories. Most folks are absolutely shocked to find that out. We will look at that later. The book does provide a recommended reading section, titled, "A Note On Sources."[7] I was disappointed because, in my opinion, it reminded me of a state-run media PR stunt. There were questions and points made which others have asked and answered; frankly, with different answers and in a far more scholarly and accurate fashion.

In my opinion it seemed like a double standard. I expected more from professors teaching college students. Imagine my second shock as I spoke with young adults who have mortgaged their first-born children to get an education, only to find in reading such a book and taking classes from these kinds of professors, they were signing on for the morphine drip in propaganda from a state-run media crusade. Dumbing down the population is easy if they don't know their history.

If you want an unbiased opinion, not framed by state-run media PR, we need to look at historians who researched the constitutional process. It was a process which took 150 years. Most folks have the attitude the Declaration of Independence somehow flowed from Jefferson's pen. Once they find out he was among a committee of five assigned the task, and most of what he wrote had been published in public newsprints previously for years, they are surprised. They become even more surprised to learn these public documents had a large number of sermons which were written before being preached in churches. They are equally surprised to learn the churches were the "TV" and "Internet" conduits for disseminating the information of freedom and liberty. It was a process which actually started in 1619 and continued through 1791. For that process one must include the documented covenants and charters, state constitutions as well as the other Federal documents. Those would be the Declaration of Independence and the Bill of Rights. Some believe the Articles of Confederation should be included as well and I would not disagree.

I would have no problem with a godless document if that were the totality of the truth and sum total of the evidence. It really would have no bearing on this book for outlining our covenant. But that really is not the sum total of the evidence. There are many books out there trying to tell you something based on a small portion of evidence to make a point for a certain conclusion; while the sum total of the evidence proves a very different fact.

Again, my purpose is not to prove God in all our documents. My finding is not in a 'godless' Constitution. My research has lead me to believe the Constitution (the one part of our three-part governing document) is a 'color-blind' document, and not necessarily 'color-blind' as we define the term today. In other words, it adds a dimension of non-partisan orthodoxy— non-sectarianism— smack in the middle of the other two documents, but as a perfection of the previous Articles of Confederation which came before it. It does this in an effort to show justice and equal federal covenant to the various states, religious faiths at the time (Judaism, Christianity and the myriad of various denominations of Christianity), the various political parties as well as mankind in general (women, children, slaves, religious dissenters). I believe that was a critical desire (among many) in framing a constitution for the various founders. It was the result of hundreds of years of history that no form of government would hinder the people or the rights God gave them. No form of government would hinder the public flow of ideas or hinder religious belief and practice. That protection afforded by a governing body to the different groups (or denominations) in existence at that time would not be based on government, but on non-biased covenant fidelity, based on inalienable rights.

Inalienable rights are rights given by God, not man, not government. They are not based on what any group collective viewed within social media think. Those rights cannot be taken away by anyone either. They go way beyond the secularist definition of "universal rights." When we covenant and exchange an inalienable right for the protection of the larger group, we do so judiciously, cautiously and at a great expense to our freedoms. They are not exchanged cheaply. In the "universal" method everyone has a right. Inalienable rights are a sacred trust and gift. The reason why any group can claim covenant rights now, is because there were so many church denominations who wanted *their* rights. The governing compact had to be "colorblind" or non-sectarian. Governmental history is that governments cannot be trusted. That idea is not an old idea from some crusty century where documents were written on vellum (cow hide). It's being written before our eyes.

Recently, the Environmental Protection Agency just wrote the 2015 Clean Water Rule.[8] If you just read that sentence and glossed over it without a thought crossing your mind that something had to be wrong with the sentence, then YOU have been dumbed down by the same media-morphine laced drip our college students are hooked up to. Our Constitution is clear that only Congress can write laws. But something very scary has gone on within our political parties and with our elections. With each one, the people's body (Congress) has lost more and more power and presidents have consolidated more tyranny by allowing these federal departments to write what started out as "guidelines" to function by.

Those regulations have now become their own laws whereby an American can be charged with a crime without ever needing to make the case for their own innocence. Innocent until proven guilty is a cliché instead of a rule of law. That's because federal departments like the EPA now write their own regulations. We have a federal legal system the likes of which not even the lawyers can count how many laws it contains. Continue reading to view the stories of heartache for those caught in its clutches.

Our founders were so careful with our rights and our documentation that today atheists have inalienable rights because early Christians fought for their own rights. Some historians would find it odd I would include atheists in the group, since it is historically hard to find an atheist in this country at that time. In early America it is much easier to find those who didn't believe in organized religion, but they believed in a god.

Furthermore, many countries routinely persecuted atheists to the point of death, especially in pagan societies. Atheists were more prevalent overseas in Europe from about 1740 on. What I found concerning our founders was that these folks were reading their Bibles, and it affected their thinking in ways we do not appreciate. More than once we see within those pages God's hand extended to the "stranger" (Psalm 145:9;146:9). That term meant more than just an ethnically different traveller. It was a term which meant *not part of the covenant people,* or in many of the Bible-reading population of the time, a non-believer and/or an atheist. Contrary to popular opinion, the Bible does not equate the stranger with the wicked (see the previously quoted psalms). In fact, biblically speaking, the wicked can be quite religious while the stranger can wind up with God in paradise if he relies on Him in repentance (see Jesus' treatment of the thief on the cross).

I am not a believer in the accommodationist approach which has replaced covenant in this country; so you will not see it within these pages. I mention this now so if you read something which might sound as if I am attempting to "fit" everyone in, you will understand that is not my intent. My approach is to reveal what having a true covenantal understanding would do for us, as opposed to just making us all fit in or "try" to agree with each other. I do not see divergent sides ever "agreeing" as in an accommodationist approach. Non-sectarian does not mean secular. In a non-sectarian or "colorblind" application one enacts a law to include all sects of various denominations. You could use the term "colorblind" to describe this approach. In a secular world you are specifically omitting religion. You must deny its very existence if you can! You cannot give it any credence. It is obvious from this practice that leads to bigotry and discrimination. There has been a slippery slide with the definition of the word and you have seen me employ that here already. *Secular* now meaning something that doesn't have to have a religious connotation. Unfortunately, there is a danger in using the word with that definition because this can also lead to discrimination.

As you can see, I also have no desire to be a revisionist in the study approach I took to write this book. Without the hard and exhaustive work of unbiased scholars, I don't think we would ever be able to trace the covenant, or concept of covenant I found flowing throughout the founding/framing time period to roughly the 1940s. I, and countless generations before and after me should be grateful for their work. You might ask why I mention covenant and the Federal Constitution at all. The word *federal* comes from a Latin word *foedus,* which originally meant covenant.[9] If you look at the endnote and the etymology of the word, those who would wish to argue could say federal does not mean that to them now. Well, if it was you or me who chose to use the word hundreds of years ago, then it would matter. Since neither of us did that, then it is the people who did it who define the word. Its definition starts 150 years BEFORE they used the word; just as our definition NOW has expanded from 150 years since the framing generation applied it.[10]

This is the kind of treatment of words and documents I used in writing this book. In other words, if we started something, how did the people who started the process do it and are there still the same people involved in the process or result today? In other words, like the tribal folks of other nations who carry and embody the philosophy from their ancestors, do they still follow the same practices and belief system now, and can they prove a continuity of that practice or doctrine?

If you've been on the morphine drip of social media and socialism for any length of time, the idea of covenant holding our country together will seem odd. But I am going to ask you to disconnect from the IV for a moment— that's right, pull it out of your arm. Take a deep breath and think for just a moment before you continue reading. I've heard many of you wonder why the right for freedom of religion extends into the public square and why the right to say what you believe, especially based on your thoughts or scientific research is so important. Yet think about how often you would like to silence people whom you refuse to agree with. Some of you even want laws for college campuses that don't confront you with speech you don't like.[11]

I've read how many of you want the right to bear arms to stop. Heck, we have government writing laws to disarm us. The scientific facts prove America, with all her guns, is number one in gun ownership, per capita, out of 218 countries. So naturally, the mind would tell you that should make us number one in per capita murders, especially with all the news media coverage of all the massacres, right? Well, not exactly. America ranks per capita in murder rates, somewhere near the middle at 111. The top ten countries in per capita murder belong to socialist-leaning and socialist gun controlled countries. In point of fact, it is those states and regions of America where gun control is the *highest* which allows high murder rates. In those places in our country where guns are controlled based on our original Constitution and traditional Second Amendment rights, the murder rates are much, much lower.[12] Many argue the reason for that is more guns mean more citizens have the right to protect themselves. It is a compelling argument possibly backed by research. Though I have not read a study asking criminals if they feel more compelled to rob the store owner with no firearms and firearms' training as opposed to those who have both. I will continue to look for that research.

My argument is that the "tech" of covenant keeps the crime rate down in those sections of the country like nothing else can. Covenant bases itself upon the biblical mandate of "do unto others as you would have them do unto you." In other words, I want to be able to protect myself with a firearm, and so should my neighbor. I don't want to get shot, and I'm assuming my neighbor doesn't want a bullet either. Culturally, children should be taught all the rigors and responsibilities of this ethic. When laws codify that requirement, as our originally written Bill of Rights has, you step into covenant accomplishment, securing health and protection for the largest group of people. You will always have the mentally ill as well as criminal deviant in any society. It is not our originally written Bill of Rights which expose us to their sickness, but the socialist controlled federal rules and regulations preventing all of us— including gun shops— from knowing who these people are. These newer rules and regs are creating chaos and destroying what was a covenant-based and prosperous country. Let's take a look at the history of how we got to where we are now.

ENDNOTES

1   AZ pastor thrown in jail for housing a church in his house: <http://www.foxnews.com/us/2012/08/05/arizona-man-sent-to-jail-for-holding-bible-studies-in-his-home/> MS church denied the right to lease a building in the town square: <http://www.foxnews.com/us/2012/08/09/miss-congregation-fights-town-square-church-ban566512/> Business leader threatened with economic losses by elected officials and pro-liberal groups because of voicing his religious beliefs:<http://www.foxnews.com/politics/2012/07/26/politician-plan-to-block-chick-fil-is-unconstitutional-legal-experts-say/> Same business' employee harassed by customer because of the business leader's religious beliefs: <http://video.foxnews.com/v/1777258215001/sandra-fluke-us-chick-fil-a-employee/?playlist_id=86856&intemp=obnetwork> Street preacher threatened with murder in Semmes, AL, for preaching, two good Samaritans come to his rescue and are stabbed: <www.wkrg.com> site accessed 8/10/12; preacher's name: Gene Duffy, good Samaritans: Kenneth Cushman and Steven Stuart. GLAAD convinces CNN to withdraw airtime from guests who cite pro-family scientific research: <www.cbn.com/cbnnews/us/2011/February/Faith-Groups-Challenge-Gays-to-Debate-not-Hate/> KY clerk jailed for religious beliefs in marriage: <http://www.cbn.com/cbnnews/us/2015/September/Jailed-Clerk-Becomes-in-Faith-Freedom-War>In Canada the persecution is outlined in an article by Michael Coren entitled, "Canadian Crackdown," June 11, 2012, © The National Review, Inc. In Britain a Muslim leader says Christians are under attack: <http://www.cbn.com/cbnnews/world/2010/April/Muslim-Speaks-Against-Attacks-on-UK-Christians/> Home schoolers are fleeing Sweden because of religious persecution: <www.cbn.com/cbnnews/world/2012/April/Swedish-Home-Schoolers-Flee-Parental-Inquisition>also click on related links. German family is granted US asylum because of homeschooling:<http://www.cbn.com/cbnnews/us/2014/March/High-Court-Rejects-Home-Schoolers-Bid-for-Asylum/>All sites accessed 2/15/16. These are in no way the only persecutions I have read documentation for in Western countries. They are only a minuscule sampling of what I have found.

2   <https://www.fbi.gov/about-us/cjis/icr/hate-crime/2013/topic-pages/victims/victims_final> Accessed 1/27/16

3   <http://www.cbn.com/cbnnews/us/2012/September/Most-Christians-Dont-Read-the-Bible-Much/> accessed 1/27/16.

4   Some of these cases have just been reported, others are still in litigation, so there is no outcome. For the first two an Internet search would reveal more specifics. They are Jenkins v. Community College of Baltimore County where a lawsuit was filed in the U.S. District

Court in Maryland on behalf of student applicant Brandon Jenkins after the community college mentioned denied his application because of his Christian faith. <http://www.cbn.com/cbnnews/us/2014/April/Md-College-Student-Denied-Admission-over-Faith/><http://onenewsnow.com/education/2015/07/19/colleges-reject-fail-expel-students-for-faith> The second case cited would be Enstrom v. UCLA in which the plaintiff was fired after a successful 35 years at the university because of his criticism of certain regulations and unethical practices in air pollution research. UCLA fired him for his criticisms. <https://www.thefire.org/pdfs/41bead8455fb5b5a0f7415a3b970a8a0.pdf> and <http://dailybruin.com/2015/03/05/former-ucla-researcher-james-enstrom-reaches-settlement-with-uc> A charter school in Temecula, CA, told library attendants to remove all books with a Christian message, authored by Christians, or published by a Christian publishing company. The Pacific Justice Institute sent them a letter basically informing them that they violated the First Amendment and they cited a 1982 Supreme Court ruling in "Board of Education, Island Trees Union Free School District No. 26 v. Pico," that said "local school boards may not remove books from school library shelves simply because they dislike the ideas contained in those books and seek by their removal to prescribe what shall be orthodox in politics, nationalism, religion, or other matters of opinion." <http://politichicks.com/2014/09/california-charter-school-reverses-decision-ban-christian-books> Although the news headline says they reversed the decision, this was anything but a reversal. Accessed 1/22/16.

5   <http://www.foxnews.com/opinion/2016/03/16/giant-texas-cross-sparks-atheist-lawsuit-and-wont-believe-why.html> accessed 3/19/16

6   Lutz, Donald S. 1988. "The Origins of American Constitutionalism." Baton Rouge, LA: © 1988 Louisiana State University Press. 152

7   Kramnick, Isaac, and Laurence R. Moore. 1997. "The Godless Constitution." New York, NY & London: © 1997 & 2005. W.W. Norton & Company

8   <http://www.foxnews.com/politics/2016/01/25/senators-seek-doj-probe-into-epas-covert-propaganda-on-water-rule.html> accessed 1/26/16

9   Here is the etymology of the word: "1640s as a theological term from Fr. federal, from Latin foedus [gen. foederis] 'covenant, league, treaty, alliance,' related to fides 'faith.' Meaning 'pertaining to a treaty' [1650s] led to political sense of 'state formed by agreement among independent states' [1707], from phrases like federal union 'union based on a treaty,' popularized by formation of U.S.A. 1776-1787." <http://www.etymonline.com/index.php?allowed_in_frame=0&search=federal> Online Etymology Dictionary © 2001-2016 Douglas Harper. Accessed 1/22/16.

10   Lutz, Donald S. 1988. "The Origins of American Constitutionalism." Baton Rouge, LA: © 1988 Louisiana State University Press. 153

11   <http://www.nationalreview.com/article/426979/safe-spaces-colleges-campus-incompatible><http://www.nationalreview.com/article/426853/yale-student-protest-safe-space-political-correctness> accessed 1/19/16

12   This is a YouTube clip titled "Number One with a Bullet" <https://www.youtube.com/watch?v=pELwCqz2JfE> accessed 1/20/16

SECTION THREE

Section Three:

HISTORICAL FACTS

Chapter One

WITH AN EYE TOWARD COVENANT
(FOR ALL WHO CHOOSE TO READ)

Getting back to our church relocation program, I really did try to do an 'archaeological dig' of history by using those researchers who did as much balanced work as I could find. I started by counting ships landing in North America proper and the United States mainland specifically. I also counted expeditions, especially coming up from South America.[1] I searched for as consolidated a timeline as possible concerning the history of events in this land from about 1500-1850.[2] As I continued the dig, I realized "dirt and brushes" are not something I have a passion for. That's because I started to realize with the exception of St. Augustine in Florida during the 1500s, none of these ships or expeditions produced lasting colonies which affected or made their way into our current laws or government structure until the 1600s. For sure you had native cultures in North America, but none of them produced a lasting governmental or religious effect. I am not saying there are no vestiges of them here today. Instead, that they produced no foundational pathway to govern-ment except in the laws molding specific covenants made with them by the latter Federal authorities. Those authorities had already been formed by then. In fact, today's compacts with various Indian tribes are a direct result of those early covenants.

Of the more modern expeditions (1500 through 1850), most were religious and some had elements of religion attached to them. There seem to have been a few whose desire was economic only and solely. It seems the Spanish were more involved with that practice than the French or the English. While little archeological evidence exists of them, most recently a site in northwestern North Carolina has been excavated within those parameters. The garrison was built by Captain Juan Pardo and was settled around 1567. It was inhabited for only two years and, like others of its kind, produced no lasting results in foundational governing structure.[3] I was surprised to find an attitude in academia within some circles of ignoring a religious attachment to any of our founding expeditions. To me it would be important to be mentioned as history. This would give a more comprehensive overview of who these folks were.

An example of this would be Columbus' 1492 expedition. In fact, Christopher Columbus was so religious he is quoted writing about the how and why of his voyage: "I found our Lord well-disposed toward my heart's desire, ...Who doubts that this illumination was from the Holy Spirit? He, with marvelous rays of light, consoled me through the holy and sacred Scriptures, a strong and clear testimony .... encouraging me to proceed and continually without ceasing for a moment, they inflame me with a sense of great urgency."[4] I read many modern voices who said Columbus kept his first voyage secular in nature because there were no clergy on the three ships. The standard for the definition of secular seems to be the lack of clergy. I tend to disagree. That's because they did keep what they called daily vesper services.[5] These are nightly prayer meetings. My thought is if they kept nightly prayer meetings, why would you say they were strictly secular? By any standard a nightly prayer meeting is not secular. We never hear about Columbus' faith. His faith might seem remote to some now, but it was the overriding reason he undertook his voyages: He believed God was sending him on a mission.

I would like to debunk some other myths I have read and heard over the years. The crown of Spain did not take forever to sign Columbus up for the journey because they were afraid to mess with the church over the flat-earth myth. First of all, the crown of Spain had just taken areas back from Muslim domination and they were still struggling militarily and financially. They didn't have the money to waste. The Muslims had blocked a safe way to the East and Africa. In an effort to basically kill two birds with one stone (promote the Catholic Gospel of Jesus Christ and get the goods they needed in a cheaper and safer way), the monarchy agreed to support Columbus' voyage. Oh, and the flat-earth myth? It was promoted by two atheist authors of great influence in the late 1800s in an effort to shame and cause hatred for the church (Andrew Dickson White and John William Draper). That myth had been around for many decades before they put it in print. They, as well as many before them, ignored documented medieval scholars of the time such as Venerable Bede, Roger Bacon and Thomas Aquinas who built on the ancient Greek's knowledge of the earth's circumference by debating the size of the oceans and the earth's mass.[6]

The scholarly and educated within the church and outside the church believed in the concept of "Orbis Terrarum." This meant water made up most of the **GLOBE** with small land masses spread out around it.[7] They understood the word globe meant *round*, not flat! What the church tried to keep quiet was the thought of large people groups who had not been evangelized. They wanted to boast that the church at Rome had reached the entire world with the Gospel, thus hastening Jesus' Second Coming. Remember what I said about kids with loaded guns? Columbus ran into a similar problem as Galileo will after him: jealousy and power struggles. The church was only a player in those struggles along with many other courtiers and financiers of the time.

The flat-earth myth doesn't show up in text books pre-1870s. It was Earth, NOT as-the-center-of-the-Universe (Copernican theory), which gave the ignorant of the clergy ulcers. The scholars of Columbus' time knew full well the earth was round. Finding other continents with masses of people groups was one target for heresy. For me, this "flat-earth" myth is proof of the sad fact hatred or disrespect for the thoughtful ideas of others, even when we disagree with them, produces stunted discoveries in research. Of course, even Columbus thought he landed in Japan and Malaysia. Discovery through research is a process. We don't always "arrive" immediately to the truth. By the third journey, he knew something was wrong with his theories and figured he hit the Garden of Eden!

Other explorers were coming upon this new land and finally, in 1507, a German monk by the name of Peter Martyr had his theory published which suggested another continent existed between Europe and Asia.[8]

Over time, this sent the church into the reality they could evangelize more souls. Hence, with many an expedition, especially from Spain and France, monks and other clergy were sent to evangelize the natives. Even if treasure was the real goal, there was no dividing line between church and state for the goal of evangelization and treasure— both equally greedy for their own desires— both equally stated as the reason for the voyage.

Saints, scoundrels and many others came to these shores leaving behind great stories of adventure. Many made lasting claims on the memorial stones placed in their memory. For me there are countless stories to tell, but I had to restrict them to what made a lasting effect on our structural systems in the form of covenant. One could argue the colonization by the Spanish of the states we now know as Florida, Texas, New Mexico and California contributed mightily to our nation. I would agree. The Spanish left a lasting effect on the nation, especially through the promotion of Catholicism. We very often forget— or worse, are never told— that the first two Thanksgiving meals held in this country were not held by the Protestant New Englanders but by the Catholics in St. Augustine, Florida in 1565, and in Texas in 1568.[9] We call Native Americans "Indians" because many at the time thought Columbus had landed in the lands loosely termed *indies*. Of course, the Catholic French as well as the Protestant English left many customs and traditions behind for all of us as well.

Unfortunately though, reading the colonization period can be like reading a book of fiction written by a serial killer! So many murdered over settlements by the natives, the Spanish, the French and the English. By the way, believers and non-believers alike! In the mayhem of colonizing the continent so much can be lost by the bloody conquests, grants, land purchases and other dizzying history, both of religious customs and non-religious stories about the people, their countries of origin and the leaders who governed them.[10] Until the empire building by the countries of England, France and Spain dies down during the late 1800s, you really might miss the flavor and the lasting structural mores anchoring what was by then a vibrant and mostly civil society (compared to what it had been before).

I know some might say by searching religious structural foundations that I miss the sound of crashing waves onshore for a single molecular structure of H_2O. I thought so at first too. But it was that single droplet of water which turned into millions of them which produced the sound on the beach. That's what got my attention. If you will hold on for those two hydrogen and one oxygen molecule, I will prove the framework of this book as well as the nation.

For those waves, history seemed quite emphatic to me. There seemed to be only three colonies with original intent to colonize which were successful in making an effect on the structural framework of the nation. Those effects made their way through charters, compacts, state constitutions and eventually our three-part Federal documents, which our Federal Constitution is a part of. Surely many principles influenced laws later. We will look at them as well, specifically when they built upon the original work. Any school child could tell you the names of the three: Jamestown in 1607; Plymouth Colony in 1620 and Massachusetts Bay Colony in 1630. The last colony having much more in number of colonists and resources than the other two. While many dislike the fact the New England Protestants get the bulk of the credit for founding our nation, there are reasons why they get that credit. Their work was lasting and foundational. With these three, the formation of self-rule government, charters, compacts, towns and cities were made. This is the basic framework for what we see today.

Because of our autonomy from a crown, we don't always realize what impact various monarchies had on our original laws. From the time of the late 1400s to Jamestown's first self-governing assembly in 1619, none of what went on was done without one of the three countries monarchy's say-so (Spain, France and England). Generally, the custom was to give the explorer or emissary a stake in the land or some other decision-making rule for governing. The monarchs, especially in England, did their best to control what, over time, was becoming an unruly continent. In varying degrees they were able to do that until the Revolutionary War. Spain and England played a game of football with Florida at the Treaty of Paris in 1763, turning it over to England; and then, in the Treaty of 1783, it was turned back over to Spain. France finally gave up Louisiana in 1803. The 'football game' stopped when the United States purchased Florida from Spain in 1819 and it was surrendered in 1821.

So you can see to draw a sweet line in the sand and say it all went down on this date and we all had the same mindset and voila!— It HAPPENED— is just not how history played out. Those "drops of water" I talked about before became the idea for freedom. These played out over time, and became the sound of waves crashing on our shores. Those ideas of freedom, like pennies from heaven, are what we will travel through history to look at.

ENDNOTES

1   <http://www.packrat-pro-com/ships/shiplist.htm> © 1996-2015 Sharry Anne Stevens Packrat Productions. Accessed 2/25/16.

2   <http://wsu.edu/~campbelld/amlit/timefram.html> © 2015 Washington State University; timeline pages authored, written & updated by Donna M. Campbell, Ph.D., 1997-2012; accessed 2/25/16.

3   <http://www.foxnews.com/science/2013/07/27/medieval-spanish-gold-hunters-fort-found-in-north-carolina/> accessed 3/17/16

4   Christopher Columbus. "Book of Prophecies," Fols. 5 revs., 4; There are several sites that quote this. Text can be found at this site by scrolling down and clicking on the link to the aforementioned book <http://www.christianheritagemins.org/articles/> There are several good history sites that take into account the recent evidence found concerning Columbus. One of the least religious but accurate is <http://history-world.org/christopher_colum-bus.htm> accessed 3/17/16

5   <http://www.christianchronicler.com/history1/colonization_of.html> site articles written by Michael Hines; accessed 2/25/16

6   <http://www.eagleforum.org/educate/columbus/columbus.shtml> "The myth about Christopher Columbus," by Phyllis Schlafly; accessed 3/21/16.

7 <http://www.christianchronicler.com/history1/colonization_of.html> site articles written by Michael Hines; accessed 2/25/16

8 Ibid.

9 <http://www.traditioninaction.org/History/B_024_Augustine.html> © 2002-2016 Tradition in Action, Inc.; article by Marian T. Horvat, Ph.D., accessed 2/25/16.

10 <http://www.sonofthesouth.net/revolutionary-war/colonies/original-thirteen-colonies.htm> © 2003-2014 Son of the South; accessed 2/15/16. Much of the history on this site is repeated elsewhere. I use it because of the ease of consolidation. Sites are overflowing with northern as well as middle colonial "flavor." Even with those that mention southern colonies, Virginia usually dominates their discussion— and for good reason. This site's example of representing the southern colonies and history from that vantage point, presents more balance in reporting the history in general.

Chapter Two

JAMESTOWN

I don't intend to write a history lesson on Jamestown. Books have been written for that and you can read them. My question was what made these folks decide a self-governing assembly— the first in the nation— was the way to go? Atheists as well as non-believers may or may not be interested in the religious climate of the time and how it influenced government. Believers may or may not be interested in the economics of "all things colonial." When it comes to the colonial mindset it is important to view the religious, economic as well as the pertinent monarchies. I may center on the religious, but economics and the monarchies cannot be ignored.

Spain was Catholic and so was France. England was Protestant with persecuted Catholic minorities along with a group called Non-Conformists. Pilgrims, Quakers and the like— all dissenters— these are the folks who would not be a part of the Anglican Church, also known as the Church of England.[1] Because I'm generalizing, I don't want to leave the impression history happened quickly. This evolved as hatreds and persecutions lead to massacres and murders. Religious groups starting in one location would move, change their name or both. The English killed the French. The French killed the English. The Spanish killed the French. The English hated the Catholics. You get the idea. Eventually, the religious got onboard and started killing one another as well. Each was governed by their monarchy's rule back in Europe, which is where these animosities originated. In fact, to the English monarchy, the papacy looked too much like a competing empire demanding the people's adherence. To them, this simply could not be tolerated, thus the persecution of Catholics. And to say religion causes all the problems is also inaccurate. Murder and hatred are equal-opportunity warmongers. Just because a monarch or some other used the premise of religion for the violence, does not make the whole of religion the culprit. Quite often, money was the motivator.

The other difference was the way each country looked at their colony. The Spaniards and French were more successful at early colony building because of their Catholic way of wanting to work with the natives in an effort to evangelize them. The English, on the other hand, had a doctrine known as 'plantation' building. It is how they conquered Ireland. It basically means to settle a place under pressure by driving off the natives or capturing them and subduing them into a work force. Well, you can imagine the Native Americans were not going to put up with that.[2]

Jamestown advanced as well as suffered due to all of the aforementioned, along with severe hardships of many kinds. Several factors helped it to stabilize and eventually thrive. One was the cash crop of tobacco. Tobacco was the 'pot' of its day, and these good Christian folk were desperate to survive and saw no problem with its growth. Preaching of the day did not prevent certain vices; it did, however, restrict those vices as well as drunkenness, inebriation and the like. Remember what I said before about revelation and the Bible? It is a progressive thing. Like history, it is not something happening all at once. So you have to look at the customs of the time and interpret events based on those customs, not what the practice is now.

All the various charters given for Jamestown's establishment were organized under the Virginia Company. While they were a company of merchants, all members of the company were members of the Church of England. That meant they owed their allegiance to the King of England and received no authority in their lives from the Pope. There was no separation of church and state. Both had the same goals. In fact, in the original charter granted by King James I in 1606, one main goal for the colony in the realm of the 'church and state' was to further the "Christian religion."[3] As time went on though, it is obvious the settlers had the mindset of English indentured servitude. This attitude allowed them to receive the Dutch ship in 1619, which brought cargo as well as 20 black slaves. These were initially treated the same as the English indentured servants, but that didn't last long. The monarchy of England discouraged such slave trade in the colonies, but the settlers realized they had to do some things on their own. I am not excusing the practice, just stating the facts.

In 1610 they were put under the English mandate of martial law (military rule) through a document made in England naming Sir Thomas Gates the governor.[4] By the time he arrived, the permanent governor, Lord De La Warr was almost within docking distance of the shoreline.[5] This meant with the new governor's arrival, attendance at religious meetings was mandatory. Services were held fourteen times a week. Sermons were preached twice on Sunday, once on Wednesday and two prayer services were held once in the morning and evening, Monday through Saturday. I've always thought some of these practices went back to early church customs, which went back to Judaism. Jews of Jesus' time fasted twice a week and the early church did as well, only the days were changed. Jamestown's services used the Book of Common Prayer. The minister also held a catechism in the afternoon on Sunday. At one of these services they read the civil law so everyone was aware of what was required. Anyone caught not attending services was denied rations.[6] I found no historic records indicating punishments were ever given out relating to church attendance.

Their religious services became one of the cohesive forces which kept them going, whether you or I think they were too frequent. This is also what was known as the "starving time." What some of them did to survive was certainly drastic and barbaric. I'm not sure what many of us would have done to remain alive, but it is obvious the colony fell into some form of neglect. After reading many historical accounts, it seems each time the colony fell into disrepair, a new ship with a new charter would arrive, rebuilding the church. There are records of church rebuilding three times.[7] One such arrival in 1611 brought Alexander Whitacre (we now spell it Whitaker). He became known as the "Apostle of Virginia." He was a zealous evangelist and preacher. He traveled up and down the area to the different settlements we call Jamestown and cared for the spiritual needs of the colonists. Unfortunately, he drowned in the James River in 1617.

He was not the only fiery minister. Later in time the British sarcastically referred to these men as the "Black-Robed Regiment." Preachers wore black robes in those days. As the Revolutionary War progressed, England would rue the day she let these preachers flourish. An 1833 magazine, The American Quarterly Register wrote: "As a body of men, the clergy were pre-eminent in their attachment to liberty. The pulpits of the land rang with the notes of freedom."[8] Historians catalog six ministers from the Jamestown Colony as some of these "Black Robe Regiment" ministers: Robert Hunt, Richard Burke, William Mease, Alexander Whitaker, William Wickham and Rev. Bucke.[9] As part of the Church of England, they were not as fiery in their desire to separate from the English monarchy as their later brethren were (Pilgrims in particular); but sermons for freedom in Christ as a means of self-government are well documented (see future chapters). Even the "secular" leaders of a colony like Massachusetts had an everyday life with Christ. Governor John Winthrop writes back to his wife and says, "We here enjoy God and Jesus Christ, and is not this enough?"[10]

Atheists may find it difficult to understand the premise of freedom in Christ with government by the people and for the people as biblical, but that is exactly the nature of the understanding from the Bible. I am not saying a secular understanding did not reveal itself. When one does these historical studies, if you are only looking at secular research material, it may seem hard to tell which fact helped the colonists more: The arrival of the cash crop of tobacco or the cohesive ministry of their religion. But something gave them the idea of self-government, and I would submit you cannot ignore the ministry of religion from the Bible.

In 1619 Lord De La Warr died. With his death, the Virginia Company gave what was called Virginia (Jamestown settlements) more self-rule in an attempt to encourage immigration and local development. "Burgs" or different towns up and down the estuaries sent representatives who became known as *burgesses*.[11] These formed into the first assembly, known as the House of Burgesses. The first meeting took place in what we would say was church rebuilding number three. On July 30, 1619, the then governor, George Yardley convened the meeting to abolish martial law and "establish one equal and uniform government over all Virginia." It was to provide "just laws for the happy guiding and governing of the people there inhabiting."[12] Remember that church and state were one.

This first meeting of the self-governed was opened with prayer by Rev. Bucke.[13] Many laws enacted in 1624 dealt with church matters. One of the penalties concerned derogatory comments made about ministers. I actually got a kick out of that thinking if I had to spend 14 church services a week with the same group of people every single week for years, I might have made a derogatory comment or two myself! The ministers seem to have been paid well in tobacco and corn.[14]

These few and brief time periods of relative success were short-lived. In 1621, the friendly relations made with the native tribe led by Chief Powhatan ended when he died. Relations with the Indians had been tenuous over the years, when it was good. When Powhatan's brother took over he viewed the settlers as a threat. On March 22, 1622, the natives slaughtered 25 percent of the Virginia settlement; what we know as Jamestown. This attack caused the outlying settlements to close and move down the river to a more defensible area. With these trends the colony went through an economic shockwave which caused losses to the Virginia Company. It eventually went bankrupt and the monarchy in England revoked the charter thereby making Virginia a royal colony. It came under the king's direct control. He confirmed Anglicanism as Virginia's state religion and placed the church under the colonial governorship's direct oversight.

While this may seem like no big deal to us, the effects, in my opinion, sowed some of the seeds for revolt and action. The Virginia Company was what we today would consider a Christian business. These joint stock companies are viewed by some scholars as precursors for our modern corporations.[15] They cared for the religious growth and economic concerns of Jamestown. Under the monarch's oversight, these issues were not his pressing care. He appointed ministers but they turned out to be the bottom of the pack. In other words, if a minister could not cut it in England, they sent him to the colonies. The Virginians were not going to put up with this. They relied on their ministers in a way we have totally forgotten nowadays. They also had another problem: Because they were no longer self-governed, they had no control to remove incompetent ministers and ordain new ones. These folks had the best of the best minister to them and now they had the worst of the worst.

What they did reminds me of what it is to be American. They ignored the crown by simply failing to inform them when a clergyman vacated his post. This opened a position for people they called *readers*. Readers couldn't do anything official like baptize or hold communion. They could still read, pray and worship. This relates straight back to biblical Christianity, which relates straight back to Judaism. During Jesus' time you had temple authority but you also had local synagogues. In those synagogues were folks who read the Scriptures, but they were not the "nasi" or administrator of the synagogue. Biblical Christians of today rely on the Old Testament for that which has not been made obsolete by the New Testament. But Christians of yesteryear relied on the practices of the Old Testament in ways we do not today. So it makes total sense they created this new post in the manner they did as a solution to their 'governmental-crown' problem.[16]

This learning experience has been a process which has taken hundreds of years. But there are some practices we can follow today where there are Old Testament connections or symbolisms which are not counterproductive to our New Testament life, or have been abrogated by the New Testament (see previous endnote). An example of that would be how early colonial Anglican churches functioned in hierarchy. Early colonial Anglican churches typically appointed a board of twelve men selected from the congregation to act as trustees. For those not particularly religious, the number twelve may not seem significant. Within the pages of the Bible, twelve describes spiritual governance with secular as well as ecclesiastical effect. There were twelve tribes in Israel and twelve disciples for the early church. From the book of Revelation we are told there is a future where these authorities combine to form 24 seats of influence (Revelation 4).

Anglican twelve-member board of trustees then selected the readers. They nominated new preachers to the Virginia governor for approval. These trustees became known as the *vestry*. Over time their power grew and Virginia came to rely on its vestry. Some vestry were studious, others were not. George Washington was a vestryman for the congregation and for an area in which Pohick Church was located in Virginia. The vestry often served as a training ground for representatives to the House of Burgesses. Historians viewed the vestry system as the beginning of American republicanism.[17] We are a republic and our present government functions like one. Jamestown remained the capitol of Virginia until the statehouse burned in 1698. The capitol was moved to Williamsburg that year and Jamestown itself began to slowly disappear from above ground, almost lost to history.

ENDNOTES

1   Dissenters included all of the religious minorities that landed on our shores. It wasn't until the 1700s the term also included deists and a small minority of atheists. Atheists were not well represented except in France.

2   Harding, David, 2005. "Objects of English Colonial Discourse: The Irish and Native Americans." Nordic Irish Studies, Vol. 4 (2005) pp. 37-60. by Dalarna University Centre for Irish Studies. Accessed 2/25/16. <http://www.jstor.org/stable/30001519> A second site for information is <http://www.mckinneyandstewart.com/genealogy/histories/Plantation%20of%20Ulster.htm> Accessed 2/25/16. A site that looks at a politically correct version <https://www.apstudynotes.org/us-history/outlines/chapter-2-the-planting-of-english-america-1500-1733> accessed 3/17/16. There are many scholarly discussions on the mindset of the three nations when it came to their colonial empire building, and subsets of their mindsets within different years, century to century. This is a long discussion with an involved academia. So reader beware. Academia can go from Rome to the Catholics and then end in England with Protestants. I am not sure that is helpful when it comes to the economics of this issue, century to century. You can search

this subject on your own and come to the decision as to whether the statements I made are supported by your research.

3   <http://avalon.law.yale.edu/17th_century/va01.asp> © 2008 Lillian Goldman Law Library, New Haven, CT and <http://www.historyisfun.org/pdf/Background-Essays/RegionatJamestown.pdf> © Jamestown-Yorktown Foundation; accessed 3/23/16.

4   Donald S. Lutz, Colonial Origins of the American Constitution: A Documentary History, ed. Donald S. Lutz (Indianapolis: Liberty Fund 1998). [Online] available from <http://oll.libertyfund.org/titles/694>; accessed 2/25/16; Internet. Scroll down the contents page and click on "Articles, Lawes, and Orders, Divine, Politique, and Martiall for the Colony in Virginea; first established by Sir Thomas Gates Knight, Lieutenant Generall, the 24th of May 1610."

5   <http://www.nps.gov/jame/learn/historyculture/a-short-history-of-jamestown.htm> There is a short bio with links to the left of the page. You can click on it to view a truncated politically correct history. Accessed 2/25/16.

6   Donald S. Lutz, Colonial Origins of the American Constitution: A Documentary History, ed. Donald S. Lutz (Indianapolis: Liberty Fund 1998). [Online] available from <http://oll.libertyfund.org/titles/694>; accessed 2/25/16; Internet. Scroll down the contents page and click on "Articles, Lawes, and Orders, Divine, Politique, and Martiall (etc.) See items numbered 1, 6, 7.

7   <http://www.nps.gov/jame/learn/historyculture/jamestown-churches.htm> The U.S. Park Service maintains this site. Their history consists of 5 church buildings and one temporary tent-like structure. This is an extremely secular site containing almost no mention of the religious practices of Jamestown. Accessed 2/25/16.

8   "The American Quarterly Register," (1833) Volume 5. 217. In the public domain.

9   Anghis, Roger. 2011. "Chapter 6: The Pastors." In "Defining America's Exceptionalism." © 2011, 2012 R. Peter Anghis, Jr. Bloomington, IN: WestBow Press, a Division of Thomas Nelson. also <http://teachinghistory.org/history-content/ask-a-historian/24635> accessed 2/25/16.

10   "Life and Letters of John Winthrope," (from 1630-1649) by Robert C. Winthrop, (Boston: Ticknor and Fields, 1867) 48. In the public domain.

11   <https://en.wikipedia.org/wiki/Burgess_(title)> see "Etymology." Accessed 2/25/16.

12   <http://www.nps.gov/jame/learn/historyculture/the-first-legislative-assembly.htm> <http://www.ushistory.org/us/2f.asp> accessed 3//18/16

13   <http://www.ushistory.org/us/2f.asp> accessed 2/25/16

14   <http://www.christianchronicler.com/where_to_go.html> Click on Anglicanism, author Michael Hines; accessed 2/25/16. This chronicler has exact amounts of the corn and

tobacco. I scoured sites for early laws. I have noted one source for you already <http://oll.libertyfund.org/titles/694> Scroll down to [340] #6. I found many laws concerning fines to be paid to the church for lack of morality, including derogatory statements, and fines for the minister if he failed to work, but nothing concerning the exact pay as the first source states.

15   Cairns, Earle E. 1981. "Christianity Through The Centuries." Grand Rapids, MI: © 1981, The Zondervan Corporation. 359

16   To realize how differently we interpret the Bible and history today as Christians, we need look no further than the system the Pharisees of the New Testament set up. Today we view them as this "evil" bunch. Though I make no excuses for their attempt to thwart Jesus, it was actually the Pharisees who spread Judaism throughout the countryside of Jerusalem. They and their theology would have set up the synagogue system and taught in them. It was the Pharisees who went about evangelizing for the Mosaic covenant. In fact, Jesus' own theology was classically Jewish and as such would have been more in line with the Pharisees' teaching. He was sort of "preaching to the choir" when he addressed their idiosyncrasies in the New Testament. For a good read on this, a book by Brad H. Young, "Jesus The Jewish Theologian" would help. (Published by Hendrickson Publishers, Inc., Peabody, Massachusetts, © 1995) Today we have turned Jesus into someone who misrepresents Judaism. But Jesus was not only a Jew, but he was a good Jew and his theology was classic in its Jewishness. Today many Christians have this idea the Old Testament is totally obsolete. Then you have groups who follow varying obsolete aspects of The Law. Finally, you have folks with a proper understanding of what has been made obsolete and what has not and follow those directives. Let me give an example, though it may not be the best of examples, it is something practiced by those who understand the difference between obsolete and relevant. We know Passover and Pentecost were fulfilled by Jesus (He was the Passover Lamb) and Pentecost was fulfilled by the coming of the Holy Spirit to the church, seen in the book of Acts. So we no longer acknowledge those holidays as Jewish folks would. I have had Christian friends who have attended Passover meals with Jewish friends and family. Certainly there is no harm in that, but they realize Jesus is seen throughout the symbolism of the whole meal. It is more of a learning experience and celebration for our Savior than anything else. But the third feast, beginning with Rosh Hashanah and continuing for eight days has not yet been fulfilled. In Hebrew the word literally means, head (rosh) or beginning of the (ha) year (shanah). There are many evangelical churches today who celebrate this feast because it embodies the Second Coming of the Lord with all of the new things that will take place afterwards. There are others who earnestly look forward to the holiday, but do not necessarily celebrate it in an outward way. Instead they

will look for the actual Second Coming of the Lord. Neither methods (or a combination) violate our New Testament lifestyles. This is one example. But there are other examples that violate our New Testament mandate. These would be to kill or harm someone who sins. The New Testament makes it clear we are to point out sinful behavior and reveal Christ's love and repentance in order to leave these old habits behind. There are other methods of prayer as well in exposing this to spiritual forces. In cases where such behavior is causing harm to the church, asking the individual to leave or step down from a place of authority in order to be restored, is also good New Testament policy. But 400 years ago, Puritans viewed broken covenant (because that's what sin is) from a more Old Testament narrative and treated it as such. Of course, if someone has broken a civil law, that must be reported to the relevant civil authorities. Four hundred plus years ago, in the Puritan sections, that was the church. As such, they could, though not always, apply Old Testament methods of correction. Today many Christians hold offices in civil government. Many choose to show mercy where the law allows it (like some judges or police officers). This is where we see covenant responsibility in action for Christians as they apply it in their daily lives. They can also pray for, and in, the situations they see or find themselves in.

17   \<http://www.christianchronicler.com/where_to_go.html> Click on Anglicanism, author Michael Hines; and \<http://www.mountvernon.org/research-collections/digital-encyclopedia/article/george-washington-and-religion> accessed 3/18/16

Chapter Three

PLYMOUTH COLONY

If Jamestown was the torch which lit the fuse for the founding of our flavor of government in our nation, Plymouth Colony was the fuse. Those on the ship which landed in what we call Plymouth Colony were way beyond self-government. Their idea was government answered to the people and the people answered only to God. This is the idea we see in our founding documents, and this goes directly to biblical covenant. Things back in England were not going well for those who would not belong to the Church of England, known as the Anglican Church. As with Jamestown, I can't do a complete history on Plymouth Colony. As fascinating as that history is, it's not the purpose of this book. I view Plymouth Colony as the fuse igniting our revolutionary bomb for one reason: Covenant. With the idea of the people beholden to God and government beholden to the people emanating from Scripture, it is not hard to see and understand the significance of the theology of covenant forming a more perfect union. Let's look at a short historical overview to see why.

We may not like it, but our thinking in America, both believer and non-believer has more to do with the Bible and history than either believer or unbeliever want to know. The Renaissance and the Reformation had an impact on both the believer and the nonbeliever. I was surprised to find an archaic teaching that the Renaissance got people away from all things "God" now being taught to our school children. So let's debunk that myth. The Renaissance started because of two major factors: The Black Death (two different types of plague) and the printing press. The first book printed was the Gutenberg Bible.[1] In a time before people read the Bible, Catholic priests could and did tell them whatever the church wanted people to believe the Scriptures said. Unfortunately, whether out of ignorance for what the Scriptures really said, or plain old misrepresentation, what was told the people was not always the truth. The Plagues killed large people groups. This had a dire effect on economies. As people started to repopulate, economies started to recover even more broadly. Bibles were being printed and the people could read the classics of antiquities, including the early biblical works as well as the early church fathers.[2]

All throughout this book, you will notice a running theme of economics and biblical truth as concurrent factors for our form and flavor of government. This is the nature of the argument between groups at odds as to whether our government and its documentation was founded as a result of religious or secular reasons. Unfortunately for both sides, the reasons and the documentation developed as two sides of a coin or two halves of ONE heart. You can't separate them. If you try, a "nothingness" develops. This is why covenant is necessary.

The center for the resurgence of all things biblical, classical, and in some cases economic, was Italy. To try to separate men like Galileo and Columbus from the Scriptures, or Michelangelo from his own words of faith is plain bunk and not good history. To try to put these men into the cloth of the modern-day Christian is just as wrong— or modern-day "anything" for that matter. It is important to understand the time period they lived in. They questioned the Catholic church's teachings but that doesn't mean they had no faith. Hence you had the protestation or Protestants in Germany and other places in Europe erupting in revolt: John Hus, Joan of Arc, Martin Luther, among others.[3] Even Leonardo Da Vinci called for a priest to make confession on his death bed.[4]

The classics and the sciences as well as the arts emboldened many who could now read the Scriptures for themselves, along with other works of antiquities. Most folks ignore the fact the Bible was originally written in Hebrew and Greek, not English. We have a small portion of Daniel written in Aramaic. The ancient church Fathers all wrote in Greek. Many secular scholars ignore how the resurgence in reading their works affected the Reformation. Christian writers have made the point it was the Holy Spirit who was involved in this. Fast-forward some 200 years to the framing time period and we see Greek taught to those who would write our governing compact. Lost to history is the reality that the Bible was read by many of them in its original languages. This influenced how they interpreted the book.

While this impact is playing out in history and societies, two men came up within Christianity: John Calvin and Jacobus Arminius. There were many other leaders and thinkers in the Reformation who had a huge effect on society at the time, which extends to our thinking today; but for the purpose of understanding Plymouth Colony and early colonial America, these two are paramount. Both lived during the Reformation period and the Renaissance (John Calvin, 1509-1564 and Jacobus Arminius, 1560-1609; his Dutch name was Jakob Hermandszoon). I am now going to do what every theologian will scream at me for. I'm pretty much going to oversimplify the argument the two of them and their followers had.

Calvin believed God so Sovereign nothing is made without Him and no one can be saved unless He says so, thus predestination is determined. Arminius (his followers were called Arminians) said God gave mankind human responsibility to choose whether to get saved and stay saved and to make good and bad decisions about things on the planet. In this way, man carries responsibility and can influence salvation. While this is an oversimplification, the Bible describes both as totally true and accurate. Remember what I said in the last section about Jesus being 100 percent God and 100 percent man, and that messing people up? Well, there are ten of those truths in the Bible. As I said before, they have been given names, but even naming these truths evoked wars. Ridiculous, yet true. Let's just say they are not contradictions as so many suppose. They are two equally true facts which must be given equivalent weight, but when you give equal weight to both, it goes against the law of our human reasoning. Well, when it comes to divine sovereignty and human responsibility you must do just that. And that is where the wars started. (See endnote one from "Covenant and the Kingdom.")

Thankfully, as I said before, folks know better than to go to war over this stuff. But back then, the kids were playing with a very big "gun" and lots of folks got shot. It is also, as one might expect where *one* of the streams of theology flows toward a difference in church and state. We will continue to review this in future chapters. There was no separation as a "high wall" as one modern justice opined. As a practice in the Old Testament, Aaron maintained the priestly and Moses the civil or civic— but they were brothers. To say they never participated with each other or helped the other is ridiculous. They were different people but both had responsibility in governing Israel. Divine sovereignty and human responsibility are different in application yet both one in an understanding of how our lives are governed. Let's not forget our two sides of one coin or two halves to one heart. Of course the monarchies of the day ruled in an understanding of God divining them to do so; or in some cases, the monarchy as God manifest in the flesh. So there would be no separation. Church folk were beginning to see these monarchies were as mortal as anybody else. Church theology was taking a hit from monarchists' doctrine of divinity. Thus the birth for and desire in a separation of church from state.

The monarchs had their own perverse understanding of the Scriptures. The Bible makes it clear Messiah—Jesus Christ, for us Christians—is the embodiment of the government (King) and the High Priest (sacred) here on earth. The monarchies tried to portray their deviant and abnormal practices as examples of the true expression of biblical orthodoxy. In many instances they used the Bible, or church hierarchy to give them legitimacy. It was this practice folks fought against and wanted separation from. This one tenet of the Reformation was influenced as well by the protestation against the Catholic Church. To many a reformer the Catholic hierarchy of the time, with their penchant for fascism and despotism reminded them of earthly kings (the papacy) and not the Kingdom of God they saw reflected in the Scriptures. Many of the British monarchs agreed; hence the persecution of Catholics.

This was also a dogmatic firestorm within the French Revolution, which took place comparatively in a timeline with our own American revolt from Britain. Unlike the American Revolution, France's was totally secular and as a result far more bloodier, costlier and with a more muddled outcome. One of its desires was to remove God (Catholicism was the religion of France) from government totally because the monarchy and the church were one in practice as well as subjugation.

When you study this historical episode, you come away with the differences in how our early American founders and framers viewed the theory of separation as opposed to the European (French) view because you see the original Reformation's doctrines, which both continents spring from. In most instances of human mimicry of the Divine Monarch, tyranny becomes the end result— beware the Federal government, cried the Anti-Federalists. (Have their fears been realized?) So the study of Scripture as well as other principles and examples of the brotherly division of the state from the church's business, was fundamental to those historical Americans. It is not so for us today. We have lost the basics of this philosophy.

This is where philosophy takes us to history and where history takes us back to the Pilgrims and the Puritans. Actually, *puritan* was a slang and derogatory term for two dissenting groups. Both groups, the Pilgrims of Plymouth Colony and Massachusetts Bay Colony, were Puritans. But all Puritans were followers of Calvin, not Arminius. So you would think all would go smooth in our world, right? Not so fast. Arminius' ideas came in through the Dutch Reformed which settled in many parts of New England, but especially in New York. Calvin's ideas were imported through all of the Puritan areas. Over time, a blending of the original ideas of Calvin and Arminius would ensue. For the Pilgrim time period, the question was separation or non-separation from the Church of England. Fast-forward to Virginia, circa 1776, and we can see this heritage play out as Virginia keeps a closer relationship with the Crown. (More on that later.)

Both groups considered the church to be made up of only "proven" saints: Those people who had a true conversion experience. Such people confessed their faith to one another and then bound themselves together by a covenant. The idea of covenant was essential to their,

- ✦ church government,
- ✦ government outside the church, which was not separate as we view separation today,
- ✦ family,
- ✦ community organization into townships and,
- ✦ other communities.

This idea of covenant was significantly developed by the time they sailed for the colonies. It was so developed they had society and government planned out by it. Everything in their lives was done by covenant-making; by writing out their agreements and by inviting God into the equation. These agreements would become the binding laws necessary for their societies to function by. The premise of covenant was the backbone of the early governing documents we see in colonial America.

Back-tracking slightly, the difference between separatist puritans and non-separatist puritans is in how they viewed the Anglican Church or the Church of England (same thing, different name). Pilgrims were separatists. The separatists believed every church was a distinct unit independent of all outside Anglican hierarchy and forms of control like you see in Catholicism. As a result, separatists refused to recognize their congregations subservient to outside organizations. This doctrine would become critical in how the states came to view themselves in a federalized system, and why it is so deadly when the Federal government infringes upon states' rights today.

The separatist puritans did not believe the Church of England had done enough to rid itself of Catholicism. As a result, they believed they had a divine directive to separate from Anglicanism. They believed in the church influencing England, but not England influencing the church. Remember that Anglicanism is the divine outreach of the monarchy. You can imagine the King of England was not happy with these folks. In fact, he routinely tried to arrest them. Fleeing to Holland kept them out of his reach. Leaving Holland, they formed Plymouth Colony.

The Massachusetts Bay Colony were non-separatists. Non-separatists agreed with separatists on matters concerning the Bible and covenant but disagreed in their view of the Church of England. They believed true believers existed in these churches no matter what form the church took and to bring about change from within the established church was more Scriptural. Thus they were called non-separatists. Jamestown (and by inference, Virginia) as well as Massachusetts Bay Colony were non-separatists. Plymouth Colony (The Pilgrims) were separatists.

Both sides had slightly different views on separation of church and state. These views birthed various strains of thought, especially on economic separation. They both agreed the state is unable to influence the church on biblical and covenantal matters. They both agreed the church had the duty to influence the state on matters of spiritual as well as social norms. That included moral and economic fidelity. The argument over economic fidelity played out with England's James I in matters of taxation.[5] They disagreed in how to do that. The separatists wanted economic separation. The non-separatists did not.

While this is going on, Reformation thinking is playing out in Holland, Germany, Sweden and many other places where large groups of folks will eventually resettle in the colonies which become our first thirteen states. Thus the groundwork and practice of church covenant-making as forms of government would already be socially imprinted on these folks. In those places where the Catholics settled, there will be an underlying tone of Renaissance thinking— Catholicism will remain— although the puritan form of covenant will eventually take over. Persecution of the Catholics will remain as well, and keep their numbers smaller by comparison.

Getting back to Plymouth Colony, both Pilgrims (Plymouth Colony) and Massachusetts Bay Colony were firm in their covenant of relationships one to another and to the idea of the structure of family units. Even if a family unit could not be found, they put folks in one so they would remain connected and in covenant. Covenant was key in all things, including political life. This is also one of several fundamental reasons why you see so many groups coming to the colonies under charters and the charters mentioning God. They were making an agreement and bringing God into the equation for success, they just didn't always word it the same. Plymouth Colony was the first in this country to apply covenant, as it is in the Bible, directly to secular politics.[6]

They also looked on "unbelievers" as the Old Testament did by calling them "strangers." The Old Testament uses different words which our English Bibles translate as *strangers* or *alien*. One idea translates as an ethnic foreigner, another means a sojourner. In other words, these folks are not part of the covenant people. While these 'strangers' may have believed in God, they were not part of their Puritan covenant (church). Even in this decision by a person to not be a part of the covenant people, Puritans would still try to make some type of covenant with them because the God of the Scriptures did with the people of Israel and the *strangers* who lived among them (2 Chronicles 6:32 & 33).

Puritans did not view some things spiritually as Christians do today. Marriage was more of a civil-civic rather than a religious custom. Arranged marriages were made, but a girl could veto the choice made for her. Love was not as we see it today. It meant to physically care for someone so romance was not necessary. But several myths remain. One is they dressed to be unfashionable; not true. Their dress was fashionable when necessary but practical also when necessary. Another is they spent hours and hours preaching; not true either. Their services were much shorter, usually no more than an hour and most of them leaned toward the practical instead of the purely spiritual. In other words, where the rubber meets the road kind of stuff.[7]

A third myth is they were somehow devoid of understanding human sexuality and rigidly self-righteous; not so either. They saw healthy human sexual relationship as normal. They just believed obsession was unhealthy and to be discouraged. I think we could all agree with that after viewing our own modern history of sexuality. They did practice the custom of courting. With that custom came the odd practice of *bundling*.[8] This is where a courting couple comes into the home of the bride-to-be and a sleep-over may possibly happen. Well, they would put them in sacks and sew the sides up to the neck of one, usually the man, or both of the pair. As you can imagine, girls got pregnant. For some odd reason, they didn't view this as a problem; namely because they would make sure all was made right by the covenant of marriage! Even when a girl did get pregnant without such a history, Puritans still tried to establish a family unit in an effort to maintain covenant.

Remember what I said before about not understanding their Bibles fully? Like little children with a loaded gun? Their theology was not perfect and as a result their practices were not perfect. But looking at us as a nation now— atheist and religious alike— I would say exactly the same of us. Adultery and homosexuality were punished severely, mainly because covenant had been broken and in their eyes there was no turning back from that. Later with the Massachusetts Bay Colony, we will see how covenant extended to town structure. But the idea of covenant and it governing people was central to the puritans of Plymouth Colony.

I will debunk one other myth: The witch trials— not that they didn't happen or they were somehow okay— but that these people were more evil or intolerant than other groups all across Europe who routinely slaughtered 'witches.' While the Pilgrims never signed on to the trials— they occurred in Massachusetts Bay Colony only— I mention them here to confront some of the mis-stated facts we learn. To read the stories of how the whole affair of the "Salem" trials took place is to ask oneself, "Could this really have happened?" It is so ridiculous and sad.

What is seldom taught in schools is that all across the world witch trials were taking place. In Europe alone thousands died. Compare that to the 19 or 20, plus two dogs, (depending upon what source you read), who were murdered here, and I submit it's still bad, but not the mass murders we see in Europe. In Europe this kind of thing went on for years. Here they lasted four months.[9] The much shorter duration in Massachusetts Bay Colony is because Christian leaders like Reverend John Wise, Reverend Increase Mather and Thomas Brattle challenged the trials because Biblical Rules of Evidence and Due Process were not being followed. Of course you never hear colonial courts had such rules. We will discuss this briefly later.

In October 1692, Governor Phipps formally stopped the trials. Later the Massachusetts Court publicly repented and set apart a special day of fasting and prayer to ask for forgiveness for "the late tragedy raised amongst us by satan." Those involved publicly repented.[10] Again, it doesn't excuse those in the name of Christ who committed atrocities, but thankfully the influence of real Christian leaders didn't allow it to become the massacre it did for the rest of the world. I realize that's little solace for those and their families who were victims, but history is full of the religious and non-religious doing this kind of stuff. Early church historian Charles Galloway said when the Puritans "are compared to their brothers in England and all Europe, they stand out as reformers of the most advanced and majestic type."[11]

Turning our attention back to the Pilgrims, when they left England for refusing to be a part of the Anglican Church, they relocated to Holland. When that was not progressing well, they decided to emigrate to the New World. As a religious group they brought together money and funding for the ships from their own pockets but that was not enough. So they had to join with those they called *strangers*. While not connected to their church, the strangers were willing to pay for passage to the New World for whatever reason of treasure, fortune and adventure. The Virginia Company had secured a legal charter for land settlement north of Jamestown in northern Virginia. The Pilgrims worked under the Virginia Company's charter and northern Virginia was their destination. So while not holding their own charter, the Pilgrims believed they "covenanted" with the Virginia Company and agreed to go where the charter told them to go.

As they brought covenant with them, there are some who believe they also brought an early form of capitalism with them. The evidence for both covenant and capitalism should not be ignored, though the evidence for covenant is far stronger. Many look at the economic atmosphere in Holland and Amsterdam as early forms of capitalism.[12] Early merchant guilds functioning in commerce and trade would have been hard to avoid for these Pilgrims who needed cash. While there is solid evidence for their covenantal ways, the evidence for their economic methods will have to be left for another book.

The harrowing tale of the ocean adventure is well documented. We all know the story, except one little, but major part some forget. Two ships set sail, the Speedwell and the Mayflower. The Speedwell became unseaworthy and both ships returned to England. Eventually all crowded onto the Mayflower: Saints, as the colonists called themselves; and strangers, as they called those from the crew, officers and others who were not part of the church. The journey was nearly the end of them. The upper decks leaked and the ship cracked a main beam. The strangers wanted to turn back, but the beam was secured by a giant screw miraculously provided by the saints. They brought it thinking they would need it for their building program once onshore in their new home. (I couldn't make this stuff up.)[13] Yet even then, the strangers threatened to leave when they came ashore. The Pilgrim leaders understood they were not landing in their appointed and legally chartered (covenanted) destination. Therefore, nothing was keeping the group together. To separate meant certain death for all. What did they do? They did the only thing a good puritan would do. They covenanted with the strangers as Israel did in the Old Testament with the strangers among them. Thus the Mayflower Compact was born. In the Pilgrims' mind if they brought God into the equation, He would give them success.

I know the atheist among you as well as the non-religious are not going to like what I am about to say. I apologize ahead of time. If there really is a God and if He really did birth the nation of Israel and do all that *covenant* stuff back then— guess what? If you're an American citizen, your atheist or agnostic forebears covenanted with that God and with the believers that landed here. But you say, "We are under a Federal Constitution." Yes, we are; but did the concept of covenant find its way throughout, and do we have memorials to that idea of covenant and do we have the people groups with federal or fidelity or 'fides' (faith) left in this country? Read on and let's see.

Those Native Americans who understood the "English" and understood their religion, understood covenant and even its effects. You can read about the agreement made between the Pilgrims and Massasoit, who was the chief and Grand Sachem of a number of Indian groups living around Narragansett Bay to Cape Cod. These Native Americans lived from parts of Massachusetts to Rhode Island. They were also known as the Wampanoag Indians. The covenant made by Massasoit and the Pilgrims remained in effect during his lifetime. Why only his lifetime? His son broke the covenant and they were driven out of the land.[14] Although, in reading the history it is easy to see how William Bradford technically broke the covenant in delaying the handover of the Indian Squanto.[15]

The Mayflower Compact remained a part of their constitution until Plymouth was incorporated with the Salem settlements into Massachusetts in 1691. Because the Pilgrims landed in the location they did and settled in the former tribal land of Indians who had been wiped out by disease, they were able to be taught how to survive by the Indian Squanto. It is doubtful any of them would have made it without his help. His own story is an amazing tale the hand of Providence played in this nation. Captured, taken to London, almost sold into slavery in Spain, spared by Spanish friars and taught Catholicism, he travels back to England and eventually makes his way back to the land of his birth.[16] This is where he meets the Pilgrims and their God.

The reality and another 'miraculous fact' is if the Pilgrims had landed in Virginia or the northern parts thereof, as their charter had designated, they would have been vehemently persecuted because of their separatist and non-Conformist practices. The fact of their lasting influence could easily have been called in to question. Thus their idea of covenant and its specific outreach of separation, would have been a doctrine without a foothold in our nation.[17]

There are always benefits to covenant for both parties as there were back then. It carried weight far beyond the landing party, as all covenants with God do (think Moses). It invited God by name into the agreement and said they were colonizing for His glory and the furtherance of Christianity (my paraphrasing). It also made sure all were in agreement to this as a covenant in the presence of God "mutually in the presence of God and one another, covenant and combine ourselves together into a civil body politick." It also made clear that out of this formation they would "enacte, constitute and frame shuch just and equal laws, ordinances, acts, constitutions, and offices, from time to time, as shall be thought most meete and convenient for the general good of the Colonie, unto which we promise all due submission and obedience." It was signed at Cape Cod, November 11, Anno Dom. 1620.[18] I submit to you that covenant had spiritual ramifications, as well as civic ones, for every charter and constitution we see for the next 150 years, and even longer.

It also follows another biblical principle those who do not study their Bibles ignore, and that is: As the beginning is, so is the rest of the group. As Christians we tithe or give God a tenth of the beginning of our income to represent the whole came from Him, and so He takes care of all of it. Israel celebrated the feast of first fruits by waving a portion of the crop before the Lord; in effect saying, "As is this portion in its bounty, so is the rest bountiful." There are many other biblical examples. As a republic (not a democracy) we take a portion out of the society and elect them as representatives. Why? To say these are the first out of many who will do what the rest of us want them to do. It is not supposed to be "us" and "them" but WE are the government. As brothers and sisters in Christ in secular and/or non-sectarian covenant with non-believers, WE are Americans covenanting for the best of the nation.

John Robinson, pastor of the separatist colonists we now call Pilgrims, charged the colony before they left Holland to elect civil leaders who would not only seek the "common good" but who would also eliminate special privileges and status between governors and the governed. That had never been done before. Where did he get the idea? He got it from the Bible. They followed their minister's advice. By 1636 they had organized representative government and held annual elections and laws as well as enacting a type of rights of the freeman (citizen). It was generally thought of as an early bill of rights.[19] It also helped that those onboard were all men of the common type in society and no aristocrats had made the journey. The practice back home would have been to allow the special men of stature to govern. Yet within the pages of the Bible, that was not always the case. So they had an example to follow when only common folk could be found.

I don't want to leave any confusion here. The Mayflower Compact was only for the colonists within their district. Yet there is proof this practice found its way throughout 150 years of document writing. But there is an added dimension here. The practice of the God of the Bible is different from my human rules. He made a Covenant with one man— Abraham— and his descendants have experienced the blessing of following and tragedy of ignoring Covenant for thousands of years. Were all of Abraham's descendants covenant people? Ethnically, yes; in practice, no. Yet the rules were still applied to the covenant nation. Why? Because the God of the Bible wants to bless, not curse. He searches the earth to find whom He may help (2 Chronicles 16:9). His word given is placed with the weight of gravity. Like gravity, once a universal function is in place, not even God will break the effects of the breach.

Thankfully, not all of His laws function the same. Time and gravity are different; covenant functions differently than space. In the case of covenant, a party to the covenant who has been faithful, can, on certain conditions, turn around the unfaithfulness of the other party. (See the history of the nation of Israel.) Even to this day, many who are Abraham's seed refuse the Covenant, yet God is still bound to the nation of Israel. While this is the Divine principle I am following in writing this book, there are still legal applications I can follow to prove the covenant form our government took. The Mayflower Compact of Plymouth Colony was only the beginning.

ENDNOTES

1   You can see the two surviving copies at the British Library's website on Gutenberg:<http://www.bl.uk/treasures/gutenberg/homepage.html> accessed 3/18/16

2   A truncated and informative history of the Reformation and its effects on the Pilgrims/Puritans that came to this country can be seen at a site © Westminster Theological Seminary and produced by Capstone Films <http://theprotestantrevolt.com> These short DVDs can be seen for free. There are eleven of them. They have books that can be purchased as well. I use no information from them, but they are quite informative, especially if religious history is something you are new to.

3   Cairns, Earle E. 1981. "Christianity Through The Centuries." Grand Rapids, MI: © 1981, The Zondervan Corporation. 259-342

4   Gillet, Louis. "Leonardo da Vinci." The Catholic Encyclopedia. Vol. 15. New York: Robert Appleton Company, 1912. 1 Aug. 2012 <http://www.newadvent.org/cathen/15440a.htm> <http://www.adherents.com/people/pd/Leonardo_DaVinci.html> accessed 3/18/16

5   Cairns, Earle E. 1981. "Christianity Through The Centuries." Grand Rapids, MI: © 1981, The Zondervan Corporation. 339

6   Ibid., 338

7   <http://www.christianchronicler.com/where_to_go.html> Click on "The Puritan Scene," author Michael Hines; site accessed 2/25/16

8   Ibid.

9   <http://xroads.virginia.edu/~CAP/Puritan/purhist.html> © American Studies at the University of Virginia. There are other sources which include the 7 folks placed in jail as well as other sources that differ on the time duration. I have not included them here because you can search them out for yourself. The statistical difference is minimal when answering the broader question of why there was such a huge difference between here and Europe. Accessed 2/27/16.

10   <http://www.wallbuilders.com/libissuesarticles.asp?id=89988> © Wallbuilders, LLC; scroll down under the title "Modernism;" page accessed 2/27/16. If this moves, it may be accessed by <http://www.wallbuilders.com> then click on Articles, then click on "John Adams, Was He Really An Enemy of Christians?" There are sites noted in this book that have thousands of original documents relating to our American history. This site boasts over 10,000. It is one of the smaller sites, but you can call them up and request to see a document. That is unlike any of the others with a much larger inventory, even though the larger sites put up all or most of their documentation.

11   Bishop Galloway, Charles B. "The Quillian Lectures, 1898." In "Christianity and the American Commonwealth." "Delivered at the Chapel at Emory College, Oxford, GA, March 1898." Nashville, TN: Publishing House Methodist Episcopal Church, South, Barbee & Smith, Agents. 90.

12   <https://en.wikipedia.org/wiki/History_of_capitalism> accessed 2/28/16

13   <http://www.pilgrimhallmuseum.org/william_bradford.htm> article written by Dorothy Honiss Kelso, accessed 10/25/15. You can read more concerning the Pilgrims by clicking on the links embedded within the aforementioned article, as well as all the links on this site. This museum also houses original documentation from circa 1600 for historians who wish to book appointments.

14   <http://xroads.virginia.edu/~CAP/Puritan/purhist.html> American Studies at the University of Virginia; accessed 2/27/16.

15   <http://mayflowerhistory.com/tisquantum> site copyrighted © 1994-2015 MayflowerHistory.com. Accessed 2/28/16.

16   Ibid., <http://www.native-american-indian-facts.com/Famous-Native-American-Facts/Squanto-Facts.shtml><https://en.wikipedia.org/wiki/Squanto> accessed 2/28/16

17   You can also read the Mayflower Compact or the copy William Bradford made afterwards. The original has not survived. <http://www.pilgrimhallmuseum.org/bradford_william.htm> There is an article by Dorothy Honiss Kelso and links to the Mayflower Compact. There is also a site maintained by American Studies at the University of Virginia that also has a copy of the Mayflower Compact. <http://xroads.virginia.edu/~CAP/Puritan/purhist.html> accessed 2/27/16. One last site that has copies of all of our founding documents<http://www.lonang.com> To link to a copy of the Mayflower Compact after the initial address add </library/organic/1620-mc/>

18   <https://en.wikipedia.org/wiki/Mayflower_Compact><http://avalon.law.yale.edu/17th_century/mayflower.asp> See previous endnote. Another site displaying the compact is <http://xroads.virginia.edu/~CAP/Puritan/purhist.html> site maintained and © by American Studies at the University of Virginia; accessed 2/27/16.

19   <http://www.histarch.illinois.edu/plymouth/laws1.html> New Plymouth, November 15, 1636 © 1998-2011 Patricia Scott Deetz and Christopher Fennell and J. Eric Deetz. Accessed 3/18/16.

Chapter Four

MASSACHUSETTS BAY COLONY

If Jamestown was the torch and Plymouth Colony the fuse— you can guess where I'm going with this— BOOM! We reviewed differences between Plymouth Colony and Massachusetts Bay relating to the separation issue. As with Jamestown, there was no separation between church and state in Massachusetts Bay Colony. They believed similarly in covenant and covenantal family groups, all covenanting with one another and God. They did do something different or maybe just more intensely than Plymouth Colony, and that was in forming new towns. This could be because they came over with far more people than Plymouth did. In some ways Plymouth opened the door for their expansion. They did have a group settlement in Salem of non-separatist Puritans in 1626. Francis Higginson and Samuel Skelton helped to form the non-separatist Puritan church. It did not succeed.

Massachusetts Bay also learned from Jamestown's mistakes, even though their history is different. Due to questions over various land holdings and who was going to receive and compete for them in the New World, along with the attitude concerning puritans in general, the commercial company which owned land rights in "Salem" secured a charter from Charles I. Assuming this was a commercial venture, like the Virginia Company, Charles I granted the Massachusetts Bay Company the charter. It's not clear how well known it was that an overwhelming majority of puritans were involved in these business ventures. It's also assumed Charles I would not have known that the annual stockholder meetings were not going to take place in England, as other commercial trading companies did. In an interesting maneuver which moved the charter and the management, lock, stock and barrel, to Massachusetts, they made a fiat decision that the commercial company and its charter was now a political endeavor with a legal document instituting their decision.[1]

This, and the fact Plymouth's original charter and this charter were commercial charters, makes some secularists claim we started as a secular nation. This ignores the fact church and state were one. That claim ignores the religious climate and what these puritans did with the charters they received. It also ignores what they did with the documentation they made on their own. And it ignores their initial government and their lifestyles. Remember my contention that we are two sides to one coin? Without the ability to see that, we are going to have to agree to disagree.

There are some folks who feel these puritans pulled the wool over the monarchy's eyes. Maybe and maybe not. By my reading of the March 4, 1629 charter, they were "... vnder the Blessing of Almightie God, and the support of our Royall Authoritie ... att all tymes forever hereafter be, by Vertue of theis presents, one Body corporate and politique in Fact and Name, by the Name of the Governor and Company of the Massachusetts Bay in Newe-England, ... one Bodie politique and corporate in Deede, Fact and Name ..."[2] (excerpted). All they did was take advantage of the omission of a location for the stockholder meetings and took full advantage of the wording for a body politic. Other corporations conducted their meetings to make laws and function in their colonies as bodies politic, so that in and of itself was not unusual.

While it was understood this related to their business venture, as it did with other companies, there is nothing to say they can't be in New England conducting this endeavor. An attitude that only looks at the secular also ignores what the puritans from Plymouth Colony did with their documents. We will look at establishment documents and then bills of liberties (Bills of Rights), along with the constitutions in the next few chapters. But something in addition to English common law gave Plymouth the ideas of establishing themselves, attaching institutional documentation and bills of liberties. As we shall see, church governmental documentation gave them one avenue toward establishment, institutionalization and rights. The puritans of Plymouth Colony immediately formed a covenant with the strangers when their charter was no longer relevant. They then formed documents of liberties and institution. This was done nine years before this charter of 1629.

Massachusetts did other things differently than Jamestown. Their first voyage brought 700 settlers. Throughout the 1630s anywhere from 10,000 to 30,000 settlers came, depending upon your sources.[3] By 1645 they had established 23 churches arriving with 65 ministers.[4] They were also different in that they had a plan for expansion the other two colonies, as well as the southern colonies in general, did not have. For one thing, they arrived in complete family units. This was a direct result of their covenant theology. In these units were men with complimentary skills— and they stayed together, based on covenant— they moved as a unit. This gave them great success in colonizing, although an outbreak of small pox among Native American tribes didn't hurt either.

In short order they platted out towns. When one town became too large they followed an orderly plan. Three to five prominent men would request a charter from the colony's governor. The governor would only grant the charter if these men could prove they had covenanted families who had complimentary skills and, most importantly, a minister. They also had to have an agreed upon government, a method of land distribution, a church, a system in place for future citizenry and an elected leadership.[5] Even as they disagreed theologically (among other things, remaining some form of Anglican) and formed other states, they brought this method with them.[6] Scholars have termed this method, which affected every aspect of their lives, the "New England Way."[7] In a future chapter we will look at the various church documents which support this governmental approach.

Massachusetts Bay Colony churches were like all Puritan churches in that they were congregational. All decisions happened within local congregations. In their minds, for God's word to function freely, it had to be built on a foundation of each member feeling a part of the body. In order for that to happen each congregation had to be self-sufficient, exercising self-regulation. I wonder, when looking at us today with our attitudes of 'everybody belongs' that this is not where we get it from?

In short order by 1641, they had a representative form of government like Plymouth Colony. They held annual elections and instituted a bill of rights. It was called the Body of Liberties. It was a document which outlined individual rights and was drafted by devout Puritan lawyer, Nathaniel Ward.[8] The importance of their congregational way of forming churches is directly mirrored in their organization of forming towns. What informed the Puritans, in both legal and religious spheres, was God's word.[9] This tradition continued for at least the next 125 years. That understanding gave weight to covenant and extended covenant throughout the locality. This did something other settlements outside of the Puritans did not do. It minimized an attitude of "I don't need you" or "I'll go it alone." Citizenship was also tied to church membership, also minimizing that 'to-hell-with-you' attitude we see so often in political discourse today. It also gave the conversion experience civil as well as spiritual benefits. Even Christians today view salvation similarly. It is not just limited to spiritual matters. It extends to every aspect of our lives, including political aspects. It governs us.

Moses affixed a written, political-social law to the covenant governing Israel. Israel is still governed by this covenant today. Its laws have changed, been modernized and secularized when necessary. The Puritans understood the necessity for this because it is what governed them. As we shall see in future chapters, the documentation providing for these governing bodies and/or the philosophical treatises they were formed from and put into writing have been maintained by some of our colleges and universities as original documentation. That many of these documents are being disintegrated and lost to the ravages of time is a tragedy. It is a travesty they are not studied and compiled as foundational courses taught to our school children, along with the reason why they were secularized by the religious who formed this country. It was the religious who first demanded separation from the state (monarchy). In like manner, the first secularized covenantal document for government was written by those religious Christians who objected to put God's name on such a document. This was not because they hated God or did not invite Him into their government, but because oath-taking and other such avenues were viewed as sin. See the Providence Agreement of 1637 (Rhode Island).[10]

As this covenant form of government spread in the colonies, many of the religious had to make sure English common law was adhered to, without which, they could lose their charters. This happened to some. We shall see in the next chapter as the territories that were formed became states, eventually all of them adopted the same template of covenantal-compact government. They did so because it worked. It was efficient, effective— and lasting, as long as everyone understood covenant— whether they wanted to follow it or not. And it did something else no future ideology, secular or otherwise had done before: It allowed the largest number of people to be a participant in liberty, freedom and the pursuit of happiness the world has ever seen. We are losing this precious gift covenant gave to all, even for those who don't believe in God. By comparison only a tenth of the population of Athens (Greece) were considered citizens with attached rights.[11]

Please don't think I want us all to become Puritans to relive some kind of supposed utopian society, like modern-day progressives want to live out socialist paradise. That would be absurd. I write this as history so we can understand what produced our later statesmen, our Bill of Rights, Constitution and Declaration of Independence. It is why both sides of the aisle used to be able to reach out to one another. They had a common bond in whatever their background of Christianity or Judaism was— and they understood covenant— especially because they were people of one Book (the Bible).

This produced a common goal for the benefit of the country. It benefited the whole country, not solely and severally, the federal government, an individual, an institution, a department or whatever other imaginary group of humanity who wants to get "in" on the gravy train of taxpayer funds. I was very young when I remember those remnants left of that kind of statesmanship in our government. It was statesmanship which benefited the whole country. What I do remember is it was a much better system than the divisiveness displayed now. The divisiveness that has formed in our country recently is not because our template of covenantal laws do not work. It is because we have a foreign ideology that has crept into our government which does not work at all with the template we were formed from.

Said again, I have no thoughts of "Puritan paradise," like progressives trying to recreate Elysium. If Christians today had to live with the Puritans of yesteryear, one group would probably extinguish, jail or somehow diminish the other! I write this truncated religious history because there is a very real calamity which happens to a nation which loses its true story. Secularists object to the large role of religious history in the founding of the nation. I will admit it takes talent to develop courses which teach the truth of history through the centuries. In some stages of history it is largely religious and in others it is blended with murder and mayhem, possibly with some form of excuse for religion mixed in! In other portions of time it becomes more cerebral and secularized, with and without the murder and mayhem! For the sake of history and truth, I have outlined these three colonies. As we shall see, while they may have been first in foundational government, they were also first in a long line of a very similar train of thought, which produced a cohesive nation who understood covenant thought and understood it was the secret to success.

ENDNOTES

1   <http://avalon.law.yale.edu/17th_century/mass03.asp> site © 2008 Lillian Goldman
     Law Library, New Haven, CT. accessed 3/18/16.

2   Ibid.

3   <http://www.ushistory.org/us/3c.asp><https://en.wikipedia.org/wiki/Massachusetts_
     Bay_Colony><http://www.britannica.com/place/Massachusetts-Bay-Colony><http://
     www.study.com/academy/lesson/massachusetts-bay-colony-religion-history-economy.
     html><http://www.historyofmassachusetts.org/history-of-the-massachusetts-bay-
     colony> accessed 3/18/16. See also next chapter where we review a modern scholar's
     numbers for all the colonies.

4   <http://www.christianchronicler.com/where_to_go.html> Click on the "Puritan Scene." author Michael Hines; accessed 3/18/16.

5   Ibid.

6   Lancaster, Daniel. 1845 "Proprietary, Civil, Literary, Ecclesiastical, Biographical, Genealogical, and Miscellaneous History, from the First Settlement to the Present Time; Including What is Now Gilford, To The Time It Was Disannexed," Gilmanton: Printed by Alfred Prescott. 28 for a sample covenant and 46-59 for the proprietary way they settled, as they had originally in Massachusetts, with clergy among them. Public domain but can be seen in pdf through New Hampshire State's Archive. Archive accessed 1/28/16.

7   Campbell, Donna M. "Puritanism in New England." Literary Movements. Dept. of English, Washington State University, last modified 7/4/13 © 1997-2010 Donna M. Campbell <http://public.wsu.edu/~campbelld/amlit/purdef.htm> accessed 3/18/16. Another good start at a reading list would be with the "Selected Secondary Bibliography on Puritanism in New England." You can find that at <http://public.wsu.edu/~campbelld/amlit/purbib.htm> accessed 2/26/16.

8   Lutz, Donald S. and Jack D. Warren. 1987. "A Covenanted People: The Religious Tradition and the Origins of American Constitutionalism" Providence, RI: © 1987, The John Carter Brown Library at Brown University, and sponsored by The Lily Endowment, Inc; The Rhode Island Committee for the Humanities. 25

9   <http://xroads.virginia.edu/~CAP/Puritan/purhist.html>site maintained and © by American Studies at the University of Virginia; accessed 2/26/16.

10   Donald S. Lutz, Colonial Origins of the American Constitution: A Documentary History, ed. Donald S. Lutz (Indianapolis: Liberty Fund 1998). [Online] available from <http://oll.libertyfund.org/titles/694>; accessed 2/25/16; Internet. Scroll down the contents page and click on "Providence Agreement."

11   Lutz, Donald S. 1988. "The Origins of American Constitutionalism." Baton Rouge, LA: © 1988 Louisiana State University Press. 14

Chapter Five

THE FORMATION OF STATES

Some would say it is a waste of time to look at early state constitutions. I would say no one can accurately understand our Federal documents, especially the Federal Constitution unless and until you view the early state constitutions. We all know, somewhat subconsciously, we are a member of the state we reside in as well as the country we live in, but we may not know why. The Federal Declaration of Independence creates independent states and a unity or "marriage" of states. There are state documents declaring independence from Britain as well. Many are incorporated into their early constitutions.[1] Because of this, Article IV, Section 2 of the Federal Constitution makes every citizen one of both the United States and the state in which they reside— a dual citizenry. There is, as well a dual court system— one at the state level and one at the Federal level— a dual police system, governmental budgetary system and dual bureaucracies, among other dualities. The Federal senate was originally chosen by the state assembly they were sent from, not by a vote of the people residing in the state, as it is now. Through many decades the states' documentation shaped and informed the Federal documents we have now. One scholar put the proficiency of that generation in governmental affairs in a statistical way which is enlightening. The people living in the states in 1780 put out three constitutions every two years for 22 years.[2] They wrote some 1,300 pamphlets and newspaper articles on political theory a year during that same time period.[3] So what was it about them which drove such a flurry of documentation?

As I started to research how each state was formed, I realized the religious depth and desire for covenant with God each state decided to make. Initially, a few did form for strictly economic reasons, with only a minority mention of God. I did an overview of the individual states early governmental documentation by reading each constitution and/or charter. Because of the wealth of information and bulk of it, I am not going to look separately at the thirteen original, individual states (colonies) simply because every single charter or early document mentions either God, Jesus Christ, Christianity, Protestantism, the preaching of the Gospel and the state or territory.[4] It took me quite some time to read them. Some are charters and constitutions are not formed until later. I tried to get the earliest possible documents. Even the later ones mention God and/or Christianity.

To say they are purely secular documents is absurd. To say every document is a singularly religious one is equally inaccurate. Many could be described as quite religious, but certainly not all. Each one mentions God as the right of the people to worship Him as they see fit. That alone makes the document non-secular and places an emphasis on religion. I did not say the WHOLE emphasis. I mention ONE emphasis on God. Remember I need only one, from a biblical-covenant point of view. Obviously the main emphasis for all of them is to govern, thus bringing in every single one of their secular aspects. But remember, the word constitution is a derivative of the Hebrew word mitzvah. Mitzvah is covenant and **covenant is government**, biblically. Moses affixed a written law to the covenant governing Israel. In fact, Massachusetts' early constitution mentions covenant specifically while others mention it in principle.

A developed idea of covenant is what separates many colonial-American charters, compacts and early constitutions from the rest of the world. I can almost hear many screaming, "But what about Greece, Rome and Britain?" To say there is nothing similar in our formation of government to the ancient Greeks or Romans would be untrue. To say revisions made to the governing documents over time before the Revolutionary War did not bring some of these documents more in line with English legal procedure, would also be untrue. Human beings learn from one another.

In fact, one of the lessons taught in seminary is that Moses had very similar concepts carried over from ancient Sumerians and Hittites. But to say all the concepts of governing which ancient Israel possessed were identical to the other ancients would be inaccurate. As there are differences with ancient Israel and her neighbors, there are differences with our early documents of statehood and our European neighbors, as well as similarities. I don't intend to go into them. Our colleges and other schools are overwhelmed with those similarities and totally bereft of the biblical elements which helped to shape our government. We will look at the atmosphere early thinkers lived in which could have had some influence on our founders shortly. I just ask the simple question, "Was the idea of bringing God into the discussion evident?"

The documentary formation of states (colonial) has several different aspects to it. In its first respect we have charters granted by the presiding king of England to commercial ventures; religious groups hiding under a commercial venture; commercial groups with religious understanding, or aristocrats who also had some type of religious language within the charter. At some point in time (usually immediately) they then either formed church covenants or other governmental documentation. Those documents most often would have biblical underpinnings of covenant understanding which would create governing bodies. Sometimes these were theocratic only, as in the case of New Haven.[5]

In many cases, they were extremely religious— even church based— with civil outreach, as in the case of the Massachusetts Body of Liberties. In other cases they were governing bodies created by the same structural underpinnings of biblical covenant theology, but written for a secular approach, as in Rhode Island. The reason for their secular language was because of their religious belief that this type of covenant documentation was taking an oath and by placing the Lord's name in it they were using His name in vain (Matthew 5 & 6). Yet they still covenanted secularly to obtain their stated goals. In a later segment we will review the only two charters issued in England by the king to create bodies politic or colonial charter governments solely and specifically.

All these charters would be operational at the same time as a colonies' own documentation. The charters issued by England were establishment documents, giving a reason for why these people existed. These would then be, in effectual practice, compacted with what documentation the colonists wrote, or their own 'American' governmental documents. In New England many colonies formed because religious people, persecuted from one area, left to form a new one, which would eventually form what we now call states. In some cases they left England or Holland or another European area. When they did, they brought with them a system of governmental documentation which were known as compacts. Within these they infused the covenantal-biblical method, as we have seen with the Mayflower Compact. The covenantal-biblical method invited God into the equation and then covenanted with those who did not belong to their church, to function in certain ways.

Compacts got their names because they can, but may not always, pull together different peoples, geographic areas and structures of government into one document, thereby compacting the desired result. The beauty of the compact-covenant method is you did not have to declare a "people" all over again. You could make your establishment documentation (initially those were usually charters); be functioning under them, and then compact whatever institutions/laws (what we now view as constitutions) with the establishment or declaration documents, and even compact whatever else you wanted with them later in time; as they did with bills of liberties or what we call our Bill of Rights.

Taking the Mayflower Compact as an example, all compacts were agreements; but the religious used them to express a covenantal understanding by joining disparate groups. Since the Pilgrims were not landing in their designated area, they could not rely on their charter to hold the group together. The strangers in the group threatened to leave when they landed and since they were no longer bound to the designated area, that meant certain death, probably for all. So they had to rely on a new document. The compact method employed the biblical covenant but now placed it in a different venue. The ease of the compact was that they did not have to go back to the strangers to re-form when they got together to create other liberties or institutions or ordinances, as they did years later with the Pilgrim Code of Law. This method of covenant-compact came from their church governmental documents. We shall look at some of them in this chapter and the church-political theory documents which contributed to them in another chapter. Almost all of these compacts contain the covenant element which describes the people, the bills of liberties and/or code of laws (constitutions) within them. Over time this is what has come to describe a compact.

During the colonial time period in America, compacts were seen as covenants. In almost all cases— there are some exceptions we will review later— many of these religious governmental documents infused the language as well as the aspects of English common law simply because they had to. These colonists were still the subjects of the king. An example I have already mentioned would be the Pilgrim Code of Law, where charter and covenant language are interwoven.[6] What makes this document so unusual for that time period, is the attitude seen within it that the colony's general assembly was equal to Parliament and it had the same relationship to the king, therefore, it was not under Parliament's control. The colonists saw themselves covenanting directly with the king. One hundred and forty years later all the colonies would make the same legal case.[7]

The land mass the colonists occupied was vast. If we take a year like 1640 as an example, we will see approximately 25,000 Europeans occupy what we now view as the thirteen original colonies. Plymouth Colony had about 1,000. The Boston area had about 2,000. There were about 7,000 scattered inland up to what we would consider Maine. Virginia had about 10,000 and the coast of Maryland would have another 500. The colonies we now consider as Connecticut had about 1,500 people. The Dutch Reformed who settled what we know as New York had about 2,000 people. There were roughly 600 Africans, about 150 each in Virginia and Massachusetts and more than 200 in New York.[8]

It was during the mid-early to late 1600s that much of our ancient theory and practice in government documents took place. We can trace this theory throughout our governing documents, especially the religious aspects. Because of the upheavals in England during this period of time, little help or communication flowed to the settlers. They were basically on their own. Equally telling, much of the upheaval in Europe produced more disenfranchised religious groups arriving in the colonies. Initially, those who came for fortune had a hard row to hoe, to put it mildly. Facing extinction events, they barely had enough in labor, production for goods and equipment. In other words, items needed for success. It would take 50 or more years to claim any profit. To say life was not easy would be an understatement. We have already reviewed some of the problems: hunger, disease, bad weather and warfare with the natives. Church and their individual belief in God was in fact their only source for strength. That belief affected their ability to work, to govern, to socialize and eventually to prosper. It created a psychological welfare— and I would submit, miraculous spiritual effect— which enabled them to eventually succeed.

To give you an idea of the impact this had on the settlers, let's look at what it took to get a house and form a neighborhood. I've already mentioned early theological arguments among church leaders and the connection those had in the formation of some states. We looked at the practice of covenanting families and the requirements needed in skills, a minister, a form of government and a plan for making new neighborhoods even before one started. What we now call New Hampshire was a vast sea of land with wolves, bear and natives who were quite willing to kill and capture, when they could. While our time frame right now is circa 1640s, here is an overview of what it took for a young married couple to get a plat of land in a new town called "Gilmanton" in New Hampshire, in 1761. This would be a little over 120 years later, while New York and Philadelphia were bustling cities:

> "During the summer of 1761, several individuals had selected their lots, commenced clearing, built a camp and laid in some provisions, with the design of attempting to pass the winter in town. Benjamin and John Mudgett, two brothers from Brentwood, were of this number. They

had erected a camp on lot No. 3, third range, first division of 100 acre lots, a little Northwest of the spot where the school house in district No. 1, now stands, and late in the fall went down to bring up their families, but their removal was for some time delayed by the deep snows of that winter. They at length however commenced their journey, and on the memorable evening of 26th of Dec. 1761, Benjamin Mudgett and his wife arrived in town, having come that day from Epsom, a distance of not less than 12 miles, on foot, and if tradition be correct, on snow shoes also. It is related of Mrs. Mudgett, that she became exceedingly wearied long before they reached the camp, and often halted to rest. At length when about a mile from the end of her journey, she came to the conclusion that she could go no further, and sat down upon the cold snow saying to her husband, 'I may as well die here as any where; if I attempt to go farther it will kill me, and if I stop here I shall but die.' We can but faintly imagine the feelings which possessed their bosoms at this moment. In the waste howling wilderness, separated from all friends, who could assist them, by many a weary mile travelled over, the shades of night now drawing around them, and yet at an oppressive distance from the poor shelter which had been provided for their accommodation. But they had hearts not easily subdued by discouragements like these; and after a little respite, she made one more effort, and they at length reached their 'home in the wilderness.' Mrs. Mudgett was the first white woman, who set foot on the soil of Gilmanton, and she passed one night in town with no other woman nearer than Epsom! On the next day Dec. 27th, John Mudgett and wife with great weariness reached town, having found little better traveling than their predecessors. On the 10th of January following, about 15 days later, Orlando Weed and wife joined them and here these three families remained through the winter; their nearest neighbors being in Epsom, at that time a day's journey removed from them. How dreary their situation must have been, will appear from the following entry, made in a journal kept by Mr. Benjamin Kimball of Concord, 'The winter of this year (1762) was very severe. Snows were so frequent and so deep as to prevent passing in any direction for two months, being nearly six feet on the level.' Had they been visited with sickness, or had fire consumed their provisions, their sufferings must have been intense, even if they had not perished. The arrival of the first family has heretofore been fixed on the 27th of Dec., but this point is settled by the following certificate made by Mrs. Mudgett at the age of 78, the original copy of which is still preserved. 'I, Hannah Mudgett the wife of Benjamin Mudgett, hereby certify that I was born in the town of Brentwood, on the 9th of June, 1739, was married to Benjamin Mudgett on the 21st of Dec. 1761, and arrived in Gilmanton on the evening of the 26th of Dec. that same year, where I have lived ever since. I moreover state that I was the first white woman who ever set foot in Gilmanton, was the first woman who ever came here to settle, and that I passed one night in town before any other woman arrived. This, I now state in my 78th year.' her Hannah X Mudgett mark (Nov. 3, 1817)."[9]

After reading this, I realized this trek occurred during what we today would have considered her honeymoon, as a woman of 22! She had the first male son born in the town, on February 15, 1764, and named him Samuel. This record states by the time she left the town before "Gilford was disannexed," it had grown to 5,000 souls. She lived to the ripe old age of 95, dying near Pickford's Mills, where she lived with one of her sons, on July 9, 1834.[10]

It was quite difficult to vote or hold office or even become a freeman in certain areas without taking oaths certifying either church attendance or some other oath of character. Acts of Tolerance were enacted in 1689, which divorced citizenship from specific church membership. I say that because by 1765, church attendance was no longer mandatory. Yet just a few years after our "trekking honeymooners" settled their land, one of their neighbors missed church:

"Mr. Morrison settled on No. 3, of the first gore. . . . Being much engaged in clearing up his land, he lost his reckoning, and mistaking the Sabbath for Saturday, continued his work through the day. When Monday morning came, he put on his Sabbath suit, which, at that time, was not very much superior to his every day one, and being prepared for meeting, made his way by spotted trees to the house of his nearest neighbor, Joseph Philbrook, who lived on his route to the place of worship. To his surprise, he found him at work in his blacksmith shop, and immediately reproved him for breaking the Sabbath. Mr. Philbrook assured him it was not Sabbath day, but Monday. Mr. Morrison repeated with certainty of its being the Sabbath day, and re-asserted his sin of Sabbath breaking; and it was not until Mr Philbrook assured him that he attended meeting on the preceding day, and informed him who preached, that his mind became convinced of his error. He immediately returned home, called his family together, and told them the mistake; and 'now,' said he, 'let us strictly keep this day to the Lord in return for the Sabbath which we have profaned by our labor.' The day was accordingly devoted to acts of worship in the family, and Mr Morrison was never known again to fall into a similar error while he resided in town."[11]

Even though church was not mandatory by 1765, it was still critically important. When we look back to the mid-1600s we can see why. There were the adventurers among them who cared little for religion, as we saw with Plymouth Colony. The need for keeping them in check and society orderly could only be solved by their individual covenants. This thought of seeking the common good, as we shall see in specific documents later, is the groundwork for all religious covenants which became secular ones, and society as a whole later (within the colonies). To view this ideology in any way other than addressing the pressing need at that time ignores basic human survival instincts. These folks were on the verge of death at any given time. Heading to the hospital or doctor for antibiotics or to the grocery store for supplies was not a thought. Calling in the military for airstrikes or deploying the National Guard for help was not an option. Each member had to work for what was best for all. This was the biblical model of Christian fidelity seen throughout the New Testament.

Surely all societies understand this. But attending church in centuries past was a survival technique. Many today view it similarly. Its benefits are more than psychological, they have spiritual applications with physical benefits. To mock this idea by using the exceptions of human nature which did take place is to ignore the principles all biblical societies strive for. My mother used to have a saying which applies and finds its foundation in the referenced truth: "Shoot for the stars, if you fall short of the stars and only hit the tree tops, at least you have made it farther than you would have otherwise."

Expecting everyone in a society to do what is best puts all on notice that behavior which puts life, the next generation or the welfare of society at risk, puts everyone at risk. This overriding reality of extinction, survival and its solution in stable communities through spiritual tasks (church attendance)— in other words, covenant— is a truth for all foundational peoples, or people in nature or a natural state. The solutions the Bible presents is what applied more or less to the different thirteen colonies (those who, within 130 years' time follow nature's God).

This practice of covenant is seen even in an "outback" area like New Hampshire in 1765, well over 100 years outside of its implementation within the colonies and roughly 75 years after church attendance was no longer mandatory for citizenship (1689). Yet the practice of covenant may have looked different in different places. That's because the "flavor" or culture and tradition seen in various states is different. This also found expression in the governments and documents and found a voice in our three Federal documents today. Scholars usually divide them into the northern colonies (New England), the middle colonies and the southern colonies.[12]

The middle colonies form somewhat later in time from either the south or the north. Virginia, the largest southern colony set the tone for the south. Even though it became a royal colony, it formed quasi-independently. Developing its own form of government with elements of the current religious ideology, it would still keep a flavor of aristocracy, yet would really have no aristocrats. It would also keep the practice of land ownership for citizenry requirements, as was done in England. This idea gave those with "skin in the game" the responsibility, since laws and taxes would affect them the most. Approximately 25 to 35 percent of white males met the requirements (see next endnote).

While the southern colonies leaned toward a more aristocratic viewpoint, they were still similar in Calvin-puritan worldview. As was mentioned before, the Church of England was protestant with many non-separatist puritans. In other words, their ideas of Reformation theology connected to puritanism were kept quiet, so having a Calvin-puritan worldview would have also been followed, but kept quiet. Yet it was their idea of non-separation which allowed their formation of government to attempt to work within English mandates more easily than we see in the northern colonies (New England). This contributes to our ignorance of where many governmental ideas stem, like roots from a large tree. We see the huge tree, but never the hundreds of connections which enable it to function.

In the south, all of these connections leaned toward tradition: in church, in government and in culture. The effect of land owners and plantation economics gave these colonies, and especially Virginia, a more English manor-estate feel. But if you were to ask most Americans today which one of the thirteen original colonies would have given more of the population citizenship and which one was the most secular, you would probably get answers including almost all of the middle colonies and none of the southern; yet you would be wrong. Georgia was probably the most secular and least enfranchising colony of the bunch and was located in the south.[13] It would be the northern colonies (New England) who were the most religious with the most enfranchised citizenry. This is where most who ignore true spiritual effect miss the effect.

True Holy Spirit effect is seen on our attitudes and on the attitudes of the children born under that anointing. Humans, without the indwelling Holy Spirit cannot maintain that effect because they refuse the continued covenant connection needed to maintain it, which is indwelling in Word and Spirit. Nevertheless, an effect is still seen. This is *one reason* why it was the northern colonies who would fight to see all people set free and why the southern colonies would maintain their desire for slavery. Without the "indwelling," money matters more than anything else. This is where the practice of one's covenant obligations differ. Let's review the three groups of colonies to view some more connections to our modern world and our modern governing documents.

SOUTHERN COLONIES:

Virginia, South Carolina, North Carolina and Georgia were considered southern colonies. It is believed John Locke wrote the 1669 "Fundamental Constitutions of Carolina." It has traditional Church of England language for control and outreach in preaching the Gospel within the liberties section of the document. It was never fully functional and was abrogated by the lord proprietors in 1693. North Carolina's electoral process is advanced. But little within three of the southern colony's documentation made headways toward our present Federal documentation. In fact, it was the northern and middle colonies which made more of an impact upon them. So it is Virginia's documentation we will review as an example for the southern colonies.

Once martial law, or military control was relinquished in Jamestown, the colony as a whole over time developed a more covenantal practice. We have already reviewed some of its governmental practices in representative government and some of its religious connections to that practice. Oddly enough, this was after it was forced back into the "fold," so to speak, of England by becoming a royal colony. Before that took place, the Virginia Company (the charter holder) realized the need for the colonists to have more involvement in their own government. The state-mandated church was the Church of England, so you will see more Old Testament practices for punishment within the laws than in New England (northern colonies) documentation. You also don't see as much documentation. In New England every church had a covenant creating civil laws. In the early years of settlement in Virginia (as well as the south in general), there was only one church led by whatever king sat on the British throne.

Initially, the aristocracy and the clergy itself were strictly associated with the state church (Church of England). It was the common people who were more linked with the ideas of non-separatist Puritans. Over time this would change. What also would change was the fact that here in the colonies the aristocrats were non-existent. The huge numbers of dissenters with foundational puritan-Reformation practice became obvious in 1690 when the Crown wanted to send an Anglican bishop from England to Virginia. Every single pastor in the colony sent a letter asking the Crown do no such thing. Over time, almost all of the south and most of Virginians would become Protestant dissenters of one form or another, yet remain within the umbrella of the Anglican Church (Church of England), until toleration acts were enforced. They were able to remain dissenters with a "puritan streak" simply because of the distance in sea travel and/or the preoccupation of the throne with continental issues. The northern colonies used this distance and monarchal distraction for the creation of self autonomy. The southern colonies and Virginia in particular stayed within English law but enacted some creative solutions.

We reviewed how they solved the problem of receiving ministers from England once the Crown took over. This solution of bringing their own choice before the presiding governor for approval developed a more puritan-covenant-like-Reformation theology within the colony over time because that's what these men preached. Many scholars point to a document enabling that practice. There are other scholars who suggest the practice was a fait accompli. In my opinion, this is a chicken and egg riddle. Whatever your opinion is, this document was the first compact adopted in the colonies creating self-government.

Enacted in 1619, "Laws Enacted by the First General Assembly in Virginia" lasted until 1624.[14] It created a legislature, the House of Burgesses with a governor as head. It was under the subordination of the Virginia Company (the Council of State was created for it back in England). After this document was created a constitution was enacted in 1621. The "Constitution for the Council and Assembly in Virginia" basically ratified what was done in the previous document.[15] It was written in England and affirms the local assembly's subordination to England. It also defines the structure of the local government more clearly. There is a governor along with the council, under the English authority within the charter of the Virginia Company. While these were constant, the people's representatives (House of Burgesses) would assemble once a year from the various locales within the colony proper to form a General Assembly. As with many colonial documents, it calls for "divine assistance, to settle such a form of government there, as may be to the greatest benefit and comfort of the people. . ."[16] This covenantal-type language is in addition to other language establishing a people in New Testament practices.

In 1624, a code of laws, "Laws and Orders Concluded by the Virginia General Assembly" was passed.[17] It was very much like others passed in the colonies. It restricted some of the governor's authority, as well as making him subject to the assembly in levying taxes. Eight of the laws deal with church, three are quasi-church and state (in my opinion), and twenty-four are civic or secularly necessary. It was right after this in the same year that the king mandated Virginia a royal colony. The House of Burgesses was technically disbanded, but as with her religious practices in solving England's mandates, that never happened. The governor continued to rely on the House of Burgesses for unofficial consultations while gaining formal approval for whatever was done from the council appointed by the king in London. This unofficial practice in quasi-self government lasted until 1638 when the governor was ordered to call an official session of the House of Burgesses.

The upheaval with the monarchy and Parliament in England gave room for creative solutions for the settlers with their government. In Virginia's case, this lower house of what was in practice a bicameral system would gain the control over the governor and the council in London by gaining the power to levy taxes. Once that took place, it did not take long for it to gain control over all the laws enacted within the colony. Over time these practices would become similar to that of New England's and the middle colony's innovative governmental "fixes," finding their way into our national documents. The idea of a branch of government "controlling the purse" by levying taxes, thus making it the true power of the government, is why our Constitution requires the "peoples' house" (Congress) to do so, not the executive or judicial branches.

For Virginia the process to allow the people's representatives to control and not the king, was gradual. Their practice was to write a law and then when they changed it "to re-enact it," introduce the amendments and repeal all former laws. They would "re-enact" them exactly or employ the amendments, whatever was necessary.[18] The practice was then to read the whole of the law publicly. But there would only be one copy in each county. This left them with an oral understanding but scant few copies of their history. In fact, it was the post-Revolutionary Assembly wanting to make copies of Virginia's earliest laws, especially those relating to land issues, who made the observation that quite a few of her written laws were ready to crumble.[19] What we do know is the governor was elected by the House of Burgesses during the upheaval in England with the Crown.[20] It seems this practice was then approved by Charles II.[21]

The oath administered to the Burgesses was also more covenantal: "LAWS OF VIRGINIA April, 1652— 3rd OF COMMONWEALTH. The oath administered to the Burgesses: and every of you shall swear vpon the holy Evangelist, and in the sight of God to deliver your opinions faithfully and honestly, according to your best vnderstanding and conscience, for the general good and prosperity of this country and every perticular member thereof, and to do your vtmost endeavor to prosecute that without mingling with it any perticular interest of any person or persons whatsoever."[22]

Whenever you read the language "swear upon the holy Evangelist(s)" it means to place your hand upon the Bible while making an oath. They also called themselves "the representatives of the people" (Act IV). They pretty much took government into their own hands, as much as was in concert with the laws of England, until the Crown-issue in England could be settled. On paper, they may have given some authority back, though scholars disagree about that, but in practice it was the House of Burgesses who was in charge.[23] Whether they liked it or not— or were even paying attention to Virginia in some years— Parliament and the Crown had surrendered more and more of its authority in Virginia and the southern colonies over time.

The earlier laws deal with church matters, especially rooting out non-conformists (puritans as well as other protestants). Catholics could not hold office and Catholic priests were not allowed to stay in the colony more than five days. Quakers were dealt a heavy blow as well. Usually imprisoned until they could leave, the ship or vessel bringing them to the colony was fined 100 pounds for each one who debarked on land.[24] Virginia was a colony which prided itself in following laws. It enacted many and varied, covering all sorts of subjects. In 1643 the first act regulating attorneys was passed. Their fees were twenty pounds of tobacco for the county courts and fifty pounds for the quarter courts (those were when the governor and council attended). In 1657 they gave the vote to all freeman, but in 1670, Charles II restricted the vote to Freeholders only (enfranchised land owners).[25] The laws dealt with local as well as colony wide necessities. When toleration acts were enforced, oaths changed somewhat because Quakers would be allowed to become freeholders. During the pre-Revolution years, laws were enacted concerning that conflict as became necessary.

As most states did in 1776, Virginia wrote her own constitution. It is a compact, as mentioned in the same sentence as the people's inherent rights:

> "I. THAT all men are by nature equally free and independent, and have certain inherent rights, of which, when they enter into a state of society, they cannot, by any compact, deprive or divest their posterity; namely, the enjoyment of life and liberty, with the means of acquiring and possessing property, and pursuing and obtaining happiness and safety."[26]

We can easily see how the words compact and covenant become interchangeable within the documentation of our forebears by 1776. We see popular sovereignty, the form of government with separate powers, elections, trial by jury, along with others in the first section, which would be a bill of rights. As with other constitutions of the time, Item XVI states:

> "That religion, or the duty which we owe to our Creator, and the manner of discharging it, can be directed only

by reason and conviction, not by force or violence, and
therefore all men are equally entitled to the free exercise of
religion, according to the dictates of conscience; and that it
is the mutual duty of all to practice Christian forbearance,
love, and charity, towards each other."[27]

The second section is termed as the constitution proper. It describes
the present trouble with England and why they are doing what they are
doing. It's similar to what they did as states united in the Declaration of
Independence. It dissolves the former government and declares a new
one (item II). It then goes on to describe the form of government they
are now adopting. It is very much in line with what we would soon see in
our present Constitution. The House of Delegates and the Privy Council
(Council of State) along with the governor make up the branches of government.[28] It is a remarkable document for its rights and expressions of
institutional government.

What is even more remarkable is those items are little changed in today's
document. Added are sections which describe criminal prosecutions
and the rights of victims of crime, along with more involved due process
rights, marriage and religion. As in the 1776 document, Section 16 language in Virginia's present constitution is similar, with some differences.

Present-day document: "That religion or the duty which we owe
to our Creator, and the manner of discharging it, can be
directed only by reason and conviction, not by force or
violence; and, therefore, all men are equally entitled to
the free exercise of religion, according to the dictates of
conscience; and that it is the mutual duty of all to practice
Christian forbearance, love, and charity towards each other.
No man shall be compelled to frequent or support any religious worship, place, or ministry whatsoever, nor shall be
enforced, restrained, molested, or burthened in his body or
goods, nor shall otherwise suffer on account of his religious
opinions or belief; but all men shall be free to profess and by
argument to maintain their opinions in matters of religion,
and the same shall in nowise diminish, enlarge, or affect

their civil capacities. And the General Assembly shall not prescribe any religious test whatever, or confer any peculiar privileges or advantages on any sect or denomination, or pass any law requiring or authorizing any religious society, or the people of any district within this Commonwealth, to levy on themselves or others, any tax for the erection or repair of any house of public worship, or for the support of any church or ministry; but it shall be left free to every person to select his religious instructor, and to make for his support such private contract as he shall please."[29]

You can see the echoes of yesteryear's ideas in the present constitution. Today's document is obviously more involved with institutional practices and the oath is more in line with modern practices as well:

"All officers elected or appointed under or pursuant to this Constitution shall, before they enter on the performance of their public duties, severally take and subscribe the following oath or affirmation: 'I do solemnly swear (or affirm) that I will support the Constitution of the United States, and the Constitution of the Commonwealth of Virginia, and that I will faithfully and impartially discharge all the duties incumbent upon me as _____, according to the best of my ability (so help me God.)' "[30]

Like other documents today, it is not short. I still marvel at the brevity of yesteryear's documentation. As you can imagine, it has been updated many times since 1776. Yet I was surprised to see the same compact-covenant method still in practice, only in an updated form.

NORTHERN COLONIES:

We have reviewed New England's (northern colonies) practices in more detail than the southern or middle colonies probably because the connection to independence is so strong. The trading companies that formed them along with the religiously persecuted who executed function within the colonies worked easily with what was a radical Calvinistic worldview.

It was morally based and so the view that prosperity was a sign of God's blessing on an adventure— whether that was strictly economic or blended in its desires— was a theme for whatever they did. Not only did the idea of separation from the Church of England (and England's laws) affect their function, it also made an effect on their governmental documentation. Initially church membership was the requirement for citizenry. This would enfranchise almost all adult white males.[31]

This would also do something else in an ever so slightly greater fashion than the other two colonial groups: It would create an attitude of civic community involving all citizens in self-government. Moral fidelity in community was the foundation for whatever they did. This allowed more of the "people" to become involved. Connecticut, Massachusetts, New Hampshire and Rhode Island were considered northern colonies (New England). Within the northern colonies we have reviewed the Mayflower Compact and the Pilgrim Code of Law, which are examples of covenantal compact agreements extending to a governing document. So let's look at a different northern colony other than Massachusetts.

We already looked at the settling honeymooners from New Hampshire. By the time they settled, Boston was a city. So let's stay with New Hampshire.[32] Exeter was in New Hampshire and was settled by puritans who would come to be known as Congregationalists. Exeter became the county seat. In 1639 the settlers in Exeter wrote an agreement under the authority of King Charles. It is a typical church covenant extending to government (excerpted):

> "Wee, his loyal subjects, brethren of the church of Exeter, situate & lying upon Piscataquacke, wth *(with)* other inhab-itants there, considering wth ourselves the holy will of god and our owne necessity, that we should not live whout *(without)* wholesome lawes & government amongst us, of wch *(which)* we are altogether destitute; doe in the name of Christ & in the sight of god combine ourselves together, to erect & set up amongst us such government . . . . ."[33]

The elders and the rulers had an oath. It started off:

> " You shall swear by the great and dreadful Name of the High
> God, Maker and Governor of Heaven and earth and by the
> Lord Jesus Christ, the Prince of the Kings and rulers of the
> earth, that in his Name and fear you will rule and govern
> his people according to the righteous will of God . . . ."[34]
> (excerpted).

The people had their own oath:

> "We do swear by the Great and dreadful Name of the High
> God, Maker and Governor of heaven and earth, and by the
> Lord Jesus Christ, the King and Saviour of his people, that
> in his Name and fear, we will submit ourselves to be ruled
> and governed according to the will and word of God . . . ."[35]
> (excerpted).

After reading this 'peoples' oath, can you see echoes in our much later
"Pledge of Allegiance"? New Hampshire's settling was quite tumultuous.
That is reflected in their documentary history.[36] They received a charter
from England. After writing various governmental documents, they then
wrote a similar style of document within the compact-covenant method.
They wrote what was viewed as bills of rights or liberties with basic
descriptions of institutions, which we now view as early constitutions.

Written in 1679-1680, "The Generall Lawes and Liberties of the
Province of New Hampshire, made by the Generall Assembly in Portsmo
(Portsmouth, NH) the 16th of March 1679/80" seems to have been an
agreement England did not entirely "agree" with. As it was submitted
to her, "Attorney General Sawyer" marked off items of law unnecessary
within England's legal viewpoints.[37] Nevertheless, it seems England
approved it, and it applied to the whole colony (see previous endnote).
It had 16 capital laws, 27 criminal laws and 45 general laws in the town-
ship (including naming institutions). It reflected much of her religious
zeal, and a real deviation from English common law. This is probably
why notes are made in the copy sent to England of refusal for some of
the ordinances. That New Hampshire enacted the laws is not in question
because it was approved by the *President* and Council.[38]

Back then the term *president* was defined as a celebrant at a eucharist (or communion ceremony). It is later in time from the previous agreement. After reading all these laws, you can see a progression in the ideas of the colony for law. Much of what England disagreed with here had to do with autonomy and religion. New Hampshire had no desire or connection to the Church of England and its adherence to English authority. This document showed that penchant for self-government, especially in its religious views.

After reading a few of these early colonial documents, the similarities between the states in the northern colonies, Virginia, and some middle colonies comes into view. With the exception of William Penn (see Middle Colonies), we know they never read those men who would become champions of compact, legal or political theory: John Locke, (he would have been about six) Montesquieu, Blackstone or Hume (not born yet). We know the English documentation they knew was different from what we see here. To my reading, with the exception of Virginia, some of the documentation started to resemble England's more. That's probably because of the colonist's need to keep their charters. But earlier in time, we know contact between colonies (states) was limited, so in most cases (see Pennsylvania as the exception) they did not copy one another. The connection is the biblical covenant-style method in church documentation.

Since we are following New Hampshire, it was during the upheavals in 1776 that there was a flurry in the writing of state constitutions. New Hampshire wrote as well. It was a temporary document basically describing the need for it and the institutions desired. It contained no bill of rights. It also does not establish a people but it does describe the need of the people to explain the disruption of their connection to England. No mention of God is made in the 1776 document. So this could explain its temporary status in an establishment clause. In a future chapter we will review the covenant mention of God in New Hampshire's ratification document. With this document from 1776, it seems obvious they felt their own previous documentation, which we have reviewed here, would suffice in both regards. In other words, there was a compact between what they had already written and the 1776 document.

In 1784 New Hampshire wrote a new constitution. Part I contains 38 articles, declares a people and is a bill of rights with the fabric of institutions overlaid and infused throughout. Part II describes the institutions and is the constitution proper with the appropriate oaths necessary, giving exemptions to Quakers. The words covenant (see Article 3), popular sovereignty (see Article 1) and an amendment process (see Article X) are not mentioned, nor is specific behavior beneficial for the common good, (except morality and piety grounded on evangelical principles); but the ideas are implied within the first ten articles. Think of the force used today by the Federal government to make its citizens comply with its orders as you read these words from 1784: "The doctrine of non-resistance against arbitrary power, and oppression, is absurd, slavish, and destructive of the good and happiness of mankind."[39]

The first update was made in 1792-1793. Many updates have taken place since, but it has basically kept this same constitution and is still in use today. As most states did in time, New Hampshire disestablished its religious denominations in 1813. Yet oaths and covenantal understanding toward the people as part of the state is still seen even in today's document.[40]

MIDDLE COLONIES:

The middle colonies of New York, Maryland, Delaware, Pennsylvania and New Jersey were more mixed in their religious endeavors, yet there was still a strong connection to the Reformation worldview, especially the teachings of Arminius. Pennsylvania and New Jersey form later in time. Within the middle colonies, Catholicism and a slightly different train of thought in Reformation teaching is seen. This, in connection with a better flow in economic stability by this time, gave these colonies a more individualistic outlook than either northern or southern colonies. Because of persecution, Catholics would always seek some form of isolation. With Catholic populations lower, individuals were paramount. But it was the direct teaching of Jacobus Arminius among the Protestants in the middle colonies which made the idea of individualism so strong here.

As we reviewed in the last chapter, Calvin's overriding idea of Divine Sovereignty pushed the cards in Another's Hand. But Arminius saw an individual responsible for his own salvation in the sense that human responsibility played a huge role in whether or not someone decided for or against salvation. In other words, free will and choice in our relationship to the Divine. This is one of those places in which the two different Reformation teachings will affect government. The Dutch Reformed, who were closely linked with Arminius' teachings settled in what would become New York and New Jersey. The Quakers' doctrine, seen through the ideas of William Penn in Pennsylvania only reinforced Arminius' teaching. Penn was a friend of Locke and Locke was a fan of Descartes, who was a friend of Arminius. Their documents stress individual, not just morally structured communitarian responsibility.

New York's documentation would not exhibit the same covenant style seen in either Pennsylvania or a northern colony like Connecticut, but would still create representative government. This was due to a governor or governor as representing an English aristocrat or charter-holder. Because New England's colonies were either theocratic (church-government controlled) or blended, from the start it was a grassroots effort, like self-government on steroids! The middle colonies granted government from the top down instead, using their English charters and following English common law. But because help from England was minimal, these colonies still had to rely on the "people" for a representative government, like the northern and southern colonies. New York's later documentation is more secular (1683) than its earliest church documents. Unlike New England, New York's church documents are separate, with little or no functionality with their charter government, except that they are "confirmed" churches (especially after toleration acts are passed in Europe).

New Jersey is somewhat blended and becomes more covenant based. In 1681 they write the "Fundamentals of West New Jersey."[41] It declares a religious people in a geographic area who come in agreement with the governor and charter holders. It is different from others I have read. It puts a set of limits on the governor's, and by extension, the charter's proprietors' power. Instead of talking about the people's rights, it talks about what the governor shall not do. So rights are received because the governor's power is restricted.

Maryland becomes more religious because of the Catholic influence and the Protestant debate. Like Penn in Pennsylvania, this is because of Lord Calvert, a Catholic and the charter holder (along with his heirs). Maryland's later documentation would also influence our present day Federal documents with the innovation of an electoral college (it elected their senate). There is a similarity here with the New England colonies in that order and polite exchange were stressed as paramount within the governing body. With Catholics and Protestants being forced to function as one, I found language used by St. Paul in 1 Corinthians 14:27-33 similar to language used within New England and Maryland's documents in conducting an orderly and deliberative debate while meeting.[42] I've never seen such restraint exhibited within the British Parliamentary system today. I don't know how long after free speech was enacted it took to get as boisterous as it is now. So within the colonies it is the Christian influence which restrained their passions. Within Maryland's 1649 Toleration Act you read a pluralistic-religious type of covenant of protection for various religions.[43] All citizens within all the colonies had to swear allegiance to the king, yet different groups had different ways of solving religious objections to oath-taking.

The elephant in the room of the middle colonies was, without a doubt, Pennsylvania. Though it formed later than Virginia (Jamestown) or Massachusetts, because of Penn's influence concerning religious liberty and his practical as well as published desire to give generous benefits to those who would come to settle, it became the most populated colony, with Philadelphia as the largest city in the colonies. This statement does not count slaves since the Quakers and Mennonites would outlaw slavery. Later in time, Philadelphia would be chosen as the site of the Constitutional Convention.

We will review Pennsylvania's documentation for a number of reasons. Eventually, like New England, it contributed a number of practices finding their way through to our present Federal documentation. Unlike New England, Penn did review the documentation in place from

Massachusetts, New York and Virginia in composing his charter of liberties (bill of rights).[44] Like Lord Calvert's desire in Maryland to find a home for Catholics, innovation in solving problems had to be made. Penn's desire to find such a home for the Quakers, and his economic need for settlers of all types, produced some innovations not seen in the colonial documentation in existence at the time. The elected officials sat continuously (like we do today). Its term limits were spread out so a third of the members were elected each year. It resembles our present senate more than any other earlier document. It also had specialized standing committees, a practice not seen in the colonies or England, but seen in our federal legislature today. Also not seen elsewhere at that time was the creation of a formal amendment process.[45] Many of these innovations found their way to our present day Federal documents.

The Northern Colonies were upfront about religious aspects in their documentation (except Rhode Island). The preface of Pennsylvania's document is a piece of biblical legal theory, so subtle in its application, unless you were a student of theology as well as history, you might miss it. By inference Penn uses the theological and legal teachings of God's invisible laws and God's revealed laws for its need. Using the same style of understatement, he establishes the Divine right of government through man's disobedience. Mentioning this reveals two more points of legal theory: It establishes the need for laws because of the depravity of man, *and* proves that man only discovered the law by breaking it. Next, by mentioning Adam and Eve, Penn touches on the Scriptures which afford the most authentic account of the origin, history and multiplication of societies, thereby reinforcing the need and theory of social compacts. This mention of Adam also infers one of the first orders of God's laws: Do good, multiply, subdue and do no evil. This establishes God's law as a rule of action to govern what God created; inferring the principle that God's laws are already fixed and universal. He touches on the fact that man will always justify his own disobedience, thus the need for the law Penn is creating. (Hinting at this by talking about its detractors.)

Lastly, by mentioning the Second Adam (Jesus Christ) and linking his rule of law to the end of government, he is establishing another principle of biblical legal thought: God's legitimacy in preaching the Gospel to all nations, causes light and revelation to dawn on all. In other words, it does the most good for the most amount of people. I could go on, but the subtlety of his wording reveals my own verbosity. Though it does not specifically mention these terms, by discussing several biblical events, it is alluding to developed legal theory of his day.[46]

I think his understatement makes sense. His audience would have known and understood law from its biblical roots. We have lost that knowledge today, thinking that law emanates from us; refusing to admit we only discovered what the Divine had already created. We will look at church documents which discuss biblical legal theory in detail in a future chapter. Penn's preface was written decades after many of those church documents for legal theory. I discuss the Pennsylvania preface now, so you can get an idea of the legal theory of the day and see how it transferred to what would become their statewide governing documents.

The 1682 "Charter of Liberties and Frame of Government of the Province of Pennsylvania in America" continues with "The Frame" which consists of 24 articles establishing and describing institutional practices. It is compacted with the next 39 articles which were laws agreed upon in England. To my reading these are more a bill of liberties with ordinances included. The last aspect to this document was added in December 1682, the same year the others are signed. Titled "An Act for Freedom of Conscience," it is six chapters long with an introduction which describes the colony's religious toleration and the limits of that toleration. There were updates and newer versions in 1683 and 1696.[47]

In 1701 a new Frame was made and remained in effect until 1776. It is a covenant and is predicated upon belief in Jesus Christ:

> "Pennsylvania Charter of Liberties. . . . . First. BECAUSE no people can be truly happy, though under the greatest Enjoyment of Civil Liberties, if abridged of the Freedom of their Consciences as to their religious profession and worship. And Almighty God being the only Lord of Conscience, Father of Light and Spirits, and the Author as well as the object of all divine Knowledge, Faith, and Worship, who only does enlighten the minds and persuade

and convince the Understandings of People, I do hereby grant and declare that no Person or Persons inhabiting in this Province or Territories, who shall confess and acknowledge One almighty God, the Creator, Upholder and Ruler of the World; and profess him or themselves obliged to live quietly under the Civil Government, shall be in any Case molested or prejudiced in his or their Person or Estate because of his or their conscientious Persuasion or Practice, nor be compelled to frequent or maintain any religious Worship, Place, or Ministry contrary to his or their Mind, or to do or suffer any other Act or Thing contrary to their religious Persuasion. AND that all Persons who also profess to believe in *Jesus Christ,* Saviour of the World, shall be capable, notwithstanding their other Persuasions and Practices in Point of Conscience and Religion, to serve this Government in any Capacity, both legislatively and executively, he or they solemnly promising, when lawfully required, Allegiance to the King as Sovereign and Fidelity to the Proprietary and Governor, and taking the Attests as now established by the Law made at New-Castle, in the Year One Thousand and Seven Hundred, entitled *An Act Directing the Attests of Several Officers and Ministers,* as now amended and confirmed this present Assembly."[48]

It continues with further articles. As with the previous documents, one had to profess belief in Jesus Christ to vote and hold office. This document, as with other middle colony documents, was successful in its attempt at removing some of the charter holder's power, or in this case the proprietor's legislative veto. The citizens wanted more control in self-government and this is how they removed what they saw as obstacles to that end. It also creates a unicameral legislature. Penn takes great care in writing this while documenting its history with the history of the previous documents that went before it.

In 1776 Pennsylvania wrote a document which resembles our three-part Federal documents. We see a compact with the establishment of a people describing a broken relationship with England, a bill of rights (called a declaration of the rights of, etc.) and a frame (constitution proper). It also contains specific wording within an oath for its elected representatives. It is in covenant form, both with the people and the acknowledgement of belief in a deity:

> (under Section 10, second paragraph) "I do swear (or affirm) that as a member of this assembly, I will not propose or assent to any bill, vote, or resolution which shall appear to be injurious to the people; nor do or consent to any act or thing whatever, that shall have a tendency to lessen or abridge their rights and privileges, as declared in the constitution of this state; but will in all things conduct myself as a faithful honest representative and guardian of the people, according to the best of only judgment and abilities. And each member, before he takes his seat, shall make and subscribe the following declaration, viz: I do believe in one God, the creator and governor of the universe, the rewarder of the good and the punisher of the wicked. And I do acknowledge the Scriptures of the Old and New Testament to be given by Divine inspiration. And no further or other religious test shall ever hereinafter be required of any civil officer or magistrate in this State."[49]

It contained only one single assembly, no upper house but it did have a council and president with no veto powers. What it did have, which also resembled church government was a review process. The people had to review each law approved. Every piece of legislation had to be passed by two consecutive sessions of the legislature. The bill had to be publicly posted for a period of time so the citizens could go to their representative between elections, for fact-finding missions (Section 15). There was a Section 45, which encouraged virtue and used religious societies to help in teaching morality and help in charitable purposes. There was also a Council of Censors, created as a sort of "watch" to make sure the constitution was followed and the lawmakers and other officers behaved accordingly. In other words, the "Government Accountability Office" of its day.

In 1790 a new constitution replaced the 1776 document. The 1790 document came more in line with the Federal documents in place at the time. It had an upper and lower house, along with a governor. The oath contained no specific mention of God. Instead, within a bill of rights, under Article IX is contained 26 rights:

> "Section IV. That no person, who acknowledges the being of a God and a future state of rewards and punishments, shall, on account of his religious sentiments, be disqualified to hold any office or place of trust or profit under this commonwealth."[50]

A change of documentation was made again in 1838, with amendments in 1850, 1857, 1864 and 1872. The oaths and Section IV were retained. African Americans were disenfranchised. In 1874 another Constitution was formed. It re-enfranchised African Americans and changed the wording in its establishment section:

> "WE, the people of the Commonwealth of Pennsylvania, grateful to Almighty God for the blessings of civil and religious liberty, and humbly invoking His guidance, do ordain and establish this Constitution."[51]

By doing so, the document became more covenantal than even the previous one. The oath became more non-sectarian and longer. It remained in effect until 1968. Like most state constitutions, Pennsylvania made amendments in 1901, 1909, 1913, 1915, 1920, 1922, 1923, 1928, 1933, 1937, 1945, 1949, 1951, 1955, 1956, 1957, 1959, 1963 and 1967 to bring it more in line with the state's needs and Federal law. This is similar to what we see the colonies do earlier with their own documentation to come in line with English common law. In 1968 the present day Constitution was made. No changes were made to the establishment section, except it is now called a "preamble" and no changes were made to Section IV. Presumably, by naming it a preamble you would make it legally non-binding. I would mention though, what man considers so, God does not, as we have already reviewed. I would also mention our early founders combined preambles with establishment documents, thus making all of it legally binding. This 1968 oath became shorter but remained as non-sectarian as before. Like the previous document it was amended many times for the same reasons, none of which affect the elements we are concerned with here.

While there are differences between the three groups of colonies, there were great similarities and/or events which blended the colonies, forming practices and ideologies, which made them more alike than different. I still marvel at the careful debate concerning the laws enacted within the thirteen colonies. The practice has "church" written all over it. It was important back then (as it is now) to make sure all understood the fullness of a law and agreed to it. This takes time. It is the practice today among those of the socialist leaning to quickly slide something by the people, or to just take a pen in hand and do what one wishes; even treating the people's representatives perversely.[52] That is not what our present Federal documents make legal. The process is meant to take time for a reason and that reason is the ultimate brain child of the churches (I am referring to the early colonial practices). The goal was to enact the most amount of liberty for the most amount of people. This was always the biblical model. God warned Israel things would change if they wanted a human as their king instead of God (1 Samuel 8:1-22, see the NIV). Our early American ancestors wanted nothing to do with the governmental processes of kings.

I want to be careful in writing this book that I do not look at an effect and because we see some group or author have the same ideas at an earlier time, make the assumption the idea came from that group or author. Some could say that is exactly what I am doing, like the example I use of William Penn. Much influenced Penn, especially his own experiences with persecution. But that is not to say there are no scientific or exacting methods to base a value of influence on a concept. There is a relevant method because there is a perfected science to it. In our case here, we have the unique capability of seeing total isolation as a test tube for our early colonial documentation. We can know and see that the colonists had almost no connection with one another in discussing the formation of their documentation and yet we see the exacting similarities. We know there were only two exacting connections to these documents: church covenants, which relies heavily on Reformation theology, and by extension the Bible, and English common law (through Magna Carta). England played a role, especially in the idea of charters, compacts, contracts, oaths and other definitions and practices. We have to remember the idea of a compact was different on our shores than in Europe from that time period. The people in Europe and especially those living in England would have no need of something like the compacts written here. That's because they were already in settled towns and cities with the king and Parliament as their leaders.[53]

Tracing the connection for what is English is easy, especially during this period of time. The science of this is called appropriation. Scholars view appropriation in all sorts of ways. I came across some rather odd viewpoints on the subject. But the more scientific models look at early peoples within isolated environments and then review documentarian history and follow exacting influences. A good example of this method would be to review the first ten amendments (our original Bill of Rights). We see 27 rights within the document. Six, or 20 percent were first seen in the Magna Carta. Twenty-one, or 75 percent are first written in colonial documents *before* the 1689 English Bill of Rights (Acts of Toleration). Only one, the 9th Amendment is found in early state constitutions written between 1776 and 1787.[54] One could then apply this method to Magna Carta, if you were so inclined to review Greek, Roman and even biblical influences. In later chapters we will review the data from such an exacting method for our Constitution. So to make the assumption church covenantal documents, based on biblical underpinnings and written within colonial documents, sometimes made within a compact form, played a majority influence in writing the Bill of Rights, would not be factually or scientifically wrong.

ENDNOTES

1   Lutz, Donald S. 1988. "The Origins of American Constitutionalism." Baton Rouge, LA: © 1988 Louisiana State University Press. 116

2   Ibid., 97

3   Ibid.

4   <http://avalon.law.yale.edu/default.asp> © 2008 Lillian Goldman Law Library; you can read the bulk of them on this site; accessed 3/16/16

5   Lutz, Donald S. 1988. "The Origins of American Constitutionalism." Baton Rouge, LA: © 1988 Louisiana State University Press. 47

6   Donald S. Lutz, Colonial Origins of the American Constitution: A Documentary History, ed. Donald S. Lutz (Indianapolis: Liberty Fund 1998). [Online] available from <http://oll.libertyfund.org/titles/694>; accessed 2/25/16; Scroll down the contents page and click on "Pilgrim Code of Law."

7   Lutz, Donald S. 1988. "The Origins of American Constitutionalism." Baton Rouge, LA: © 1988 Louisiana State University Press. 39

8   Ibid., 23, see Footnote on the same page.

9   Lancaster, Daniel. 1845 "Proprietary, Civil, Literary, Ecclesiastical, Biographical, Genealogical, and Miscellaneous History, from the First Settlement to the Present Time; Including What is Now Gilford, To The Time It Was Disannexed," Gilmanton: Printed by Alfred Prescott. 65-66. Public domain but can be seen in pdf through New Hampshire State's Archive. Archive accessed 1/28/16.

10   Ibid., 67

11   Ibid., 72

12   Lutz, Donald S. 1988. "The Origins of American Constitutionalism." Baton Rouge, LA: © 1988 Louisiana State University Press. 50-58

13   Ibid., 10; the enfranchisement opinion is within this cited source, but the secularity is mine after a review of documentation.

14   SOUTHERN COLONY ENDNOTES: Donald S. Lutz, Colonial Origins of the American Constitution: A Documentary History, ed. Donald S. Lutz (Indianapolis: Liberty Fund 1998). [Online] available from <http://oll.libertyfund.org/titles/694>; accessed 2/25/16; Internet. Scroll down the contents page and click on "Laws Enacted by the First General Assembly in Virginia."

15   Ibid., scroll down the list and click on the "Constitution for the Council and Assembly in Virginia." See the essay paragraph before the document proper.

16   <https://archive.org/details/statutesatlargeb01virg> accessed 2/27/16

17   Donald S. Lutz, Colonial Origins of the American Constitution: A Documentary History, ed. Donald S. Lutz (Indianapolis: Liberty Fund 1998). [Online] available from <http://oll.libertyfund.org/titles/694>; accessed 2/25/16; Internet. Scroll down the list and click on the "Laws and Orders Concluded by the Virginia General Assembly." See also <https://archive.org/details/statuesatlargeb01virg> Turn to 121. Accessed 2/27/16.

18   All of Virginia's early laws can be seen <http://vagenweb.org/hening/vol01-00.htm> look at page vi; © Freddie L. Spradlin, accessed 3/3/16.

19   Ibid., pages iv-xi.

20   All of Virginia's early laws can be seen <http://vagenweb.org/hening/vol01-15. htm#Page_371>; © Freddie L. Spradlin, accessed 3/3/16.

21   All of Virginia's early laws can be seen <http://vagenweb.org/hening/vol01-23. htm#Page_530>; Scroll down to 531 and up to 528 for the essay. © Freddie L. Spradlin, accessed 3/3/16.

22   All of Virginia's early laws can be seen <http://vagenweb.org/hening/vol01-15. htm#Page_371> © Freddie L. Spradlin, accessed 3/3/16.

23   All of Virginia's early laws can be seen <http://vagenweb.org/hening/vol01-23. htm#Page_530> Scroll down from 530 to 532. © Freddie L. Spradlin, accessed 3/3/16.

24   All of Virginia's early laws can be seen <http://vageweb.org/hening/vol01-00.htm> look at page xv; © Freddie L. Spradlin, accessed 3/3/16.

25   Ibid. page xx

26   All of Virginia's early laws can be seen <http://vageweb.org/hening/vol01-02.htm> © Freddie L. Spradlin, accessed 3/3/16.

27   Ibid.

28   All of Virginia's early laws can be seen <http://vagenweb.org/hening/vol01-02. htm#bottom> © Freddie L. Spradlin, accessed 3/7/16.

29   <http://law.lis.virginia.gov/constitution> site © Commonwealth of Virginia 2016, accessed 2/27/16.

30   Ibid, see Article II, Section 7.

31   NORTHERN COLONY ENDNOTES: This statement is not seen in this source reference, it is mine after a review of history and quite a lot of documentation. Becoming a freeman usually included a certain amount of accumulated funds and an age requirement. But viewing these pages may also help to arrive at this assumption: Lutz, Donald S. 1988. "The Origins of American Constitutionalism." Baton Rouge, LA: © 1988 Louisiana State University Press. 10 see footnote 8, 53

32   Within the public domain is an interesting history of New Hampshire's documentation from an English legal code and point of view: <https://archive.org/details/government andla00batcgoog> accessed 2/28/16

33   <http://avalon.law.yale.edu/17th_centurynh06.asp> © 2008 Lillian Goldman Law Library, New Haven, CT, and see also <http://www.constitution.org/primarysources/ covenants.html#exeter> site © constitution.org; sites accessed 3/17/16

34   Ibid.

35   Ibid.

36   See Endnote 32 and this site from the University of London. <http://www.british-history.
      ac.uk/cal-state-papers/colonial/america-west-indies/vol11/pp37-49> scroll to "98"
      accessed 3/23/16

37   <http://www.british-history.ac.uk/cal-state-papers/colonial/america-west-indies/vol11/
      pp37-49> accessed 3/23/16

38   Donald S. Lutz, Colonial Origins of the American Constitution: A Documentary History,
      ed. Donald S. Lutz (Indianapolis: Liberty Fund 1998). [Online] available from <http://
      oll.libertyfund.org/titles/694>; accessed 2/25/16; Internet. Scroll down to "The General
      Lawes and Liberties of the Province of New Hampshire." Scroll down to read oaths from
      various colonies.

39   <https://www.nh.gov/constitution/billofrights.html> accessed 2/28/16.

40   <http://www.nh.gov/constitution/constitution.html> accessed 2/28/16. See the various
      articles with the amendment dates; Article 84 spells out the oaths.

41   MIDDLE COLONY ENDNOTES: <http://avalon.law.yale.edu/17th_century/nj08.
      asp> © 2008 Lillian Goldman Law Library, New haven, CT; you can read all of the origi-
      nals on this site; accessed 2/28/16.

42   Everstine, Carl, N. 1951. "The Establishment of Legislative Power in Maryland." 12 Md.
      L. Rev. 99 (1951) 110 <http://digitalcommons.law.umaryland.edu/cgi/viewcontent.
      cgi?article=1411&context=mlr> accessed 2/2/8/16

43   Maryland has an extensive archival system for early documents. They have an interactive
      digital tribute for their Religious Toleration Acts. Click on the arrows to scroll through it.
      Eventually you will see an original copy of the Acts. <msa.maryland.gov/msa/speccol/
      sc2200/sc2221/000025/html/toleration.html> accessed 2/28/16

44   Donald S. Lutz, Colonial Origins of the American Constitution: A Documentary History,
      ed. Donald S. Lutz (Indianapolis: Liberty Fund 1998). [Online] available from <http://
      oll.libertyfund.org/titles/694>; accessed 2/25/16; Internet. Scroll to document 59, see
      editor's notes.

45   Ibid.

46   Ibid. As you read the document, think of why Penn would bother mentioning those biblical
      characters/events. This is why many of today's theologians would be able to clearly see his
      legal train of thought and secularists would ignore it as religious gobbledegook.

47   Donald S. Lutz, Colonial Origins of the American Constitution: A Documentary History,
      ed. Donald S. Lutz (Indianapolis: Liberty Fund 1998). [Online] available from <http://
      oll.libertyfund.org/titles/694>; accessed 2/25/16; Internet. Scroll from 59 through 60.

48 <http://avalon.law.yale.edu/18th_century/pa07.asp> © 2008 Lillian Goldman Law Library, 127 Wall Street, New Haven CT, 06511; accessed 2/25/16

49 <http://avalon.law.yale.edu/18th_century/pa08.asp> © 2008 Lillian Goldman Law Library, 127 Wall Street, New Haven CT, 06511; accessed 2/25/16

50 <http://mariettapa.com/pa_pacon_1790.html> accessed 3/29/16

51 <https://archive.org/details/constitutionofp00penn> accessed 3/29/16

52 To see several articles on the paid consultant for the 2010 Affordable Care Act and his comments about the need to make the law difficult to understand and the need to push it through quickly: <http://www.foxnews.com/politics/2014/11/14/despite-dem-claims-trash-talking-gruber-was-well-paid-adviser-for-obamacare-and/?intcmp=trending><http://www.washingtonpost.com/blogs/fact-checker/wp/2014/11/14/did-jonathan-gruber-earn-almost-400000-from-the-obama-administration><http://video.foxnews.com/v/3888172771001/gruber-remarks-put-obama-administration-on-defense-/?intcmp=related#sp=show-clips> Some of these articles initially came with videos and links attached. This caused them to have more views from both sides of the political aisle. I am not sure they will be connected when you view them, so viewer beware. To see the argument and consequences of unbridled executive action of a modern example from a liberal constitutional lawyer <http://video.foxnews.com/v/3892456666001/jonathan-turley-on-obamas-expected-immigration-overreach/?intcmp=related#sp=show-clips> To read articles and links <http://www.foxnews.com/politics/2014/11/15/obamas-immigration-overhaul-could-put-burden-on-states> To see some studies from a liberal think tank report, click on the accompanying links in this report <http://www.brookings.edu/research/opinions/2014/07/08-daca-renewals-ramp-up-svajlenka-singer> What these do not divulge is criminal, cultural and/or church environmental impacts. Accessed 3/5/16.

53 Lutz, Donald S. 1988. "The Origins of American Constitutionalism." Baton Rouge, LA: © 1988 Louisiana State University Press. 31

54 Ibid., 62

Chapter Six

RELIGIOUS ATTITUDE FORMS COLONIES ATTITUDE INFORMS STATES' DOCUMENTATION

As already mentioned, these folks were surviving extinction events. What helped them to survive, and do more than that, to eventually thrive? I can prove the covenant method within the documentation. But for documents to have survived from our ancestors, and for us to be able to celebrate them and that documentary history as viable today, it and they had to be successful. We can see from other native peoples they had to have skills of some kind or another to survive. If they constantly fight, they weaken themselves. If they are corrupt, they weaken themselves. If they remove the impetus to "have and to hold" they remove success from what it is which makes humans biologically monogamous in their ability to pass skills, traditional values and accumulated wealth to the next generation, even reproducing that generation. If they are able to learn from native peoples who have skills to survive in specialized environments, they are successful. Whatever Platonic arguments one would like to make for socialism and its various offsprings (fascism, communism, progressivism, multiculturalism, etc.), there is something biologically innate in humans— even at our very core brain function— that needs to worship a creator and love another human being to the point of reproduction.

Legally the Creator has bound us in this action. In other words, we are built for immortality and reproduction. Whatever arguments are made to the contrary, humans do not thrive in systems which espouse pluralisms. I did not say they could not survive, I said thrive. We do our best when we have close family units who live at peace and share enough common values which cause them to share survival skills. After societies are created and goods and services are established, harmony for the common good must still be maintained or the societies will fracture. Socialism/progressivism does this by force. Communism does this by force at the point of a gun.

Societies based on Christian or biblical ethics do this based on the concept of love— and not just any love— first based on love legally bound by the Creator (God to man, see Deuteronomy 5; 6:5; Matthew 22:38, 39; Mark 12:30, 31; Luke 10:27) and then love bound to mankind: "Love thy neighbor as thyself." Contrary to popular opinion, the Bible does not encourage communal property holdings as, or over and above, private holdings. Love, from Old to New Testaments, belongs to the Creator first, then to husband and wife (family), and then to the community (even the created environment). So goods and services (in a much smaller amount) are given for worship needs. Fidelity in economics is shared to reproduce the family and its generations. The Bible is a book about generations (and economics). In fact, it is a good man who leaves wealth for his children's children (Proverbs 13:22)!

Finally, and in a much smaller fashion, and based on biblical mandates of consensus, brotherly love and immediate need (or on an as-needed basis), goods and services extend to the society as a whole. These services are to always meet the local need first. In the first act of giving, to support priests (Jewish temple worship) and/or the churches (New Testament requirements). Even a large portion of that support is given to help the community at large. Under biblical mandates we are encouraged to be a giving people whenever we see the need. The New Testament reveals an added admonition to give as the Holy Spirit directs (see the whole sorry affair in Acts 2:1-5). In other words, He may ask you to give all, or He may not, or you may not want to, but it is still yours, given by God so you may be a good steward of His blessings.

Doing what is right in God's eyes will also be an extremely critical part of such a society. As seen within the biblical model, even a biblical society may not understand or agree with everything you do, (think Old Testament prophets, Jesus and the early apostles) but the New Testament does not violate another's health and wellbeing. Eventually this attitude will help the greater good. It is not God's plan or will to harm His messengers. Their words are shared to promote the larger good within the community.

This is the rudimentary basics of the biblical New Testament modeled by attitude which the early settlers followed. The settlers of early America incorporated what they needed to survive. You can argue they weren't perfect Christians and they disagreed with one another. You can blow up the errors which led to combativeness. You can deny a Deity is needed to live peacefully. Under the tradition these Christians founded, you have the right to do so. You can't change their attitude, the history or what they experienced. They realized the practices of harmony, Christian fidelity in law and brotherly love, were survival techniques (covenant) which helped them to thrive, over time.

Let's revisit the neighbors of our "honeymooning settlers" from New Hampshire again. Remember Mr. Morrison, the neighbor who swore to the town's first blacksmith (Mr. Philbrook) it was Sunday, not Monday and they should have been in church? Well, his wife became ill. Mr. Philbrook's wife (the blacksmith) decided to visit her and see to her needs.

> "She went out, leaving her husband, who was fatigued with labor, at home. It began to be dark as she left her own door, and she had no path to follow but one indicated by spotted trees. On a sudden there came up a dense fog or sea turn, and ere she was aware, she was unable to discern the spots on the trees. She hurried along, however, hoping to keep the direction, and reach the house at which she was aiming. But in this she was disappointed. When she supposed she had gone far enough, she began to hallo, with the hope of being heard, and relieved from her embarrassing situation.

But this hope was not realized. She then attempted to retrace her steps; but here her perplexity was as great as before. Having become bewildered, she was doubtful what course she had come. To go back in the dark was utterly impossible, and to remain in the woods, through the night would be perilous. She therefore continued to call for help until she could call no longer; and to wander on, feeling her way in the dark, until exhausted with fatigue. She now made up her mind that she must here pass the night, notwithstanding her dread of wild beasts, which she heard prowling at no great distance around her. She dared not to sit down, or think of taking repose, lest she should become their prey. Having therefore found a short space, where she could walk back and forth, she determined to keep all harm at a distance by vocal prayer, and singing psalms and hymns, with which she had stored her mind. Thus early was this wilderness, the midnight hour, made to resound with the praises of God, and thus was her soul sustained in the perils of darkness, while prayer and praise were made her defense! Her husband, supposing that she had found the woman more ill than she had anticipated, and had concluded to pass the night, retired quietly to rest. But as she did not return in the morning, he early repaired to his neighbor's house, and learning that she had not been there, he immediately conjectured her situation; and started forth to rescue his lost wife. By the sound of his horn, she was enabled to ascertain the direction of her home; and turning her steps thitherward, she arrived in season to eat a joyful breakfast with her husband, for which she had now a sharpened appetite. This circumstance she related but a short time before her death, in her 94th year, with a minuteness and interest which showed that it made, as well it might, a very deep impression upon her mind."[1]

By the way, in today's church we call what she did by praying, singing and pacing, intercession. Like prayer and singing, intercession is a form of covenant fidelity connection. Our early ancestors believed in the supernatural power of God to provide for them in practical ways. Because they invited God in, He showed up in the ways they wanted Him to help them in, as this story from circa 1766 suggests. In fact, during the blizzard of 2016, busloads of Catholic high school and college students were returning from the March for Life in Washington, D.C.[2] They shared supplies while holding a worship service for stranded motorists on the Pennsylvania Turnpike.[3] Some could argue if they were listening to God in the first place, no one should get stranded. That is an interesting point, but not the one I'm making here to show traditional covenant fidelity. As I've mentioned, we are human and certainly don't do everything "right." Thankfully when we do mess up, or the unforeseen takes place, the belief then, as it is now, whatever area we decide to let the Almighty into, He can show up to help. Deuteronomy 8:18 says, "You must remember the Lord your God, for he is the one who gives ability to get wealth; if you do this he will confirm his covenant that he made by oath to your ancestors, even as he has to this day." (NET Bible®)

Then as now, the majority were not looking to walk on water or turn water into wine. They were just looking for good crops and weather and shelter and love and kindness. Covenant and its parameters gave them that and much more. The Bible and its teaching lessons helped them create societies which promoted honesty and integrity and a form of supernatural reproduction in money (the tithe). Even a secular covenant provides similar effects. These facts are important. Kings use up a substantial portion of a peoples' goods and services. Corruption and ineptness wastes a lot of time and money. We see this in our present system today. That's because it has strayed from its roots. A system which ferrets out both corruption and ineptness shows itself superior. A frugal government run by frugal people in fidelity to the greater and common good (especially biblically) uses up less of the peoples' time and energy. More is left over for those families who are intact and able to pass these techniques of fidelity in both law and love to the next generation. The tithe is God's supernatural economy based on faith. You give a portion (ten percent) and He promises to pour you out a blessing you cannot contain.

The question can be asked, "Then why can't socialism or progressivism, as it is now called, be used in the same fashion?" In later chapters I will prove scientifically and biblically why it cannot and will never be able to enfranchise a majority. Over time, it only and always will create an elite minority who must control the majority in order to function. Whatever attempts we make to solely and only control human nature by secular means, will never be able to control human nature, except by force.

Let's look at the various concepts which made our early state documentation what it is today. In some state constitutions you couldn't be anything but Protestant in order to hold office (Delaware and South Carolina) or Christian (Maryland). In some states we see a clear separation of the branches of government. This premise is also in the Bible (Isaiah 33:22; Jeremiah 17:9, because of our untrustworthiness). This is carried over into many Christian teachings of the day, but especially the Puritans where Calvin's teachings preached the *depravity of man*. This is still taught in seminaries today. It basically proves without Divine Intervention, mankind follows a state of moral decay instead of moral betterment. As it relates to government, the understanding is taught too much power held in the hands of one man (or group) will result in tyranny, unless the group is controlled by the Holy Spirit.

You actually see that thought in the earliest constitutions of Connecticut, Delaware and South Carolina. These people lived this with the King of England and other monarchs, courtiers, sycophants and the like. Should it be any wonder they embodied an understanding of the separation of the state from the church? The understanding is quite old and predates the colonies by hundreds of years. The phrase itself came out of the Reformation and a time period before, where church leaders were tired of the monarchs controlling them and their theology. Many of these regime's rules were coercive and brutal. In fact, in countries like France and Spain, they would have been connected with the Catholic hierarchy in coercive government. This is one reason why we have an elaborate system of checks and balances, along with explicit language defining institutional limits. These protestants needed this to survive. If that were not enough, we have an independent judiciary which is unique from the Britain of old.

What you never see in this country (until 1947) or taught in our schools about the founding of our nation, is an idea that church must have no mention in or voice to the state, or any vocal display in public. The idea was to keep the state from dictating the theology and affairs and ideas of the state to the religious. It is impossible to maintain the kind of separation we see by interpretation now, without institutionalized persecution. The evidence for this persecution is seen when books written by Christians are removed from schools, or when Christian speech is banned, or the wearing of messaged T-shirts, as well as other restrictions of our First Amendment rights.[4]

Early on, the separation issue morphed into an idea the state should not have to pay for the church's upkeep. There was a primary purpose to the state and a primary purpose to the church. Eventually and functionally they separated during the 1700s surrounding the upkeep issue. But there were established state-sanctioned churches in some areas up until the 1800s. That was what forming the new territories which became states was all about. One group would disagree in a biblical area of theology and off they would go and get a charter and form their new church-state or stated church which became a territory which became a state.

Three states formed as a direct result of not being able to abide by the Puritans' rigid adherence to all aspects of what they believed to be doctrinal purity. Religious freedom was fine for the Puritans, but their attitude was that it was not "as fine" for everyone else! Those states were Rhode Island, New Hampshire and Connecticut. The most religious out of the three constitutions was Connecticut. It is called the Constitution State because it was the first state to have adopted an early form of constitution. You might argue it was actually Virginia. Virginia's were written under direct British oversight. Even in those northern colonies which had charters, they still wrote in autonomy.

Looking at Connecticut's document, our Federal Constitution has some of the same principles laid out in it. Thomas Hooker, a Puritan minister influenced its genesis.[5] New Hampshire's mentions God as well. Even though Rhode Island kept its charter made with King Charles II for quite some time, Roger Williams assisted in writing the Providence

Charter (1644) and the "Acts and Orders of 1647" and the Rhode Island Charter of 1663.[6] In similar fashion William Penn forms Pennsylvania for the Quakers.

Much of this autonomy was the direct result of their theologies. The average British citizen would have believed government should rest within the purview of the nobleman. These Protestants read in their Bibles God gave government to man to govern the earth and instill God's blessings among their fellow man. As a result, this idea of popular sovereignty becomes an active part in our documentation. Many would argue it began with Greece and Rome. It is doubtful these early settlers read much about Greek and Roman ideas of democracy. The colonist's connection to popular sovereignty was found in Reformation ideas connected to the Bible. Our idea of popular sovereignty is based more on biblical values than we realize. It is now and was then, far more intense than those seen in England at the time, or even now. Europeans still have a hard time understanding why we eschew a monarchy and cry "We, the People" incessantly.

In mentioning Connecticut, most of us don't realize the separation issue and toleration acts start in a constitutional form in this country with Connecticut's formation. Rhode Island has earlier laws, and practiced separation earlier, but no form of constitution. The right of all, not just church members, to participate in civil government (at least in the colonies) comes from a dispute over theology (the science of God) between John Cotton (supported by Massachusetts' colony) and the Reverend Thomas Hooker. Cotton believed only proven saints, evidenced by church membership, should have a voice in civil government. Reverend Hooker believed the social covenants they drew up as civil documents instructing governments (early constitutions) should be "chosen by all." In other words, the rights were inalienable: All humans were born with them. The disagreement continued to progress to the point Hooker is quoted to have made the statement "I should neither choose to live nor leave my posterity under such a government."[7]

Reverend Hooker then moved his congregation to set up their own government outside of the jurisdiction of the Massachusetts Bay Colony.

They formed three towns. Within three years' time of settlement in dealing with civic issues, their general court instituted a constitutional covenant governing them. Thus the Fundamental Orders of Connecticut of 1638-1639 was born. It afforded the right to vote to any freeman living within one of the three towns, as long as they were proven to be of high moral character by a magistrate. By removing the need for church membership as a requirement for participation in civil government, these Puritans became heralds for toleration as well as the separation issue long before England's 1689 Toleration Acts.

When you look at the history of each state, almost without exception they all eventually develop one aspect, to lesser and greater degrees, of religion in mind. Was treasure and fortune there as well? You bet it was and with equal effect. But in their minds, there was no dichotomy. Why should there be? God blessed financially. Among many, including the Puritans and especially the Puritans, a sign of the blessing of God was financial.

Speaking of the Puritans, they morphed into two groups: the Presbyterians and Unitarians. Present-day Universalist-Unitarian is not the same as the early founding of Unitarian. As we shall see, eventually they did become anti-Christian, but initially they were not. Unitarians were considered Christian. They were non-Trinitarian Christians. Many puritans were Congregationalists. Congregationalists would form from different covenant-based church groups.

Another fact establishing theological divisions which helps to explain the need to separate power, has to do with the wholeness of human beings. In those days, their theology did not extend to an understanding of emotional wounding in the sense it does for some churches today. Today we view wholeness biblically as health within realms of spirit, soul and body. In those days, you believed, got saved and lived accordingly. It was, in many respects, more legal and practical as opposed to a more spiritual view like we hold now. Today we actively seek healing. This minimizes new churches or new sects forming, unless God specifically speaks to start a new church. In those days, unless your body was in rough shape, there was no need for healing. They did not equate bad behavior and the need for transformation in our souls as some churches equate it today.

In those days, you obeyed or else. For them it was not something to be discussed and worked out. You either agreed with the group or you got booted.

This is why the Puritans were so interesting. To have two different groups within their ranks, one understanding the need to change from within and the other understanding the need for separation in a healthy respect, is further proof they were reading their Bibles. To make it sound like they 'did lunch' on a regular basis is incorrect. When one side could not see the logic of the other sides' argument, they kept their distance. That distance sometimes went so far as to form a new state. By way of example today, we see the same attitude among atheists concerning the faithful, the religious when they avoid atheists and the non-religious when they won't discuss politics or religion.

Divisions among Protestants were not the only catapult for legal solutions. Maryland's long struggle with Catholicism and Protestantism led her leader, George Calvert (Lord Baltimore), to put down a rebellion from the Jesuits. They attempted to undermine his ownership in the colony by trying to make a deal with the Indians for land. The Jesuits insisted only Canon Law was supreme and all civil government was subservient.[8] In an effort to stop this rebellion you have a law in Maryland declaring no one can obtain land for religious purposes unless the legislature approves it. Secondly, no priest or clergy can hold elected state office (yet as I wrote previously, you also had to be a Christian to be a citizen and hold office).[9] Calvert was a convert to Catholicism from Protestantism. That fact alone and his ability to work with the English Crown, in my opinion, makes him somewhat of a gifted ambassador-diplomat. He was a religious man, making the colony and eventually what became the early State of Maryland, a very tolerant place for public as well as private religious practice. Surprisingly enough, by the Jesuits going directly to the native land owners, they were reinforcing the idea of nature's God and people found in nature as subservient to that God, and not the king. Although, Calvert could not tolerate the Jesuits' attempt at takeover.

The need for separating the powers and the language we see in the documents enunciating the thought was there to protect religion and individuals from the abuse of a government run amok. They had a personal history with that in their time. I think every one of us, looking at what's gone on in our nation in the past 50 years can agree. The memory from dissenting religious groups of persecution was alive and well. After all, that's what they were fleeing as they started a new state. We have developed, what would be for the colonists, an odd thought process that government was separate from the people. These church folks were the government. The idea of popular sovereignty for them was the fact that *they* were the government.

There were some odd religious sects showing up on our shores as well. That's why you have a guy like Roger Williams forming Rhode Island and keeping his distance, both spatially and doctrinally and forming government to reflect that. He wrote a political tract which called for religious freedom and freedom of conscience called "The Bloody Tenent."[10] The very first documents for civil government (unhindered by England and not demanding church attendance) were written in 1637 by Roger Williams in what we now call Rhode Island.[11] It was written as a covenant but without a religious oath because Williams viewed such a thing a sin because it took the Lord's name in vain. Instead of relying on the oath, it is structured on the biblical values of popular sovereignty seen at the time. In fact, on our shores Williams himself became involved with one of the different sects which emerge later on. The fight Williams had with other religious sects has even played itself out in modern times because of our lack in understanding his idea in separating church and state.[12] Rhode Island kept her charter in place from England. I can't help but think this must have been a reminder of the tyranny of a monarch as well as a protection from any future bondages his later progeny would know as the new Federal government.

In fact, Rhode Island was the last state to ratify the United States Constitution. The Federal government itself under the Articles of Confederation almost collapsed because of a fear of despotism (among other things). Enlarging the powers of Congress was not something the states wanted to do. There were internal arguments for non-ratification peculiar to each state. For instance, Rhode Island delayed ratification for reasons other than the bill-of-rights issue, though that was a primary concern. Another reason was its size in comparison to other states. Why ratify when the larger states will force their will on you anyway? And then there was the paper money issue. Not without merit, many argue this was more of an issue for Rhode Island than any other, including a bill of rights.

This was more than a thought for concern for some in other states as well, not just Rhode Island. Hard currency is how debt was paid off. But in more agrarian districts devaluing money by tendering debts—a bartering system of some kind or other either in paper or trade in kind—made it cheaper to pay off those debts. A strong central government would hinder that cause. Many make a worthy argument this was the real reason for Anti-Federalist's attitudes within some states. With the issue of debt also owed to England under Article IV of the Treaty of Paris, most states as well as most Americans, resented the thought a strong Federal government would require them to pay for British pre-Revolutionary War debt. Personally, I've often thought this was issue number one against ratification for the majority of those Americans so inclined, with the lack of a bill of rights as either a twin or close second for non-ratification. In point of fact, the Revolution was fought for economic reasons. The history supports the argument. I've already used the example of liberty and religious freedom, as one side of the coin of Revolution, with economic reasons on the other side. The Bill of Rights (with the first right as religion) is part of the liberty and freedom side of the coin.

Nevertheless, the whole notion of a Federal constitution almost fell on its face because many states refused to ratify because it held no bill of rights. All of these initially church-run groups (states) had one. The Anti-Federalist's argument to control a powerful and unbridled Federal government was one many felt could be solved with a bill of rights. Some did not. It came to a head and the fact of the whole thing collapsing— government, constitution, one single nation— without a bill of rights was obvious, so fragile was the reality of a Federal government. So, voila! We now have The Bill of Rights of the United States of America.[13] The arguments concerning these two documents were so fierce, not only in protecting our freedoms but in making sure we did not become a tyrannical form of government.

This should not be read as a timeline for the arguments either. Mine is not a linear approach. Our Federal government was in session when the last state ratified the Constitution. It took from May 25, 1787, when the first Constitutional Convention met, to May 29, 1790, for the Constitution to be ratified by the last of the thirteen states: Rhode Island, with the mention of commercial annulment![14] On December 15, 1791, the Bill of Rights (or first ten amendments to the Constitution) were ratified. I don't know if these men could have gone far enough in protecting us from how reprobate the government has become. They couldn't have foreseen how bad it has gotten. But they did leave behind thousands of documents letting us know their experience told them to worry, and to let us know to be vigilant.

As long as covenant was practiced, vigilance against tyrants was not as great a problem. Because the formation of states was done by so many different religious Christian groups, there seemed to be an underlying understanding of the need for unity, even though human nature seems to adore divisiveness. The covenant method, which gradually turned governmentally civic and non-sectarian is what was employed early on. States forming for mainly economic reasons rather quickly became infused by the covenant blueprint. We can see over time documents which enunciated covenant clearly, were replaced by specific language for the actions which would reproduce the same result.

For example, when church membership roles were no longer used as citizen roles, the property ownership rules became more pronounced. In other places, freemen with certain definitive requirements filled the void. We will review other ideas encouraged by biblical covenant and reinforced by English, Greek and Enlightenment influences in future chapters. But within state constitutions you see a desire to have men who owned *something* involved in government. The idea was to have folks with an inherent interest involved. Just as the Pilgrim leaders knew they needed everyone involved, the states understood the same principles. English monarchs fostered this approach as well.

Free will was as strong an idea among the Arminians as covenant was among the Calvinists. Both are aspects of our covenant with God.

Property owners are people who are independently minded (free will) with skin in the game so what works for one tract of land within the community works for the other (covenant). In other words, what is good for the community is ultimately good for everyone or the largest number of people. This came directly from the preaching of the gospel in the colonies. It came directly as a practice in England. Connected to needs already mentioned, is the need to pay for community expenditures. If an expenditure is not necessary or can be settled in a less expensive way, because you are an owner and will be paying for the tax or tax hike, you have a keen interest in preserving integrity in this area. All the Christian sects within the colonies were frugal in this regard. It was also a religious necessity learned from church affairs. Economics comes in to play here as well: One cannot deny gravity! The connection of being a freeman and/or property ownership to voting rights is seen in all the state constitutions at some point in time. In some cases it became a secularized answer to the need for a covenant of community.

Another attitude the biblical group brought over here was an attitude of excellence. This permeated what they did. Some of it may have stemmed from their desire to show those back in England their way of governing worked best.[15] We know they saw it taught in the New Testament (Colossians 3:17, 23, 24; Ephesians 6:7). We know this attitude infected our founders and their respective governmental agencies well into the 1800s. Quite possibly it had something to do with the attitude among the majority religious population of virtue and piety—almost as a form of worship for the deists—and even the various societies and orders (freemasonry). We know the English had a history of inebriation and "excellence" was not a necessary desire for the commoner, the same way it was here in the colonies. Whatever the exact causes, this attitude was the reason why our military was dedicated to a spirit of excellence. It was why, until the last 50 to 100 years, you could trust the Federal government.

In fact, it was a rarity to see a court decision made in violation of a voter's, Christian group or state's rights. Now, it is rare that a decision is made to protect us from the Federal government. In fact, our Constitution specifically makes the judicial branch the weakest of the three. The thought of impeaching a justice, including a Supreme Court justice, when they ruled against the will of the people or ruled based on foreign law, thus obfuscating American Constitutional law, or were involved in behavior "unbecoming" was common knowledge. It was well known that it was not an office for life in the sense they were unimpeachable. Early on there were attempts at removing justices for some of the above offenses. Though when it comes to the Supreme Court, impeachment proceedings have not met with success.[16] My point is, whatever factions joined to produce it, formerly our spirit of excellence came from sources extending from the Bible, since the population was overwhelmingly Christian and Jewish.[17]

Obviously, you don't have to be a follower of the Bible in order to function in a spirit of excellence. This is mimicked by example, which is why it is quite possible various groups exhibited such an attitude. The saying, "it's more caught than taught" would apply here. Within the Old Testament in Jeremiah 35, there is a story told of a group called the Rechabites (see also Jeremiah 34 for the back story). They were strangers who decided to live peaceably among Israel. Jeremiah is called to preach captivity to the Israelites because they have repeatedly broken God's covenant. The Lord sends Jeremiah to the Rechabites and tells them because of their obedience in following their forefather's commandment they will never cease to have a blessing from the Lord's presence. What is this story saying? If you decide to live among the people God's covenant extends to and you do no harm— like removing their money, symbols or encroaching on their rights to practice their beliefs— and you do what is excellent, as you are commanded to do, even if God's people go into captivity, you will be spared! Stories of excellence abound, both in religious and non-religious circles in America. Why? We first saw it in the early colonists, then in the early founders and later as the country got into her early youth.

In these few, short paragraphs we see several possible reasons why we, as Americans today, have such an independent, and sometimes damaging attitude when we don't agree with one another. Yet we also see how the atheist, as well as everyone else has had the benefit of living in a country which valued the rights of individuals in matters of conscience to live peacefully, accordingly. It's better than a great experiment. It is now a scientific fact.

ENDNOTES

1   Lancaster, Daniel. 1845 "Proprietary, Civil, Literary, Ecclesiastical, Biographical,
        Genealogical, and Miscellaneous History, from the First Settlement to the Present Time;
        Including What is Now Gilford, To The Time It Was Disannexed," Gilmanton: Printed
        by Alfred Prescott. 73-74. Public domain and can be seen in pdf through New Hampshire
        State's Archive. Archive accessed 1/28/16.

2   <http://www.nytimes.com/live/winter-storm-jonas/> see "No Longer Stranded in
        Pennsylvania" article by Ashley Southall. Accessed 1/30/16.

3   <http://www.post-gazette.com/news/state/2016/01/23/Archdiocese-of-Omaha-
        students-celebrate-Mass-on-snow-altar-while-stranded-on-PA-Turnpike-due-to-snow-
        storm/stories/201601230125> accessed 1/30/16

4   <http://www.foxnews.com/opinion/2014/09/23/school-accused-purging-christian-
        books><http://www.washingtonpost.com/local/education/christmas-stricken-
        from-school-calendar-after-muslims-ask-for-equal-treatment/2014/11/11/f1b789a6-
        6931-11e4-a31c-77759fc1eacc_story.html><http://radio.foxnews.com/toddstarnes/
        top-stories/texas-lawmakers.html><http://radio.foxnews.com/toddstarnes/top-stories/
        parents-call-textbook-anti-semitic.html><http://radio.foxnews.com/toddstarnes/top-
        stories/students-told-to-call-9-11-hijackers-freedom-fighters.html> accessed 3/19/16

5   Lutz, Donald S. 1988. "The Origins of American Constitutionalism." Baton Rouge, LA:
        © 1988 Louisiana State University Press. 120

6   Ibid, 120 (see note)

7   Edward Hooker, Commander, U.S.N. "The Descendants of Rev. Thomas Hooker, Hartford,
        Connecticut, 1586-1908." Edited Margaret Huntington Hooker. (Rochester, NY: E.R.
        Andrews Printing Co. 1909) Introduction xxi. Public domain and can be seen <https://
        archive.org/details/descendantsofrev00hook> accessed 3/23/16

8   <http://www.christianchronicler.com/where_to_go.html> Click on the "Other Religious
        Groups." Michael Hines, author; accessed 3/16/16.

9   <http://avalon.law.yale.edu/17th_century/ma02.asp> Maryland Declaration of Rights,
        Article XXXIV and Maryland Constitution, Article XXXVII; © 2008 Lillian Goldman
        Law Library; you can read all of the originals on this site; accessed 3/16/16.

10   <http://www.constitution.org/bcp/religlib.htm> site © constitution.org; accessed
        2/27/16.

11   Donald S. Lutz, Colonial Origins of the American Constitution: A Documentary History,
        ed. Donald S. Lutz (Indianapolis: Liberty Fund 1998). [Online] available from <http://oll.

libertyfund.org/titles/694>; accessed 2/25/16; Internet. Document 32, titled "Providence Agreement."

12   The old source of contention between the Massachusetts puritans and Roger Williams' brand of religion extended the separatist argument among the puritans in relation to their colonial government, not just the government in England. See a proper theological understanding of the use of Roger William's "wall" metaphor in a "Bloody Tenet" <http://www.americanminute.com/index.php?date=02-05> (accessed 3/30/16)

13   <http://law2.umkc.edu/faculty/projects/ftrials/conlaw/billofrightsintro.html> ©2001-2011; University of Missouri-Kansas City Law School; Doug Linder, author; accessed 3/15/16.

14   <http://avalon.law.yale.edu/18th_century/ratri.asp> © 2008 Lillian Goldman Law Library, 127 Wall Street, New Haven CT, 06511; accessed 1/26/16. Look especially at the language of the various amendments to see the flavor of what troubled Rhode Island.

15   Campbell, Donna M. "Puritanism in New England." Literary Movements. Dept. of English, Washington State University, last modified 7/4/13 © 1997-2010 Donna M. Campbell <http://public.wsu.edu/~campbelld/amlit/purdef.htm> accessed 3/18/16 <http://www.christianchronicler.com/where_to_go.html> click on "The Puritan Scene." Michael Hines, author; accessed 2/25/16

16   <https://www.washingtonpost.com/news/answer-sheet-wp/2015/12/12/can-a-supreme-court-justice-be-forcibly-removed-from-the-bench-a-quick-civics-lesson/> accessed 2/16/16

17   98.4% Protestants; 1.4% Catholics and .2% (Other) mainly, Jews; "One Nation Under God;" © 2005 Coral Ridge Ministries; The DVD is still available on Amazon and EBay. I do not know where they got that breakdown from, though they are not out of line with the 1790 census or other sources I list here. There is a 'hard copy' source on the Library of Congress' website. They claim "Between 1700 and 1740, an estimated 75 to 80 percent of the population attended churches…." <http://www.loc.gov/exhibits/religion/rel02.html> accessed 1/26/16. The census of 1790 should also play a role in this discussion and those numbers are comparable to the previous ones quoted. Those census numbers are available online to download. There is also military study guides which use a 1775 date for statistics on religious affiliations and beliefs: "Define White-American as defined by DoD Dir. 1350.2.2. Describe the origins of White American and the different groups in Colonial America." Lesson 13 from the U.S. Army @ Fort Bliss, page 10, section c. dated 2001 produced by the Department of Defense. While their figures are slightly different compared to the other sources, [98% Protestant; 1.4% Catholic and .12% Jewish] they are

similar enough in expressing majority Christian-Jewish populations. This source is more helpful in that it goes back further than the census statistics.

Chapter Seven

COVENANT AND IGNORED HISTORY

We have talked about some of mankind's historical response to God in the colonies and their desire to maintain a covenant relationship. But were there any responses from "Above" to this early nation and our tether-corded cousins in Europe? The answer is yes. The next question is, do we see a counter-culture and/or in some cases, a response from those who are uncomfortable when God gets so close? The response, again, is yes. Was a mid-wife called to cut the cord and deliver the different responses within the various groups to the culture, counter-culture and the various social functions in between? Again, the answer is yes. Obviously I cannot go into the detailed history taking place between the 1700s and 1800s in Europe and America. Neither can I go into a detailed history of revivals and other supernatural occurrences in this country during the same time period. But do we see a pattern similar during Israel's Covenant building as a nation?

Each time God wanted Israel to take a portion of land that was to become hers— land created by God and given legally to Israel some 4,000 years ago (David made Jerusalem the capital over 3,000 years ago)— someone (even within Israel herself) would say, "not so fast" and start a war. When Moses wanted to move the Israelites farther along, Korah said, "no" (Numbers 16). When Israel asked for neighborly help in ancient times, the Moabites and Ammonites said, "no." Even after Israel settled in her land in 1948 other nations said, "no;" Saudi Arabia, Muslim Brotherhood, Iran, to name a few. Many more can be named.

You could argue this struggle has been going on with many different people groups for quite some time. While that is true, you don't see the same hatred and dogmatic zeal to murder and annihilate not only the people, but even the memorials of an entire culture. Both China and Egypt predate Israel as a nation and had to occupy their land for a far less time period before everyone else got the idea they were there to stay. This has not been so for Israel. China, Egypt and Israel are some of the oldest, perpetually named societies to occupy relatively the same land mass with a similar ethnic government in place through the history of mankind.[1] I would submit the very existence of tiny, little Israel makes a case for the God of the Bible. You can disagree. What no one can deny is the history of miraculous occurrences which have taken place when a covenant is made with the God of the Bible.

Many events in Europe, and Britain in particular, had an effect on our culture here. Some of those affected the furtherance of, and our desire in, maintaining our beliefs in God. As Puritanism's influence was waning, 1689 toleration acts were enacted (English Bill of Rights). Broadly speaking, they removed legal and other restrictions placed on Protestant groups who would not be part of the Anglican church. Eventually these benefits made their way to the colonies. Some received the benefits sooner than others. In places like Virginia where Anglicanism was the state church, it took longer. Making their way throughout the colonies, Presbyterianism filled the void Puritanism was leaving. Many Puritans became Presbyterians as other groups started to spring up. State and church were not separate; the states paid for the churches. Because there were so many different groups migrating and competing for state money, a separation is seen in this crucial area of finance throughout the 1700s. This was their act of separation of church and state. It was never antagonistic or persecutory as we see more recently.

From the 1600s on, denominations needed schools to train their ministers and pass on religious learning. Quite a few colleges were formed to do just that: Harvard in 1636; William and Mary in 1693; Yale in 1701. What would eventually become Princeton was founded by the Irish minister William Tennent, Sr., in 1726. King's College (Columbia) came into existence by royal charter in 1754. The Baptists set up an institution in 1764 which became Brown University. Dartmouth was founded in 1770, and Rutgers came into being in 1825. These and many others were founded to provide leaders in the church as well as the state.[2] All of the schools were founded upon one denomination's religious learning with courses structured around subjects taught through the lens of their particular biblical worldview. The first school to change this was founded by Thomas Jefferson. The University of Virginia was meant to be non-sectarian. All denominations were welcome.[3] It was founded in 1819, with classes starting in 1825.[4]

As we saw with Reformation and Renaissance, this time period of roughly 1650 through 1800 affects our own thinking today in ways we may not all wish to acknowledge. It is during this time we see the beginnings of revivals or awakenings (The Great Awakening), along with what's called the Enlightenment period. The Reformation was tilted toward developing theological reform from the Catholic Church. We see spiritual awakening but not to the extent we see later with the great revivals. The Renaissance also awakened folks classically, opening up their eyes to new and different arts, sciences and philosophies. Renaissance was also more involved with denying the Catholic Church as opposed to refuting God or opposing Protestant protesters, which Enlightenment came to symbolize in some countries as it denied divine revelation and Protestant theology. I understand this is not even close to explaining the differences. But mine is not that purpose. I merely wish to draw quick generalizations in this specific area in order to show a pattern.

The various awakenings happened almost simultaneously, as did the various Enlightenment movements. It was not always or necessarily a targeted response. But it was almost as if an unseen hand was drawing a line in the sand. Protestantism produced a very dry and cold orthodoxy in theology. There was little to no fervor in spiritual experience. In the colonies a decline in spiritual awakening was taking place. In some places people were becoming downright heathen! They were now following

England down a path of drunkenness and debauchery. Pressures from westward expansion, the work of separating the state from the church, along with the breakout of different skirmishes (wars and mini-wars) took a toll on a psyche where the dry and cold theology of Protestantism showed itself inadequate for the spiritual task. This evidenced a decline in moral as well as religious effect.

In answer to this, the revivals started small, within various rural and congregational areas from the 1720s on. The colonies were being warmed to the idea of spiritual awakening, so when the revival which started in Jonathan Edwards' church began in 1734, nothing could stop it. Samuel Davies (1723-1761, Presbyterian) carried the revival to the South. The Baptists moved in revival in the South as well through the preaching of Shubal Stearns (1706-1771) and Daniel Marshall. Early forms of Episcopalians and Methodists got on board also. George Whitefield came over from England during seven visits from 1738 to 1769 and unified the different efforts of the various revivalist preachers.[5]

This was the first Great Awakening in the colonies. There was a second one later in time. In New England alone the first one produced 30,000 to 40,000 new converts and 150 new churches out of a population of roughly 300,000.[6] Those figures do not take in to account the middle or southern colonies. This was no small bout with miraculous occurrences. Maybe that's because of the widespread decline in religious fervor. I found more than one source which mentioned the fact that some of our early founders, including Benjamin Franklin looked favorably upon the Great Awakening.[7] Besides colleges, many missionary endeavors took place with philanthropy and conversion in mind. It is said the colonies looked like a different place in the home, work and entertainment after this time period than immediately before it.[8] Most books and historians place this as the origins of our present day evangelicalism, though the term itself predates the Great Awakening in the colonies by more than 200 years.[9]

Revival fires were not limited to the colonies. Quietism had been ebbing and flowing in Catholic circles in both Spain and France since the early 1600s. It became a life for many in England as well in the 1700s. (See the

Church of the New Jerusalem in London, 1788.) The Quakers and the various offshoots of them have their origins on the European Continent during this time period. The manifestation of the Divine was in their involuntary "quaking," thus the name. There are modern Quaker examples of this manifestation. They are different from the various revival 'shaking' seen in the last 100 or so years.[10] Quite a few manifestations of the 'shaking' type have been produced during revivals in between. This cannot be attributed to mankind's example since, in some cases, hundreds of years have separated this one manifest illustration of the Divine.[11]

One of the largest and most influential revivals was seen in England, Ireland and Scotland with the preaching of John Wesley and the music ministry of his brother, Charles. John started preaching in 1739 and continued until his death in 1791. Thereafter, the Methodist Church was formed and formally broke with the Anglican Church. By the time of Wesley's death he had 70,000 followers and a Methodist Church in America was started. In 1746 he opened the first free medical dispensary in England. It is said because of Wesley, the same bloody and violent revolution which took place in France because of Enlightenment thinking did not bring about another bloody war in England. Many of the English workers were won to Christ because of Wesley as the various labor leaders of Ireland, Scotland and England got their training in speaking at his class meetings (Bible study societies).[12] He opposed liquor, slavery and war. The lower classes of England were transformed by Methodism, but because Wesley would not break with the Anglican Church, the upper classes were also affected. Some historians attribute this miraculous transformation as helping—along with so much other history—to make England the great leader of nations and keeper of world peace we see during the 1800s.[13]

Miraculous revival occurrences had its detractors within the churches. The detractors existed somewhat abroad but especially in the colonies. In fact, the greater response to schism was seen in the colonies. Some of the churches wished to kick the revivalists along with their "bad habits" of ordaining ministers based on spiritual gifts and not intellectual, theological learning out on their butts. This was not unlike their puritan-Christian forebears' practice of starting new states. The Wesleyan revival minimized this attitude in England. But with the rise of worldwide English colony building, there was also a backlash toward the idea of English Christianity and thus revivalism in particular.

Unitarianism also developed during this time and became codified after the Second Awakening in protestation over that revival.[14] They were originally part of the Presbyterians but had roots far before that in Arianism and Socinianism (300 AD and Reformation, respectively). This was one of the first schisms developed in protestation over the Great Awakening. Originally they believed the Bible, emphasizing the goodness of man, the unity of God and the humanity of Christ, but the Trinity was out. As time went on, salvation by character culture was seen in their midst. Unitarians at first considered themselves Christians— as did many other Christians— and were not hostile toward the orthodox. But this liberal, quasi-biblical outlook would not last. By 1865 all mention of Christ would be struck from their doctrines, clearing the way for what is now basically an anti-Christian group. Many confuse Unitarians with deists because their beliefs seem similar. But early on they were very different groups and people. Some of our founders were Unitarians and leaned toward it. As a result, many nowadays place them as deists. This is a mistake, as we shall see shortly.

As I mentioned before, there wasn't just one "not-so-fast" response to God's idea of covenant-keeping among His people. There was also an 'Ishmael' growing up somewhat before, and simultaneously with, the 'Isaac' of the church (metaphorically speaking). Several church historians I read drew a distinct line between the orthodoxy of Protestantism along with its cult-like obsession to rationalism, and the formation of two responses. One was inside the church. The other was from those who may or may not have believed in a God. Both groups wished to move the world with ideas of rationalistic thinking in everything from the sciences, politics, arts and to somewhat of an unfortunate degree, theology.[15] When it came to theology, if there ever was a period of time proving the thesis of the depravity of man, this was it.

The rationalism movement of this time period produced English Deism, the illuminati, the French Enlightenment period, the German Aufklärung and, by the time it found its way to the colonies, a mix of these different ideas, infused with our own brand of colonial thought. This thought was influenced by the covenant God of the Bible, who was preached consistently from many different pulpits.[16] Popular culture today places a huge role of the illuminati on Enlightenment thinking. But history tells a different story.[17] Clearly rationalistic thinking became the fulcrum of the movement. It developed in many different locales. In most cases rationalism as a result of what could be observed was at its core, with virtue and piety ruling above all, especially here in the colonies.

In fact, here in the colonies, the idea of virtue and piety among the deists became one of the agreements between them and the majority Christians which could form a "more perfect" union. In Europe, rationalism was also fueled by the work of scientists like Copernicus, Galileo and Newton, all of whom believed in the God of the Bible, though almost equally treated by the Roman Catholic Church as heretics.[18] As with the Renaissance, folks were seeing the Roman Catholic Church was not infallible. While the natural laws of science were not in conflict with the Bible, they were so for some in the Catholic Church during this period. This started the antagonistic trend that fueled the bloody Revolution in France, though it was not its only source. Even today, many forget the theology of Roman Catholicism and Protestantism is vastly different. Natural laws discovered by reason in science led to similar applications in political science, economics as well as religion.

John Locke applied many of these applications within the realm of political science. He was a Christian as well as an Englishman who wrote with the signage of his times.[19] While he was a leader in the thinking of natural laws and reason, his was toward liberalizing the common man and the inner workings of government as it related to the laws of nature and nature's God. When many tried to take his work out of context by using it to build the antagonistic trend of the state toward Christianity, he wrote three works: "The Reasonableness of Christianity (1695); A Vindication of the Reasonableness of Christianity" (1696) and "A Second Vindication of the Reasonableness of Christianity" (1697). The last two he wrote to vindicate his work from some prominent church folk and the antagonism he experienced from them.[20] It seems he also wrote these in the hopes they would quell the discussion of him being a deist.[21]

Locke lived between 1632 and 1704. Many of the religious dissenters preferred to have their governmental structures within compacts. In matter of fact, our three-part Federal documents are not social contracts. They are governmental social compacts. We will review the difference shortly. Locke was what those who wrote our Constitution would have called a compact theorist.[22] Locke's parents were puritans. When he was exiled from Great Britain because of his collaboration with Shaftesbury, he lived among French and Dutch Calvinists.[23] His compact theory of government was a secularized version of covenant theology.[24] His ideas confirmed a good fit for those who would sign their names to the Declaration of Independence. It was Jefferson who named Locke as one of four individuals who influenced the writing of the Declaration of Independence. Yet it is wholly and independently a document which is our own:

> "Not to find out new principles, or new arguments, never before thought of, not merely to say things which had never been said before; but to place before mankind the common sense of the subject, in terms so plain and firm as to command their assent. . . Neither aiming at originality of principles or sentiments, nor yet copied from any particular and previous writing, it was intended to be an expression of the American mind. . . All its authority rests then on the harmonizing sentiments of the day, whether expressed in conversation, in letters, printed essays, or the elementary books of public right, as Aristotle, Cicero, Locke, Sidney, etc."[25]

These ideas of government were what Jefferson said were common or elementary books among the public, one of which was Locke. On the French side of this equation in the political sciences was Charles-Louis de Secondat, Baron de Montesquieu. He is an interesting character. He was not antagonistic against Christianity at all, but definitely felt the Catholic Church did not fit in with any of the natural laws of reason. For that matter, the absolute monarchy with its governmental trappings had fallen far short as well. He leveled much of his ridicule against the Catholic

Church and the monarchy in his fictitious "Lettres Persannes." Yet many years later he writes, "What a wonderful thing is the Christian religion! It seems to aim only at happiness in a future life, and yet it secures our happiness in this life also."[26] Even stranger, is the preparation for his death, which he did by receiving the sacraments of the Catholic Church.[27] If he were a deist, this is not how he would have done this.

Many ideas of separating executive, legislative and judiciary powers, abolishing slavery and torture, toleration in religious belief and freedom of worship are seen in the teachings of these men. Yet they are different. If I had to sum up what difference we see within our own framework of documentation, I would say Montesquieu wrote concerning institutional genesis within constitutions. Locke wrote about the genesis of countries in general. Locke was used for declaration purposes but Montesquieu would have been used for constitutional purposes. Montesquieu wrote in favor of placing the known conditions of time and place on enacted laws and including experience and traditions in its developments. He, as well as Locke wrote in favor of Christianity but Locke supported the separation of church and state. Montesquieu did not:

> "I have never claimed that the interests of religion should give way to those of the State, but that they should go hand in hand."[28] "The Christian religion, which ordains that men should love each other, would, without doubt, have every nation blest with the best civil, the best political laws...."[29]

He never wrote as Locke did on theological matters and was decidedly no churchman, especially in his earlier years. But it is obvious at some point in his life, he believed and that belief, to whatever extent we can read in his writings, lent itself to Christianity.

It is also important to realize the difference in our definition of the separation of church and state and the definition during the different times these men wrote in. The Toleration Act of 1689 was meant to allow different church groups certain freedoms they otherwise would not have. Those in support of the separation of church and state would define their position in those terms. Later in time, the definition (especially and particularly in France) would lean toward the removal of church (the

Catholic Church) and God from any public life. In different countries and in different time frames, the definition would be limited to money, in the sense the state would no longer support churches financially. The antagonism seen most recently was not the definition understood in our American colonial founding era.

I did come across a statement in my research which said Montesquieu borrowed much from Locke as it related to Montesquieu's Spirit of Laws ("L'Esprit des lois").[30] In over 15 different research sources of these two men, I found no one else who suggested that Montesquieu borrowed from Locke. Since it does appear in our National Archive, I could not discount the statement entirely as false. It is obvious many of these thinkers read one another and/or had the opportunity to listen to or read various debates by contemporaries. In fact, this digestion is where ideas from one generation flow to the next, become upgraded, redefined and/or even thrown out and rebuilt.

Later in time (1765 and 1769) and right smack in the middle of the debate over rationalism, the laws of nature and of nature's God, and their effect on the governments of nations, the great English law professor, Sir William Blackstone wrote his "Commentaries on the Laws of England." He lived between 1723 and 1780 and he was not a deist. His work was infused with Judeo-Christian principles.[31] It was the primary legal reference for our Founding Fathers and remained such for lawyers and judges until the mid-Twentieth Century. It was then that a successful attack was levied at the heart of our Constitution and our nation's heritage of biblical covenant.[32] While Blackstone was not the political science theorist others were, his work was timely. He did a great service to this country in the sense he consolidated the common laws of England, even where no consolidation could be found.[33] Here is an amazing fact concerning Blackstone and how influential he was to the men who wrote, debated, and lived during the writing of our three-part Federal documentation: When an argument ensued concerning some aspect of law or theory, if Blackstone was cited, the argument ceased so the one citing Blackstone was the victor.[34]

It seemed to me when it came to the period of time many call "Enlightenment," these mentioned and some others were more in line with many of their Renaissance elders as it relates to the church. In other words, they brought the thinking of their day into their belief system. They were men of their times, using contemporary terminology for their specific area of rational thinking. While it would be bad history to say they were all deists or atheists, it would be equally bad history to say they were all orthodox in their Christianity. Just as equally poor in history to say they were like Locke, who wrote on biblical studies in an effort to promote and/or defend Christianity. Such was not the case; these were different men.

The time period called "Enlightenment" produced other political science buffs who came to very different conclusions from the previous mentioned. Scholars divide the movement called "Enlightenment" into different categories and time periods. As a general reference when talking about "Enlightenment thought," these thinkers usually refuted any other way to get knowledge except by discovering truth according to reason, without any divine revelation. There are lists of what many refer to as Enlightenment thinkers; some we have mentioned. There were others: Rene Descartes, Edward Herbert, David Hume, Charles Blount, John Toland and Lord Shaftesbury in England, among many others.

Some became what we call deists. Deism was a religion without written revelation which said the moral law was within man and the natural laws of religion were discovered by reason. Most of them believed in a transcendent God who caused creation and left it to operate under natural laws. They believed in virtue and piety, almost as a form of worship to God. They also believed the Bible was an ethical guidebook. Deism in England was limited to the upper classes, who traveled to France, melding the thought with the French. When listing the men above, it must be mentioned after involved studies on some of them, the clear line between them and deism is not so clear. In some cases it is, but in others it seems they did not sign on to deism. I think what may confuse some or allow others to claim them for their own, is their Christianity may not have been orthodox in its theology.[35]

Under the French, deism became an argument against the Catholic Church and the monarchy. Men like Rousseau, Voltaire (Francois M. Arouet), D'Alembert, Diderot and Montesquieu provided political cover for the right of popular revolt against Louis XVI and the Catholic Church. The bad economic conditions in France, coupled with the aftermaths of the successful 1689 civil war in England and revolution in 1776 in the colonies, produced a fevered desire toward what they thought would be an unbridled utopian freedom. It was not. This tinderbox brewed for years, decades even.

Decidedly bloody and chaotic, these ideas of Enlightenment in France produced more of an atheistic hatred and desire to remove all mention of God from their governmental structure. Mine is not to absolve the Roman Catholic Church in France from its murderous and thieving guilt; just to broadly overview the story for our understanding of colonial thought and highlight some differences between a true godless revolt taking place almost at the same time. It reached a frenzied pitch in 1793-1794, during what came to be called the 'Reign of Terror,' when the Catholic Church and the French State separated. The atheistic leaders tried to force a religion of reason on France in which they crowned a young actress the goddess of reason in Notre Dame Cathedral.[36] They changed the calendar so every tenth day rather than Sunday was a day of rest. It was adopted on October 7, 1793, and lasted until 1804. Its specific purpose was to eliminate all mention of God, thus Sundays and the various saints' days would have to go as well.[37] Hence the practice in Christian nations of inviting and cataloging the Lord into legal documents by the term *Anno Domini* ceased.

Of course, the hearts of the people were not as easily changed. In 1801 Napoleon proposed a settlement of sorts between the French State and the Roman Catholic Church; whose pope, by the way, they captured and held in a French prison, where he died. The Concordat of 1801 recognized Roman Catholicism as the "religion of the great majority of French citizens." Bishops were named by the state and consecrated by the pope. They were paid by the state but the property which had been confiscated by the state during the 1790s was not to be returned to the church. Papal bulls (letters or decrees from the pope) as well as synods, which were council or meetings of church leaders, mostly bishops, could not be published nor held in France without the express consent of the state.[38]

Deism and revolution in the colonies (as well as England) was of a very different type. Already mentioned was the effect of Wesley's revival in England. In the colonies deism never gained any traction among the 'common folk' as it did in France, only among the upper classes, and that, not in great number. The Library of Congress states: "Deists, never more than a 'minority within a minority,' were submerged by evangelicalism in the nineteenth century."[39] In America the upper classes were a true minority. Many Americans shunned an upper class superiority produced by bonds of royalty, as it was in England. Instead, ours was one produced through higher education and knowledge, which, quite often produced wealth; yet they were still a minority. The type of deism seen in early America is usually not of the variety leaning toward atheism. There were those that were very anti-religion (think, Thomas Paine). Remember our best example for a godless Constitution, and an attempt by leaders for a godless government, is the French Revolution. In that they were successful. But that was never the desire here. If it had been, that is what we would have gotten. Anybody reading our founding documents can see very well that is not what we have.

What we should not be confused by is the terminology used centuries ago. Some use this vocabulary to depict someone as a deist. The term "nature and nature's God" (as well as other rationalistic language) is used by all: orthodox Christians, non-sectarian Christians, those who were of some variety of deist and atheists of that day (think France). They all used the same terminology. The terms used are quite consistent with a very religious Judeo-Christian worldview, wishing to include all by not forcing certain beliefs on all.[40]

As Renaissance ideas and terminology are no indicator for a person's belief in the God of the Bible, the same can be said of the use of Enlightenment thinking and terminology. If Bibles and copies of the classics of antiquities could be accessed, they were dutifully read by our ancestors in the colonies. Their time period of rationalistic thinking melded quite well with many who held orthodox Christian and Jewish doctrine. Remember that rationalism came out of the Reformation. It gave many hope they could develop a more perfect union, learning from the mistakes of those who had gone before them.[41] Enlightenment thinking and terminology only strengthened their biblical worldview of God granting power to the people and the people granting limited and specified power to the state. But remember, there was an 'Ishmael' growing up at the same time. That thought was that the STATE was sovereign and all powerful, without God at the head. This idea had taken full root in France, where poetry and artistic license was growing more and more decadent in its expression. Modern socialism-communism has its evolution in these ideas, and would later be developed through Kant to Marx.[42] It is now termed as 'progressivism' and is embraced by the Democrat Party in America.

While I don't intend to go in-depth into Enlightenment's effects on the arts, I would like to make mention of one such response from Heaven to it. We all know Georg Friedrich Handel (George Frideric Handel, Anglicized) and his work, the "Messiah." Many may not know that by 1741, while he was living in London he had somewhat of a career crisis. Heavily in debt, and with the threat of a life in debtor's prison, he became so discouraged some scholars think he was contemplating a return to Germany. It was during this time that a man by the name of Charles Jennens was troubled by deism's teachings. As a response, he selected various texts from the Old and New Testaments on the Christian Messiah and took them to Handel to set to music. The text Jennens gave to Handel consisted of 42 verses from the Old Testament and 31 verses from the New Testament. In total, seventy-three verses from the King James Version describing the biblical Messiah. Additionally, a charity in Dublin, Ireland, paid to have him write a new work for a humanitarian performance. With this convergence of events, the musical performance of "Messiah" was born. Within 24 days Handel had a 259-page score. Even today, scholars marvel over the scanty amount of errors for a work of its size. Handel is quoted as saying, "I did think I did see all Heaven before me and the great God Himself."[43]

They viewed this piece as an outreach for evangelism. So instead of relegating it to the churches to perform, they took it to secular artists. Its effects were grand. In fact, the practice of standing during the "Hallelujah" chorus is because when it was played for the King of England a year later, he stood. There are several different stories as to why he stood, but the result was the same. Since no one could be seated while the King stood, all stood. He said it was because God was so strong in presence all should stand. They used the proceeds to provide for those in debtor's prison as well as orphans. Handel himself was so moved while writing it he refused to sign his name, wishing to give the glory to God. So he signed it, "SDG" or Soli Deo Gloria meaning, "To God Alone the Glory."[44]

Humans, being what we are without influence from on High frequently resort to decadence within, and sometimes especially in, the church. The history of this nation has been a spontaneous and miraculous religious revival when those conditions arose. There are too many to enunciate over the 200-plus years of our existence. But they are evidence to the covenant-keeping abilities of God.[45] There are specific promises in the Scriptures which apply. Whether because a war is coming and the people need encouragement or when decadence is in control, our early Bible-reading forebears would have understood these revivals or awakenings as specific help from on High. The decline or decadence would be viewed as an attack from spiritual enemies as well: "When the enemy shall come in like a flood, the Spirit of the Lord shall lift up a standard against him." (Isaiah 59:19, see full verse. Psalm 68 is also a good overview to this biblical teaching. There are many others.)

Whether we are reviewing the Reformation, Renaissance or Enlightenment, attempting to draw exact belief systems of everyone involved based upon what we see today of the belief systems which bear the same name, is poor history. We have to evaluate them based on their own words, along with the totality of what they said. It's important to learn about episodes which may have produced a certain document or thought. Even though we can make those connections, we must realize people are not all ONE thing. While God does not change and the Bible does not change, belief systems evolve and change. Not even the revivalists of this time period can be said to believe exactly as revivalists of today. People can have interests in agriculture, theology and science— be true saints, total demons or something in-between to live with— but people are not always ONE thing. Another condition evident upon us as humans is time. Some folks form a relationship with Jesus at an early age, but decide not to follow Him as they get older. It can be just the opposite with other people, or you can see every experience in between.

Let's illustrate the point when it comes to this period of time and rationalism. We've talked about the Calvinistic influence of the Puritans on our country. Through Anglican households, that doctrine was infused from childhood to men like Washington and Jefferson. We did not speak as much about Arminius and his followers. His followers migrated through the teachings of the Dutch Reformed Church. The influence of his doctrine was seen in the colonies much later, just about the time of rationalistic thinking in Enlightenment (pre-Revolutionary War). The struggle between the two spiritual camps is fleshed out among the Methodists (who came from the Anglicans) and the Mennonites (who have doctrinal connections to the Quakers), along with other groups. The struggle between the two doctrines was thought to be inseparable. With the migration of rationalistic thinking, the rationale for both spiritual trains of thought became both/and, instead of either/or. This awareness is playing out while rationalistic thinking produces many ideas, from deism to atheism.

I mention this because these ideas are flowing and moving among our founding fathers, influencing as well as training their way of thinking, coupled with an enduring understanding of Christian covenant. Calvin's ideas demanded only divine sovereignty toward covenant— God was in control, no one else— thus He should also receive the blame when we fail. As a result of that kind of thinking, Arminius argued for human responsibility toward covenant, thus absolving God of our faults. Rationalism demanded that you think about what can be proven all around you through observation, including the Scriptures. Covenant government— the Christian way— proved by observation that action in this area produced virtue and piety. These were traits our founders demanded and wanted followed, whether orthodox Christian, colonial deist or full-blown atheist—by the way, a rare individual during that time period in this country. It had been thought Calvin and Arminius could never live in the same house, yet through rationalism they could. By observation they could see that following the Scriptures as a guidebook, certain positive benefits were elicited from society as a whole and from the "Unseen Hand of Providence."

I have often thought the difficulty in understanding our ancestors for students and scholars of today has to do with this synthesis. We want them to be "one thing:" either perfect Christian or perfect atheist. Certainly I don't mean to make it sound as if they were all biblical scholars, or this time period of rationalism was an end to itself for the production of our form of government. It only built upon centuries of thought which went before it. What also makes it difficult for fans of American history today is our ignorance of the colonists' biblical literacy. To understand the struggles and differences for them, we have to understand the times they lived in as well as the religious events and thoughts which swirled around them. When we do, we understand their desire of freedom for everyone to practice their religion. We also understand why they all condoned, and in many cases agreed with the Judeo-Christian ethic and the Bible as that guidebook. We would understand the plethora of, and varying concepts for, biblical interpretation of the day.

In understanding these ideas, we can then see the individuals in which these patterns found like-minded souls. We can also understand how Unitarians were still considered some form of Christian and Quakers were viewed somewhat suspiciously. When we don't look at the depth of the history, we would assume Unitarian means anti-Christian; Quaker means spiritual giant and ALL deists of the time were hostile toward Christianity. Even though none of that was true. We would even understand the political parties of the day better (Whig, Federalist, Anti-Federalist). If we do not have an understanding of their lifestyle of church attendance, of their various forms of work and work ethic—so different from our own—of their reading material and other social structures, we could understand nothing. We would assume piety and virtue was an after-thought for these forebears and that they believed those could be attained outside of the parameters of biblical/religious constructs. Also, not true. We would never be able to accurately ascertain the real beauty and truth sought in our founding documents. Lastly, our assumptions of those documents would be tainted, our thinking corrupted by that taint, and our interpretations eventually would render us unable to maintain those documents and their pure effects on our society as a whole.[46]

ENDNOTES

1   Contrary to popular myth, Israel has never left the land. Even in the 1920s when the League of Nations, official pre-cursor to the UN, gave her land and her people member status and other rights under the San Remo Resolution, approximately 60,000 Jews lived in Israel. See <http://www.jewishvirtuallibrary.org/jsource/History/jewpop2.html> © 2012 The American-Israeli Cooperative Enterprise. Their source is the Israeli Bureau of Statistics. I used this site because of the chart which looks at Jewish inhabitants of Israel compared to Jews living worldwide. See a DVD for purchase at this site <https://www.cbn.com/special/landdvd/landdvd.aspx> Accessed 3/19/16.

2   Cairns, Earle E. 1981. "Christianity Through The Centuries." Grand Rapids, MI: © 1981, The Zondervan Corporation. 366

3   Hutson, James H. 2000. "Religion and the New Republic: Faith in the Founding of America." James H. Hutson, ed. Lanham, MD: © 2000 Rowman & Littlefield Publishers, Inc. 49-52

4   <http://uvamagazine.org/articles/1825_old-school/> Accessed 2/29/16.

5   Cairns, Earle E. 1981. "Christianity Through The Centuries." Grand Rapids, MI: © 1981, The Zondervan Corporation. 367

6   Ibid., 368

7   <http://www.christianchronicler.com/where_to_go.html> click on "The Great Awakening" Michael Hines, author; accessed 2/16/16.

8   Cairns, Earle E. 1981. "Christianity Through The Centuries." Grand Rapids, MI: © 1981, The Zondervan Corporation. 368

9   <http://www.loc.gov/exhibits/religion/rel02.html> accessed 2/29/16

10   See also the Revival at Brownsville in Pensacola, Florida, from 1995 to 2004 for examples of the 'shaking' type. <https://en.wikipedia.org/wiki/Brownsville_Revival> For the 'laughing or joy' type of revivals see Dr. Rodney Howard Browne from 1992 to the present <https://en.wikipedia.org/wiki/Rodney_Howard-Browne> and the "Airport" Church in 1994. <https://en.wikipedia.org/wiki/Toronto_Blessing> accessed 1/26/16. While Brownsville would be more involved with the 'quaking' manifestation, the other revivals would also see folks 'shake' as well. None of them have been connected to the Quaker religion of today.

11   There are two different stories of how Quakers were named. See: <http://www.sonofthe-south.net/revolutionary-war/pilgrims/quakers.htm> and <http://www.wisegeek.com/what-is-the-religious-society-of-friends.htm> for a modern-day quaking experience that is very different from what the modern-day revival 'shaking' experiences are like—even though they may look the same to outside observers. <http://hystery.blogspot.com/2008/04/do-liberal-quakers-quake.html> accessed 2/16/16

12   Cairns, Earle E. 1981. "Christianity Through The Centuries." Grand Rapids, MI: © 1981, The Zondervan Corporation. 384

13   Ibid.

14   Ibid. 418

15   Ibid., "Christianity Through The Centuries," 373-375

16   Hamburger, Philip A. 1993. "Natural Rights, Natural Law, and American Constitutions." The Yale Law Journal. Vol. 102: 907. 916 , 917

17   Almost all sources credit Adam Weishaupt of Westphalia with starting the secret society in 1776. After his death it was clearly absorbed by the broader 'Age of Enlightenment.' Sources as common as Wikipedia will give you an overview of this. A more in-depth review of Weishaupt's life can be read at <http://www.newadvent.org/cathen/07661b.htm> accessed 2/5/16. Others follow the trend of Weishaupt's group in different directions, from Kantian philosophy to socialism. <http://plato.stanford.edu> accessed 2/5/16. This site's search engine connects the illuminati to other such individuals. But for our purposes here looking at a moment in history, the illuminati morph into Enlightenment thinking.

18   It is not my purpose to review the exact minutiae of these individuals' religious beliefs. Many claim it was their beliefs that labeled them heretics by the church and not their discoveries. The argument may have value for the academic, but for my purposes in writing this book, it does not.

19   There are those who claim Locke was not a Trinitarian Christian. While the discussion certainly has merit, it is not relevant for my argument of covenant, namely because Locke was heavily influenced by covenant theory and secularized its application when it came to political science. The other reason I won't review his religious beliefs is because when I read what I have of his body of works, I find quite a developed idea of salvation inconsistent with non-trinitarianism. And that may very well be the case: he may have had beliefs inconsistent with, but his belief was. So it seems that if evidence can be had for both sides of the debate, it would and should be a healthy and lengthy one; which debate would not be necessary to engage here. The next endnotes give you sites to view his religious as well as political theory works from.

20   There are many sites you can read Locke's bodies of works from. <http://oll.libertyfund. org/people/john-locke> © 2004-2014 Liberty Fund, Inc. <http://www.libraries.psu.edu/ tas/locke/bib/ch0i.html#Reas> and <http://www.libraries.psu.edu/tas/locke/bib/ch0i. html#controv> © 2015 John C. Attig; accessed 3/6/16. Or Google your own.

21   Ibid.

22   Lutz, Donald S. 1988. "The Origins of American Constitutionalism." Baton Rouge, LA: © 1988 Louisiana State University Press. 18

23   <http://www.fee.org/freeman/john-locke-natural-rights-to-life-liberty-and-property> see © Foundation for Economic Education; accessed 2/29/16.

24   Lutz, Donald S. and Jack D. Warren. 1987. "A Covenanted People: The Religious Tradition and the Origins of American Constitutionalism" Providence, RI: © 1987, The John Carter Brown Library at Brown University, and sponsored by The Lily Endowment, Inc; The Rhode Island Committee for the Humanities. 53

25   Carl Lotus Becker, The Declaration of Independence: A study on the History of Political Ideas (New York: Harcourt, Brace and Co., 1922). 25, 26. In the public domain.

26   You may also read many of Montesquieu's works and many of his positive statements concerning Christianity in general at: <http://www.constitution.org/cm/sol_24.txt> accessed 3/17/16. See next note also.

27   Dégert, Antoine. 1911. Charles-Louis de Secondat, Baron de Montesquieu. In The Catholic Encyclopedia. New York: Robert Appleton Company. Retrieved 3/29/16 from New Advent<http://www. newadvent.org/cathen/10536a.htm> " © 2012 Kevin Knight. Dedicated to the Immaculate Heart of Mary."

28   See note 26 and 27

29   <http://www.constitution.org/cm/sol_24.txt> © constitution.org; accessed 2/29/16.

30   <http://www.archives.gov/exhibits/charters/constitution_q_and_a.html>National Archives, page 5, Constitution of the United States, Questions and Answers, written by Sol Bloom; site accessed 2/29/16.

31   Charles J. Reid, Jr. 2004. "The Unavoidable Influence of Religion Upon The Law of Marriage." 23 Quinnipiac Law Review 493 (2004). 1. See William Blackstone, Commentaries on the Laws of England: of the Rights of Persons 54 (1765) the legislature "acts only . . . in subordination to the great lawgiver, transcribing and publishing his precepts. . ."

32   You may access Blackstone's writings as I did at Lonang Institute: <http://lonang.com/ library/reference/blackstone-commentaries-law-england/> While this next reference is unabashedly Judeo-Christian, the importance of studying Blackstone, especially for those having no frame of reference for biblical covenant in law and thus Blackstone in particular,

is made in simple argument and thus the reason for this reference: <http://www.black-stoneinstitute.org/index.php> If you click on the William Blackstone tab on top of the site and then click on the "downloading this" article written by Virginia C. Armstrong, Ph.D., you will be able to read the debate. Site © 2012-2015 Blackstone Institute, Abilene, TX, USA; accessed 2/29/16.

33   <http://www.britannica.com/biography/William-Blackstone><http://avalon.law.yale.edu/subject_menus/blackstone.asp> accessed 2/29/16

34   Donald S. Lutz, "The Relative Influence of European Writers on Late Eighteenth-Century American Political Thought," American Political Science Review, Vol. 78, No. 1 (March 1984) 196, 197

35   <http://www.britannica.com/biography/Rene-Descartes> accessed 2/29/16. For example, it seems to me that Descartes' theology was more in line with that of Jacobus Arminius, who was an associate. Arminius was one of the leaders of Reformation thought, whose ideas have infused modern-day Christian theology in many different ways, including our political landscape of freedom for religion. Descartes also wrote in favor of the existence of God, actually making an attempt to prove His existence by reason of thought. John Locke was a great fan of Descartes. See <https://www99.libraries.psu.edu/tas/locke/bib> site accessed 2/29/16.

36   Cairns, Earle E. 1981. "Christianity Through The Centuries." Grand Rapids, MI: © 1981, The Zondervan Corporation. 390

37   Ibid.

38   Ibid., "Christianity Through The Centuries"

39   <http://www.loc.gov/exhibits/religion/rel02.html> accessed 2/29/16

40   Hamburger, Philip A. 1993. "Natural Rights, Natural Law, and American Constitutions." The Yale Law Journal. Vol. 102: 907. 916, 917. See also Lanshe, James. 2009. "Morality and the Rule of Law in American Jurisprudence." Rutgers Journal of Law & Religion. Volume 11, Part 1, 18

41   Lanshe, James. 2009. "Morality and the Rule of Law in American Jurisprudence." Rutgers Journal of Law & Religion. Volume 11, Part 1, 10-14

42   Cairns, Earle E. 1981. "Christianity Through The Centuries." Grand Rapids, MI: © 1981, The Zondervan Corporation. 378

43   <https://en.wikiquote.org/wiki/George_Frideric_Handel> To view a small clip on these stories or read the article you can go to <www.cbn.com/cbnnews/us/2011/December/Handels-Messiah-Inspires-Listeners-Transcends-Time> accessed 3/16/16. You can also read noted Handel scholars Tim Brown, Ruth Smith as well as a book with many of these historical facts by Calvin R. Stapert titled, "Handel's Messiah, Comfort for God's People."

Another book, while not solely concerning Handel, mentions some stories surrounding Handel's work. Patrick Kavanaugh's "Spiritual Lives of the Great Composers." Some of the facts noted can contradict one another in these various works, like the story as to why King George II stood.

44   Ibid., news clip

45   Schmitt, Charles P. "Floods Upon the Dry Ground." Shippensburg, PA: © 1998, Destiny Image Publishers. 129-246

46   Lanshe, James. 2009. "Morality and the Rule of Law in American Jurisprudence." Rutgers Journal of Law & Religion. Volume 11, Part 1, 18-23

Chapter Eight

GODLY COVENANT: A STRUCTURE FOR THE FOUNDERS AND "WE, THE PEOPLE"

Historians today have to make analyses of people living from the 1600s to the early 1800s through the lens of our modern-day personal experience. I've often believed this makes it difficult to speak accurately about the practices, ideas, lifestyles and countless people having an influence in the founding of our nation. If the folks living in 500 or more years' time only read news clips of today's media, they would know nothing about the majority faith of this nation (70 percent Christian). They would think Hollywood was all we paid attention to and "twerking" is what a majority of us did. They would think a large segment of our population were homosexual (only one to three percent). They would think all those working in the sciences were geeks, a majority were bullies, people who believed in the Second Amendment were gun-toting nuts, and we were all socialists. When told exactly what socialism is, an overwhelming majority don't want it, even though they vote for it consistently.[1] You may disagree with my examples but the fact remains if future generations have a limited pool of evidence to get a grip on our society, their view of our society is going to be quite fallacious.

With our inability to be "flies on the wall" of previous centuries, we must narrow down the influencers to those whose names made it through centuries of documents. Because of that, we will need to look at the specific ideas or documents which birthed a covenant approach. Up until now I have tried to give a broad religious approach to history, with a broad-stroked approach in revealing a governmental covenant directive. Obviously, a thorough history of the 200 years leading up to 1791 would be volumes and volumes of books. To the end of writing about our three-part Federal documents, we did not take an in-depth look at specific British, Greek, Roman or European influencers. They all influenced our government and Federal documents, some more than others. It's not my purpose in this chapter to look at exact percentages. There is research material out there which attempts to do that.[2] We will look at that shortly.

There is a great depth of material proving various influencers on our documents. My purpose is the influence of covenant specifically and religion in general. In this chapter, I would like to look at some specific church documents which formed the understanding for the churches, then communities, then state, confederal and finally our federal documents. These early documents were written by the religious to answer political theory issues and questions. Some were in response to other ministers' apologies. Some were sermons preached by ministers. We reviewed some early colonial documents and we will review some documents written by the religious which reveal similar principles seen in present-day federal documents as well as precursors of federal governance. I also suspect some were written to prove to those in England their idea for the formation of government was more perfect than what Europe was experiencing.

These documents are filled with political ideology which formed governmental structures like early covenant-compacts, early constitutions, early legislatures and voting blocks, early ideas of our distinct republicanism and early forms of freedom for religion, including direct ideology from the Reformation for inalienable rights. This was "Theology 101" for politics. Politics which became church governments, that became church-civil governments, which eventually became civil governments with a penchant towards religious ideals. As I have mentioned previously, constitutional concepts morphed and evolved as a result of environmental influences, both within our country and outside of it. Yet the same covenantal structure of documentation remained. There were specific

English common law practices which found their way to our Federal documents. We have constructs and principles seen in our present Federal documents which started as a biblical ideology but later morphed into what we have now because of influences made decades later.

One striking difference between researchers looking at history and researchers who try to specifically omit religion as a major contributing factor is the depth of research. Those reviewing all the history without omitting religion, rely on a huge amount of source material. After much time spent in reading, I came across so many books and researchers who told the truth about the contribution that religion made and specifically Christianity and Judaism, that it would be quite impossible to include them all. I will only be mentioning a handful. What I did come away with was the revelation, at least for me, that the specific teaching and preaching of Old Testament covenant theology was in their heads as well as their hearts, even before the Puritan settlers sailed to the colonies. This was their blueprint for a new government. So in a real sense, this specific type of religious teaching actually birthed and was intertwined with the politics of the early settlers.[3] I knew the Pilgrims did this, but I never realized until this research Massachusetts Bay Colony did the same thing and how much they influenced the rest of the colonies. I had always thought that the "cat just kinda got outa' the bag." In other words, the practice of church just flowed into society. But that kind of thinking is tainted by my modern experience.

In fact, the Massachusetts General Court was a court controlled by church hierarchy and was applied secularly to all. The truth is they made every intention and successfully did start their civil politics with only Christians and only bound by written covenants framed by their religious theology.[4] In other words, the practice of covenant governing them in church was intentionally applied to covenant governing them civically— and it was **secularly** applied— *not in an attempt to omit religion,* but to protect it and their human rights, **as well as** their governmental and economic policies. Rules of evidence and due process are critical in any court. In Massachusetts they were Biblical Rules of Evidence and Due Process.

Massachusetts General Court governed a land between the Connecticut River and the Atlantic, from roughly Maine to Springfield inland and somewhat south of Boston on the coast. Over time this changed with the additions of New Hampshire, Rhode Island and Connecticut. Plymouth Colony was absorbed into Massachusetts in 1691. Nevertheless, over time, as they wrote specific secular civil documents, they applied the exact same form of covenant to those documents. One such document describing this was written by John Cotton in 1642, titled,

✝ "The True Constitution of a Particular Visible Church, Proved by Scripture."[5] He was passionate in his position that all government had to be based on Scriptural principles.

Noted historians agreed it was the different theologies among the church groups which birthed their specific different church covenants. These theologies became a major influencer in our own peculiar form of government in early America. Government by the consent of the governed, reliance on a written constitution, and belief in a higher law is what separated us from Europe at that time.[6] These people were told over and over again they were special to God and they were chosen to start over in a new land— a land given by God, just like ancient Israel— and here were the Scriptures to prove it. Those preachers turned to the Old as well as the New Testaments to teach and show proof of their doctrine.[7]

It was because of their belief in a higher law that they were told by their preachers to obey that law. The Bible is a book of law, with consequences for disobedience. Because of this, these church-government covenants held certain bills of rights, or statements of fundamental values and principles which formed the basis for the covenant. All bills of rights are covenantal through basic theory. In essence the people are listing rights not given up, as they list what government (through constitutions/institutions) must do. In likewise fashion, many community, state and finally our federal documents have a bill of rights. The Bible revealed the doorway for these principles. Magna Carta held the door open, allowing our early settlers to walk into biblical revelation. Let's look at the continuing thought of these doctrines through two centuries.

John Winthrop said in the 1600s: "The eies of all people are uppon us, soe that if wee shall deal falsely with our god in this worke wee have undertaken and soe cause him to withdrawe his present help from us, we shall be made a story and a by-word through the world."[8]

Look at the understanding of this doctrine infused into John Adams' language over 150 years later:

> "The people in America have now the best opportunity and the greatest trust in their hands, that providence ever committed to so small a number, since the transgression of the first pair; if they betray their trust, their guilt will merit even greater punishment than other nations have suffered, and the indignation of Heaven."[9]

I have no intention of putting words in the mouth of our second president, but why would a nation suffer the "indignation of Heaven" if there were not some type of understanding that the nation— the "We, the people"— had made an agreement or "trust" that could be broken? This idea of the covenant of our Federal documents was not something misunderstood. It may now be understated, but it was then well understood. So much so that over 125 years after Adams' quote, historian Bishop Charles B. Galloway, when speaking for the inclusion of slaves among the citizenry says:

> "The time has come, therefore, for us to claim and demand the full *fellowship* and absolute *confidence* of our great *national brotherhood*. The *fidelity of our people to their political covenant* and their loyalty to the flag that floats over them have been attested by the valor they have displayed and the blood they have freely spilt."[10] (Italicized to show covenant thought.)

Government by the consent of the governed was never done to the extent it was done in this country. Bills of liberties or rights were an integral part of church covenant documentation. The idea was not new. The example for these ministers' parents and great-grandparents had been Magna Carta. They were Englishmen along with various other Europeans who knew of the Magna Carta document. But bills of rights or liberties had never been used to the extent the church groups who came to this country used them. These were written and enacted *before* the 1689 English Bill of Rights (or toleration acts). Because very few political scholars today understand the nature of the Bible as a book of political thought and what exactly the worldview of both Jews and Christians is and how that view affects government, whenever you talk about the "We, the People" apparatus, their brain immediately translates into all things Greek. There is no argument influencers outside of Christianity employed consent of the governed as a form of function. More immediate sources did as well: Locke, Blackstone, Enlightenment thinkers. But these initial settlers had a more immediate problem neither Greece, Rome, England or Enlightenment could or would solve.

Aristocrats had always controlled the government and the monarchy was its head. As we have seen, the Puritans in this country could not stand a church with even the hint of aristocracy; hence their refusal of Anglicanism (non-separatist Puritans or dissenters) and Catholicism. This presented a challenge for them. Who and how would their civil government run if the elite, the special, the aristocrats or the noble born did not do it? As in all challenges for Christians of many different sects, a major source for answers is the Bible. Do humans also incorporate and copy other solutions as well? Of course, they do. Yet these Puritan ministers knew anointing extended to ALL in the Scriptures (Galatians 3). Eventually, and over time, the teaching and instructions for living and government reflected that understanding. Look at what Pastor John Robinson wrote to the Pilgrims as they were leaving for the colonies:

> "Lastly, whereas you are to become a body politic, using amongst yourselves civil government, and are not furnished with any persons of special eminency above the rest to be chosen by you into office of government, let your wisdom and godliness appear, not only in choosing such persons as do entirely love, and will promote the common good, but also in yielding unto them all due honour and obedience in their lawful administrations . . ."[11]

The idea that men without special aristocracy, elitism or noble birth could and should govern themselves, stayed with them throughout the writing of our Federal documents.

Look at the sentiment of George Washington some 160 plus years later concerning the state of the confederacy when he wrote to John Jay in an August 15, 1786 letter:

> "What astonishing changes a few years are capable of pro-
> ducing! I am told that even respectable characters speak of
> a monarchical form of government without horror. From
> thinking proceeds speaking, thence to acting is often but
> a single step. But how irrevocable & tremendous! What a
> triumph for our enemies to verify their predictions! What a
> triumph for the advocates of despotism, to find that we are
> incapable of governing ourselves, and that systems founded
> on the basis of equal liberty, are merely ideal and fallacious!
> Would to God that wise measures may be taken in time
> to avert the consequences we have but too much reason
> to apprehend."[12]

These ideas produced many other concepts. The first is our own form of republicanism. I am not saying two legislative houses or choosing representatives from the people to a senate of sorts did not appear on history's shores previously, most notably in the Roman form of government. Americans did not invent bicameralism. But there was a more immediate ancestor on our own shores. This one was very different from the England these settlers came from. Remember we are a republic and NOT a democracy. This distinction is important in that democracies (in theory) are more corrupt in outcome. The majority can be bought or otherwise hoodwinked. Mob rule and constant use of protestation and subtle and outright bullying by name calling with the suggestion the 'other' side is insensitive, hateful because of their disagreement— "doesn't care for the common man or the poor"— is in constant use by those who want social-ist and/or communistic democracies. They control, by many different means, what a people hear and know. Today's control of mass media by the ideology of progressivism is one example. When you do find out how much truth is being withheld from "We, the people," it makes you realize we have truly crossed over to a state-run media— at least in proactive ideology— while leaving the hope of a free press behind.

In contrast, republics are run by representatives who are picked by population count or some other identifying class. They are elected or appointed by a means of decision of the people to "BE the people" and act on their behalf. A truly free and unbiased theological presbytery and press tells the truth and does not use its position to filter what the people hear. Instead, it just tells the 'news' or preaches the truth and lets the people decide. Thus the truth influences churches and/or elections or the decision-making process— not special interests— not those on public dole or churches which corrupt the biblical truth. This is why our first two rights are freedom of religion and speech, both for religion and a free press.

In 1643 Richard Mather wrote,

✝ "Church-Government and Church-Covenant Discussed."[13] Notice the hyphens in the title of this document. This was a discourse concerning what many Puritans viewed government must contain as a three-part system. Christ as the monarchal element, church elders as the aristocratic element and the church members were the element from the republic. As previously mentioned, this blended system was not new. Aristotle had written about a similarly blended system of government. Both Old and New Testaments reflect such systems before Aristotle was born. Think of Father, Son & Holy Spirit from the New Testament and God, Moses & Aaron from the Old Testament. Thereafter they would replace God with a king. Before Israel replaced her Heavenly King for a human one, we see prophet/judge as the executive arm, the priesthood as the aristocratic arm and the fathers/elders as the arm of the republic. Of course it was Isaiah who wrote: "For the Lord is our judge, the Lord is our lawgiver, the Lord is our King; he will save us" (Isaiah 33:22).

But who do you think was closer in the minds and hearts of this covenanted people; Rome, England, Aristotle? Or the Bible? They formed individual states which had three-part systems long before the framers of the late 1700s were born. Even today at the Federal level, the House of Representatives is more closely associated with the people, while the Senate is more closely associated as a relatively cultured and educated bunch. Our present practice for choosing the senate was not how it was originally done. It was changed. In church practice the elders are picked from the people. The senate was formerly chosen by the state legislatures and sent to the Federal forum. That is no longer the case.

Another extension of our form of republic is a system of checks and balances. Again, an understanding of checks and balances is seen in many governmental systems. The Pilgrim/Puritans had a very interesting system of checks and balances. There are those today who have made total abuse of executive and judicial power and complain our system of checks and balances is too extensive. I would disagree. Our system of checks and balances was far more intense than any other the world over at that time. After I review the system the Puritans set up, many of us would understand our tradition of redundancy in this area.

Their first requirement was that the individual would confess and share their salvation experience to the local congregation. By the way, this is still done in almost all Bible-believing churches today. I dare say, if any of you have ever listened to what must be learned and the oath taken to become a citizen of these United States, the principles echoed in a "testimony" meeting is not that far a leap in similarity.

Next was the election of church elders to officiate the distribution of power. A pastor was chosen to preach; a teacher was chosen to make sure proper doctrine was adhered to. Elders were chosen to oversee spiritual procedural issues. Finally, deacons were elected to take care of the everyday needs of the church, which would include the care of the poor and needy. Again, this is not so very different in Bible-believing churches today.

Lastly, each of the households held interlocking covenant with their minister/churches, which became towns. These church members (at that time, male only) voted to elect what they called "selectmen" to run the towns' daily needs. Additionally, town meetings were held to vote on the needed legislation within each town. I dare say, it is not hard to see the election process, the system of checks and balances, and the individual requirements of responsibility toward community evident in the systems of almost half the early settlements, spreading to the rest of them. In fact, the Puritan system concerning factual proof for conversion is what eventually did them in, as well as their strict adherence to their view of biblical life. As I have mentioned before, even in those communities where Puritanism was not appreciated or followed, their practice of government showed itself superior. Eventually, all individual state governments reflected their systems. Many sources traced this system back to the Puritans, but one in particular mentioned a sermon preached in Salem, Massachusetts, in 1636, by John Cotton as describing this system specifically belonging to Puritan theology.[14]

Another outcome we have already reviewed, produced from the Pilgrim/Puritan methods and echoed in the previous quote attributed to Pastor John Robinson, is the idea of leaders formed from a body politic to look for the "common good" of all the people. A "common" people produced the "common" good. This thought of sacrificing what you want for the betterment of the community is what this country was founded on. This is why virtue and piety was so important to all: Christian, Jew, some sect of Christianity and deist. It allowed for the idea of an impartial third party in covenant with, for and over the nation.

This is what the Federal government was supposed to be. The states had their desires and the people had theirs. The Federal system developed in this country was supposed to be impervious to special interests because of its virtuous character. It was supposed to act for the health of individual communities as well as the states and the nation as a whole. It was and still is *supposed* to stay out of regulating religious practices and enacting laws which could hurt the practice of an individual's belief system. I believe it was an unspoken thought the Federal government could become like "God" which made many demand a Bill of Rights. Some felt it was redundant. Can you imagine what the "Feds" would have done to us already if we did not have a Bill of Rights?

Remember Robinson's quote from the 1600s? Look at similar thoughts expressed in applications of government by John Adams, first vice-president and second president of the United States:

> "Upon this point all speculative politicians will agree, that the happiness of society is the end of government, as all divines and moral philosophers will agree that the happiness of the individual is the end of man. From this principle it will follow, that the form of government which communicates ease, comfort, security, or, in one word, happiness, to the greatest number of persons, and in the greatest degree, is the best. All sober inquirers after truth......have declared that the happiness of man, as well as his dignity, consists in virtue......That, as a republic is the best of governments, so that particular arrangement of the powers of society, or, in other words, that form of government which is best contrived to secure an impartial and exact execution of the laws, is the best of republics."[15]

Adams, in talking about the length of time the representatives of the people should serve wrote:

> "This will teach them the great political virtues of humility, patience, and moderation, without which every man in power becomes a ravenous beast of prey.....or make any other alterations *(in term limits)* which the society shall find productive of its ease, its safety, its freedom, or, in one word, its happiness."[16] Italics are mine.

Even more telling is Adams' musings to create "sumptuary" laws, which deal with food and drink. Though he does mention his doubt the people would have the wisdom and virtue to submit to them for the betterment of all: " . . . curing us of vanities, levities, and fopperies, which are real antidotes to all great, manly, and warlike virtues."[17]

'The depravity of man' doctrine, seen within the pages of the Bible predestines any similar concepts seen in Greece, Rome or similarly taught in Europe. In 1651, Thomas Hobbes wrote his discourse, "Leviathan."[18] In it he wrote men originally lived in a state of nature, free from the restraints of civil society and when they did create those societies they did so by entering into a compact. His opinion was men were essentially sinful, thus making it necessary for self-preservation to subject themselves to the will of a sovereign. It was Hobbes' theory of the original social compact which said because men turned over their original compact to a sovereign they actually abrogated their individual autonomy which existed when they lived in a state of nature. This view lost its proponents when Locke's material started to be published. But it was in America it gained an audience again as the climate of the 1780s flowed to the French Revolution. Look at this idea from the depravity doctrine, seen within Hobbes, quoted by John Adams, who quotes Niccolò Machiavelli: ". . . that whoever would found a state, and make proper laws for the government of it, must presume that all men are bad by nature. . . ."[19]

I have already discussed the Fundamental Orders of Connecticut of 1638-1639, influenced by the Reverend Thomas Hooker. It covered the settlements of Windsor, Wethersfield and Hartford. Written in covenant form, it was the first constitution (compact) in the colonies which allowed all to participate in government, not just those involved in church membership. The one requirement was to be a freeman of good, moral character. This idea of those of high moral character involved in civil government influenced the founders as well as framers of our Federal documents centuries later. While the minority deists in the colonies took virtue, piety and high morals to levels of worship, this was no schism in thought nor application for the rest of the civically minded population. The majority of that population were Christians of one form or another. Some 120 years after the Reverend Hooker's influence, the Greek understanding of arete` (meaning virtue or excellence) would become blended with the early settlers' biblical practices and would influence the notion that to follow self-interest or the desires of a minority was at the very heart of corruption.[20]

In 1643, Richard Mather published another work,

✝ "An Apologie of the Churches in New England for Church-Covenant." It was a discourse encompassing church covenant as it dealt with the organization of church government. Some scholars see the organization of church government Richard Mather described as similar to the organization of our government under our constitution.[21] In this document, Mather describes covenant from biblical thought and expounds the human side of the equation as an agreement to be bound to God and each other. So many wonder why our three-part Federal documents are so important to us as a people and why we go back to them constantly in order not to break the bonds by which they sustain and restrain us. We've already talked about the Puritans' practice of making everyone feel included and a part of the covenant. That's because the early church covenants were agreements which could not be broken. Unless the mutual parties decided to amend the agreements, their thought was that they were mutually binding for eternity. That's because God was the overseer. It is no secret some of the amendments to the Constitution are still not agreed upon by all. But the core concepts are still intact, so the covenant or foedus (Federal) is still in effect. We all still honor it. Our American ancestors practiced a sort of "mutual consent on steroids" in theory, if not always in practice.

Let's look specifically at the core of church covenants and the mirrored affect and effect in American Constitutionalism or our American government. Church covenants as well as civil governments defined by compacts use the same formation and process of structure. They both:

1. Define the covenanted people,
2. Make a political body out of the people,
3. Detail the common goals and values which bind them in covenant together, and
4. Describe those institutions by which the people will function.[22]

English charters held similar structures, though rarely mentioning institutions in the way colonists did. At that time English common law was a maze of various rules, roles and regulations. It was the church covenants and governments which exampled these four tenets. Church covenants existed within the religiously minded state territories (many had their original charters). These existed before the formation of the secularized states, which existed before the national federal structure was formed, and which also contains the same four parameters.

Next is the similarity in ratification. In 1646 the Massachusetts General Court convened an electoral body consisting of clerical as well as lay delegates elected from the different churches throughout New England to develop a platform of church discipline. After two years and three meetings later, in 1649 they published "The Cambridge Platform." It was then called upon individual churches to either vote to ratify the document as the true form of church government established from the word of God or not. Over several decades ministers would read the Platform to their younger congregations as their "constitution" and used that term to describe it.[23] Only seven copies are known to have survived. The church government it described and the way it was ratified among individual churches is a federal system seen later between the states in the United States Constitution.[24]

Another connection is seen in the echoed thought of civil government as part of a Christian's communion and duty to mankind. In 1663, John Cotton wrote:

✝ "A Discourse About Civil government in a New Plantation Whose Design is Religion."[25] It conveyed two expressions of government seen in the Scriptures, thus what should be seen in their common times. This was seen in the Mayflower Compact and echoed in many early state constitutions. It was that "Christian Communion" had two forms: the ecclesiastical and the civil state. Cotton said they both existed by divine decree and both pursue "God's glory." The secondary purpose of the ecclesiastical government was for "conversion, edification, and salvation of souls;" while contemporaneously "civil government is preservation, honor, justice and peace."[26]

Multiplied millions in this country have that same understanding passed down to them within their families. I know those who have served in my family in branches of the military, police, as well as one superior court judge (now deceased) felt it was their duty to preserve and protect the peace and our justice— it was a civic as well as privately maintained religious duty— for God & Country.

196

When the President takes his oath he swears to "preserve, protect and defend" the constitution. (Herbert Hoover swore to "preserve, maintain and defend.") We have a similar vestige in our early documents. The Northwest Ordinance finalized on July 13, 1787, states under Section 14, Article 3:

> "Religion, morality, and knowledge, being necessary to good government and the happiness of mankind, schools and the means of education shall forever be encouraged. The utmost *good faith shall always be observed towards the Indians; their lands and property shall never be taken from them without their consent; and, in their property, rights, and liberty, they shall never be invaded or disturbed,* unless in just and lawful wars authorized by Congress; but laws founded in justice and humanity, shall from time to time be made for preventing wrongs being done to them, and for *preserving peace and friendship with them.*"[27] (*Italicized to highlight thought*; it is done "in the year of our Lord 1787.")

The first article makes it clear that "No person, demeaning himself in a peaceable and orderly manner, shall ever be molested on account of his mode of worship or religious sentiments in the said territory." Section 14 states, "that the following articles shall be considered as articles of compact between the original States and the people and States in the said territory and *forever remain unalterable, unless by common consent,........*"[28] (*Italicized to highlight thought.*)

The Northwest Ordinance was a temporary document, stated so in Section 1. It is no longer binding. Obviously later generations of settlers, as well as the Federal government, did not behave accordingly concerning Native Americans; they broke covenant. Nevertheless, you can see this idea of *preserving, protecting and defending* in covenant-compact form from circa 1663 echoed and documented 124 years later in 1787. You can see the idea of compacting and covenanting for eternity ("forever remain"). These are ideas which still function for many today; unfortunately, not applied by all. Might you find similar thoughts with other systems? Possibly. These folks did not grow up inside other systems. Their parents attended church together, their ministers preached and printed the sermons, and their newspapers or pamphlets wrote about it. It must have happened frequently enough for the ideas to still reverberate from the 1600s through to 1787 (and beyond).

I have mentioned the reality the Scriptures promote liberty and freedom for all and the same reality was embraced by the religious settlers. The rest of the world was not as free a place and this ideology was dangerous teaching in some places. Mentioning again the Massachusetts Body of Liberties, it was an attempt governmentally (in a church-civil document) to promote that freedom for all. Adopted in 1641, compiled by prominent Puritan lawyer Nathaniel Ward, it was updated many times over many years, incorporating more and more English common law. Initially Ward relied heavily on biblical principles within English common law. In it we see some rights for women, children, servants, foreigners, animals and prohibited slavery, torture and cruel punishment.[29]

Our specific three-part Federal documents do not mention slaves or slavery (as originally written), but just like the apex document— the U.S. Constitution— does not mention God, we can see all the principles adopted and affirmed in the temporary Northwest Ordinance. This included religion in schools (which would imply Bill of Rights protections for children), the prohibition of slavery—implying Bill of Rights protections for slaves—inheritance rights for both women and children, trial by jury, prohibition of torture and cruel punishment, along with any subrogation of religious liberties or confiscation of property—which animals or livestock would be considered part of as well as any other personal property. We see the similar principles specified in the temporary document of 1787 (1789) as we see some 146 years earlier in the Puritan document. Many of these ideas were also seen in English common law. This should not surprise us, nor negate the biblical connection between the ideas seen in the Massachusetts Body of Liberties and the same ideas seen later in the temporary document for westward expansion.

Americans perceive the Bill of Rights are connected with the Constitution and somehow the Declaration of Independence is connected to the other two. What we are not as clear about is how and why the documents belong in a compact. All of the church covenants enunciated a bill or body of liberties or "rights." These documents described, declared or otherwise established, a group of people who were in covenant. The documents then either flowed through a body of liberties or enunciated some form of institutional requirements. Things like when they will meet, who will meet and/or how those so called will function for the community. In that sense they were early forms of the national compact documents we have now. But before those documents existed, the principle of a higher or fundamental law was brought over with the Puritan settlers as a direct thought developed by Protestant theologians of the Reformation.

With the church and the monarchy as the magistrates— judge and executioner, if you will— those of the Reformation were going to have an impossible road for dissent. Remember when we talked about the Puritan's adherence to the teachings of John Calvin? Well, a disciple of his, Theodore Beze, developed an idea of fundamental law or political rights. Remember that they were also religious rights. They were one in the same. Church and State were not separate at that time. Beze believed these laws should establish the covenant between the people and the state. His work was titled,

✝ "Du droit des magistrates."[30] Basically, his ideas said man was called upon by God to obey a higher law, one higher than that instituted by mankind, whether just or unjust. This is what we now term as inalienable rights. As you can imagine, this did not endear him nor his followers to the civil authorities of his day. This is one reason for the English monarchy's persecution of the Puritans. This led to the persecution of many of the different groups who wound up on our shores: Puritans, Quakers, Baptists, Catholics, to name a few.

Trial by jury, due process as well as others, were liberties prescribed under English common law. But rights "inalienable" were not made law until the colonies. Even though these rights sprang from Reformation thinking, and back further through the nation of Israel to the Bible, they had to have a people which agreed or "covenanted" and identified with them to be a conduit to flow to the next generation. We have already reviewed the importance of this fact. If a group thought of these ideas, and might have even applied them in various parts of the world, but they did not translate to other domains, then the idea died. It was the people of the one Book (Bible) which did this in a comprehensive and consistent way on our shores.

God still chooses to flow and function with humans. After all, He gave the planet to Adam and his seed after him. Adam gave it over to the devil; Christ bought it back, and gave us the right to become heirs, joint heirs in His kingdom. This is how the religious from the Reformation tradition think. This is how Bible believing Christians of today still think. Within that tradition it was their book, the Bible, that showed them the way. When those of a majority biblical thought control a geographic area these rights or liberties will become evident. They were when Israel controlled certain sections of what we now term the Middle East. As Israel has taken back her homeland, these concepts are once again evident.

When Bible-following Christians begin to have influence over monarchal rule, these liberties begin to be seen in those areas as well. What makes this original train of thought harder for the secularist in this country to see as flowing from the Reformation through the early Puritans to the rest of the country's generations, is the active engagement in the late 1700s of the idea of social contract, which was developing and being executed most notably in France. Yet our method was already written in binding documents within colonial governments before the engagement of the French national document. Our idea was not one of social contract, it was one of social compact. We will discuss the difference shortly.

As in all things "colonial," our final documents became part of a long process of thought proceeding to action. By the mid-1600s the Puritans who settled Massachusetts were concerned the magistrates here could become what they were in England. With the reality that their charters from England had to remain in effect, they were concerned their religious liberties would be truncated because they certainly were not following English common law *religiously*. These realities helped to birth the first Body of Liberties adopted by the Massachusetts General Court in 1641. Ward kept the tradition of English common law, without which their charter would be in jeopardy. The charter was revoked in 1684, and was restored, in part, in 1689. The rights were not yet inalienable. They could be changed by decision of the court. It took time for "all" the dissenting Christian sects to be included in the idea of inalienable rights. Persecution still took place. As our governmental documents morphed, so did our rights to eventually become those rights which are neither given by man, nor taken away by man.

Church covenants with their rights were changed and revised and then published so all knew what they were. The same practice was followed with secular governmental documents later in time. While this habit or practice gave the people the right to know, as well as protection from arbitrary or subjective judgments, it also, in some cases helped the specific colony to maintain some traditions of English common law. If they did not, their charters would be lost. Each update of the Massachusetts document became more and more linked to English documentation.

From "The Maryland Act of Toleration" (1649) to the practice of the state of Rhode Island, civil rights (which were also religious rights) were enunciated, printed, revised and reprinted. Rhode Island was the first to keep the practice of a separation of state from the church's business. We have already reviewed William Penn's code of laws (bill of rights), contained in "The Frame of Government of the Province of Pennsylvania" (1682). It enunciated a limited government and defined the electoral system, the prohibitions of taxation without representation, trial by jury, due process, regulated inheritance, land tenure and the performance of marriage. It also guaranteed religious freedom for those who believed in God.[31] The New York Charter of Liberties and Privileges (1683); the Connecticut Code of Laws (1650); the Puritan Laws and Liberties (1658); the General Laws and Liberties of New Hampshire (1680), all these and many more give heed to the earlier covenants and the Bible, which undergird them, framed by the "cup" of English common law.

An early confederation document was made in 1643 between Massachusetts, Plymouth, Connecticut and New Haven. It has come to be called the New England Confederation of 1643. But they actually titled it "*The Articles of Confederation* of the United Colonies of New

England" (May 19, 1643).[32] Notice the similarity in title with the Articles of Confederation written some 133 years later. That is not the only similarity. Within this document we see each separate area maintained their own independence through their own documentation and governments. It lasted until 1684. New Haven was a theocracy (government totally controlled by the church, requiring church membership for citizenry). It was eventually forced to become part of Connecticut's territory. The other three were quite religious with a religiously-controlled civil government.

Before that time in 1641, the settlements of Providence, Pocasset, Warwick and Portsmouth came together and wrote a compact called the Organization of Government of Rhode Island.[33] Scholars have noted this was most likely one of the first federal systems in our country.[34] While not what we would expect compared with the developed compacts we see in the late 1700s, it is in covenant form (Item 1). It does allow for the election of a common representative body (Item 2). It spells out its covenant agreement man to man (Item 3). Finally, it spells out an early form of freedom for religion in the sense that no one would be held delinquent in doctrinal matters (Item 4).

These are two examples of early federal-type documents made by very religious people to preserve economic as well as security protections. The New England document names as a reason for why they came to the land as spreading the Gospel of Jesus Christ in the beginning of the document (establishing or describing a people), and ends with the signature of the year as Anno Domini 1643. It is a confederal document built on the covenant tradition in compact form. Our present three-part federal documents echo the purpose, form and structure of these early (con) federal documents.

Another interesting occurrence took place in both Connecticut and Rhode Island with their documentation. Because of events in England and the dissent among religious groups who would form those two territories, neither Connecticut or Rhode Island had English charters. The restoration of Charles II on the throne in 1660 would change and challenge the new territories' autonomies. Almost immediately, (one year apart) they sent leaders to secure charters for their areas. Connecticut sent John Winthrope, Jr., and Rhode Island sent both Roger Williams and John Clarke. What came out of these independent negotiations were two charters from England, with the King's seal on them which basically ratified the religious colonist's own documentation (1662 charter for Connecticut and a 1663 charter for Rhode Island). All the early forms and ideas we have discussed are now, in effect, ratified by the King. Instead of granting the land for treasure or religious endeavors, it said it was "graciously Pleased to create and make them a Body Politick and Corporate."[35]

Whether knowingly or not, Charles II now sanctioned governments engrossed in religious freedom, popular sovereignty, executing and electing their own laws and leaders, based on biblical covenant foundations for their governments. Both these states— and New England in general— functioned much like independent republics. Concerning Connecticut, it generally did not follow English practice in its legislative proceedings. Years later, this would court the ire of King James II, as he wanted more control over New England. He sent his emissary to collect the charters. As the story goes, when he came to Hartford in 1687 to demand surrender of the 1662 charter, the colonial leaders hid it in an oak tree. It became a landmark known as the Charter Oak.[36]

As time went on, ideas which were church-civically applied became semi-secularly applied and eventually applied in non-sectarian orthodoxy. This metamorphosis is easily seen through the ideas of John Locke. With Puritan parents and living among Dutch and French Calvinists, he was also a friend to William Penn. He enjoyed reading Rene Descartes, friend of Jacobus Arminius.[37] So the arguments of both Arminius and Calvin would find root in Locke. As we have seen, compact forms of government were not new to him. They were in use before he was born.

They found a home and synthesis among our early framing generation of Americans, simply because their parents and grandparents functioned under compacts and bills of liberties. Among their great-grandparents, we see fluent ideas of rights of conscience were already written within the documentation of many colonies. Locke would have only been ten years old. We have already seen how great distances encompassed land masses, with few people on them. So these religious-civic practices placed within covenant-compact documentation were not copied. They were digested through biblical preaching and teaching, especially concerning covenant and the theology pertinent to various forms of Puritanism and Protestant Reformation. This was the practice of a super majority of the colonies.[38]

Locke's ideas were brought into the colonies mainly through Election Day Sermons.[39] We will look at the practice in depth in following chapters. But for now, they were sermons with engaged political theory ministers preached to their congregations as well as to politicians. Initially these holidays were only enacted in Massachusetts for the official swearing-in of politicians who had won their elections, hence the name. Over time the practice grew to other colonies. Locke's "Two Treatises of Civil Government; An Essay Concerning Human Understanding; Four Letters Concerning Toleration" were all works which consolidated the ideas of freedom of religious conscience with liberty in the secular realm and then secularized the compact-covenant form of governmental documentation.[40] Freedom of religious conscience and the compact-covenant form of document writing were not Lockean. Locke took those ideas, digesting them from his Reformation experience. His compact theory of government was a secularized version of covenant theology, coupled with another Reformation idea from Beze: inalienable rights.

We've looked at the role Reformation theology played on this process (bills of liberties or rights). Let's look at an effect from the Great Awakening. If you'll remember from the last chapter, not all the religious in the colonies signed on to the revivals. Some felt they were acts of the devil. This came to a head in Connecticut, where they felt these meetings and the itinerant preachers they produced were attacks on public order. The Connecticut General Assembly passed a law placing severe restrictions on the preachers. Many in the colony were aghast at the restriction. In 1744, a minister by the name of Elisha Williams, who had served as rector of Yale University, published one of the most eloquent apologies for inalienable rights titled,

✝ "The Essential Rights and Liberties of Protestants. A Reasonable Plea For The Liberty of Conscience, And The Right of private

Judgment, In Matters of Religion, Without any Controul from human Authority."[41]

He wrote this in response to what was viewed as an assault on religious liberties, inalienable rights and the rights of conscience. We've mentioned that the process of reason employed by the minority deists in the framing era was not in a battle with any of the factions of Christians during the same time period. The concept as well as the terminology was used by all. Since the Reformation time period, Christians had been taught reason was like all of God's gifts to humans: It needed to be used as a tool. Seen in Thomas Hooker's

✝ "A Survey of the Summe of Church-Discipline" (1648), reason was used as a philosophical explanation for church government.[42] This understanding of reason was employed to view the universe, God's creation on Earth, the science of working within the human race, as well as many of the other sciences.

Some 100 years later the same language of reason is employed by the minister, Elisha Williams, in defense of inalienable and natural rights and the liberty of conscience. This is 32 through 47 years, respectively, *before* our Federal documents are finalized. While Williams based his policy on Scripture as well as Locke's "Two Treatises of Government," these were concepts flowing from Scripture and read by many. His voice in print just rose to the occasion experienced by all. This doctrine of reason emanates from the Reformation to Calvinism and Arminianism. Calvinism is followed by the Puritans. Arminianism is followed by the Dutch Reformers. It's then blended into the rest of the colonies. We see it in their government and it is employed as a practical explanation for what good government looks like. Finally, and in a widespread manner, it is propagated through Election Day Sermons, reinforcing these ideas. If that were not enough, it's reinforced by John Locke (and others), who himself fuses Calvin covenantal ideas with Arminius' liberty of religious conscience. All of this produces a religiously-minded and secularized, non-sectarian offspring, seen within the pages of our founding Federal documents. While the humans involved take on the doctrines of many ingrafts— stoicism, illuminati, Enlightenment, deism, etc.,— it is easily traced early on through Protestantism and the Reformation.

I hope after our review here, you can see the irony of this quote from Federalist 51. The subject is titled, "The Structure of the Government Must Furnish the Proper Checks and Balances Between the Different Departments. From the New York Packet. Friday, February 8, 1788."[43] The arguments take twists and turns for the subject matter so stated. My use here is only as an observation:

> "In a free government the security for civil rights must be the same as that for religious rights. It consists in the one case in the multiplicity of interests, and in the other in the multiplicity of sects. The degree of security in both cases will depend on the number of interests and sects; and this may be presumed to depend on the extent of the country and the number of people comprehended under the same government. This view of the subject must particularly recommend a proper federal system to all the sincere and considerate friends of republican government, since it shows that in exact proportion as the territory of the Union may be formed into more circumscribed Confederacies, or States oppressive combinations of a majority will be facilitated: the best security, under the republican forms, for the rights of every class of citizens, will be diminished: and consequently the stability and independence of some member of the government, the only other security, must be proportionately increased. Justice is the end of government. It is the end of civil society. It ever has been and ever will be pursued until it be obtained, or until liberty be lost in the pursuit. In a society under the forms which the stronger faction can readily unite and oppress the weaker, anarchy may as truly be said to reign as in a state of nature, where the weaker individual is not secured against the violence of the stronger; and as, in the latter state, even the stronger individuals are prompted, by the uncertainty of their condition, to submit to a government which may protect the

weak as well as themselves; so, in the former state, will the more powerful factions or parties be gradually induced, by a like motive, to wish for a government which will protect all parties, the weaker as well as the more powerful."[44]

We have been wooed by judges, politicians and historians that claimed victory for the Federalists, but we forget the Federalists were not correct about a great many things. We did need a representative republic which was in covenant with the people: a federal government. In that they were correct. But there were a great many on the other side of the Federalists (Anti-Federalists) who voiced coherent objections which have come to pass. The problems are still there and we have done nary a thing to fix them. When we have made attempts to do so, we enact more laws, instead of striking down what has caused problems. We get sidelined by the lawyers and regulator-bureaucrats.

Why mention this? The Federalist Papers were written to get a populace, unhappy with a federal government to realize they needed one and it could work. As you read the above, in light of the illustrative samples of documentation I have shown you, what ironies show themselves extant? First, the very reason this particular paper needed writing was because of the fear of power concentrated in one branch of government or one faction of people. Why? Because men are inherently sinful and checks and balances must be enacted. This is foundational in biblical understanding, thus the need for a Savior.

Secondly, the religious congregations that birthed the conceptional theory which gave our American government form, must now argue to have the same rights as civil rights and that the very heart of the argument— multiplicity of sects— is the very constituency now demanding religious freedoms be curtailed to only church buildings. The truly frightening desire now made obvious by the various "sects" is those with religious freedoms have no right to show forth scientific or religious proof that is contrary to whatever dialog is labeled *good* by controlling liberal factions within media, education and government. I will continue to prove this dangerous trend in future chapters.

Contrary to popular thought, the framers did not think it necessary to obliterate or weaken a majority. If they thought that then the majority referenced in Federalist 51 would have been non-existent. In other words, why bother mentioning how to work within a majority if a majority were not expected to exist? What we have today is a minority who controls media, government and education, who demands a subservient majority. This is tyranny. I find it odd we consider Americans those who view our traditional form of republican government an enemy. I will prove how socialism/communism, or progressivism as it is now called, is not a friend of our government as it was originally written.

But for now, I hope we can begin to see why the idea and need for covenant is even greater. Our earliest settlers of Anglican, Puritan, Dutch Reformed, Quaker and others were not perfect in either theology or in practice. That is not the argument. In order to survive when the wolves were at the door, they knew something had to keep them as a cohesive unit, in spite of the huge gulf between their beliefs. They may have made new states, with identifying documentation, but they understood there was only so far they could travel before all their backs were up against the proverbial wall AND that their enemies were in common united against them.

ENDNOTES

1   <http://thefederalist.com/2016/02/15/why-so-many-millennials-are-socialists/> Article and research by Emily Ekins and Joy Pullmann. <http://www.theatlantic. com/politics/archive/2012/05/americans-have-no-idea-how-few-gay-people-there-are/257753> Article by Garance Franke-Ruta, see research cited.<http://www.pewforum. org/2015/05/12/americas-changing-religious-landscape> © 2016 Pew Research Center. Accessed 3/1/16.

2   Donald S. Lutz, "The Relative Influence of European Writers on Late Eighteenth-Century American Political Thought," American Political Science Review, Vol. 78, No. 1 (March 1984) 189-197

3   Lutz, Donald S. and Jack D. Warren. 1987. "A Covenanted People: The Religious Tradition and the Origins of American Constitutionalism" Providence, RI: © 1987, The John Carter

Brown Library at Brown University, and sponsored by The Lily Endowment, Inc; The Rhode Island Committee for the Humanities. Preface, 1. (For documents used in this chapter this source shows all the face pages and some of their contents from the originals. Brown University is a steward and holder for many of these original-sourced documents. They can be seen in person by contacting the University directly. They have not been made available by them online. Though some sources have been reproducing them online.)

4   Ibid., 14-15

5   Ibid., "A Covenanted People," 14

6   Ibid., Introduction, 1

7   Ibid., Introduction; Chapter 1; 3, 5, 7, 13

8   This is from John Winthrop's famous "City on a Hill" sermon. It can be accessed on many and various different websites and encyclopedias. Pick your favorite. For the Internet, here are some of my favorites <http://www.pilgrimhallpimuseum.org><http://www.mayflowerhistory.com/museums-and-societies/> The first is the website of the oldest public museum in the US for the Pilgrims. If you are ever in Massachusetts, a visit is worth your travel time. If you are traveling with young children, Plimoth Plantation, also in Massachusetts is a re-creation of a Pilgrim village with actors and activities that should keep the attention of the energetic ones.

9   John Adams, The Works of John Adams, Second President of the United States: with a Life of the Author, Notes and Illustrations, by his Grandson Charles Francis Adams (Boston: Little, Brown and Co., 1856). 10 Volumes. Vol 4. 290. Public domain

10   Galloway, Charles B. 1849-1909. "Great Men and Great Movements, A Volume of Addresses." Nashville, TN: © 1914 Publishing House Methodist Episcopal Church, South, Simth & Lamar, Agents. 141, 142. In the public domain.

11   John Robinson, The Works of John Robinson, Pastor of the Pilgrim Fathers, with a Memoir and Annotations by Robert Ashton, 3 Vols (London: John Snow, 1851). Vol. 1. In the public domain. l (Roman numeral 50)

12   "From George Washington to John Jay, 15 August 1786," In "The Life of George Washington, Commander In Chief of the American Forces." compiled by Bushrod Washington, 2nd ed., Vol 2. 109. There is an interesting deviation here. Our National Archive omits a line Ingersoll as well as many other works add. The line would be following: "But how irrevocable & tremendous!" Then the added sentence is: "What a triumph for our enemies to verify their predictions!" I deviated from the National Archives concerning the sentence.

13   Lutz, Donald S. and Jack D. Warren. 1987. "A Covenanted People: The Religious Tradition and the Origins of American Constitutionalism" Providence, RI: © 1987, The John Carter

Brown Library at Brown University, and sponsored by The Lily Endowment, Inc; The Rhode Island Committee for the Humanities. 16

14   Campbell, Donna M. "Puritanism in New England." Literary Movements. Dept. of English, Washington State University, last modified 7/4/13 © 1997-2010 Donna M. Campbell <http://public.wsu.edu/~campbelld/amlit/purdef.htm> accessed 3/2/16

15   John Adams, The Works of John Adams, Second President of the United States: with a Life of the Author, Notes and Illustrations, by his Grandson Charles Francis Adams (Boston: Little, Brown and Co., 1856). Vol 4. 193-194.

16   Ibid. 197

17   Ibid. 199

18   <http://www.iep.utm.edu/hobmoral> See this site for a quick yet involved and comprehensive outlook on Hobbes. Accessed 3/1/16.

19   John Adams, The Works of John Adams, Second President of the United States: with a Life of the Author, Notes and Illustrations, by his Grandson Charles Francis Adams (Boston: Little, Brown and Co., 1856). Vol 4. 408

20   Lutz, Donald S. 1988. "The Origins of American Constitutionalism." Baton Rouge, LA: © 1988 Louisiana State University Press. 28-29

21   Lutz, Donald S. and Jack D. Warren. 1987. "A Covenanted People: The Religious Tradition and the Origins of American Constitutionalism" Providence, RI: © 1987, The John Carter Brown Library at Brown University, and sponsored by The Lily Endowment, Inc; The Rhode Island Committee for the Humanities. 15 under Fig. 2.3

22   Ibid., "A Covenanted People," 13

23   Ibid., 17

24   Ibid., "A Covenanted People," 19, Fig. 2.5

25   John Cotton. 1663. "A Discourse About Civil Government In A Plantation Whose Design Is Religion." Cambridge: MDCLXIII Printed by Samuel Greene and Marmaduke Johnson. 5-7. Public Domain.

26   Ibid. 7

27   <http://avalon.law.yale.edu/18th_century/nworder.asp> © 2008 Lillian Goldman Law Library, 127 Wall Street, New Haven, CT. You can read all of the originals on this site; accessed 3/1/16. The technical name was "An Ordinance for the Government of the Territory of the United States, North-West of the River Ohio." It was adopted by the Continental Congress July 13, 1787, and signed by George Washington after affirmation by the US Congress on August 7, 1789.

28   Ibid.

29   Lutz, Donald S. and Jack D. Warren. 1987. "A Covenanted People: The Religious Tradition and the Origins of American Constitutionalism." Providence, RI: © 1987, The John Carter Brown Library at Brown University, and sponsored by The Lily Endowment, Inc; The Rhode Island Committee for the Humanities. 25. See also <https://history.hanover.edu/texts/masslib.html> site © History Department, Hanover College, P.O. Box 108, Hanover IN 47243

30   Theodore de Beze, "Du Droit des Magistrats." 1573 (1574). It can be seen on many sites as a result of reprinting. Pick your favorite.

31   Ibid. "A Covenanted People." 31, 32. This source contains a photograph of an early copy of this document (two pages).

32   <http://avalon.law.yale.edu/17th_century/art1613.asp> © 2008 Lillian Goldman Law Library, 127 Wall Street, New Haven, CT. You can read all of the originals on this site; accessed 3/1/16.

33   <http://avalon.law.yale.edu/17th_century/ri02.asp> © 2008 Lillian Goldman Law Library, 127 Wall Street, New Haven, CT. accessed 3/1/16.

34   Lutz, Donald S. 1988. "The Origins of American Constitutionalism." Baton Rouge, LA: © 1988 Louisiana State University Press. 32

35   <http://avalon.law.yale.edu/subject_menus/17th.asp> © 2008 Lillian Goldman Law Library, New Haven, CT. Scroll down to the respective charters; accessed 3/1/16.

36   <http://www.city-data.com/states/Connecticut-History.html> accessed 1/26/16

37   <https://en.wikipedia.org/wiki/John-Locke><http://sites.torahacademy.org/john-locke/home/influences-1><http://www.britannica.com/biography/Jacobus-Arminius><http://www.britannica.com/biography/Rene-Descartes> accessed 3/1/16

38   Lutz, Donald S. 1988. "The Origins of American Constitutionalism." Baton Rouge, LA: © 1988 Louisiana State University Press. 153, 165, 166

39   Ibid., 68, refer to footnote 16

40   Ibid., p 140-144, 149. See also this text's Future Reading section: William Jackson Johnstone, "George Washington, the Christian," (New York: The Abingdon Press, New York & Cincinnati, 1919), 24-235; at this site <http://www.constitution.org/primarysources/george.html>

41   Lutz, Donald S. and Jack D. Warren. 1987. "A Covenanted People: The Religious Tradition and the Origins of American Constitutionalism." Providence, RI: © 1987, The John Carter Brown Library at Brown University, and sponsored by The Lily Endowment, Inc; The Rhode Island Committee for the Humanities. 35. The title page is printed in original form in this work. Please see the language used in Matthew 22:21; this is the Scripture this minister based the thesis on.

42   Ibid. 17

43   <http://avalon.law.yale.edu/18th_century/fed51.asp>© 2008 Lillian Goldman Law Library, New Haven, CT accessed 3/29/16 Some archives attribute this to Madison. The Library of Congress lists Hamilton or Madison as its author.

44   Ibid.

Chapter Nine

FEDERAL DOCUMENTS

If you are of the modern school which minimizes the founding of the states' documentation into the Federal documentation, you are not alone. So I thought I was going down a rabbit trail in trying to find covenant within the state documentation and thus the Federal thought when I came across scholars who had already done so. As I started the research, I discovered without mentioning certain principles within the state constitutions, the Federal refers to those documents either directly or indirectly over 50 times within 42 sections.[1] The federal document never specifically mentions things like federalism, the extended republic, virtue, legislative supremacy, checks and balances, separation of powers, mixed regime or rights, but the concepts are inherent, from start to finish.[2]

What was reinforced to me over different sources, was that in order to understand the federal documents we have, we must include the tradition and documents which produced the state constitutions and/or documentation in effect at the time. This is not to the omission of studying the British and European traditions which were also infused in our documentation. But there are strong arguments because of differing constructs, you have to view our American tradition separately from Greece, Rome, Europe and even Britain.[3] First, you have the separation from the motherland, the degree of autonomy the monarchy gave to the New

England colonists, and the distraction of the monarchy due to historical events in Europe. Add to that the religious tradition of document writing among these settlers.

For now, let's look at some very basic linguistics of what we term today as contract law. You might ask, "Why bother?" Well, it is perfunctory to understanding constitutional literature. Trust me, you won't need a law degree to understand this. A contract is when differing parties agree to undertake specified obligations and form some type of understanding or remuneration by means of a formal or informal agreement. In times past, these understandings could be informal; sealed with a word or a hand shake. Today they must be done by signature of all parties involved with proof and some type of permanent record kept by all.

In Abraham's time they were called covenants. The parties to the covenant would cut birds or sacrifices in half and both parties to the agreement walked between the pieces. In effect this would say, "As these birds were once whole, so we are in the center of the whole by blood." They then sacrificed the birds in the presence of witnesses. The old-time phrase "to cut a covenant" gives the understanding from the Hebrew of cut-and-seal. So to break a covenant meant to break one another, literally.[4] Other ancient cultures had their varying customs. Of course no covenant is binding unless a higher authority officiates. Thus the need for elders in a region to act as witnesses and/or some other token necessary to prove the agreement exists.

Higher authority was always brought in to officiate or oversee these agreements. In a time frame after Abraham, when a deity was enlisted, the idea of a covenant is used as opposed to a contract. Though the understanding would still be the same even if no deity were enlisted. There is evidence covenants were around before biblical times, but the shading of meanings render them slightly different from the biblical ones. That agreements have existed from the time of man on earth is not in debate. The debate is whether they use the same definition as our Bible does, thus predating the covenants in the book of Genesis. Most notably these would have to do with the Hittites and possibly Sumerians, which some texts predate Egypt as well as Abraham.

The idea of a biblical covenant with the God of the Bible is not an idea of mutual equals in negotiation. It is very different from a contract. God's Covenant originates with Him and ends with Him. Humans can agree and receive the blessings or benefits associated with that covenant. They can reject the covenant in its entirety but they cannot negotiate or alter it in any way. The covenants we see in the Old Testament, especially the Mosaic Covenant, is tied directly to God's Laws, or The Law (Torah). Torah is generally understood as the first five books of the Bible (see also an understanding of the Tanakh). The word covenant is also employed when two or more human parties to an agreement use terminology asking (usually as a witness), inviting, evoking or invoking divinity into the equation with some language stating its existence.

By the way, that is all that is needed. When we look at Abraham's covenant in the Old Testament, there is not a huge dialog of repetitive prayers and extensive and explicit language of inviting God to covenant with Abraham. God does most of the talking and Abraham is actually asleep— or "knocked out" by the power of God (Genesis 15:1-15). It should be mentioned Jewish scholars view Genesis 12-17 as three covenantal aspects of one whole covenant. The same is true in the New Testament (see John 20:24-29, esp. v 28; Romans 10:9 & 10). Yet within human to human in the divine it can be as extensive as marriage covenants, the covenant of the priesthood or church covenants among people in general. In that sense negotiation is seen or in some cases brokered settlements between the humans.

There is also another difference between contracts and covenants within human agreements. In a contract an agreement is made for a price. It is cut and dry. A covenant is used to describe the giving up of something sacred or priceless. In the case of our founding generations, they refused to give up inalienable rights. These, in our minds as well as theirs, are rights given by our Creator which can be given by no other but God Almighty. These are rights we are born with. They are not exchangeable for, or at any price. This is why we call marriage a covenant or the priesthood a covenant, or our right to own land as a covenant. These are sacred choices, but one does not have to give up one's God-given rights to be married or own land. These covenants are sacred trusts, human to human and/or human to environment. They can invoke the biblical God or not. The main idea is they are not cheaply done like a contract is for money. While priceless, they are private decisions which have the potential to affect communities for better or for worse. In that sense they can be viewed as contractual, and in some cultures they are.

This is why the colonists as well as the monarchy viewed what they were entering into as a charter. This has a slightly different definition. Of course there were always the political science buffs who premised since a king was the expression of the divine on earth, he or she could grant certain benefits to those within his or her domain in place of the deity. In that sense our charters for colonial America were born. Charters are basically grants by a country's legislature or sovereign given to a person, institution, company, college, etc., for the purpose of creating rights and privileges. In our case it was for the land to be used as a settlement or colony of the king, in what we now call America. These were on paper, thus the Old English term from the Latin for paper (charta). The idea extends from the Magna Carta, which was the charter of liberty and political rights given to the barons at Runnymede in 1215 by King John of England. It came to be seen as the groundbreaking document of English constitutional practice. In our colonial charters some could be seen as covenantal between the monarchy and the grantee, as well as divine, in that God or Jesus was mentioned. More commonly, the spreading of the Gospel or Christianity was elicited as one reason for the particular charter, along with those "all important" economic needs. Almost all of them mentioned God in some form.

In a similar sense a treaty can be born. For example, like a charter grants, a treaty conveys an agreement. A charter, like the one with the barons at Runnymede was covenantal between what they considered as equals, though the King did not consider it so. It was the King with the one conveying a right. The understanding of charters was someone of greater authority was conveying to someone of lesser authority a *right*. In a treaty, like the ones we see between nations, it is of mutual equals (nations) agreeing to terms set out and negotiated. It can be covenantal, especially if one invokes or mentions a deity. In more modern 21st Century language, they most often have a contractual purpose. Yet even modern treaties which end wars carry a covenantal element or understanding. So treaties, depending upon what they are agreeing over will either be contractual and/or covenantal, and in some cases, both.

Next is the term known as the compact. We have reviewed some of them already. As its name suggests, it holds an agreement and/or covenant within several different ideas, groups, documents or affected geographies into one compilation. The Mayflower Compact was a covenant, but because it made the agreement between two parties (strangers and saints) who were not the same and placed them in a more potentially spread out (and different) geography from their original charter, it had to be called a compact. We've already reviewed how consistently the compact form was employed by the settlers to the colonies.

The term we are most familiar with is the term "constitution." This is a body of fundamental principles which define and sometimes establish a certain group of people (usually, but not always, geographically based) into a political body. Constitutions as we understand them usually define the institutions that the people will authorize to function, like the judiciary or the legislature. A mention should be made of the term "confederal." As you might imagine, it relates to federal in that it is something that is "like" federal. It denotes a group of parties which form an alliance or league. I have mentioned the Articles of Confederation. They attempted to form a confederal (like federal) government mainly for the purposes of conducting the war with England. The weakness of the confederal form was understood immediately because it could not compel the states to do much of anything they didn't want to do.[5]

Today we confuse the term social contract for social compact. Our constitution is a social compact, not a social contract. Compacts almost always contain a covenantal element or understanding. Contracts rarely, if ever do so.[6] Furthermore, our constitution was viewed as a part of a compact by those who wrote it (more on this later). Our three-part Federal documents compact the Declaration of Independence, the Constitution and the Bill of Rights, tying all of them together. Again, contracts rarely, if ever, do this. By adding the term *social* in front of either of them, the definition means to incorporate agreements within societies of people.

As a quick guide, contracts are more legal. They almost always involve the exchange of money in kind for services or some other remuneration. Where compacts are more covenantal. In our earlier centuries, contracts could be enforced by law, but did not have the status of a law; whereas compacts were just like a standing rule. Even if a compact was not a law, they always had the same effect as one.[7]

Early on in this book, we reviewed the definition for federal and its covenantal aspect. Again, groups can unite as one, but when they employ the term *federal* they always employ a covenantal element. It is inherent in the definition of the word. Various centuriates from the 19th and 20th centuries, especially in Europe, would remove the definition and understanding of the covenantal nature of the words compact and federal; namely because European societies did so to enact constitutions and various other governing documents. In my opinion, they wanted to copy us, but not totally. When they did this, they would use the term social contract in forming their governing documents.

They also wanted to describe inalienable rights, because we were the first to employ them, practically through gestation and birth. Europeans began to call them "universal" rights. There is a huge difference. Obviously, inalienable are God-given and sacred. Everyone has a universal right, so they are human birthed. Unfortunately, they are not priceless. Even if you demand that category, somehow a shift always takes place, removing the demand. With inalienable rights, the status of sacred remains. They become tied to life itself. By engaging foreign ideologies and law attached to those ideas, a transfer or slippery slope began within our definitions concerning compact, covenant to contract, inalienable rights to universal rights, and even the word *federal*.

Our understanding of these words as they relate to our documents seems to have been lost in one generation. The definition of associating contract or social contract is different from the framing generation employing those terms, who formed our Federal compacting agreements. They would not have seen them as a contract, but a covenant. One glaring proof is seen when they use examples of our documents for political theory, they very frequently use biblical examples to do so. They also frequently use "providence" or the "Almighty" as examples in various references of political and social outreach. While Federalists, as a political group did not do so for political theory in framing Constitutional institutions like the Anti-Federalists do; we will see in future chapters how often this was done by everyone when defining social, political and economic activities.

This generation did not waste words or paper (as they understood it) like we do today. Our medium frequently is digital, so we have an unlimited supply. They didn't use a name understood as God, or a biblical reference in speech or other form of political dialog or communication because they were so religious. They didn't do so because they were somehow inferior in intellect to us. The reference had meaning to them through various elements of political, social and economic activities, and it would have to have meaning to their hearers, or else they would not be understood. Very often that unspoken meaning related to the covenantal aspect of who Providence was in their political, social, and to a lesser extent, economic colloquy.

After reading up to this point, a forgotten fact of matter should be obvious. Unfortunately lost to our present generation, Christian and atheist alike, is the Bible itself can be seen as a compact. It brings together by a covenant two very different groups of people (Jews and Gentiles) into one understanding within two separate covenants (Old Testament and New Testament). Both covenants contain separate ordinances and define separate and several different institutions to govern them. The generation who made the early church covenants and then turned them into civil governmental covenants understood this all too well. It is one of the reasons they settled on the form of government they did. It makes equal sense when their children's grandchildren read Locke, they could agree with his pattern for a social compact which was secular. Just because it had secular outreach, did not remove the covenantal nature within it. I will prove this shortly.

We have reviewed the dynamics of the circumstances which conceived our Federal compact. We have already looked at some specific and ancient church documents. Their history can then be traced all the way to the Declaration of Independence, the United States Constitution as well as the Bill of Rights. In fact, we can see the exact same symbolism used in those early covenants in our Declaration.[8] We have reviewed on-the-ground circumstances which contributed to how those documents were formed. The large land mass, with lack of communication between them and in some cases, their sovereign, lent itself as a platform for our compact today. Their need to survive extinction events produced, by no small turn of events, the mutual consent we saw employed by these people. This morphed into the popular sovereignty we employ today.[9]

While that history helps us to see our modern compact in a new light, there is another way we can discern how the framers viewed what they were writing was covenantal and not necessarily contractual. Instead of being legalistic to language as a contract would be— and then become argumentative as when a contract is broken— these compacts would celebrate community and trust with covenantal fidelity. This is one difference between a covenant-compact and a contract. Over time, these compacts or covenants, through years of understanding within the community would need to be updated for whatever purpose, like renewing the oaths or some other covenantal understanding the communities relied upon. That process is rarely done for a contract. Usually a whole new document is required.

These "updates" would be termed as organic acts. Examples of early colonial organic acts would be the "Laws and Liberties of Massachusetts" (1647), the "Connecticut Code of Laws" (1650) and the "Puritan Laws and Liberties" (1658).[10] They contained both religious as well as secular ordinances. Much later in time and moving toward our recent time line, we reviewed how each state updated its compact by updating its constitution. We saw the beauty in the compact design by not having to establish or declare a people all over again. Their declaration or establishment documents would remain and then be compacted with whatever updated constitution or bill of rights they needed.

I have heard arguments this was just a style of writing showcasing the time frame they lived in. That premise does not take in to account the seriousness with which the founders viewed what they were doing in forming governments. I hope I have shown in a truncated form, these were a deeply religious people. To make exact assessments on the specific religious beliefs of our forebears and then transform that assessment into our Constitution when no connection exists, is not good history. I equally hope I have shown that they were, in actuality quite religious in a belief God existed. That belief did have an affect on our founding documents. Its impact was seen as a continuation of *a desire* for a covenant among the people to their differing and respective beliefs in the God of the Bible to form a government and constitute a people in a geographic area. While this was *a desire*, it was not the **only** desire.

One desire among many concerned safety for the same people to live without fear of reprisal in what form of worship they deemed fit and what speech they desired to use to express their belief in that God. Governments affect economies, money, trade, international relations, war, etc. If your life depended upon the documents which governed you, might you take the wording those documents contained seriously? This is our problem today. Many do not understand the words in your governing document produces an attitude to govern. Desires were enunciated that were secular (and/or economic) in nature for strictly governmental purposes. These people were so careful in writing their documents they even omitted God's name in them on occasion. Frequently that was because in their specific interpretation of the Bible, taking an oath was sacrilege. In some cases they omitted God's name because they were not part of a church. Because of history like this, the framers of the 1770s and 1780s had a clear path to move forward when the need arose to write our modern compact.

Some have said it was because of their isolation they wrote the kind of documents they did. Certainly the lack of interference from England made writing the way they did expedient. As isolation wore off and the colonies became more populated, they still could have used the British form of constitution writing, but they did not. In fact, coming from England initially, they should have used England's form of document writing exclusively, but they did not. Not only did these folks have choices in how they wrote their documents for governmental affairs, human nature would tell us they should have done it the way they knew best and even should have gone back to doing it that way once more settlers from England came over and more adherents and loyalists to the monarchy settled here. But that is not what they did.

I have shown you documentary evidence supporting this. We do have oral history and tradition from many thousands of families with personal ancestral history. The religious tradition in document writing is not some myth or fantasy. I might add the oral tradition supporting the documentation is not some obscure myth either. Up until the 1960s this understanding was well known. So much so those who had been trained legally or militarily were taught *some* of the minutia of this history. Listen to these words:

> "For I have sworn before you and Almighty God the same solemn oath our forebears prescribed nearly a century and three quarters ago. . . And yet the same revolutionary beliefs for which our forebears fought are still at issue around the globe— the belief that the rights of man come not from the generosity of the state, but the hands of God. We dare not forget today that we are the heirs of that first revolution. Let the word go forth from this time and place. . . that the torch has been passed to a new generation of Americans. . . tempered by war. . . proud of our ancient heritage— and unwilling to witness or permit the slow undoing of those human rights to which this Nation has always been committed, and to which we are committed today at home and around the world."[11]

Many might think I am quoting from some radical preacher or some other conservative "trouble maker" from the 1960s. Well, not exactly. I quote from the late President John F. Kennedy as he spoke in his inaugural speech from 1961. It is amazing how much national history has been lost inside of two generations.

Just as telling is the deist's (atheist) control of constitution writing in France with the French Revolution. We have seen how this was contemporary with our own constitution writing. We have no argument: our Constitution is not a religious, Christian document. Yet even when you single out the one document (the Federal Constitution) from the

Declaration of Independence and the Bill of Rights, you still have two oblique mentions or references to religious traditions you would never, ever have in the contemporary French document if you were looking for a godless constitution.

The French made every effort to remove the mention of Sunday from all their everyday documents as well as their national ones (see Chapter 7). They especially removed the words Anno Domini, translated *"in the year of the Lord."* Before Christ (BC) and AD [Anno Domini, *in the year of the (our) Lord]* were more than "writing habits" and styles.[12] They were direct references in Christian nations of inviting and acknowledging Jesus Christ in their documents, as well as evidencing Him in their time line. If you are an atheist you would have no such history, desire or understanding for this. If you were a dissident in the train of thought of France (many of whom were atheist and deist), you never, ever make such references of God— and they didn't. The French document is a godless constitution on paper and in tradition.

Our early history proves even when they were quite religious, our forebears wrote strictly secular documents when they wanted to.[13] Yet they do no such thing with our three-part Federal documents. Are they religious treatises? Not at all. Are they Christian documents? No. They are governmental documents built on the framework of religious covenant writing, compacts, English common law and European thought. They make references, not only acknowledging God specifically by name— acknowledging these people have a history of worshipping Him as they see fit— but our Federal government, specifically in this country has no rights, whatsoever, to interfere with the people's faith (or other inalienable rights). In fact, the Federal government must covenant to protect the states, the people and their faith (and other inalienable rights). They make sure those documents reference the fact that faith functions in other areas of their lives such as speech, happiness, safety, economics, and others. These documents acknowledge a pattern of covenant the people have with their God and establish a covenant-compact, people to people and continue that understanding with the people to the new Federal government. The three-part Federal documents follow a similar, yet slightly different pattern of covenant-acknowledgement of God as all the early state documentation make. Ours is not a "godless" tradition. The framers, like their early colonial forebears, danced around many issues when it came to religion in their documentation.[14] The reasons for this are different and varied.

Even the Articles of Confederation were birthed from this practice of independent communities organizing in a covenant way by federation [foedus (federal) meaning to covenant]. This was not something which just "happened" or "appeared" in 1776 and 1787, but came from a long history of document-making.[15] We reviewed those (con)federal documents already. Many of those early documents mention God, including Jesus Christ by name in the early confederal document.[16] Fast-forward to the 1781 Articles of Confederation and we see a similar expression in writing a document as the previous pattern for document writing.[17] Even the fact they called the document our Constitution replaced, "The *Articles* of Confederation," proves the history and pattern they already knew and followed.

There is no argument our present Federal documentation is more non-sectarian, especially so with the Constitution from its predecessor. Nevertheless, it is in covenant form— with the Constitution itself in a compact and oaths evident within it.[18] In foundation pedigree, our Federal documents come directly from church covenants. While all other constructs of outline, form, institutional language blend, secularize and morph through several avenues (British, Greek, Rome as well as Enlightenment era) to become what we have today, the foundation is clear. What gives the people the right to form? Those rights are unalienable, given by the Creator to whom, in practice, the people covenanted with. What gives them the right to constitute institutional government? Those same rights. So the right to make a constitution and the rights within it, whether specified or implied are given by God, not anyone else. The exception happens to be acts of violence or those of miscreants. Obviously God gives no one the right to murder or harm anyone else or their own body or other ungodly acts. The people then covenant (foedus— federal) among themselves and give rights to an institution which has limits— the Federal government is a limited government by design and constitution.

There are deeper arguments made by academics as to what exactly framed American Constitutionalism. When scholars exercise these discussions they look at framing systems. In other words, there was a shared and proven intellectual structure which gave an underlying support for the next structure of intellectual concepts, which would become proven to be a support for a more nuanced structure. Like a larger cup can hold a cup somewhat smaller in size and a third cup even smaller in size than the last. If the first cup is not round but square and the second cup is not square but round, it would be impossible for the first to have a frame for the next cup. Of course, when speaking about American Constitutionalism, the cup analogy ends there. Folks have their own charged debates in this area. I like the tree with roots analogy, but in much research, the term most often used was "frame," hence my decision to use cups.

Described in this way, we can see the original charters and English common law given to the colonies made a frame for the settlers' practice of writing church governmental covenants. So specific biblical concepts are now grafted in, even standing on their own and changing the earlier "tree" or frame. Those had civil outreach and became civil governmental covenants. These made a frame for some of the varied European Enlightenment theories to emerge. Scholars can get quite intense and become a little fanatical when discussing these issues. But I never read an early academic who did not mention the influence of Greek, Rome and the Bible within the larger framework of the British tradition; and then the direct application of the Bible within the covenant framework, and then employ the final framework of Enlightenment ideas.[19]

If you still have a problem with my argument for three-part Federal documents, let's look at the Declaration of Independence first. After defining a compact you can understand our Constitution to be within a compact. Many find it hard to realize its covenantal aspect. Federal government documents start with the Declaration of Independence and end with the Bill of Rights.[20] Some might say that cannot be the case since there are 11 years separating the signing of the Declaration of Independence and the Constitution. Well, the Declaration of Independence and the first constitution, the Articles of Confederation were written in covenant form as a governmental social compact. Many would then say the Articles were replaced by our Constitution. Of course, that would be my point. The 28 grievances listed in the Declaration of Independence were not new. Jefferson did not have to search the world over to find them. They were printed in newspapers of the day and many state constitutions.[21] The terminology used "nature and nature's God" was not new either. Locke, among others at an earlier time, had used the term. It describes a group of people before they form themselves into government. At that point they are found in nature, under the direction of the God who made nature. They are found in a natural state.[22]

The Declaration declares (or establishes) what kind of people we are and why we are declaring our freedom from what should have been a just government. It describes who these people are and what their purpose must now be in declaring their independence. All of the early state documentation have this type of element, with and without declaring independence and grievances. It is then compacted with Articles which will frame or constitute what the new government will and will not do— under a fact of separate, equal, yet united states.

Once the war was over, it became obvious the Articles were not adequate enough. So a new and stronger federal document would have to be made. But the Declaration would never be abolished. It would declare for the history and entirety and for the duration of the nation the 'Why' and 'Where' of the existence of these people and 'Who' gave them the right to form; and the 'What' these people should expect from the government they were forming (what government should never do to cause the grievances listed). This Declaration for Independence would always be covenanted and compacted with what constitutes the government it was forming; i.e., the United States Constitution or 'How' the government would operate. These would then, in turn, be compacted with specific rights belonging to these covenanted people; i.e., the Bill of Rights.[23]

Today we view the Declaration as a champion of individual rights. We aren't wrong when we do that. But Jefferson and his readers would understand it to be rights belonging to civil societies or societies of men— groups of people within individual, yet united states. It was understood the colonists would be expected to have the same rights as those belonging to British citizens.[24] It also included, for the first time, an understanding of an agreement between the people, the states and the states united into a Federal government.[25]

If you are looking for all these framers to be particularly religious or "wear their religion on their sleeves," the religious as well as the atheist will be disappointed. Some were, some were not and some simply would not show the depth of, or lack of, faith they espoused. This was not the immediate issue. The question for many was to what degree the new federal government would be limited. Would it affect their state's rights? How about the condition of revenue and debt? How about their particular religious denomination? How would they be affected? All of these states had one predominant Christian denomination closely linked with them; in other words, an establishment of a religious church. In some cases those denominations even described the religious atmosphere of the state. More to the point, was the thought no particular denomination of covenanted people of the one Book (Bible) should control and tyrannize the federal process— as their parents experienced and some of them knew personally the Church of England could do or Catholicism might do— And to a large degree, the states also had several "dogs in that fight." By the time of 1787, there were so many different church denominations within the states that chaos could ensue to obfuscate majority rule. The Federal covenant had to be "colorblind" or take a non-sectarian approach to any favoritism from them in vying for Federal affections.

We view these partisan issues in a different way and from a whole different vantage point in time. We need to remember our federal compact included far more peoples as affected citizenry than any other up to that time period, anywhere on the globe. Secondly, by stating all men are created equal and they are endowed by their Creator with certain unalienable rights includes all those humans created. While these founders may not have specifically mentioned unaffected covenant people, they created the framework for all human beings to be affected and granted rights. I find it hard to believe after reviewing the history of these people, they thought covenant could not extend to all eventually. In their thinking a later generation could deal with that specific citizenry, which is exactly what later generations did.

I would also make a point of our linear thinking today in document writing. The thinking of yesteryear was not as we think today. From the time the colonists first settled they would rewrite documents, but have declaration documents or establishment documents in place. The necessity of this element of the covenant-compact form was so you never had to re-establish, as it were, the "how and who" these people came to be. Their institutional language document— or what we now call a constitution could be updated and changed, leaving intact the establishment portion— or in our case, the declaration portion. This way the people would never be hurled back into a state of nature. The process would be streamlined and stable. It was implemented in practice as soon as the first English charters declared who the people were or established their reason for being. Then the settlers wrote church covenantal governing documents. All of these documents functioned at the same time. They never went back to the drawing board, as it were.

This had been their practice for 150 years before the Declaration was written and some 50 years before John Locke was writing treatises. So the stable element of covenant and establishment or declaring has always remained. In other words, our modern lawmakers and elite groups in media and education cannot remove the faithful and our most cherished rights of religious covenant from our Declaration document.

You might be asking the question, what covenant are you talking about? I refer you to the Declaration of Independence. Granted, it is not the usual format of declaring the covenant with God in the very beginning of the document that we have seen. Instead, read it as if you lived then. You have made biblically founded covenant government in your respective communities, for over one hundred years. The monarch, who granted your land also made these agreements. In many cases charters were issued stating the spreading of the Gospel of Jesus Christ (or Christianity) as one motive in your occupation and settling of the land and giving you rights to government on that land. Your families and relatives might still live on the "mainland" or mother country. But the monarchy's dealings with you presently are breaking that agreement or covenant every day. Fed up, it is incumbent upon your communities to declare why you must take the action you must.

Your Declaration document starts off with the fact separation must occur. Since God has already been named in previous documents, it stands to reason all must be reminded that all parties to the former agreements (charters) are viewed equally with rights coming from that same God (unalienable). You have a relationship or covenant with the King directly. You have the legal right to by-pass Parliament (even though Parliament didn't see it that way). The King has violated that bond. Next is a list proving (grievances) the ways in which that agreement has been broken.

Lastly, and the crux of my argument are these words: "We, therefore, the Representatives of the UNITED STATES OF AMERICA, in General Congress, Assembled, *appealing to the Supreme Judge of the world for the rectitude of our intentions, do, in the Name, and by the Authority of the good People of these Colonies,* solemnly publish and declare, That these United Colonies, are and of Right ought to be Free and Independent States; that they are Absolved from all Allegiance to the British Crown, and that all political connexion between them and the State of Great Britain, is and ought to be totally dissolved; and that, as Free and Independent States, they have full Power to levy War, conclude Peace, contract Alliances, establish Commerce, and to do all other Acts and Things which Independent States may of right do. *And for the support of this Declaration, with a firm reliance on the Protection of Divine Providence, we mutually pledge to each other our Lives, our Fortunes and our sacred Honor."*[26]

I italicized words to highlight the two areas in question. Whenever you call or appeal to God by common names used during the times, or by names all generations should and would understand Him by, it is in covenant form. Because they had previous agreements with the King invoking Deity, it stands to reason they would appeal to that Deity. When you then state your reliance is upon Him to establish (declare) the nation, along with those you are covenanting with; namely the signatories as well as the "good" people you are uniting with, the deal is done. They are declaring the establishment of a nation. This is our establishment document. I have already proven this is a social governmental compact with both our final Constitution as well as our Bill of Rights.[27]

In case you may not see it spelled out plainly, it says so plainly within the Declaration that you have the right to form the government, with all the abilities of an independent country. Logically, and in fact, they then did form one. They constituted it with the Articles of Confederation. Deciding a specialized and additional constituting governmental document needed to be ratified, they gathered to do that. They decided against additional regulations to the Articles of Confederation, and instead by a majority, ratified a specialized replacement document. This would constitute the institutions within the country. Then deciding that was not enough to ensure godly, religious and other freedoms, they compacted another document. History tells us that as this began, the King of England, and England herself understood exactly what these colonists were doing: That's why they sent troops to try and stop them.

We have another pedigree continuation from documentation made by early church groups. This practice, as we have seen, did come from church practice in oath taking, but it also came from England. An argument could be made that the church groups got it from Europe. The Bible discusses all sorts of oaths throughout the book. So whether English or biblical, our early settlers engaged oaths in taking governmental offices. England used the taking of oaths as a sort of test to restrict certain religious groups from office or to allow accepted groups access. State constitutions did basically a very similar thing. We have reviewed them and reviewed the fact you had to believe in God to hold office. The Federal Constitution was meant to allow everyone to participate in government. One difference between England and America is the covenantal responsibility of the Federal government to the states and the people.

Article VI itself bans religious tests for "any office or public trust under the United States." The history is quite clear that our founders wanted no part of the Federal government to prevent the people from being able to function in government, yet they were sensitive to state's requirements in religious tests. It wasn't until 1961 that states were included in the ban of religious tests.[28] The proof for covenant is clear: Why ask the representatives of the people to promise (covenant) to "support and defend the Constitution . . . against all enemies, foreign and domestic" . . . in "faith and allegiance" . . . as an "obligation" . . . with no "purpose of evasion"

... when you "faithfully discharge" your duties, if you are not agreeing to a promise or covenant with the people? It is in this environment that Article VI, Clause 3 has oaths applicable to the various offices and those last four words, "So Help Me, God."

No wonder no in-depth language is used to describe God in the Constitution body proper. Why would you if you were writing a document for constituting a government you previously declared through a declaration or establishment document? You've already done it in the very beginning. Yet, let no one forget we won't be doing certain 'things' on Sunday. There is no reason to state why. All is done in the year of our Lord, one thousand seven hundred and eighty-seven. Just in case there might ever be any confusion for future generations, let's also add a Bill of Rights, even though rights seem to already have been stated in our grievances within our Declaration.[29] Just to be sure no one is confused, let's make it clear that there are rights we do not negotiate which are attached to and given by our Creator. Enunciated as the *first* one is the right to worship Him freely without Congress attaching any law, tax or speech behavior or other regulatory endeavor. There should be nothing which inhibits the people's ability to assemble and petition Government when they attempt to do so. Let's make that as the **first** one so no one gets confused. I realize some try to separate free speech and free press and assembly away from religion, but it cannot be and it has never historically been so.

These people held these truths to be self-evident. It is a shame in this country at this time, many do not understand the totality of what were self-evident facts and truths. So who were these folks and who were the people they put forward to represent them?

ENDNOTES

1   Lutz, Donald S. 1988. "The Origins of American Constitutionalism." Baton Rouge, LA: © 1988 Louisiana State University Press. 2. It was hard for me to pick just one researcher, because earlier scholars concurred in varying degrees about their inclusion of religious influence. Getting their books and research would be quite hard if you did not have them

already, was part of a university library system, or subscribed to book and/or research-paper sharing sites, as I do. For me the most recent and prolific scholar was Dr. Lutz. In my opinion he is more than a prolific writer. He has an extended as well as in-depth experience of research. Lastly— and this was just as important as my two other prerequisites— his books and works are available quite easily today, especially on the Internet.

2   Ibid. 4

3   Ibid. 5-12; 62-66

4   Sites as common as Wikipedia will have this information, or you can view your own favorite religious site for the meaning of the Jewish covenant.

5   For a scholarly definition of these terms see Lutz, "Origins," 16-22. My purpose in these definitions is not to copy the professorial but to engage our present understanding of these terms. While my loose descriptions will do no exact harm to the academic, they definitely will not totally describe how the ancients viewed these terms or how academics define them. My purpose is to help all of us understand what it is about our documents today which help them to be described by the terms I have mentioned.

6   Modern compacts made today, especially with Indian tribes on tribal land concerning their gaming enterprises have quite extensive contractual language within them. In that sense they are quite different from what we see in our three-part Federal documents. But that these standing rules/law/agreements contain quite a few elements we have already discussed in describing a compact, is evident through an example made by the State of Florida with the Seminole Indian Tribe in 2010. <https://www.flsenate.gov/PublishedContent/Committees/2014-2016/RI/Links/2010%20Compact-Signed1.pdf> accessed 2/16/16. This example clearly describes a people under separate location (land) and multiple jurisdictions (tribal government, and Federal government, and state government) page 1 Part II; and combines or incorporates other agreements that would not be altered by the compact page, 52 (F); along with an added dimension of time expiration, page 49. There are covenantal attitudes seen and stated in the compact, more or less incorporated into contractual language. Because of that it has covenants, page 32, and covenantal aspects of solutions and conflict solving, pages 28, 43-46; and defense, page 46, (E). Though arguably, this is far removed from what we see as covenantal from our own Federal three-part documents. Because it is a contract in money and in kind, it has contractual agreements, page 31 (and all throughout the document). That money is the main goal and understanding, thereby incorporating contract into the modern-day compacts, can be seen by the discussion surrounding the new compact moving through the state legislature, promising a larger payout to the state <http://www.politifact.com/

florida/statements/2016/feb/11/seminole-tribe-florida/new-gaming-compact-offers-florida-biggest-guarante/> accessed 2/16/16.

7   Lutz, Donald S. 1988. "The Origins of American Constitutionalism." Baton Rouge, LA: © 1988 Louisiana State University Press. 16, 17

8   Ibid. 23-27; see also Chapter 2

9   Ibid. 27

10   Ibid. Lutz, "Origins," 18, 19

11   John F. Kennedy: "Inaugural Address," January 20, 1961. Online by Gerhard Peters and John T. Woolley, The American Presidency Project <http://www.presidency.ucsb.edu/ws/?pid=8032> and other info concerning the speech can be seen at <http://www.bartleby.com/124/pres56.html> © 1993-201 Bartleby.com, Inc. accessed 3/3/16.

12   <http://www.britannica.com/topic/anno-Domini-Christian-chronolgy> click on the various other topics associated under the title, especially the one "Christian Chronology;" accessed 1/22/16.

13   Lutz, Donald S. 1988. "The Origins of American Constitutionalism." Baton Rouge, LA: © 1988 Louisiana State University Press. 28-31

14   Ibid. 124

15   Ibid. 32

16   <http://avalon.law.yale.edu/17th_century/art1613.asp> © 2008 Lillian Goldman Law Library, 127 Wall Street, New Haven, CT. accessed 3/1/16.

17   <http://avalon.law.yale.edu/18th_century/artconf.asp> © 2008 Lillian Goldman Law Library, 127 Wall Street, New Haven, CT. accessed 3/1/16.

18   Lutz, Donald S. 1988. "The Origins of American Constitutionalism." Baton Rouge, LA: © 1988 Louisiana State University Press. 34, 41, 43-44

19   Ibid. 67-69. See also Lutz's footnote on p 68 in Election-day Sermons by the clergy bringing Locke's ideas into the colonies.

20   Ibid. 111-115

21   Ibid. 114-115

22   Ibid. Lutz, "Origins," 111, 113, 114

23   Ibid. 115-118

24   Ibid. Lutz, "Origins," 78-80; especially 80 and its footnote on the preaching of a colonial sermon.

25   Ibid. 116, 117; see also references to biblical covenant thought on 117-120.

26   I have already noted and documented sites in which you can get copies of the Declaration of Independence as well as so many of our early documents. Our Library of Congress has a site in which you can click on either the Declaration in the Journals of the Continental

Congress of 1776, or a Broadside. That site is <https://www.loc.gov./rr/program/bib/ourdocs/DeclarInd.html> One site for many of our federal documents <http://avalon.law.yale.edu/subject_menus/18th.asp> for the Declaration in particular <http://avalon.law.yale.edu/18th_century/declare.asp>

27   Lutz, Donald S. 1988. "The Origins of American Constitutionalism." Baton Rouge, LA: © 1988 Louisiana State University Press.121-124

28   <http://www.heritage.org/constitution/#!/articles/6/essays/135/religious-tests>accessed 4/2/16

29   Ibid. Lutz, 122

Chapter Ten

A WORD ABOUT THE FOUNDERS
VERSUS THE FRAMERS

If we look at the governmental environments which existed globally before the settlers came and the systems which were placed upon them by England to function here; then we look at the systems they created and implemented, we have a much clearer definition of why our government was shaped the way it was. Up until this point, I have attempted to look at some of those religious sources which made a direct impact. This is considered by many as the founding period; and those within that timeframe are considered the "founders." Let's say it's the period in which our American pie (cake) was made and baked. If I was deciding to make an analogy out of it, I would say, "No cake tastes the same without a good frosting, or pie without some topping." The framing period could be termed as the frosting on the cake or the topping on the pie. Many countries just "eat cake" or pie, but here in America, everything can be better.

I have read those which define the "framers" as only the 55 men who were delegates to the Constitutional Convention. I have read others who place everyone from 1600 on as a founder. While others describe only those from 1740 to 1800 as a founder. I have seen other terminology which makes it clear the framing time period is a period of time from roughly the 1760s (some go back to the 1740s) through the early part of 1800 (usually 1805). They do this to include influencers within the thinking minds of the populace who framed our final three federal documents. Some of the difficulty here is because you have men like Thomas Paine, who did not write any of our documentation, was not a delegate to the Convention, yet did make an impact through public discourse in his writings. He lived during the framing period, but would be considered a founder. Then you have other individuals like Jefferson, who could not attend the Convention sessions, yet wrote the Declaration of Independence, thus framing our three-part Federal documentation. Some find it heresy to label him a founder and not a framer as well. All told, 70 individuals were appointed by their states to attend, but they either did not accept or could not attend. Rhode Island sent none. Fifty-five delegates attended sessions but only 39 actually signed the Constitution.[1]

To understand the founders and/or framers, some go back to what the framing population was taught in school or how they were raised or what they read by evidence of their private libraries. Quite often I've seen people review a few individuals and call them the founders. Those who do that usually use three, or at the most, five individuals; namely, Jefferson, Hamilton, Adams, Madison and possibly a combination of some aspects of Washington, Franklin and Paine. While all of the above is helpful, it doesn't even come close to an understanding of the framers, let alone even remotely portraying the founders. Because many omit the history of the 150 years (or more) time period of the founding era, you also wind up omitting the influencers from that era which affected the framing period. Many scholars term all those who had a coherent influence in shaping political theory and/or development of our country as a founder. I would agree with that definition.

That definition would have us reviewing close to 300 individuals (possibly more), spanning four centuries. So it can get confusing, and with good reason. For our understanding within these pages, I would define the founding era of time between 1600 to 1760 and the framing era of time between 1760 to 1805, mainly because it was the period of time with events influencing our federal compact. For the purposes of this book, I will also define those who could be delegates to the Constitutional Convention as 'framers.' Not all the delegates attended, but I will refer to those 70 men who had the potential to attend as framers. This narrow definition does not have the majority of support, yet it does have its followers. For me personally, I would define all of these individuals as founders— and many folks do. Yet there is a need to delineate framers from founders. Although any attempt to be dogmatic in this area will probably fall flat on its face because history as well as the individuals involved don't always conform to neat labels.

In researching what influencers contributed to this period of time it is essential to view earlier historians. The reason is earlier scholars and historians took in more history in their analysis; which is great if you can access their books. Unfortunately, most are out of print and quite often they are specialized, leaning to one topic. While not all research done today is skimpy and/or biased, it does leave you needing to go to twenty or more different sources to try to get the older books. Unless you have access to a university's library system, which would then give you access to such systems across the country, it can be quite difficult to view original documents or read the early historians who did. I have tried to review the influence of *covenant history* during the founding era, which was influenced solely by religion. Religion also had some influence on English common law as did Greek and Roman influencers.

There were many factors influencing the founding period of time. I have only reviewed a handful of them. There seems to be less of an argument as to the influencers during the founding era. There seems to be less of an argument concerning the huge influence Christianity and Judaism made during that period of time. But the argument becomes more heated when we get to the framing era. The bulk of the disagreement usually revolves around what European thought was involved in forming our Constitution. This is also with good reason. Because any attempt to place the framing period into the same box as the founding period will have its problems.

I have already looked at definitions of framing influencers. I have mentioned English common law and the original English charters, which produced a framework for the Puritan covenant theory of government forming community, specific state, as well as Federal documents. What

I have not done is look at specific European Enlightenment thought influencing the last document, the Constitution. Even though the Bill of Rights or the first ten amendments to the Constitution was written last and is a part of the framework of structure for our American system, its influence had already been in place for centuries prior. The Bill of Rights was influenced heavily by covenant theory, Reformation theology, and to a great extent as a response within English common law, which had Greek/Roman influencers as well. Many feel our Bill of Rights is descended from England's 1689 Bill of Rights. This is not true. As you have already read within these pages, we had bills of rights or liberties up and running early in the 1600s, decades before the British.

The argument could be made because of the controversial nature of what many at that time felt was the implementation of a strong federal system, the Bill of Rights was added as a protection to the last piece of framework to our federal documentation. While that is absolutely true, I believe the history proves the Constitution would never have been ratified had it not been for the addition of a Bill of Rights. It was the very nature of covenant theory a Bill of Rights embodied, coupled with the various and countless ways previous bills of rights or liberties had functioned within community and state governments. The framing generation and the specific framers at the Convention sessions knew bills of rights had a history of working and functioning with various governments already settled on our continent. This made many of them feel comfortable enough to sign on to this new constitution. While the Declaration of Independence certainly mentions specific rights; a document titled such and spelling out exactly which rights must be adhered to, specifically by attachment to a constitution within compact design, could certainly (in their minds) put the brakes on what had the possibility to become a tyrannical federal government. There should be no controversy when influencers to one or two documents are not the same as influencers for another. This is precisely one of the reasons why the influence of religion in the history of one document is different from another.

Yet the framers did not have to be religious men in order to come to the conclusions they did concerning the federal documents they signed. In fact, Jefferson, who could not attend the Convention sessions because he was in France at the time, made clear statements in support of a bill of rights or liberties. His listed religion was Episcopalian, although the reality of that statement may be questionable. He could simply be listed as such because he was born into an Anglican household and attended Episcopal services during his lifetime. It is quite easy to find comments he made in favor of Unitarianism, as well as Jesus. It is clear he did not view Jesus as God, nor did he agree to many tenets Christians hold dear, but he also was not an atheist. He made every attempt to keep the Federal government a non-sectarian setting, yet allowed for religious events within a public setting.[2]

This dichotomy, as it were, for historians, troubles many today. I really don't understand why. Classical deists believed firmly in a 'God.' Most of them had no conflict with the moral convictions of Judaism or Christianity, at least in this country. Unitarians of Jefferson's day did consider themselves Christians. There were differences between the two we have already reviewed. We will review Jefferson's odd religious history in a future chapter. It is my opinion this same inability to understand how a president can wish to keep the Federal government non-partisan with respect to church denominations, yet support religious Christian tenets within public government, is what I think is also the same inability to see the threads of different influencers within the framework of our Federal documents. As a general rule, the founders mentioned religion or some term used or agreed upon by all for God more frequently than the framers did. Many have made the argument this is because the framers were atheists or deists. They then use that hypothesis to say the Constitution is godless. While the evidence is clear some were deists, there is skimpy evidence for them to be atheist.

I do think we are missing the forest for the trees with that argument for three reasons. The time period in which they lived and the specific role producing a federal government made on the framers and the seemingly incessant attempt to gain favor by many different Christian denominations. Many of the framers believed in God, though their comments did not specifically mention religion as their source for the decisions which would have to be made in writing a constitution. Why would it? When I go to get my motor vehicle paperwork filled out or my taxes done, I don't mention God to anyone. That is not my focus at the time. Getting the insufferable paperwork done is. If anyone spoke to me about the paperwork, they would have no knowledge of my belief or lack of belief. As we shall see shortly, they did erect monuments and pray at many other political events. Not everyone will want to mention God as they are trying to work out the internal framing of the institutions constituting how a people function in government. Not to mention the fact political ideologies of Federalist, Anti-Federalist— as well as remnants of Whig theory— are floating around these deliberations.

Another problem here has to do with all the different "Enlightenments" and who specifically influenced what. In studying many of them, it became clear quite a few were non-orthodox and/or orthodox Christian (Blackstone, Locke, Montesquieu, among others) and quite a few were atheist and/or deist (Hume, Voltaire, Rousseau, among countless others). Then there is the very confusing task of separating all the letters, papers (Federalist) and other documents written by founders as well as framers— though for the framing period one would probably limit sources from the framers themselves— and I have already mentioned the difficulty in narrowly defining them!

As we have seen, this group of individuals, as well as the framing period itself, was one of the best in the history of mankind, to date, in producing constitutions. Their experience in writing many of the state documents, as well as their research and books read, especially from the Enlightenment period was huge, from our perspective. Not all of the Enlightenment sources read by the American framing generation was antagonistic of religion. Certainly some were. The framers' practical experience of what worked in a constitution and what did not, as well as their literary political experiences made them experts, by our standards, in what they were about to do in writing a federal constitution.[3]

Getting to what was in the hearts of, as well as what influenced founders and framers can almost certainly write itself into its own encyclopedia. As I looked at personal letters, published political statements, the sessions of different political conventions, as well as published sermons, several thoughts hit me. First, the people in this generation (in the colonies) were a very religious people by our standards, with some exceptions. Secondly, the proceedings of the Constitutional Convention itself were dedicated solely to governmental nuances within ideologies in an attempt to form the new government. And finally, wouldn't it be nice if someone took all these documents, threw them into a computer and came up with percentages as to who influenced what? I was overjoyed when I found *ONE*— and dismayed I only found one research paper which attempted to do something close to that (in a non-partisan way).[4]

Because of our chosen subject matter, it stands to reason that we have centered on religious influences up until now. But when it comes to the Constitution, those influencers become more focused on secular governmental theory and in our particular compact, quite non-sectarian. What produced the institutional make-up of the Constitution still had to rest or nestle in a structure, but the Constitution institutionalizes government in very clear-cut ways. Let me share with you what I found to be the difficulty in coming to conclusions as to the exact influencers for the Constitution.

Many of the sources I read had a penchant for either one of the two political factions in existence at the time. Those were the Federalists and the Anti-Federalists. Even the names are filled with prejudice. Let me share an example. In our world today we have the pro-abortion groups and the anti-abortion groups, right? Wrong. Regardless of where you stand on the issue, the anti-abortion groups refer to themselves as pro-life. By reducing our early political factions to "something" and "anti-something," negates the true dynamics within the groups. It also ignores what influenced them from the two political parties in England, who brought their fights to the colonies (Whig and Tory). There is so much history within these factions alone which leant an influence, and that's even before one gets to our first two political parties of Federalist and Democrat-Republicans.

Next you have all the theories spilling out from the various Enlightenment thought from Europe. When you start reading about them, there is this dizzying way modern scholars take the context of one founders/framer's paperwork and attribute it to a certain European writer, while another would take the same founder/framer and opine in favor of a totally different writer. Then they base that opinion solely on the amount of times that writer or the idea espoused upon by the founder/framer was mentioned, without any real proof the idea came from a single sourced European writer! If you broadened the category, you could probably find hundreds of these writers!

Finally, you have thousands and thousands of pages from letters, pamphlets, books, political meetings, as well as newspaper publications and sermons. You might balk at any thought of including sermons. I would too, except the sermons preached during the period of roughly 1760 to 1805 were filled with political theory. Pastors of yesteryear did not self-censor themselves from political theory within biblical matters as they do today. In fact, quite a lot of education went on from pulpits concerning political thought, legal matters and the theory surrounding those from the Bible. These sermons were used as part of the dialogue concerning the formation of the government, the argument for Revolution, whether or not a federal government could be trusted, among so much else. Many of the clergy were in support of a constitution. The sermons were printed in pamphlet form as a means of public education and discourse.

Whether clergy or political hack, they disseminated these pamphlets much like a school teacher hands out homework. Like TV, Internet news, magazines or Internet blogging of today, the pamphlet was how they got "their news" out. Many of the sermons in print which have come down to us contained political theory and influenced how the people thought about politics and why. You can't exclude them just because they are sermons, without understanding the history which produced them. This helps you understand why these folks were so involved in their politics and government. In my opinion, they would be shocked at the apathy seen in today's modern voter by how often we DON'T vote. Even though the sermons should not be excluded, they still need a representation among the documents by the amount of documents included. If you don't do that properly, then you skew the history. I realize I take a chance in leaving that impression with this work, but I have explained my need to stick with what proved a covenant pattern.

The researcher I reviewed looked at 15,000 writings. In the end, their research used one-third of all public political writings with political theory, which held 2,000 words or more, published from 1760 to 1805. This wound up rating 224 different *individuals/writers* of *European* thought.[5] They excluded private material and biased content like legislative and convention proceedings, so the sample drew equally between Federalist as well as Anti-Federalist. Percentages were received based on the frequency of citation. In analyzing citations, writers mentioned got a count whereby you can break down their influence in different decades. Unfortunately, you can't know whether a writer was cited because framers agreed or disagreed with the writers' theories. Because their method took in a large sampling of historical documents from the time period, the Bible is represented as a writer or author. It accounted for ten percent of all pamphlets written.[6] Any unbiased research should include it proportional to its citation, as you would any other writer.

I don't think we realize the influence the Bible had on this generation. But that influence did change. Dramatically so much, you cannot use it as an exact source for our Constitution. During the 1760s, Enlightenment beat out the Bible.[7] Its mention falls off the map, as it were, during the years of 1787-1788.[8] That means in any critical analysis of the Constitution an understanding of Enlightenment thinking is important. So folks are not wrong to study Enlightenment theory in analyzing the Constitution. Any in-depth study of our compact means you have to view the influences separately for each document.

The top four Enlightenment writers for the time period from 1760-1805 are, in order of prominence: Montesquieu, Blackstone, Locke and Hume.[9] (I have only mentioned the top four, so I would encourage you to review the endnote source.) We have already looked at the first three. While much is said today about Montesquieu and Locke, very little mention is made about Blackstone. His focus on law was based on a moral code. This could be the reason for the lack in mentioning him nowadays.[10] His work deals with the governmental process and that process within institutions. He consolidated England's laws where no consolidation took place. Without understanding his influence, as well as others, I'm not sure we can have a balanced viewpoint of our governing documents.

We have not reviewed David Hume (Home). His influence centers around the time period our Constitution was written. Born in 1711 in Edinburgh, Scotland, he died in 1776 in the same city. He was a philosopher, historian and sometime economist.[11] He was a fan of Cicero, Virgil, Rene Descartes, among others. His passion was writing and in that he was prolific. Some, among his many works are: "A Treatise of Human Nature; Essays, Moral and Political; An Enquiry Concerning Human Understanding; An Enquiry concerning the Principles of Morals; Political Discourses (which became incorporated into Essays, Moral and Political); Natural Religion; The History of England." His "History of England" was well read in the colonies, being the most "Hume" cited in the research.[12] During his day, he lost potential appointments because of claims of atheism. Many contest that claim, citing that he was a skeptic.[13] I will say after much research, I find him either a deist or atheist. It seems he may have leaned more toward atheism, but I suppose fans and critics of the man could argue that point for another two centuries.

Many of the colonists viewed Hume a covert Tory.[14] This makes sense because the book our framers cited the most, Hume's "History of England," leans in line with the Tories.[15] His philosophies made attempts at carrying on the thinking of Aristotle down through Kant. Many quote his "A Treatise of Human Nature" as a work which leant advice for framing our Constitution. Whether well read or not, this is where many find Hume reinforcing the thinking free speech is essential and a constitution is needed to prevent bad government. While Hume may have been sympathetic toward the Tories in his "History of England," the work had a subtitle theme showing the beginning of liberty in England.[16] He uses England's common law, and eventually what became an independent judiciary, as being a foundation for liberty. It's easier to see Montesquieu, Locke and Blackstone's influence than Hume's. Maybe that has to do with the volume of work he did on matters other than politics. Some even see his works relating to economics as formatively conservative. In our time, he has many fans and critics alike. Love or hate Hume, one must consider his works when viewing influences on our Constitution.

The founding generation read a wide library of works.[17] The argument whether the Bible through covenant theory influenced our Federal documents is a silly one. It can only be a source of contention if one does not review the history. By the time the framers convened, that ship had already sailed. They were not reinventing the "governmental wheel." One can argue with my example, but it's my opinion they were inventing new material for the treads of the wheel in order to support an upgraded vehicle. What they were doing was inventing a system in which the people, states and the Federal government could coexist in a real way in which one did not make the others impotent. The Articles of Confederation were shown to be inadequate for that task. This was not done in a vacuum. The Constitution would be applied to and in the context of documents which existed. (The Declaration of Independence and the state constitutions.)

In reading the Constitutional Convention's proceedings, the word compact is defined as well as how they defined foederal, with the old English way to spell it, meaning covenant. It was spelled that way to describe foetus for the executive branch as well as federal (with and without the 'o') for the legislative branches.[18] The words "great confederated republic" are used to describe state involvement.[19] Words like "federal pyramid" are used as well.[20] Madison described their definition of federal, not as a national "unlimited or consolidated" government but as a federal government operating "within the extent of its authority thro' requisitions on the confederated States, and rested on the sanction of State Legislatures, the Government to take its place, was to operate within the extent of its powers directly & coercively on individuals and to receive the higher sanction of the people of the States."[21]

We should also understand the "coercively" used by Madison here is not the same as we see power used today as it has become unlimited: Involved in our health, personal and social networking through the access to our Internet, phone and banking; data collecting where we send our mail and looking into our credit card records and mortgage information. As well as laws passed in 2010 to collect information on students' voting records, medical records, among so many other extremely private information concerning them— Or the attempt by the EPA to control land where the smallest of temporary waterways or puddles exist.[22] Along with the ridicule to our free speech and the economic procurement attached to our religious and scientific beliefs, if they do not conform to the government's ideology and plans.[23] I seriously doubt Madison would have approved of laws invading citizens' privacy and the snatching of our inalienable rights.

I have already expressed why I believe the Constitution to be 'color-blind,' with only two oblique mentions toward Christian tradition. Some have made the argument the real reason why the Constitution makes no mention of God is because the framers intended it so. When I find researchers who have looked at the fullness of the history and make that argument, I certainly listen. Why? Because for those individuals I see no bias and hatred toward religion, just a desire to know the truth. They openly acknowledge covenant history in the documents. But accurately see the framers as men who did not necessarily bring their faith (or lack thereof) into the wording of the Constitution, as we see it in The Declaration of Independence, or even the Bill of Rights.

As I have already mentioned, the proceedings of the sessions were not religious. I dare say they had barely the pastime to develop the inner workings of the Constitution itself. Unbiased scholars look at questions which came up by folks along the same lines immediately after the Constitution was published. That research is telling. For one thing, it certainly lets us know the wider public was, as a general rule, seemingly more religious than the framers— Or for some reason, the framers were not as willing to allow denominationalism in the form of any religion into their midst. For over a century a "story" has floated around of Hamilton's response to a question by a minister as to why God "had not been suitably recognized" in the Constitution. Hamilton's response? "We forgot."[24] On the other side of the coin is the well documented, eyewitness deathbed account of Hamilton's rededication and partaking of communion.[25] (See the next chapter.) Even when Franklin called for prayer during the Convention (in an effort to stop the rancor), it was not adopted.[26]

In reading the material which came out of the Convention and the rancor surrounding the adoption of the Constitution, some have made mention of the miracle in its adoption. Frankly, a miracle would describe an immediate event. This just is not so. It took years (1787-1791) for the final ratification by the last of the 13 states. I see the work as more of a healing, whether by the hand of God or in the normal course of events, can be left to the individual reader of history. For me personally, after reading the history, it is a marvel we even have a country. Any unbiased reading of the history certainly cannot attribute the founding of our nation to solely human endeavors. Some other "unseen" factor was at work. Call it Providence, fate or GOD, but you cannot omit its existence. I reference that history for the *fullness* of the timeframe, not just the framing period.

The other fact constantly before me when I read the history is the vying for favor from the different Christian groups. While there certainly were deists at the Convention; the greater problem for them, besides writing the Constitution, was in maintaining neutrality from one sect over another. I don't believe any delegate hated God or believers, as many atheists do today. The evidence does not support that. The evidence does support a super-majority Protestantism. But there is evidence because of Franklin's late request for prayer, it would be viewed as an embarrassment for the delegates in that they were having problems.

These sessions were closed door and not open for public viewing, all in an attempt to allow them to deliberate without ridicule or pressure. In that they seemed adamant. Hamilton made mention if prayer was called for at that late date, it would be viewed as if they were in trouble, which of course they were (my opinion). Lastly, they were in Quaker territory. Quakers were still viewed with suspicion by many, in no small part because of their refusal to go to war on behalf of the nation (Revolutionary War). This also added a desire to keep the proceedings non-sectarian. After reading quite a lot of material, this "non-sectarian" desire becomes quite apparent to the religious student. Madison seems to confirm that by making mention of it in a letter explaining some of the historical inaccuracies which took place surrounding the Convention's sessions: "The Quaker usage, never discontinued in the State & the place where the Convention held its sittings, might not have been without an influence as might also, the discord of religious opinions within the Convention, as well as among the Clergy of the Spot."[27]

The fact they might have considered Franklin's request had it been at the beginning of the sessions, would be in line with the practice of prayer, even to this day, at the opening of meetings. Isn't that why we hear so much of the frequency some freedom-from-religion groups make in going to court to stop any prayer at public events, including governmental ones?

There really is a larger issue here and that is the difficulty the attendees faced in completing the assignment set before them. Even a short review of the history will show these men faced obstacles within their ranks at every turn. Reading any number of sources who quoted Washington or Madison or Hamilton will show they all despaired of the nation becoming any more than a handful of disparate states. The founders, and especially the framers, were people of different backgrounds as well as different specialties. While the founders, in general, were much more adamant in their faith, the framers were not all as convincing. Yet they were smart enough to realize a people became more than they could ever be when they were admonished in the ways of virtue, piety, harmony and working together. Instead of being antagonistic toward the Bible, the devout as well as those who were not, along with those of varied opinions, worked on the common goals shared amongst them.

In my opinion, this *proves covenant* like nothing else can. The disparity between even those who were not religious didn't stop them from working with the religious, as is evidenced by a framer like Hamilton. His early beginnings, coupled with what seem to be inclinations toward a "playboy attitude" don't make him what anyone could call a choir boy.[28] Even though Hamilton may have had a late-life conversion (or rededication; see the next chapter under "New York"); at the time of the writing of the Constitution, he seemed more in line with deism or indifferent "belief." After Christianity, freemasonry was another group adherence. You couldn't get any more different in attitude concerning religion than Hamilton and say a guy like Franklin, neither of them Christians. While Hamilton was probably a deist at this point in his life (as was Franklin), he seems to have been okay with prayer at the Convention had Franklin called for it earlier. We view all these today as vagaries probably because we dismiss common covenantal bonds. I believe it was *because* of their differences they made efforts to work together for a common goal in writing a constitution. It was what would be best for what would be the newly formed nation. This idea is covenantal.

As a result, they spread the net far and wide to review governmental documents from many different international sources. Benjamin Franklin is quoted as saying to the delegates of the convention: "We have gone back to ancient history for models of Government, and examined the different forms of those Republics which having been formed with the seeds of their own dissolution now no longer exist. And we have viewed Modern States all round Europe, but find none of their Constitutions suitable to our circumstances."[29] While these specific comments by Franklin are made within the context of his request for prayer at that time, it does show the attitude as well as the steps they were taking to complete their task and their own diversity in a belief for the covenant-keeping benefits of prayer.

There are delegates that don't care what the opinion of others happens to be, they want prayer; and then there are those delegates who are more worried about the opinion of others, than a desire to make a request to God. For their specific task, both decisions have merit. One, in support of Godly intervention; the other, in support of stability and harmony among the general population. Collectively, it seems they did not see their governmental responsibility in Franklin's request as an and/or but as an either/or. But doesn't this also go to the very heart of the human condition? And yet they rose above it— not by ignoring the call to prayer— they prayed often privately and at later dates and public events; but by working together to accomplish the task at hand. For that, Franklin states they literally searched the world over.

This attitude of attempting to work together and searching far and wide to complete their goal, while still staying true to their individual beliefs as well as whatever state they each represented, is also seen as an 'attitude of covenant' or thought which permeates our U.S. Constitution. I don't wonder this is precisely why we have so much documentation by these delegates as well as other founders within the framing time period concerning the different literature they read and/or discussed. Two facts become apparent when viewing Franklin's statement: Our Constitution as originally written is like nothing else the world over. They couldn't find any "suitable to our circumstances."[30] Covenant psychology— non-sectarian and religious, within a secular outreach— like nothing else, pushed them forward in completing a near Herculean task.

ENDNOTES

1   <http://www.archives.gov/exhibits/charters/constitution_founding_fathers.html> accessed 2/26/16

2   <http://www.adherents.com/people/pj/Thomas_Jefferson.html> site accessed 10/31/15. I find this site mostly accurate. Because their research is limited, they do concede to errors on the home page. But they also do the best they can at non-partisanship, which for me means they are simply trying to get at the truth with whatever research they can find. I use them frequently when we look at the religious affiliations of the framers as well as founders. Much of the same research can be found in our National Archives and the Library of Congress. Accessed 2/28/16.

3   Lutz, Donald S. and Jack D. Warren. 1987. "A Covenanted People: The Religious Tradition and the Origins of American Constitutionalism" Providence, RI: © 1987, The John Carter Brown Library at Brown University, and sponsored by The Lily Endowment, Inc; The Rhode Island Committee for the Humanities. 51-61

4   Donald S. Lutz, "The Relative Influence of European Writers on Late Eighteenth-Century American Political Thought," American Political Science Review, Vol. 78, No. 1 (March 1984), pp. 189-197

5   Ibid. 191

6   Ibid., Lutz, "The Relative Influence. . ." 192

7   Ibid., 192. see "Table 1"

8   Ibid., 194

9   Ibid., 194. see "Table 3"

10   <http://www.blackstoneinstitute.org/index.php> If you click on the William Blackstone tab on top of the site and then click on the "downloading this" article written by Virginia C. Armstrong, Ph.D., you will be able to read the debate. Site © 2012-2015 Blackstone Institute, Abilene, TX, USA; accessed 2/29/16. You may access Blackstone's at Lonang Institute: <http://lonang.com/library/reference/blackstone-commentaries-law-england/>

11   My favorite site for a quick biography <http://www.britannica.com/biography/David-Hume> My favorite site for everything "Hume" <http://www.davidhume.org> Something

closer to the first, and slightly more involved, but nowhere near as complete as the second <https://en.wikpedia.org/wiki/David_Hume> accessed 3/5/16. I include Wikipedia because many like it. I hesitated because we must understand that even though they should be commended for their work, it can be quite fallacious if the sources are inaccurate or nonexistent. This is why I usually will give other sources, if necessary if I give you a Wikipedia source.

12   Lutz, "The Relative Influence. . ." 196.

13   <http://plato.stanford.edu/entries/hume-religion/#WasHumAth> accessed 3/5/16

14   Lutz, "The Relative Influence. . ." 196.

15   Hume, David. 1776 (1777) "My Own Life." South Australia: eBooks@Adelaide, University of Adelaide. 2015. Online <https://ebooks.adelaide.edu.au/h/hume/david/life-of-david-hume-esq-written-by-himself/> accessed 3/16/16. See paragraph 15.

16   Ibid.

17   <http://oll.libertyfund.org/pages/founding-father-s-library> This is a list of 37 of the top works read by the founding generation. Accessed 3/6/16.

18   <http://avalon.law.yale.edu/subject_menus/debcont.asp> and click on the respective dates of 5/30; 5/31; 6/1; © 2008 Lillian Goldman Law Library, 127 Wall Street, New Haven, CT accessed 3/6/16.

19   Ibid., Click on the date of 6/1.

20   Ibid., Click on the date of 5/31.

21   <http://memory.loc.gov/cgi-bin/query/r?ammem/hlaw:@field(DOCID+@lit(fr003379)):> Library of Congress, accessed 3/6/16.

22   There are so many newspaper articles documenting the 2013 information leaked by a recent whistleblower (some term as illegal and many term as a hero) and follow-up information released by the NSA and other governmental bureaucracies— unfortunately controlled by administration sympathizers who implemented the more coercive and sinister aspects of these laws (from 2009 on). Any Internet search engine can help you reveal hundreds, if not more of them; both conservative as well as liberal. <http://thehill.com/policy/energy-environment/210130-fears-of-epa-land-grab-create-groundswell-against-water-rule>You can take your pick as to which you prefer to view. One of the best descriptions of what was done in 2010 to our students can be seen at this site, accessed 1/23/16 <http://video.foxnews.com/v/2686994216001> Search material concerning the thousands of new regulations enacted by the administration of the 44th President can also be viewed at many sites. One site that has several different links to the information can be seen here <http://www.foxnews.com/politics/2014/11/24/

white-house-quietly-releases-plans-for-3415-regulations-ahead-thanksgiving> If you click on the links you can read the information supporting the article from both the left and the right.

23   I refer to the demand through "ObamaCare" that everyone pay for someone's birth control pills, abortions, sex change operations when it comes to psychological gender preferments. (As opposed to those through physical birth defects, which would demand physical medical intervention as opposed to psychological/psychiatric care.) The demotion and criminalization of members of the military concerning their private religious beliefs as they share them on bumper stickers or Facebook pages. The rights of businesses involved in marriage ceremonies, to refuse specialized business advantages based on religious convictions. This list could go on and on. For that reason, I encourage you to do an Internet search. It shouldn't take long for you to find these instances and more. There is a blogger by the name of Todd Starnes that has cataloged quite possibly hundreds of them. Once you get out of the U.S. Internet protocols and are lucky enough to be able to search this overseas, you can see how much bias is made in this country in tainting research and news. But with some detective sleuthing, any comprehensive search should be able to reveal the biased sources as well as unbiased, and help you, the reader draw your own conclusions in this area.

24   Lutz, Donald S. and Jack D. Warren. 1987. "A Covenanted People: The Religious Tradition and the Origins of American Constitutionalism" Providence, RI: © 1987, The John Carter Brown Library at Brown University, and sponsored by The Lily Endowment, Inc; The Rhode Island Committee for the Humanities. 63

25   Ibid., 68 (see next, "The Framers" and endnote 57).

26   <http://avalon.law.yale.edu/subject_menus/debcont.asp>click on the June 28, 1787, date. It can also be accessed at <http://avalon.law.yale.edu/18th_century/debates_628. asp> © 2008 Lillian Goldman Law Library, New Haven, CT, accessed 2/22/16.

27   <http://memory.loc.gov/cgi-bin/query/r?ammem/hlaw:@field(DOCID+@ lit(fr003416))> Library of Congress, accessed 3/6/16.

28   There is a quote attributed to him that he once recommended a military chaplain with the words, "He is what I should like for a military parson, except that he does not whore or drink." Lutz, Donald S. and Jack D. Warren. 1987. "A Covenanted People" 68. There seems to be some controversy over the wording here. I could not find it in any original sources, but if it can be found, it would not surprise me. You can see where the argument goes here <http://americancreation.blogspot.com/2008/11/alexander-hamilton-died-newbie. html> Accessed 3/6/16.

29   <http://avalon.law.yale.edu/18th_century/debates_628.asp> © 2008 Lillian Goldman
      Law Library, New Haven, CT. accessed 1/21/16. An original facsimile of a book titled
      "The Works of Benjamin Franklin containing Several Political and Historical Tracts. . .
      Volume 5" by Jared Sparks, from the Harvard College Library from the Library of Ernest
      Lewis Gay, dated June 15, 1927, can be seen <http://books.google.com> as an ebook.
      You must sign in; accessed 2/16/16.

30   Ibid., June 28, 1787 Convention debate.

Chapter Eleven

THE FRAMERS

Let's look at the specific framers who attended the sessions and what they stated their religion, or lack thereof to be. There were 55 delegates able to attend some or all of the Constitutional Convention's sessions. As mentioned before, you couldn't get a more different group of men. Yet they had similarities. They were also, almost as a whole, a remarkable group of men. By comparison, I believe I belong to a generation of slackers! After the Convention, many worked within their own states and at the federal level to create the foundational institutions/departments and regulations of those bodies the Constitution birthed. Almost to the man they had all taken some part in the Revolution. Twenty-nine had served in the Continental forces, many in positions of command.[1]

Their political experience was extensive as well. At the time the Convention was held, 41 of them had been or were members of the Continental Congress. Only 14 of them lacked congressional experience. Eight of them had signed the Declaration of Independence (Clymer, Franklin, Gerry, Robert Morris, Read, Sherman, Wilson and Wythe). Six had signed the Articles of Confederation (Carroll, Dickinson, Gerry, Gouverneur Morris, Robert Morris and Sherman). Almost all of them had experience in colonial and state government; with eight having been governors (Dickinson, Franklin, Langdon, Livingston, Alexander

Martin, Randolph, Read and Rutledge). Thirty-five were lawyers or had legal training. Many held dual occupations.

Most were involved in some form of business or commercial land and/or agricultural venues. Only nine received a substantial portion of their income from public office (Baldwin, Blair, Brearly, Gilman, Jenifer, Livingston, Madison and Rutledge). Three were retired (Franklin, McHenry and Mifflin), although Franklin along with Williamson were scientists. Along with their other pursuits, McClurg, McHenry and Williamson were also physicians. One, Johnson, was a university president and one, Baldwin, had been a minister. The majority of them had seminary or theological education because all colleges were schools for a particular denomination. Except for eight, they were all born in the thirteen colonies (Butler, Fitzsimons, McHenry, Paterson: Ireland; Davie, Robert Morris: England; Wilson: Scotland; and Hamilton: West Indies). Sixteen of them had already lived or worked in more than one state or colony. Several of them had studied or traveled abroad.[2]

It can be quite easy to find the religious convictions of some of these men; others can be more nuanced. In most cases, a church would not accept an individual for burial if they were proven to be antagonistic toward Christianity or their specific church/denomination. This is common knowledge, but especially so for some, as in the case of a founder like Thomas Paine. Paine's writings are notorious for his animosity for organized religion and support for deism. His Will made a request for burial at the Quaker cemetery. The Quakers refused the body. Knowing they might do this, he requested burial on his farm.[3] Bodies were moved from initial interment, and lack of church burial does not mean the individuals were not believers, as church burial also does not mean they were not Unitarian or possibly deist.

In mentioning political party, it does not always equate a Federalist was a deist. On the other hand, I could find no evidence of an Anti-Federalist being a deist. I am not saying some were not, just that I could not find conclusive facts they were. Whereas, with Federalists, the evidence seemed easier to find. Party affiliation also changed within a man's life as well as religious affiliations. Regarding education and matriculation at certain colleges or universities, as has been previously mentioned, almost all of these bodies in the colonies were started as seminary-based institutions. During the period of time these men attended, all of them were heavily centered upon theological studies, being a school of one Christian denomination or the other. The first secular, non-sectarian college is not seen until 1825 with Jefferson's University of Virginia.

It would be quite impossible to do any of these men justice by a biography here. I cannot find the space. Books could, and have been written concerning these men's lives. I limited my overview to what might or did prove religious affiliation. I believe we should be careful though in interpreting their beliefs based upon what denomination they espoused. I have already made my objections noted concerning any attempt to place them into any modern ideology we see today. The politics, the work history and their habits are quite alien to our century. In fact, the reason why we can define or place them is because of their biblical, classical and agrarian studies. Where I could show a dichotomy with their practices and professed beliefs, I attempted to do that. Although, because of the times they lived, such practices which conflicted with a study of the Scriptures did not always translate into society. As well, certain habits did not make them unbelievers. Preaching of the day did not always eschew alcohol and especially tobacco, as it does today. Though it did decry over-indulgence. Of course, the Quakers rejected the use of alcohol— and forbid military endeavors which involved violence. Please also remember the Quakers of today, as with other Protestant denominations, are not the Quakers of the 1700s.

The other difficulty is in making many of them out to be deists. Without a doubt, there was a higher concentration of deists in the upper classes. Many of these men were from that group. The deism in this country was different from, let's say a country like France. Quite a few deists abroad leaned toward or were atheist. That was not the case in this country. In fact, within the colonies, every deist, or an individual who leaned toward deism or Unitarianism believed in a god, just not necessarily the Triune God. They usually found the Bible to be a good system of religion for a country to espouse. As well, most also felt Jesus to be a good character figure for people to emulate, but that "religion" had changed the Bible, and not always for the better. These tenets (as I have related them, loosely) were followed by many who espoused some form of deism in America.

We should also remember the change in belief over a man's life and to what degree, can be hard to find. I did notice quite often marriage affected these men concerning their belief systems, and the death of a wife affected them as well. If I could find that firmly, then I noted it. In one or two cases, it was rumored an individual was a deist, but then I would find mention they regularly attended church and/or was buried in that church's or denomination's churchyard. In that case I made no mention, simply because the evidence did not show it conclusively one way or the other. I have also noted the theological doctrine from Protestantism of rationality and rational thinking. Many forget this started with the Reformation, linking it only with deism or Enlightenment thinking. In fact, it is possible a few of the delegates may not have been aware of rational thinking's origins or of its extension in covenant theology. Though I was pleasantly surprised when I realized a super majority of them did have an understanding of the latter. To use either one of these concepts as proof of an individual's belief system is faulty at best. Many churches, especially Presbyterian and Episcopal denominations would adhere to rationalism quite religiously. So to use that concept as proving a deist or a Christian, for that matter, has its problems as well.

It can be difficult to be totally exhaustive in searching for their religiosity or lack thereof. In other words, I did not search all universities nor all rare book sites. I did not make an extensive search of every family history, which many times will tell us more of what these men believed than anything else can. It wasn't that I didn't try. But quite often, these archives would not necessarily be available for view if a university or other organization did possess them. You would physically have to travel to those locations. I also made use of a state's archives, when it was available. I did my best to read many of the older books to find the history of a man's life.

There is a practice today of making someone out to be a deist if they belonged to a freemason organization or other type of societal or university group. That also has its problems because when I attempted to do that, I could find statements the individual made or others of their contemporaries made, which would contradict a penchant for deism. I believe the reason why many erroneously attribute belonging to scientific or other membership-based societies as a deist is due to the lack of understanding concerning the science of the day and its connection to theology. Theology is the scientific study of God. The Bible is quite a scientific book, if you actually study it. Many of these men did and they brought that understanding of the cosmos, creation and their world view to what they saw as cause and effect. It affected their different studies and the results ascertained from those studies. As we have already read, there were many different professions which belonged to this group. The majority of these men believed in God and the majority of them were Christian. In fact, if they lived today, they would be like the many Israeli scientists in studying the Bible and correlating it to their professional findings. They would be overjoyed to find recent research on the "God particle" as well as other recent discoveries (especially in cold fusion).

Another mistake is to place a deist as a member of the Unitarian Church. The Unitarian Church of yesteryear is very different from the Unitarian-Universalist denomination of today. Unless I could prove both facts extant in an individual, I would not place a Unitarian as a deist. They may have agreed in non-trinitarianism, but deism and unitarianism were two very different belief systems. In other words, I tried to make no assumptions but looked for hard evidence by direct quotes and what went on for the entire duration of a man's life. Concerning the delegates themselves, none were atheists. If we keep a loose definition on their Christianity; in other words, don't try to make them all out to be devout modern-day believers— by my count— out of the 55, I found three during the writing of the Constitution to be a deist, possibly three or four more that *seemed* to be deists. Two were confirmed Catholics. The remainder followed some form of Protestant Christianity. I found none who were of the Jewish faith.

CONNECTICUT:

Concerning the delegates to the Constitutional Convention, Connecticut sent three men: Oliver Ellsworth, William Samuel Johnson and Roger Sherman.

Oliver Ellsworth had degreed in theology but then switched his study to law. He was a Congregationalist, a strict Calvinist and personally experienced his election by God for salvation.[4] He did not sign the Constitution. He was buried in the cemetery of the First Church of Windsor (CT), 1807.

William Samuel Johnson's father was a prominent Anglican clergyman, the first President of King's College (Columbia). The son would eventually follow into the same job. The father urged his son to enter the ministry, but he became a lawyer. In reviewing a biography of Johnson in 1877, it mentions that Johnson's opinions and character were strongly affected by the conservative influences of "English churchmanship." And that even though he remained a layman, he was a deeply religious man.[5] He was buried at Christ Episcopal Church Cemetery, Stratford, CT, 1819.

Roger Sherman was a Congregationalist and was educated by his father's library, as well as by the Harvard educated parish minister, Rev. Samuel Dunbar. Among his accomplishments, he was appointed treasurer of Yale College and awarded an honorary Master of Arts degree. He was a professor of religion for many years, corresponding with many of the great theologians at that time.

DELAWARE:

Delaware sent five men: Richard Bassett, Gunning Bedford, Jr., Jacob Broom, John Dickinson, and George Read.

Richard Bassett was a devout Methodist who held religious meetings at his home, Bohemia Manor, and supported the church financially. He died in 1815 and is buried at the Wilmington and Brandywine Cemetery in Wilmington, DE.

Gunning Bedford, Jr., was a Presbyterian. He was also a freemason. I have no desire to change what a man believed, but his daughter Henrietta, who I dare say, knew him well enough to write what she did with certainty on the monument she placed over his remains wrote: "In Hope of joyful resurrection through faith in Jesus Christ here rests the mortal part of Gunning Bedford. . . ."[6] It then goes on to list his accomplishments, at the end of which it says, "Reader, may his example stimulate you to improve the talents— be they five or two, or one— with which God has entrusted you."[7] He died in 1812 and was buried in the First Presbyterian Churchyard at Wilmington. When the cemetery was abandoned, he was moved to the Masonic Home on the Lancaster Turnpike in Christiana Hundred, DE.

Jacob Broom's earlier convictions were Quaker, but he did surveying work for Washington during the Revolution. Among his many pursuits, he was heavily involved in his community's religious affairs and was a layman at Wilmington's Old Swedes Church, an Episcopal church since 1791. It is now known as the Holy Trinity Church in Wilmington, DE, and claims it is the oldest church building in this country, still in use as originally built (1698-99). In a letter sent to his son, dated, February 24, 1794, he tells him, "don't forget to be a Christian, I have said much to you on this head (*topic they must have previously discussed*) & I hope an indelible impression is made."[8] Italics are mine. While in Philadelphia on business in 1810, he died and was buried at the Christ Church Burial Ground. Several sources trace his religion as Lutheran, others Quaker and still others as Episcopalian.[9]

John Dickinson was known as the "Penman of the Revolution" because of his writings in support of colonial rights. He came from a wealthy Delaware family, whose forebear, Walter Dickinson, came to the colonies as an indentured servant. After gaining his freedom, he built the estate on the tobacco crop, which generations later, John would come to benefit from. John's mother, Mary Cadwalader Dickinson, was a Quaker with strong convictions she instilled in her son. His wife, also a faithful Quaker, exhorted him frequently in letters concerning religion. His convictions may not have been that of his mother or wife since he held positions in Pennsylvania's militia. But he was a man of convictions, since he refused to sign the Declaration of Independence for political reasons as well as hoping for reconciliation with England. Also because of those convictions, he remained an ardent supporter of abolition, and tried in vain, to include language in our founding documents abolishing the slave trade. I must say he put his money where his convictions were. In 1776, the Quakers in Philadelphia made a decision that all Quakers should free their slaves. Owning 5,587 acres in Delaware and 1,279 in Pennsylvania, this would be a drastic financial situation, since each time a slave was freed, a bond payment would have to be made to the county. By 1786 all his slaves were unconditionally set free.[10] One source placed him as both a Quaker and an Episcopalian.[11] William Leigh Pierce's short bios of his fellow Convention attendees say that he "was bred a Quaker."[12] In a political address concerning the Stamp Act and civil rights he says: "Kings or parliaments could not *give* the *rights essential to happiness*, as you confess those invaded by the Stamp Act to be. We claim them from a higher source— from the King of kings, and the Lord of all the earth. They are not annexed to us by parchments and seals. They are created in us by the decrees of Providence, which establish the laws of our nature. They are born with us; exist with us; and cannot be taken from us by any human power, without taking our lives."[13] (Italics are not mine.) Decidedly, these are not the words of a deist. He died in 1808 and was interred at the Wilmington Friends Meetinghouse Burial Ground (*Quaker churchgrounds*), Wilmington, DE.[14]

George Read was an Episcopalian. His wife, Gertrude, was the daughter of Rev. George Ross, the first Anglican rector of Immanuel Church in New Castle, DE. He was listed as a member of Immanuel Episcopal Church. Read died in 1798 and was buried at the same church he was a member of and attended, and his father-in-law was the first rector of. Immanuel Episcopal Church still exists today in New Castle, DE. Though its buildings have been remodeled, burned and remodeled again, it still remains.[15]

GEORGIA:

Georgia sent four men: Abraham Baldwin, William Few, William Houston (sometimes spelled Houstoun) and William Leigh Pierce.

Abraham Baldwin had been a tutor and minister at Yale. He served as a chaplain in the Continental Army. After the war Yale offered him a professorship of divinity. Instead of accepting, he became a lawyer. His father died and Baldwin paid off his debts, as well as taking on the raising, housing and education of his six half brothers and sisters— alone. He never married. Among his other accomplishments, he became the founder of the University of Georgia. He died in 1807. Because he was serving in the Senate at the time, he was buried in Rock Creek Cemetery, Washington, D.C.[16]

William Few was a devout Methodist who contributed to many philanthropic causes. He died in 1828 while in Fishkill-on-the-Hudson, NY (Beacon). He was buried at the local Dutch Reformed Church. He was later reinterred at St. Paul's Church in Augusta, GA.

One source places **William Houston** as an Episcopalian.[17] He did not sign the Constitution. He died in 1813 and was interred at St. Paul's Chapel, Manhattan, NY.

William Leigh Pierce is listed as an Episcopalian.[18] He wrote notes at the Convention sessions concerning short character bios of his impressions of the delegates he had the occasion to know about. They are quite interesting and should be read by any student of U.S. history. For one thing, they tell me what he thought was of importance to get the job they were tasked with accomplished. Education, manner and style of speaking, the ability to make political points of theory, and in some cases, the religious and/or character and personality of the attendee. In my opinion, it is representative of what was assumed important for the work at hand. While religion is mentioned, it is not pre-eminent. A good character, education and the ability to bring forth coherent political theory is of utmost importance in what they were doing and what they had done and what their present occupation was.[19] He did not sign the Constitution. He died at his plantation in 1789, but I was not able to find any record stating exactly where he was buried.[20]

MARYLAND:

Maryland sent five men: Daniel Carroll, Daniel of St. Thomas Jenifer, Luther Martin, James McHenry and John Francis Mercer.

Daniel Carroll was a Catholic from an influential Roman Catholic family. His older brother, John was the first Roman Catholic bishop in the United States. He died in 1796 and was buried in St. John's Catholic Cemetery.

Daniel of St. Thomas Jenifer is listed as an Episcopalian.[21] In Pierce's bio concerning Jenifer he mentions, "From his long continuance in single life, no doubt but he has made a vow of celibacy. He speaks warmly of the Ladies notwithstanding."[22] Today's vows concerning celibacy are usually associated with the priesthood or Christians, pre-marriage. But yester-year's had those such vows made for life. They were not common, but were far more frequent than the practice today. Maryland's archives state he was an Anglican, was a member of All Hallow's Parish and sold slaves. So his religious convictions did not conflict with this venture, as it did for some.[23] He died in 1790, probably at his estate, but the exact location of his grave is unknown.[24]

Luther Martin is listed as an Episcopalian. Yet this is one of the nuanced of the framers when we talk about religion. Here is where most of us forget God remembers the thief on the cross as much as the righteous, if they both repent. He was taken in by Aaron Burr, whom he defended against acts of treason. He died paralyzed by stroke. While there are those during his lifetime who contested newspaper reports, it is a shame during his life and since, those reports printed, mentioned alcoholism.[25] This overshadows probably the most prescient of the political science voices concerning non-ratification. Without reading what this man's warnings were to us concerning a run-away federal government (not without merit, based upon ratifying the Constitution), we are doomed to repeat a history of tyrannical governments. His convictions were strong. He never signed the Constitution. From an 1879 biographical encyclopedia, within the section on Martin, and in his own words, it says: " 'During this period,' he says, 'I also studied the Hebrew language, made myself a toler-able master of the French, and among many other literary pursuits, found time fully to investigate that most important of all questions, the truth and the divine origin of the Christian religion.' . . . 'From my parents,' he says, 'I received a sound mind, a good constitution and they deeply impressed on my young mind the sacred truths of the Christian religion, the belief of which is my boast.' "[26] It goes on to state, "Mr. Martin was a regular member of what was in those days known as the Old English Church, now known as St. Paul's Protestant Episcopal Church. He erected the family altar, and prayed in private. . . . He indulged in the use of ardent spirits as was the habit of his time, but seldom to excess. Reports and newspaper stories greatly exaggerated what his friends considered as his one fault."[27] He died in the care of Aaron Burr and was buried in an unmarked grave somewhere on the site of the Trinity Churchyard, Manhattan, NYC, NY, in 1826.

James McHenry was born in Ireland. After coming to the colonies in 1771, he continued his education, eventually studying medicine under Dr. Benjamin Rush. He is listed as a devout Presbyterian, who upon his retirement held the office of president of a Bible society. He died in 1816. His grave is in Westminster Presbyterian Cemetery, Baltimore, MD.[28]

John Francis Mercer is listed as an Episcopalian.[29] Like Luther Martin, he did not sign the Constitution and was a staunch Anti-Federalist. In 1821 he became ill and traveled to Philadelphia to consult his doctor, where he died. He was temporarily buried in a vault at St. Peter's Church in Philadelphia. He was later reinterred to his family's estate, Cedar Park, at a graveyard at the foot of the garden.[30]

MASSACHUSETTS:

Massachusetts sent four men: Elbridge Gerry, Nathaniel Gorham, Rufus King and Caleb Strong.

Elbridge Gerry's current usage in common English is the term "gerrymander." It developed because of a redistricting in Massachusetts, which produced a district shaped like a salamander (combining gerry and salamander). As a result today, when redistricting is done to create a voting advantage for one party over another, it is called "gerrymandering."[31] Like most Anti-Federalists, he made cogent arguments against the Constitution, which unfortunately, have turned out to be prescient as well. One of his objections was the lack of a bill of rights. Years later, his opinion changed concerning the document, as he thought it could be made better by amendments. He did not sign the Constitution. He is listed as an Episcopalian.[32] As I have already mentioned, I have not found an Anti-Federalist who was a deist. While a governor in Massachusetts, Gerry made several proclamations for prayer mentioning Jesus Christ. While these in and of themselves might not prove a faith in Jesus, his attendance in his church certainly confirms he was a Christian. In 1814, he died while in office, serving as Vice President of the United States. As a result, he is buried in the Congressional Cemetery in Washington, D.C.

Nathaniel Gorham is listed as a Congregationalist.[33] He wrote a letter to a minister named Timothy Dwight concerning this man's search for what would become his eventual ministerial home at the Congregational church at Greenfield Hill, CT, in July of 1783. I am supposing you would care less if you were not truly of that persuasion where a minister would officiate. Though, that is my supposition entirely.[34] I could find nothing which showed he was anything but a good Congregationalist. He died in 1796 and is buried at the Phipps Street Cemetery in Charlestown, MA.

Rufus King is listed as both an Episcopalian and Congregationalist.[35] As a few others did, he made notes on the proceedings of the Convention settings. They have provided insight for historians.[36] He was also a champion of emancipation, having uttered these words on the senate floor: "I have yet to learn that one man can make a slave of another. If one man cannot do so, no number of individuals can have any better right to do it."[37] He died in 1827 and is buried near his estate home at the cemetery of Grace Episcopal Church, Jamaica, Long Island, NY.

Caleb Strong is listed as a Congregationalist. Among his many accomplishments, he was president of the Hampshire Missionary Society and the Hampshire Bible Society. He was also one of the founders of the Academy of Arts and Sciences and a member of the Massachusetts Historical Society.[38] He did not sign the Constitution. He died in 1819 and was buried in the Bridge Street Cemetery in Northampton, MA.

NEW HAMPSHIRE:

New Hampshire sent two men: Nicholas Gilman and John Langdon.

Nicholas Gilman belonged to an old Puritan family who got their first tract of land, eight miles square, granted to them by the Plymouth Colony in 1641.[39] Nicholas himself is listed as a Congregationalist.[40] The whole family settled an area named Gilmanton. This is the same area our honeymooning settlers (the Mudgetts) were clearing in 1762. This is the same area in which the blacksmith's wife, Mrs. Philbrook, got lost and spent the night interceding. Nicholas Gilman was born in Exeter. Gilman's early education was local and as such, he was probably taught by the Rev. William Parsons.[41] New Hampshire, like the other colonies had regular prayer requested by their officials. When it was time to pick the New Hampshire representatives, the governor called them to assemble at Exeter. He "appointed a day of fasting and prayer, on account of the gloomy aspect of the times, which was observed with religious solemnity in most of the towns."[42] Nicholas also served in the New Hampshire contingent of the Continental Army during the Revolution. His brother, John Taylor Gilman, was a governor of the state.[43] John made a proclamation for public thanksgiving, "The Sovereign LORD, and Benevolent Parent of the Universe. . . .be observed as a day of PUBLIC THANKSGIVING through this State, and I have thought fit, by and with the Advice of Council to issue this Proclamation, exhorting Ministers and People of every denomination, religiously to dedicate said day. . . .to praise the name of Almighty God, our Supreme and Bountiful Benefactor, as the free Giver of all Good which we enjoy."[44] It is true that the religious beliefs of siblings can be vastly different, yet I was not able to find any disagreement between them in this matter. The Puritan-Congregational denomination was the earliest in Exeter, especially during Gilman's youth. In 1814, while serving in the U.S. Senate he died. He is interred at the Winter Street Cemetery in Exeter, NH, as is his brother and sister-in-law's father.

John Langdon was appointed to the second Continental Congress. He was also sent, along with Gilman as a delegate to the Convention.

Being a man of some means, he paid for both their fare to Philadelphia, since New Hampshire was unwilling to do so. As a result, both men arrived late by July 21. In New Hampshire, once the state constitution had been approved, it went into operation "at the proposed time, the Government being organized at Concord, accompanied by a religious service called the Election Sermon, which service was annually repeated until 1831, nearly half a century." (In 1793 no sermon was preached.)[45] It is true that just because you are elected to a state, does not mean you approve of its religious traditions, current or otherwise. He is listed as a Congregationalist, which usually meant he had no aversion to such religious proclamations; I could find none. He died in 1819 and is interred at the Old North Cemetery in Portsmouth, NH.

NEW JERSEY:

New Jersey sent five men: David Brearly, Jonathan Dayton, William C. Houston, William Livingston and William Paterson (Patterson).

David Brearly was an Episcopal. Among his many accomplishments, he served as a delegate to the Episcopal General Conference in 1786, helping to write the church's prayer book. He died in 1790 and was buried at St. Michael's Church, Trenton, NJ.

Jonathan Dayton was a Presbyterian and then changed his religious affiliation to Episcopalian.[46] Dayton, Ohio, is named after him, since, at one time he owned 250,000 acres of the "Ohio lands." He died in 1824 and was buried at St. John's Episcopal Church, Elizabeth, NJ.

William C. Houston was a Presbyterian.[47] It seems his early education was given by the Presbyterians as well as their ministers.[48] In fact, it was probably from the advice of these Presbyterian missionaries who were graduates of Princeton, that he went to Princeton, where he also graduated.[49] He did not sign the Constitution. In 1788 he died of tuberculosis while in Franklin, PA. He was buried at the Second Presbyterian Churchyard in Philadelphia, PA.

William Livingston as a youth spent a year with a missionary living among the Mohawk Indians. Mixing religion and politics in government was second nature, as he rejected the Anglican influence and supported the Calvinist influence in the colonial assembly. As was mentioned before, the Puritans' split between Presbyterian, Episcopal and finally Unitarian, forced people to make a choice in those areas where Congregationalists had no representation. Livingston chose to be a Presbyterian. Chosen governor of his state, he retained that position for 14 years. He was active in the anti-slavery movement as well. In 1790 he died and was originally buried in the local Presbyterian Churchyard. A year later his remains were moved to a vault his son owned at Trinity Churchyard in Manhattan. Finally, in 1844 he was reinterred to Brooklyn's Greenwood Cemetery, NYC, NY.

Anyone who knows something about New Jersey knows the name **Paterson**, where both the William Paterson University (formerly known as Paterson State College) as well as the City of Paterson are named after our next delegate from New Jersey. William Patterson is also one of our eight delegates who was not born in the colonies. He is listed as a Presbyterian.[50] Among his accomplished career, he was also governor of the state for three years. The university site which boasts his name carries this quote from him on his bio page: "The education of children is a matter of vast importance and highly deserving of our most serious attention. The prosperity of our country is intimately connected with it; for without morals, there can be no order, and without knowledge, no genuine liberty."[51] Ballston Spa, NY, as well as many other such sites in New York, are known for healing waters, spas and springs. In Paterson's day and for decades after him, many traveled to partake in order to find a cure for what ailed them. While on his way to Ballston Spa in 1806, he died and was buried at his son-in-law's Rensselaer family vault. Anyone knowing New York, knows the Rensselaer name. As a result, the city purchased the property and relocated the cemetery. He is now laid to rest at the Albany Rural Cemetery in Menands, NY.

NEW YORK:

New York sent three delegates: Alexander Hamilton, John Lansing, Jr., and Robert Yates.

I have already made mention of **Hamilton's** quotes. There is evidence for his rededication to Christ on his death bed.[52] He lived in the home of William Livingston as a teenager, who we see had no problem with religion in politics, to some extent. Yet it does seem Hamilton's beliefs changed over his life time. Of course, among his many accomplishments, we can thank him for the two-party political system we now have. I'm not sure if he were alive today, he would be satisfied with the way that turned out. He is, of course, better known today as one of the authors of The Federalist Papers.[53] It is odd how frequently he is brought to mind today as a champion of the Constitution. Yet his influence was not as well rehearsed during his attendance at the Convention. It was his fellow delegate from New York, John Lansing, who wrote that Hamilton "was praised by everybody, but supported by none."[54] But he does have his fans today— and for good cause. He was a trusted aid to Washington during the Revolution. His economic policies helped to shape our country and its posterity in no small part by instituting a National Treasury, outlining municipal institutions for the payment of the public debt, establishing banks, the Mint and much of the revenue system of the country. He is, of course, pictured on the ten dollar bill. He is also credited with starting what eventually became the Coast Guard. He is listed as a Huguenot, Presbyterian and Episcopalian, evidencing much of the experience different religions had on him, as well as his own changing beliefs.[55] His mother was a Huguenot and his first education was by a Presbyterian minister. Many know of his own experience as a deist, for he certainly was one during the conventions. But in the end it was the Episcopalians who claimed his body.

In a fated duel with Aaron Burr in Weehawken, NJ, he was mortally wounded. It is the Reverend Benjamin Moore who wrote to the editor of the Evening Post in New York relating how he administered Holy Communion to Hamilton on his death bed. The Reverend Dr. John M. Mason wrote similarly in the same paper in an effort to clear up rumors which had obviously circulated. He relates how he led Hamilton in assurance of redemption through Christ's sacrifice. These ministers did not sugar-coat salvation. They both received assurances from Hamilton of his acceptance of Jesus' sacrifice. Both letters are quite long, but relate the firsthand accounts in detail.

The Daily Advertiser wrote a piece about Hamilton and mentions these words: "As a Christian, we are happy to add, he has not left the world to doubt of his faith and hope. In his last hours he has put a seal on his character, by declaring his firm belief in the merits and atonement of a SAVIOUR; by avowing his trust in the Redeeming grace, and by requesting and receiving in attestation of his faith, the sacrament of the Lord's Supper."[56] He died on July 11, 1804. He was buried in Trinity Churchyard, NYC, NY. You could not get more different in a delegation than New York's. While Hamilton signed the Constitution and rallied for it back in New York, these next two men (Lansing and Yates) refused to sign it. In a letter they wrote to the then governor, among other issues they said, that the kind of government the convention was proposing could not "afford that security to equal and permanent liberty which we wished to make an invariable object of our pursuit."[57]

John Lansing was a member of the Dutch Reformed Church (Christian Reformed).[58] His death, like his prediction concerning our liberty is, unfortunately, very much in line with modern times. While on a visit to New York City in 1829, he left his hotel room to mail (post) some letters. He was never heard from again. The supposition has always been he had been murdered. There is a cenotaph at Albany Rural Cemetery, Menands, NY.[59]

Roberts Yates and John Lansing were related by marriage. As well, they were both members of the Dutch Reformed Church (Christian Reformed).[60] In the 1780s Yates had been recognized as the leader of the Anti-Federalists. He also published letters and signed them "Brutus" and "Sydney," as many signed their "papers" or letters with pseudonyms. He also made notes of the convention under the title, "Secret Proceedings of the Federal Convention of 1787, Taken by the Late Hon. Robert Yates, Chief Justice of the State of New York, and One of the Delegates from That State to the Said Convention."[61] They were originally published in 1821. He died September 9, 1801. Where he was originally buried is unknown. But he was reinterred at the Albany Rural Cemetery, Menands, NY.

NORTH CAROLINA:

North Carolina sent five men: William Blount, William R. Davie, Alexander Martin, Richard Dobbs Spaight and Hugh Williamson.

William Blount holds the achievement of being the first man to be expelled from the Senate. That should not take away from his other achievements. Although the reason was for a plan to win the Spanish portions of Florida and Louisiana for Britain by using, among other things, Indians, frontiersman and British naval forces. While his early career in politics was for North Carolina, it was in Tennessee he made his mark, elected as one of their first senators (1796-1797). It seems the change in states was also a life change in religions. He started off as an Episcopal and later became a Presbyterian. When the plan which caused his expulsion from the Senate had been exposed by a letter he wrote, one author from 1884 wrote about the facts surrounding the whole episode: "Governor Blount made no claim to what is known as modern Christian statesmanship; but he did claim to be a man of honor and to regulate his official life by those principles which were accepted as honorable by the public men both of England and America; and judged from these standards and the report of the Committee, the Carey letter was very far from being sufficient cause for his expulsion."[62]

The reference to the practice of "Christian statesmanship" comes from the tradition and religious belief service to God carried both governmental (civil and/or secular) as well as ecclesiastical (spiritual and/or philanthropic) obligations, and both should be accomplished together or singularly, whatever the individual felt. It is the theological and doctrinal side of the history from whence we get the phrase, "For God and Country." We have already reviewed this doctrine in a previous chapter. It is interesting that one of his supposed "conspirators" wrote him a letter of which the complimentary closing reads: "Adieu: God bless you and preserve you where you be."[63] Obviously this individual knew him well enough to know the blessing would not offend, and might comfort Blount in whatever he was doing.

What is also interesting is that in taking depositions of this matter in 1797 before the House Committee, the record of the proceeding starts this way: "Dr. Nicolas Romayne, being sworn on the Holy Evangelists of Almighty God, doth depose and say. . . ."[64] There is also mention of another man complaining that Quakers advised him not to drink whiskey and that "Blount laughed and said, 'Never mind it; when I come to Knoxville I will give you two kegs of whiskey.' "[65] This seems to have been made mention of as trying to prove that was payment for some nefarious deed. Arguably, that was a stretch, but it does show whatever his particular beliefs were, they included the occasional imbibe. Over and over again, within the pages of resources I read, it was made mention of what a generous and hospitable man Blount was. The final resolution on the affair concerning the Articles of Impeachment states the month and the date, "in the year of our Lord one thousand seven hundred and ninety-seven. . ."[66] All five Articles date the same way, and several times within some.

Behind the scenes, political shenanigans were afoot. The Federalists made it impossible to see Tennessee as a state. With Adams having won election, the hope of such for the then western citizens of the continent was lost. With Spain causing problems for commerce on the Mississippi River and France no better, since they were attempting to purchase the land, England was, in their minds, their only hope. Without statehood these folks were experiencing hideous as well as life threatening consequences. The Federalists were ignoring their pleas. Spain and France would have compounded their problems. Whatever Blount did, it was not criminal in nature (see the next two endnotes). The Senate eventually dismissed the Articles of Impeachment on premise of jurisdiction. These proceedings also showed the practice of bringing the phrase "year of our Lord" into the literature, as well as swearing in deponents upon the "Holy Evangelists" (Bible). It was a common practice we will review shortly.

It seems there had been evidence which exonerated Blount entirely.[67] Unfortunately, this is not always noted in modern accounts. True is the axiom that the victors write history. There is a real bias today in favor of all things "Federalist." As in any unbiased review of history, sometimes that is merited, sometimes it is not. This affair shows an extreme amount of political hooliganism by the Federalists, and as such, Blount is rarely vindicated in any short bio. Blount was quite popular in Tennessee, with his wife and daughter being granted places of nomenclature, as well as Blountville and the County of Blount being named after him.[68]

He was received back in Tennessee with much fanfare. When the Federal government wanted him arrested and brought back to Philadelphia, the sergeant-at-arms was sent and hospitably treated by Blount as his guest for several days. Even the citizens treated the Fed's agent with respect. But when it came time to be on their way, the officer called for a posse to accompany them back, but could not find a man willing to do so. The district marshal also proved unable to help. Convinced of the uselessness of the endeavor, he returned prisoner-less.[69] Blount probably leaves us with one of the best examples of what to do when a party within the Federal government refuses to give the citizens of the states their constitutional rights: call for states' constitutional convention.[70] While the particulars and law surrounding Blount and Tennessee's struggles are quite different from our modern times, many believe there is nothing within the Constitution which prevents states from bringing legislation to fruition through convention methods. As the Federalists of Blount's day were unable to stop Tennessee from becoming a state, those strangling state's rights today, would also be powerless. Blount died after a short illness in 1801 and is buried in the cemetery of the First Presbyterian Church, Knoxville, TN.[71]

William Richard Davie was born in England. His father brought him to South Carolina in 1763, where his maternal uncle, William Richardson, a Presbyterian clergyman adopted him and sent him to college in North Carolina and New Jersey. Although quite a few sources make it clear that he did not adopt him, but being his namesake, that they were extremely close.[72] Among his many accomplishments, one as a governor of North Carolina, he is considered as one of the founders of the University of

North Carolina and was given the title of "Father of the University" in 1810. Davie County, NC, is named after him. He did not sign the Constitution. He is one of the more nuanced of framers when we speak of religion. There are those that rumor him to be a deist. Here is one of those situations where a framer may have seen elements of truth, for them personally in both their denomination as well as deism. I could not find one bit of evidence he ever denounced the Presbyterian denomination.[73] Though, from many resources, including his University of North Carolina, it seems he clashed with the clergy over the role religion would play at the school.[74] As was the practice of his day among the elite, he said very little about his religious beliefs. Personally, I would place him as a deist during his mid-life. I would need more evidence to say so for his entire life. He died in 1820 and is buried at the Old Waxhaw Presbyterian Church in South Carolina, in the northern part of Lancaster County.[75] The churchyard and site are still there and are part of the U.S. National Register of Historic Places.

Alexander Martin is listed as a Presbyterian and was Governor of the State of North Carolina for seven years, nonconsecutive.[76] His accomplishments were many, though he never married. He did have a son, Alexander Strong Martin, whom he publicly acknowledged.[77] He did not sign the Constitution. He was politically astute. As a conservative, he navigated between Federalist and Anti-Federalist causes, seeking to build consensus. As a result, he was rewarded with years of service in state government.[78] He died in 1807 and was buried at his plantation "Danbury" in Rockingham County.[79]

Richard Dobbs Spaight, Sr., was orphaned at the age of eight. His guardians sent him to Ireland, where he had a good enough education to graduate from Scotland's Glasgow University before coming back to North Carolina. Among his many accomplishments, he served as governor of the state from 1792-1795. He is listed as an Episcopalian.[80] His son, also quite accomplished, was a vestryman of Christ Episcopal Church in New Bern.[81] While that may not be solid proof of his father's beliefs, since fathers and sons can have very different ideas concerning religion; it was less common in that day than it is today to find a huge discrepancy. In other words, it was not common to find a father a deist and a son an involved member of the same denomination his father is listed as being a member of as well. Spaight, Sr., was struck down in a duel at the age of 44 in 1802, and was buried in the family sepulcher at Clermont estate near New Bern, NC. The preaching of the day would have prohibited dueling and placed anyone so engaged as an unbeliever, since it was considered as flirting with suicide. Yet it does not seem Spaight, Sr., was an unbeliever. I could find nothing indicating it, and more in support of his belief. Nevertheless, he did die in a duel, and as such, no church would have received the body (without proof of repentance).

Hugh Williamson's parents directed their son's education to become a Presbyterian minster. He received his license to preach in that denomination, but never became ordained. Instead he pursued medicine and eventually became a scientist. He was an associate of Benjamin Franklin in this regard as well as other endeavors for the cause of liberty. In 1771 he wrote an "Essay on Comets." As a result, the University of Leyden awarded him an LL.D. He was a scholar, scientist, physician, statesman and philosopher. Among his many accomplishments for the cause of liberty, he was appointed as surgeon-general for the state troops in North Carolina. He frequently crossed battle lines to tend to the wounded and prevented further disease and sickness among the troops by spreading knowledge concerning food, clothing, shelter and hygiene. He is also known for inoculating the North Carolinian soldiers against smallpox.[82]

Some have placed him as a deist. I cannot do that. In reading a discourse on the biographical history of Dr. Williamson (public domain), delivered and written by a friend of 25 years, it seems impossible to call him a deist.[83] Besides proven statements over the years of his life,[84] at the very end he wrote his nephew, what is believed to be his last letter: "I have, as I believe, given you notice of every thing to which it is proper that you should attend; and having now, as I think, nearly finished my course through the wilderness of life, grant, O Lord! that when my feet shall touch the cold stream of the waters of Jordan, my eyes may be steadily fixed on the heavenly Canaan, so that I may say to death,'where is thy sting?' "[85]

His reference to 1 Corinthians 15:55 is telling. Firstly, no student of theology, as Dr. Williamson had been before settling on his chosen profession, would be without knowledge that the fifteenth chapter of 1 Corinthians is the 'resurrection' chapter. In other words, the theological proof of our legal right by God for resurrection based upon the sacrifice of Jesus Christ. Among so much more in the science of God (theology) than just these few points, but: a) That we have bodily resurrection because Jesus was the pure and obedient Son, made flesh; b) We have the conveyance of our spirit to the heavenly realm (described now and at that time by the terms "crossing the Jordan" or "heavenly Canaan" or "Canaan-land"); and c) Because of His divinity, He paid the full price for our redemption. I speak in loose terms here, not nearly explaining the depth of, nor all the points of the theology within 1 Corinthians 15.

Let me quote the whole of the Apostle's thought through the one Dr. Williamson quotes: "So when this corruptible shall have put on incorruption, and this mortal shall have put on immortality, then shall be brought to pass the saying that is written, Death is swallowed up in victory. O death, where is thy sting? O grave, where is thy victory? The sting of death is sin; and the strength of sin is the law. But thanks be to God, which giveth us the victory through our Lord Jesus Christ." (1 Corinthians 15:54-57, with the Apostle referencing Isaiah 25:8.) Secondly, I doubt a man as learned as Dr. Williamson would have or could have quoted this verse without knowing the full extent of the verses before and after. A dependence upon which, would have to include faith in the divinity of Jesus Christ.

In the observations that caused him to write his "Essay on Comets" he wrote this statement: "All those worlds, and every one of their inhabitants, are under the constant care of the Divine Being. Not one of them is neglected. 'Great and marvelous are his works: how terrible his power!' "[86] Deists believed in God, but not a God who takes active nor careful and "constant care" of the creation. I have mentioned I have not reviewed all his writings. I tried to find the earliest writing that gathered as much information as possible from family, friends, colleagues, as well as his own. We know his early life was not as a deist. The "Essay" was written in 1771, approximately mid-life. We also see his last communication is not as a deist. If there are communications proving he dabbled with deism's tenets, it obviously was not long-lived. As with many other delegates, his accomplishments are too many to list here. He died May 22, 1819, and is buried at Trinity Church in New York, NY.

PENNSYLVANIA:

Probably because of the location of the Convention (Philadelphia) and the size of the state, Pennsylvania sent eight men: George Clymer, Thomas Fitzsimons (also spelled as FitzSimons and Fitzsimmons), Benjamin Franklin, Jared Ingersoll, Thomas Mifflin, Gouverneur Morris, Robert Morris and James Wilson.

George Clymer was orphaned as a baby of one year old. He was taken in by a wealthy uncle, Thomas Cole, who educated him and left him his mercantile firm upon his death. He succeeded in making these business ventures prosperous. He personally underwrote the Revolution by exchanging all his own specie for Continental currency. He contributed in other ways toward the war effort. He was a Quaker. The devout of them would not actively engage in battle, but they would find ways to contribute by other means, and quite a few did. He died in 1813 and is buried in the Friends Meeting House Cemetery, Trenton, NJ. As already mentioned, if a man was received for burial by the Quakers, he proved his faith.

Thomas Fitzsimons was born in Ireland. He was a devout Roman Catholic who contributed financially as well as in a command position to the Revolutionary War effort. His many contributions to this country's early life are too numerous to list here. He died in Philadelphia in 1811. He is interred at the graveyard of St. Mary's Roman Catholic Church. This is located within Independence National Historical Park.

Benjamin Franklin's accomplishments and life have fostered many documents and books. As is the case with many of our early fathers and mothers, this man was extraordinary. He has been popularized in our culture by reference to the "Benjamins," since his face graces our $100 bills. In earlier society it was his work with electricity, since he was frequently depicted holding a key with a string to a kite. But it is his religious beliefs we are concerned with here. In the case of Franklin, his own words supports his belief in a God, but not necessarily the whole of the biblical One. He mentions his agreement with many of the teachings of deism. His autobiography carries many of his beliefs concerning religion. He was like many of the deists in this country; many of whom were pro-Bible as a system of religion. Some felt any country would find its teachings beneficial for society and the moral fabric of a nation. Many folks nowadays do not realize the cost of immorality. Earlier generations knew quite well an efficient society is one who holds high moral standards in all of its doings. Many of the deists in this country were such a people.

A little over one month before his death, he responds in writing concerning his religious beliefs to a query by Ezra Stiles, president of Yale College: "You desire to know something of my Religion. It is the first time I have been questioned upon it. But I cannot take your Curiosity amiss, and shall endeavor in a few Words to gratify it. Here is my Creed. I believe in one God, Creator of the Universe. That he governs it by his Providence. That he ought to be worshipped. That the most acceptable Service we render to him is doing good to his other Children. That the soul of Man is immortal, and will be treated with Justice in another Life respecting its Conduct in this. These I take to be the fundamental Principles of all sound Religion, and I regard them as you do in whatever Sect I meet with them.

"As to Jesus of Nazareth, my Opinion of whom you particularly desire, I think the System of Morals and his Religion, *(this phrase of his refers to the Bible)* as he left them to us, the best the World ever saw or is likely to see; but I apprehend it has received various corrupting Changes, and I have, with most of the present dissenters in England, some Doubts as to his Divinity; tho' it is a question I do not dogmatize upon, having never studied it, and I think it needless to busy myself with it now, when I expect soon an Opportunity of knowing the Truth with less Trouble. I see no harm, however, in its being believed, if that Belief has the good Consequence, as probably it has, of making his Doctrines more respected and better observed; especially as I do not perceive, that the Supreme takes it amiss, by distinguishing the Unbelievers in his Government of the World with any peculiar Marks of his Displeasure.

"I shall only add respecting myself, that, having experienced the Goodness of that Being in conducting me prosperously thro' a long life, I have no doubt of its Continuance in the next, though without the smallest of Conceit of meriting such Goodness. My Sentiments on this Head *(topic being discussed)* you will see in the Copy of an old Letter enclosed, which I wrote in answer to one from a zealous Religionist, whom I had relieved in a paralytic case by electricity, and who, being afraid I should grow proud upon it, sent me his serious though rather impertinent Caution. I send you also the Copy of another Letter, which will shew something of my Disposition relating to Religion. With great and sincere Esteem and Affection, I am, Your obliged old Friend and most obedient humble Servant. P.S. I confide, that you will not expose me to Criticism and censure by publishing any part of this Communication to you. I have ever let others enjoy their religious Sentiments, without reflecting on them for those that appeared to me unsupportable and even absurd. All Sects here, and we have a great Variety, have experienced my good will in assisting them with Subscriptions for building their new Places of Worship; and, as I have never opposed any of their Doctrines, I hope to go out of the World in Peace with them all." (Italics, mine; dated March 9, 1790, he died April 17, 1790.)[87]

He had been a Presbyterian and later related to the Quakers, but in his own words, here and elsewhere in his autobiography, he came to believe in deism at an early age. Some placed him as a Unitarian, but I found no membership in a Unitarian congregation. Deists, Unitarians and the Christians (all the different 'sects' mentioned) worked well together. One of those reasons was because of their dogmatic adherence to virtue and piety, hence Franklin's mention of the Bible as a system which produces the best societal outcome. He does mention the "dissenters" overseas. This could have different definitions, but since he is talking about religion here, we can easily assume he means those who dissent from organized religious beliefs, which would probably mean 'deist.' The definition of "dissenter" had grown by Franklin's time. Earlier they had included the Puritans and others who came to our shores. But by then they included deist and, especially in Europe, atheists. Franklin died in Philadelphia and was buried at the Christ Church Burial Ground.

Jared Ingersoll had uncles who were ministers. One was a pastor of the First Church of New Haven, CT. His father (whom he was named after) was actively involved in the same church before moving to Philadelphia, where Jared, Jr., later followed.[88] While fathers and sons can have great differences in beliefs— as is what happened with Jared and his father concerning the Revolutionary War— Jared, Jr., remained a religious man, like his father. He was a staunch Presbyterian throughout his life.[89] He held many positions of leadership, as well, throughout his life. He died in 1822. He was buried at the graveyard of the First Presbyterian Church.

Thomas Mifflin came from a family of original settlers to Pennsylvania. As such, they were devout Quakers. Mifflin himself was a Quaker and found himself in business as well as politics when the Revolution began. This left him the difficult position of disobeying the Quakers in fighting or do nothing. When the news of the battle at Lexington hit Philadelphia, a town meeting was called in which many of the leaders spoke. Mifflin gave a speech: " 'Let us not,' he said, 'be bold in declarations, and afterwards cold in action. Let not the patriotic feelings of to-day be forgotten to-morrow, nor have it said of Philadelphia, that she passed noble resolutions, slept upon them, and afterwards neglected them.' "[90] He became actively engaged and held leadership positions in the war effort. As a result the Quakers expelled him. He was an orator of the first quality. When things looked as if the nation in the womb would be aborted, he lent his voice to rouse the populace "from the pulpit of the church, from the meeting house, and the court house."[91] While never leaving the basic principles of the Quakers during his life, he did not keep ardent control over his own finances. He was elected governor of Pennsylvania and served nine years in that position. He was elected one more time to the state legislature. While it was in session in 1800 he died and was buried at the state's expense, his own finances were in such disarray his estate could not cover the funeral expenses.[92] He was buried at the local Trinity Lutheran Church.

Gouverneur Morris was probably as close as any of the delegates would get to an aristocratic upbringing. He descended from Welsh soldiers and his father inherited a large manor in Westchester County, where his economic interests extended to many other colonies as well. Gouverneur would have to wait in line to inherit. He being the only son of his father's second marriage, his share of the estate would be small. His education was upper class. He penned quite a bit of the Constitution. The phrase, "We, the People of the United States, in order to form a more perfect Union. . ." is his as well as a good portion of it, including many of the intricately framed clauses within the document itself. He introduced the idea of decimal coinage, thus inventing the use of the word "cent" in our currency.[93]

He started off as an Episcopalian but there might be evidence he leaned toward deism at some point in his life. Although, it is obvious he ended as an Episcopal. It seems as he watched the chaos of the French Revolution from his ambassadorship to France, he would later reject what he came to see as unjustified assertions of authority from the Federal government he helped framed through the Constitution.[94] During his ambassadorial capacity in France he attended Catholic mass with nobles.[95] While he may have been sympathetic toward deism as well as other religions, I don't believe he remained (if he ever truly was) a deist.

In a discourse before the New York Historical Society in 1816, two months before his death, he takes a swipe at some of the ideas of noted deist David Hume and then makes these statements: "The reflection and experience of many years have led me to consider the holy writings, *(the Bible)* not only as most authentic and instructive in themselves, but as the clue to all other history. They tell us what man is, and they, alone, tell us why he is what he is: a contradictory creature that, seeing and approving what is good, pursues and performs what is evil. All of private and public life is there displayed. Effects are traced, with unerring accuracy, each to the real cause."[96] (Italics are mine.) He then describes sinful man and alludes to the miracles which took Israel out of Egypt. He basically uses this discourse to confirm political principles seen in the Bible, undergirding the Constitution.[97]

It is most revealing, and that from the man who penned much of the Constitution. He as well references Jesus, without mentioning his name, as the "King of kings." All readers of the New Testament would know this term well, but only those that believed in Christ's deity would use it in such a manner.[98] The sentence used references King David as being favored by "the King of kings." Only if you attributed divinity to Christ could Jesus have favored a human king (David) centuries before Jesus' own human birth. Rarely would God, the Father, be referenced this way, especially when in two pages time he will again allude to the fact he is talking about a Christian nation.[99] While Jews could reference God this way, Jesus is mentioned as such in Revelation 17:14; 1 Timothy 6:14-16 and specifically explained in Revelation 19:16 as having a name written on His robe and on His thigh, "King of kings and Lord of lords." In Psalm 136:2, God is referenced as the "God of gods." He invokes the name of Yahveh (spelled Jehovah in English) as being the only God to be worshipped in a nation.[100]

In closing his discourse he makes this statement, dispelling the deist thought of a God who created and then left: "Let mankind enjoy at last the consolatory spectacle of thy throne, *(he is speaking about the throne of science here)* built by industry on the basis of peace and sheltered under the wings of justice. May it be secured by a pious obedience to that divine will, which prescribes the moral orbit of empire with the same precision that his wisdom and power have displayed, in whirling millions of planets round millions of suns through the vastness of infinite space."[101] (Italics are mine.) This discourse, given not too long before his death, is perfect in displaying the thought of harmony between the sciences, politics and religion, something which the founding generations, especially the Christians among them did frequently. He died November 6, 1816, and was interred at St. Anne's Episcopal Church Cemetery, Bronx, NY.

Robert Morris is one of our delegates who was born overseas. He was born in England in 1734 and emigrated to Maryland to join his father in tobacco exportation at the age of 13. He was probably one of the most influential financiers of the Revolutionary War effort, procuring money and supplies for the Continental Army. It has been said without his efforts the army would have run out of funds and supplies.[102] In fact, almost all of his money was taken by the young government. Morris is quoted to have said of this situation: "In accepting the office bestowed on me, I sacrifice much of my interest, my ease, my domestic enjoyments, and internal tranquillity. If I know my own heart, I make these sacrifices with a disinterested view to the service of my country. I am ready to go further, and the United States may command everything I have except my integrity."[103] Washington relied upon him to finance the troops. It is said they were close friends; and what Washington was to the military campaign, Morris was for the financial aspect of the infant nation. He asked Morris to be in his cabinet as Treasury Secretary; Morris declined. It was under his talents the Bank of North America was chartered in December of 1781, the first one incorporated by the new government. Unfortunately, though, he wildly speculated in land and this is what got him into trouble. In 1798, being dangerously overextended, his creditors requested his arrest for debt owed. He was thrown into the Philadelphia debtor's prison and remained there until 1801, when he was released under a federal bankruptcy law. He is listed as an Episcopal.[104] His brother-in-law was the second bishop of the Protestant Episcopal Church in the United States.[105] His friend, Gouverneur Morris, was able to get a pension for his wife, which they lived on after Robert was released from prison. He lived only five more years and was buried in Christ Church (Episcopal).

James Wilson is another one of our delegates born outside of the colonies. Born in 1742 near St. Andrews, Scotland in Carskerdo, he was educated at the universities of St. Andrews, Glasgow and Edinburgh. He emigrated to the colonies in 1765. He studied law under another delegate, John Dickinson and was admitted to the bar in 1768. Unlike Dickinson, he was a signer of the Declaration of Independence. It is said his influence at the Constitutional Convention was second only to James Madison and that only Gouverneur Morris delivered more speeches. Almost all sources relate his conversion from Presbyterianism to that of an Episcopal. But a few relate a further conversion to deism later in life. I believe Wilson would be one of those deism was something he researched and might have agreed with some of its tenets, but unless I can absolutely find his total agreement or philosophy concerning it or a moment from a historical account of a conversion— as we have from a

Presbyterian to Episcopalian— I will have to leave him as one who was not a deist.

He was raised within the teachings of the Scottish Moral Enlightenment tradition, and that is why some place him as a deist. He was a legal mind a century ahead of itself. He wrote a pamphlet outlining the legal right of the thirteen colonies not to be bound by acts of Parliament, but by the Crown only. His position concerning English colonies was eventually followed by England as it related to her other colonies almost a century later. In previous chapters we have reviewed how this was the legal position of the early settlers as well. Oddly enough, had England agreed with this legal position concerning the American colonies in 1774, there would have been no Revolution. Wilson's other contribution, along with John Dickinson of urging all the colonies to be in agreement forging ahead when separating from England, instead of jumping in with only half in favor, also saved us a divided house during the Revolution. It was his legal view in asserting states' rights that they were united as one: "In the Declaration of Independence the united colonies were declared to be free and independent States; independent not individually, but unitedly."[106] If this one tenet was the only one the Declaration espoused, it would be enough on its own to compact the Declaration with our other two Federal documents.

In reading his legal lectures, given many years later, I found no evidence to suggest he was hostile toward a legal system where there was a supreme law based on some form of divine justice. While many deists in this country subscribed to such a system, virtually all Christians and Jews did as well. This can make placing the exact religious beliefs of some founders difficult. In the very beginning of his lectures, he relates the beginning of America with the freedom of religion and freedom from persecution because of religious belief as the foundation of "an original compact of a society, on its first arrival in this section of the globe."[107] In a broad overview, he relates the history of the founding of the laws of this country rooted in the covenant of religious freedom by those history will never know, as well as those who receive the praise, including George Washington. (I paraphrase him here.) It was Washington who was in attendance during that particular lecture.[108]

He did talk about the law of God and the law of man. He divided law into two different classes, Divine and Human. He divided the law of God into four groups: 1) the "book;" 2) the law governing angels or spirits or "law celestial;" 3) the law by which irrational and inanimate parts of the creation are governed (philosophy of body or natural philosophy, which he broke into numerous branches); and 4) "that law, which God has made for man in his present state . . . As addressed to men, it has been denominated the law of nature; as addressed to political societies, it has been denominated the law of nations. But it should always be remembered, that this law, natural or revealed, made for men or for nations, flows from the same divine source: it is the law of God. . . . Human law must rest its authority, ultimately, upon the authority of that law, which is divine. Of that law, the following are maxims— that no injury should be done— that a lawful engagement, voluntarily made, should be faithfully fulfilled. We now see the deep and the solid foundations of human law. It is of two species. 1. That which a political society makes for itself. That is municipal law. 2. That which two or more political societies make for themselves. This is the voluntary law of nations. . . . Far from being rivals or enemies, religion and law are twin sisters, friends and mutual assistants. Indeed, these two sciences run into each other. The divine law, as discovered by reason and the moral sense, forms an essential part of both."[109]

Besides his acknowledgement of legal theory that is not "classic" deist and definitely is not atheist, he makes a statement here about law that is "revealed." This is not deist in its tradition. Wilson seems to attribute one source for revelation as divine. Deists would not attribute revelation from any source other than reason. So many verses of Scripture could be shown as examples of this worldview, but the easiest of them could be Jeremiah 31:35, 36; see the word ordinance or law. As I continued to search for a conversion to deism or other statements confirming its adherence, I did find his understanding of social covenant. In its most basic form between members in a society:

"Without mutual confidence between its members, society, it is evident, could not exist. This mutual pervading confidence may well be considered as the attractive principle of the associating contract. (*Another word for associating contract is covenant, this is not be confused with the theory from Europe in the 1900s.)* To place that confidence in all the others is the social right, to deserve that confidence from all the others is the social duty, of every member."[110] (Italics are mine.) While he relates this most basic understanding of social covenant in relation to a lecture on criminal law, it does show a knowledge of the history of biblical law and its connection to their modern application of law. He does this by quoting many legal philosophers from ancient Greeks and Romans to Blackstone, Montesquieu as well as the deists of his time: classical, biblical and Enlightenment thinking.

His thinking is more reflective of the moral biblical codes of the day. We have reviewed many in previous segments. But I will repeat some here as Wilson relates them in his lectures. The first is that punishment should meet the intent as well as commission of a crime. Another is the quick application of punishment after the commission of a crime; and finally, the biblical principle of the depravity of man.[111] Though some of his positions are as much a contradiction as his life became. It is clear his position within the Constitutional Convention was that the "sovereign" people are the source of the government and should be trusted to change as well as uphold the Constitution; yet, he opposed the addition of a Bill of Rights. Without some of these contradictions, many of his opinions reflected biblical legal thinking as opposed to the type of system we have today.

Think about how long it takes for criminals to receive punishment from the commission of a crime today as you read what was recorded as one of his lectures: "The association of ideas has vast power over the sentiments, the passions, and the conduct of men. When a penalty marches close in the rear of the offense, against which it is denounced, an association, strong and striking, is produced between them, and they are viewed in the inseparable relation of cause and effect. When, on the contrary, the punishment is procrastinated to a remote period, this connexion is considered as weak and precarious, and the execution of the law is beheld and suffered as a detached instance of severity, warranted by no cogent reason, and springing from no laudable motive. It is just, as well as useful, that the punishment should be inflicted soon after the commission of the crime."[112]

Another practice from Puritan covenant he supported (as was supported by other historic sources other than the Puritans) was the need for simple laws and laws which were well known to the populace: "Crimes and punishments too may be distributed into their proper classes; and the general principles of proportion and analogy may be maintained without any gross or flagrant violation. To maintain them is a matter of the first moment in criminal jurisprudence. Every citizen ought to know when he is guilty: every citizen ought to know, as far as possible, the degree of this guilt. This knowledge is as necessary to regulate the verdicts of jurors and the decisions of judges, as it is to regulate the conduct of citizens. This knowledge ought certainly to be in the possession of those who make laws to regulate all. . . . When a citizen first knows the law from the jury who convict, or from the judges who condemn him; it appears as if his life and his liberty were laid prostrate before a new and arbitrary power; and the sense of general safety, so necessary to the enjoyment of general happiness is weakened or destroyed. *(He is talking about citizens that do not know the law until arraignment or prosecution, which unfortunately, is now the case with many of the Federal regulations.)* But a law uncertain is, so far, a law unknown. To punish by a law indefinite and unintelligible!— Is it better than to punish without any law?"[113] (Italics mine by way of explanation.)

He was also a supporter of remonstrance, as were other legal minds of yesteryear. Remonstrance is from a medieval French and earlier Latin phrase meaning to "exhibit or present strong reasons against." It gave rise during the Reformation to an understanding of toleration in recognizing the rights of individuals in matters of faith and worship to preach and practice that faith without interference from government intervention. The 1689 Toleration Acts contained ordinances flowing from this legal premise. It was used by Wilson, Madison and other legal minds of the founding and framing era, and encouraged by men like Washington, Jefferson and Hamilton in support of many legal causes for liberty. It was used by those espousing a biblical/covenant legal tenet. It was not used extensively by atheists, as much as it was used by the religious.

I have made a case covenant theory as part of the founding laws of our country are seen in the states' constitutions as well as the founding of our compacted Federal documents. Going back to one of Wilson's first lectures, he makes a case for law schools in this country to be taught from the elements of law drawn from the United States. Here are the reasons and the documents he makes mention of training by: "Should the elements of a law education, particularly as it respects publick law, be drawn entirely from another country— or should they be drawn, in part, at least, from the constitutions and governments and laws of the United States, and of the several States composing the Union? The subject, to one standing where I stand, is not without its delicacy: let me, however, treat it with the decent but firm freedom, which befits an independent citizen, and a professor in independent states. Surely I am justified in saying, that the principles of the constitutions and governments and laws of the United States, and the republicks, of which they are formed, are materially different from the principles of the constitution and government and laws of England; for that is the only country, from the principles of whose constitution and government and laws, it will be contended that the elements of a law education ought to be drawn. I presume to go further: the principles of our constitutions and governments and laws are materially better than the principles of the constitution and government and laws of England."[114]

In support of using an American foundation in teaching a legal education as opposed to that of another country's laws, he was not averse to using a biblical example: "We have passed the Red Sea in safety: we have survived a tedious and dangerous journey through the wilderness: we are now in full and peaceable possession of the promised land: must we, after all, return to the flesh pots of Egypt? Is there not danger, that when one nation teaches, it may, in some instances, give the law to another?"[115] Unfortunately, this is exactly was is happening within the law schools of our country now. Socialists have placed people on the benches who are using foreign law and they are now interpreting the law accordingly. This is one of the reasons we are losing our freedoms. He was specific in believing the monarchal as well as ecclesiastical laws of England should not be taught in American schools (those would be laws of a king and the aristocracy as well as laws pertaining to church governing the general public). And like others in his era, he denotes God as "Providence" or makes use of the word "Divine" in other places. His lectures, while infused with moral doctrine of biblical and virtuous foundations, are still lectures for lawyers about law, not God. So these would not necessarily prove his religious beliefs.

It is said his early education in Scotland as a child was for the Scottish pulpit because he was "early on designed for the Church."[116] But he decided on a legal career. It was a grand career which helped birth a nation. Yet toward the end of his life, his speculation in land brought his finances (as well as that of Robert Morris) into ruin. He was briefly jailed for his debt, both in New Jersey in 1797, and North Carolina in 1798, all while he was a sitting justice on the Supreme Court. He was listed as a devout Christian.[117] As mentioned before, I could find no conclusive proof he ever became a deist. Yet I could find evidence for his Christianity. He died in 1798 from malaria. Due to lack of finances, his remains were not able to be sent to Pennsylvania for burial. He was eventually reinterred many years later at the Christ Episcopal Church of Philadelphia.

RHODE ISLAND:

Rhode Island sent no delegates to the convention.

SOUTH CAROLINA:

South Carolina sent four delegates: Pierce Butler, Charles Pinckney, Charles Cotesworth Pinckney and John Rutledge.

Pierce Butler was born in County Carlow in Ireland on July 11, 1744. His father was Sir Richard Butler, a member of Parliament and a baronet. Because Pierce was his third son, there was not much chance of inheriting his father's estate or title. A commission was purchased for him at the age of eleven in the British army. He was eventually assigned to His Majesty's 29th Regiment of the Foot as a major.[118] He had quite a few assignments and was posted to Boston in 1768. He met and married Mary Middleton, the daughter of a wealthy South Carolinian planter. Before long, he resigned his commission and moved to South Carolina. He became involved in quite a few business ventures and prospered.

His in-laws were a well respected family in South Carolina. His brother-in-law was one of the signers of the Declaration of Independence. As a result, he also got involved in colonial politics, supporting the colonies in their fight against Britain.

He came close to going broke because of the Revolution. It nearly cost him all of his property during the British occupation of South Carolina. Like many of our framers and founders, he contributed mightily to the war effort in cash as well as putting his physical security in danger. He was almost captured on several occasions.[119] Quite often we forget the Revolutionary War was fought on several fronts, not just in Washington's north. In fact, the British adopted a "southern strategy" when Washington's troops became better trained. We may very well have lost the southern half of the country if it were not for these brave souls from the South who fought the British there.[120]

For Butler to remain afloat after the War, he secured a loan overseas and settled into politics and business. He was an independent thinker, though. There were times he sided with the Federalists and times he sided with the Anti-Federalists. During the Convention he supported Madison's and Wilson's positions. He switched party lines after the Federal government was adopted as well. This tells me it was in his heart to do what was right for the people, not a party. He was also a church-going man. On his trip overseas to secure capital, he also engaged the services of a new minister from the British clergy, bringing him to his church back home.[121] He remained in business and politics and died a wealthy man with huge land holdings in several states. He owned a summer home in Philadelphia and spent quite some time there. One of his daughters married a local Philadelphia physician. He died in 1822 in Philadelphia and is buried at the Christ Churchyard (Episcopal). He is listed as an Episcopalian.[122]

What I found most interesting about Butler was his laser focus to help the many, while focusing on the one concept of national integrity through moral liberty. As a result, this left him outside of the Federalist "boys club." When he felt the Federalists had lost sight of the principles of liberty for the western territories in pursuit of party, he switched parties. When the Jeffersonians did the same, he became an independent in 1804.

This did not endear him to his Federal political colleagues; but then as now, such souls should be considered a national treasure.

Our next two delegates from South Carolina are related; the Pinckneys were second cousins. **Charles Pinckney** was the second youngest delegate to serve at the Convention at the age of 29. He started his government service at the young age of 22 by being elected to represent Christ Church Parish in the South Carolina General Assembly. This was the site of his family's Snee Farm, among other plantation estates. He fought in the Revolutionary War and was captured by the British when Charlestown fell in 1780; sent home on a sort of house arrest, then rearrested and remained imprisoned until 1781.[123] He served four times as governor of the state, twice as a U.S. Senator, and once as a Representative to the U.S. House. He was also a member of the Continental Congress. Like Butler, he started off as a passionate Federalist, speaking often at the Convention. But over time he broke with them and helped form the Democratic-Republican Party. Like another delegate, James Wilson, he rejected the British model of government.[124] He also argued for no religious tests in order to hold office in the new government. He was Thomas Jefferson's South Carolina campaign manager for President of the United States. When Jefferson won the election, he appointed Pinckney as ambassador (Minister) to Spain in 1801.

We know Pinckney celebrated Christmas. He owned 58 slaves according to a census taken in 1810. He was elected a parish vestryman from 1797 through 1802. Yet he only met the requirement for residency service in 1807. There is evidence his slaves converted to Christianity from their mainly animist African belief system, and in some cases, blended the two.[125] We do know he retired for a short period of time to promote educational as well as charitable endeavors.[126] He encouraged the right of slavery for the southern states, yet was a staunch supporter of religious liberties.

He is listed as an Episcopal.[127] He died in 1824 and was buried at St. Philip's Episcopal Church in Charleston, SC. He did write an epitaph to his father on a cenotaph dated 1785. The original is too weathered to read, but an exact replica was erected on the site of Snee Farm. There is no reference to God directly, though we see a common reference made by those who believed. In listing the date it says, "Anno Domini 1785" or, in English, In the year of Our Lord 1785.[128] The remarkable Pinckney family produced two of our delegates. They were prominent in South Carolina political activities. Like our previous delegates, they were also prominent in national activities.

Charles Cotesworth Pinckney, as heir apparent of his father's estate was well educated in the sciences of the time, having received his extensive education overseas. He had military as well as legal training and heard the lectures of the prominent legal authority of his day, Sir William Blackstone. Like Blackstone he was a Christian. Like his cousin, he was captured by the British when Charleston fell in 1780 but was held until 1782. He saw extensive wartime action and was discharged as a brevet brigadier general. His profession was legal. He spoke frequently at the Constitutional Convention. Like his cousin, he was a staunch Federalist; unlike him, he remained so throughout his political career. All of us can wish that his proposal to have the senate serve without pay had been adopted, but alas, we know it was not. He was influential, however, in the compromise that was reached concerning the abolition of the international slave trade. He turned down many offers to serve on the Supreme Court, as Secretary of War and as Secretary of State. He eventually accepted an offer as Minister to France (ambassador).

Unfortunately for Pinckney, the French were not happy with our treaty with the English. This developed into a Quasi-War.[129] He was refused entry, threatened with arrest and was forced to flee to the Netherlands. During negotiations the next year, he, along with the delegation Adams sent, found himself refusing to pay a bribe suggested by the French in order to facilitate normal relations. The episode was termed the XYZ affair because Adams replaced the three French agent's names with these letters. For years after this event, school children were reported to have uttered his comment to the suggestion of the bribe as a rhyme: "No! No! Not a sixpence!"

After returning to the States in 1798, he was appointed as a major general in command of the American forces in the South until 1800 when the threat of war with the French had passed. He ran as a vice as well as presidential candidate in 1800, 1804 and 1808, but did not win his elections. He returned to legal practice in South Carolina and served in his own state's legislature. He was also engaged in philanthropic endeavors; serving as a charter member of the board of trustees of South Carolina College (University of South Carolina) and chief executive of the Charleston Library Society. He was a member in the Society of the Cincinnati as well as the first president of the Charleston Bible Society. He died in 1825, at the age of 79 and was buried at the cemetery at St. Michael's Episcopal Church, Charleston, South Carolina.

John Rutledge also came from a politically active family. His elder brother, Edward Rutledge was a signer of the Declaration of Independence. He came from a large family and himself had ten children. He was educated here by his father, an Anglican minister, as well as in London at London's Middle Temple in 1760. When he came back to the colonies, he engaged in law practice and became politically active. He was governor of South Carolina when the British captured Charleston in 1780. They confiscated his property. He escaped capture and fled to North Carolina. There he was successful in rallying a force to recover the state. Aided by General Nathaniel Greene and an army of men, they reestablished the government. He resigned the governorship in 1782 and took a seat in the lower house of his state's legislature. Unfortunately, he never did recoup the losses he suffered during the war. During the Constitutional Convention he spoke frequently and was an advocate for southern interests. He served his own state's government as well as the national one, where he spent short interims on the Supreme Court. He suffered a mental breakdown due to the death of his wife. Unfortunately, this ended his political career. He is listed as an Episcopal.[130] He died in 1800 and was buried at St. Michael's Episcopal Church in Charleston, South Carolina.

VIRGINIA:

Virginia sent seven delegates: John Blair, James Madison, George Mason, James McClurg, Edmund Randolph, George Washington and George Wythe.

John Blair's maternal grandfather, the Reverend John Munro, was a rector in Virginia's St. John's Parish.[131] John Blair was also the nephew of the famous clergyman, and Doctor of Divinity scholar, Reverend James Blair, founder and longest serving president of William and Mary College. This is the second oldest institution of higher learning in the United States. The college started as "a certain Place of Universal Study, a perpetual College of Divinity, Philosophy, Languages, and the good arts and sciences. . . . . to be supported and maintained, in all time coming."[132] Religion played a long history in the lives of many of our founders, especially in Virginia. The merging of these two pastorates in the lineage of John Blair is an example of this. The college was a herald of many 'firsts' in the nation. Tradition has it the capital in Virginia was moved to Williamsburg at the request of James Blair and five of his students.[133]

The apple did not fall far from the tree of 'firsts' in his nephew, John. While not vocal at the Constitutional Convention, even though he attended religiously, he was among the first jurists in the country to decide on what would become serious precedents. It was up to these first justices to make decisions based on the laws written within the understanding of the newly minted Constitution. Alexander Chisholm was a citizen of South Carolina and was owed money for services rendered to the State of Georgia. When Georgia did not pay, his executors sued. In Chisholm v. Georgia, it was decided because the people were sovereign, power was retained by the citizens themselves, and not by the "artificial person" of the State of Georgia. As a result, controversies by individual states and citizens of other states were under the jurisdiction of the federal courts (by extension allowing citizens of one state to sue another state).[134] The decision was controversial because even the framers and founders themselves had made promises the Constitution did not allow for the citizens of one state to sue another state. Some even tried to invoke European law, stating our law in suing the state was based upon them. But the justices saw it differently. They made it clear it was the text within our Constitution— not any European models or promises made by politicians— but what the text said within the law itself which was binding.

As a result, Congress proposed and later ratified the Eleventh Amendment. This states, in part, that federal judicial power should "not be construed to extend to any suit . . . against one of the United States by Citizens of another State." Blair was also influential in setting the precedence for the Supreme Court to declare a law made by Congress unconstitutional. In his day Supreme Court justices also heard circuit court cases. In that capacity they heard the case of William Hayburn, who applied to be put on the pension list of the United States as an invalid pensioner. Congress ordered circuit court judges to serve as Pension Commissioners. But the justices ruled Congress had violated the terms of the Constitution because the supervision of a federal pension plan was not a judicial duty; and therefore, its law was null and void. In doing so, the Court asserted the separation of powers and established the principle of judicial review.[135] Blair started off as a Presbyterian but later became an Episcopalian. He died in 1800 and his tomb is in the graveyard of the Bruton Parish Church, Williamsburg, Virginia; and is part of the Episcopal Diocese of Southern Virginia.[136]

Many place **James Madison** as a deist. I simply cannot do that. We have evidence he attended St. John's Episcopal Church while he was president and evidence he was a theist.[137] The National Archives (among many others) relate his history as one who considered the ministry as a career, staying on at the College of New Jersey (later Princeton) for a year of postgraduate study in theology. Even though he embarked on a secular career, as a young man he once wrote a friend, "Nevertheless a watchful eye must be kept on ourselves lest while we are building ideal monuments of Renown and Bliss here we neglect to have our names enrolled in the Annals of Heaven."[138] In the same letter he writes that he has no doubt his friend will season his learning experiences for life with a little "divinity" (see previous endnote and letter).

As a student of theology, I doubt he would have left Christianity for deism. I have other doubts as well. Whatever arguments are made concerning Madison's disagreement with how the First Amendment was being interpreted, this is the man who would have made this the amendment: "The Civil Rights of none shall be abridged on account of religious belief or worship, nor shall any national religion be established, nor shall the full and equal rights of conscience be in any manner, nor on any pretext infringed." (See previous endnote.) Certainly Madison tried to use his prototypes for his own desire to see the states regulated by the Bill of Rights. For this reason, along with many others, Madison's version was rejected. It is often difficult for children born within the last 60 years to understand that the states were not bound by the Bill of Rights. The Bill of Rights were intended to apply only to the Federal government. It was the states who had power in regulating religious matters. In fact, the states had no "separation of church and state" until quite some time later. Remember that our establishment document, The Declaration of Independence establishes sovereign states and a unity of those states. States had rights before our Federal government became "nationalized." It is a sad fact, but in today's world, states are almost impotent to stop the Feds. We will discuss this in future chapters.

Getting back to Madison and his religious beliefs, I have seen no direct testimony nor historical account of a conversion to deism. Another concern I would have to place him as a deist would be his support of remonstrance. Like many other framers and founders who had legal as well as theological understanding, he was a proponent of remonstrance. Those who were, understood the covenant relationship between the divine, mankind and the people themselves when forming a government. We have already looked at an overview of remonstrance. It means to lay out the reason for protest or opposition. It comes from the Reformation time period and is an outward flow of Protestantism's use of protestation. It was used specifically by Jacobus Arminius in his "Five Articles of Remonstrance." In it he outlined the five reasons why he disagreed with the Calvinistic doctrine of predestination.[139] A remonstrance was a legal argument made against forcing a group to do or not do a thing. Remonstrances were quite common forms of protest, even up to the Constitutional era. In fact, it could be said the whole of the Declaration of Independence was a remonstrance or list of grievances in opposition to how England was treating her colonies.

Like many remonstrances, they use as a foundation a covenant relationship with the biblical Creator. In fact, one of two remonstrances law schools formerly used in teaching legal history from our country is from Madison. The other one was written in 1657 by the inhabitants of Flushing, NY, to the then Governor Stuyvesant. It is an amazing piece of legal treatise for religious freedom based solely on biblical covenant.[140] Madison wrote his against a law the Commonwealth of Virginia was going to enact which would have made everyone pay for religious teachers. Many use this as proof he was a deist. This, in and of itself, should not be used as such. Why? Because he appealed to the covenant between God and man and citizens one to another. In fact, in reading it, I find it hard to see him as a deist, or one who felt the "Creator" left the creation to its own devices. But think of the understanding of covenant as I have laid it out so far when you read these (excerpted) words by Madison:

"It is the duty of every man to render to the Creator such homage and such only as he believes to be acceptable to him. This duty is precedent, both in order of time and in degree of obligation, to the claims of Civil Society. Before any man can be considered as a member of Civil Society, he must be considered as a subject of the Governour of the Universe: And if a member of Civil Society, who enters into any subordinate Association, ... do it with a saving of his allegiance to the Universal Sovereign. We maintain therefore that in matters of Religion, no man's right is abridged by the institution of Civil Society and that Religion is wholly exempt from its cognizance."[141]

Madison was notorious in his support for religious freedom and his contempt for any— especially among the religious— who would persecute another for their religious beliefs. Because of this, and his connection to the Federalist Papers, his letters to and relationship with the Jefferson presidency, many attempt to place his religious views as leaning toward deism. I still believe he would not have attended an Episcopal Church, nor wrote some of the things he did as a deist. I do believe he was sympathetic toward deists in the sense he believed everyone had the right to personal belief. He and Jefferson were close allies and friends and his wife was engaged as hostess for Jefferson in his presidency. Jefferson was not a deist (see the next chapter). In point of fact, Madison was quite strict in his belief he keep the Federal government colorblind when it came to religion:

"There has been another deviation from the strict principle in the Executive Proclamations of fasts & festivals, so far, at least, as they have spoken the language of injunction, or have lost sight of the equality of all religious sects in the eye of the Constitution. Whilst I was honored with the Executive Trust I found it necessary on more than one occasion to follow the example of predecessors. But I was always careful to make the Proclamations absolutely indiscriminate, and merely recommendatory; or rather mere designations of a day, on which all who thought proper might unite in consecrating it to religious purposes, according to their own faith & forms."[142]

A man with such a deep conviction, would not have attended a church, simply to "keep the peace," or as protection from persecution, as some have implied. I also do not believe he attended a church for the same reasons as Jefferson did. They were very different men. There is another argument they did this for political reasons. Poppycock! While politics may not change, the attitude toward campaigning is like day and night or heaven and hell compared to our earliest politicians. The earliest presidents did not campaign for themselves as they do today. To attempt to make a play for an office was viewed as sheer ambition, thus making you unfit to hold that office. Would to God that attitude had not changed! Some put themselves out like media sensations, using the public's credit card as if it were limitless. I will say though the early political campaigns were still like boxing rings to draw blood. The main difference though, was surrogates did most of the "boxing."

In relation to Madison's religion, this entire letter by him reveals the real intent from him and many others for a colorblind (non-sectarian) Federal government, which was in covenant with the destiny of the people and the States. While Madison was strict in not espousing one religion over the other, what I have never read within Madison's or any other delegate's writings is a desire to see the people persecuted because of their religion, or lack thereof. What you never see is the desire to co-opt the people's faith or, for that matter, money, in order to force them to do or pay or participate in what any religious or scientifically-ruled individual would find abhorrent or fallacious. Without a doubt— and whatever his sympathies toward deists may have been— Madison was a proponent of the covenant form of government.

In 1824, Madison wrote a letter in which he dispels any thought that the English common law was America's birthright: "If the Common Law has been called our birthright, it has been done with little regard to any precise meaning. . . . . As men our birthright was from a much higher source than the common or any other human law and of much greater extent than is imparted or admitted by the common law."[143]

I am not espousing any attempt to incorporate religion into The Federalist Papers. They are discussions concerning governmental issues. But Madison made an observation in Federalist No. 37, which I thought could never have supported a personal and total submission to a belief in deism. He is writing about the circumstances of forming a nation, federal government and constitution:

"The real wonder is that so many difficulties should have been sur-mounted, and surmounted with a unanimity almost as unprecedented as it must have been unexpected. It is impossible for any man of candor to reflect on this circumstance without partaking of the astonishment. It is impossible for the man of pious reflection not to perceive in it the finger of that Almighty hand which has been so frequently and signally extended to our relief in the critical stages of the revolution."[144]

From this statement you can understand the effect he and this genera-tion had in keeping us safe from a run-amok Federal government, spitting out new regulations like cockroaches multiply: "The infirmities most besetting Popular Governments, even in the Representative Form are found to be defective laws which do mischief before they can be mended, and laws passed under transient impulses, of which time & reflection call for a change. These causes, render the Statute Book complex and voluminous, multiply disputed cases between individuals, increase the expence of Legislature, and impair that certainty & stability which are among the greatest beauties, as well as most solid advantages of a well digested Code."[145]

Jefferson asked for his help in compiling a "Theological Catalogue for the Library of the University."[146] The list he conveyed is enlightening. First, it seems from the letter Madison was going all out to convey a true theo-logical library with discussions on the merits of arguments pertaining to that science. Then Madison realized Jefferson did not want as extensive a library. During the course of time, Madison sent him a list. This list is expansive in the sense it includes various writers from various centuries, even broken down into centuries. Ninety recommendations in all. I do not mean to include what became the final theological library or any differences from the list I viewed Madison sent to Jefferson. Madison did become a rector, so there is further history here. Of the ninety works, sixty-four are based in Christian theology. Of the rest, some are extensively used as history for Christian theologians (Like Josephus and Eusebius) as well as works concerning other religions.[147] This "count" is my best guesstimate. I certainly could have added others in the Christian "column," but I erred on the side of caution.

Fourth President of the United States and a power house for functioning in many diverse duties on both a state (Virginia) and federal level. He wrote volumes of literature, letters and lent his name to other governmental documents. They can be viewed easily in our National Archives. After doing so, and looking at the history of the times in which he lived, see if you don't also come away with the sense he sympathized with many sects, was adamant in a separation of church and state, but remained true in a private belief for the God of the Bible. Though he was the eldest of twelve children himself, he and his wife had no children of their own. He died at the age of 85 in 1836 and was buried at a gravesite in the family cemetery at the then Madison family estate of Montpelier. It is now a museum owned by the National Trust for Historic Preservation. The Montpelier Foundation now manages the site in Orange County, Virginia, where Madison's Obelisk is located.

George Mason is listed as an Episcopalian.[148] As a lifelong Anglican he attended services regularly.[149] Mason did not sign the Constitution. His reasons have become prophetic— not because, in my opinion, the document itself made anything come to pass— but because we have so changed it to make it what Mason feared would happen. Among other items, one that he feared was that the states would basically lose their rights. He had many other cogent arguments directly linked to what he felt were insufficiencies in the document itself. These items have taken time to fruition, but unfortunately, we are now eating the sour grapes.[150]

He was a firm supporter of religious freedom, a signer of the Declaration of Independence and a brilliant, but forgotten legal mind that, like Wilson, was centuries ahead of itself. He was a vestryman from 1748 to 1785, the length of time of that position alone would prove he was not a deist.[151] We have reviewed what vestrymen were. These were laymen who were members of the church which had a governing position, both within the church and the locality. There was no separation between church and state. The desire for the separation between church and state originated among the religious, not the other way around. Vestrymen held both a quasi-ecclesiastical role and a local governmental duty as a result of the lack of representation to the monarchy in church matters and governmental issues.

Barely enough can be said of the tireless nature in which Mason fought to make sure the Constitution would keep the people at the helm, the states on the high seas of governmental history and the federal government in constant check and on the leash of both aforementioned. Thankfully for us, his descendants did much to keep his papers and other provenance safe through fire and other calamities, though much has been lost. They make mention of recordings in the family Bible of births, deaths, marriages, baptisms, etc. Another recording was in Mason's will and what he desired to be done with the large silver baptismal bowl used to baptize his children: ". . . in which all my children have been christened, and which I desire may remain in the family unaltered for that purpose."[152] Deists would not have purposed their descendants to baptize themselves and to keep the specific bowl designated for that purpose in tact. All Christian baptisms are done "In the name of the Father, and of the Son and of the Holy Spirit." Most ministers add "In the name of our Lord Jesus Christ." In centuries past, folks were also baptized into "The Christian religion" and even into a specific church, whether Catholic or some other Protestant denomination. No deist would request their descendants keep a baptism bowl for baptisms, knowing full well in what manner it would be done.

Because he was an ardent supporter of the separation of church and state and because his case for not monetarily supporting the churches was based, in part on reason, many try to claim him a deist. I have already proven the Reformation origins of 'reason' in political and religious argument. He encouraged Madison to write his Memorial and Remonstrance. He was the author of the Virginia Declaration of Rights and Virginia Constitution. Because of those two documents, he has been credited to varying degrees with the wording seen in both the Declaration of Independence as well as the Bill of Rights.[153] He died in 1792 and is buried at the family estate, Gunston Hall. It is a museum, declared a National Historic Landmark and owned by the Commonwealth of Virginia. It is located in Lorton, VA, 24 miles south of Washington, D.C.

James McClurg is listed as a Presbyterian even though he was buried at St. John's Episcopal Churchyard in Richmond, VA.[154] He was a noted physician of his time and served as mayor of Richmond, VA, from 1797 to 1798. He also served as a physician during the Revolution. He did not sign the Constitution and was an advocate for a monarchial type of executive.

Edmund Randolph served in many state as well as federal positions.[155] He was a strong advocate for limiting the Constitution's ability to control the states. One of his several arguments for not signing the Constitution was the lack of amendments.[156] He was a staunch supporter of religious freedom as well. There is some evidence he started life as a deist but later converted to become an Episcopal.[157] He served as an aide-de-camp for Washington during the Revolutionary War. He was not a supporter of a one-man executive, stating that such a unity was "the foetus of monarchy."[158] Since he was a lawyer (he was our first Attorney General), I find it interesting he used the word *foetus* to describe the covenant that a monarch holds in governing the people. While it was used to describe how he felt concerning a powerful executive office, it is the legal understanding of the time period that such offices and governmental endeavors were covenantal in nature. In some cases describing the covenant between the monarchy and the divine. He died visiting a friend, Nathaniel Burwell of Carter Hall, near Millwood, Clarke County, VA, in 1813. As a result, he is interred at the Old Chapel Cemetery in Millwood, VA.[159]

Our next delegate, like quite a few other founder/framers has had troves of books written about him. Yet for some unfathomable reason, some still try to claim him as a deist. As a legend, **George Washington** has become larger than life. Yet as a man, we have much recorded history he really did live a life which was larger than reality. There are well documented receipts of his attendance in church, quite consistently; even some claiming he rarely missed attendance, going to whatever local place of worship he could.[160] I wish an action movie could be made of his life and wartime experiences. Unfortunately, I'm not sure our generation could actually understand how pious as well as brave; humble as well as stoic, and steadfast as well as generous he was. In one battle he escaped injury, excepting his hat and coat were riddled with bullets and he had two horses shot out from under him![161]

There are numerous sources which prove he was a Christian. In fact, too numerous to count. Books upon books have been written. Now, I will say it again: If we are expecting him to take to pulpits and shout at public conventions about Jesus, we would all be disappointed. Before the Federal government took up his time, and battles skirted him away from his loved ones, he was a vestryman. In fact, he and George Mason were friends and neighbors, in the sense we understand the term for large landowners living during the 1700s. Washington was also a freemason. Being a freemason at that time would not have precluded Washington from being a Christian. Which is why I feel we must be careful when we try to define all these men's Christianity as we understand Bible-believing Christians of today. The fact is there were more freemasons who signed the Constitution (thirteen) than deists.

You could be a freemason and be a deist (as was Franklin) or a believer in Christ (as were many of the thirteen).[162] The preaching of the day did not find a dichotomy with freemasonry, temperate alcohol consumption, the use of tobacco, owning slaves— among other things— and belief in Jesus, as it does today. Quakers as well as other ministers would have shunned such things, but a large segment of Christian-based teaching of the time would not have. Just because we can find documentation by a minister criticizing the lack of religiosity of our founder/framers, does not mean they denied God. Some ministers of the day were quite critical if people did not show their religious convictions in traditional ways. It wasn't until the William Morgan affair of 1826 that freemasonry fell out of vogue with Americans.[163] Over time, Bible-centric theology would continue to discourage all rituals other than those based on a full trust in the atoning work of Christ. The deception of trusting in anything else would have been exposed. Before that time, I've often felt as if there was a grace period for some of those folks who practiced freemasonry yet believed in Jesus.

We still have quite a good portion of Christianity today who does not realize it is through faith alone, and nothing else that saves. American teaching of Bible-centric salvation doctrine is almost as woefully inadequate today as it was 150 years ago. About 50 percent of the churches' teaching from yesteryear would have blurred the lines between salvation and the works you do after you are saved. (That is my guesstimate, it is probably quite higher.) So to be involved in an organization of ritual which blurred the lines as well, would not necessarily have set off any alarms. I view the Morgan affair as a point in time the Lord used to expose the deception of trusting in anything else but the blood of Jesus for salvation and the word of God for life itself. There have been good historians who believe Washington was a stoic, but not a Christian. Stoicism, as well as freemasonry, would not have precluded or excluded Christianity. In point of fact, a closer look at Christianity would even enhance someone's stoic behavior, not have discouraged it.

After reviewing as much as I could concerning his actual words, I still find him to be a Christian, with caveats concerning our modern understanding. But we do have first-hand accounts from two separate individuals on two separate occasions where Washington was seen in the practice of taking devotions with his Bible open, at least daily.[164] We know when he was first sworn into office as president he did so with a Bible. It was a Masonic Bible and is still in use today.[165] Masonic Bibles of the time, like the one used during the inauguration, were the King James Version. Frequently they had an Apocrypha within them. While most lodges during that time period would not have been able to afford such a pricey treasure as a Bible, if and when they did, they all would have had some identification of Masonic use as well.

None of this takes away from his church attendance, his service to his church or the fact that Christianity, as well as freemasonry, military service, governmental service, agricultural pursuits or family life were all a part of who he was and what he believed. Since there was no format to follow when inaugurating a president, Washington's was precedent setting, as was everything he did as president. Technically, it was a private affair, though famously done as a public event. To this day, almost all of the inaugural balls and/or parties are paid for by the president-elect's campaign. They are not governmental affairs.

A first-hand account of the inauguration has been kept by the freemasons.[166] Many balk at the recount of Washington taking the oath on the Bible, and using the words, "I swear, so help me God," and then kissing the Bible when he was done. This is pretty much how many oaths were taken in that day, if you were a Christian and not one who objected to using God's name in oath-taking. In fact, many still take oaths using God in the swearing in. Record-keeping from that time is not always easy to find. The freemasonry of Washington's caliber and the lodge in New York City who handled the Bible for the inauguration, would have gone to great lengths to preserve this history. I have read some accounts who make the noise of the ceremony and the hushed voice of Washington as a case, along with some accounts which did not mention this until 65 years later as a reason why it could not have happened that way. I do not intend to solve this controversy here. I choose to believe the historical account of the freemasons in this event. This same Bible was also present during Washington's funeral procession in New York on December 31, 1799. It has been present on many other special occasions.[167]

We also have Washington's own words and actions. In 1781, he appointed a church service for the whole of the military after Cornwallis' surrender. On October 20, 1781, after the Articles of Capitulation are finalized he presents his thanks to his brothers in arms, and makes these orders: "In order to diffuse the general Joy through every Breast the General orders that those men belonging to the Army who may now be in confinement shall be pardoned released and join their respective corps. Divine Service shall be performed to-morrow in the several Brigades or Divisions. The Commander in Chief earnestly recommends that the troops not on duty should universally attend with that seriousness of Deportment and gratitude of Heart which the recognition of such reiterated and astonishing interpositions of Providence demand of us."[168]

I have read attempts to use Washington's lack of mentioning Jesus' name as some kind of proof he was a deist. While I could find only a few references to Jesus' name specifically, his use of the words Providence, Almighty, or some other reference to describe God are profuse. Far more than even those no one argues were Christian. It was quite common in so much of his communication to use the word Providence or Almighty when speaking about God. In fact, a list was made of his many references to God. A quick perusal would shun any idea of deism.[169] After reading the excerpts I am about to write, and while reading, remember there are hundreds more references made to God or the Almighty or Providence. You judge for yourself whether this man was some type of Christian.

He wrote a circular letter addressed to the governors of all the original thirteen states when the Army was disbanded. The letter is dated June 14, 1783. Its last paragraph: "I now make it my earnest prayer that God would have you, and the State over which you preside, in his holy protection, that he would incline the hearts of the Citizens to cultivate a spirit of subordination and obedience to Government, to entertain a brotherly affection and love for one another, for their fellow Citizens of the United States at large, and particularly for their brethren who have served in the Field, and finally, that he would most graciously be pleased to dispose us all, to do Justice, to love mercy, and to demean ourselves with that Charity, humility and pacific temper of mind, which were the Characteristicks of the Divine Author of our blessed Religion, and without an humble imitation of whose example in these things, we can never hope to be a happy Nation."[170]

His first inauguration address on April 30, 1789, was even more specific concerning who it was that helped to secure the nation. In part it reads:

"Such being the impressions under which I have, in obedience to the public summons, repaired to the present station; it would be peculiarly improper to omit, in this first official Act, my fervent supplications to that Almighty Being who rules over the Universe, who presides in the Councils of Nations, and whose providential aide can supply every human defect, that his benediction may consecrate to the liberties and happiness of the People of the United States, a Government instituted by themselves for these essential purposes: and may enable every instrument employed in its administration to execute with success, the functions allotted to this charge. In tendering this homage to the Great Author of every public and private good I assure myself that it expresses your sentiments not less than my own; nor those of my fellow-citizens at large, less than either. No People can be bound to acknowledge and adore the invisible hand, which conducts the Affairs of men more than the People of the United States. Every step, by which they have advanced to the character of an independent nation, seems to have been distinguished by some token of providential agency. And in the important revolution just accomplished in the system of their United Government, the tranquil deliberations and voluntary consent of so many distinct communities, from which the event has resulted, cannot be compared with the means by which most Governments have been established, without some return of pious gratitude, along with an humble anticipation of the future blessings which them past seem to presage. . . . Since we ought to be no less persuaded that the propitious smiles of Heaven, can never be expected on a nation that disregards the eternal rules of order and right, which Heaven itself has ordained: . . . I shall take my present leave; but not without resorting once more to the benign parent of the human race, in humble supplication that since He has been pleased to favour the American people, with opportunities for deliberating in perfect tranquility, and dispositions for deciding with unparalleled unanimity on a form of Government, for the security of their Union, and the advancement of their happiness; so his divine blessing may be equally *conspicuous* in the enlarged views, the temperate consultations, and the wise measures on which the success of this Government must depend."[171]

His own farewell address to the nation is telling as well. He warned of the weakening of our liberties by weakening the Constitution, by such subtle enemies that would wage a war against it. Refusing an outright attack, the battle would be waged by factional and callus indifference. He said much and I would encourage you to read it. I will only be printing a small portion that would contain references to God or religion. Here are excerpts from the farewell dated 1796:

". . . the constancy of your support was the essential prop of the efforts, and a guarantee of the plans by which they were effected. Profoundly penetrated with this idea, I shall carry it with me to my grave, as a strong incitement to unceasing vows that heaven may continue to you the choicest tokens of its beneficence. . . With slight shades of difference, you have the same religion, manners, habits, and political principles. . . . Of all the dispositions and habits which lead to political prosperity, religion and morality are indispensable supports. In vain would that man claim the tribute of patriotism, who should labor to subvert these great pillars of human happiness, these firmest props of the duties of men and citizens. The mere politician, equally with the pious man, ought to respect and to cherish them. A volume could not trace all their connections with private and public felicity. Let it simply be asked: Where is the security for property, for reputation, for life, if the sense of religious obligation desert the oaths which are the instruments of investigation in courts of justice? And let us with caution indulge the supposition that morality can be maintained without religion. Whatever may be conceded to the influence of refined education on minds of peculiar structure, reason and experience both forbid us to expect that national morality can prevail in exclusion of religious principle. It is substantially true that virtue or morality is a necessary spring of popular government. The rule, indeed, extends with more or less force to every species of free government. Who that is a sincere friend to it can look with indifference upon attempts to shake the foundation of the fabric?"[172]

There was much else that he said, but his humility was always present:

"Though, in reviewing the incidents of my administration, I am unconscious of intentional error, I am nevertheless too sensible of my defects not to think it probable that I may have committed many errors. Whatever they may be, I fervently beseech the Almighty to avert or mitigate the evils to which they may tend."[173]

It seems obvious to me Washington would not have made these statements, and called for various religious services just because it was fashionable or popular. They meant something to him personally and he knew they would benefit others as well. The type of statements made concerning "Providence" or religion were not the type a deist would make. They are of the nature that presupposes the divine involved in the affairs of men, and a God whose nature it is to save and give prosperity within individual lives, both for the people he spoke to as well as the nation he helped to birth. It seems quite obvious he knew he was speaking to the future generations of a nation. It is a shame under the guise of "religious freedom" we prevent our school children from learning in school the very words the "father" of the nation spoke. I can understand how one might review Madison's words and miss the flavor of his faith. But to review Washington and do the same, is not as easy.

It is equally as much a shame mankind could not have provided him better medical care when he became sick with what many have believed was some type of infection. He died on December 14, 1799. What I cannot do within these pages is describe how truly epic this man's character was in refusing to be a king. He could have taken any number of offerings from many, including our own government. He refused all of them.

This is certainly my personal opinion, but I do believe it impossible Washington missed these words in John 6:15, "When Jesus therefore perceived that they would come and take him by force, to make him a king, he departed again into a mountain himself alone." Instead of making himself a king, Washington gave away much in alms to the poor and time to those who were genuinely in need. He spent the good portion of his life in service to the new nation and gave his time willingly to the many visitors he entertained at Mount Vernon after his retirement. There seems to an argument concerning whether he took communion. For me, the argument ignores an ancient understanding of warriors with blood on their hands (2 Chronicles 28:3). It ignores personal fasting and oath methods (Deuteronomy 23:21; Ecclesiastes 5:4, 5). All three are seen within the Scriptures. It is uncommon to see them performed in regard to communion. While not unheard of, they are not well documented. Whatever the truth— whether of those who say he partook (especially as a young man) or those who say he did not (during his military career and after)— this ignores the mix of law and grace, Old Testament and New Testament which sometimes clouded Christianity's practice in the early colonies. Rumors are rumors and conclusive evidence in short supply. I have, as yet, seen no proof to convince me Washington was anything but a Christian.

He was first buried in the old family vault at Mount Vernon. A new vault was eventually built and this is where you can view his sarcophagus today.[174] There has been much confabulation concerning the different Scripture verses placed in and around his old and present tombs. Like the portraits we have which have come down to us from history, some are composites of the man and the personal recounting of those who knew him best. Repositories like Mount Vernon (and our national archive sites) are experts in his exact quotes and his and Martha's thoughts concerning portraits and burial. It is certainly worth one's time to go to the different sites and see for yourself what it took to birth this nation. I visited scores of them as a child (from Virginia up through New York, and many in the South as an adult). From those experiences, I can tell you without faith, morality and a far greater understanding of what the Bible says than what our population has now, this country just simply would not have come into existence. A man named George Washington told us as much!

George Wythe is the last delegate we will review. He was a lifelong Episcopalian.[175] He is the second to have died by murder. His father died when he was three. His mother, a devout Quaker, gave him excellent skills, teaching him Latin and Greek. Unfortunately, she died when young George was an adolescent. His elder brother and what family he had left eventually sent him to apprentice with another family member, a lawyer by the name of Stephen Dewey. Wythe embarked upon a program of self-education which really lasted a lifetime. He learned Hebrew in his seventies (to better understand the Scriptures). At the age of twenty he gained admittance to practice law. His career as both a lawyer and teacher of law is what earned him the title of America's first law professor. He was a member and a clerk in the Virginia House of Burgesses for many years. He was mayor of Williamsburg in 1768. He wrote a remonstrance against the Stamp Act and was a delegate to the Continental Congress from

1775 to 1776. He signed the Declaration of Independence but not the Constitution. He helped with its ratification in Virginia. He also helped to revise the laws of Virginia itself. What he will always be remembered for was in the training of law for men like Thomas Jefferson, John Marshall, James Monroe and Henry Clay. When Jefferson was governor of Virginia he appointed Wythe as the first law professor for the College of William and Mary. He was also a judge in the Virginia chancery court from 1778 to 1788, and eventually became its sole chancellor.

His legal positions were based on both Sir William Blackstone and Francis Bacon's ideologies. He had strong convictions concerning slavery as well as America's role in providing for law which maintained good social order.[176] Wythe was not a deist, but his teaching style was heavily centered upon the Classics as well as some study in the Bible. In legal theory, I would place Wythe very closely linked with James Wilson.[177] When I speak of their legal theory, many assume they must be deist or have deist tendencies to be legal scholars. The corrupting force and teaching of socialistic theory in our law schools has made many unable to understand the totality of natural rights and its link with biblical legal principles. Marx's theories have proven both economically and socially to stunt human rights as well as cause the economic decline of the countries which adhere to them. Unfortunately, the tendency to teach from a Marxist perspective (progressivism) goes hand in hand with our present generation's total misunderstanding of the link between biblical knowledge, faith and the sciences (whether political, legal, biological or any other).

For example, many of today's astronomers believe in God simply because their field of study proves to them there is a higher being who created all of this. Some have biblical knowledge as well. Their thinking then becomes informed through a vision which lifts creativity to a whole new level. For scholars from generations ago, they also found no conflict with faith and science; in fact, it explained quite a few things to them. For Wilson and Wythe's part, it was their understanding of government as a legal covenant relationship with the people and the people in a covenant relationship with God which was precious. This was the basis of natural rights; they are God-given, not given by the state. This is what formed and informed the legal opinions of Blackstone and Locke, as well as others. The very virtue of liberty being founded on the ability to worship God as one chose to— and government not interfering with religion— was foundational for men like Wilson and Wythe. From this one principle, others concerning our republic followed. Wythe taught these principles to his students (see the section on Wilson for some concepts flowing from this understanding of covenant).

He produced a generation of lawyers, judges, ministers, teachers, politicians and statesmen. He taught two United States presidents, two Supreme Court justices and over thirty governors, senators, congressmen, ambassadors and judges. His students read the classics, orally discussed what they had learned and then explained how it applied to personal life and world events. He required insight, clarity, research, writing, thinking and public speaking skills to be put in practice.

We also need go no further than the ratification documentation of the Convention in Virginia to know whether George Wythe understood covenant and considered the Constitution to be a social compact which housed covenant with the other Federal documents. He wrote it within Virginia's ratification documents itself, using the words "social compact."[178] Upon his untimely death, he left a large library of 338 titles or 649 volumes to President Thomas Jefferson.[179] The total of Jefferson's library (along with Wythe's) was to eventually become the beginnings of the Library of Congress.

George Wythe was poisoned with arsenic by his sister Anne's grandson, George Wythe Sweeney. By the age of 18, Sweeney was in debt for gambling. Unfortunately, he was in the habit of swindling his granduncle of money, while selling his cherished books right out from under his nose. The elder Wythe was on the brink of cutting him out of his will. At the same time he poisoned Wythe, Sweeney wound up poisoning two freed slaves. A cook named Lydia Brodnax survived. A young boy, who was a student of his granduncle, Michael Brown, did not survive. Because of the laws forbidding a black to testify against a white, the eyewitness testimony of Lydia having seen Sweeney put something in the coffeepot, could not be mentioned. That, in conjunction with a series of other legal missteps made by the prosecution, and the young Sweeney went free of all charges. It is fortunate for the cause of justice Wythe lived 14 days after the poisoning. This gave him enough time to call for his lawyer and cut Sweeney totally out of his will. Michael Brown succumbed within seven days.[180]

Wythe's character was of the utmost integrity. Nevertheless, as historians are want to do, Wythe's legal opinions have been picked apart and a few have made mention of the disconnect between some of his rulings and the ideologies he espoused. This does have merit. As in other cases with our founders and framers, no one is perfect. We are all, at different moments in our lives, living and breathing dichotomies. Wythe was no different. But he was a man engaged in one of the greatest governmental experiments, based in some part, on one of the oldest agreements known to man. We know from history he was adamant in keeping virtue alive by the example he lived. We can forgive him, as well as other founder-framers, if they were not as perfect as we suppose ourselves to be. Wythe is buried in the yard at St. John's Episcopal Church in Richmond, VA.

ENDNOTES

1   You can review a short biography for any founder at <http://www.archives.gov> To retrieve the information concerning the secular biographies of the framers, go to <http://www.archives.gov/exhibits/charters/constitution_founding_fathers.html>

2   Ibid., the specific site of the National Archive as noted before can be checked and there are quite a few other sites to check the information given. Pick your favorite history site and enjoy, or find a new one!

3   The religious information for the individuals listed can also be accessed easily from sites such as Wikipedia and other public encyclopedia sites. In the case of the religion of these men, I was pleasantly surprised to find the information common in knowledge. For instance, Googling Thomas Paine's Will is quite easy and can give you many sites which carry his intentions and on many, the Will itself. When I use another source, an endnote will follow the information for that individual.

4   <http://www.britannica.com/biography/Oliver-Ellsworth> accessed 2/1/16

5 "Atlantic Monthly" Volume 0040, Issue 238. August 1877; 243-245. Can be seen at <http://digital.library.cornell.edu> by entering the journal or Johnson's name into the search engine. It can also be seen at <http://memory.loc.gov> by entering Johnson's name into the Library of Congress' search engine.

6 <http://www.granite-corinthian34.org/Gun_Bed_Hist.html> © 2005-2014 Granite-Corinthian Lodge No. 34, A.F. & A.M.; Grand Lodge of Delaware; accessed 2/26/16.

7 Ibid.

8 <http://www.wallbuilders.com/libissuesarticles.asp?id=52> You can view the original letter on this site, accessed 2/15/16.

9 <http://www.adherents.com/people/pb/Jacob_Broom.html>

10 <http://history.delaware.gov/museums/jdp/jdpfamily.pdf><http://history.delaware.gov/museums/jdp/jdppolitics.pdf><http://history.delaware.gov/museums/jdp/jdpslave.pdf> accessed 3/2/16

11 <http://www.adherents.com/people/pd/John_Dickinson.html> accessed 3/2/16

12 <http://avalon.law.yale.edu/18th_century/pierce.asp> 3/2/16

13 "The Political Writings of John Dickinson, Esquire, Late President of the State of Delaware, and of The Commonwealth of Pennsylvania," Bonsal and Niles, Wilmington (Delaware) 1801, Volume 1, 111 (see also 112-113); Public domain

14 <http://www.history.delaware.gov/museums/jdp/aboutjd.shtml><http://bioguide.congress.gov/scripts/biodisplay.pl?index=D000321><http://colonialhall.com/dickinson/dickinson.php>accessed 2/16/16

15 <http://www.ohiofamilyresearch.com/GeorgeRead.htm> site © 2002 Yolander Lifter; accessed 2/16/16

16 <http://www.georgiaencyclopedia.org/articles/history-archaeology/abraham-baldwin-1754-1807> accessed 2/16/16

17 <http://www.adherents.com/people/ph/William_Houstoun.html> 3/2/16

18 <http://www.adherents.com/people/pp/William_Leigh_Pierce.html> 3/2/16

19 <http://avalon.law.yale.edu/18th_century/pierce.asp> site accessed 3/1/16

20 <http://www.georgiaencyclopedia.org/articles/history-archaeology/william-pierce-1753-1789> 3/2/16

21 <http://www.adherents.com/people/pj/Daniel_StThomas_Jenifer.html> 3/2/16

22 <http://avalon.law.yale.edu/18th_century/pierce.asp> © 2008 Lillian Goldman Law Library, New Haven, CT, accessed 3/6/16.

23 The Maryland State Archives is a repository source for this framer. Direct Internet links are not stable. Go to <http://msa.maryland.gov> in the search window enter framer's name.

24 Ibid.

25   Kauffman, Bill. 2008. "Forgotten Founder, Drunken Prophet, The Life of Luther Martin." Wilmington, DE: Publisher Intercollegiate Studies Institute. See our National Archive database.

26   "The Biographical Cyclopedia of Representative Men of Maryland and District of Columbia," Baltimore: National Biographical Publishing Co., 1879. 215. In the public domain and can be seen within the Maryland State Archives, Luther Martin, (1748-1826) MSA SC 3520-875 at this website <http://msa.maryland.gov> Search engine and site accessed 2/24/16.

27   Ibid., 216

28   <http://www.adherents.com/people/pm/James_McHenry.html> accessed 2/24/16

29   <http://www.adherents.com/people/pm/John_Mercer.html> accessed 2/24/16

30   The Maryland State Archives is a repository source for this framer. Go to <http://msa.maryland.gov> In the search window enter framer's name.

31   <http://millercenter.org/president/essays/gerry-1813-vicepresident>accessed 2/22/16

32   <http://www.adherents.com/people/pg/Elbridge_Gerry.html>accessed 2/16/16

33   <http://www.adherents.com/people/pg/Nathaniel_Gorham.html>accessed 2/22/16

34   The letter can be seen at <http://memory.loc.gov> search "Letters of Delegates to Congress: Volume 20; 5/12/1783-9/30/1783; Nathaniel Gorham to Timothy Dwight, May 21, 1783; accessed 2/16/16.

35   <http://www.adherents.com/people/pk/Rufus_King.html>accessed 2/22/16

36   <http://avalon.law.yale.edu/18th_century/king.asp> © 2008 Lillian Goldman Law Library, New Haven, CT, accessed 2/16/16.

37   "Genealogies of the State of New York." 1915. Long Island Edition, Edited by Tunis Garret Bergen. Volume 2; 926, 927. New York: Lewis Historical Publishing Company

38   <http://www.historic-northampton.org/highlights/strong.html> accessed 2/26/16

39   Lancaster, Daniel. 1845 "Proprietary, Civil, Literary, Ecclesiastical, Biographical, Genealogical, and Miscellaneous History, from the First Settlement to the Present Time; Including What is Now Gilford, To The Time It Was Disannexed," Gilmanton: Printed by Alfred Prescott. 267. In the public domain and can be seen in pdf through New Hampshire State's Archive. Archive accessed 2/28/16.

40   <http://www.adherents.com/people/pg/Nicholas_Gilman.html>accessed 2/26/16

41   Ibid., Lancaster, Daniel. 1845 "Proprietary, Civil, Literary, Ecclesiastical, Biographical, Genealogical, and Miscellaneous History ..." 145

42   Ibid., 84

43   <http://bioguide.congress.gov/scripts/biodisplay.pl?index=G000214> accessed 2/16/16

44   The proclamation of the governor is in the public domain. You can see a broadside at several sites <http://gutenberg.us/articles/John_Gilman>At the preceding site you can see documentation of the town Nicholas came from and its religiosity. Also on Wikipedia <https://en.wikipedia.org/wiki/John_Taylor_Gilman> accessed 3/16/16

45   Ibid., Lancaster, Daniel. 1845 "Proprietary, Civil, Literary, Ecclesiastical, Biographical, Genealogical, and Miscellaneous History. . . "102.

46   <http://www.adherents.com/people/pd/Jonathan_Dayton.html> accessed 2/16/16

47   Glenn, Thomas Allen. 1903. "William Churchill Houston." Norristown, PA: privately printed. 2. In the public domain.

48   Ibid. 5-7

49   Ibid. 7

50   <http://www.adherents.com/people/pp/William_Paterson.html> accessed 2/28/16

51   <http://www.northjersey.com/news/education/founding-father-stood-up-for-the-small-states-1.1379236> accessed 3/6/16. Also maybe seen at his namesake university <http://www.wpunj.edu/university/history/WilliamPaterson_Bio.dot> accessed 1/15/16. From "On Education," an essay by William Paterson, c. 1793-95

52   <http://archive.org/stream/collectionoffact00colerich/collectionoffact00colerich_djvu.txt> See pages 48-57; accessed 2/26/16.

53   The Federalist Papers can be seen at this site<http://avalon.law.yale.edu/subject_menus/fed.asp> © 2008 Lillian Goldman Law Library, New Haven, CT, accessed 3/6/16.

54   Cook, Frank Gaylord. 1889. "James Wilson." "The Atlantic Monthly, Volume 64, Issue 383 (September 1889). 327, public domain.

55   <http://www.adherents.com/people/ph/Alexander_Hamilton.html>accessed 3/29/16

56   John M. Mason, "A Collection of the Facts and Documents Relative to the Death of Major General Alexander Hamilton," (New York: Hopkins and Seymour, 1804). 48-57. In the public domain.

57   <http://www.archives.gov/exhibits/charters.constitution_founding_fathers.html> accessed 2/18/16; all of these men's bios can be accessed here; just click on their names

58   <http://www.adherents.com/people/pl/John_Lansing.html>accessed 2/18/16

59   Ibid.

60   <http://www.adherents.com/people/py/Robert_Yates.html> accessed 2/19/16

61   <http://avalon.law.yale.edu/18th_century/yates.asp> © 2008 Lillian Goldman Law Library, New Haven, CT. accessed 2/19/16

62   Wright, Gen. Marcus J. 1884. "Some Account of the Life and Services of William Blount: An Officer of the Revolutionary Army. . . ." Washington, D.C.: E. J. Gray Publisher. 22, public domain.

63   Ibid. 34

64   Ibid. 40

65   Ibid., "Some Account of the Life . . . Blount. " 64

66   Ibid., 89

67   Ibid. 110-115; 119-122, 125-126; 138-141

68   Goodpasture, Albert V. "William Blount and the Old Southwest Territory." "The American Historical Magazine." Volume VIII, No. 1. January 1903. 8-9. In the public domain.

69   Ibid., "Some Account of the Life . . . Blount. " 136

70   <http://www.northcarolinahistory.org/encyclopedia/william-blount-1749-1800/> Site copyright John Locke Foundation.

71   <http://www.northcarolinahistory.org/encyclopedia/william-richardson-davie-1756-1820/> Site copyright John Locke Foundation.

72   <http://www.northcarolinahistory.org/encyclopedia/william-richardson-davie-1756-1820/> Site copyright John Locke Foundation, accessed 2/23/16.

73   Ibid.

74   <http://library.unc.edu/wp-content/uploads/2014/07/2006_watson.pdf> accessed 2/23/16

75   <http://www.adherents.com/people/pd/William_Davie.html>accessed 2/23/16

76   <http://www.adherents.com/people/pm/Alexander_Martin.html> accessed 2/23/16

77   <http://www.ncmarkers.com/Markers.aspx?Markerid=J-15> site © 2008 North Carolina Office of Archives & History - Department of Cultural Resources;accessed 2/23/16.

78   Ibid.

79   <http://www.archives.gov/exhibits/charters/constitution_founding_fathers.html> click on the bio for Martin, accessed 2/26/16.

80   <http://www.adherents.com/people/ps/Richard_Dobbs_Spaight.html> accessed 2/26/16

81   <http://www.ncmarkers.com/Markers.aspx?Markerid=C-7> site © 2008 North Carolina Office of Archives & History - Department of Cultural Resources; accessed 2/26/16.

82   <http://www.northcarolinahistory.org/encyclopedia/hugh-williamson-1735-1819/> Site copyright John Locke Foundation.

83   David Hosack, M.D., LL.D., delivered 11/1/1819, 'A Biographical Memoir of Hugh Williamson, M.D., LL.D' In "Collections of the New York Historical Society for the year 1821," Volume 3, published by E. Bliss and E. White; J. Seymour, printer. 125-179. Public domain.

84   Ibid. 134, 140, 164, 169. 171, 172, 174-176

85   Ibid. 175-176

86   Ibid. 140

87   Franklin, Ben, "Autobiography of Benjamin Franklin," Chapter 9. Public Domain

88   "Papers of the New Haven Colony, Volume 9, Printed for the New Haven Colony Historical Society, 1863." by The Tuttle, Morehouse & Taylor Press, 1918. 211, 228-229, 234. In the public domain.

89   Ann T. Keene. "Ingersoll, Jared, Jr." <http://www.anb.org/articles/07/07-00821.html> American National Biography Online. April 2010. Accessed 3/7/16. © 2010 American Council of Learned Societies. Published by Oxford University Press.

90   William Rawle, L.L.D., "Sketch of the Life of Thomas Mifflin," Memoirs of the Historical Society of Pennsylvania, Volume 2, Issue 2. October 28, 1829. 110, 111. In the public domain.

91   Ibid. 114

92   <http://www.history.army.mil/books/RevWar/ss/mifflin.htm> accessed 3/11/16

93   <http://www.history.army.mil/books/RevWar/ss/morrisg.htm> accessed 3/11/16

94   Ibid., as well, "Scribner's Magazine," Volume 0001, Issue 1, January, 1887, 93-107, "Glimpses At The Diaries Of Gouverneur Morris; Social Life And Character In The Paris Of The Revolution," by Annie Cary Morris. In the public domain.

95   Ibid. 98

96   *"Collections of the New York Historical Society for the year 1821," Volume 3, published by E. Bliss and E. White; J. Seymour, printer, 29-30: 'An Inaugural Discourse, Delivered Before The New-York Historical Society By The Honourable Gouverneur Morris (President), 4th September, 1816.' In the public domain.*

97   Ibid. 25-40

98   Ibid. 32

99   Ibid. "Collections of the New York Historical Society for the year 1821," 34

100   Ibid. 36

101   Ibid. 40

102   Frank Gaylord Cook. "Robert Morris." In "The Atlantic Monthly." Volume 0066, Issue 397, November 1890. 607-618. Public domain.

103   Ibid. 612

104   <http://www.adherents.com/people/pm/Robert_Morris.html> accessed 3/1/16

105   Frank Gaylord Cook. "Robert Morris." In "The Atlantic Monthly." Volume 0066, Issue 397, (November 1890) 607-618. Public domain.

106   Frank Gaylord Cook. "James Wilson." In "The Atlantic Monthly." Volume 64, Issue 383 (September 1889) 325. Public domain.

107   "The Works of the Honourable James Wilson, L.L.D., Late One of the Associate Justices of the Supreme Court of the United states, and Professor of Law in the College of Philadelphia." Volume 1. 6. Philadelphia, PA: Published Under the Direction of Bird Wilson, Esquire, At the Lorenzo Press, Printed for Bronson and Chauncey, 1804. Public domain.

108   Ibid. 6-8

109   Ibid. 103-106

110   "The Works of the Honourable James Wilson, L.L.D., Late One of the Associate Justices of the Supreme Court of the United states, and Professor of Law in the College of Philadelphia." Volume 3. 23. Philadelphia, PA: Published Under the Direction of Bird Wilson, Esquire, At the Lorenzo Press, Printed for Bronson and Chauncey, 1804. Public domain.

111   Ibid. "The Works of the Honourable James Wilson, L.L.D." Volume 1. 6

112   Ibid. "The Works of the Honourable James Wilson, L.L.D." Volume 3. 34

113   Ibid. Volume 3. 45-46

114   Ibid. "The Works of the Honourable James Wilson, L.L.D." Volume 1. 17

115   Ibid. Volume 1. 26

116   Frank Gaylord Cook. "James Wilson." In "The Atlantic Monthly." Volume 64, Issue 383 (September 1889) 316. Public domain.

117   <http://www.adherents.com/people/pw/James_Wilson.html> accessed 11/12/15

118   Coghlan, Francis, "Pierce Butler, 1744-1822, First Senator from South Carolina," The South Carolina Historical Magazine. Vol. 78, No. 2 (April 1977) 104-119

119   <http://www.history.army.mil/books/RevWar/ss/butler.htm> accessed 2/12/16

120   Ibid.

121   Ibid.

122   <http://www.adherents.com/people/pb/Pierce_Butler.html> accessed 3/27/16

123   <http://www.ccpl.org/> accessed .3/10/16; © 2013 Charlestown County Public Library, 68 Calhoun Street, Charlestown, SC 29401; They have much by way of documentation for this framer. If you happen to be in the neighborhood for an appointment or directions: 843-805-6930.

124   <http://www.nps.gov/chpi/learn/historyculture/upload/CHPI_HRS.pdf>accessed 3/2/16. A biographical tour of the history and culture of the Charles Pinckney National Historic Site can be seen by the public online. Robert W. Blythe, Emily Kleine, Steven H. Moffson "Charles Pinckney National Historic Site, Historic Resource Study." August 2000. Cultural Resources Stewardship, Southeast Regional Office, National Park Service, U.S. Department of the Interior, Atlanta, GA.

125   Ibid. "Charles Pinckney National Historic Site, Historic Resource Study." 21, 22, 24, 29, 31, 35; see also footnote 40 on page 40; see also footnote 56 on page 41

126   <http://www.history.army.mil/books/RevWar/ss/pinckneyc.htm> accessed 3/2/16

127   <http://www.adherents.com/people/pp/Charles_Pinckney.html> accessed 3/2/16

128   <http://www.nps.gov/chpi/upload/Pinckney_Cenotaph.pdf> accessed 3/2/16

129   <http://www.john-adams-heritage.com/the-xyz-affair> John Adams Historical Society, <https://www.monticello.org/site/research-and-collections/xyz-affair><http://www.let.rug.nl/usa/biographies/john-marshall/> © 1994-2012 GMW; accessed 3/5/16

130   <http://www.adherents.com/people/pr/John_Rutledge.html> accessed 3/14/16

131   <http://legal-dictionary.thefreedictionary.com/John+Blair><http://www.findagrave.com/cgi-bin/fg.cgi?page=gr&GRid=84636956> accessed 3/2/16

132   <http://en.wikipedia.org/wiki/Bruton_Parish_Church> accessed 3/5/16

133   See the aforementioned sites as well as the website maintained by the College of William and Mary, especially in the history section.

134   <https://supreme.justia.com/cases/federal/us/2/419/case.html> accessed 3/2/16

135   <http://press-pubs.uchicago.edu/founders/documents/a3_2_1s31.html> site © 1987 by The University of Chicago; see also "Virginia Law Review" Volume VIII, November, 1921, No.1, © 1921 by The Virginia Law Review Association. 109-120. In the public domain. Can be seen as an ebook at<http://books.google.com> you must sign in. accessed 3/2/16

136   <http://www.adherents.com/people/pb/John_Blair.html> accessed 3/21/16

137   <http://www.adherents.com/people/pm/James_Madison.html> accessed 3/2/16

138   "From James Madison to William Bradford, 9 November 1772, in "Letters and Other Writings of James Madison in four Volumes. (Philadelphia: J.B. Lippincott & Co. 1865-67) Volume 1; 5, 6. We have papers of Madison found in the 1940s, called "Detached Memoranda." They are a series of handwritten documents discovered in 1946 among the papers of William Cabell Rives, noted Madison scholar. Undated, they are believed to have been written somewhere between 1817 and 1832. They were not published until 1946 by Elizabeth Fleet. In them we see a Madison who seems to be unhappy with the way things are turning out. Like John Locke, the debate over Madison's views could go on for centuries. What we should not do with them is bring them into governance. The very fact Madison was disagreeing over how the First Amendment was working seems to me to be the very fact that it was being legally applied through the correct interpretation of the majority of the citizens, lawyers, politicians and justices in the country. Modern Supreme Court decisions have violated former practice, tradition and law. For a good history see a quick overview of a book by Bill Federer in this article <http://www.wnd.com/2016/01/supreme-court-was-not-always-hostile-toward-faith/> I may find historical facts quoted

by both atheist and faithful questionable, but there has been a practice in this country of allowing covenant to work, both secular and religious. That which hampers either should be questioned. Intellectual arguments surrounding various historical individuals and their legal opinions must be taken in light of the whole of the legal practice, not used to tear the nation apart. This will always be my position. When persecution takes place, we must remember not all atheists are persecutors and not all the religious of various faiths are either. I may have questions and doubts concerning the modern historical narrative over Madison's faith, but those questions and doubts will remain. It is not the purpose of this book to solve them. I always enjoy listening to those who have cogent arguments in either direction, of course, omitting the hateful and disrespectful speech. See <https://www.loc.gov/exhibits/religion/rel06.html> for Madison's original notes. See also a cogent argument in favor of Madison's rights of conscious <http://www.heritage.org/research/reports/2001/03/james-madison-and-religious-liberty> accessed 3/28/16

139   <http://www.theopedia.com/five-articles-of-remonstrance> accessed 3/2/816

140   <http://www.nyym.org/flushing/remons.html> They have a new website, but this address was correct on 3/28/16. If you have trouble with it the new site is <www.flushingfriends.org>

141   "Memorial and Remonstrance Against Religious Assessments." In "The Writings of James Madison." Edited by Gaillard Hunt. Volume 2, 1783-1787. 184, 185 (New York: G.P. Putnam's Sons. The Knickerbocker Press. 1901)

142   Here is a stable pdf URL from LOC <http://lcweb2.loc.gov/service/mss/mjm/20/20_0132_0135.pdf> 3 of their pdf. James Madison's letter to Edward Livingston, July 10, 1822. Public domain, accessed 3/28/16.

143   Letter from Madison to Peter S. Duponceau. August 1824. In "The Writings of James Madison." Edited by Gaillard Hunt. Volume 9, 1819-1836. 200, 201 (New York: G.P. Putnam's Sons. The Knickerbocker Press, 1910)

144   Ibid.

145   Letter from Madison to John Cartwright. 1824. In "The Writings of James Madison." Edited by Gaillard Hunt. Volume 9, 1819-1836. 181, 182 (New York: G.P. Putnam's Sons. The Knickerbocker Press, 1910)

146   Ibid., 203

147   James Madison, The Writings of James Madison, comprising his Public Papers and his Private Correspondence, including his numerous letters and documents now for the first time printed, ed. Gaillard Hunt (New York: G.P. Putnam's Sons, 1900). Vo. 9 [Online] available from <http://oll.libertyfund.org/titles/1940; accessed 3/28/16. See footnote 1 in the letter from this site.

148   <http://www.adherents.com/people/pm/George_Mason.html>

149   <http://gunstonhallblog.blogspot.com/2014/01/george-mason-and-pohick-church.html> accessed 3/23/16

150   "The debates in the several state conventions on the adoption of the federal Constitution, as recommended by the general convention at Philadelphia, in 1787. Together with the Journal of the federal convention, Luther Martin's letter, Yates's minutes, Congressional opinions, Virginia and Kentucky resolutions of '98-'99, and other illustrations of the Constitution…..2d ed., with considerable additions. Collected and rev. from contemporary publications" by Jonathan Elliot. Pub. under the sanction of Congress. (1836), 5 vols." <http://oll.libertyfund.org/titles/1905> accessed 3/28/16. Site © 2004-2015, Liberty Fund, Inc. Public domain. Scroll down to this title: "Objections of the Hon. George Mason, one of the Delegates from Virginia in the Late Continental Convention, to the Proposed Federal Constitution; Assigned as His Reasons for Not Signing the Same."

151   <http://gunstonhallblog.blogspot.com/2014/01/george-mason-and-pohick-church.html> accessed 3/23/16

152   Kate Mason Rowland. 1892. "The Life of George Mason, 1725-1792." Volume 1, 1892. New York & London: G.P. Putnam's Sons. The Knickerbocker Press. 58. In the public domain.

153   Lutz, Donald S. 1988. "The Origins of American Constitutionalism." Baton Rouge, LA: © 1988 Louisiana State University Press. 120

154   <http://www.adherents.com/people/pm/James_McClurg.html> accessed 3/28/16

155   <http://www.history.org/almanack/people/bios/bioraedm.cfm> accessed 3/28/16

156   "The debates in the several state conventions on the adoption of the federal Constitution, as recommended by the general convention at Philadelphia, in 1787. Together with the Journal of the federal convention, Luther Martin's letter, Yates's minutes, Congressional opinions, Virginia and Kentucky resolutions of '98-'99, and other illustrations of the Constitution…..2d ed., with considerable additions. Collected and rev. from contemporary publications" by Jonathan Elliot. Pub. under the sanction of Congress. (1836), 5 vols." <http://oll.libertyfund.org/titles/1905> accessed 3/28/16. Site © 2004-2015, Liberty Fund, Inc. Public domain. Go through the list to the bottom of the table of contents to find Randolph's argument.

157   <http://candst.tripod.com/tnppage/qrandolf.htm><http://www.adherents.com/people/pr/Edmund_Randolph.html> accessed 3/22/16

158   <http://www.archives.gov/exhibits/charters/constitution_founding_fathers_virginia.html> accessed 3/28/16

159   <http://www.findagrave.com/cgi-bin/fg.cgi?page=gr&GRid=20977> accessed 3/28/16

160   <http://www.findagrave.com/cgi-bin/fg.cgi?page=gr&GRid=20977> accessed 3/28/16

161   Metaxas, Eric. 2013. "7 Men and the Secret of Their Greatness." Nashville, TN: © 2013 Thomas Nelson, Inc. 10. There are numerous other sources, both online and in various books written about Washington that tell the same first-hand accounts. I use this source because it is well footnoted and the short biography concerning Washington gives a real flavor of the man in a very concise and easily read format.

162   <http://townhall.com/columnists/craigshirley/2008/04/02/romancing_the_corner-stone/page/full> Article written by Craig Shirley, 2008; accessed 3/28/16.

163   Ibid.

164   Metaxas, Eric. 2013. "7 Men and the Secret of Their Greatness." Nashville, TN: © 2013 Thomas Nelson, Inc. 15-17. See also this © 2015 Mount Vernon Ladies Association <http://www.mountvernon.org/research-collections/digital-encyclopedia/article/george-washington-and-religion/> accessed 3/28/16

165   <http://www.stjohns1.org/portal/gwib> Site © 2014 St. John's Lodge No. 1 AYM F&AM; accessed 3/12/16.

166   Ibid.

167   Ibid.

168   <http://memory.loc.gov/cgi-bin/query/r?ammem/mgw:@field(DOCID+@lit(gw230267))> accessed 3/2/16. For additional information, these copyrighted sites (© 2003-2014 by Son of the South) also have in-depth history on the surrender of Cornwallis and the religious activities that were celebrated by our young government. <http://www.sonofthesouth.net/revolutionary-war/british/lord-charles-cornwallis.htm> <http://www.sonofthesouth.net/revolutionary-war/battles/siege-yorktown.htm> A copy of the Articles of Capitulation can be seen at <http://avalon.law.yale.edu/18th_century/art_of_cap_1781.asp> A pamphlet by Dr. Robert Selig on the campaign of 1781 would be beneficial. It can be seen at this site <http://www.history.army.mil/html/books/rocham-beau/CMH_70-104-1.pdf> Maintained by the U.S. Army Center of Military History

169   Mary V. Thompson, Research Historian. "George Washington's References to God and Religion, Together with Selected References to Death, Eternity, Charity, and Morality." Mount Vernon Ladies' Association, 2003-2010. Online <http://catalog.mountvernon.org/cdm/ref/collection/p16829coll4/id/10> Accessed 11/2/15. This historian assembled 120 pages or 642 references.

170   <http://www.loc.gov/teachers/classroommaterials/presentationsandactivities/presenta-tions/timeline/amrev/peace/circular.html> accessed 3/8/16

171   <http://www.archives.gov/exhibits/american_originals/inaugtxt.html> accessed 3/8/16

172 <http://avalon.law.yale.edu/18th_century/washing.asp> © 2008 Lillian Goldman Law Library, New Haven, CT, accessed 3/8/16.

173 Ibid.

174 You can view a short tutorial from Mount Vernon at the copyrighted site of the Mount Vernon Ladies Association. <http://www.mountvernon.org/the-estate-gardens/the-tombs/> and a reference article <http://www.mountvernon.org/research-collections/digital-encyclopedia/article/the-tomb/> accessed 3/28/16

175 <http://www.adherents.com/people/pw/George_Wythe.html> accessed 3/2/16

176 "Wythe, George (1726-1806)." American eras. 1997. Retrieved 3/2/16 from © site Encyclopedia.com<http://www.encyclopedia.com/topic/George_Wythe.aspx>

177 "George Wythe: Early Modern Judge" by Wythe Holt, 1011, footnote 10. <http://www.law.ua.edu/pubs/lrarticles/Volume%2058/Issue%205/Holt.pdf> Site © and maintained by the University of Alabama, accessed 3/3/16.

178 To see the original at the Library of Congress' site <http://memory.loc.gov/cgi-bin/ampage?collId=bdsdcc&fileName=c1201//bdsdccc1201.db&recNum=1&itemLink=r?ammem/bdsbib:@field(NUMBER+@od1(bdsdcc+c1201))&linkText=0> accessed 3/2/16

179 "Monticello" a newsletter, Volume 20, Number 2, Winter 2009. <http://www.monticello.org/sites/default/files/inline-pdfs/2009wGeorgeWytheWntr09.pdf> accessed 3/2/16

180 <http://www.history.org/almanack/people/bios/biowythe.cfm> © 2015 The Colonial Williamsburg Foundation <http://www.historynet.com/the-mysterious-death-of-judge-george-wythe.htm> © HistoryNet, LLC; accessed 3/28/16.

Chapter Twelve

JEFFERSON

This concludes our 55 delegates who had influence in writing our Constitution. There has been a clamor to make as many as twelve of the 55 as deist. I simply cannot do that. Definitely we had 3 confirmed deists. It is possible three or four more could be added to the list. Yet when I tried to do that, I found evidence contradicting deist belief. This should not be surprising. It is the continuity of a man's life and its ending I am looking at. Certainly people develop different thoughts concerning belief in the Divine during their own lifetimes. It would not surprise me to find I may have missed a change. So you, the reader, should also be aware of this metamorphosis.[1]

We have other men who were not specific framers of the Constitution and were not delegates to the Convention who were either deist or had deist leanings. There was an overwhelming majority of Christians and Catholics in this country at that time (over 98% with a small minority of Jews and even smaller minority of deists). This makes it impossible to think those considered "We, the people," would have encouraged any that hated God to stifle public acts and expressive speech of a Christian nature. As stated before, there were many and varied sects of Christians in this country at that time. Because there were so many, our Federal government had to be neutral (colorblind) to the different religious factions.

One might ask, then why is it so hard to place the framers' religious belief system? The amount of time which has passed, the scanty records available for some, and sometimes just the sheer volume of records. Another problem I noticed was when historical statements are interpreted in light of today's understanding for religious belief. For example, reading a man like Benjamin Franklin, if you were a historian who leaned toward Christian beliefs, you might say Franklin just had to be a Christian. Yet he, himself, made it very clear he was a deist. In like fashion, those today who are atheist or deist try to claim Jefferson as their own. But in reviewing Jefferson's belief system you simply cannot place him in light of today's religious standards. Thomas Jefferson could technically fit within the category of a varied Christian sect of yesteryear. Yet he would not be considered a Christian today. There were those who did not consider him a Christian then either. Let me explain why.

Contrary to the deist dialog concerning Jefferson, he himself mentioned he would have been a member of a Unitarian church had one been present in his area (the state of Virginia). He also associated with Unitarians. It is well known Jefferson had problems with Jesus' deity as well as the doctrine of the Trinity. He disagreed with other tenets of the Christian faith. Because of this many assume he was a Unitarian.[2] If he were a member of the Unitarian Church, you could, by the standards of such in 1780 consider him a sect of Christianity. But the reality is he was neither a member of the Unitarian religion nor was he a declared deist. We have already reviewed the fact Unitarianism during the time period in question was viewed as Christian. That has changed. But this is one of the nuances we forget when we view the religious beliefs of the framing generation. Many claim him a deist, but that has its problems as well. He attended Episcopal church services while president and made comments which would classify him with no religion at all, except his own form of belief in the Scriptures he approved of.[3]

I will try to ignore the arrogance of the man in my assessment of him, but Jefferson really did not allow diversity of theological thought he disagreed with to engage his agenda. Many make mention of him writing his own bible. But this statement may not incorporate all of the factual history. In his earliest work, what he did was cut out what *he believed* was

Jesus' actual words and events, from two copies of the New Testament in English. This left behind what Jefferson felt was man-created (or the corrupting influence of ministers over the years) and not original to the Bible itself. What he removed from the original Bible many called Jefferson's bible. But Jefferson did not title the two works referred to in this category as a "bible." He called his first work "The Philosophy of Jesus of Nazareth, being Extracted from the Account of His Life and Doctrines as given by Matthew, Mark, Luke and John. Being an Abridgement of the New Testament for the Use of the Indians, Unembarassed with Matters of Fact or Faith beyond the Level of their Comprehensions." The first work seems to have been completed in 1804.[4]

The second work was titled "The Life and Morals of Jesus of Nazareth." The second work was started in 1819 and seems to have been completed in 1820. Using the same process as he did for the first, it is taken from two Greek/Latin New Testaments, along with two French New Testaments and two English New Testaments. Among lay people, there seems to be some confusion as to which work historians refer to as the "Jefferson bible" simply because the first work does contain the recounting of some miracles, while the second work does not. Both these works were well known during Jefferson's lifetime. Both were works he is said to have read from privately.[5] Almost all historians refer to the second work as the Jefferson bible.

Christians today should know Jefferson did not believe in the doctrine of salvation, justification by faith or eternity in hell for the lost. Deists and atheists should know he did not believe in miracles or the miraculous intervention of God through prayer, but did believe in a benevolent God who intervened in the universe.[6] Obviously this makes him neither Christian, deist or atheist. Since he was not a declared member of the Unitarian religion, he was not a Unitarian either! It was during the presidential election of 1800 his unconventional "Christianism" was highlighted in such a way (as all elections do) to garner votes by the other side; calling him, among other things, an arch-infidel.[7]

His university was non-sectarian and open to all. He allowed religion to be taught within the department of philosophy and ethics. With all the various sects of Christianity teaching the specific doctrine necessary to train their own ministers from other universities, to bring in a minister from a specific denomination would do the same thing. So religion would have to be taught outside of a denominational setting. Yet he disagreed religious services could be held at the school because it was a public building paid by the state. It seems under pressure he agreed religious services could have free access to the building as long as it was impartial and open to all public speakers.[8] This, in conjunction with the fact he was a strong supporter of the separation of church and state, has caused many to believe he was anti-Christian. While relating to Jesus Christ, this simply is not true. He was fascinated by the person of Jesus Christ. Unfortunately for Jefferson, he could not wrap his mind around the totality of who Jesus is. Thinking binary in systems with spiritual enigma was not something Jefferson would tolerate.

Putting aside my argument of whether it was sheer hubris to believe he could edit the New Testament better than the ancients who wrote it— Many historians do not believe that was his intention; I am not so sure— he was very much like our other framers in believing that government would corrupt the church. Many believed the church needed protection from government, not the other way around. Those delegates living in Virginia were well acquainted with ministers who were paid by the state. Most were ineffective and cared little for their flocks. Ministers who were paid by the congregations were cut from a far superior cloth. Jefferson believed, like Madison, Washington and most others, the corrupting influence was the government on the church. They also believed in a federal government which was colorblind when it came to the various sects (all Christian) within the country.

Unlike Washington and Madison, Jefferson seemed to become more hardened against Christianity as he aged, but more fascinated with Jesus and his teaching. Dichotomy surrounding Jefferson doesn't stop there. Jefferson attended church quite regularly. Because of this, Christians use it to say he must have been a Christian and non-Christians use it to say that he, like others attended for social and/or political reasons. Neither pursuit takes in to account an individual founders' particular belief system, and in the case of Jefferson, that was quite different indeed.[9]

As a youth and young man, there is strong evidence he was quite traditional in his belief system. He even became a vestryman. But it was his professor in college, William Small, who started Jefferson on his lifetime trek with unconventional belief.[10] It seems this unconventional trek is what formed much of his political as well as social endeavors. As with his religious views, his political views concerning religion are varied as well. We know he firmly believed in a separation between religion and government and he rejected the presidential precedents of Washington and Adams in issuing proclamations for prayer and thanksgiving. Yet he openly prayed for divine assistance in both of his inaugural addresses.[11] In this one act he proves his belief that the government made a distinction between what responsibilities people had to their God, even in a public governmental venue and the intrusion of government into a person's private and public display of religion. He signed and confirmed a proclamation that Virginia's delegates wrote when he was governor of the state.[12] Jefferson worked on a committee of three for a seal of the United States. His version had the words: "Rebellion to Tyrants is Obedience to God" printed along with various images, one was a picture of Moses leading the Israelites from the Red Sea.[13]

In other words, there was, in Jefferson's mind, a strict separation between church and state. But there was no separation between a person's personal covenantal responsibilities to their God and their public or private life. He believed the state had no right to interfere with a person's public or private religious adherence. He also believed the state had no right to interfere with religions' institutional inner workings, even in its public outreach. He also believed that states had the right to invoke and encourage religious belief, but the Federal government was to be kept separate from denominationalism and legislating in religious matters. This was the classic historical view of the framers.

Let me prove all of this. "I consider the government of the United States as interdicted by the Constitution from intermeddling in religious institutions, their doctrines, discipline, or exercises. This results not only from the provision that no law shall be made respecting the establishment or free exercise of religion, but from that also which reserves to the states the powers not delegated to the United States. Certainly no power to prescribe any religious exercise or to assume authority in any religious discipline had been delegated to the general government. It must then rest with the states, as far as it can be in any human authority."[14]

I believe it is in that train of thought he wrote to the Danbury Baptist Association that the Bill of Rights protected them and their religious freedom from federal involvement. Yet in today's muddied translation of Jefferson's note, we have the excuse to restrict any public display of religious belief and the right by the federal system to make the public pay for services which clearly violate a majority of people's religious beliefs. Jefferson:

> "But our rulers can have no authority over such natural rights, only as we have submitted to them. The rights of conscience we never submitted, we could not submit. We are answerable for them to God. The legitimate powers of government extend to such acts only as are injurious to others. But it does me no injury for my neighbor to say there are twenty gods, or no god. It neither picks my pocket nor breaks my leg."[15]

This was the standard before the arbitrary choice of "a wall of separation" definition.[16] If we followed Jefferson's advice, my "pocket" would not be picked by the more recent regulations and the more recent decisions to place people not entitled to federal largesse on tax exemptions that the founders never envisioned when the Constitution or Bill of Rights were written.

What a slippery slope judges and bureaucrats have us careening down. There was a majority who believed in a separation between church and state, but not as strict as Jefferson's position was. There was an overwhelming majority thought which did include Jefferson. This group, which included Jefferson, believed the people had a clear and inalienable right to worship their God publicly and privately and that covenantal responsibility was one the government could not nor should ever interfere with. That inalienable right extended to their interaction publicly and privately— and it was as it crossed the public line in a governmental event— that government could not interfere.

Some make Jefferson's strict separation stance as an argument for perfection. Yet Jefferson wrote clear errors in his historical narratives as well as theological errors in his belief systems.[17] Even with all his dichotomies, he still believed in keeping government out of rights of conscience. In the same note concerning his state of Virginia, he writes about the religious tolerance of other states. While doing so, he makes statements which show a clear understanding of covenant between people; people and their God, and the acknowledgement of government to support that covenant. In other words, the covenant between government and the people was understood.

In his own words: "Religion is well supported; of various kinds, indeed, but all good enough; all sufficient to preserve peace and order: or if a sect arises, whose tenets would subvert morals, good sense has fair play, and reasons and laughs it out of doors, without suffering the State to be troubled with it. They do not hang more malefactors than we do. . . . But is the spirit of the people an infallible, a permanent reliance? Is it government? Is this the kind of protection we receive in return for the rights we give up? Besides, the spirit of the times may alter, will alter. Our rulers will become corrupt, our people careless. A single zealot may commence persecutor, and better men be his victims. It can never be too often repeated, that the time for fixing every essential right on a legal basis is while our rulers are honest, and ourselves united."[18]

Jefferson's own words clearly show the understanding of covenant (Is this the kind . . .we receive in return for. . . ?) between the people. His own words within the Declaration of Independence show his own understanding that a people can never give up the rights which are given by nature's God. This effectually affirms government's covenant to the people in maintaining and affirming their covenant to their God. It seems the whole country agreed with that understanding. That understanding **is covenant** and it stands adamant against the interpretation of today's persecutors— as well as some academics— in removing all symbols and statements of the settlers' God, their offspring and those of us who have settled here to be free from religious persecution or systems which prosecute their ability to live freely.

While Jefferson's unconventional "Christianism"[19] was one opinion among many religious opinions in this country, there is much evidence supporting the reality the founders and framers viewed covenant from its biblical roots. I could find none who did not. I am not saying they did not exist, just that I could not find *any*. Our problem today is we view their religious opinions in the light of what our religious opinions are now. We need to study biblical foundational beliefs and then track the various sects from that foundation. One might argue this is erroneous because the Bible should not be laid as the foundation. In my opinion, not doing so is erroneous. The population at that time traced all of its belief systems from the roots of the Bible, including the right not to believe. If I was looking at some of today's Muslim nations, I would go back to the Koran and trace their various sects from their understanding of that book. In fact, doing so, would give us a much clearer understanding of the violence we see globally concerning Islam.

This back-and-forth we see concerning the framers/founders who were not Christian (I include Jefferson in this group), does not take in to account the evidence we have concerning their understanding of covenant and government (a social compact). It also refuses to honor the opinion of almost everyone at that time of the divine intervention in the fight this nation undertook for its freedom. It also ignores evidence like the monuments, books and firsthand accounts left by them and subsequent generations concerning their faith in that same God; whether conventional or unconventional in its approach.[20] It is a small grouping of this evidence we will be looking at next. Including all of it, would make its own book.

ENDNOTES

1   Scholars have been doing this work for centuries. In my search, I usually stayed with the earlier historians for a reason. I discovered some of the most recent ones had a motive, while the earlier ones just desired to find the truth. I also found the more recent ones were not understanding patterns of belief from a biblical standpoint— the same standpoint

these generation of founder/framers were from. In future editions, I will update any changes I find concerning what has been written.

2   <www.adherents.com/people/pj/Thomas_Jefferson.html> accessed 3/1/15

3   <https://www.monticello.org/site/research-and-collections/jeffersons-religious-beliefs> accessed 3/1/15

4   <https://www.monticello.org/site/research-and-collections/philosophy-jesus-nazareth> You can click on the footnote sections and review some of the documentation online accessed 3/1/15.

5   Ibid.

6   <http://www.encyclopediavirginia.org/Jefferson_Thomas_and_Religion> Click on links; accessed 3/9/16.

7   Ibid.

8   Ibid.

9   <https://www.monticello.org/site/research-and-collections/jeffersons-religious-beliefs> accessed 3/1/15

10   <http://www.encyclopediavirginia.org/Jefferson_Thomas_and_Religion> accessed 3/8/16

11   Ibid.

12   <https://www.monticello.org/site/research-and-collections/day-thanksgiving-and-prayer> accessed 3/10/16

13   <https://www.monticello.org/site/research-and-collections/seal-united-states> accessed 4/2/16

14   Jefferson letter to Samuel Miller, Jan. 23, 1808. In "The Writings of Thomas Jefferson." Edited by Andrew A. Lipscomb and Albert Ellory Bergh. Volume XI. 428 (428-430) (Washington, D.C. 1905: The Thomas Jefferson Memorial Association)

15   Thomas Jefferson, "Query XVII, Notes on the State of Virginia" In "The Works of Thomas Jefferson" Edited by H.A. Washington. Volume 8; 400. (New York: Townsend Mac Coun. 1884)

16   http://www.encyclopediavirginia.org Letter_from_Thomas_Jefferson_to_the_ Danbury_Baptist_Association_January_1_1802> accessed 3/8/16

17   Thomas Jefferson, "Query XVII, Notes on the State of Virginia" In "The Works of Thomas Jefferson" Edited by H.A. Washington. Volume 8; 399-401. (New York: Townsend Mac Coun. 1884)

18   Ibid. 402

19   <http://www.encyclopediavirginia.org/Jefferson_Thomas_and_Religion> accessed 3/5/16

20   You can view the governmental correspondence as well as many of Washington's and Jefferson's papers— along with others from the framing generation at <http://founders. archives.gov>

Chapter Thirteen

DOCUMENTATION SUPPORTING COMMON COVENANT UNDERSTANDING

We have the evidence of the Virginia Convention, dated June 27, 1788. When they ratified the Constitution they did so with a report from the Committee George Wythe was on. Writing for the Committee he states, (and) in part: ". . .That there be a Declaration or Bill of Rights asserting and securing from encroachment the essential and unalienable rights of the people in some such manner as the following: . . . .That there are certain natural rights of which men when they form a *social compact* cannot deprive or divest their posterity. . ."[1] (Italicized by me to highlight the covenant concept.)

The two most learned lawyers among the delegates would be Wilson and Wythe. Here Wythe writes the word *compact* in linking what has gone before with what Virginia expects to come afterwards: Bills of Rights. We have already looked at some of Wilson's lectures to see his thoughts on the Federal social compact and how he viewed the people as sovereign within it. You can see the understanding in the use of the word "posterity" that no future government, no matter how often they *think* they are giving us "more" rights can actually do so, because inalienable rights are not given by governments. In other words, these rights are not given by man, but by the Creator Himself. All any future government can do is enunciate the rights better. This attempt has been done by the amendment process. Of course, I stress here no one has the *right* to harm other citizens (excluding physical self-defense).

To see the understanding the framing generation had of covenant we need to look no further than that famous speech, known to all and recited almost every Fourth of July: "Give Me Liberty Or Give Me Death." My recounting here is not meant to be thorough. I only mean to look at the idea of covenant held by the people. The colonists had put up with Parliament's shenanigans over taxation for well over 10 years. Since they had a covenant (charter) with the King, it was to the King they petitioned. This they did to no avail. The basis of the legal argument was since the king had a covenant with the God of Heaven and the colonies had a covenant with both the King and the God of Heaven, then Parliament had no right to tax the King's subjects without proper representation in Parliament. Without question, there were other legal arguments: Economic and political in nature which had nothing to do with the religious one I lay out here. It would take a small book to enunciate them all, along with the history. Within one generation in this nation we have almost lost the understanding for the non-sectarian/secular legal argument for covenant. I realize many might be disappointed I do not go into the secular arguments. I understand that. There are literally thousands of works out there reviewing all secular aspects of the founding of our nation.

There were many events leading up to the assault in Boston, but Virginia had a much closer relationship with the Crown than the other colonies. In fact, many of the colonies looked to Virginia to lead the way when it came to Parliament's over-reach.[2] One of the reasons the royal colonial governor of Virginia gave to disband the people's representation— the House of Burgesses— was the civil unrest. But the Crown's reasons were far deeper. For the House to meet, would have meant arrest. They met anyway— and out of his reach in a remote location— what is now known as St. John's Church, but was then known as Henrico Parish Church.[3]

In attendance over seven days were the various representatives from Virginia, up to 120 in all, including Washington, Jefferson and Patrick

Henry himself. They opened with prayer. Once they were done with prior business, they took motions for new business. On March 23, 1775, Patrick Henry proffered a motion to gather and secure a militia. Many were against it, saying the Crown was in the process of reviewing their petitions and more time was needed. As well, others felt secure Virginia was not Massachusetts and their relationship with England and the Crown was more peaceable and covenantal. This, in no small part due to Virginia's far more lengthy association with the Church of England as opposed to Massachusetts' more tumultuous past. Within the first paragraph, Patrick Henry references the covenantal responsibility the colonists have to both the Crown and God.

Henry: "For my own part, I consider it as nothing less than a question of freedom or slavery; and in proportion to the magnitude of the subject ought to be the freedom of the debate. It is only in this way that we can hope to arrive at truth, and *fulfill the responsibility which we hold to God and our country*. Should I keep back my opinions at such a time, through fear of giving offense, I should consider myself as guilty of treason towards my country, and of an *act of disloyalty toward the Majesty of Heaven*, which I revere above all earthly kings."[4] (Italicized to show concept.) Henry makes the point that past experience should tell them all what is coming next. He does this through several arguments, but makes one that is revealing: For if you had no covenant, no agreement of brotherly respect and love in Christian grace, why would you expect to have hope of reconciliation? There would and should be no expectation of brotherly love.

He says in part: "And judging by the past, I wish to know what there has been in the conduct of the British ministry for the last ten years to justify those hopes with which the gentlemen have been pleased to solace themselves and the House. Is it that insidious smile with which our petition has been lately received? Trust it not, sir; it will prove a snare to your feet. Suffer not yourselves to be betrayed with a kiss." (*Remember that Jesus was betrayed with a kiss.*) "Ask yourselves how this gracious reception of our petitions comports with those warlike preparations which cover our waters and darken our land. Are fleets and armies necessary to a work of love and reconciliation? Have we shown ourselves so unwilling to be reconciled that force must be called in to win back our love? Let us not deceive ourselves, sir. These are the implements of war and subjugation; the last arguments to which kings resort. I ask gentlemen, sir, what means this martial array, if its purpose be not to force us to submission? Can gentlemen assign any other possible motive for it? Has Great Britain any enemy, in this quarter of the world, to call for all this accumulation of navies and armies? No, sir, she has none. They are meant for us: they can be meant for no other. They are sent over to bind and rivet upon us those chains which the British ministry have been so long forging."[5]

What is in italics is mine, by way of explanation. He then goes on making more points in his argument and closes that part of it with these words: ". . .we must fight! I repeat it, sir, we must fight! An appeal to arms and to the God of hosts is all that is left us!"[6] When one side of a covenant is unwilling to work with the other side, the only appeal, other than arms is to the God who holds the covenant together.

In the next paragraph he addresses another argument the colonists are too weak to engage in a battle with England. To that he says, in part: "Sir, we are not weak if we make a proper use of those means which the God of nature hath placed in our power. The millions of people, armed in the holy cause of liberty, and in such a country as that which we possess, are invincible by any force our enemy can send against us. Besides, sir, we shall not fight our battles alone. There is a just God who presides over the destinies of nations, and who will raise up friends to fight our battles for us."[7]

Among several of his closing arguments, he makes this last one: "Is life so dear, or peace so sweet, as to be purchased at the price of chains and slavery? Forbid it, Almighty God! I know not what course others may take; but as for me, give me liberty or give me death!"[8] This is not just a statement, "forbid it, God." This is a plea to the Almighty God they opened the meeting in prayer to. This is a plea to the Almighty God he speaks about as raising up friends to help in the fight and who presides over the destiny of nations. And lastly, this is a plea to the Almighty God they covenanted with in chartering the colonies with the King of England, and whom they all understood they were still in covenant with. If not, then why would they expect Him (God) to help in the fight?

This kind of legal argument infused the minds of Blackstone, Locke and many others. It was the reason why the fight for the cause of liberty was a "holy" one. It was God who gave humans liberty or the right to choose. This is biblical and specifically New Testament entrenched in its thought. Another wholly biblical legal worldview was the fact this particular God oversaw the destiny of nations. This was foundational in being able to declare an independent nation to begin with: The Almighty God who the colonists covenanted with gave them inalienable rights— rights, not chains— not allegiance to be taxed without proper representation. Rights to life without interference of their religious beliefs. Rights which meant their money was not to be confiscated for things which were wholly against those beliefs. Rights to speak your mind without fear of reprisal because of those beliefs. The right to know the God you covenanted with was in charge of giving nations to people groups to begin with.

This argument was concerning the colonies' relationship with the then crown of England. I place it here so you can see the covenant understanding within the conception ground of our federal republic. They had their individual colonial documentation of covenant government with the people extant while their individual charters (reflecting covenant) were in force. It only stands to reason as they maintained a covenant with the crown within a charter, they would continue a foederal (covenant) government and maintain that documentation while their individual state documentation of covenant government functioned.

Proving this, probably more in principle than in using exact words— though we do have exact wording to review— we have the understanding of agreeing to the Constitution in the first place. The idea that in a covenant compacting other documents, one gives up something in order to get something is evident. George Washington seemed to sum it up in his letter to the President of Congress, transmitting the Constitution, after the Convention had ended (dated 9/17/1787).

Remember as you read his words, that federal *means* covenant: "It is obviously impracticable in the federal government of these states, to secure all rights of independent sovereignty to each, and yet provide for the interest and safety of all: Individuals entering into society, must give up a share of liberty to preserve the rest. The magnitude of the sacrifice must depend as well on situation and circumstance, as on the object to be obtained. It is at all times difficult to draw with precision the line between those rights which must be surrendered, and those which may be reserved; . . . . That it *(the Constitution)* will meet the full and entire approbation of every state is not perhaps to be expected; but each will doubtless consider, that had her interest been alone consulted, the consequences might have been particularly disagreeable or injurious to others; . . . that it may promote the lasting welfare of that country so dear to us all, and secure her freedom and happiness, is our most ardent wish."[9] Italics are mine for clarity.

We see here the understanding of the States as a party with rights which are not bound by the Federal government. We will review how the Federal government has broken its covenant in later chapters. When we do, we will see how the states have lost their rights. In this letter, not only does Washington make the covenantal understanding of the Constitution clear when he speaks of giving up something in order to secure something, but he also compacts the idea of happiness, which is found in the Declaration, and not within the pages of the Constitution as written, or the Bill of Rights. That all should have the ability to read and agree or disagree to this new addition to the compact is seen in the subsequent intent with which the conveyance of the document was made. You might counter with some of the amendments made to the Constitution since it was written. I am not talking about the changes we made. Many of those changes are proof of broken covenant. I speak only about the understanding of the founding-framing generation. If you will remember, I am not writing this book for my sake or desire, but because I feel compelled by God. I also feel a duty to the nation I, and eight previous generations of my kin, was born within to write.

We are still a majority (70 percent plus) Christian nation with a minority Jewish population. It is still my prayer the seventy-year time period appointed can be ameliorated. Let me explain why, according to the Scriptures, we can still, today, experience our own self-inflicted wound. Atheists would say they have tried to use laws and create situations removing our Christian beliefs and preventing Christian thought from the public square; in that they have been successful. So successful many claim we are no longer Christian. All throughout the Bible we have a first-fruits principle we should understand when dealing with the God of the Bible. It goes something like this, "Whatever was done at the first, will follow through to the last or the whole." In fact, there is a sacred Jewish holiday called First-fruits. You wave a portion of the first harvest of a crop before the Lord, in effect saying, "How bountiful this beginning is, will be the whole crop, because we dedicate it to you, Oh, Lord." That specific God never sleeps nor slumbers and He does not forget such vows. He always stands at the ready to perform His word.[10]

This is what the colonists were trusting in when they fought for the Declaration of Independence in the Revolution and when they constituted themselves through a Constitution. They trusted the God they individually covenanted with would bless them and generations after them. This holiday and principle was meant to be a blessing. Unfortunately, when we decide we know better than God and institute laws, making conditions which defy nature, nature's God and which persecute or frighten God's people— even jailing them— the principle becomes a snare and judgment. Let me be clear again and state God is not doing this to us. God loves His creation. This is why certain laws exist, so life is sustained. If you decide to walk off a tall building and get hurt, you can't blame the laws of gravity for working (the laws of nature and nature's God).

Getting back to specifics within the documentation, we have a "Resolution of the Federal Convention Submitting the Constitution to Congress" (9/17/1787). We have a "Resolution of Congress of September 28, 1787, Submitting the Constitution To the Several States." Finally, we have a "Circular Letter of the Secretary of Congress, Dated September 28, 1787, Transmitting Copy of the Constitution to the Several Governors."[11] You might say, "Oh, this is just perfunctory stuff, necessary in day-to-day business." Well, it would be, but the business we are talking about is an addition to the agreement the people and the states had, even adding a whole new part of the compact. If it were not so, it would not have been necessary for Washington to send his letter or for the assembled Congress of the people, at that time, to send the transmittals they did.

You also have the response of the individual states for ratification. Again, I relate these as proving an understanding of that generation for covenant or compacting documents. I am not saying there is no line concerning a separation of church and state. Once the first nine states ratified, the Constitution was binding upon all. We will review all thirteen, but look at the nine, first. In writing their ratification documents it is quite telling as to what the specific fears were for each state. Divine covenant with each other extended to many liberties, including secular ones, not just specifically religious. I won't be reviewing all of those rights. Although an in-depth review would open today's American citizen's viewpoint as to why we are in the mess we are in. We have already looked at Virginia's, where Wythe uses the exact wording explaining this understanding of social covenant which compacts, even though Virginia was not among the first nine. I would expect the wording to be so exact in its case, since Wythe wrote for the Committee, and before that time, men like Washington and Jefferson had been members of the House of Burgesses. We must also be careful to understand "social" did not mean socialism or all its other various terms used to describe basically a society which is controlled by government who gives the people their rights. (Terms like progressive, communist, fascist and others would fit the bill.)

Remembering that we are looking at the first nine because once they ratified, the document became binding: Within the first nine states, all of them, with the exception of Maryland mention either the Divine, the fact that social compacting was being done, or religious freedoms specifically, or what they are doing in ratifying is being done in "the year of our Lord." [They use Anno Domini (AD), which means the same thing]. Two of the first nine mention the Divine and social compacting. Three of the first nine mention religious rights. Seven of the first nine use AD. With the last four states, one (Virginia) mentions the Divine. Three of the last four mention social compacting and employ the use of AD in their dating. All four mention religious rights.

In the case of Massachusetts and New Hampshire, they express not only a compact with the Declaration of Independence and the Constitution but a continued covenant with the "Supreme Ruler of the Universe." Let me explain why I make such statements. Before I do, let's look at the specific language used by these two states. They both enunciate the need for religious freedom of speech and expression in worship, among other rights. Massachusetts notes it was being done in AD 1788. They both use pretty much the same phrasing in this part of their ratifying document, all you have to do is transfer the different state's name. They differ at the end of their documentation. Additionally, I italicized words to highlight my point. Massachusetts and New Hampshire:

"The Convention have impartially discussed, & fully considered the Constitution for the United States of America, reported to Congress by the Convention of Delegates from the United States of America, & submitted to us by a resolution of the General Court of the said Commonwealth, passed the twenty fifth day of October last past, *& acknowledging with grateful hearts, the goodness of the Supreme Ruler of the Universe in affording the People of the United States in the course of his providence an opportunity deliberately & peaceably without fraud or surprise of entering into an explicit & solemn Compact with each other* by assenting to & ratifying a New Constitution in order to form a more perfect Union, establish Justice, insure Domestic tranquillity, provide for the common defense, promote the general welfare & secure the blessings of Liberty to themselves & their posterity; Do in the name & in behalf of the People of the Commonwealth of Massachusetts assent to & ratify the said Constitution for the United States of America."[12]

As stated before, New Hampshire's reads almost word for word with some exceptions in a word and with punctuation and capitalization. As we see with Patrick Henry's "Give Me Liberty or Give Me Death" speech, there was an intrinsic understanding of covenanting with/or in a people and a higher power, as well as covenant among the states, the states and the people and both with the federal government. In the colonies' cases every charter mentions covenant with the King of England and the people to whom he was giving the land mass to and a very real divine right or covenant the king had with God. This was well understood that the king was divinely appointed to give land (or so he thought). We have reviewed this concept when we looked at the charters. Patrick Henry makes mention of it, but he goes a step further. Because Henry is 100 plus years outside of the charter era, a new thought or concept has emerged, and it is very American. We have been looking at it throughout this book. That thought is *the people* have a Sovereign Right to covenant with the Creator and whomever they wish, especially when a previous arrangement (the charters) was broken. This understanding lived in the hearts and the minds of the framing generation. Massachusetts and New Hampshire (roughly four and a half months apart) enunciate it in their ratifying documents.

This is why the phrase "Supreme Ruler of the Universe" is used. Instead of being chartered and given the land by an earthly king, it is being chartered and given by the Supreme Ruler. This Ruler is not just of a country or one world, but of the Universe. It is He who is giving it to the people of the whole country (specifically to the states mentioned). It is He who rules and governs. The states make it clear this is done by them in order to compact what has come before (the Declaration of Independence) with what they are ratifying now (the Constitution) amongst themselves, the states and the states' documentation. As we have reviewed, a compact is more than just a contract. A compact puts together multiple agreements possibly in multiple locations, even various people groups.

What had gone before at the Federal level among the states had been the Declaration of Independence. This idea of a Creator granting the rights because He created the land and the people, is inherent in our system of government. When that is lost, we are lost. Substituting an alien system like socialism (progressivism, communism, fascism or Sharia Law) will not and simply cannot work. I will explain more clearly why in subsequent chapters. But for now, there was always the understanding that subsequent generations would amend the Constitution to include what this framing generation could not. That generation understood as the majority of its people, and I might add what subsequent generations have understood, that when we accept God by faith and see the God of the Bible within its pages through faith, we gain, as part of our covenant with Him, an insight and open a door to a spiritual realm which quickens our mortal minds into a dimension of immortality. That ethereal yet literal *quickening* brings with it a wisdom in amending and governing ourselves the framing generation understood was necessary to a sovereign people's governance.

Coupled with that is the definition of the word *Providence* used so often by them. Inherent in the word is an understanding of covenant. That God took care and had special insight into the careful consideration of those He was *providing* for. Why would you use that word if there was not some expectation of an agreement He was called upon to care for those who asked Him? Some say, "Oh, they believed it was nature they were asking." Not in this country. Some may have used it to describe a higher being, which is the definition of *God*, but not necessarily the God of the Bible. The majority of those would be deists. The overwhelming use was for a biblical understanding.

In reference to Massachusetts and New Hampshire's documents, there are some who would say, "Oh, they're just thanking God." Not so. Remember the king granted them the land God previously granted the king. This is a basic covenant understanding. God grants land and makes agreements or covenants when He does the 'granting.' (See Genesis 17:7,8; along with New Testament teachings that the promises of God in the Old Testament are ours also in Christ Jesus; 2 Corinthians 1:19 & 20.) You can easily read sermon after sermon during that time period of preachers telling their congregations that God granted them the land. (As well as politicians who use the phrase "providence.") If the people were not in a covenant with the God that grants land, then why are they thanking Him for doing so and likewise thanking Him for allowing them or "affording" them an "opportunity" to covenant with one another? If they aren't in covenant with Him, then why bother? It is plain they believe He holds the other end of the covenant together. Of course, this makes no impact upon the non-sectarian/secular covenant: It only strengthens it.

I have already proved this concept of the Divine in statements made by Washington and others concerning how God fought on their behalf. We will look at others who made such statements. This concept among the religious is foundational in our understanding of covenant. It is one of the by-products of biblical covenant. It's not that we do nothing or work minimally. To the contrary, often the work is quite hard and more frequently, even dangerous. But there is this intent understanding within our inner being something supernatural was helping in the work. Both Massachusetts and New Hampshire enunciate it while thanking the

"Supreme Ruler" for his providence in giving them the opportunity. There are so many other concepts inherent in the minds of this generation listed in these ratifying documents, but I only mention this one.

Later on in these ratifying documents, they, as well as South Carolina mention other rights the individual states feel need to be enunciated. Again, both Massachusetts and New Hampshire mention religious rights of freedom. Three of the "non-binding" states, Virginia, North Carolina and Rhode Island mention both the demand for religious rights of freedom, among other rights, and the understanding of the documents representing social compacting agreements.[13] They use those exact words; while New York is concerned with all rights, including religious ones. This understanding of compacting covenants was not alien to that generation as it is to ours today. Even someone with an odd "Christianism" like Jefferson understood not only the need for such a concept, but made it a very plain legal case for independence when he wrote the Declaration, in addition to the "rights" which had been broken (the grievances listed in that document).

It was also mentioned within Virginia's ratifying document. In fact, within the first paragraph Virginia lays out the simple fact the people are Sovereign, and they can and will resume that sovereignty and those rights when or if the agreement becomes "perverted." (A precursor understanding for the Tenth Amendment.) Let me quote it exactly:

> "Delegates of the People of Virginia duly elected in pursuance of a recommendation from the General Assembly and now met in Convention having fully and freely investigated and discussed the proceedings of the Federal Convention and being prepared as well as the most mature deliberation hath enabled us to decide thereon Do in the name and in behalf of the People of Virginia declare and make known that the powers granted under the Constitution being derived from the People of the United States may be resumed by them whensoever the same shall be perverted to their injury or oppression and that every power not granted thereby remains with them and at their will: that

therefore no right of any denomination can be cancelled abridged restrained or modified by the Congress by the Senate or House of Representatives acting in any Capacity by the President or any Department or Officer of the United States except in those instances in which power is given by the Constitution for those purposes: & that among other essential rights the liberty of the Conscience and of the Press cannot be cancelled abridged restrained or modified by any authority of the United States. *With these impressions with a solemn appeal to the Searcher of hearts for the purity of our intentions and under the conviction that whatsoever imperfections may exist in the Constitution ought rather to be examined in the mode prescribed therein than to bring the Union into danger by a delay with a hope of obtaining Amendments previous to the Ratification,* We the said Delegates in the name and in behalf of the People of Virginia do by these presents assent to and ratify the Constitution recommended on the seventeenth day of September one thousand seven hundred and eighty seven by the Federal Convention for the Government of the United States hereby announcing to all those whom it may concern that the said Constitution is binding upon the said People according to an authentic Copy hereto annexed in the Words following; . ."[14]

I italicized words to highlight the passage we will be reviewing. As she had been with England, Virginia's tone is more forceful in legal argument but as appealing to its relationship with the new government than the other two states. Very much like a carrot-and-stick approach. It does not connect their impressions (the revocation of the aforementioned rights) with an appeal to the covenanted "Supreme Ruler of the Universe" as Massachusetts and New Hampshire does. Instead, they make a solemn appeal to the "Searcher of hearts" to enter therein to search out whether or not their intentions for entering into this agreement is in good faith or not. This is another by-product of covenant. They do this by acknowledging the Constitution is imperfect and they will work those imperfections or future amendments out within the confines of the methods described within the document itself instead of bringing "the Union into danger" by some other method, most notably delaying ratification. There would be no need to ask the Divine to search ones' heart if there were no understanding of Him involved within the compact or covenant to begin with. It is within the "Videlicet" Virginia continues with enunciating social compact and religious as well as other rights. Telling as well, is the demand no denomination be adversely affected or have its rights put in jeopardy by the Federal government and its representatives. These "denominations" were church denominations.

This may sound odd to some, but probably why Massachusetts was where the first shot was made in Revolution was as much an attitude of a religious nature as any other, if not in a subconscious reality. I realize this may be my opinion only and economics played a huge role as well, but let me explain my position. We have already seen how Massachusetts' governmental practice of covenant and religious freedom already muddied the waters with England early on, enough to revoke its charter (technically twice). Because Virginia kept its nature as a royal colony, it kept its relationship with the Church of England (Anglican Church) and its vestries vibrant. Although, by the time of the Revolution there was a majority of dissenters from the Church of England (Presbyterians, Episcopalians, Quakers, etc., as well as some deists). Totally lost to history has been the argument that Virginia and its church, its hierarchy and the people aligned to it, had been fighting the revolution for some 150 years prior to 1776: "The vestries had been fighting the battles of the Revolution for a hundred and fifty years. Taxation and representation were only other words for support and election of ministers."[15]

This quoted attitude is directly related to the nature and understanding of covenant. As the children of Puritans, Massachusetts' patience with England was limited. Covenant— which was ingrained in their psyche— had, in their minds, already been broken. We have already reviewed the Puritan attitude when a covenant was seen as broken. Virginia came to that realization more slowly, and over a much longer period of time. The vestries were the representatives between the people, the Church (the Divine) and the Crown, thus the expression of the House of Burgesses. Because Anglicanism (their churches) was important to them in that sense, they had a resemblance of representation; they felt they could work it out. By the time Patrick Henry made his speech, the majority of land owners and freeman realized the facade of representation was just that: All smoke, no mirrors, with great big guns pointed their way. All Henry did was verbalize what many already knew in their hearts. I can hear many shouting far more in economic and social entanglements were involved. I would agree, but my focus here is the religious and covenant. Books have been written concerning the other issues circling revolution and many are excellent reading material. Even a short Internet search will reveal the many arguments made for and against revolution as well as the volumes of literature which exists concerning what went on at the Federal level and within the states concerning ratification.[16]

I have seen an argument by many which tries to make an attempt to say religion or covenant or how the national government treats people must be seen differently pre-Constitution than it is today. Before the Constitution was ratified and even while the Articles of Confederation were still active, the government was viewed as a federal (*foedus-covenant*) government. We see a dialog within the Virginian ratification process which takes place on June 7, 1788. It is an argument to counter Patrick Henry, who was against ratification. Francis Corbin, one of the delegates to Virginia's Ratifying Convention has heard the arguments around calling the new government "federal" or consolidated and counters by saying it is "a representative federal republic."[17] Why is this statement important? It proves, not only arguments for and against ratification, but what had been desirous in the pre-Constitutional government would be desirous in the nature of the post-Constitutional government. In other words, the people needed to be in charge and in covenant. Corbin may not have been exuberant in his desire for the Constitution, but after reading his arguments, it seems obvious he agreed it was necessary. Not only is our Federal government, by definition of the word *federal*, a covenant, it is a representative republic! How's that for redundancy? It seems Madison acknowledged the legitimacy of the argument (see previous note).

I realize there was so much more going on in all the different states concerning ratification. I have already mentioned I felt economic reasons may have outweighed even the religious freedom arguments in many states. Yet there was such an outcry for religious freedom. It was mentioned specifically in the ratification documents in seven out of the thirteen states, that a Bill of Rights had to be added. Whatever other factors contributed to the name given the new government, the idea of it covenanting with the states and the people— people who covenanted with God— cannot be ignored as part of its history, tradition and **functionality**. This idea of terming the government the same term which had been used before the Constitution is also seen one hundred years later by historians:

> "In all these troubles the weakness of Congress, under the old articles of confederation, was seen and deeply felt— a want of power to act strongly and effectively. The confederation produced no security against foreign invasion, Congress not being permitted to prevent a war nor to support it by its own authority. The Federal Government could not check a quarrel between States nor a rebellion in any, not having the constitutional power nor the means to interpose; nor could it defend itself against the encroachments of the States, not even being paramount to the State constitutions."[18]

Let's review some of the individual statements made concerning God, the people and the founding of the nation. These support documented covenant understanding. This may sound redundant, but I am not proposing there is no line separating church and state. Nor am I using this documentation to support such an argument. Whatever the minutiae of each individual's belief system may have been, we see many quotes supportive of the biblical system of belief (at least in our country). For the first 75 years of our young Federal government, this understanding of the biblical system of belief understood covenant, in its basic form; that form being a people on an individual basis covenanting and worshipping their God. That basic form then views the belief that God specifically gives nations their boundaries and land. (See Genesis 9:1, 19, 26, 27; 10:1-11:9; 17:1-21; 21:14-18; 26:4; Psalm 2:7, 8; Isaiah 45:1-13; Isaiah 65:1.) That basic understanding assumes this Federal government will be in non-sectarian covenant with the people and states. That basic form then becomes the basis of many of these individual's reflections on the ability of our form of government prospering, thriving or even being able to continue or function. Functionality *speaks* to documentation. The biblical belief system is always looking towards or for the next generation, thus the need for documents. So you will see wording reflecting that as well.

I have mentioned this before, but it deserves repeating here. There is a difference between understanding covenant from a biblical point of view and believing that humans are born with inalienable rights, no matter what they believed. This was one of the divisions early on between the Puritan church groups within the colonies. If you will remember Rev. Thomas Hooker believed only believers could vote and hold office while Rev. John Cotton found that abhorrent. He believed all humans had rights given by the Creator. Their dissension was so great that Cotton founded another state! Biblical covenant belief certainly supports inalienable rights. Yet it is still a different tenet from experiencing covenant blessings. In other words, when a nation as a whole leaves its covenantal responsibilities, even though they have inalienable rights, there is a potential that covenant blessings can be diminished or disappear totally. I have included quotes here which reflect both aspects of this subconscious thought process.

One last reality is crucial. Atheists or socialists (progressives) have an inherent inability to see law from our nation's founding thesis. This is because the ideas of morality, self-worth, dignity and inalienable rights are tied to a Creator, not to the State. The artificial entity of *state* or *government* is only an obedient servant to the people's sacred trusts. Socialists (progressives) do not believe this and atheists will not always acknowledge it. With those kinds of understandings, can there even be a sacred trust to honor? Although, some atheists frame it within an understanding of "nature." In that case they are able to shift a sacred trust to "nature" instead of God and that can be our avenue to agree in non-sectarian covenant. I will show in later chapters atheism as well as socialism are religions. They may not worship in a specific building, but they do worship. Any covenant, non-sectarian, religious or otherwise, seen within the Federal system must protect the citizens from these two religions and their secular ideologies, as well. Judges who refuse to because they are either progressives or atheists must be recused from cases— this includes the Supreme Court; which is no longer impartial, but severely political and biased.

Whenever you see italics within the following quotes, they are mine to highlight that thought and covenant thought, unless I mention otherwise. I have done that in some cases because the individuals were not writing treatises in support of Christianity, but were making reflections while, in some cases addressing other issues or reasons for why the statements or writings were made.

We have already reviewed many of George Washington's statements and reflections. He said it very clearly: "...And let us with caution indulge the supposition that morality can be maintained without religion. Whatever may be conceded to the influence of refined education on minds of peculiar structure, reason and experience both forbid us to expect that national morality can prevail in exclusion of religious principle. It is substantially true that virtue or morality is a necessary spring of popular government. The rule, indeed, extends with more or less force to every species of free government. Who that is a sincere friend to it can look with indifference upon attempts to shake the foundation of the fabric?"[19]

John Adams made a similar observation when he wrote an October 11, 1798, letter to the officers of the First Brigade of the Third Division of the Militia of Massachusetts:

> "While our country remains untainted with the principles and manners which are now producing desolation in so many parts of the world; while she continues sincere, and incapable of insidious and impious policy, we shall have the strongest reason to rejoice in the local destination assigned us by Providence. But should the people of America once become capable of that deep simulation towards one another, and towards foreign nations, which assumes the language of justice and moderation while it is practicing iniquity and extravagance, and displays in the most captivating manner the charming pictures of candor, frankness, and sincerity, while it is rioting in rapine and insolence, this

country will be the most miserable habitation in the world; because *we have no government armed with power capable of contending with human passions unbridled by morality and religion.* Avarice, ambition, revenge, or gallantry, would break the strongest cords of our Constitution as a whale goes through a net. *Our Constitution was made only for a moral and religious people. It is wholly inadequate to the government of any other.*"[20]

John Adams was a Unitarian, but as I have already explained, they were considered some form of Christian. That has not been the case for over 140 years. I use the quote to show how Adams' communication to the regiment was viewed. There must have been common knowledge and agreement on the subject for the statement to have been made or there would have been no understanding of what Adams was saying.

There is another quote many use to show the government is not based on the Christian religion. Many attribute it to Adams, some even attribute it to Washington. Both are incorrect. It is found within the pages of the 1797 Treaty of Tripoli, Article XI. The Article states:

> "As the government of the United States of America is not in any sense founded on the Christian religion,— as it has in itself no character of enmity against the laws, religion or tranquility of Musselmen,— *(Muslims)* and as the said States never have entered into any war or act of hostility against any Mehomitan nation, it is declared by the parties that no pretext arising from religious opinions shall ever produce an interruption of the harmony existing between the two countries."[21]

There is an involved history concerning this treaty. I would suggest you look at the endnote for further reading on this subject. The history of war between the rest of the world and the Muslim pirate nations regarding sailing vessels had been going on for hundreds of years. At some point many countries paid to have their vessels pass through the areas unharmed. Prior to the Revolutionary War, American ships were included under the English agreements and were allowed to sail unmolested as well. But after the Revolution, America was now on her own. Since France, England and Spain all had connections with the heads of their government and the church in Rome or, as in the case of the King of England, he was the head of the Church of England, these Muslim pirate nations (and there were various different sects of them) assumed all the countries had the same setup. They assumed heads of state and the church were one and/or connected. Even within their own ranks, their imams controlled many governmental-type functions, or what we might consider as some type of legal and governmental influence. Sharia law had been an integral part of Muslim nations since the tenth century and imams were involved since at least 872 AD.[22]

As our Federal government had never been set up with the church in charge of any governmental cabinet or other function as a head of state, we operated differently from Spain, France and England. Ours was a government of "We, the People." It was a government not seen on the planet before. It was a covenanted, united government which covenanted with independent states made up of independent people, whose individual covenant with the God they worshiped *was* cherished, honored and respected. It "just so happened" the God they worshiped, created a system in which integrity, honesty and freedom of choice was a by-product of covenanting with Him. This produced an atmosphere of trust and moral integrity which has the *potential* to create unbridled wealth and health for the affected citizenry. These Muslims had never before encountered such a system— except in Israel— but their contact with Jewish governmental affairs would be nonexistent at that time. They can hardly be blamed for not understanding our government. Their primary contact with "Christian" nations was with monarchial ecclesiastical systems with established churches. Since these Muslims now believed they were dealing with just another Christian nation, they assumed we had the same form of government as all the rest.

The man in charge of writing this treaty was a secularist; some have even said he was an atheist. So he was not a Christian. It is not hard to imagine he came up with a solution (negotiated treaty) which worked with his personal narrative and the problem at hand. Some have made this as a point for Article XI. Yet, there seems to be no in-depth records concerning the finer points of how the wording was conceived in this document. So we do not know. There is also a mystery surrounding why the Article XI itself is different in its Arabic copy than from its English copy. The Arabic copy has no such language and seems to be some form of a letter instead; it is totally different. This was not uncovered until 1930.

Obviously, we have the potential of this man changing documents, based upon his personal narrative. Others have made the legal argument if one party has one copy of an agreement and another party has a different copy, then that part of the agreement is void. Others have made the simple argument the Congress who ratified would have had those copies. We made other treaties with different sects of Muslim pirate nations and this type of wording was never used. While it is dated 1797, it was not ratified until 1799 and remained in effect for eight years, at which time it was renegotiated without Article XI language. No treaty before, during or after ever contained similar language. Because of all the hatred and bullying tactics seen against Christians nowadays, there seems to be no common ground for discussion any longer, and no trust among the faithful when they find a possible atheist was in charge of writing something like treaty language.

Frankly, I am not surprised many interpret this article as suggesting our nation is not Christian. Yet when one reads it, you can see that is not what it is saying. It says, quite correctly, our Federal government is not founded as a nation in which Christianity is its head. Also note the article makes a distinction between the government and the States, because many states were founded as one sect of Christianity or another within their documentation. In fact, at that time states still had established churches. It then assigns an element of history that the States have never engaged in war with any of the other Muslim (Mehomitan) nations. Add to the confusion for these Muslims the fact the Federal government was bound to a Bill of Rights that the states were not bound by. This was not going to be an easy "sell" to these Muslims. I think the negotiator did the best he could within his own narrative and the situation at hand. Since we do not know what negotiations contributed exactly to this language, I imagine it was going to be difficult to explain to Muslims how it was that we had been one with England; over 98% of the people in the country were Christian; the states were in majority founded with Christianity in their charters, had establishment churches, and yet our Federal government was colorblind when it came to religion and would not deal falsely with another nation based upon its religion, or lack thereof.

As it is today, so it was in the past. Today folks are beheaded and jailed in Muslim nations because they are not Muslim. It is a majority situation in Muslim nations. This is not something new. It is also something which is not well told in today's press. Some would disagree. If all the instances of persecution were properly recorded, we would band together and demand a different approach to our world from what we are doing. There is a long history concerning this type of persecution. I should also be clear to mention there is **specific history** stating the Muslims attacked the ships *because* they worshipped a different God than the Muslims did, and they were *specifically* attacking Christian ships.[23] It would make sense to me the negotiators would attempt to make a distinction between our Federal government, the states, and the governments of other nations.

All of this *assumes* Article XI is in fact a bona fide part of the treaty. There are those who do not believe it is and then there are those who feel differently. Whether it is or not really makes no difference for my argument of covenant. Nevertheless, I have found it odd when one brings up the Northwest Ordinance and the Treaty of Paris of 1783, both which state Christianity as some influence for the functionality of their documentation— thus extending to the government— folks on the other side argue one was never really enacted with any effect and the other has been updated, so they 'don't count.'[24] That reasoning seems a bit mercurial to me. History is black and white; the methods you use to interpret one event must be used to interpret all events. If it were reversed, and the history proved you had a slim minority Christian population with little or no documentation proving Christian patterns and traditions in ancient government— and yet you have this one treaty, whose history in one of its articles has mystery and questionable provenance connected to it; which article seemed to suggest the Federal government was run by the Christian religion— well, I dare say folks would take exception to it— and for good reason.

It still seems quite clear to me there should be no controversy in under-standing Article XI when you read the entire history of Muslim pirate nations with the nations of the world at that time, and our history of treaties with them. It states clearly the Federal government is not run by Christianity, and the states, who had been run through Christian docu-ments (within some of their original documentation) with established churches, would have no desire to fight with these Muslim pirates, and neither would the United States government. By the way, after this was renegotiated— which was after the writing of the First Amendment— if it had been the desire of the government to keep such language, it would have been included, but it was not. After all, Jefferson was president by that time and since his idea of separation was such a big "wall" and supposedly others in Congress felt the same way, then it should have remained in the treaties, but it did not.

Much like the Northwest Ordinance, it never made much impact because it was breached quite quickly (see Jefferson's first address to Congress). In 1801 Tripoli (located in modern-day Libya) declared war on the United States.[25] Like the Northwest Ordinance, it should not be used to show the Federal government is somehow Christian or Atheist, or it is antago-nistic to either one. Although, I would not have a problem if someone wanted to mention it to show the understanding of a "colorblind" or non-sectarian Federal government. In my mind, it certainly does show that.

I have already mentioned the Northwest Ordinance in previous chapters, but let's repeat Section 14, Article 3: "Religion, morality, and knowledge, being necessary to good government and the happiness of mankind, schools and the means of education shall forever be encouraged."[26] It was finalized on July 13, 1787. It is defunct; but it does show what the thoughts and desires of our early Federal government was when new states were added, to suggest to them that religion, morality and knowledge are so necessary to government, wellbeing and our schooling that all three should "forever be encouraged." The ordinance has a history of twists and turns as well. It was most notably a document revealing the intentions of those seated, on how they would deal with Native Americans (Indians) and how future states should be formed. My purpose of showing it here is not to prove somehow the Federal government was Christian, even though most legislators were. Its use here only shows an understanding of the people's desire for future relations to continue a covenantal religious commitment towards each other. Since they would assume to become part of the independent united states, they would have rights not bound by the Bill of Rights. So they could make their own decisions in that regard. It seems this Congress felt the need to enunciate their desires in what decisions those states would make surrounding these areas. It seems to have carried no other weight, except to show examples of political theory and thinking of the day based on the reality of inclusion at the Federal table.

We have not looked at the Treaty of Paris of 1783. This was negotiated by John Adams, Benjamin Franklin and John Jay for the United States and David Hartley for King George. It formally ended our war for independence from Britain and recognized the thirteen colonies as free and independent and the United States as a sovereign country. It is one of our early treaties as a nation, and starts off with these words: "In the name of the most holy and undivided Trinity. . ."[27] So clearly we invited God, and specifically the Trinity— the Christian God found within the pages of the Scriptures— into the agreement as a party to the covenant with England. The effect was intended on the United States as a sovereign country, its affect was on the people as well. The people are still the people, with or without a Federal government. Whether it was updated or not, historically the intent is seen to covenant, so changes made would not influence the covenantal example.

Another example of helping the people within the confines of the federal-covenant understanding was made by the first Congress (pre-Constitution). It made a resolution to discuss the printing of Bibles at the request of three ministers. There are twists and turns to this story as well. Those specific Bibles the first Congress made a resolution to discuss were never ordered. At least I cannot find any action taking place on that resolution. Some claim it was really price regulation as to why the Bibles were requested and others claim they were intended to be reimbursed so, it doesn't matter anyway. They did probably desire price regulation and they would want to be reimbursed. Would to God modern-day

Congresses had the same agenda! Again, the arguments should not exist. The Bibles were never ordered.

But it is the Bible we are talking about, not grapes or leather for shoes. It does show a desire to maintain help and fidelity for the people, whether it was grapes or leather or Bibles. And of course they would want to reimburse the people's money; after all, they were to be good and faithful servants entrusted with the people's funds. This due, in no small part, because they were broke. As with other documentation from that time period, we have no hard evidence as to why they were never ordered. Was it price regulation, lack of funds, various aspects of war, state's rights (they were under the Articles of Confederation), chicanery on the part of someone using the Bible as cover— or some other issue— or aspects of all of them?[28] We can make some deductions, but for a fact, we will never know. If state's rights and/or price regulation played important roles, then that is part of the federal forum's duty and an outward display of covenant-keeping, both on a state and individual basis. Our modern Federal government has foisted a $19 plus trillion debt on the people. When the Federal government balances the budget, it proves its covenant-keeping ability. In this case, it was a commodity. All we can know is there was a desire to help the people— and they had no problem discussing the order of a commodity which had religious value— even though it was just discussing its order.[29]

While they never ordered or received Bibles, in 1781, colonial printer Robert Aitken petitioned Congress regarding many aspects in the printing of his copies of the Bible. This also has some twists and turns but eventually what they did do was make two resolutions and a report on the matter.

In order as it appears; with punctuation as I viewed and copied it exactly: "THURSDAY, *September* 12, 1782. Whereas James Innes, esq. who was on the 9th day of July last, elected to the office of judge-advocate, has not signified his acceptance, and it being intimated to Congress that he declines to accept the office: *Resolved,* That Wednesday next be assigned for electing a judge-advocate. The committee, consisting of Mr. Duane, Mr. McKean and Mr. Witherspoon, to whom was referred a memorial of Robert Aitken, printer, dated January 21st, 1781, respecting an edition of the holy scriptures, report, "That Mr. Aitken has at a great expense now finished an American edition of the holy scriptures in English; that the committee have, from time to time, attended to his progress in the work: that they also recommended it to the two chaplains of Congress to examine and give their opinion of the execution, who have accordingly reported thereon: The recommendation and report being as follows: "PHILADELPHIA, September 1st, 1782. *Rev. Gentlemen,* Our knowledge of your piety and public spirit leads us without apology to recommend to your particular attention the edition of the holy scriptures publishing by Mr. Aitken. He undertook this expensive work at a time, when from the circumstances of the war, an English edition of the bible could not be imported, nor any opinion formed how long the obstruction might continue. On this account particularly he deserves applause and encouragement. We therefore wish you, reverend gentlemen, to examine the execution of the work, and if approved, to give it the sanction of your judgment and the weight of your recommendation. We are with very great respect, your most obedient humble servants, (Signed) JAMES DUANE, Chairman, In behalf of a committee of Congress on Mr. Aitken's memorial. Rev. Dr. White and Rev. Mr. Duffield, chaplains of the United States in Congress, assembled." REPORT "*Gentlemen,* Agreeably to your desire, we have paid attention to Mr. Robert Aitken's impression of the holy scriptures, of the old and new testament. Having selected and examined a variety of passages throughout the work, we are of opinion, that it is executed with great accuracy as to the sense, and with as few grammatical and typographical errors as could be expected in an undertaking of such magnitude. Being ourselves witnesses of the demand for this invaluable book, we rejoice in the present prospect of a supply, hoping that it will prove as advantageous as it is honorable to the gentleman, who has exerted himself to furnish it at the evident risk of private fortune. We are, gentlemen, your very respectful and humble servants, (Signed) WILLIAM WHITE, GEORGE DUFFIELD. Hon. James Duane, esq. chairman, and the other hon. gentlemen of the committee of Congress on Mr. Aitken's memorial. PHILADELPHIA, September 10, 1782." Whereupon, *Resolved*, That the United States in Congress assembled, highly approve the pious and laudable undertaking of Mr. Aitken, as subservient to the interest of religion as well as an instance of the progress of arts in this country, and being satisfied from the above report, of his care and accuracy in the execution of the work, they recommend this edition of the bible to the inhabitants of the United States, and hereby authorize him to publish this recommendation in the manner he shall think proper."[30]

The first American version of the Bible was printed with roughly 10,000 copies. It is now even rarer to find than copies of the Gutenberg Bible.[31] The time frame here is pre-ratification. So my use of this example is in showing the idea of covenant responsibilities to the people. I'm assuming because it was the Bible, Congress wanted to make sure it was printed accurately with no falsehoods. They did not pay for it, but asked the chaplains to review it for accuracy. This is covenantal. That mindset of keeping all covenant responsibilities continued post-ratification as well.

Another example of similar thinking during that time frame came when Washington retired from the War and became a private citizen. He saw the need to secure the western boundaries, in no small part by surveying important rivers. He spearheaded initiative among the states in this endeavor, ultimately seeing legislation in Virginia and Maryland passed authorizing the Potomac Company and the James River Company to shepherd whatever steps were necessary to realize the goals of security and commercialization. This resulted in the legislature of Virginia giving 150 shares of the two companies to Washington. He graciously refused them. Because they were shares and could not be given back, a compromise was reached. He asked it be put to use making seminaries for higher learning within the districts of the rivers that were being opened. The legislature acted upon his wishes and used the moneys for seminaries in the vicinity of each of the western rivers they discussed.[32] This attitude, once again evidences a desire to maintain covenant responsibility to the people.

Individual statements made revealing the practice of acknowledging the people's covenant with God and/or stating Christianity as a benefit for the nation as a whole are quite prolific. One founding father we have not looked at is Dr. Benjamin Rush. He is quite an interesting character in that he was a patriot yet tried to get Washington removed from his position as general. Some have even noted he was viewed as a gossip, thus causing controversy. He was a passionate man who believed the army hospitals and the care of our soldiers was not up to par, and was willing to fight an uphill battle to have Washington removed for it![33] But he was also a celebrated physician of his time; the first to believe mental illness is a disease of the mind and not a possession of demons.[34] He was a well known abolitionist; a signer of the Declaration of Independence; Treasurer of the U.S. Mint; elected from Pennsylvania to the Continental Congress in 1776; appointed Physician General of the Military Hospital of the Middle Department, American Army in 1777. He was also an instructor and physician at the University of Pennsylvania in 1778 and elected to the Chair of Institutes, Medical and Clinical Practice of the University of Pennsylvania from 1791 to 1813, the year of his death.[35]

As a doctor one of his more famous quotes while teaching his students had to do with attending the poor, and them being good patients because God was their "paymaster."[36] He was a noted chemist and once out of politics set up a dispensary in Philadelphia to provide medical care for the poor, the first in the nation. He was committed to promoting education and was a founder of Dickinson College in Carlisle, Pennsylvania in 1783. He proposed a national system of public education with a federal university to train public servants. Somewhat uncommon for his time, he helped to establish and finance the oldest "Negro church" in the country and promoted the education of women. He was also a proponent of the tragic medical practice of bloodletting. He became involved in politics again by promoting the ratification of the Constitution, along with his ally in that endeavor, James Wilson. The two also encouraged and successfully saw the makeover of the Pennsylvania constitution.[37]

It was as an educator that he said: "I shall proceed in the next place, to enquire, what mode of education we shall adopt . . . the only foundation for a useful education in a republic is to be laid in Religion. Without this there can be no virtue, and without virtue there can be no liberty, and liberty is the object and life of all republican governments. . . . . But the religion I mean to recommend in this place, is that of the New Testament. . . . recorded in the Old Testament, is the *best refutation that can be given to the divine right of kings, and the strongest argument that can be used in favor of the original and natural equality of all mankind.* A Christian, I say again, cannot fail of being a republican, for every precept of the Gospel inculcates those degrees of humility, self-denial, and *brotherly kindness, . . . for his religion teacheth him, that no man "liveth to himself." . . . for his religion teacheth him, in all things to do to others what he would wish, in like circumstances, they should do to him."*[38]

I place in italics the foundational belief of popular sovereignty and the right of the people to covenant, not only with one another, but with God. This covenant understanding informed the documentation.

John Jay, our first Chief Justice of the Supreme Court said:

> "It certainly is very desirable that a pacific disposition should prevail among all nations. The most effectual way of producing it is by extending the prevalence and influence of the gospel. Real Christians will abstain from violating the rights of others, and therefore will not provoke war. Almost all nations have peace or war at the will and pleasure of rulers whom they do not elect, and who are not always wise or virtuous. Providence has given to our people the choice of their rulers, and it is the duty as well as the privilege and interest of our Christian nation to select and prefer Christians for their rulers."[39]

The letter is in answer to a question concerning whether war is prohibited by the gospel. It is within that context he mentions the understanding at that time, that we are a Christian nation, and that Christian rulers are preferred.

He also wrote: "With equal pleasure I have as often taken notice that Providence has been pleased to give this one connected country to one united people— a people descended from the same ancestors, speaking the same language, professing the same religion, attached to the same principles of government, very similar in their manners and customs, and who, by their joint counsels, arms, and efforts, fighting side by side throughout a long and bloody war, have nobly established general liberty and independence. This country and this people seem to have been made for each other, and it appears as if it was the design of Providence, that an inheritance so proper and convenient for a band of brethren, united to each other by the strongest ties, should never be split into a number of unsocial, jealous, and alien sovereignties. Similar sentiments have hitherto prevailed among all orders and denominations of men among us."[40]

Jay was answering those who wished to break the union into separate countries. So his main topic was not a discussion concerning God or Christianity. Nevertheless, you can read the idea that the country was given to us by God, thus the understanding of covenant in which the God of the Bible gives lands to nations, and especially blesses those nations whose people covenant with Him.

Some last quotes showing the legal understanding of covenant, both non-sectarian and biblical playing a role in government, come from two early legal power houses birthed on our shores and the compiler of dictionaries. James Madison is giving a long answer to a question in Federalist 43. The question asked what principle supersedes federation without consent (I loosely frame it for brevity's sake). His answer is lengthy and takes some twists and turns, but he seems to base all those on this foundation:

"The first question is answered at once by recurring to the absolute necessity of the case; to the great principle of self-preservation; to the transcendent law of nature and of nature's God."[41] In other words, when—in his case he was talking about dealing with states that did not ratify—you have a disagreement between those states located on our shores who had been under confederal agreement and not under the Constitution, what is the appropriate legal basis for working out a disagreement. He gives three foundations: the specific case, its affect on self-preservation and finally to the all-encompassing law of nature and nature's God. That law embodies covenant, for it is what establishes a people found in nature; i.e., the reality that God makes His agreement with a people with or without manmade laws.

My point in the preceding quotes is to show how covenantal responsibilities were viewed. Religious and civil rights stem from the same covenant. Following the law of nature and nature's God is viewed as one responsibility with several aspects to it which cannot be mitigated nor duplicated. It is viewed as a responsibility humans take on to remain faithful to laws seen in nature, that nature was created by God. For the overwhelming majority of the religious, those responsibilities are adopted in an effort to remain faithful to that God. Those responsibilities are covenant based. You cannot separate "We, the People," from our covenant responsibilities to nature's God; Pre, or Post Constitution. To make it clear you could not, the Bill of Rights was written. Even atheists who do not believe that there is a "god" that created nature— nature itself exists; so laws seen in nature must be viewed as covenantal— even for atheists. In other words, you must remain faithful to laws governing gravity, space, time, reproduction and survival. If you do not, you will not exist. It is not my purpose in this book to view the causal relativity of time within planetary travel. Even those laws which exist naturally within that sphere must be "covenanted" with or obeyed.

One powerhouse of legal review, Supreme Court Chief Justice John Marshall, who served for 34 years, the longest of any chief justice, wrote these words in response to an opinion by a minister concerning Christianity and the common law (as well as other topics): "The American population is entirely Christian, & with us, Christianity & Religion are identified. It would be strange, indeed, if with such a people, our institutions did not presuppose Christianity, & did not often refer to it, & exhibit relations with it."[42] This is the public outreach of the covenant where it crosses both non-sectarian/secular and religious lines in civil matters; in other words, institutions. Marshall thought it would be strange if the institutions did not presuppose their religious covenant outreach. If religious covenant was not understood or practiced, then it wouldn't be strange to think otherwise.

Whether for public or private discourse, God was frequently invoked in the conversation, which is another extension of covenant outreach. In a letter dated November 1821, from Noah Webster to John Jay mentioning the compilation of his dictionary, Webster mentions his reliance upon God for his health. As well, he mentions how he worships:

> "Making my past progress the basis of calculation, it must require the constant labour of four years to complete the work, even if my health should be continued. For this blessing I rely tranquilly on the goodness and forbearance of that Being, whose favor I desire to seek in the way which he has prescribed, and which I trust I value above any temporal good."[43]

In response from John Jay to Noah Webster concurring the writing of a dictionary, Jay closes with this comment:

> "Your intention to favor me with a visit next summer gives me pleasure. Whether our lives will be prolonged to that period, depends on that good Providence on which you happily and wisely rely, and whose beneficence I hope you will continue to experience."[44]

Even in a private hope to finish a public document as helpful as a dictionary, reliance is made on covenant example and understanding to extend to his good health to finish the job.

Conservative lawyer and recurrent senator from Massachusetts (first elected 1822 and 1827-1841) as well as Secretary of State under three presidents (William Henry Harrison, John Tyler and Millard Fillmore), Daniel Webster, said this:

"The religion of the New Testament— that religion which is founded on the teachings of Jesus Christ and his Apostles— is as sure a guide to duty in politics and legislation as in any concern of life."[45]

"And let us remember," says Webster, "that it is only religion, and morals, and knowledge, that can make men respectable and happy under any form of government. Let us hold fast the great truth that communities are responsible, as well as individuals, and that without unspotted purity of public faith, without sacred public principle, fidelity, and honor, no mere forms of government, no machinery of laws, can give dignity to political society. In our day and generation let us seek to raise and improve the moral sentiment, so that we may look, not for a degraded, but for an elevated and improved, future."[46]

ENDNOTES

1   <http://avalon.law.yale.edu/18th_century/ratva.asp><http://memory. loc.gov/cgi-bin/ampage?collId=bdsdcc&fileName=c1201//bdsdccc1201. db&recNum=1&itemLink=r?ammem/bdsbib:@field(NUMBER+@ od1(bdsdcc+c1201))&linkText=0> accessed 3/10/16

2   Croft, Lawrence M., R. Bruce W. Laubach, and Virginia Richmond. "All America Looks Up to Virginia;" Virginia and the Declaration of Independence." 2

3   A DVD of an enactment of this convention can be had by logging onto St. John's Church Foundation's website. As well much of the background history can be read there <http:// historicstjohnschurch.org/meet-the-man> accessed 2/5/16

4   <http://avalon.law.yale.edu/18th_century/patrick.asp> Public domain. All copies of this speech are not from the pen of Henry himself. They are garnered from the memory of those in attendance and reconstructed in a biography by William Wirt of Patrick Henry published in 1817. Site © 2008 Lillian Goldman Law Library, New Haven, CT. Accessed 3/2/16.

5   Ibid.

6   Ibid.

7   Ibid.

8   Ibid.

9   <http://avalon.law.yale.edu/18th_century/translet.asp> Public domain. Site © 2008 Lillian Goldman Law Library, New Haven, CT. Accessed 3/2/16.

10   Leviticus 23:9-14; 1 Corinthians 15:20-23; <http://www.hebrew4christians.com/ Holidays/Spring_Holidays/First_Fruits/first_fruits.html> accessed 2/2/16. I know nothing about this ministry, as is the case with quite a few of my endnote sources. But it is one of the most concise accounts of this holiday, especially as related to Christianity that I could find. Other Scripture references for the last two sentences are: Psalm 121:3, 4; Jeremiah, 1:12; Isaiah 55:11; Genesis 28:20, 21; Psalm 65:1; Psalm 50:14; Psalm 22:5.

11   <http://avalon.law.yale.edu/subject_menus/constpap.asp> Site © 2008 Lillian Goldman Law Library, New Haven, CT. Accessed 3/2/16. You can click on the title of each of these documents to view the document itself.

12   <http://avalon.law.yale.edu/18th_century/ratma.asp> Public domain. Site © 2008 Lillian Goldman Law Library, New Haven, CT. Accessed 3/2/16.

13   <http://avalon.law.yale.edu/subject_menus/constpap.asp> Site © 2008 Lillian Goldman Law Library, New Haven, CT. You can click on the title of each of these documents to view the document itself.

14   <http://avalon.law.yale.edu/18th_century/ratva.asp> Site © 2008 Lillian Goldman Law Library, New Haven, CT. Accessed 3/5/16.

15   Kate Mason Rowland. 1892. "The Life of George Mason, 1725-1792." Volume 1, 1892. New York & London: G.P. Putnam's Sons. The Knickerbocker Press. 32. In the public domain.

16   <http://teachingamericanhistory.org/ratification/virginiatimeline> site © 2006-2015 Asbrook Center; accessed 3/1/16. You can use this site as well as many others, including our National Archives to view the literature and the timelines in the formation of the Federal Government. This particular site has an easy-to-read timeline available, while sites like our National Archives tend to be more difficult to navigate, possibly due to the sheer volume of material on them.

17   <http://teachingamericanhistory.org/ratification/elliot/vol3/june7> site © 2006-2015 Asbrook Center; accessed 3/1/16.

18   Daniel Dorchester, D.D. "Christianity in the United States From the First Settlement Down to the Present Time." New York: Phillips & Hunt, Cincinnati: Cranston & Stowe. (1888) 272. In the public domain. It uses discussions from Edmund Randolph of Virginia in Madison's Works, Volume 2, p 730. Yet the term for the national government was seen as federal before the Constitution came about.

19   <http://avalon.law.yale.edu/18th_century/washing.asp> Site © 2008 Lillian Goldman Law Library, New Haven, CT. Accessed 2/5/16.

20   Charles Francis Adams, "The Works of John Adams, Second President of the United States: with a Life of the Author, Notes, and Illustration." Boston, 1854: Little, Brown and Co. Volume 9. 228, 229. In the public domain.

21   <http://avalon.law.yale.edu/18th_century/bar1796t.asp> Site © 2008 Lillian Goldman Law Library, 127 Wall Street, New Haven, CT. Accessed 3/5/16. For Further Reading <http://avalon.law.yale.edu/18th_century/bar1796n.asp#n1> is an explanation of the odd Article 11, as not an article at all and here is the menu for the other Barbary Treaties<http://avalon.law.yale.edu/subject_menus/barmenu.asp>Please look at this site for a concise history surrounding the Treaty and Article 11<http://www.tektonics.org/qt/tripoli.php>Here is a good article that takes a critical look at claims made by some <http://www.politifact.com/truth-o-meter/statements/2010/may/11/keith-olbermann/count-down-host-says-founding-father-reached-out-mu/> Wikipedia has a good and concise history for those that like that site<https://en.wikipedia.org/wiki/Treaty_of_Tripoli>

22   <http://www.crf-usa.org/america-responds-to-terrorism/the-origins-of-islamic-law.html><https://en.wikipedia.org/wiki/The_Twelve_Imams> Accessed 3/16/16.

23   <http://www.tektonics.org/qt/tripoli.php> Accessed 3/6/16.

24   <http://2001-2009.state.gov/r/pa/ho/time/ar/14313.htm> Accessed 3/30/16; you can click on the links to read the updates.

25   <http://www.tektonics.org/qt/tripoli.php> Accessed 3/6/16.

26   For the timeline see <http://franklaughter.tripod.com/cgi-bin/histprof/misc/nwtimeline.html> For the full wording of the ordinance see <http://avalon.yale.law.edu/18th_century/nworder.asp> sites accessed 5/23/16.

27   <http://avalon.law.yale.edu/18th_century/paris.asp> Site © 2008 Lillian Goldman Law Library, New Haven, CT. Accessed 2/5/16.

28   Irvin, Benjamin H. 2011. "Clothed in Robes of Sovereignty: The Continental Congress and the People Out of Doors." New York, NY: © 2011 Oxford University Press, Inc. 250, 251. I site this source because this Assistant Professor of History at the University of Arizona has a good argument for lack of funds.

29   <http://www.loc.gov./exhibits/religion/rel04.html> Accessed 3/10/16. You can click on the page to see the exact resolution. In viewing the previous note and viewing the Library of Congress' site here noted, I also find a discrepancy. Either they are mistaken as well, or they have information we are not privy to. But this discrepancy should be noted. I could not find any documentation where they ordered or received Bibles. The LOC may correct their web page by the time you view the site.

30   "Journals of the American Congress from 1774-1788: In Four Volumes, Volume IV: From April 1, 1782, to November 1, 1788, inclusive. Also, The Journal of the Committee of the States, from the 1st Friday in June, to the 1st Friday in August, 1784, with an Appendix." Washington: Printed and Published by Way and Gideon. (1823) 75, 76. In the public domain.

31   <http://www.invaluable.com/auction-lot/robert-aitken,-printer-the-holy-bible,-con-tainin-276-c-9bc154c659> For further reading on family Bibles and printing <http://mobia.org/resources/American_Spirit.pdf> Accessed 2/8/16.

32   <http://www.earlyamerica.com/lives-early-america/ramsays-life-washington/life-george-washington-david-ramsay-chapter-ten><http://founders.archives.gov/documents/Madison/01-08-02-0117><http://vagenweb.org/hening/vol11-28.htm><http://oll.libertyfund.org/titles/washington-the-writings-of-george-washington-vol-xi-1785-1790> On this site the letter is dated October 29, 1785, to Patrick Henry, Governor of Virginia, accessed 3/1/16.

33   <http://www.ushistory.org/declaration/signers/rush.html> accessed 2/5/16

34   <http://www.uphs.upenn.edu/paharc/features/brush.html> © The Trustees of the University of Pennsylvania; accessed 3/10/16.

35   Ibid.

36   Lillian Ione Rhodes, "The Story of Philadelphia." New York: American Book Company. 1900 © Lillian Ione Rhodes. 303 (see Proverbs 19: 17; Proverbs 22:2)

37   <http://www.archives.upenn.edu/people/1700s/rush_benj.html> © 1995-2013 University of Pennsylvania University Archives and Records Center; accessed 3/10/16.

38   "The Historical Notes of Benjamin Rush" First published in "The Pennsylvania Magazine of History and Biography." Vol. XXVII, no 2. 1903. 129-150. Taken from print published before 1923.

39   Letter from John Jay to John Murray, Jr., dated October 12, 1816. In "The Correspondence and Public Papers of John Jay." Edited by Henry P. Johnston, (NewYork: G.P.Putman's Sons, 1893). Vol. IV, 392, 393. In the public domain.

40   "The Federalist Papers No. 2; Concerning Dangers from Foreign Force and Influence For the Independent Journal," by John Jay. <http://avalon.law.yale.edu/18th_century/fed02.asp> Site © 2008 Lillian Goldman Law Library, New Haven, CT. Accessed 2/5/16.

41   "The Federalist Papers No. 43; The Same Subject Continued (The Powers Conferred by the Constitution Further Considered) For the Independent Journal," by James Madison. <http://avalon.law.yale.edu/18th_century/fed43.asp> Site © 2008 Lillian Goldman Law Library, New Haven, CT. Accessed 2/5/16.

42   W.A. Whitehead. "Alleged Atheism of the Constitution" In "The Northern Monthly" edited by Allen Lee Bassett (New York and Newark: Allen L. Bassett. 1868) Volume II November-April. 66. Citing a letter from John Marshall to Rev. Jasper Adams dated May 9, 1833. Public domain.

43   Letter from John Jay to John Murray, Jr., dated October 12, 1816. In "The Correspondence and Public Papers of John Jay." Edited by Henry P. Johnston, (NewYork: G.P.Putman's Sons, 1893). Vol. IV, 392, 393. In the public domain.

44   Ibid., letter from John Jay to Noah Webster, dated December 3, 1821. 459

45   Benjamin Franklin Morris. "Christian Life and Character of the Civil Institutions of the United States, Developed in the Official and Historical Annals of the Republic." (Introduction by Byron Sunderland, Washington, D.C., April 16, 1863) Philadelphia: George W. Childs, 628 & 630 Chestnut St., Cincinnati: Rickey & Carroll, 1864. 3. In the public domain.

46   Ibid., 277

Chapter Fourteen

WE THE PEOPLE: COVENANTAL UNDERSTANDING PRODUCES COMMON PRACTICE

I could include many other documents and specific quotes, but that would become redundant. The previous are samplings of a tradition of covenant-keeping among our "We, the People," apparatus. There are practices and monuments erected which have displayed the tradition of our government to keeping covenant with a biblically inspired people. It is usually what a people understand that they practice. When it comes to covenant-keeping, those practices are many. As we have reviewed, the faithful practice covenant-keeping through secular events: They work, clean, raise children and keep their economics in order to evidence how God rules in their lives— and develop nations. Many forget atheists must also keep these practices in order to remain in covenant with their own surroundings. Just because many folks fail at some of the above practices, does not mean they intend to or, in the case of the religious, they disbelieve in God. Quite often, the non-religious only think of the religious practicing covenant in their prayer or preaching or reading of the Bible or church attendance, worship or giving of time and money. But the religious as well as the non-religious must covenant to live. The practices themselves might be the same, but the attitude in which one does them and what we say while we do so, are different. Whether it is military, police or civil service, each individual is performing a duty to fulfill a covenant obligation. Some do it secularly in a non-sectarian way, while many do so to fulfill the covenant of service to God and Country.

During our founding era, one of those practices that we see among the people, celebrated by the clergy and totally encompassing politics was the Election Day Sermon. Frankly, I believe it to be a practice we should reinstitute among us as clergy. But it lasted roughly 250 years from as early as 1633 to as late as 1884. It was first done in Massachusetts Bay Colony. They would appoint one of the clergy to preach on the day those who were elected were installed. "By the charter of William and Mary, October 7, 1691, the last Wednesday in May was established as 'election day,' and it remained so until the Revolution."[1]

Over time it became an institution which instructed on political theory, various questions of government and the ground rules for forming political parties. Ethics in government and the character of those running were popular topics as well as the nitty-gritty of institutional practices. It spread throughout New England and was picked up sporadically throughout the thirteen colonies. In some places it marked a pre-election. But in New England it was more like an inauguration day commencement. There was a formal address to the newly assembled legislature, preached in the statehouses with the elected officials present. It eventually became a public holiday as it was picked up by other localities, primarily in Middle as well as other New England colonies. Schools and stores would close and folks held parades and picnics. At that point the sermons were also preached in the churches as well as the statehouse.

"These discourses were a remarkable feature in the opening of the war of the Revolution."[2] In a speech in 1775, Edmund Burke said:

> "It contributed no mean part toward the growth of the untractable spirit of the colonies— I mean their education. In no country in the world, perhaps, is the law so general a study."[3] "The annual election sermons widely promoted the study of political ethics, which had become a prominent feature in New England history in the middle of the

last century, and laid the foundation for that 'earnestness which consciousness of right begets, and those appeals to principle which distinguished the colonies.'

The highest glory of the American Revolution, in the estimation of Hon. John Quincy Adams, was the ripe fruitage of this old custom: 'It connected, with one indissoluble bond, the principles of civil government with the precepts of Christianity.' "[4]

Sermons with titles like "A Discourse Concerning Unlimited Submission and Non-resistance to the Higher Powers" (1750 by Rev. Jonathan Mayhew, D.D.), "Civil Government for the Good of the People" (1770, Rev. Samuel Cook, D.D.) and "Christian Duty of Resistance to Tyrants; Prepare for War; Appeal to Heaven" (1774 by Rev. William Gaden),[5] were preached to all. Here are a few more samplings of the sermon titles: "Arise O God! Plead thine own Cause by Abraham Keteltas, Newburyport, 1777, Psalm 74:22."[6] "Scriptural Instructions to Civil Rulers, and all Freeborn Subjects, by Samuel Sherwood, 1774."[7] "A Sermon on the Day of Commencement of the Constitution, by Samuel Cooper, Boston, 1780; Their Congregation shall be established before me: and their Nobles shall be of themselves, and their Governor shall proceed from the midst of them, Jeremiah 30:20, 21."[8]

"Occupying a position of such eminent respect and influence in society, it is not strange that the clergy shared the sympathy of the people in the civil struggles through which they were passing, and that 'The Pulpit of the Revolution' came to be one of the great factors of the times in the Middle and the New England colonies. God was invoked in the civil assemblies, and the teachers of religion were called upon for counsel from the Bible. Sermons were preached, religion and politics were closely united, and with Bibles and bayonets they entered into the struggle."[9]

This practice birthed the British term, "Black Robe Regiment." Before the Revolutionary War, these sermons preached ideas Britain was not necessarily happy with. "This was the secret of that moral energy which sustained the Republic in its material weakness against superior numbers and discipline, and all the power of England. To these sermons the State

fixed its *imprimatur,* and this they were handed down to future generations with a twofold claim to respect."[10]

The British made the churches pay for their practice of disloyalty. Those
ministers who were rumored to be Loyalists left for England, where in
some cases, they went on a tirade in print against the colonists and their
clergy. Not all the English clergy disagreed with the American cause.
Though viewed suspiciously by many patriots, the Methodists had a zeal
for preaching in the colonies. In England, their leader, John Wesley, wrote
to Lord North and the Earl of Dartmouth after the battles of Lexington
and Concord: "I am a High Churchman, bred up in my childhood in the
highest notions of passive obedience and non-resistance; and yet, in spite
of my long-rooted prejudices, I cannot avoid thinking these an oppressed
people, asking for nothing more than their legal rights, and that in the
most modest and inoffensive manner that the nature of the thing would
allow. But, waiving this, I ask, is it common sense to use force toward
the Americans?"[11]

Many of the clergy espousing liberty fought in the war or preached to
the troops. This usually landed them in an English prison. A large portion
of those buildings confiscated for prisons and stables for British horses,
were the clergy's very own churches! All the younger men in pulpits
or destined for them, took up arms. They suffered the same loss of life,
property and family as the rest of our new nation did. In New York City,
out of 19 churches, only nine were in decent enough shape for worship
when the war ended. In Boston all of their pastors, save two, from
Congregational churches, left during the siege of that city. In Virginia, the
Episcopal church alone recorded its own denomination's losses:

> "When the colonists first resorted to arms Virginia in her
> 61 counties contained 95 parishes, 164 churches and
> chapels, and 91 clergyman. When the contest was over, she
> came out of the war with a large number of her churches
> destroyed or injured irreparably, with 23 of her 95 parishes
> extinct or forsaken, and of the remaining 72, 34 were des-
> titute of ministerial services, while of her 91 clergymen 28
> only remained who had lived through the storm; and these

with eight others, who came into the State soon after the struggle terminated, supplied 36 of the parishes. Of these 28, 15 only had been enabled to continue in the churches which they supplied prior to the commencement of hostilities, and 13 had been driven from their cures by violence or want."[12]

It seems if we do not study the truth of our history, we do not respect some of the practices which made it possible. I have proven the covenant-puritan form of government was inculcated into our governing documents, but it was also within the practice as well as the understanding of the American people. It was within their own minds and psyches that this fact brought forth liberty, country and then finally Federal documents. Let me quote a historian who documented the sentiment: (Concerning the Congregational Churches of New England)

"This form of church-government is democratic. It was of Puritan birth, and, like the faith of the Puritans, it came fresh and vigorous from the word of God. It is the embodiment and practice of the American doctrine of popular sovereignty, applied to church-government, as it is to all the civil affairs of the nation. Each Church is an independent Christian democracy, where all the members have a right to a voice in the government of the Church, and whose decisions are subject to no reversal by any other ecclesiastical tribunal. The Bible is regarded as the text-book in theology and politics, in Church and State, as it is in its form of church-government; and, holding the Bible as the standard of form as well as of faith, the Puritans and their descendants constituted their ecclesiastic form after the pattern set them in the Bible. The fruits of their faith and polity everywhere abound. 'The principles of their religious system have given birth and vigor to the republican habits and republican virtue and intelligence of the sons of New England.' The Congregational churches were not only schools of Christian faith, but of freedom, in which the ministers were the teachers and the people the pupils, and whence came the men and women to fight and pray for freedom and the battles of the Revolution. During the Revolution there were in New England 575 ministers and 700 Congregational churches, almost all of which were in active sympathy with the cause of liberty... It is no violence to truth to affirm that without the devotion and earnest activity of these churches the Revolution never could have been effected. Their faith and form of church-government were in harmony with the reigning spirit of liberty, and energized all the efforts of patriots with piety and ardor, and infused into that great conflict those Christian ideas and principles which impart a divine dignity and grandeur to a people struggling to be free. The Congregational form of church-government suggested to the philosophic mind of Mr. Jefferson our present republican form of government. Near his residence, in Virginia, several years previous to the Revolution, there existed a Baptist church on a congregational basis of government, whose monthly meetings Jefferson often attended. Being asked how he was pleased with their church-government, he replied that it struck him with great force, and interested him very much; that he considered it the only form of pure democracy that then existed in the world, and had concluded that it would be the best plan of government for the American colonies. If Jefferson confessed himself indebted to the business meetings of a church in his neighborhood, substantially Congregational in government, for his best ideas of a democracy, much more were John Adams and his New England compatriots beholden to their ecclesiastical surroundings for the republican tendencies of their politics. The churches of New England had been for a century and a half educating their people, in their Christian and political democracies, to love liberty, so that when the trial of their faith came at the Revolution, they were ready to enter with soul and energy into the great conflict, and to carry it to a happy consummation... 'The lowly men who now met ... accustomed to feed their own cattle, to fold their own sheep, to guide their own ploughs; all trained to public life in the little democracies of their towns; some of them captains in the militia, and officers of the church according to the discipline of Congregationalists; **nearly all of them communicants under a public covenant with God.' "**[13] (Highlight is mine.)

This historian displays the common understanding of the time with the common practice of the time. For a covenant people, everything done, is so done with integrity to display covenantal practice. While preaching or sharing the God of the covenant with another human is one of the most well known practices extending from that covenant, there are many other elements that are practiced. One ignored element in the religious history of this nation is the practice among the people that is called *prayer*. From pastry chefs to presidents and janitors to jewelers, the People have maintained this covenant practice. History records a regular prayer from President John Quincy Adams:

> "Mr. Adams said, only a short period before his death, that he never retired to rest without repeating the simple prayer which his mother taught him in childhood:— Here I lay me down to sleep; I pray the Lord my soul to keep; If I should die before I wake, I pray the Lord my soul to take."[14]

Prayer is the most basic of our covenantal responsibilities. Quite frequently coupled with prayer is action:

> "... 'The heroism of the females of the Revolution has gone from the memory with the generation that witnessed it, and but little remains upon the ear of the young of the present day but the faint echo of an expiring tradition.' ... And yet enough of the noble deeds and influence of the women of the Revolution remains to show their piety, their patriotism, and their self-denying efforts in the cause of their country. Their piety and labors are thus referred to by Mrs. Ellet, the historiographer in this field of the Revolution. 'I have been struck,' says she, 'by the fact that almost all were noted for piety. The spirit that exhibited itself in acts

of humanity, courage, patriotism, and magnanimity was a deeply religious one. May we not with reason deem this an important source of the strength that gave success to the American cause? To inflame the fires of freedom by mutual interchanges of feelings, and to keep them burning in the hearts of all around, they formed freedom-associations, and entered into written pledges *(covenants)* to make every sacrifice they could for their country.'"[15] Italics are mine.

In Edenton, North Carolina, on October 25, 1774, fifty-one women signed a covenant to do all in their power to help the American cause.[16] Throughout New England they refused to drink tea and signed pledges (covenants) to bind them together in their resolve. They even entered into written pledges to refuse the attentions of young men who would not volunteer to defend their country.[17] Covenants were still common enough that these women did not hesitate to enter into them in support of their wartime purpose.

In a morning church service in Litchfield, Connecticut, news arrived that St. John had been taken by the Americans. While shouts of victory rang out, it was made known by the messenger the army was suffering and destitute, without clothing, stockings or shoes. The women of the congregation immediately went into action:

"... the result was that, when the congregation assembled in the afternoon, not a woman was to be seen... their earnest, noble wives and daughters had taken down their hand-cards, drawn forth their spinning-wheels, set in motion their looms, while the knitting and sewing needles were plied as they never were before. It was a strange spectacle to see that Puritan Sabbath turned into a day of secular work... and the voice of prayer and hymns of praise ascended as usual from devout and solemn hearts; but all through the usually quiet streets of Litchfield the humming sound of the spinning-wheel, the clash of the shuttle flying to and fro, were heard, making strange harmony with the worship of the sanctuary... eyes... were over their work, and lips moved in prayer for the destitute and suffering soldier."[18] They sacrificed cloth for coats; sheets and blankets for shirts and flannels into "men's habiliments." "Weights of clocks, pans, dishes, pewter services of plate, then common, were melted by the women and given to the army to be used in defence (sic) of freedom."[19]

Prayer with hard work was not the only thing these ladies contributed. A letter from a Mrs. Reed of Philadelphia to General Washington tells the story:

> ". . . which make in the whole, in paper money, $300,634. The ladies are anxious for the soldiers to receive the benefit of it, and wait on your directions how it can be best disposed of. We expect considerable additions from the country; and I have also written to the other States in hopes that the ladies there will adopt a similar plan to render it more general and beneficial. Philadelphia, July 4."[20] This quoted work also records the monetary offering of the ladies of New Jersey and Maryland.[21]

The British knew what they were up against with the women. A British officer is quoted as saying to Mrs. Pinckney, wife of Charles Pinckney,

> "It is impossible not to admire the intrepid firmness of the ladies of your country. Had your men but half their resolution, we might give up the contest. America would be free."[22]

There had been a long standing practice of making banners for their state militias. In 1745, the New Hampshire Regiment had eight companies with 300 men. Col. William Pepperell commanded the forces and had the following motto inscribed on one of their flags, "Nil desperandum Christo duce," which means, "Nothing need be despaired of where Christ takes the lead."[23] During the Revolution they also made banners or flags for the various regiments within their different locales. They inscribed them with Christian symbols and mottoes. "On the other side, in the centre, an emblem, representing the all-seeing eye, with the words, *Non allies regit*, — 'No other governs.' This banner, symbolical of woman's faith in God and her devotion to the cause of liberty, was borne by the brave Polander *(Pulaski)*, in all his battles, till he fell, in 1779, on the field, a martyr to liberty."[24]

"Prayer does avail with God; and the women of the Revolution were almost all praying women, and hence their powerful and beneficent influence during the scenes of the Revolution."[25] There are too many stories to include in one section.[26] Not unlike our towns today, prayer was made for their sons at war: "While the battle was raging on the heights of Charlestown, as it was afterwards ascertained, the anxious wife of Lieut. Eastman, together with the people of the town, was attending public worship at the usual place."[27]

There is another famed role these covenant sharing, praying ladies played: that of spy. In 1777, the British took control of Philadelphia. Washington spent the winter in Valley Forge. These women formed an association for transporting the information they overheard while the British soldiers were quartered in their homes. The British never paid much attention to the ladies' intellect and would easily share with each other their future campaign plans while the ladies overheard. The ladies would then run point from one woman's house to another in a line of female couriers until Washington received the information at Valley Forge. They did all this under the guise of visiting each other as women have occasion to do as friends and neighbors. The British seemed to be oblivious to the women's effect.[28]

The western lands should not be left out of this. This story was told to the author herein cited, directly (see endnote):

> "The history of twelve years' suffering in Tennessee, from 1780 to 1792, when the inhabitants succeeded in conquering peace without the aid of Federal troops; and of sixteen years' carnage in Kentucky, from 1774 to 1790, when the first effectual relief began to be extended, would require volumes of detail for which we have no time, and powers of description for which I have no talent. Then was witnessed the scenes of woe and death, of carnage and destruction, which no words of mine can ever paint . . . Then was seen

the Indian warfare in all its horrors— that warfare which spares neither decrepit age, nor blooming youth, nor manly strength, nor infant weakness. . . when the slow consuming fire of the stake devoured its victim in the presence of pitying friends, and in the midst of ploughed, (sic) the crops were gathered, the cows were milked, water was brought from the spring, and God was worshiped under the guard and protection of armed men; when the night was the season for traveling, the impervious forest the highway, and the place of safety most remote from the habitation of man; when every house was a fort, and every fort subject to siege and assault. Such was the warfare in the infant settlements of Kentucky and Tennesee, (sic) and which the aged men, actors in the dreadful scenes, have related to me so many times."[29]

I have no desire to wade into the carnage of Indian and settler warfare, but the eastern states also experienced much of the same and documented it. It should also be noted the natives were fighting to keep their land. The adage, "war is hell" applies here. But there was also a common knowledge that the British, during the Revolutionary War days were behind some of this conflict, inciting the Indians to war against the settlers.[30] To what degree, I have not researched. Although, if a British member of the House of Commons mentions it in a speech to his constituents, (see endnote) I can imagine it was widely done.

Furthermore, there is history the English were not alone in this habit. The French did so in the 1700s. As recorded by the New Hampshire settlement of Gilmanton:

"Col. Thomas Westbrook of Portsmouth, was ordered in the depth of winter, 1721, with a party of men to surprise Norridgewock, and seize upon Sebastian Ralle, a Romish priest, who was there residing with the Indians as a Missionary; but who, it was found, was secretly corresponding with the French, and instigating the Indians to commit depredations on the new settlements of New Hampshire.

Ralle himself escaped from their hands; but they obtained a 'strong box' of papers; among which were letters from the Governor of Canada, showing a conspiracy in exciting the Indians to hostilities."[31]

I have related these stories to show that the early experience of the western settlers were the same as other settlers. In the midst of all the hell, they still practiced a covenant responsibility: "God was worshiped under the guard and protection of armed men."[32] It shows they did not forget Him. This account of the settlers was told directly to the author I have quoted by those who experienced it. As a result, I have no reason to doubt his veracity.

Not to be confused with Election Day Sermon "holidays" was the practice of sermons and speeches made on the Fourth of July celebrations, thanksgiving days, fast days or other days of proclamations, which were quite common by our presidents as well as governors of the various states. In fact, it was not unusual for the people to hear a sermon given by the clergy after an elected official called for a day of fasting and prayer or other celebration.

John Quincy Adams, sixth President of the United States and son of President John Adams said in a speech celebrating the 61st Anniversary of the Declaration of Independence:

> "Why is it, Friends and Fellow Citizens, that you are here assembled? . . . Is it not that, in the chain of human events, the birth-day of the nation is indissolubly linked with the birth-day of the Saviour? That it forms a leading event in the progress of the gospel dispensation? Is it not that the Declaration of Independence first organized the social compact on the foundation of the Redeemer's mission upon earth? That it laid the corner stone of human government upon the first precepts of Christianity, and gave to the world the first irrevocable pledge of the fulfillment of the prophecies, announced directly from Heaven at the birth of the Saviour and predicted by the greatest of the Hebrew prophets six hundred years before? . . . The sublimest of

the prophets of antiquity with the voice of inspiration had exclaimed, 'Who hath heard such a thing? Who hath seen such things? Shall the earth be made to bring forth in one day? Or shall a nation be born at once' (Isaiah 66:8)? In the two thousand five hundred years, that had elapsed since the days of that prophecy, no such event had occurred. It had never been seen before. In the annals of the human race, then, for the first time, did one People announce themselves as a member of that great community of powers of the earth, acknowledging the obligations and claiming the rights of the Laws of Nature and of Nature's God. The earth was made to bring forth in one day! A Nation was born at once! . . . . *One People* . . . unfolded the principles upon which their national association had, by their unanimous consent, and by the mutual pledges of their faith, been formed. It was an association of mutual covenants. . . Thirdly, the Declaration of Independence announced the *One People*, assuming their station among the powers of the earth, as a civilized, religious, and Christian People,— acknowledging themselves bound by the obligations, and claiming the rights, to which they were entitled by the laws of Nature and of Nature's God."[33] (Italics are NOT mine.)

Of course, modern theologians look to the fulfillment of what Adams was talking about in Isaiah 66:8 as the beginning of the modern nation of Israel in 1948. But theologians of Adams' day would not yet have that history. They had the history of our nation in mind, and they would not, theologically be wrong, though proving that is not my purpose here. When "new" people of nations make covenants with the God of the Bible, it must seem to them like they are birthed "overnight," even though the process takes a bit longer.

Proclamations by governors and presidents in the appointment and observation of days of public prayer, fasting and humiliation were quite common.[34] Some modern presidents have shunned the need for repentance and fasting, which is exactly what this nation does need to do. This might be the result of either a total ignorance of the covenant foundation of the country and its present need within our borders; or it might be the result of a lack of respect for the covenant people. Past officials understood covenant and the breaking of it. They understood the need to repent when war and conflict was so prevalent and imminent. The understanding that it was God who oversaw the people's covenant one to another and that breaking it could have the effect of wars as well as other calamities upon the nation was well known, even interwoven within the psyche of the American public.

It was well understood and preached by the clergy the way back to right fellowship (covenant) with one another as well as the Maker was to proclaim a fast, confess sin, to mourn and observe the need to ask The Supreme Ruler of the Universe to forgive sin and intervene on the people's behalf. Theologically we now understand it is not God who is causing the potential calamities, but humans. I'm not so sure that was as clear in the minds of yesteryear's people. I also do not mean to infer a man like Jefferson would have believed in the total experience of a New Testament understanding of covenant-keeping. His was more of an Old Testament understanding with a secular, non-sectarian agreement in mind (see the chapter "Jefferson"). Nevertheless, it was still covenantal. To imagine we no longer need to seek God's counsel is to ignore realities. Men like Jefferson and George Wythe signed their names to them, and George Washington and George Mason followed it through fasting, prayer as well as exhorting their families and constituents to do the same.[35] Every state did this, the Continental Congress did this; the Federal Senate and House of Representatives have done this; former presidents as well as modern presidents have done this.

Look at the wording that a president like Madison gave to one of these proclamations:

> "I do therefore recommend the third Thursday in August next, as a convenient day to be set apart for the devout purposes of rendering to the Sovereign of the Universe and the Benefactor of mankind, the public homage due to his holy attributes; of acknowledging the transgressions which might justly provoke the manifestations of His divine

displeasures; of seeking His merciful forgiveness, His assistance in the great duties of repentance and amendment; and especially of offering fervent supplications, that in the present season of calamity and war, He would take the American People under his peculiar care and protection; that he would guide their public councils *(that means speak to elected officials)*, animate their patriotism, and bestow His blessing on their arms; that He would inspire all nations with a love of justice and of concord, and with a reverence for the unerring precept of our holy religion, to do to others as they would require others to do to them; and finally, that, turning the hearts of our enemies from the violence and injustice which sway their councils against us, He would hasten a restoration of the blessings of Peace. Given at Washington the 9th day of July, in the year of our Lord one thousand eight hundred and twelve. James Madison. By the President. James Monroe, Secretary of State."[36] (Italics are mine.)

On February 18, 1815, Madison conveyed the official notification of peace with Great Britain. The next day the Senate as well as the House made the following resolution:

"It being a duty particularly humbly and devoutly to acknowledge our dependence on Almighty God, and to implore his aid and protection, and in times of deliverance and prosperity to manifest our deep and undissembled (sic) gratitude to the Almighty Sovereign of the Universe; therefore, Resolved, by the Senate and House of Representatives of the United States of America, in Congress assembled, That a joint committee of both Houses wait on the President of the United States, and request that he recommend a day of thanksgiving to be observed by the people of the United States, with religious solemnity, and the offering of devout acknowledgments to God for his mercies, and in prayer to him for the continuance of his blessings."[37]

Madison issued the requested proclamation. I would like you to read part of that and see whether or not these men and women understood covenant and its practices:

> "No people ought to feel greater obligations to celebrate the goodness of the Great Disposer of events and of the destiny of nations *(In other words, God.)* than the people of the United States. His kind providence originally conducted them to one of the best portions of the dwelling-place allowed for the great family of the human race. He protected and cherished them under all of the difficulties and trials to which they were exposed in their early days. Under his fostering care, their habits, their sentiments, and their pursuits prepared them for a transition in due time to a state of independence and of self-government. In the arduous struggle by which it was attained, they were distinguished by multiplied tokens of his benign interposition. During the interval which succeeded, he reared them into strength, and endowed therewith the resources which have enabled them to assert their national rights and to enhance their national character in another arduous conflict, which is now happily terminated by a peace and reconciliation with those who have been our enemies. And to the same Divine Author of every good and perfect gift we are indebted for all those privileges and advantages, religious as well as civil, which are so richly enjoyed in this favored land."[38] (Italics are mine.)

Madison reiterates what all covenant people know intrinsically, that it is God who places people in a land and it is God who will allow them to be taken out of that land and it is God who gives them the practices of civil and religious advantages. It is up to them as to whether they practice them or not. This proclamation occurred after the War of 1812. The next time our nation was attacked on its own land was 2001. We then experienced a long stretch of peace on our land from the War on Terror. This lasted from 2001 through 2008. Our most recent memories of attack on our own land again are Fort Hood, Texas; the Benghazi attacks (On the soil of the American Consulate in Libya, which is American soil.), the Boston Marathon and quite recently in San Bernardino, California and Orlando, Florida. There have been smaller, isolated incidents but all of these modern ones happened between 2009 and 2015. I have not included the attacks on the USS Cole in 2000 or our consulates in Beirut in 1984, 1998 and Kenya in 1998. For a list of consulate attacks see the endnote.[39]

Let's see if some modern presidents understood some small aspect of the need for covenant understanding in practice. All are excerpted.

John F. Kennedy: " . . .In the General Congress assembled they appealed the rectitude of their intentions to the Supreme Judge of the world, and 'with firm reliance on the protection of Divine Providence' they mutually pledged *(that means to covenant)* their lives, their fortunes, and their most sacred honor. During the deliberations in the Constitutional Convention they were called to daily prayers, with the reminder in sacred Scripture it is written that 'except the Lord build the house, they labor in vain that build It,' and they were warned that without the concurring aid of Providence they would succeed in the political building 'no better than the builders of Babel' . . . Conscious of our continuing need to bring our actions under the searching light of Divine Judgment, the Congress of the United States by joint resolution approved the seventeenth day of April 1952 provided that 'The President shall set aside and proclaim a suitable day each year, other than a Sunday' . . . Let us all pray, inviting as many as may be visitors in our country to join us in our prayers, each according to his own custom and faith . . . For Divine guidance in our efforts to lead our children in the ways of truth; . . . and to the end they may be at their best in their day as the responsible trustees of the great heritage which has come to us from those who went before us; . . .in awareness that this Nation under God has achieved its great service to mankind. . . Recognizing our own shortcomings may we be granted forgiveness and cleansing, that God shall bless us and be gracious unto us, and cause His face to shine upon us as we stand everyone of us on this day in His Presence. . . DONE at the City of Washington this twenty-eighth day of September in the year of our Lord nineteen hundred and sixty-one, and of the Independence of the United States of America the one hundred and eighty-sixth."[40] Italics are mine.

Jimmy Carter in 1980: ". . . Our forebears, drawing from a faith in the people rooted in a firm faith in God, launched this grand experiment in responsible self-government. . . . Recognizing our need for prayer, the Congress, by Joint Resolution, approved April 17, 1952 (36 U.S.C. 169h; 66 Stat.64), has called upon the President to set aside a suitable day each year as a National Day of Prayer. . . I further ask that all who so desire make this a Day of Fast as well. On that day, I ask Americans to join me in thanksgiving to God for His blessings and in earnest prayer to Him for His protection in the year ahead. . . ."[41]

George H. W. Bush: "While we owe constant praise to Almighty God, we Americans have added cause for thanksgiving . . . This is because, as Alexander Hamilton once noted, 'the Sacred Rights of Mankind are not to be rummaged for among old parchments or musty records. They are written, as with a sunbeam, in the whole volume of human nature, by the Hand of the Divinity itself, and can never be erased or obscured by mortal power.' Almighty God has granted each one of us free will and inscribed in our hearts the unalienable dignity and worth that come from being made in His image. Because our dignity and freedom are gifts of our Creator, we have a duty to cherish them, always using the latter to choose life and goodness. . . As an elevation of the soul's eyes to Heaven, prayer helps us to distinguish between liberty and license— to recognize that which is the grateful exercise of free will and that which is its corruption. Through prayer, we turn our hearts toward their real home and, in so doing, gain a sense of proper direction and higher purpose. Faith and prayer are as important to guiding the conduct of nations as they are to individuals. We Americans, Abraham Lincoln once wrote, 'have been the recipients of the choicest bounties of heaven.' A nation so richly blessed has equally great responsibilities. Indeed, we have recently been reminded that 'much will be asked of those to whom much has been given.' The crucible of war has once again tested our Nation's character, and it has shown us both the need for and the power of prayer. On this National Day of Prayer, let us acknowledge with heartfelt remorse the many times we have failed to appreciate the Lord's gifts and to obey His Commandments. *(His commandments are other words for the Bible, the book the covenant is written in.)* Giving humble thanks for His mercy, let us vow *(Vow is an oath and an oath is a covenant.)* to fulfill not only our responsibilities but also our potential as one Nation under God. Most important, let us make our prayers pleasing to Him by the regular practice of public and private virtue and by genuine renewal of America's moral heritage. As Scripture says, 'righteousness exalteth a nation, but sin is a reproach to any people.' In Witness Whereof, I have hereunto set my hand this 25th day of April, in the year of our Lord nineteen hundred and ninety-one, and of the Independence of the United States of America the two hundred and fifteenth. George Bush."[42] (Italics are mine.)

Look at **George W. Bush's Proclamation** after September 11, 2001: "Since our Nation's founding, Americans have turned to prayer for inspiration, strength, and guidance. In times of trial, we ask God for wisdom, courage, direction and comfort. We offer thanks for the countless blessings God has provided. And we thank God for sanctifying every human life by creating each of us in His image. As we observe this National Day of Prayer, we call upon the Almighty to continue to bless America and her people. . . ."[43]

And again in 2006: "Throughout our Nation's history, our citizens have prayed and come together before God to offer Him gratitude, reflect on His will, seek His aid, and respond to His grace. On this National Day of Prayer, we thank God for His many blessings and His care of our country. God has greatly blessed the American people, and in 1789, George Washington proclaimed: 'It is the duty of all nations to acknowledge the Providence of Almighty God, to obey His will, to be grateful for His benefits, and to humbly implore His protection and favor.' Americans remain a prayerful and thankful people. . . . Through prayer, our faith is strengthened, our hearts are humbled, and our lives are transformed. May our Nation always have the humility to trust in the goodness of God's plans. The Congress, by Public Law 100-307, as amended, has called on our Nation to reaffirm the role of prayer in our culture and to respect the freedom of religion by recognizing each year a 'National Day of Prayer.' . . . I ask the citizens of our Nation to give thanks, each according to his or her own faith, for the freedoms and blessings we have received and for God's continued guidance and protection. I urge all Americans to join in observing this day with appropriate programs, ceremonies, and activities. In Witness Whereof, I have hereunto set my hand this third day of May, in the year of our Lord two thousand six, and of the Independence of the United States of America the two hundred and thirtieth. George W. Bush."[44]

The last two proclamations do not offer repentance for national sin or our transgressions— as other presidents have done— both after war, before war, or in peacetime. I am sorry to say not all of our modern presidents have understood this need. While prayer is a vehicle for maintaining covenant, repentance is the method for its maintenance because repentance sustains the covenant when we neglect it. It has only gotten worse among our nation in that respect. I found nowhere within recent proclamations where repentance or an understanding of national sin was made. The last such proclamation with the word "sin" in it was quoting Abraham

Lincoln: " 'it behooves us then to humble ourselves before the offended Power, to confess our national sins and pray for clemency and forgiveness' for any injustice we perceive in our midst." Bill Clinton quoted Abraham Lincoln, adding his own eight words to end the sentence. He did this in 1995, the year of the Oklahoma bombings.[45]

Besides presidents, and our first president in particular, the American people have covenanted as well as committed this nation to God. This is a part of their covenant responsibilities. The religiously covenanted people in this country have not gone or left our land. We are still here covenanting with God, sharing Jesus and committing this nation to God. We are now indigenous and have been active in this nation continuing the practice of liberty under Jesus Christ. Our liberties within the Bill of Rights were placed there by the religious and all others who love liberty. The covenanted people should not have to sue in order to keep their rights. OUR ancestors fought long and hard for them. This tradition is not based upon color or race— the blood of Jesus knows no color or race— it is activated by faith and thus covenant is produced. If you worship the same God as the founders did, and you are a citizen of this country, then men like Washington are your ancestors, based upon the blood of Jesus. This is your covenant. This is how Christianity is displayed in a nation. Those not of the original covenant people maintain a secular covenant with them. When you attack one party of the covenant, you attack all parties. This is not something alien in practice or understanding to the people first affected by the Federal government.

When Washington was inaugurated in New York City, a newspaper article ran this:

> "As we believe in an overruling Providence and feel our constant dependence upon God for every blessing, so it is undoubtedly our duty to acknowledge him in all our ways and commit our concerns to his protection and mercy. The ancient civilized heathen, from the mere dictates of reason, were uniformly excited to this; and we find from their writings that they engaged in no important business, especially what related to the welfare of a nation, without

a solemn appeal to Heaven. How much more becoming and necessary is such a conduct in Christians, who believe not only in the light of nature, but are blessed with a divine revelation which has taught them more of God and of their obligations to worship him than by their reason they ever could have investigated! It has been the wish of many pious persons in our land that at the framing of our new Constitution a solemn and particular appeal to Heaven had been made; and they have no doubt but Congress will soon call upon the whole nation to set apart a day for fasting and prayer for the express purpose of invoking the blessing of Heaven on our new Government. But this, in consequence of the distance of some of the States, cannot immediately take place: in the meanwhile, the inhabitants of the city are favored with the opportunity of being present on the very day on which the Constitution will be fully organized, and have it thus in their power to accommodate their devotions exactly to the important season. In this view, it gave universal satisfaction to hear it announced last Sunday from the pulpits of our churches that, on the morning of the day on which our illustrious President will be invested with his office, the bells will ring at nine o'clock, when the people may go up and in a solemn manner commit the new Government, with its important train of consequences, to the holy protection and blessing of the Most High. An early hour is prudently fixed for this peculiar act of devotion, and it is designed wholly for prayer: it will not detain the citizens very long, or interfere with any of the other public business of the day. It is supposed Congress will adopt religious solemnities by fervent prayer with their chaplains, in the Federal Hall, when the President takes his oath of office; but the people feel a common interest in this great transaction, and whether they approve of the Constitution as it now stands, or wish that alterations may be made, it is equally their concern and duty to leave the cause with God and refer the issue to his gracious providence. In doing this, the inauguration of our President and the commencement of our national character will be introduced with the auspices of religion, and our enlightened rulers and people will bear a consistent part in a business which involves the weal or woe of themselves and posterity (*well-being, prosperity and happiness; or misery, affliction and mournfulness*). I have heard that the notification respecting this hour of prayer was made in almost all the churches of the city, and that some of those who omitted the publication intend, notwithstanding, to join in that duty; and, indeed, considering the singular circumstances of the day, which in many respects exceed any thing recorded in ancient or modern history, it cannot be supposed that the serious and pious of any denomination will hesitate in going up to their respective churches and uniting at the throne of grace with proper prayers and supplications on this occasion. 'I was glad when they said unto me, Let us go into the house of the Lord.' — (David)"[46] (Italics are mine.)

We know after this date in time an "alteration" called the Bill of Rights was made to the Constitution. The first clause enunciates our freedom of religion and freedom to speak to those issues concerning everything religion affects. It also enunciates freedom of speech to the press. We also know Congress did ask for a day of prayer and thanksgiving:

"Mr. Boudinot said, he could not think of letting the session pass over without offering an opportunity to all the citizens of the United States of joining, with one voice, in returning to Almighty God their sincere thanks for the many blessings he had poured down upon them. With that view, therefore, he would move the following resolution: — *Resolved*, That a joint committee of both Houses be directed to wait upon the President of the United States, to request that he recommend to the people of the United States a day of public thanksgiving and prayer, to be observed by acknowledging, with grateful hearts, the many signal favors of Almighty God, especially by affording them an opportunity peaceably to establish a Constitution of government for their safety and happiness."[47]

There seems to be a tenet among those espousing Jefferson's hardliner argument that asking for covenant protection and fulfillment under our compact is illegal. Nothing could be further from the truth. The covenant fulfillment I speak of concern days of thanksgiving and prayers. After Rep. Boudinot (NJ) asked for the resolution there was a disagreement from those representing South Carolina that asking for a prayer of thanksgiving would be a "mimicking of European customs" and that the people should not be directed to do anything, especially since they did not know how the Constitution would affect them (my words). That's an attitude I wish we saw today from Congress! Rep. Tucker (SC) also made the correct legal argument that matters of religion should be left to the states to decide.[48] That's an attitude I wish the Supreme Court and Congress had today!

> How was the problem resolved? "Mr. Sherman justified the practice of thanksgiving, on any signal event, not only as a laudable one in itself, but as warranted by a number of precedents in holy writ: for instance, the solemn thanksgivings and rejoicings which took place in the time of Solomon, after the building of the temple, was a case in point. This example he thought, worthy of Christian imitation on the present occasion; and he would agree with the gentlemen who moved the resolution. Mr. Boudinot quoted further precedents from the practice of the late Congress; and hoped the motion would meet a ready acquiescence. The question was now put on the resolution, and it was carried in the affirmative."[49]

This is quite interesting, because those refusing to acknowledge covenant rights to the religious under the guise of the hardliner's fear that church and state are somehow violating the Constitution if the "state" acknowledges its own covenant, would have lost the argument early on by the invocation of covenant! If you read the entire dialog, (see the Library of Congress sourced endnote) the objection was not to prayer or the religious praying, it was in remaining "colorblind" (my words), and not trampling the covenant the Federal government had to the states. This took place *before* the Bill of Rights was compacted through ratification. Although events were moving rapidly and the First Amendment had been debated. In other words, this was based solely on the understanding inherent in the Declaration and the Constitution. In addition, we do not know exactly what the vote tally was, but it had to be by simple majority. Why would Rep. Sherman (CT) justify Solomon's dedication of the Jewish Temple of antiquity with prayers of thanksgiving for the inauguration of the Constitution and our Federal government if no understanding of covenant existed? This was not by simple example, this was a legal argument in a debate over Constitutional law. Solomon was dedicating more than the Temple: He was invoking the covenant made to Moses, and to David, and then down to the Jewish people. I realize many wish these events did not take place, but they did.

This surface argument which denies the religious their rights of covenant is just that; it is on the surface. The argument I make is at the very foundations of the compacting agreement and at the very bedrock our covenant stands on. This one example shows it was the practice of covenant understanding, even to members of Congress, that was paramount. Even without knowing the tally of the majority votes, those who brought up the desire for debate did so with covenant arguments. The first by Rep. Burke (SC) was seeking a realized harmony (covenant) between the political parties—probably those signing the Constitution and those not signing—since he mentions the mockery of European parties at war to sing "te deum" even though victory meant one party's defeat. The other arguments for covenant by Rep. Tucker (SC) were in maintaining the Federal government's covenant for the people by not seeming to force the people to do or not do a thing. The third argument was in not seeming to force or trample on the covenant the Federal government had with the states in violating their authority in religious matters. The states were not bound by the Bill of Rights, the Federal government was the entity that was bound. These are all secular covenant arguments, even the one involving religion. Which argument won the day? The one involving the secular rights of the religious to covenant all on their own, without states' authority. Why? Because it is the first of our inalienable rights, even an atheist's inalienable right. And it trumps all others because it is neither given by government, nor taken by government, nor taken away by man.

Washington complied with the request from both Houses. He did more; he affirmed his dedication of this nation and its Constitution to God when he made an October 3, 1789, Thanksgiving Proclamation. Here are excerpts:

"Whereas it is the duty of all nations to acknowledge the providence of Almighty God, to obey his will, to be grateful for his benefits, and humbly to implore his protection and favor; . . . .to be devoted by the people of these States to the service of that great and glorious Being who is the beneficent Author of all the good that was, that is or that will be— that we may then all unite in rendering unto him our sincere and humble thanks— for his kind care and protection . . . for the peaceable and rational manner in which we have been enabled to establish constitutions of government for our safety and happiness, and particularly the national One now lately instituted— for the civil and religious liberty with which we are blessed; . . . . And, also, that we may then unite in most humbly offering our prayers and supplications to the great Lord and Ruler of Nations, and beseech him to pardon our national and other transgressions— to enable us all, whether in public or private stations, to perform our several and relative duties properly and punctually— to render our national government a blessing to all the people, by constantly being a Government of wise, just, and constitutional laws, discreetly and faithfully executed and obeyed— to protect and guide all Sovereigns and Nations (especially such as have shewn kindness to us) and to bless them with good governments, peace, and concord— To promote the knowledge and practice of true religion and virtue, and the increase of science among them and us— and generally to grant unto all Mankind such a degree of temporal prosperity as he alone knows to be best. . . Go. Washington."[50]

I find it illuminating Washington included "all Mankind" in this proclamation. Once the news got out, this Thanksgiving Day was "widely celebrated" by our nation. Feasting and celebrating wasn't the only thing that was done. It also became a time for the churches to feed the poor.[51]

Getting back to the inauguration events in April, thousands participated all along the route Washington took to get to New York. Some inauguration accounts from eye witnesses have survived. This note was said to arrive in Philadelphia from New York after the events of the inauguration. (Please see the endnote.)

"New York, May 3, 1789: I was extremely anxious to arrive here, in order to be present at the meeting of the president and the two houses. That even, however, did not take place till Thursday last, when the President was qualified in the open gallery of the Congress House in the sight of many thousand people. The scene was solemn and awful, beyond description. It would seem extraordinary that the administration of an oath— a ceremony so very common & familiar— should, in so great a degree, excite the public curiosity. But the circumstance of his election— the impression of his past services— the concourse of spectators— the devout fervency with which he repeated the oath— the reverential manner in which he bowed down & kissed the sacred volume— (*in other words, the Bible*) all these conspired to render it one of the most august and interesting spectacles ever exhibited on this globe. It seemed from the number of witnesses, to be a solemn appeal to heaven and earth at once. Upon the subject of this great and good man, I may, perhaps, be an enthusiast; I confess, that I was under an awful and religious persuasion, that the gracious Ruler of the universe was looking down, at that moment, with peculiar complacency on an act, which to a part of his creatures was so very important. Under this impression, when the

Chancellor pronounced, in a very feeling manner, "long live George Washington," my sensibility was wound up to such a pitch, that I could do no more than wave my hat with the rest, without the power of joining in the repeated acclamations which rent the air."[52] (Italics are mine.)

Let me ask this question, Why was an oath a "common and familiar" ceremony? Oaths were covenantal and they were regarded as sacred in keeping them. They were made constantly for business, as well as minor agreements. They had been handed down the custom from father to son, from mother to daughter. They were frequently done in England and other countries as well.[53] I have already quoted excerpts from Washington's inaugural speech. He invites the blessing of God, which you cannot do unless there is an expected understanding of covenant already in place. Just to confirm again, what I have already shown, here is another excerpt from Washington's closing comments:

"Having thus imported to you my sentiments, as they have been awakened by the occasion which brings us together, I shall take my present leave; but not without resorting once more to the benign parent of the human race, in humble supplication that since he has been pleased to favour the American people, with opportunities for deliberating in perfect tranquility, and dispositions for deciding with unparallelled unanimity on a form of Government, for the security of their Union, and the advancement of their happiness; so his divine blessing may be equally *conspicuous* in the enlarged views, the temperate consultations, and the wise measures on which the success of this Government must depend."[54] (Italics are NOT mine.)

There is the ceremony and divine celebration of the President of the United States taking his oath of office. These directions were explicitly written (excerpted):

"The Committees of both Houses of Congress, appointed to take order for conducting the ceremonial of the formal reception, etc. of the President of the United States, on the Thursday next, have agreed to the following order thereon, viz. . . . Both Houses having resolved to accompany the President after he shall have taken the Oath, to St. Paul's Chapel, to hear divine service, to be performed by the Chaplain of Congress, that the following order of procession be observed, viz. The door-keeper and messenger of the House of Representatives. The Clerk of the House. The Representatives. The Speaker. The President, with the Vice-President at his left hand. The Senators. The Secretary of the Senate. The door-keeper, and messenger of the Senate. That a Pew be reserved for the President - Vice President- Speaker of the House of Representatives, and the Committees; and that pews be also reserved sufficient for the reception of the Senators and Representatives. That after divine service shall be performed, the President be received at the door of the Church, by the Committees, and by them attended in carriages to his residence."[55]

It is obvious they had no problems or quandaries with writing a formal visit to a church as part of the federal government's function, among its first functions. This function kept covenant.

The services that day weren't solely divine. They had festivities that evening. But before that, Washington dedicates this nation to God Almighty on April 30, 1789. There is a comparison in Solomon's dedication of Israel when the Temple was dedicated. Solomon gathers the leaders in prayer and he speaks of God's hand on the providence of the nation and he prays for the future generations if or when they turn from God. Washington does the same thing, only in different words. We have already read it. This is on the consecration ground or the dedication ground. This was not done for America only by the Puritans. It was done by the newly minted government—Constitutionally federated government—in New York on April 30, 1789. Here are excerpts of Washington's words, similar in concept to what Solomon did:

"Such being the impressions under which I have, in obedience to the public summons, repaired to the present station, *it would be peculiarly improper to omit in this first official act my fervent supplications to that Almighty Being who rules over the universe, who presides in the councils of nations, and whose providential aids can supply every human defect, that His benediction may consecrate to the liberties and happiness of the people of the United States a Government instituted by themselves for these essential purposes, and may enable every instrument employed in its administration to execute with success the functions allotted to his charge.* In tendering this homage to the Great Author of every public and private good, I assure myself that it expresses your sentiments not less than my own, nor those of my fellow-citizens at large less than either. *No people can be bound* to acknowledge and adore the Invisible Hand which conducts the affairs of men more than those of the United States. *Every step* by which they have advanced to the character of an independent nation seems to have been distinguished *by some token of providential agency;* and in the important revolution just accomplished *in the system of their united government* the tranquil deliberations and voluntary consent of so many distinct communities from which the event has resulted can not be compared with the means by which most governments have been established *without some return of pious gratitude, along with an humble anticipation of the future blessings which the past seem to presage.* These reflections, arising out of the present crisis, have forced themselves too strongly on my mind to be suppressed."[56] (Italicized by me to highlight thought.)

God will neither bless nor consecrate His blessings on something which has not been given to Him as an offering in the first place. In order to be a charge or receive the "charge" of something and expect future blessings, it has to be dedicated. Since the American people are the government, they did it in services all over New York. I'm sure New York wasn't the only locale for prayer of that nature, but New York is the account that we have here. It doesn't matter whether Washington knew of those services.

Whether he did or not, he calls the people and the government and the workings within the government God's "charge." I also submit these excerpts of the same inaugural address for your review. Washington now alludes to the secular/non-sectarian covenant or agreement between the people themselves and mentions the "smiles of Heaven" over it. In excerpted fashion:

"By the article establishing the executive department . . . to recommend to your consideration such measures as he shall judge necessary and expedient. . . to substitute, in place of a recommendation of particular measures, the tribute that is due to the talents, the rectitude, and the patriotism which adorn the characters selected to devise and adopt them. In these honorable qualifications I behold the surest pledges *(Oaths in covenant; in other words, guarantees.)* that as on one side no local prejudices or attachments, no separate views nor party animosities, will misdirect the comprehensive and equal eye which ought to watch over this great assemblage of communities and interests, so, *on another, that the foundation of our national policy will be laid in the pure and immutable principles of private morality,* and the preeminence of free government be exemplified by all the attributes which can win the affections of . . . the world. . . . since there is no truth more thoroughly established . . . . *between virtue and happiness; between duty and advantage; between the genuine maxims of an honest and magnanimous policy and the solid rewards of public prosperity and felicity; since we ought to be no less persuaded that the propitious smiles of Heaven can never be expected on a nation that disregards the eternal rules of order and right which Heaven itself has ordained;* and since the **preservation of the sacred fire of liberty and the destiny of the republican model of government** are justly considered, perhaps, as deeply, as finally, **staked on the experiment entrusted to the hands of the American people.**"[57] (Italicized and highlighted to reflect concept, in parentheses mine by way of explanation.)

Since "Heaven" cannot be considered to oversee a covenant among the people when the people are not in covenant to begin with and are not in covenant with God firstly, I submit to you it was common practice as well as knowledge this "experiment" was committed to God. It was also common knowledge that "an equal eye" in the Federal government would watch over the people. In other words, the Federal government would remain non-sectarian in its application of its duty. It would remain in covenant to the people, not party or faction.

John Adams, as president of the Senate wrote to congratulate Washington and assure him of the Senate's desire to work for the good of the nation. Washington's response was expected, but also interesting. In it he dedicates the organization to God:

> " . . . that Heaven, which has done so much for our infant Nation will not withdraw its Providential influence before our political felicity shall have been completed; and in a conviction, that the Senate will at all times co-operate in every measure, which may tend to promote the welfare of this confederated Republic. Thus supported by a firm trust in the great Arbiter of the Universe, aided by the collected wisdom of the Union, and *imploring the Divine benediction on our joint exertions in the service of our Country*, I readily engage with you in the arduous, but pleasing, task, of attempting to make a Nation happy. Go: Washington."[58] (Italicized by me.)

As mentioned, we have the practice of oath-taking as well as the practice of taking the oath of "so help me God" in court. Oath-taking is covenant, from a biblical perspective, and this is the perspective which it originates from in this country. I did not say you could not find avenues of English as well as other European descent for sources other than the biblical one. The English formerly took oaths for everything. I refer to the original history from the Bible for the Puritans, and then other Christians after them follow suit for our country. This perspective for Americans predominates all others.

Genesis 22:15-18, Old Testament: "And the angel of the LORD called unto Abraham out of heaven the second time, and said, 'By Myself have I sworn, saith the LORD, for because thou hast done this thing, and hast not withheld thy son, thine only son: that in blessing I will bless thee, and in multiplying I will multiply thy seed as the stars of the heaven, and as the sand which is upon the sea shore; and thy seed shall possess the gate of his enemies; And in thy seed shall the nations of the earth be blessed; because thou hast obeyed My voice." From the New Testament in Hebrews 6:13, 14: "For when God made promise to Abraham, because He could swear by no greater, He sware by Himself, saying, 'Surely blessing I will bless thee, and multiplying I will multiply thee.' "

Oath-taking is covenant, from our earliest Puritan settlers. The practice and understanding for a solemn religious observance of covenant continued in this country. It continued straight through to post Bill of Rights, and much further. From Washington in his farewell address to the nation in 1796: "Let it simply be asked: Where is the security for property, for reputation, for life, if the sense of religious obligation desert the oaths which are the instruments of investigation in courts of justice?"[59]

John Adams made a similar observation when he wrote an October 11, 1798, letter to the officers of the First Brigade of the Third Division of the Militia of Massachusetts:

> "An address from the officers commanding two thousand eight hundred men, consisting of such substantial citizens as are able and willing at their own expense completely to arm and clothe themselves in handsome uniforms, does honor to that division of the militia which has done so much honor to its country. *Oaths in this country are as yet universally considered as sacred obligations.* That which you have taken and so solemnly repeated on that venerable spot, is an ample pledge of your sincerity and devotion to your country and its government."[60] (Italicized by me.)

Remember the word *pledge* was a sign of the covenant or agreement; i.e., oath, you were taking. When you invoke or invite God into the oath or covenant you are making, the deal is sealed, since you can swear by no higher authority. Its understanding has continued in this country even to the present day. Did you know we entered into a covenant with Japan by inviting God into the equation in 1945? Here is the exact quote of General MacArthur accepting the surrender of the Japanese on September 2, 1945:

> "I now invite the representatives of the Emperor of Japan and the Japanese Government and the Japanese Imperial General Headquarters to sign the Instrument of Surrender at the places indicated. Let us pray that peace be now restored to the world and that *God will preserve it always.* These proceedings are closed."[61] (Italicized by me.)

I can hear some say, "Oh, that's ridiculous. He was just saying that. He was just expressing a wish." The announcer in the preceding end-noted video clip says so, but you never hear MacArthur say that. If that were the case, he would have said, "It is my wish that God. . ." Your opinion is what it is, but I can tell you clearly the God of the Bible does not view it thus. I will ask this: Are we at peace with Japan? It is almost 70 years to the day, as I am writing this we are still at peace.

In this country, whenever an oath was taken, God was frequently brought into the sentence. How do I know? I swore in so many people I cannot count all of them. Very few of them 'affirmed' to tell the truth. In fact, I can only remember three. There may have been more, but not too many more. You might say, "Oh, you worked in some backwater Podunk." No, I worked in the New York City metropolitan area. Back in the 1980s we never thought of refusing to bring God into the equation: not the lawyers or the judges or even the witnesses. In fact, as I have already stated and shown, it was the Christian religious of various persuasions who refused to mention God's name in an oath because they felt it was sin. This is in part because of Jesus' words in the New Testament, housed within a portion of Scripture which is viewed as Him affirming a New Covenant (Matthew 5-7) with those who believe:

> "Again, you have heard that it was said to an older generation, 'Do not break an oath, but fulfill your vows to the Lord.' But I say to you, do not take oaths at all— not

by heaven, because it is the throne of God, not by earth, because it is his footstool, and not by Jerusalem, because it is the city of the great King. Do not take an oath by your head, because you are not able to make one hair white or black. Let your word be 'Yes, yes' or 'No, no.' More than this is from the evil one" (Matthew 5:33-37; NET Bible®).

The birthing of secularized non-sectarian documents is because these religious were so adamant about not putting God's name into a covenant or any oath. Yet they still made the agreements (or covenants). They just refused to place God's name within it. They did invite Him into their lives, even into everything they did. (See the multitude of previous end-notes on this subject where these documents are mentioned in previous segments of this work.)

ENDNOTES

1   Daniel Dorchester, D.D. "Christianity in the United States From the First Settlement Down to the Present Time." New York: Phillips & Hunt, Cincinnati: Cranston & Stowe. (1888) 262. In the public domain.

2   Ibid.

3   Ibid."Christianity in the United States. . . "

4   Ibid.

5   Ibid. 263; See the section on Future Reading where a collection by Ellis Sandoz, "Political Sermons of the American Founding Era, Vols. 1 & 2;" is listed and can be seen <http://oll.libertyfund.org/groups/54> © Liberty Fund, Inc., 2004-2016; scroll down the page to the titled work and click on the link.

6   Ellis Sandoz, "Political Sermons of the American Founding Era: 1730-1805, 2 Vols., Foreword by Ellis Sandoz (2nd. ed. Indianapolis:Liberty Fund, 1998). Vol. 1. May 31, 2015, available <http://oll.libertyfund.org/titles/816> or <http://oll.libertyfund.org/groups/54> © Liberty Fund, Inc., 2004-2015, scroll down the page to the titled work.

7   Ibid., scroll down the page to the titled sermon.

8   Ibid., scroll down the page to the titled sermon.

9 Daniel Dorchester, D.D. "Christianity in the United States From the First Settlement Down to the Present Time." New York: Phillips & Hunt, Cincinnati: Cranston & Stowe. (1888) 262-263. In the public domain.

10 Ibid., 263

11 Ibid., 268

12 Ibid., 267

13 Benjamin Franklin Morris. "Christian Life and Character of the Civil Institutions of the United States, Developed in the Official and Historical Annals of the Republic." (Introduction by Byron Sunderland, Washington, D.C., April 16, 1863) Philadelphia: George W. Childs, 628 & 630 Chestnut St., Cincinnati: Rickey & Carroll, 1864. 421-423. In the public domain.

14 Ibid., 410

15 Ibid., 391

16 Ibid.

17 Ibid., "Christian Life and Character. . ." 392

18 Ibid., 393

19 Ibid., 394

20 Ibid., 395

21 Ibid., "Christian Life and Character. . ." 396

22 Ibid.

23 Lancaster, Daniel. 1845 "Proprietary, Civil, Literary, Ecclesiastical, Biographical, Genealogical, and Miscellaneous History, from the First Settlement to the Present Time; Including What is Now Gilford, To The Time It Was Disannexed," Gilmanton: Printed by Alfred Prescott. 49. It is now in the public domain but can be seen in pdf through New Hampshire State's Archive. Archive accessed 1/28/16.

24 Benjamin Franklin Morris. "Christian Life and Character of the Civil Institutions of the United States, Developed in the Official and Historical Annals of the Republic." (Introduction by Byron Sunderland, Washington, D.C., April 16, 1863) Philadelphia: George W. Childs, 628 & 630 Chestnut St., Cincinnati: Rickey & Carroll, 1864. 401-402. In the public domain.

25 Ibid., 402

26 Ibid., "Christian Life and Character. . ." 402-406; see Chapter 17

27 Lancaster, Daniel. 1845 "Proprietary, Civil, Literary, Ecclesiastical, Biographical, Genealogical, and Miscellaneous History, from the First Settlement to the Present Time; Including What is Now Gilford, To The Time It Was Disannexed," Gilmanton: Printed

by Alfred Prescott. 85. It is now in the public domain but can be seen in pdf through New Hampshire State's Archive. Archive accessed 1/28/16.

28   Ibid. "Christian Life and Character. . ." 403-404

29   Gen. Marcus J. Wright. "Some Account of the Life and Services of William Blount: An Officer of the Revolutionary Army. . . ." Washington, D.C.: 1884. E. J. Gray Publisher. 129. In the public domain.

30   This reference does NOT document this. What I refer you to here is a sermon by Samuel Cooper, "A Sermon on the Day of the Commencement of the Constitution." (Boston 1780) In it Cooper makes mention of this fact by quoting Mr. Hartley of the British House of Commons for Hull. See Ellis Sandoz, "Political Sermons of the American Founding Era: 1730-1805, 2 Vols., Foreword by Ellis Sandoz (2nd. ed. Indianapolis:Liberty Fund, 1998). Vol. 1, © Liberty Fund, Inc., 2004-2015<http://oll.libertyfund.org/titles/816> or <http://oll.libertyfund.org/groups/54> scroll down to the titled work and click on the link, or go to 641-642, Accessed 3/15/16.

31   Lancaster, Daniel. 1845 "Proprietary, Civil, Literary, Ecclesiastical, Biographical, Genealogical, and Miscellaneous History, from the First Settlement to the Present Time; Including What is Now Gilford, To The Time It Was Disannexed," Gilmanton: Printed by Alfred Prescott. 34. It is now in the public domain but can be seen in pdf through New Hampshire State's Archive. Archive accessed 1/28/16.

32   Gen. Marcus J. Wright. "Some Account of the Life and Services of William Blount: An Officer of the Revolutionary Army. . . ." Washington, D.C.: 1884. E. J. Gray Publisher. 129. In the public domain.

33   John Quincy Adams, "An Oration Delivered Before the Inhabitants of the Town of Newburyport at Their Request on the Sixty-first Anniversary of the Declaration of Independence, July 4, 1837" (Entered according to an Act of Congress, in the year 1837, by Morse & Brewster, In the Clerk's office of the District court of the District of Massachusetts). 1, 6, 12, 13, 14 and 17. In the public domain.

34   <http://www.john-uebersax.com/plato/proclam.htm> site © 2011-12 by John S. Uebersax, site accessed 3/11/16. Scroll down the page to "1. Virginia, 1774"

35   Ibid., scroll down to the image of the first document and text, with the quotes by Washington and instruction of Mason.

36   Ibid., No.13; scroll down to the image of the document and text, also see the links. Public domain documents of this nature can be seen in LOC and National Archives, as well as other works of each president.

37   Benjamin Franklin Morris. "Christian Life and Character of the Civil Institutions of the United States, Developed in the Official and Historical Annals of the Republic."

(Introduction by Byron Sunderland, Washington, D.C., April 16, 1863) Philadelphia: George W. Childs, 628 & 630 Chestnut St., Cincinnati: Rickey & Carroll (1864) 549-550. In the public domain. See also page eight for the long list of original sources the author consulted.

38   Ibid., 550

39   <https://en.wikipedia.org/wiki/Attacks_on_U.S._diplomatic-facilities> accessed 2/5/16

40   John F. Kennedy: "Proclamation 3436-National Day of Prayer, 1961," September 28, 1961. Online by Gerhard Peters and John T. Woolley, The American Presidency Project. <http://www.presidency.ucsb.edu/ws/index.php?pid=24157> accessed 3/30/16

41   Jimmy Carter: "Proclamation 4795-National Day of Prayer, 1980," September 22, 1980. Online by Gerhard Peters and John T. Woolley, The American Presidency Project. <http://www.presidency.ucsb.edu/ws/index.php?pid=45102> accessed 3/30/16

42   George Bush: "Proclamation 6280 -National Day of Prayer, 1991," April 25, 1991. Online by Gerhard Peters and John T. Woolley, The American Presidency Project. <http://www.presidency.ucsb.edu/ws/index.php?pid=47294> accessed 3/30/16

43   George W. Bush: "Proclamation 7547 -National Day of Prayer, 2002," April 26, 2002. Online by Gerhard Peters and John T. Woolley, The American Presidency Project. <http://www.presidency.ucsb.edu/ws/index.php?pid=61843> accessed 3/30/16

44   George W. Bush: "Proclamation 8012 -National Day of Prayer, 2006," May 3, 2006. Online by Gerhard Peters and John T. Woolley, The American Presidency Project. <http://www.presidency.ucsb.edu/ws/index.php?pid=72885> accessed 3/30/16

45   William J. Clinton: "Proclamation 6777-National Day of Prayer, 1995," March 14, 1995. Online by Gerhard Peters and John T. Woolley, The American Presidency Project. <http://www.presidency.ucsb.edu/ws/index.php?pid=51103> accessed 3/30/16

46   Quoting "The Daily Advertiser, New York, Thursday, April 23, 1789," In Benjamin Franklin Morris. "Christian Life and Character of the Civil Institutions of the United States, Developed in the Official and Historical Annals of the Republic." (Introduction by Byron Sunderland, Washington, D.C., April 16, 1863) Philadelphia: George W. Childs, 628 & 630 Chestnut St., Cincinnati: Rickey & Carroll, (1864) 271-272. In the public domain. See also page eight for the long list of original sources the author consulted.

47   Ibid., "Christian Life and Character of the Civil Institutions of the United States, Developed in the Official and Historical Annals of the Republic." 274

48   "Annals of Congress, Debates and Proceedings, 1789-1824," in the "History of The Proceedings and Debates of The House of Representatives of the United States," by Joseph Gales, Senior, Washington: printed and published by Gales and Seaton 1834, Volume 1. 949-950, proceedings of September 25, 1789. It can be seen at the Library of Congress'

site by clicking on the 1st Volume and going to "image" 949 <http://memory.loc.gov/ammem/amlaw/lwaclink.html> accessed 3/30/16

49 Ibid., "Annals of Congress. . ."

50 Library of Congress and can be seen at their site <http://lcweb2.loc.gov/ammem/GW/gw004.html> site accessed 11/2/15. As well see Ibid., "Christian Life and Character. . ." 275

51 See the Hudson Institute's article "Thanksgiving, 1789," by Melanie Kirkpatrick, Senior Fellow at this © site <http://www.hudson.org/research/9385-thanksgiving-1789> accessed 13/30/16. They quote the "Papers of George Washington, compiled by the University of Virginia."

52 "The American Museum, (Philadelphia), for May 1789." This is an auction house showing the original. No one can guarantee this original will be available for public viewing at the publication of this book. But the auctioneer can be contacted for its provenance: Timothy Hughes, Rare & Early Newspapers. P.O. Box 3636, Williamsport, PA 17701, (570)326-1045 <http://www.rarenewspapers.com/list/us_presidents?page=2> See also in "The American Museum: or Repository of Ancient and Modern Fugitive Pieces, etc." Vol. 5; 506. Philadelphia: Mathew Carey 1789. This is also excerpted in "Christian Life and Character of the Civil Institutions of the United States, Developed in the Official and Historical Annals of the Republic." 272-273. See also a modern-day account by author Ron Chernow excerpted in the Smithsonian Magazine <http://www.smithsonianmag.com/history/george-washington-the-reluctant-president-49492/?no-ist> all sites accessed 3/12/16. See next endnote.

53 Benjamin Franklin Morris. "Christian Life and Character of the Civil Institutions of the United States, Developed in the Official and Historical Annals of the Republic." (Introduction by Byron Sunderland, Washington, D.C., April 16, 1863) Philadelphia: George W. Childs, 628 & 630 Chestnut St., Cincinnati: Rickey & Carroll, (1864) 271. In the public domain. See also page eight for the long list of original sources the author consulted. It has been said by many that the account of Washington saying "So help me God" could not have been audibly heard and that the addition of those words were not found until some 65 years later. This has been a point of controversy, since it was quite common for someone to repeat those words following an oath, unless one was a Christian dissenter. We have many eyewitness accounts of him with his hand on the book, and kissing the Book. I make no intent to solve the controversy. See also the freemason account here <http://www.stjohns1.org/portal/gwib> site © 2014 St. John's Lodge No. 1 AYM F&AM; accessed 3/12/16.

54   Ibid., "Christian Life and Character. . ." 274. The entirety may be seen at our National Archives site <http://www.archives.gov/exhibits/american_originals/inaugtxt.html> accessed 3/30/16

55   Library of Congress <http://memory.loc.gov/ammem/amlaw/lwaclink.html> go to Volume 1 and click on "image" 25. See also pictographs of the pew from the New York Public Library's Digital Collections at this copyrighted site <http://digitalcollections.nypl.org/items/510d47e2-8bc9-a3d9-e040-e00a18064a99> accessed 3/30/16

56   <http://avalon.law.yale.edu/18th_century/wash1.asp> Site © 2008 Lillian Goldman Law Library, New Haven, CT. Accessed 2/5/16.

57   Ibid.

58   <http://congressarchives.tumblr.com/post/86106625865/225th-anniversary-of-the-first-congress-well-be> This is handwritten, you will have to click the arrow forward to see the second page. Accessed 3/30/16. "The American Museum, (Philadelphia), for May 1789." This is an auction house showing an original publication of this account. The sales price is $2,875. See former note concerning the availability of the source and contact of Timothy Hughes, Rare & Early Newspapers. P.O. Box 3636, Williamsport, PA 17701, (570)326-1045

59   <http://avalon.law.yale.edu/18th_century/washing.asp> Site © 2008 Lillian Goldman Law Library, New Haven, CT. Accessed 2/5/16.

60   John Adams, The Works of John Adams, Second President of the United States: with a Life of the Author, Notes and Illustrations, by his Grandson Charles Francis Adams (Boston: Little, Brown and Co., 1856). Vol. 9. 229

61   <http://sageamericanhistory.net/worldwar2/docs/Macarthurtokyo.html> accessed 3/30/16

Chapter Fifteen

WE THE PEOPLE: IN COVENANT PRACTICE WITH COMMON SYMBOLS

There are so many various religious symbols and monuments erected because of the history surrounding the founding of this nation. They would have no religious content if the Christian-covenanted people and the covenant the people had to their God did not exist. Isn't that why "they" try to remove them? It is an effort, under the guise of public funds going to a religion— or a religion on public lands— to remove the covenant people and their remembrances. If that were not the case, these same people would be out in the streets protesting as well as suing to stop government funding abortions and Planned Parenthood. All Muslim religious interference in our public schools would meet with lawsuits. They rarely do. In fact, the "big three" news stations never let anyone know how often it happens. They strain at a gnat, but let the horror of our national debt choke and strangle every man, woman and child in the country. That debt, and the purposeful and willful "blind" eye media and many politicians have toward it is, depending upon whom you talk to, the ugliest example of covenant breaking of the Fed toward "We, The People," foisted upon us, our children and their great-great grandchildren. That *might* be the generation to see freedom if we start to change now. Alas, when you have one party addicted to our money, and administrations gleefully rejoicing and bathing in our money, with members from the opposite party as enablers, change is hard to come by.

It was not my purpose to write all the areas in which covenant by the Federal government against the People has been broken. If I were to do that, volumes would be written. In "Broken Federal Covenant" we will look at solutions to this mess. For now, let's look at the symbols the people erected to show the covenant they have with their God and one another. Like the example of the national debt, the successful attempts to remove the monuments are part of the proof of broken covenant. They are also proof of the sinister attempt to take away the true history of this nation. A people who do not know their true history, can never arrive at the truth of their liberty or their captivity.

Let's take a look at some of the tokens and remembrances and monuments which modern as well as previous generations left. Even before the Puritans sailed, thanks was given for the safe voyage, and dedication to the land was made by even the earliest settlers. This list is no where near all-encompassing. I have included a sampling of the whole. What we know as the earliest token (a cross) is recorded on a site as common as Wikipedia. It comes from original documentation within the Jamestown Colony that on April 29, 1607, upon landing at Cape Henry, the chaplain of the group, Robert Hunt offered a prayer and the group set up a cross near the site of the current Cape Henry Memorial. They then progressed up the bay to the general area we now call the Jamestown settlement. "The nine and twentieth day we set up a cross at Chesupioc Bay, and named the place Cape Henry," according to an account by George Percy.[1] The Memorial is within the Joint Expeditionary Base East, but is an isolated unit of Colonial National Historic Park.

Also in Virginia within Jamestown they have unearthed the foundations of the various church buildings, as well as a church tower.[2] In Yorktown you can see the Grace Episcopal Church.[3] This church is one of the oldest, historical churches in our nation. The original building is no longer standing, but they do have a written history which can be viewed to learn about historical events in the country and the church.[4]

The original building in New York, which was the site of our nation's first Capitol building and Washington's first inauguration is now gone. But they have made a monument called the Federal Hall National Memorial Building. It is on Wall Street, on the site of the first building. At some point in time Washington's inaugural Bible was on display there.[5] Also on display is the stone Washington stood onto take the oath. After that time the early government went over to St. Paul's Chapel to pray. In St. Paul's we have the ornamental design of the "Glory" over the altar. It is by Pierre L'Enfant, who designed Washington, D.C. The "Glory" tells the story of Mt. Sinai in clouds and lightning with the Hebrew word for "God" in a triangle, and the two tablets of the Law with the Ten Commandments. Then on the Broadway side of the chapel is an oak statue of St. Paul. Below the east window is a monument to General Richard Montgomery, who died at the Battle of Quebec during the American Revolutionary War.[6] Washington's pew is located at St. Paul's Chapel as well as a painting of the Great Seal of the United States.[7]

Our past historians and leaders had no problem with dedicating church pews and designing religious as well as national scenes interwoven with our history. It is a shame public schools cannot teach these truths to our children. After all, every time they are taught math and money, the money says, "In God We Trust." If that isn't "public" use, I don't know what is. There are Bible verses all over Federal Buildings and Monuments in Washington, D.C.

In the Library of Congress we have the Gutenberg Bible on display as well as the Giant Bible of Mainz (within the Great Hall East in the Thomas Jefferson Building).[8] Among many sayings, exhibits and quotes we have in the Great Hall on the second floor in the West Corridor John 1:5: "The light shineth in darkness, and the darkness comprehendeth it not."[9] In the North Corridor is Proverbs 4:7: "Wisdom is the principal thing; therefore get wisdom; and with all thy getting, get understanding."[10] In the Northeast Pavilion are quotes by many notables. Abraham Lincoln, The Gettysburg Address, Gettysburg, PA, November 19, 1863:

"That this nation, under God, shall have a new birth of freedom; that government of the people, by the people, for the people, shall not perish from the Earth."

Daniel Webster, Address at Charlestown, Massachusetts, June 17, 1843, at the dedication of the Bunker Hill Monument: "Thank God, I also am an American."[11]

Within the main reading room of the Library of Congress, inside the Jefferson Building are statues, each representing different fields of study. Representing religion are statues of Moses and St. Paul with the inscription of Micah 6:8: "What doth the Lord require of thee, but to do justly, and to love mercy, and to walk humbly with thy God?"[12] Above the figure of History is this inscription:

"One God, one law, one element, and one far-off Divine event, to which the whole creation moves." (Tennyson, In Memoriam)[13]

Above the figure of Science is this inscription from Psalm 19:1:

"The heavens declare the glory of God; and the firmament sheweth His handiwork."[14]

Inside the dome of the Main Reading Room is a round mural with twelve figures representing twelve countries which the artist (Blashfield) felt contributed to American civilization. One is religion and the country is Judea. On the pillar is inscribed in Hebrew "Thou shalt love thy neighbor as thyself." (Leviticus 19:18)[15]

Within the Members of Congress Reading Room (visit by permission only), along the center of the ceiling are panels representing some phase of achievement, human or Divine; the center panel is yellow and the subject is the creation of light: "The Divine Intelligence, sitting enthroned in the midst of space, utters the words, 'Let there be light' (Holy Bible, Genesis 1:3). The cherubs in the corners represent Physics, Metaphysics, Psychology and Theology."[16] Theology is the science and the study of God. On the panel representing "The Light of Truth (Blue), The Spirit of Truth tramples the Dragon of Ignorance and Falsehood and reaches to heaven for a ray of light with which to inflict the final wound. The cherubs hold the level, the plumb, the square, and the Bible, each considered an agent in the presence of Universal Law."[17]

Among various marble relief figures within the Supreme Court Building's architecture we have a marble relief of Moses holding the Tablets containing the Ten Commandments.[18] Each day the Court is in session an announcer calls for the opening of the Court and then ends the call with these words: "God save the United States and this Honorable Court."[19]

The Rotunda of the Capitol Building has several paintings depicting among other things, William Brewster (Pilgrim) with an open Bible printed "The New Testament of our Lord and Savior Jesus Christ," and on the Pilgrims' ship's sail, the words "God With Us" (printed on the left side) as they are praying on the Speedwell.[20] There is also a painting of the Baptism of Pocahontas.[21] In the chamber of the United States House of Representatives, behind the House Speaker's rostrum are the words "In God We Trust."[22] There are 23 marble relief portraits over the gallery doors of the House Chamber and they depict "historical figures noted for their work in establishing the principles that underlie American law... the eleven profiles in the eastern half of the chamber face left and the eleven in the western half face right. The effect looks towards the full-face relief of Moses in the center of the north wall."[23] The Prayer Room, would, of course, contain an open Bible sitting on the altar, but behind it is a stained glass window showing Washington in prayer, with the words "Preserve me, O God, for in Thee do I put my trust" (Psalm 16:1).[24]

The floor of the Rotunda of the National Archives contained medallions and one for the Ten Commandments.[25] In the White House is an inscription with a quote by John Adams on the fireplace of the State Dining Room, "I pray Heaven to Bestow the Best of Blessings on THIS HOUSE and on All that shall hereafter Inhabit it. May none but Honest and Wise Men ever rule under this Roof."[26]

On the east face of the aluminum cap on top of the Washington Monument are the Latin words "Laus Deo," which translate to "Praise be to God." Inside the structure of the Monument are (roughly) 194 commemorative stones donated by states, cities and various individuals, groups (churches) and countries from around the world. Here are some of the sayings: "Holiness to the Lord; Search the Scriptures; The memory of the just is blessed; May Heaven to this Union continue its beneficence; In God We Trust; Train up a child in the way he should go, and when he is old, he will not depart from it," as well as a quote from Luke 17:6.[27]

The Jefferson Memorial has many sayings from Jefferson. On Panel Three, similarly done on other panels, are excerpts from Jefferson's writings: "God who gave us life gave us liberty. Can the liberties of a nation be secure when we have removed a conviction that these liberties are the gift of God? Indeed I tremble for my country when I reflect that God is just, that his justice cannot sleep forever. . ."[28]

The Liberty Bell in Philadelphia has Leviticus 25:10 displayed on it: "Proclaim liberty throughout the land, to all the inhabitants thereof."[29] Within Washington, D.C., at 17th and Constitution Avenue on the property of the Organization of American States building, is a deteriorating statute of the Prophet Daniel from the Old Testament with the inscription of "Liberty."[30] The building is partly funded by Congress (see previous endnote).

There are inscriptions on the Daughters of the American Revolution building and a quote from George Washington from the Constitutional Convention in 1787: "Let us raise a standard to which the wise and honest can repair. The event is in the hands of God." And Proverbs 22:28: "Remove not the ancient landmark which thy fathers have set."[31] Inscribed on the Great Seal of The United States, on the reverse side, above the "Eye of Providence" is the Latin, "Annuit Coeptis," and is translated as *He [God] has favored our undertaking.*[32] It can be seen in the Senate Chamber over the east doorway.[33]

Another example for a practice of covenant-keeping by the people is in song. Song is one expression of worship, thus one expression or practice of covenant-keeping. This nation has many songs evidencing that statement; but two well known ones are "America" (the first verse starts with "My country 'tis of thee. . .) and "The Star Spangled Banner." Written by the Rev. Samuel Francis Smith, the fourth verse of "America" has these words: "Our Fathers' God, to Thee, Author of liberty, to Thee we sing:

Long may our land be bright, With freedom's holy light; Protect us by Thy might, Great God, our King!" The story of how Francis Scott Key came upon the "The Star Spangled Banner" is an awesome one, and worthy of any student's study. The words to the last verse: "O! thus be it ever, when freemen shall stand, Between their lov'd home, and the war's desolation, Blest with vict'ry and peace, may the Heav'n rescued land, Praise the Power that hath made and preserv'd us a nation! Then conquer we must, when our cause it is just, And this be our motto— 'In God is our Trust;' And the star-spangled banner in triumph shall wave, O'er the land of the free and the home of the brave!"

The statehouses have even more mentions of the religious founding of this nation. The successful revision to remove the religious heritage from our nation within the states' symbols, unfortunately, can be seen when a photo was taken of the Pennsylvania Supreme Court. They had published a brochure with the justices in front of Moses and the Ten Commandments mural which is right behind the bench. The *only* item purposely blurred in the photo are the **words** of the *Bible— the Ten Commandments themselves.*[34] Many would try to argue symbols revealing the Christian as well as Jewish connection to the founding of this country is somehow a violation of the First Amendment. If this country were founded on Buddhist, Hindu or some other religion, then you could have a debate. But it was founded on Christian as well as Jewish principles. Any modern symbol to reveal this history is not and should not be decided as a violation. The only reason to make it such is bias and prejudice. Every generation has a right to celebrate its history.

Several state mottos, some in Latin reference God. Other states have Christian symbols. Many states make reference to moral integrity, whether the source is Christian or otherwise. In alphabetical order (this list is not all-encompassing): One of Alabama's symbols is the State's Bible.[35]Arizona's State Motto is "Ditat Deus." Translated it means "God Enriches."[36] Colorado's motto in Latin is "Nil sine Numine," which translated* means "Nothing without Providence."[37] Connecticut's State Motto in Latin is "Qui Transtulit Sustinet," or "He Who Transplanted Still Sustains."[38] The motto for the State of Florida, as well as within its seal (and on license plates, if requested) is "In God We Trust."[39] Georgia's

State Creed is quite interesting. It upholds many honorable principles, including religious ones and applies the "Golden Rule" in action and by name.[40]

Hawaii's Liberty Bell is an exact replica of our National Liberty Bell. The official motto of the state, in Hawaiian is Ua Mau ke Ea o ka ʻĀina i ka Pono. Translated it means, "The life of the land is perpetuated in righteousness."[41] Maryland is one of the few states in the United States to have a dual-sided official seal. The reverse side is what is used by the state in its official capacity. Among images and the State Motto are the Latin words, "Scuto bonae voluntatis tuae cornasti noss." Translated it means, "With favor wilt thou encompass us as a shield." The Maryland State Flag bears the colors and coat of arms of both the Calvert and Crossland families who originally founded the state. The red and white sections bear crosses, which many family designations from England at the time did.[42]

The state capital of Minnesota is St. Paul. Minnesota's State Photograph depicts an elderly man bowing his head and giving thanks; it is titled "Grace."[43] Among New Hampshire's ten state songs, the first, the official song is "Old New Hampshire" (1949). It references God as making many of the wonderful attractions New Hampshire is known for. The rest of her ten songs are honorary songs. Songs Two, Three, Five and Seven, all reference God.[44]

The State Song of North Dakota, "The North Dakota Hymn" has four verses. The last verse references God in a prayer-request.[45] Ohio's State Motto is "With God All Things Are Possible."[46] Oklahoma is the only state with a "State Gospel Song." It is the famous "Swing Low, Sweet Chariot."[47] Both the "Father and Mother of Oregon" were Christians.[48] Dr. John McLoughlin was born Catholic, raised Anglican and chose to follow Catholicism as an adult. He received the Knighthood of St. Gregory by Pope Gregory XVI in 1847.[49] Tabitha Moffatt Brown, designated the "Mother of Oregon" in 1987, was married to the Reverend Clark Brown, who died in 1817. She went on to start an orphanage and was one of the founders of the Tualatin Academy with the Rev. George H. Atkinson. The Academy eventually became Pacific University.[50]

Pennsylvania is named after William Penn (Penn's woods), a dedicated Quaker. The second verse of Pennsylvania's State Song references God and the attributes of the state.[51] In Rhode Island it is said the state flag is inspired by the seal first adopted by the colony in 1664, which was an anchor with the word "Hope" above it. The seal is believed to have been brought about by the biblical phrase "hope we have as an anchor of the soul."[52] South Carolina designated "The Spiritual" as South Carolina State Music in 1999. South Carolina's First State Song (1911) has five verses. The fifth verse encourages the people on in prayer. South Carolina's Second State Song (1984) has three verses. The third verse thanks God for life within the state.[53] The State Motto of South Dakota is "Under God the People Rule."[54]

Tennessee has, among her many official state poems and poet laureates, a State Poet Laureate of Christian Country Music. Colonel Hugh X. Lewis of Nashville was designated as such in 2006. Among Tennessee's thirteen official State Songs, two of them make mention of God.[55] Texas' State Song has three verses. The chorus declares God's blessing on Texas.[56] The last verse of Utah's State Hymn references God. The first verse of Utah's State Song declares her blessed from heaven.[57] The first verse of Washington's State Song (1959) references God by quoting part of the Lord's Prayer.[58] West Virginia has four official State Songs.[59] Two reference God directly as well as indirectly.[60] Wisconsin has three songs: a ballad, a song and a waltz. The second verse from the song, "On, Wisconsin," includes a motto of how God will give them might.[61] This short list does not include the statues commemorating God-fearing pioneers as well as many other symbols erected by the states. Unfortunately, many are becoming victims of lawsuit frenzied, court-enabled social engineering, even when a majority of a states' population wish to honor their history. It is an inconvenient truth that quite often the history involves mention of the God of the Bible.

ENDNOTES

1   <http://www.nps.gov/came/index.htm><http://www.nps.gov/came/cape-henry-memorial-cross.htm> accessed 3/30/16; you can view other accounts of basically the same instance in Wikipedia.

2   <https://pastinthepresent.wordpress.com/2015/05> accessed 3/30/16. The sites used in these notes are used because the information sourced for that note is either good or will give you good photographs in a concise location. Any other information or opinion is the sole opinion of the site and/or its owners/overseers.

3   Ibid.

4   <http://www.gracechurchyorktown.org/history> © 2016 Grace Episcopal Church Yorktown, accessed 3/30/16. Click on the links to view the history sections.

5   <https://pastinthepresent.wordpress.com/2013/08/20> accessed 3/30/16. The sites used in these footnotes are used because the information sourced for that note is either good or will give you good photographs in a concise location. Any other information or opinion is the sole opinion of the site and/or its owners/overseers.

6   Many photos can be observed at this site <http://www.armedtoserve.com/BUCKLER/StPaulsChapel.html> accessed 3/30/16. See also previous note with a photo of Montgomery's memorial.

7   See also pictographs of the pew from the New York Public Library's Digital Collections at this copyrighted site <http://digitalcollections.nypl.org/items/510d47e2-8bc9-a3d9-e040-e00a18064a99> You can click on all the various other historical items they have listed; accessed 3/30/16.

8   <http://www.loc.gov/exhibits/bibles> accessed 3/30/16

9   <http://www.loc.gov/loc/walls/jeff2.html> accessed 3/30/16

10   Ibid.

11   Ibid.

12   <http://www.loc.gov/pictures/resource/highsm.02120>and<http://www.loc.gov/pictures/resource/highsm.02103>and<http://www.loc.gov/loc/walls/jeff1.html#mrr> accessed 3/30/16

13   Ibid.

14   Ibid.

15   Ibid., and <http://www.loc.gov/loc/walls/wa038001.jpg> accessed 3/30/16

16   <http://www.loc.gov/loc/walls/jeff1.html#mrr> accessed 3/30/16

17   Ibid.

18   <http://www.wnd.com/2006/11/38823><https://en.wikipedia.org/wiki/United_ States_Supreme_Court_Buidling><http://www.supremecourthistory.org> accessed 3/30/16

19   <http://www.supremecourthistory.org/history_oral_arguments.html><https:// en.wikipedia.org/wiki/Oyez> accessed 3/30/16

20   <http://www.aoc.gov/capitol-hill/historic-rotunda-paintings/embarkation-pilgrims> accessed 3/30/16

21   <http://www.aoc.gov/capitol-buildings/capitol-rotunda><http://www.loc.gov/exhibits/ religion/obj-list.html> accessed 3/30/16

22   <http://www.house.gov> accessed 3/30/16

23   <http://www.aoc.gov/capitol-hill/relief-portrait-plaques-lawgivers/moses> accessed 3/30/16

24   <http://chaplain.house.gov/chaplaincy/chaplain_brochure.pdf> accessed 3/30/16

25   <http://www.supremecourt.gov/opinions/04pdf/03-1500.pdf><http://www.cbn. com/tv/1375790266001?mobile=false><https://en.wikipedia.org/wiki/Charters_of_ Freedom><https://www.govtrack.us/congress/bills/111/hres397/text> Bill not enacted; this Bill is used here as evidence of history, where other sources confirm the historical significance as well: <http://aclj.org/in-god-we-trust/complete-idiots-guide-religious- heritage><http://columbiadailyherald.com/opinion/columns/religion-and-government- monuments>sites accessed 3/30/16

26   <https://www.whitehousehistory.org/history/white-house-facts-trivia/tour-state-dining- room.html> accessed 3/30/16

27   <https://www.nps.gov/wamo/learn/historyculture/index.htm><https://en.wikipedia. org/wiki/Washington_Monument#Memorial_stones><http://providencefoundation. com/?page_id=1962><http://www.cbn.com/tv/1375790266001?mobile=false> accessed 3/30/16

28   <https://www.monticello.org/site/jefferson/quotations-jefferson-memorial> accessed 3/30/16

29   <http://etc.usf.edu/clipart/3700/3792/liberty-bell_1_lg.gif><https://www.govtrack. us/congress/bills/111/hres397/text> Bill not enacted; it is used here as evidence of history, where other sources confirm the historical significance as well. Sites accessed 3/30/16.

30   <http://www.cbn.com/tv/1375790266001?mobile=false> accessed 3/30/16

31   Ibid.

32   <http://www.state.gov/documents/organization/27807.pdf> accessed 3/30/16

33   <http://www.senate.gov/history/instdev.htm><https://www.aoc.gov/facts/quotations>
      Sites accessed 3/30/16.

34   <http://www.wnd.com/2006/11/38906> accessed 3/30/16

35   <http://www.statesymbolsusa.org/states/united-states/alabama> accessed 3/30/16

36   <http://www.statesymbolsusa.org/states/united-states/arizona> accessed 3/30/16

37   <http://www.statesymbolsusa.org/states/united-states/colorado> accessed 3/30/16. *It
      seems there is a committee report that makes specific reference to the members requiring
      it to be translated in English as "Nothing without the Deity." I was not able to confirm that
      this report exists, or what the original circumstances were to change a language's meaning.

38   <http://www.statesymbolsusa.org/states/united-states/connecticut> accessed 3/11/16

39   <http://www.statesymbolsusa.org/states/united-states/florida> accessed 3/11/16

40   <http://www.statesymbolsusa.org/states/united-states/georgia> accessed 3/11/16

41   <http://www.statesymbolsusa.org/states/united-states/hawaii> accessed 3/11/16

42   <http://www.statesymbolsusa.org/states/united-states/maryland> accessed 3/11/16

43   <http://www.statesymbolsusa.org/states/united-states/minnesota> accessed 3/11/16

44   <http://www.statesymbolsusa.org/states/united-states/new-hampshire> accessed
      3/11/16

45   <http://www.statesymbolsusa.org/states/united-states/north-dakota> accessed 3/11/16

46   <http://www.statesymbolsusa.org/states/united-states/ohio> accessed 3/11/16

47   <http://www.statesymbolsusa.org/states/united-states/oklahoma> accessed 3/11/16

48   <http://www.statesymbolsusa.org/states/united-states/oregon> accessed 3/11/16

49   <https://en.wikipedia.org/wiki/John_McLoughlin> accessed 3/11/16

50   <https://en.wikipedia.org/wiki/Tabitha_Brown> accessed 3/11/16

51   <http://www.statesymbolsusa.org/states/united-states/pennsylvania> accessed 3/11/16

52   <http://www.statesymbolsusa.org/states/united-states/rhode-island> accessed 3/11/16

53   <http://www.statesymbolsusa.org/states/united-states/south-carolina> accessed
      3/11/16

54   <http://www.statesymbolsusa.org/states/united-states/south-dakota> accessed 3/11/16

55   <http://www.statesymbolsusa.org/states/united-states/tennessee> accessed 3/11/16

56   <http://www.statesymbolsusa.org/states/united-states/texas> accessed 3/11/16

57   <http://www.statesymbolsusa.org/states/united-states/utah> accessed 3/11/16

58   <http://www.statesymbolsusa.org/states/united-states/washington> accessed 3/11/16

59   <http://www.statesymbolsusa.org/states/united-states/west-virginia> accessed 3/11/16

60   <http://www.netstate.com/states//symb/songs/wv_my_home_sweet_home.
      htm><http://www.netstate.com/states//symb/songs/wv_hills.htm> accessed 3/11/16

61   <http://www.statesymbolsusa.org/states/united-states/wisconsin> accessed 3/11/16

Chapter Sixteen

THE FIRST TIME ONE MODERN-DAY ARGUMENT WENT NATIONAL

My goal was to end our historical section before this chapter. But in our topsy-turvy world, there is a bit of history that took place which has continued to sow the seeds for division, threatening our political/governmental covenant and opening a door for a foreign ideology which will eventually, if allowed to fester and boil, send us all into captivity. Early on we begin to see a distinct delineation form, contriving our federal documents among three political opinions concerning religion. The discussion which took place back then (pre-1820s) seemed to be divided into two camps, with no middle ground. But it did not take long for three distinct groups to form, and from there, practices imperiling our covenantal compact start to take place. It can be argued there were always three groups. In my opinion, there was no real need to form themselves until time proved our social covenant-compact was going to be successful. Once that realization hit, the desire for power and control manifested from the minority opinion. The subject matter was very different from our subject matter in this book. The subject matter back then was the involvement Christianity played within the common law of the land, history within that law and what, if any legislation could be enacted to protect Christianity. The question then asked how the government should continue contributing toward Christianity in society.

Many have made the assumption because the argument arose at all is because people began to believe differently. My introduction of this reality in this chapter is to review how it wasn't the majority's practice and belief concerning religious protections which changed— or that their covenantal compact changed— but because a vocal and powerful minority started a practice (or not so hidden agenda) of assault on the religious protections in the country for sheer political power. I believe it is when a president assumes office (in this case Andrew Jackson) that the practice becomes governmental outreach to discriminate. Some would argue Jefferson was president before Jackson, so it started then. Yet I read of no real attempt by Jefferson to discriminate while president, but I believe Jacksonian democrats tried to. I believe they just used Jefferson's own prejudices and stubbornness for effect, much the same way it has been done today.

Discrimination, in and of itself, is a practice which produces a result. Many argue they are just telling the truth. The reason we know that is NOT the truth is because of how the history is framed. Once we see the set up, we then see the effect. The effect is how you know it is discrimination. This "practice" of changing historical truth changed the religious majority, not in ways of belief, but in numbers; hence, the "agenda factor." When you:

a. Make it governmentally harder to publicly share religious beliefs or when you,
b. Refuse to respect the rest the founding religious segment pays to one day of the week [or other practices to maintain covenant] or when you,
c. Create an antagonistic environment for the religious by refusing them access to the press or,
d. Free speech within the public square by system-wide "rules," or when you,

e. Use the legislative authority of a state or the federal government to enact pecuniary damages against them for their belief because they refuse to "obey" or you,

f. Attempt to control through legislative authority how a religious institution hires or fires based on the practiced belief or practiced behavior of the employee, in effect controlling who they hire or fire, **YOU DISCRIMINATE.**

When you discriminate you do so for a purpose. That purpose is to change behavior and thus change the numbers of people who practice that behavior. When it comes to religion, this, in practice, is decidedly what the First Amendment prohibits. Let me be clear and state that I do see two sides to one coin of both secular, non-sectarian and religious history within our nation. It is the practice of discrimination I would like to address. Many atheists, agnostics and those of minority religious opinions have experienced discrimination in America. Christianity has as well. Until we can remove the chains of "us-versus-them" mentality, I'm not sure we can avoid any possible captivity we place ourselves in.

Quite poignantly, without addressing the specific issue at hand, Washington did address the practice:

"All obstructions to the execution of the laws, all combinations and associations, under whatever plausible character, with the real design to direct, control, contract, or awe the regular deliberation and action of the constituted authorities, are destructive of this fundamental principle, and of fatal tendency. They serve to organize faction, to give it an artificial and extraordinary force; to put, in the place of the delegated will of the nation the will of a party, often a small but artful and enterprising minority of the community; and, according to the alternate triumphs of different parties, to make the public administration of the mirror of the ill-concerted and incongruous projects of faction, rather than the organ of consistent and wholesome plans digested by common counsels and modified by mutual interests. However combinations or associations of the above description may now and then answer popular ends, they are likely, in the course of time and things, to become potent engines, by which cunning, ambitious, and unprincipled men will be enabled to subvert the power of the people and to usurp for themselves the reins of government, destroying afterwards the very engines which have lifted them to unjust dominion. . . . One method of assault may be to effect, in the forms of the Constitution, alterations which will impair the energy of the system, and thus to undermine what cannot be directly overthrown. . . that for the efficient management of your common interests, in a country so extensive as ours, a government of as much vigor as is consistent with the perfect security of liberty is indispensable. . . "[1]

Let's take a look at the three groups and see what history can show us. Simply put, we have what I will call a liberal group. They would include those who saw a line within our documents between church and state. In other words, they saw a separation, but believed there was a necessity, at times, for government and religion to work with one another. I hope not to intrude on Washington's beliefs too much here, but it is my opinion Washington would have been within this side of the argument.

We have a second or middle group I will call the moderates. I will place men like Madison within the group of moderates because they saw a distinct line between church and state, preferring it be crossed minimally, if ever, or never. The first two groups agreed on the history of religion within the founding documents and agreed on history's secular elements, but disagreed on any need for legislation encouraging the relationship. In fact, it could be said the moderates believed in the need to discourage it.

Finally, we have a group I will call the hardliners. I would place men like Jefferson within this group. The reason I have these three groups, placing certain men within the groups is because of a bit of history which started to take place when a man like Jackson and his "Jacksonian democrats" come into power. I hope not to make this seem as linear history because several historical events are taking place and even events which occurred earlier in linear time may not have had an effect until later. Men like Washington have passed on into eternity by then, but I believe he had a prescient understanding these arguments would take place. Although it would seem he thought it would take place more along the lines of secular politics (see previous excerpted Washington quote).

In 1824 Thomas Jefferson sent a private letter to a Major John Cartwright of England. In it he discussed his views concerning church and state; specifically whether Christianity is part of the common law. Mr. Cartwright published it in that country.[2] Eventually, it was published after Jefferson's death here in the States; partially due to its controversial conclusions. Against so much history and one tendentious Jeffersonian translation (in error, I might add) concerning a French jurist's legal opinion that Christianity is a part of the common law, Jefferson asserts Christianity was never a part of the common law. In his usual bravado, he issues a defiant proclamation to any lawyer to prove him wrong.[3] Lawyers took up Jefferson's challenge.

Obviously, it had to be published after his death. The uproar would have eventually surrounded Monticello. Many believe Thomas Jefferson's beliefs against religion were hardened from the start. I hope I have proven, to some extent, that was not the case. Jefferson credited four individuals with influencing the Declaration.[4] He was one of five on the committee to write and draft it. All Jefferson did was pull the ideas gossiped, taught from pulpits and printed frequently, into one document for a stated purpose of declaring independence, thus establishing a people. He did so eloquently, even elegantly. The document has withstood the test of time, and is needed now more than ever. Yet to my mind, it seems we see a *"somewhat"* different man in 1776 than we do during and after his presidency. Some would say that was because he was "hiding" what he truly believed. That may very well be the case. He was out of the country for a long period of time during the writing of the Constitution as well as the Bill of Rights. It is my opinion from the history I reviewed for this book, his beliefs concerning religion softened during his marriage but then hardened again, to the point we have a "wall," which sums up his life's work on separating church and state.

To prove exactly when his positions evolved— or if they even did— is not the purpose of this book. Though it would seem from the age of 21 (and probably before that time) his opinions concerning religion and government were set toward a collision course with the average citizen, especially as the full extent of his opinions would be made known.[5] I use the ballpark age of 21 because the private letter he sent to Cartwright contained many ideas Jefferson had already written in a legal opinion when he was 21 years of age.[6]

This argument Jefferson uses shows a practice of changing the truth and history to suit one's own interpretation. Jefferson was not alone in this habit. As time went on, and probably even before Jefferson's death, Jacksonian democrats, inspired by the minority's efforts in this area under the guise of "religious liberty," did the same with a subsequent debate concerning mail delivery on Sunday. Jackson also refuses to issue days of proclamation of thanksgiving, fasts or any other religious proc- lamations. The practice I refer to by those who aligned themselves with Jefferson (Thomas Cooper, Andrew Jackson and others) was to deny or omit historical truth. Frankly, I have no problem with a Federal official deciding for or against their own personal decision to proclaim prayer or fasts. Frankly, give everybody Sunday off! By denying historical truth, the effect has the intention of discrimination written all over it.[7]

I took three years of French. When I reviewed the argument over what constituted an older understanding of our English words and usage for "ancient Scripture," I couldn't believe Jefferson based his whole argument on such an error. Had he admitted to that portion of history in which the Bible did play a part in the common law, and then worked out the branches from the Anglo-Saxon, Norman, etc., into whatever secular dynamic he needed to explain, I'm not sure the uproar would have gained the same traction it did. I cannot believe Jefferson, Cooper or Jackson knew or studied different history than the moderates or liberals did. Both the moderates and liberals agreed on the history as well as the French language debate.[8]

As a result of Jefferson's challenge, lawyers and ministers wrote concerning the historical as well as linguistic error he committed.[9] One such lawyer, Associate Supreme Court Justice Joseph Story wrote an article titled, "Christianity a part of the Common Law."[10] It took him less pages to refute Jefferson's claims than it did Jefferson to write them. Story included French Norman and Anglo-Saxon branches. He also commented upon Jefferson's conclusions when he delivered the Inaugural Discourse on taking the chair of Dane Professor at Harvard (1829).[11] Justice Story had just published his "Commentaries on the Constitution of the United States." It further lay bare Jefferson's history as incomplete.[12] It is unfortunate in arguments such as this for power and influence how "the forest for the trees" happen to be missed. Talking past one another usually helps no one. Unfortunately, much of the damage had already been incurred by Jefferson's erroneous theories as well as the rancor involved in disunity. Once an erroneous wall is plastered, the true line which actually does exist between religion and government becomes buried.

I place Associate Justice Story within the liberal group of jurists, ministers and others which existed at that time. I do so because a minister by the name of Jasper Adams wrote a sermon. It was more like a thesis. In it he made cogent arguments as to why Christianity should be viewed as part of the common law (among other arguments). He did this specifically within the history of the American colonies. Rev. Jasper Adams was a member of the Massachusetts' family of Adams, who claimed John as well as John Quincy as their own. He sent his sermon to many influential and respected luminaries of the day to receive input to the validity of his history and argument.[13] Justice Story was sent a copy of Rev. Adams' thesis with a request for a response. In the response, Story seems to allude to the damage already done by Jefferson and his cohorts on the public by their "egregious error."[14] Story mentions that *bigotry* from the hardliners has led them to their error in history. An anonymous review was made in a legal journal rebutting Rev. Adams' thesis. Unfortunately, most of the same arguments had already been made by Jefferson and friends, which did not add to their cause.

Associate Justice Story was considered a Unitarian. His son seemed to believe so: "It has been seen, that my father was a Unitarian in his religious belief."[15] Here is Justice Story's letter of March 6, 1824, (excerpted) outlining what he believed to be the principles of the Unitarian Church at that time:

> ". . . What you say of the false statements in the prints respecting Unitarians does not surprise me; for I well know that bigotry, and misapprehension, and ignorance are very like to lead men to the most extravagant opinions. The Unitarians are universally steadfast, sincere and earnest Christians. They all believe in the divine mission of Christ, the credibility and authenticity of the Bible, the miracles wrought by our Saviour and his apostles, and the efficacy of his precepts to lead men to salvation. They consider the Scriptures the true rule of faith, and the sure foundation of immortality. In short, their belief is as complete of the divine authority of the Scriptures, as that of any other class of Christians. It is a most gross calumny, therefore, to accuse them of treating the Bible and its doctrines as delusions and falsehoods, or of an union with Deists. In sincere unaffected piety, they yield to no persons. They differ among themselves as to the nature of our Saviour, but they all agree that he was the special messenger of God, and that what he taught is of Divine authority. In truth, they principally differ from other Christians in disbelieving the Trinity, for they think Christ was not God, but in the Scripture language 'the Son of God.' . . ."[16]

As I have previously mentioned, during this time period Unitarians were considered one sect of Christianity. That is no longer the case. It seems from the justice's own pen, he believed in the need for a savior, so salvation was necessary. It also seems he believed in the Bible as the word of truth, so covenant was understood. Something else was understood: "The first and fundamental rule in the interpretation of all instruments, is to construe them according to the sense and the terms, and the intentions of the parties. Mr. Justice Blackstone has remarked that the intention of law is to be gathered from the words, the context, the subject-matter, the effects and consequence, or the reason and spirit of the law"[17]

Jefferson: "On every question of construction, carry ourselves back to the time when the Constitution was adopted, recollect the spirit manifested in the debates, and instead of trying what meaning maybe squeezed out of the text, or invented against it, conform to the probable one in which it was passed."[18]

In what we have reviewed of Jefferson's beliefs and Story's beliefs, we can see there seems to be an ocean of difference, as well as a political viewpoint which places Jefferson within the hardliners' camp and Story within the liberals' camp. But we also see they carried similar DNA when interpreting the Constitution. We have reviewed many dichotomies within these men, in general. None of this should surprise us: They were HUMAN. But they did define words and concepts used in the Constitution similarly. We have reviewed the liberals and hardliners. We have yet to review the moderates' position. Some would place Madison within Jefferson's "wall." I do not believe the evidence points that way. Madison's viewpoint on a great many things seemed within realms of moderation and they seemed more moderate than Jefferson's on this subject.[19] We can be thankful Rev. Adams wrote this sermon-thesis out and documented the response from the dignitaries he sent it to.

James Madison was one of those dignitaries. In Rev. Adams request to Madison (as well as others), he asks the recipient to write a few words basically commenting on his argument as well as his history.[20] Madison's reply is cordial. In it he seems to agree with Adams' history, sharing a brief few paragraphs of old world exchanges in religious affairs. These exchanges most decidedly define Madison's as well as the framing generation's use of what "establishment" means. Remember that this is the man who wished the amendment concerning religious liberty be worded thus: "The Civil Rights of none shall be abridged on account of religious belief or worship, nor shall any *national religion* be *established*, nor shall the full and equal rights of conscience be in any manner, nor on any pretext infringed."[21] (I italicized the thought.)

Within his reply to Rev. Adams, Madison takes another few, brief paragraphs to address American colonial history, again seeming to agree with the Reverend's history and further defining what "establishment" meant to them. While they agreed on history, each side of liberal and moderate would then use that history effectively to arrive at their own conclusions. Madison does so here (in excerpts):

> "Waiving the rights of Conscience, **not included** in the surrender implied by the social State, and more or less invaded by all *religious Establishments*, the simple question to be decided is whether a *support* of the best & purest religion, the Xn (Christian) religion itself ought not so far at least as *pecuniary* means are involved, to be provided for by the Gov.'t rather than be left to the voluntary provisions of those who profess it. . . .

> "In the Colonial State of the country, there were four examples, R.I. N.J. Penn.'a and Delaware, & the greater part of N.Y. *where there were no religious Establishments*; the **support of Religion** being left to the **voluntary associations & contributions** of individuals; and certainly the religious condition of those Colonies, will well *bear a comparison with that where establishments existed*. . . .

> "It is true that the New England States have *not discontinued establishments of Religion* formed under very peculiar circumstances; but *they have by successive relaxations advanced toward the prevailing example*; and without any evidence of disadvantage either to Religion or good Government.

> "And if we turn to the Southern States where there was, previous to the Declaration of independence, a *legal provision for the support of Religion*; and since that event a surrender of it to a spontaneous support by the people, it may be said that the difference amounts nearly to a contrast in the greater purity & industry of the Pastors and in the greater devotion of their flocks, in the latter period than in the former. In Virginia the contrast is particularly striking,

to those whose memories can make the comparison. It will not be denied that causes other than the abolition of the *legal establishment of Religion* are to be taken into view in the account'g for the change in the Religious character of the community. But the existing character, distinguished as it is by its religious features, and the lapse of time now more than 50 years since the *legal support of Religion was withdrawn sufficiently prove that it does not need the support of Gov.'t* and it will scarcely be contended that *Government has suffered by the exemption of Religion from its cognizance, or its pecuniary aid. . . .*

"Whilst I thus frankly express my view of the subject presented in your sermon, I must do you the justice to observe that you very ably maintained yours. I must admit moreover that **it may not be easy, in every possible case, to trace the line of separation between the rights of religion and the Civil authority** with such distinctness as to avoid collisions & doubts on essential points. The tendency to a usurpation on one side or the other, or to a corrupting coalition or alliance between them, *will be best guarded against by an entire abstinence of the Government from interference in any way whatever, beyond the necessity of preserving public order, & protecting each sect against trespasses on its legal rights by others.*"[22] (I italicized and highlighted to show concept. What is in parentheses is mine by way of explanation.)

Madison mentions those who can remember what it was like before the dis- "establishment" took place. The church benefited from the removal of governmental interference. He makes a clear definition of establishment: MONEY and governance. The church or religion was supported by the public's money and it was in charge of government or had legislative and other influence because it was the "established" or preferred denomination or "religion" in that region (state or country). We have seen the history of this in previous chapters. In fact, this was the definition a mere 50 years ago. Now "establishment" means any public speech, actions of belief at work and actions of the courts to force people to participate in practices their religion abhors.

Watch the slippery slope, because atheists will be next. They are a religion. They are demanding chaplains. They have a specific belief and belief pattern with specific behavior associated. They even gather or "associate" with one another as opposed to other religious believers. Why should they expect free speech rights when Christians are being denied theirs? Why should they expect their religion to be the established practice in a state or country? We have now established atheism as our national religion and all other religions must bow to it. If we do not, we must pay or be sent to jail. From the moment Clinton removed and replaced U.S. Attorneys, and the last eight or so years since socialism has become embedded in our laws, cases have been decided to establish atheism or atheistic secularism as the Federal government's established religion. Some say cases are decided based on science. That can hardly be so, since many decisions fly in the face of even *basic science*. This is why we must all guard each other's covenant rights. We will review this more closely in the next section.

Our two majority opinions also agreed on a history of seeing corruption within both government and religion. Today's events would demonstrate the need for covenant has not changed. Not only do we see a corruption of judicial definitions, we see the use of this corruption to effectuate discrimination.[23] Madison also evidences covenant responsibility here when he mentions "public order and protecting" the sects against each other. This has been a clear problem in modern times. Today the "sects" have decided to use the courts to deny rights of covenant to people of faith. This is discrimination.

Madison also makes a clear point of a "*line* of separation between the rights of religion and the Civil authority." The "wall" metaphor is not accurate history. It was first seen as a theological argument by Roger Williams against his nemesis John Cotton.[24] This is still the same spirit from the same argument Cotton had with Thomas Hooker. If you will remember the argument became so heated that Hooker moved and started another state (Connecticut). Williams did the same thing when he started Rhode Island. I would say we need a national stronghold removed and healing effectuated in this area because in today's world some are still arguing over it! The argument continued with various Baptist separatists. It's been going on for so long most modern secularists have lost the ability to accurately interpret the biblical theology Williams was using and why (see the previous endnote). The fact remains that Williams had a radicalized (for that time) view on the separation of church and state and practiced it.

Most folks will have no memory in a reality that the framers viewed the Bill of Rights as binding on the Federal government only. The states were not bound by the Bill of Rights. The Bill of Rights were intended to apply only to the Federal government. It was the states who had power in regulating religious matters. This contributed to a sovereignty the states possessed which they have lost today. Many events contributed to this loss including those surrounding the Civil War, among others we will review in the next section. By not applying the Bill of Rights to the states, it protected the states from the meddling of the Federal government in matters of religion; the people were also protected. After the Civil War, it became obvious that once African Americans were enfranchised, various states still had the right to deny them basic due process protections. The 14th Amendment was created only and solely to give due process to former slaves.[25] The 14th Amendment, within the simplicity of intent, rightfully stopped the practice of withholding due process and Bill of Rights protections from African American citizens.

There were early attempts for all sorts of practices and desires to be included under the 14th Amendment provisions, but they were stopped. That's why it was necessary to go the proper route by adding the 19th Amendment, giving voting rights for women, instead of jumping on the bandwagon of the 14th (see previous endnote). It was constantly promised within its debate in the 1860s that the states would not be subjected to the establishment clause as the Federal government was within the First Amendment and that the states would continue to retain their sovereignty because the 14th Amendment was supposed to be limited in its scope. That reality and promise was broken as soon as historical memory could no longer serve as an argument to stop a runaway Federal government. This is probably one of the reasons there is a fear and constant fight over historical accuracy. Fast-forward to our current history, this amendment has been used to allow anyone birthed on our shores to become a citizen, in Roe v. Wade to murder children, in Bush v. Gore (concerning the 2000 election) and more recently in Obergefell v. Hodges regarding states and same-sex marriage. As time has gone on, more and more power has accrued to the Federal government, destroying states' rights, and in a more harmful and exacting revenge, the rights of covenant citizens.

Before some of these more modern cases could have the potential to endanger our republic by potentially reneging on the Federal government's distinct role in maintaining covenant, a very odd history played out. Remember that up until 1947, states were sovereign in a way which gave them rights because they were not bound by the establishment clause of the First amendment. Originally, they had a direct position at the Federal "table" by appointing senators (before the 17th Amendment). In 1947 a man by the name of Arch R. Everson, with various ties to discriminatory groups (see next endnote) sued New Jersey because a state law allowed reimbursements of money to parents who sent their children to school on buses operated by the public transportation system. Children who attended Catholic schools also qualified for the transportation subsidy.[26] But remember that states, under the establishment clause were not bound by it as the Federal government was. In order for Everson to win, he had to maintain that the states were bound by the First Amendment, thus undoing what had been roughly 150 years of Constitutional history and understanding. The courts decided against him. No big deal, right? All remains as the framers intended and life can go on. Well, not exactly.

Supreme Court Justice Hugo Black in writing for the majority decided the states were now bound by the Bill of Rights. He gave no explanation as to why he believed the states were now bound by the establishment clause, except he used the precedence of the 14th Amendment. The very amendment those who enacted it promised could not circumvent state's sovereignty. Black then bound his opinion in a neat little bow by using the letter Jefferson wrote to the Danbury Baptists. Jefferson stated he couldn't grant favors because the Federal government was supposed to stay non-sectarian by a "wall of separation" between church and state. Many have made a mention because Hugo Black had been a member of the KuKluxKlan as a boy in Alabama, he was unable to understand the need for accommodation, stability and protection for the states which the previous 150 years worth of interpretation afforded. I am not so sure. I think something else was afoot (progressive socialism).

At the time, because the court decided in favor of the state, and by inference, the Catholics, Black and court came out looking like the voice of moderation. I suppose folks thought it would be easy to ignore a letter written by Jefferson 140 plus years before. After all, it wasn't law and we were still "free" citizens. That didn't last too long either. Black's history was suited to his own platform and narrative within the same strict separatism that puritanism birthed, even though many puritans functioned theocratically. During the 1960s the idea of "neutrality" set in. Most of us would breathe a sigh of relief in reading that history, thinking, "Okay, let's be neutral." But Black made the line of separation a "high and impregnable" wall in which America could supposedly not "approve the slightest breach." With that kind of language it did not take long for what had been a minority opinion, now turned judicial majority, to interpret law to the effect of making a new established religion out of atheistic secularism.

The judicial history since then would have most Americans feeling as if they were on a roller-coaster ride. Various Supreme Courts have jumped from different "rules and tests" to interpret what is a simple and easy jewel of an amendment for defining our freedoms, unless, that is, if you are trying to dismantle those freedoms. Realizing the mess we were in, Congress passed the Religious Freedom Reformation Act (1993). At this point some of you may have noticed that Jefferson's wall has been plastered over and Madison's line is so buried, maybe the only obvious notion of it is a "dip" in the sand! Maybe, like other ancient lines, it can be seen from "outer space" through high image satellite footage. Because frankly, folks, with this nonsense that seems to be the only place any of us will be able to practice religion in twenty years' time. It was so simple for almost 150 years.

Chief Justice William Rehnquist: "There is simply no historical foundation for the proposition that the framers intended to build a wall of separation that was constitutionalized in Everson."[27] The wall metaphor has never been beneficial to the republic. We see the fights from various colonial factions in this regard from past centuries. It attempts to deny the covenant people their right to practice that covenant in the "public square." It also prevents the Federal government from respecting their own admitted part in protecting the covenant people. Madison's line does neither. A line allows for change and compromise, especially to protect the covenant. It seems to me from Madison's response to Rev. Adams this was understood. It also seems it was well known if the Federal government would not protect the covenant people in their most basic right, and in any way abridged that right, the covenant would be broken and the union should be dissolved.

From our historical account of Rev. Adams' thesis and the response from various luminaries of the day, the liberals also understood the need for a line. While crossing it was a much more fluid affair than the moderates would ever allow, it also did no injury to the covenant people. The moderates and the liberals then form a super majority within the understanding of historical truth. Of course, then each side uses that history quite effectively to maintain their own positions, again for political effect—at least the result might have a political effect. Although that effect would not deny numbers for or against belief (within the moderates' camp) and would not minimize numbers within the liberals' camp. Within either the liberal or moderate camps coercion is not involved. But the effect from the hardliners ("a wall") would result in coercion because of the practice of discrimination.

Even using subtle societal attitudes to mock or minimize practices of morality from religious sources creates discrimination, like the Sunday mail delivery argument and days' of proclamation argument. If it did not, then why do the purveyors of the pornography industry today scream every time a governmental official tries to even define obscenity? Some would take offense at my example. I mean none, except to show the practice creates the same problem regardless of the merits of the subject. It is the same issue: If you create legislation to diminish what pornography is seen and what kind is seen by the public in a public forum, you do so to minimize content and audience. It is no different for healthy and moral segments of the populace. We all remember the attempt by New York City to stop the oversized soda dispensary. Today's state-run media— that is in effect what we have when the media is overwhelmingly associated with one political party or one ideology like socialism— practice the same discrimination. By showing only the news from one historical viewpoint or one viewpoint alone, they discriminate. They do so for a result. That result is to minimize the numbers of people associating with the political party or ideology or morality they do not agree with.[28]

By way of example, in the presidential election of 2012, a CNN reporter injected herself into the debate by telling one of the candidates his history (and then, he, by inference) was wrong.[29] She did so, not because she was right— it was later proven she was wrong in her history— she did so to minimize the success of the candidate she did not agree with, thus minimizing the numbers who would potentially vote for him. An argument can always be made as to whether this is done subconsciously or not. Whichever side one agrees with in that argument, is really not my point. The effect is the same. If you are not trained specifically in balanced journalism, which, in my opinion, our present schools do not do that any longer, you will never be able to overcome your own prejudices.[30]

Another powerhouse of legal review was sent Rev. Adams' thesis, with the same request for a response. Supreme Court Chief Justice John Marshall, who served for 34 years, the longest of any chief justice, wrote the Reverend a response.[31] Marshall was raised a Christian. His daughter related he had a problem with the divinity of Jesus his entire life, until he reached old age. He then changed his mind and wanted to take public communion before his death, which death occurred first. Marshall did have a life-long relationship with the Episcopal Church.[32] I say that because it seems Marshall's opinion may have closely resembled

Madison's line, but Marshall seemed to be willing, like Story, to cross it on occasion; although "legislation on the subject is admitted to require great delicacy, because freedom of conscience & respect for our religion both claim our most serious regard."[33]

We will never know what Marshall would have done with any hypothetical legislation. Whatever their opinions on legislation, Marshall, Madison, Story (to name a few) agreed with Rev. Adams' history. There are two questions one might bring up at this point. If our covenantal compact was in early jeopardy, what kept it together for so long? From my review of history, I have come to the conclusion the two parties I call "liberal and moderate" joined together to keep covenant, even though their opinions on quite a few subjects differed. They had enough in common to realize the disaster of disbanding.

One might also question why I mention this bit of history at all, since the subject matter of this book is not what the previous argument entails. More recently, it has been a common practice from many sides of this argument to change history. Yet it seems only one side does so to attempt to circumvent our First Amendment Inalienable Rights. These individuals (more recently now, the whole Democrat party[34]) try to say those rights don't apply to an individual in business or don't apply to active military, or to children. There are various answers given for each, usually based upon the activity each is a part of, not based on the fact they are human. What used to be a limited loss of inalienable rights for, let's say, a marine who must kill an enemy on the field of battle, has now morphed to the desk sergeant who decides to keep a Bible handy during lunch hour and the private who wants to keep a private Facebook® page witnessing their love for Jesus. God help the airmen who decides the family's car needs a bumper sticker extolling political issues concerning the Bible.

If you took my advice early on while reading this book and turned off the morphine drip of today's modern culture, you might be formulating another question. This question should ignore what you believe, what the color of your skin is or any other identifiers "they" use to keep American citizens fighting one another. The question we should all be asking— atheist, agnostic, religious (yellow, black, red, white and "blue")— is WHY? Why have our free speech rights along with our religious beliefs become a target for political activists? What slippery, slithery slope have Americans fallen into?

ENDNOTES

1   <http://avalon.law.yale.edu/18th_century/washing.asp> © 2008 Lillian Goldman Law Library, accessed 3/30/16.

2   <http://www.princeton.edu/~ereading/TJChristianity.pdf> accessed 3/10/16

3   Daniel L. Dreisbach, editor. "Religion and Politics in the Early Republic: Jasper Adams and the Church-State debate." Lexington, KY: © 1996 by The University Press of Kentucky. 12-13

4   Carl Lotus Becker. "The Declaration of Independence: A study on the History of Political Ideas" (New York: Harcourt, Brace and Co., 1922). [Online] available from <http://oll. libertyfund.org/titles/1177> © 2004-2015 Liberty Fund, Inc. 25, 26. Accessed 3/11/16.

5   See in its entirety: Thomas Jefferson, "The Works of Thomas Jefferson," Federal Edition (New York and London, G.P. Putnam's Sons, 1904-5). 12 vols. [Online] available from <http://oll.libertyfund.org/titles/1734> © 2004-2015 Liberty Fund, Inc. Accessed 3/11/16.

6   <http://www.princeton.edu/~ereading/TJChristianity.pdf> accessed 3/30/16

7   Henry Whiting Warner. 1838 "An Inquiry into the Moral and Religious Character of the American Government." New York: Wiley and Putnam. 1838, G.F. Hopkins & son, Printers. See 10-21 and 186-198 for the influence of Jefferson and the hardliners and 36-109 for a rehearsal of widely known historical evidence. In the public domain.

8   Carl Lotus Becker. "The Declaration of Independence: A study on the History of Political Ideas" (New York: Harcourt, Brace and Co., 1922). [Online] available from <http://oll. libertyfund.org/titles/1177> © 2004-2015 Liberty Fund, Inc. 25-80. Accessed 3/11/16. See especially 72-80, where, after a quick 47 pages of then almost 400 years of history he proves that Locke's ideas came to the colonists through the hearing of sermons. I find it impossible to believe Jefferson and his supporters within the (circa) 1820s argument did not know this history or of the religious history of the documents that were produced for governance within the various states.

9   Henry Whiting Warner. 1838 "An Inquiry into the Moral and Religious Character of the American Government." New York: Wiley and Putnam. 1838. G.F. Hopkins & son, Printers. 10-21, 36-109, 186-198. In the public domain.

10   *"Life and Letters of Joseph Story, Associate Justice of the Supreme Court of the United States, and Dane Professor of Law at Harvard University." Edited by His Son, William W. Story. Boston: Charles C. Little and James Brown, 1851. Volume 1. 431-433. See also pages 429 & 430 where it seems that Story knew nothing about the Jefferson letter until he was told about it.*

11   Ibid., 431

12   Joseph Story, LL.D. "Commentaries of the Constitution of the United States: with A Preliminary Review of the Constitutional History of the Colonies and States Before the Adoption of the Constitution," In Two Volumes, (Volume 1) 4th Ed., with notes and additions by Thomas M. Cooley. Boston: Little, Brown and Company, 1873. I refer to the pages of the preliminary review of the constitutional history of the colonies and states, which would be pages 1-138 of this edition.

13   Daniel L. Dreisbach, editor. "Religion and Politics in the Early Republic: Jasper Adams and the Church-State debate." Lexington, KY: © 1996 by The University Press of Kentucky. 1-2

14   Ibid., 116-117

15   "Life and Letters of Joseph Story, Associate Justice of the Supreme Court of the United States, and Dane Professor of Law at Harvard University." Edited by His Son, William W. Story. Boston: Charles C. Little and James Brown, 1851. Volume 1. 441

16   Ibid. 441-442

17   Joseph Story, LL.D. "Commentaries of the Constitution of the United States: with A Preliminary Review of the Constitutional History of the Colonies and States Before the Adoption of the Constitution," In Two Volumes, (Volume 2) 4th Ed., with notes and additions by Thomas M. Cooley. Boston: Little, Brown and Company, 1873. Chapter 5, "Rules of Interpretation." (295 in this edition, 400)

18   Jefferson to William Johnson, 1823 In "The Jeffersonian Cyclopedia, A Comprehensive Collection of the Views of Thomas Jefferson." Edited by John P. Foley. (New York & London: Funk & Wagnalls Company 1900) 844. Public domain.

19   James Madison, "The Writings of James Madison, comprising his Public Papers and his Private Correspondence, including his numerous letters and documents now for the first time printed," ed. Gaillard Hunt. (New York: G.P. Putnam's Sons, 1900). 9 vols. See in its entirety. Even after reading ten or twenty pages, one begins to understand the difference between the two men.

20   Daniel L. Dreisbach, editor. "Religion and Politics in the Early Republic: Jasper Adams and the Church-State debate." Lexington, KY: © 1996 by The University Press of Kentucky. 2, 113, 121. We can also be thankful to Mr. Dreisbach for this book. It brings a much needed response from history to many of these questions now posited today.

21   "From James Madison to William Bradford, 9 November 1772, in "Letters and. Other Writings of James Madison in four Volumes. (Philadelphia: J.B. Lippincott & Co. 1865-67) Volume 1; 5, 6

22   Madison letter to Rev. Adams (Chic. Hist. Soc. Mss. 1832) In "The Writings of James Madison, comprising his Public Papers and his Private Correspondence, including his numerous letters and documents now for the first time printed," ed. Gaillard Hunt. (New York: G.P. Putnam's Sons, 1900). Vol. IX. 485,486, 487 (see 484-488 for the entire specific response). Public domain.

23   See a concise argument <http://www.thefederalistpapers.org/current-events/what-freedom-of-religion> accessed. I also refer to attempted religious discrimination of a military chaplain from the Naval Weapons Station, Joint Base, Charleston, SC, for his biblical views. The same city where Rev. Jasper Adams transformed the tiny grammar school into the College of Charleston. Rev. Adams was also a chaplain and professor at the U.S. Military Academy, West Point, NY. The term "rolling over in one's grave" would apply here. See Dreisbach, "Religion and Politics. . ." 164. See also "today's" news <http://www.cbn.com/cbnnews/us/2015/June/War-on-Chaplains-Demise-of-the-US-Military> accessed 3/11/16. An update is in order. The military has decided the chaplain was not in violation of his duties. <http://www.washingtontimes.com/news/2015/nov/4/wes-modder-navy-chaplain-resumes-ministry-after-fi/?page=all>

24   See a proper theological understanding of the use of Roger William's "wall" metaphor in a "Bloody Tenet" <http://www.americanminute.com/index.php?date=02-05> accessed 3/30/16

25   See how the 14th amendment was originally intended to be interpreted and how it has become interpreted to allow anyone born on our soil access to citizenship and anyone with a grievance the ability to harm covenant citizens <http:www.federalistblog.us/mt/articles/14th_dummy_guide.htm> accessed 3/30/16.

26   <https://www.oyez.org/cases/1940-1955/330us1> accessed 4/2/16. Some sources place Everson as a member of the Order of American Mechanics who was dedicated to the exclusion of Roman Catholic institutions in American life. <http://www.city-journal.org/html/yes-vouchers-are-constituional-12075.html> accessed 4/2/16. This "Order" filed an amicus curiae brief with the court in this case.

27   Dissenting opinion in Wallace v. Jaffree (1985). See the argument and the quotes in Congressional Record, Proceedings and Debates of the 105th Congress, Second Session. Volume 144—Part 5 (April 21, 1998 to April 30, 1998) Washington, D.C. 1998: United States Government Printing Office. April 28, 1998. pages 6989 to 7002. See further debate Congressional Record, Proceedings and Debates of the 107th Congress, Second Session, Volume 148— Part 2 (February 14, 2002 to March 8, 2002) Washington, D.C. 2002: United States Government Printing Office. February 28, 2002. page 2244. See the debate from one side <https://www.gpo.gov/fdsys/pkg/GPO-CHRG-REHNQUIST/pdf/GPO-CHRG-REHNQUIST-4-24-2.pdf> See another debate, along similar lines <http://www.nhinet.org/jb-cray.htm> accessed 4/2/16

28   <http://www.mrc.org/media-bias-101/journalists-admitting-liberal-bias-part-one><http://www.mediaite.com/online/cbs-chief-les-moonves-partisanship-is-very-much-a-part-of-journalism-now> Some disagree that this is the reason for the bias. Some view it slanted toward advertisers and uniformity. See <http://ivn.us/2015/06/09/bias-media-just-not-liberal-bias> While I disagree with them because they usually do not cite percentages, which, in my opinion, would prove my point, the effect is still the same. This type of bias is an attempt to affect belief, thereby affecting numbers within the populace. accessed 3/11/16.

29   <http://www.uspresidentialelectionnews.com/2013/02/debate-commission-co-chair-says-candy-crowley-was-a-mistake> accessed 3/11/16

30   <http://www.publiusforum.com/2015/03/12/this-dirty-little-secret-is-one-neat-trick-why-journalism-schools-are-hopping-mad-at-me> <http://archive.frontpagemag.com/readArticle.aspx?ARTID=32928> for a more in-depth read <https://journalism.utexas.edu/sites/journalism.utexas.edu/files/attachments/reese/mediating-the-message.pdf> accessed 3/11/16

31   Daniel L. Dreisbach, editor. "Religion and Politics in the Early Republic: Jasper Adams and the Church-State debate." Lexington, KY: © 1996 by The University Press of Kentucky. 113

32   <http://www.phc.edu/gj_editorv11n1.php><http://www.let.rug.nl/usa/biographies/john-marshall> accessed 3/11/16

33   W.A. Whitehead. "Alleged Atheism of the Constitution" In "The Northern Monthly" edited by Allen Lee Bassett (New York and Newark: Allen L. Bassett. 1868) Volume II November-April. 66. Citing a letter from John Marshall to Rev. Jasper Adams. 1833. Public domain.

34   <http://www.cbn.com/cbnnews/us/2015/July/DNC-Chair-businesses-Dont-Have-Rights-Like-Churches/><http://blogs.cbn.com/thebrodyfile/archive/2015/07/08.aspx> accessed 3/11/16. Pease review the comments section if they are still available. It

seems many folks disagree with the democrats and almost all realize the only reason they did an interview was to "soften the blow" when millions finally realize they have made a successful attempt at destroying our inalienable rights.

BROKEN FEDERAL COVENANT

Section Four

A BROKEN FEDERAL COVENANT (TO ALL CITIZENS WHO CARE)

Before we look at the proof of a broken Federal Covenant, I can't help but write these words again, to make it plain as day: God is not judging America. God is not harming us nor is He desirous to see us go into a seventy-year period of bondage. In fact, as I have written previously, the Lord has shown me awesome times of revival, renewal and healing for the church and His other people, Israel, before, during and after any possible period of American captivity—or attempts made at Israeli annihilation. These experiences are not only for the believing. They can help many folks who find themselves in need of a miracle. God loves humanity and God loves America. While I have not made as much mention of this fact, I have received awesome promises from God that if we, as the religious, would but turn back to Him and follow His word— if those of the agnostic and atheist persuasion would do no harm to the faithful— and vice versa, we will receive restoration of our land, our fortunes and times of great technological innovation, the kind we have never seen before. It is unfortunate, but we, Americans, are doing ourselves harm. We are the only ones who can choose to turn this situation around.

America stands at a precipice. There is so much at stake for all of us. So forgive me if you find me unaccommodating in writing this work. I will probably step on many political toes with this next section. What some call accommodation is a mistaken application of covenant. If we divergent opinions are just trying to be nice or trying to fit people where they do not belong, it will not sustain the republic. There are palpable and real benefits to keeping covenant. There are real differences between accommodation and covenant. The eventual and devastating effects between the two ideas becomes quite apparent when the "wolves" are at the door. The early settlers to this nation realized quickly, and more so in New England, that without one another, they would not survive. So to keep a covenant meant more than to accommodate. Originally it meant the need to work with one another whether they liked each other as neighbors or not. It meant instead of backbiting your neighbor, keeping your opinions to yourself might actually keep you alive. Biblical understanding was then added so hatreds, jealousies and other divisions would be minimized. It meant particular behaviors or demands might not be beneficial to the whole.

Now we have systemized murder of children which has become more like an assembly line of slaughter. We have state-sponsored sanctions which remove tens of thousands of dollars from private citizens, businesses and especially the religious because they will not comply with the religion— excuse me, political ideology of the Federal government or that of a particular state. We have a system which rewards refusal to work, lying, fraud, as well as other immoral acts. That system takes the money from the hardworking and successful and then calls them guilty or unfair or any other number of expletives.

Because our laws were formerly anchored on principles seen in the Bible, we did not condone legal murder, except in the case of self-defense and capital punishment. Our system was based on hard and principled work, whether you were a laborer, management or an executive. Under that system, government had no right to steal from you to give it to someone else, except under extreme circumstances. That included helping the infirm, the infirm elderly, orphans, those who, for whatever reason find themselves in sickness and job loss. Under that system we understood faith and biblical faith and how it worked inside and outside of our bodies. Most people would be shocked to learn socialism, progressivism or any other number of its names, is not condoned by the Scriptures. These systems are in opposition to the Bible. When these systems are in place, their ultimate goal is to remove the Bible and the people who follow it from society. By the time you finish this book, you will read the proof for yourself.

Societies with biblical knowledge, or based on the Bible, experience practices of higher education and knowledge concerning healthy economics. They also experience something else: A real, up close and personal demonstration of the miraculous. By way of example, most folks reading this can turn on daily Christian news/programs and experience healing as the hosts pray in the Holy Spirit and receive a word of knowledge concerning healing as whole groups of people with that specific ailment are healed.[1] (See 1 Corinthians 12.) This is only one example. There are other benefits.

My point is that my Bible tells me, and my everyday experience proves to me that it is in Him that I live and move and have my being (Acts 17:18-32, see v 28). I could no more separate my business and everyday working life from my life and spirit in Christ than I could remove my heart or lungs in order to go to work. As a blood-bought, Spirit-filled believer, it is impossible to remove the working of the Holy Spirit in my life from my life! The proof of this is that I can point to people who have been healed in either mind or body or people I have shared the prophetic word of the Lord with in which that word has come to pass for them. I have shared the salvation message of Jesus Christ to folks who have accepted it, and their lives were changed. These are some of the effects of covenant. This is not in me, this is because God keeps covenant (Colossians 1:25-29).

There are secular benefits to keeping covenant. Not everyone believes or wants this type of biblical hope. The reality is the God of the Bible gives every single human the right to choose: The right to believe in Jesus and the right not to believe in Him. Choice is a great freedom. Hard work is a great freedom. Those freedoms have been built into the framework of our covenant with God and our covenant with one another as humans. Choice contains consequences and/or responsibilities. When we decide as humans to remove choice from our fellow Americans, we remove the effectiveness of our founding documents, removing covenant benefits.

When we ignore foundations encouraging what is good and beneficial hard work from our fellow Americans so that they can benefit their communities, we all suffer. One of the biggest lies out there is this "mantra" of fairness. When we reward the refusal to choose thriftiness and reward the lazy and fraudulent, we create a system which is based upon what is unfair. Hard work for all, levels the playing field. Hard work produces different results. The reason for that is because of our differences and because of diversity, not because the government hands out checks to those willing to work less. You cannot ignore all of the foundations a country is built upon and you cannot treat as irrelevant the foundational peoples which anchor them.

It may start as removing crosses, but it ends with a local mayor refusing to allow the residents to speak at public meetings because the citizens disagree with him.[2] No one wants to be a part of that system. That is broken covenant and that is what is destroying our compact. Calling what is theft, "equality" and what is good, bad; calling what is criminal "fairness" and what is totalitarianism good government, ruins what had been a gem of Western republican government. Let's look at proof of broken covenant and let's define the ideology behind it. So we understand how to never be taken captive again, I will review some history which got us to this place. As with my examples of American history, you can choose to listen; you can also understand I could not include all history and forgive my imperfection in that regard. Or you can use my lack in "perfection" in recounting historical events to attack the message. Whatever your choice, there is a reality which none of us can escape. It's that old adage: "Those who fail to learn from history are doomed to repeat it." Learning that lesson could help all of us escape captivity.

ENDNOTES

1   There are many groups who function this way, so I am not trying to endorse nor highlight just one; but sometimes it is easier to pick the most prevalent and easily accessible group to

reflect what it is I am trying to convey. The following site is such an example <http://www.cbn.com> (also known as the 700 Club); see your local listings for times and dates of on-air viewing, or pick your favorite ministry example from several TV stations nationwide.

2   <http://www.foxnews.com/politics/2015/03/04/new-jersey-mayor-decides-public-cannot-ask-questions-at-council-meetings/> accessed 3/6/16

Chapter One

PRESENT EXAMPLES OF
MODERN-DAY CAPTIVITY

"... If the leaders are divided into parties, will not one prevail at one year, and another the next? and will not this introduce the most wretched of servitudes, an uncertain jurisprudence?" John Adams, *A Defence of the Constitutions of Government of the United States of America* ...[1]

(Excerpted) ... "The consequences arising from the continual accumulation of public debts in other countries ought to admonish us to be careful to prevent their growth in our own." ... John Adams, *First Annual Message November 22, 1797*[2]

"... For the jaws of power are always opened to devour, and her arm is always stretched out, if possible, to destroy the freedom of speaking, thinking and writing." John Adams, *Dissertation on the Canon and Feudal Law*[3]

We research all sorts of things nowadays: What movie to see, what cell phone to buy, what school to attend. Yet the very nature of the law and its history is seen as somehow unnecessary. When a people do not know their history and the history of the laws which keep them free, they are easy prey for subjugation. In writing this book, indeed this chapter, I had to deal with my own ignorance of history. Initially I thought I knew what

God was talking about when He called me to write. I thought I knew our Constitutional history well enough to know what was wrong. I later came to realize I knew very little. Initially I thought it was those pesky progressives— all democrats— who were to blame for our bureaucratic police state, as well as the considerable mess we find ourselves in.

While that holds some truth in today's climate, it was yesteryear's history which surprised me. It wasn't until I discovered the first progressive was a republican, many early democrats practiced honest monetary policies, and the loss of many freedoms was encouraged by some religious and atheist alike, that I realized how doomed we are to repeat history. Of course, our modern experience has turned all history on its head. Now bad monetary policy is good. Religious freedom is bad— and you better watch out— because if you cry out with your free speech and freedom to *not participate* in someone else's lifestyles, some police-state entity (Federal or otherwise) will arrest something from you in the form of cash and/or freedom. So I thought some modern-day history would serve all at this point.

I really don't care what persuasion you adhere to. After reading some of these true stories, you would really have to be inhuman not to cry, or at the very least, be horrified for what our fellow Americans have had to endure at the hands of one of the bureaucracies controlled by one of our fifty states as well as Federal, bureaucratic police apparatus. The sad reality is there are too many true stories and court cases which have not only denied innocent American's their civil rights, but have jailed them, denying them their freedom.[4] I had to go in some kind of logical fashion, else this section alone would be thousands of pages. So we start with the First Amendment and continue from there.

There is also another danger in writing this: Too many true stories begin to desensitize us to the horror of a police state; OR printing stories of trivial and perceived trespasses upon our rights turn us deaf, as well as nonchalant about the issue. It becomes so large, we believe the lie we can't do anything about it. An inevitability sets in that it's just a matter of time before every single American knows we are in a socialist (progressive) state which has given birth to a hybrid communist state— one that is American in name only.

Throughout this book, if you have reviewed the endnotes, you will see many instances of our First Amendment freedoms of religion and speech being denied. So before I go into the examples, practices, and the ideology enabling us to go down the road of captivity, let me say from the start if you are a Christian reading this section, there is a command from our Lord that, if followed, can free our fellow Americans from bondage. I wrote about it in the beginning of this work. It is called the Lord's Prayer. Without going into a whole teaching concerning it, the section I want to refer to here has to do with forgiving others. If we, as Christians, can forgive those who violate our inalienable rights, we can release a whole generation from bondage.

Remember also, if you are a Christian, this problem and its solution is spiritual first. Forgiveness, prayer and spiritual action (especially through repentance) are not what the nonbeliever would assume as first solutions. Yet if those who feel they have had their rights infringed upon, but now realize them again can forgive as well— whether they claim Christ or not— America can be set free. One last thought for all Americans is that God forgives sin. As Christians we are told to whom much is forgiven, much is required. So before you begin this section, remember a non-sectarian covenant based upon our founding compact of religious freedoms should involve the ability to forgive each other our grievances. One does not have to believe there is a God in order to forgive. This one fact alone: **Forgiveness** can turn the tide of a broken covenant. It can start a dialogue where those who disagree can still remain faithful in practice to their religion and those with no religion can still practice their beliefs.

You may disagree with what I am about to write, but in a prolonged time of research, I have come to believe one of the worst policies ever enacted is the ability for the President of the United States to implement "executive orders." They started off innocuous and helpful enough; but have turned downright sinister. In their genuine and necessary role, they are defined as a presidential policy directive which implements or interprets a federal statute, a constitutional provision or a treaty. They do not require congressional approval. Historically they executed the mundane administrative matters concerning the internal operations of federal agencies. More recently, though, they have been used to carry out legislative policies and programs which have really belonged within the purview of the legislature. This has the potential to infringe and eliminate American's civil rights because these presidents obfuscate "The People's House."

Some executive orders have been used honorably enough: To end racial discrimination in federally funded housing or to enact a 90-day freeze on rents, wages and salaries to combat rising inflation and unemployment.[5] Usually those are issued under specific statutory authority from Congress. They have the effect and force of federal statutes; although most courts dismiss lawsuits brought when an order is violated.[6] Executive orders from honorable executives— people who honor and cherish, not only the true history of our constitutional republic, but the premises upon which it was birthed— would never violate the parameters surrounding our inalienable rights. Unfortunately, we have not always known how corrupt our politicians truly are.

Throughout this work I have shown how politics was front and center in many church pulpits. I limited writing all those instances because it would have encompassed many books. There is not, nor ever was any constitutional ban on pastors' speech from their pulpits concerning politics or candidates. In preaching from the pulpits concerning political theory and politicians, they rang out with the premise of just attitude, as well as unbiased and morally competent service. In other words, to serve and protect. Long before anyone reading this book was born, that idea was still mouthed from many, but the reality was changing.

The First Amendment states clearly: "Congress shall make no law respecting an establishment of religion, or prohibiting the free exercise thereof; or abridging the freedom of speech, or of the press; or the right of the people peaceably to assemble, and to petition the Government for a redress of grievances."

In 1954 one of our more corrupt and emotionally damaged politicians, who eventually became President, was facing re-election to the Senate.[7] In 1948 Lyndon Johnson was fraudulently elected as a U.S. Senator from

Texas. The election was known as "Landslide-Lyndon" because he was elected by only 87 votes. His opponent, Coke Stevenson, produced evidence hundreds of votes for Johnson were faked. Johnson used court injunctions to block Stevenson's success in overturning the fake result. So when Johnson was up for re-election in 1954, he knew he was in trouble.

Two anti-Communist groups came out against Johnson's agenda. To stop them, Johnson inserted language into the IRS code which prohibited non-profits from endorsement for, as well as opposition to, those running for political office. As a result, churches think there is a "gag" order which attempts to stop conservative pastors in their pulpits from free speech. I say conservatives because it is rarely, if ever, used against progressives for their cozy relationships with churches.[8] Executive orders have now been used in the same way (see next endnote). Executive orders have the potential to demolish our rights. When they are used to prop up one group or harm another, we have lost covenant and totalitarianism is in American living rooms. You can certainly disagree with my opinions and conclusions, but it is getting more difficult in light of recent cases to deny there is an attempt to silent religious speech, as well as an opponent's political speech.[9]

We don't have to look too far back in current history to view modern political hacks' successes at curbing free speech. Most Americans remember the recent debacle with the IRS and what, for want of a better term, is called "Tea Party groups." As I poured over the history of these groups and this case, it seems to me they started as a grass-roots protest against big government and the corruption that money brings to the table. Taxed Enough Already was their moniker (tea). As a whole (I only found a few exceptions) they were not politically connected. They were housewives, businessmen, grandparents and regular citizens.[10] Progressives, realizing they were in trouble before the 2010 mid-term elections, used many bully tactics, like calling the tea partiers racist, dangerous and downright unAmerican.[11] I remember the hyperbole and decided to do some inquiry as to who they were. That's when I realized how truly frightening the name-calling was. Dehumanizing and marginalizing your opponent personally is a tactic performed by most socialist regimes. All of us Americans not involved in politics and watching this nonsense assumed things would settle down and people would be able to see through the dirty politics. I don't think we could have been any more mistaken in our belief. What had looked like "politics as usual" became an attempt to criminalize what was a normal political process, using phony criminalization to deny access to one group (conservatives).

In this particular case the conservatives were the minority party and opponents of the administration in power at the time. The progressive supporters used the IRS to crush their detractors, who were the opponents of that sitting president and his administration.[12] It seems someone took a maneuver from Lyndon Johnson's playbook— and it worked. For years, in fact, over two election cycles, the conservatives were marginalized as a result of being denied access to IRS tax exempt and organizational status under the 501c(4) Code. If you were like me, you knew nothing about this exemption. I had always known religious or other charity groups could have tax exempt status, but I had no idea political groups could as well. I also had no idea how many groups from all sides of the aisle use this code. If you cannot form to organize a political group and receive the funds necessary to function without having to pay taxes on those donations, winning elections and getting your political ideas out to the rest of society is difficult. It is especially so in an environment where the media allow minimal airtime to political groups they disagree with. The hard facts prove this. To those of us watching TV, it's so obvious it looks like a glaring deficit.[13]

To date, no one has been formally charged. From what I can read of the internal workings of this, it seems to me there are more than enough legal avenues to get to the bottom of it. In my opinion, republicans have proven useless and democrats proven downright fraudulent. I had thought the courts had proven themselves incapable of redress, just as in 1948, when a Federal judge just recently told the IRS that it can't hide emails the White House wrote to the IRS during the 2010 and 2012 election campaigns.[14] Those emails had to do with the White House requesting tax return information about conservative, as well as tea party groups; in other words, the then administration's opponents.[15] You would think protecting the voters from fraud would be something a court would like to address. Hopefully the truth will be made known to the rest of us, along with the collusion of the FBI and Justice Departments (before the statute of limitations is up).[16]

Asking the Justice Department of the administration involved in the incident to investigate whether or not the IRS and the White House colluded, is like asking the German Socialists of 1939 to investigate incidents of prejudice against Jews. I don't use this example cavalierly or to incite, but to inform. Think about it: The administration in charge (from 2009 to 2017) were socialists who were notorious in their prejudice against Christians and Jews.[17] The tea partiers mainly consisted of everyday Americans. A majority of them were Christians, although other conservative groups (Jews) were also denied access. When the Justice Department was asked to investigate, they sent it over to a person who donated money to the then sitting president's campaigns.[18] Predictably, the Justice Department "found" nothing was that bad, just incompetent people, doing bad things (my words).[19] It reminded me of Dorothy in Oz going to talk to the wizard, only to find a little man hiding himself behind a curtain and telling everybody, "nothing to look at here. . . move along now. . . go away."

Reading the history on "Landslide Lyndon," I think that crusty old Texan would be quite pleased with himself. The modern day use of his tactic kept an incumbent president in office, although it had less success for the majority party in power in holding the House of Representatives and the Senate. You might say, "Well, it doesn't matter anyway, politics as usual." Unfortunately, it breaks covenant and contributes to the attitude of injustice, mistrust and corruption. Transparency in government is mandatory (see the Solutions segment). This situation smacks of fraud. It is a cog in the wheel toward the destruction of our governing compact. All of us Americans, no matter what political persuasion, should be screaming and banding together to get to the bottom of this. The reason becomes obvious when you see the further abyss we fall into. If a commander in chief gets away with activity which proves criminal or at the very least, suspicious, everyone else figures they can get away with it. There is then a disrespect for authority, and crime then goes on the rise because you obliterate the morale of law enforcement.[20] It becomes a cycle in which cops feel battered, so they get tougher and the criminals feel empowered because those involved in civil unrest feel it is their "right" to attack people. Lopsided from the start, it only gets worse.

All of this proves specifically when you start with abridging the free exercise of religion and political speech, especially through "executive" action, you walk yourself down a path which is progressivism, which is socialism, and I will prove those paths always lead to communism. In 2015 a socialist president, who did very little except by imperial action or executive order, was encouraged by another socialist running for what would be the 2016 elections, to make a threat to raise corporate taxes by executive order.[21] Putting aside the obvious breach of limited power and the separate powers enshrined within the Constitution, you can clearly see what starts as prohibiting the free exercise of someone's free religious as well as opinionated speech, ends with a president attempting to raise taxes by executive order.

Human beings are never satisfied with one power grab. If you allow them that *one,* then they will always go for more. This is not isolated to just the executive and legislative branches. There is a basic civics lesson inherent in our system: Congress makes the laws—because they are to be the people's representatives and originally states' representatives—the Executive branch enforces the law made by Congress, *and only law made by Congress.* The Judicial branch weighs and decides whether laws enacted line up to the Constitution— but they cannot "make" law— even if they decide a law is unconstitutional, they decide it in one specific case. Congress, or the legislative bodies of a state must now make a new law.

Nowhere was this basic breach of law more glaring than in the case of a Kentucky clerk who was sent to jail for refusing to issue genderless marriage licenses.[22] It matters very little what side of this argument you fall under, whether the clerk's religious rights stop at her desk or whether she has those rights at work. The fact remains she broke no written law. Can you imagine telling people their Fifth Amendment rights stop at the door of their jobs? That their Fourth Amendment rights do not apply as they commute to and from work? Add to this reality the fact the human genome has already been mapped. There is no homosexual gene.[23] The impassioned attitudes on both sides of this issue ignore science. Many supporting issues concerning homosexuality do not realize the science surrounding many of those issues is so tainted as to prove fraudulent.[24] Then you have the folks who truly are bigoted against homosexuals. You will be surprised to know I feel the Constitution gives homosexuals rights of association. I also believe firmly the God the Bible describes also gives every human the right to decide their own way and destiny. He does have an awesome destiny for every human. It is our decision whether we choose what He has decided we were created for is what we want. We can reject what God says about us. If that were not the case, the episode of Adam and Eve would not have been recorded. Those are my two reasons for refusing bias toward homosexuals. My third is that God loves people.

Marriage will always carry religious, legal connotations and ceremonial aspects through oaths as religious.[25] Sadly, anyone with cogent arguments labeling something scientifically and politically a civil union or genderless union and not a marriage are labeled as racist and haters. I'm sure there are those who will attempt to label me such. Not only do I reject that attempt, I will label it for what it is. It is communism, plain and simple. In the next few chapters I will prove progressives/socialists-communists all must degrade, dehumanize and label people who disagree with their positions in the most base and profane way so as to win the argument without ever presenting scientific or logical proofs. Progressivism/socialism must remove traditional roles and families from the next generation. They must make sure parents and political/religious values of a nation which contradict socialism are nullified in that generation. The best way to do that is to remove the identity of male and female within the next generation and to remove religious and political freedoms. Calling people who resist that attempt haters when they especially reject the hate is quite successful.

Progressive/socialists must also resist all male and female identifying practices, hence the "bathroom" debate. It's fine for men to be easy with a woman who identifies as a man to walk in and use their facility. It presents no bodily harm for the men. The same cannot be said for women. Any woman older than 25 will have some experience, either personally or from a friend, who has had a man try to follow her into the bathroom to commit a crime. I understand true transgendered are not thinking to commit a crime by using a woman's facility. But therein lies the problem. It is nearly impossible to differentiate between a true transgendered who is in counseling and probably on some form of medication/hormone therapy from a man who wants to use the transgendered situation to commit a crime. Whether the progressives or others like it or not, women need the protection— NO, WE DEMAND the protection. You will not call us haters for that and you will not call the men who understand our need for protection haters. In fact, if you continue with that nonsense and continue to bully states with economic withdrawal, I feel all citizens in that state have a right to class action lawsuits against any commercial or other enterprise demanding that kind of assault in an effort to force a bathroom policy which ignores basic safety issues. I frequent many establishments which have family unit bathrooms. These are safe, and no one I know or I have ever seen cares if a transgender walks into them. They are even safer for the transgender since they are single units and they can be locked to protect the occupant.

My next position, based on human genome mapping, is basic science. My scientific research tells me marriage is not a genderless institution. Other forms of association very well can be, but scientifically marriage cannot be. Science is the practical activity in which one arrives at conclusions based upon observation and experiment; cause and result. The "experiment" of heterosexual sex is very different from the "experiment" of homosexual sex. Based upon that experiment the outcome is very different as well. On all sorts of levels the outcome is very different; but on one stunning observation, a child is the potential outcome. If the sex is not the same, and the outcome is not the same, you must find a different basis for calling a practice something. Based on the fact we murder children regularly in this country, I am not hopeful my scientific argument will win the day. This is what happens when we cheapen inalienable rights with a foreign ideology like progressivism/socialism. But let me try to make a reasonable case for children anyway.

Research proves to me children are irreparably harmed when they are denied access to their mothers and fathers (or the image of male and female),[26] and it is not based on the circumstances of gendered or genderless marriage. This has nothing to do with hate, since many homosexuals agree with the same research.[27] Since that is the case, then all of us must act quickly to protect the next generation. In France homosexuals marched arm in arm with Christians (1 million strong, both Catholics and Evangelicals) in solidarity against marriage denying a child access to their mothers and their fathers—the image of male and female. This is true covenant. It is a secular one, but European nations understand children have inalienable rights.[28] I would also be willing to march arm in arm with those believing in the necessity for the rights of children and the religious. The UN Treaty of the Child protects children in this manner.[29] In fact, lesbians are denied insemination in some European countries.[30]

You might say, "Well, you're religious anyway, so you would think that." Actually, I thought, as many people do, all a child needed was stability, safety and love. I never thought research would ever prove a child suffered when you withhold the access to mom and dad (both genders). I was quite surprised that kind of research existed. I was also shocked there is biased research out there trying to prove just the opposite; but in order to get that result, they must add data. In other words, they must change the facts. There are some newer models which seem to show differences in how both boys and girls fare in genderless unions. I will continue to research this issue, as more and more studies which refuse to add or otherwise tamper with the data become available.[31]

There is a media black-out among almost all outlets, preventing true data from being known to the public on this subject. In fact, where colleges should be leading the charge in getting this information out, they are being bullied by students who don't want to hear any truth.[32] We constantly let people know the results from all sorts of studies about all kinds of things— both for and against coffee, steak, trans fat, sugar— you name it. Why we refuse to let folks know how our children are doing is insane. It is the same problem when it comes to the law. Very few know the law and the facts of the law surrounding the recent Supreme Court issue on states' rights and genderless marriage licenses and the injustice committed by the judge who jailed this clerk.

Just because the Supreme Court decides a certain case, does not make that case the entire law of the land. Congress, or the people's representative legislative body, must now write new law based on the High Court's decision. No new law was written in Kentucky. Even scarier in this case was that a senator from Kentucky asked the Federal judged who sentenced the clerk to give them a stay and give them time to write new law. The judge also had another option, one that the clerk's attorney asked for to simply accommodate her religious beliefs: Just remove her name from the licenses.[33] She objected to her name attached to or involved with genderless unions. It was a simple request and, ironically, one which wound up happening anyway by throwing her in prison.[34] In fact, the licenses which wound up being handed out had no signature on them.

So what was this judge really trying to do? He was abrogating to himself— to a court— judge, jury and executioner. This, my friends should have gays, the religious, those espousing the communist and/or socialist rule of law very frightened. Why? Because the double standard in this case already exists. Courts have already decided what I have just written is true. In other words, they will ignore a Supreme Court ruling when they don't like it because *they say* a law written for/against it is not clear. "When have they done that," you say? Oh, fellow citizen, they have done it already with the Second Amendment (see the next section on the Second Amendment[35]).

Many states already allow the religious to opt out of selling abortion-inducing drugs and from signing or participating in a genderless union. That new law was needed was clearly obvious when a senator from Kentucky asked the judge to give them more time because so many laws in Kentucky concerning marriage could be construed as invalid going forward, including the one genderless couples got their licenses issued from. What do I mean? In order to get a marriage license in Kentucky you had to go to the county in which the "female" resides.[36] Well, it is obvious from these cases there are either two "females" or no female. Other laws regarding this specific case were also not clear going forward. Kentucky, as well as many other states needed time to work this out. Since the legislature was in recess for the summer, and the governor refused to call them back for that issue only, more time was needed.

Did all this start with Lyndon Johnson? Well, not really, but it certainly hasn't ended with him. More modern day Texans will remember the recent attempt to seize the sermons preached from the pulpits of Houston pastors. The mayor, who is a lesbian, wrote a bill which protected grown men who *identify* as a woman to walk into a woman's bathroom. They called the bill the Equal Rights Ordinance, but the citizens called it the "Bathroom Bill." The opposition gathered 50,000 signatures to protest it, thus petitioning the city to put the issue on the ballot. The city attorney threw out the petitions, claiming they were not legitimate. He then issued a subpoena for five local pastor's sermons, some of whom were not even involved in the litigation. Eventually, the mayor had to back down since it became obvious the actions were conducted strictly to intimidate and bully the pastors in to silence, in clear violation of their First Amendment rights.[37] But suppose this were a small town, with less money and less ability to fight? Suppose a similar case is directed at only one tiny church or religious group or one individual? Well, it already has.

In January 2013 a Christian couple by the name of Aaron and Melissa Klein owned a bakery by the name of Sweet Cakes by Melissa. Like most small business owners they worked hard and long hours. A repeat customer asked to have a wedding cake made for a lesbian wedding. As Melissa tells it, her cakes are a creation of artwork, love and faith. The business declined to become involved in the wedding, citing their religious beliefs.[38] It did not take long before they were forced out of business. Their children (they have five) were threatened and a group of activists harassed their vendors.[39] The vendors themselves became worried for their own businesses and asked to be removed from their referral lists. Those referrals accounted for 65 to 70 percent of the bakery's yearly income. As a result the bakery was forced to close and posted a sign on the closed door.[40]

The State of Oregon didn't like what the sign said. They also didn't like what the Kleins said about their religious beliefs in media interviews. The Oregon Bureau of Labor and Industries had already brought a complaint against them from the gay couple, Rachel Cryer and Laurel Bowman-Cryer. The Kleins were fined $135,000 and have *been ordered* not to *talk to the press* or to *anyone* citing the reason for their refusal to bake the cake *because of their faith.* They have basically been told not to talk about their faith (see previous endnotes). The gay couple claimed medical problems as a result of the Klein's failure to bake them a wedding cake, yet no medical specialists were made available at the bureaucratic agency's hearing of the case. The Civil Rights Division of the Oregon Bureau of Labor and Industries is not a court, so the case is heard through an administrative law judge. The final say will come from the state's labor commissioner, a man by the name of Brad Avakian.

In fact, in states all across the country "human rights commissions" are staffed by political hacks who mete out justice by applying rules filled with bias and idealogical envy.[41] It is no different in this case. A GoFundMe® site was started immediately to help the Kleins with the litigation, since their business was shattered and unable to function due to the protests and threats made to the couple. GoFundMe® shut them down after more than $100,000 was raised.[42] How much of this double standard is as a result of fear and how much is an attempt to deny fellow citizens their free speech and free access? Whatever the answer, the reality is that a true understanding of our secular covenant is needed.

Even if you disagree with the premise that making a wedding cake or supplying photos and a place to honeymoon mean you are a part of a wedding, or that it constitutes using your God-given talent for something which makes a mockery of your God, you would still have to be horrified at the State of Oregon's treatment of this couple. The State's success will eventually remove the Kleins from their home, remove food and clothing from their children and leave them otherwise penniless. But, I suppose they can look on the bright side: There is always welfare! Of course, if the two or so percentage of homosexuals in this country were willing to treat their neighbors as they want to be treated themselves, they could go to any number of bakeries who would be delighted to accommodate them. Knowing the entrepreneurial spirit in this country, I can see whole industries of bakers, florists, photographers and hoteliers placing advertisements trumpeting their competent services to the homosexual.

It is the action of the free marketplace which would balance out choice in these areas— not bullying tactics by big corporations to intimidate states who allow for that free market to function— and not the intimidation (bludgeoning) we see of harassing the faithful in to silence. Those practices are what lead to captivity. They are decidedly the goal of progressives to force government into every aspect of humanity. This goal is not what our compacting documents reveal as good government. What started off as two or so percent of the country demanding a wedding has turned in to denying people their religious beliefs. Yet this is not the only problem. It is the communist-like "re-education" demands which should horrify all of us.[43]

There are basic biological science answers which should impact the decision. The politics of the socialist/progressives should not be seen in this discussion. There are political science questions needing to be answered as well, AND at least five Supreme Court Justices refused to professionally answer those political science issues. The Supreme Court says homosexuals can call something a marriage when the science says something different. At least one judge based the opinion on love. Okay, but what about the legal overlap the institution of marriage presents within religious and secular laws? How about those with scientific objections? Can we ignore the political science reality to that? The only way to do that is to have those who are not violating their conscience available to perform genderless unions.

There is another clear political science reality we cannot ignore. When you demand people violate their religious and scientific conscience— against their will— to make you a business client, aren't you violating their rights? Forcing people into that kind of violation is coercion. Why would you want to force someone with a religious objection to participate in any aspect of your wedding? What about those with clear scientific reasons for objecting to children being abused in this fashion? Why would you want them going around telling people at your reception the scientific reasons why the children are in danger? The clear answer is to give rights of conscience for these situations. This is covenantal. Frankly, I would have far more respect for the argument if they did. When you sue a state or an individual because of their own inalienable right, even though well qualified professionals were available to service your wedding plans, and you take by force or some other avenue their inalienable right, you weaken all rights and you weaken our nation. Something else becomes obvious: These are the effects of communism, not covenant. By doing these things it becomes proof positive the real desire is to remove religious rights as well as other rights of conscience from people, thereby making a clear play to remove First Amendment rights from all Americans. There can be no other reasons, since states and many others are going to great lengths to make sure the rights of all are honored.

If the homosexual argument has the right to deny citizens free speech based upon research or free speech based upon their religious beliefs, does it have the right to deny a child their inalienable right to a mother and a father—the image of male and female? There are countless adults who have been raised in homosexual unions and they discuss the deep pain in not having their mother and father available.[44] They talk about the love they have for the LGBT community, but they also know the need—firsthand— a child has for its mother and father. These adult children have been placed in an untenable position. All they want is to have the scientific and psychological studies which prove their dilemma validated and made publicly known, so other children do not have to go through what they have endured. Yet their own free speech has been marginalized by denial and harassment.[45] In a strange spate of irony, all they want is the same affirmation their LGBT parents have demanded, but the very community they grew up in denies them. My exhortation here is not to deny secular rights of compact to homosexuals, but to say to them, denying those same rights to the religious, to children and to others, will deny humanity itself.

There are always exemptions to every rule. I have had to counsel people in divorce and death. Whether under heterosexual or homosexual parenting, children do not do well when they see their newly singled parent in sexual relations. We will review these issues more closely when we look at the covenant of marriage. I mention this now because I have seen single, homosexual family members, who normally would never take a child under their care, have to make the hard decision to raise a deceased family member's child (children). This is a very difficult and painful experience. No one should add to their misery. But like the heterosexual, I have advised the divorced (or newly parented) to remain celibate, simply because children do not do well in environments where "partners" are coming in and out of those children's lives.

My mother was a young, divorcee. We all lived with her mom and dad (my grandparents). Looking back, I now realize the care and dedication my mom took in making sure we never had to experience any difficulty in this area. In fact, I was kind of surprised to be introduced to the man my mom wanted to marry. I was older by then. I had no idea she was even dating and had already booked the church with the reception in the planning! Looking back now after years of counseling others who were not as fortunate when it came to living through their single-parents' dating issues, I am so grateful my mom was so adamant about not exposing us kids to the three or four men she went on a date with. It wasn't until I was a young adult I found out she even dated a few young men before she remarried!

Children of all ages do not do well with a revolving door of adult relationships based on their single parent's sexual conquests. By suppressing the publication of the research into children's welfare, especially in light of their need for male and female reflection, those who find themselves newly parented as a result of catastrophe lose the benefits that research could give them in raising their new charges. As a result, the whole society loses benefits from its new generation of healthy citizens. This goes to the very heart of covenant. No man is an island. We are all in this together.

Another sad effect of this systemic muzzling, is when those who, for many and varied reasons are no longer homosexual talk about their newly found freedom. The treatment these folks get in the press and from the LGBT community is horrendous.[46] I love teaching and preaching the word of God, but sometimes just one experience from the love and glory of God to the human heart can set a soul free from all sorts of entanglements all my preaching could never accomplish. God loves people and God loves the homosexual. Following Him through this love experience will change folks. If people cannot share those experiences without ridicule or if they are refused the same 'airtime' from the major media outlets their homosexual counterparts receive, something is wrong and very unAmerican. Obviously this is about more than businesses, because folks who have nothing to do with a business are receiving the same horrendous treatment— even being jailed.

I believe everyone living in Christian environments—that includes homosexuals—should experience the love and dignity those environments foster, whether they themselves are Christian or not. But causing the financial ruin of businesses, suppressing the pain the children of homosexuals experience, as well as silencing ex-homosexuals concerning their new-found freedom is anything but loving and dignifying. If homosexuals and their supporters have the right to deny a child its inalienable right, then does everyone else? Do they have the right to deny people their First Amendment rights? Do three people in a "marriage" or four people have the right to deny citizens their inalienable rights? Under "re-education" orders, research and other findings could be denied based solely on the outcome of that research. This goes to the very heart of our governing social compact, to the heart of covenant and to the heart of our First Amendment rights.

Should the scientists, researchers, authors, pastors and parents with differing opinions be forced into "re-education" camps? (Sometimes called "retraining classes" or "counseling.") Should they be forced in to silence concerning their research which conflicts with the political correctness of the socialists? Must they be bullied and threatened by those who disagree with their scientific positions and religious beliefs? Must they be threatened and fined by states' officials who disagree with them? Should they be called names and have other derogatory comments made about them by the same state officials their public dollars go to fund?[47] Soldiers volunteering for military service stand up for, among other things, Americans' Inalienable Rights, particularly those embodied in the First Amendment. I think many would refuse to volunteer if they knew a business conglomerate like Planned Parenthood colluded with the governor of a state to have that same governor force and threaten a medical board in the state to deny First Amendment rights to only certain businesses which practice their First Amendment rights.[48]

It gets even worse. The California case which challenged Proposition 8 told the voters in California their vote making marriage between a man and a woman was invalid. It was eventually decided by a judge who was in a ten-year long genderless relationship. He kept this fact from the litigants, revealing it only upon his retirement, after he decided the case. His decision was challenged because he is homosexual and therefore would have benefited from overturning the voter initiative, which is what he did. Historically courts have decided judges who share a fundamental characteristic with a litigant or a member of a religion should not be recused based solely on that association.[49] They ruled similarly so in this case.

So you can imagine, if some court said a judge were unfit to rule in a case concerning genderless marriage or refused to perform a homosexual marriage because he or she shared a fundamental characteristic with a segment of the population disagreeing with the premise of genderless unions, then we would all say a double standard is in place and something is horribly wrong. Well, an Ohio Supreme Court's Board of Professional conduct has come quite close to saying exactly that.[50] Other states have made allowances for state employees to opt out of performing gay marriages and made allowances so that all marriages are performed in a timely manner.[51] But if states and even the Supreme Court decides a double standard is equal protection and equal rights, then America is broken and our Ninth Amendment has been destroyed. The socialists have finally overcome our Constitution and they did so through the abuse of the homosexual argument, and at such a time when we could have solved the issue in a covenantal and harmonious way. In fact, this is the practice of the progressives. They have done this with the 14th Amendment, the 17th Amendment and now in this issue. In creating a crisis where none exists, they use whatever issue is at hand, having an easy solution, but instead bludgeon our Constitution. In this way, the present crisis goes quietly off into the sunset— while our Constitution has been hacked to pieces— so when they come in with tanks and a communist style takeover years later, the people will not even know or remember how it all happened. I will prove this shortly.

Those of us over the age of 25 should have full memory of the multitudes of varied attempts made at ruining our Second Amendment rights. I am not ignoring them in this section, just choosing brevity. If I were to include even a small grouping of them, as with our First Amendment rights, this section would contribute hundreds of pages. It seems every time some mentally deranged individual, convicted felon or terrorist shoots multiple innocents, the politicians feel the Second Amendment is the culprit and criminalizing law-abiding gun owners out of owning guns is the answer. There are multiple examples of this in the media at any given time.

Obviously, the victims' family members are distraught and feel the need to "do something" to avenge their loved ones. Unfortunately, they make pliable minds in the hands of the politically motivated. Like the wizard in Dorothy's Oz, let's pretend the real problems of mental illness, criminality and the breakdown of society by varied and foreign ideologies don't exist. With no palpable healing-balm experience of the Holy Spirit, society is lawless. When the religious are not allowed to witness to people on the job (as requested) or in the public square, because they are prevented equal access— or their monuments are removed by court order— a society forgets the multiple benefits of the power of the Holy Spirit which the religious and secular covenant in that society can portray.

There should be no argument: People with mental illness should not have access to guns. We can all agree to that. It is the Federal government, especially under ObamaCare, which makes it difficult to find out who is mentally ill, thus making it difficult to keep a gun out of their hands. Being a law-abiding gun owner in some states is akin to having your name and address published like a convicted sex offender would be forced to have their private information published.[52] This is not covenant. It is heartbreaking to watch innocents die at the point of a gun. The gun is not the murderer. Targeting the gun is senseless. The church, over time targets the elements of criminal behavior, so less murders take place. When government and media continues to marginalize the religious, they marginalize the positive effects they and their churches produce. Unfortunately, no church can get every criminal, or stop all the mentally ill. Government must target the criminal and make it obvious who is mentally incapable of gun ownership. That means doing some things which will make liberals very angry. But who is more important in a covenant situation, the citizen or the criminal? The criminal should not expect covenantal outreach, except to remedially bring them back in covenant. That means arrest, in addition for the drug addicted, medical and mental help.

The attitude in some states is that the legal gun owner is a criminal. This attitude clearly does not understand covenant. In point of fact, it has gotten so dangerous to exercise your Second Amendment rights those who desire to remove them will call the police on you if you have a license-to-carry and decide to do so.[53] It is called "swatting." This is where someone, not exhibiting any untoward behavior has a side-arm, and a person calls police, telling them someone is brandishing a weapon. You can imagine the danger for life and limb which can ensue when the police themselves are used as weapons to try to enforce "your social" agenda.

The Second Amendment states clearly: "A well regulated Militia, being necessary to the security of a free State, the right of the people to keep and bear Arms, shall not be infringed."

There are states clearly denying our Second Amendment rights. In Maryland it is illegal to wear, carry or transport a firearm in public without a permit. The State then makes it difficult to get a permit.[54] October 2007, Charles F. Williams, Jr., was arrested for transporting a legally purchased firearm without a permit.[55] Courts that want to deny and marginalize our Second Amendment rights have clearly ruled against already established Supreme Court cases stating citizens have a right to bear Arms.[56]

It is shear nonsense to ignore the context of the framing generation, the punctuation commas in the sentence itself by delineating a militia, an individual state and the average citizen in gun ownership— all three are included in the right to bear arms. This is not "difficult" legal theory. The framers did not intend these Amendments should be hard to understand. The only time you have to make it hard is when you want to curtail the people's rights. After studying the framing generation— indeed the founding generation itself— they wrote in terse and limited language. One obvious reason was the cost of pen and paper (in this case vellum). They spoke in limiting parameters; or said another way, they wrote what would be considered the outside limit of an institution or the demarcation line of exemplar, standard or even precedent. For example, we have limited government. That means branches of government are not allowed to go over a certain line. Because government was the highest human authority, it was the government who is limited in the First Amendment. (Initially the Federal government; see previous section.) This means that free speech, both religious and political or otherwise is permitted in government, on the job and in the public square. Why? Because government was the boundary line for the First Amendment— government itself and everything under the authority of human government— business, job, public square, etc., is where the people can exercise their First Amendment rights.

In the Second Amendment we have three demarcations: a militia, the state and the individual (the people). The Third Amendment sets its boundary for the military in "times of peace." The Fourth Amendment carries even more boundary lines: persons, houses, papers and effects, (places and persons), etc. The limitation is upon the court and/or those carrying out law. Government has tried to exclude various technologies, especially covering Internet-capable technologies, saying this was not included. But the courts have reasoned against that, saying that a person's effects, though not specifically stated as a cellphone, is still their "effect." And so this goes down the line with the first ten amendments—some have included even those amendments written before 1850 to 1880, others include all 27.

Those infused with socialist-leaning legal theory try to make the Second Amendment have a "preamble" argument. They try to make it seem you have to be in an army or militia in order to own a gun. Unfortunately for them, it matters very little whether you buy into the preamble argument. The subject matter is the people; it is the people who staff the militias. Secondly, some have used the "times" or practices of 1791. This argument finds no solace either since many militias were staffed by those who owned guns privately, very much like militias today. Americans have always owned guns privately. Much like the thought process throughout the entire compact, America was a country filled with private owners, full of those loving liberty and freedom from government control. It would be uncharacteristic of the Bill of Rights if the Second Amendment were to mean only the government could keep and bear arms. Can you imagine the outrage the framing generation would have exhibited if someone tried to take their guns or limited their ownership rights?

The framers gave us an avenue for updating the Constitution: They are called Amendments. Amendments that are outside of the first ten can be altered when necessary. Why only the first ten? Because the majority of us refuse to negotiate on the first ten. When you want to encroach upon the people's inalienable rights, it seems reasoning goes out the window. Have you ever heard the nonsensical phrase "The Constitution is a living document"? It is concocted by those who want the document to say what they want, and not what it actually says. They then follow that up with the fact it was written long ago and times have changed and it needs updating. Well, it seems to me when the framers wrote the word "effects" it included elements the framers did not understand, but felt would be interpreted by those in whom English was their native-born language. Giving us the amendment process is a reasonable human thing to do with something which does not have a life. Only the people who adhere to the covenantal tradition it embodies are living.

The only Book ever mentioned and proven as a "living document" by those who read, cherish and obey or follow it, is the BIBLE. Why is that? Because the Holy Spirit gives revelation as you read. The Constitution does not do this. You can, with your mind, parse out what the document means. You can logically read the words and engage your understanding. Conversely, the Bible does not need to be read by the mind singularly, but with your spirit. This is why so many read it and cannot understand the book: They are trying to read it solely through human understanding. It must be read through the living Holy Spirit. The Holy Spirit engages our spirit and then understanding is given to the mind. This is a living Book.

The Constitution does not do this. Gee, whiz, does that mean the folks who think the Constitution is a living document also think it followed biblical principles? Well, if they feel that way, then let's really follow biblical principles strictly concerning Constitutional law. Ah, there it is, screaming voices shouting: "That's Not What We Mean!" And that, my friends, is an example of the much talked about, but seemingly never seen "double standard." For some who make the argument the Constitution is a living document, they try to use as their source for life, the people as Sovereign. Since the people are living, they then say the document is living. It's odd, but if those who use the living document argument were genuine, none of these contrary judicial decisions would ever go against the people and their covenant. Our rights would never be in jeopardy, as they are. By the very fact our rights are in jeopardy is proof the "living document" thesis is a lie.

Here is the problem with that aspect of the thesis, along with the rest of the "living document" ideas. Words are, what Madison said, explanatory. Here is Madison in The Federalist 37:

> "The use of words is to express ideas. Perspicuity, therefore, requires not only that the ideas should be distinctly formed, but that they should be expressed by words distinctly and exclusively appropriate to them. But no language is so copious as to supply words and phrases for every complex idea, or so correct as not to include many equivocally denoting different ideas. Hence it must happen that however accurately objects may be discriminated in themselves, and however accurately the discrimination may be considered, the definition of them may be rendered inaccurate by the inaccuracy of the terms in which it is delivered. And this unavoidable inaccuracy must be greater or less, according to the complexity and novelty of the objects defined. When the Almighty himself condescends to address mankind in their own language, his meaning, luminous as it must be, is rendered dim and doubtful by the cloudy medium through which it is communicated."[57]

So the living God communicates to the living people, using a descriptive medium, even an object, or for some folks a "cloudy medium." Of course, this is why the Holy Spirit is engaged when reading the Bible: He embodies the words, making them alive and giving them meaning. This concerns God's word. The words contained in the Constitution or the document itself are not alive. People, God, other beings on the planet are living. Words are used to explain life, death and all sorts of things.

Are the people what anchor the Constitution? Or is it the compact that anchors it? It is the establishment document (Declaration of Independence). That document establishes the people. What establishes that document; what anchors it? The connection the people have to whomever has the legal authority to establish them. So are the words living or is it the living people who covenant with the living God (Creator) which establishes them? Are not the people just living agents of the covenant? When you need a boat to be anchored, one must throw out a weight greater than the forces against it. This is mass and volume working against the forces of gravity to keep a person alive. After all, if nothing living is on the boat and it perishes, it can be replaced. The Constitution can be amended. The anchor, or the establishment document, must carry greater weight. But even if that is lost, it is the people in a natural state in covenant with the Creator of nature who are alive or living. The words on the vellum just describe this and the outer limits by which this functions.

Whatever my opinion about Jefferson, while talking about the religious tolerance of other states, he touches on similar facts: "But is the spirit of the people an infallible, a permanent reliance? Is it government?"[58] In other words, what is the anchor and who is infallible or sovereign? He then talks about the covenant: "Is this the kind of protection we receive in return for the rights we give up?"[59] While not addressing my specific topic, he does make a statement which trumps all the arguments: "Besides, the spirit of the times may alter, will alter. Our rulers will become corrupt, our people careless. A single zealot may commence persecutor, and better men be his victims. It can never be too often repeated, that the time for fixing every essential right on a legal basis is while our rulers are honest, and ourselves united."[60]

So that is what they did. They fixed already revealed inalienable rights on the legal basis of the Creator who granted the people existence, land, and rights. "We, The People," then covenanted, giving ourselves a document called the Bill of Rights. Jefferson, whether fairly or not, is described as the constant religious equivocator. These words, (in excerpts) attributed to him are on our monument to him: "God who gave us life gave us liberty. Can the liberties of a nation be secure when we have removed a conviction that these liberties are the gift of God? Indeed I tremble for my country . . ."[61] (See endnote for the exact excerpted pattern.) The proof of my point is in our present sickened condition. We can add no rights because we are deeply divided, not united (as Jefferson says).

The press has done a great job at spinning this fact for socialism's benefit. They also lie about gun statistics. It is not gun ownership which causes more murders because America rates number one in the world of countries with gun ownership, yet comes in at 111 among 218 countries in murders per capita. We have 4.7 murders per 100,000 citizens. What places our rates even that high are those strongholds of progressive gun controlled areas. Those areas with the highest rates of gun ownership in our country have the least murders per capita.[62]

Everyone screams background checks are not exhaustive enough. The reality is the criminal and the mentally ill will almost never apply for a background check. There is another study which proves the fallibility of the background check argument. "States with universal background checks have had 124% more mass public shootings" and much higher rates of death and injury from guns since 2013.[63] Not only does the rate per capita of deaths and injuries from guns increase when a state enacts stricter and more expensive background checks, but law-abiding poor minority gun owners in high crime areas are then priced out of gun ownership because of the expense.[64] In a city like New York, where they actually had a policy of targeting criminals for gun possession that worked, the courts struck down the law.[65]

If there are no benefits to expanding background checks, what could possibly be the benefit of going after the law-abiding gun owner? When you try to enact a policy catching the criminal before they kill someone with a gun, but socialist judges strike down the laws, what is really going on here? Obviously there are no benefits when we take away guns from the law-abiding public. So there must be an ulterior motive in attempting to bully citizens and remove their ability to protect themselves.

In order to do that one must go after the Second Amendment. Instead of aggressively targeting the criminal and mentally ill in an effort to keep guns out of their hands, the effort is made to undermine our Second

Amendment as the problem or cause of the problems. The Second Amendment, like our First Amendment is not the problem. It is the practice of socialism to lie and undermine any law which has the potential to deny socialism its supremacy. It is those with progressive (or socialistic) intent who claim the Constitution is a "living" document. This is a lie in order to ruin our Bill of Rights.

Here is the proof socialism is lawlessness: By functioning in a way making the one document of the compact "living," you wind up with contrary rulings, because you bring deceit, loss of energy, mistrust, as well as confusion into the process. When you refuse to treat all the covenant people accordingly in order of their inalienable rights, you bring confusion into the system. This has to set the stage for contrary rulings, which always produce mistrust. You must then enter into deceit to maintain the rule of the elite who bring the confusion into the system.

These contrary rulings are concocted not by the ignorant or the uneducated, but by people with either an agenda, a political motive, or by those who have fallen so far down the rabbit hole of judicial and bureaucratic largesse in making law, that no one should be surprised some judges refuse to read history and the law as cause and effect.[66] They forget it is not their job to make law, but only rule based on what is already written. Only when the language is ambiguous, which is hardly the case with our compacted documents, must they interpret for a ruling. The effect of this dual and muddled action has already taken place with our First Amendment rights.[67] Stemming from muddied thinking, it just proves the waves of history, time and space are placing a demand on the anchor (The Declaration of Independence) and stirring up the sea bed. When that happens the safety net of the "second boat" (the Bill of Rights) keeps all the people safe. It reminds all that God (living and active) gives to the people (living and active) rights that none can take away. To say otherwise is to lie or misconstrue the fact in order to gain and steal away the people's power and rights.

Jesus said it clearly in Matthew 23, to the lawyers of his day: "Woe unto you, scribes and Pharisees, hypocrites! For ye pay tithe of mint and anise and cumin, and have omitted the weightier matters of the law, judgment, mercy and faith: these ought ye to have done, and not to leave the other undone . . . for you make clean the outside of the cup and of the platter, but within they are full of extortion and excess . . . Even so ye also outwardly appear righteous unto men, but within ye are full of hypocrisy and iniquity" (Matthew 23:23-28).

By criminalizing or treating as criminals law-abiding citizens simply because they engage in their First and Second Amendment rights, and take those rights seriously, endangers our secular compact. By using the bureaucratic force of a state or the Federal government or a court to do so, endangers all citizens— the atheist, agnostic and religious— the gun owner and gun-rights opponent— the homosexual and heterosexual ones, alike. No one wants to see innocents killed by guns. This is a no-brainer. Hopefully common sense and decency will win the day, allowing those who own guns legally to remain free to practice their First and Second Amendment rights without fear of reprisal, the loss of life, money, home and freedom. So I will move on to the next amendment.

The Third Amendment has to do with quartering soldiers during peace time: "No Soldier shall, in time of peace be quartered in any house, without the consent of the Owner, nor in time of war, but in a manner to be prescribed by law."

It is straightforward and the Supreme Court cited it once in Griswold v. Connecticut in 1965 (381 U.S. 479). We solve the quartering problem in this country by paying communities to host military bases. There have been historical violations of the Third Amendment.[68] Most other violations fall within any one of the next seven amendments. It can be argued some of the cases I have already cited have violated the Fourteenth Amendment. So I will group the next seven as a whole because they are our original, inalienable rights contained in the Bill of Rights. Once you read the next stories, as with the previous ones, it will become obvious they have been trampled on and broken by our states as well as Federal government, egged on by a run-away political junta, controlling judicial oligarchy. I will prove this is by design. It is an actual conspiracy from a foreign ideology to deny us our rights.

The Fourth Amendment: "The right of the people to be secure in their persons, houses, papers, and effects, against unreasonable searches and seizures, shall not be violated, and no Warrants shall issue, but upon probable cause, supported by Oath or affirmation, and particularly describing the place to be searched, and the persons or things to be seized."

The Fifth Amendment: "No person shall be held to answer for a capital, or otherwise infamous crime, unless on a presentment or indictment of a Grand Jury, except in cases arising in the land or naval forces, or in the Militia, when in actual service in time of War or public danger; nor shall any person be subject for the same offense to be twice put in jeopardy of life or limb; nor shall be compelled in any criminal case to be a witness against himself, nor be deprived of life, liberty, or property, without due process of law; nor shall private property be taken for public use, without just compensation."

The Sixth Amendment: "In all criminal prosecutions, the accused shall enjoy the right to a speedy and public trial, by an impartial jury of the State and district wherein the crime shall have been committed, which district shall have been previously ascertained by law, and to be informed of the nature and cause of the accusation; to be confronted with the witnesses against him; to have compulsory process for obtaining witnesses in his favor, and to have the Assistance of Counsel for his defence."

The Seventh Amendment: "In Suits at common law, where the value in controversy shall exceed twenty dollars, the right of trial by jury shall be preserved, and no fact tried by a jury, shall be otherwise re-examined in any Court of the United States, than according to the rules of common law."

The Eighth Amendment: "Excessive bail shall not be required, nor excessive fines imposed, nor cruel and unusual punishments inflicted."

The Ninth Amendment: "The enumeration in the Constitution, of certain rights, shall not be construed to deny or disparage others retained by the people."

The Tenth Amendment: "The powers not delegated to the United States by the Constitution, nor prohibited by it to the States, are reserved to the States respectively, or to the people."[69]

ENDNOTES

Because of the nature of the Internet and its fluidity, email address references may not be the same as listed. If you find that to be the case, you can Google the article or legal review along with the server's URL. This will frequently give you the listed source.

1   John Adams, The Works of John Adams, Second President of the United States: with a Life of the Author, Notes and Illustrations, by his Grandson Charles Francis Adams (Boston: Little, Brown and Co., 1856) Vol 4. 584. Public domain

2   <http://avalon.law.yale.edu/18th_century/adamsme1.asp> © 2008 Lillian Goldman Law Library, accessed 3/12/16.

3   John Adams, "The Works of John Adams, Second President of the United States: with a Life of the Author, Notes and Illustrations, by his Grandson Charles Francis Adams" (Boston: Little, Brown and Co., 1856). 10 volumes. Vol. 3, 457

4   <http://www.foxnews.com/opinion/2015/09/04/christian-intimidation-kentucky-judge-does-with-gavel-what-bull-connor-did-with-dogs-and-fire-hoses.html> accessed 4/2/16

5   <http://legal-dictionanary.thefreedictionary.com/Executive+Order> accessed 4/3/16

6   Anderson, Leanna M., 2002: "Executive Orders, The Very Definition of Tyranny and the Congressional Solution, and the Separation of Powers Restoration Act." Hastings Constitutional Law Quarterly 29 (spring): 589-611. <http://www.hastingsconlawquar-terly.org/archives/V29/13/Anderson.pdf> Sterling, John A.; 2000, "Above the Law: Evolution of Executive Orders." University of West Los Angeles Law Review 31 (annual); <http://law.jrank.org/pages/6656/Executive-Order-FURTHER-READINGS.html> accessed 4/2/16

7   <http://www.theatlantic.com/magazine/archive/1998/04/three-new-revelations-about-lbj/377094><http://www.statesman.com/news/news/local/longtime-lbj-aide-mildred-stegall-finally-tells--1/nRXXK/>sites accessed 11/15/15. "Mutual Contempt: Lyndon Johnson, Robert Kennedy and the Feud that Defined a Decade," © 1997 Jeff Shesol, published by W.W. Norton & company, 500 Fifth Avenue, NY, NY

8   <http://www.freerepublic.com/focus/news/765344/posts> accessed 4/4/16

9   <https://www.nraila.org/articles/20150605/stop-obamas-planned-gag-order-on-firearm-related-speech> <http://aclj.org/free-speech/two-issues-to-watch-fec-efforts-to-regulate-political-internet-speech-and-the-fccs-net-neutrality-litigation> accessed 4/4/16

10   <http://www.britannica.com/topic/Tea-Party-movement> accessed 4/4/16

11   <http://www.nationalreview.com/article/243475/naacp-hurls-false-racism-charge-tea-party-movement-deroy-murdock> accessed 4/4/16

12   <http://www.judicialwatch.org/blog/tag/lois-lerner/><http://www.newsmax.com/Politics/lois-lerner-irs-tea-party-gop/2015/05/29/id/647452/><http://www.nationalreview.com/article/420277/irs-scandal-house-republicans-impeaching-commissioner-koskinen> accessed 4/4/16

13   <http://www.weeklystandard.com/Content/Public/Articles/000/000/004/143lkblo.asp> accessed 4/4/16

14   <http://aclj.org/free-speech/good-sign-for-acljs-tea-party-lawsuit><http://www.washingtontimes.com/news/2015/jan/12/irs-keeps-albuquerque-tea-party-in-limbo-5-years-a/?page=all><http://christianpatriots.org/2015/02/28/tea-party-groups-suing-irs-call-for-independent-prosecutor> accessed 4/4/16

15   <http://www.foxnews.com/politics/2015/08/31/judge-tells-irs-it-cant-hide-white-house-emails/?intcmp=hplnws> accessed 4/3/16

16   <http://www.judicialwatch.org/press-room/press-releases/judicial-watch-new-documents-reveal-doj-irs-and-fbi-plan-to-seek-criminal-charges-of-obama-opponents/> accessed 4/4/16

17   <http://www.youngcons.com/40-mind-blowing-quotes-barack-obama-islam-christianity/> This next site is hated by many progressives. Whatever you may think of them, please listen to the attached video clip to listen to a constitutional lawyer, who has won these battles and will prove the statement I made concerning the timeline of 1939. Searching a university research paper supporting the statement, landed me on this site. Where universities should be leading the way in this thought I found silence. My own limited research was proving that history is repeating itself, but not having the time to do that kind of thesis, I expected someone else had done it. But I found nothing, until I came upon this clip. Please listen to it with an open ear to the legal theory and non-racist, rights-for-all approach this lawyer takes <http://allnewspipeline.com/Why_O_Declared_War_On_Christianity.php> accessed 4/4/16

18   <http://www.washingtontimes.com/news/2014/jan/8/feds-pick-obama-supporter-lead-irs-tea-party-probe/?page=all> accessed 4/4/16

19   <http://www.cnn.com/2015/10/23/politics/lois-lerner-no-charges-doj-tea-party/> accessed 4/4/16

20   <http://www.foxnews.com/politics/2015/09/02/summer-crime-killings-soar-in-big-us-cities-amid-debate-over-policing/?intcmp=hpbt1> Concerning the disrespect for authority: <http://foxnews.com/us/2015/09/02/arby-apologizes-after-officer-is-denied-service-for-being-cop/?intcmp=hpbt1> Concerning the downward spiral in law and order and how it affects the recruiting of new law enforcement: <http://www.foxnews.com/us/2015/09/02/who-needs-this-police-recruits-abandon-dream-amid-anti-cop-climate/?intcmp=trending> accessed 4/2/16

21   <http://foxnews.com/politics/2015/03/03/white-house-eyes-executive-action-way-to-hike-taxes/?intcmp=latestnews> accessed 4/3/16

22   <http://www.foxnews.com/opinion/2015/09/04/christian-intimidation-kentucky-judge-does-with-gavel-what-bull-connor-did-with-dogs-and-fire-hoses.html> 4/3/16

23   <https://www.geneticliteracyproject.org/2015/10/12/despite-what-you-may-have-read-theres-no-gay-gene/> The previous is a quick and unbiased article. The second one is more involved with various overtones, but the science is still good. <https://www.trueorigin.org/gaygene01.php> accessed 4/9/16

24   <http://www.drjudithreisman.com/the_kinsey_coverup.html> <https://www.drjudith-reisman.com/archives/Kinsey_Sex_and_Fraud.pdf> accessed 4//9/16

25   Charles J. Reid, Jr. 2004. "The Unavoidable Influence of Religion Upon The Law of Marriage." 23 Quinnipiac Law Review 493 (2004).

26   This is only a tiny fraction of the research: "New Family Structures Study," done by Professor Mark Regnerus of the University of Texas at Austin, published in "Social Science Research," Volume 41, Issue 4, July 2012, Pages 752-770. An article entitled "Same-Sex Parenting: Unpacking the Social Science," by John B. Londregan, The Witherspoon Institute, February 24, 2015, and can be seen at <http://www.thepublicdiscourse.com/2015/02/14465/> Also a study done in Denmark of 6.5 million Danes over 30 years revealing the health benefits for all involved in intact traditional marriages: "International Journal of Epidemiology," Volume 39, Supplement 2, December 2010. Evidence from Canada <http://www.thepublicdiscourse.com/2013/10/10996/> Sites accessed 4/4/16

27   Mainwaring, Doug. March 8, 2013. "I'm Gay and I Oppose Same-Sex Marriage." <http://www.thepublicdiscourse.com/2013/03/9432> accessed 4/9/16

28   <https://www.lifesitenews.com/news/estimated-1-million-march-in-paris-against-gay-marriage-plans> accessed 4/4/16

29   See Article 6.1; Article 8.1; Article 9.1-4; Article 10.1-2; Article 13.1-2; Article 14.1-3;<http://www.ohchr.org/en/professionalinterest/pages/crc.aspx> accessed 4/4/16

30   <https://en.wikipedia.org/wiki/Sperm_donation_laws_by_country><http://www.foxnews.com/world/2012/04/13/fertility-treatment-bans-in-europe-draw-criticism.html.

The first site has more updated information than the second, since laws are constantly changing, accessed 4/9/16.

31   See the YouTube clip of an interview with Professor Robert Oscar Lopez at the copyrighted YouTube site of TotalLivingNetwork1 <https://www.youtube.com/watch?v=t4wJz5c5GXo> site accessed 4/4/16. At or around minutes 15 he speaks in depth concerning the tainted effects of adding data when conflicting or nonconforming results appear. If you have the time it is worth your while to listen to the cogent arguments this man has. They are certainly not based on hate. I think we can all support the protection of our children. If you want to read the science behind this in a pdf form <http://www.familywatchinternational.org/fwi/policy_brief_ss_parenting.pdf> site accessed 4/4/16

32   <http://video.foxnews.com/v/4610150912001/alan-dershowitz-students-dont-want-diversity-of-ideas/?#sp=show-clips><http://www.nationalreview.com/article/426853/yale-student-protest-safe-space-political-correctness> accessed 4/4/16

33   Ibid.

34   <http://www.foxnews.com/politics/2015/09/05/jailed-kentucky-clerks-calls-issued-marriage-licenses-to-gay-couples-void/> accessed 4/5/15

35   <http://www.supremecourt.gov/opinions/09pdf/08-1521.pdf> accessed 4/4/16

36   <http://www.usnews.com/news/us/articles/2015/09/02/kentucky-clerk-gets-help-from-gop-state-senate-president> accessed 4/4/16

37   <http://time.com/3514166/houston-pastors-sermons-subpoenaed/><http://www.foxnews.com/opinion/2014/10/29/houston-mayor-drops-bid-to-subpoena-pastors-sermons.html>accessed 4/4/16

38   <http://popehat.com/2015/07/08/lawsplainer-so-are-those-christian-cake-bakers-in-oregon-unconstitutionally-gagged-or-not/><http://dailysignal.com/2015/04/27/exclusive-bakers-facing-135k-fine-over-wedding-cake-for-same-sex-couple-speak-out/><https://ricochet.com/oregon-bakers-statements-to-national-media-were-unlawful/>accessed 4/4/16

39   <http://www.cbn.com/cbnnews/us/2015/February/Christian-Bakery-Must-Pay-Damages-to-Gay-Couple/> accessed 4/4/16

40   <http://dailysignal.com/2015/07/06/sorry-slate-oregon-did-put-a-gag-order-on-those-christian-bakers/>see previous noted sites; accessed 4/4/16

41   <http://www.nationalreview.com/article/420865/do-christians-even-have-chance-against-oregons-bureaucracy-david-french><http://www.foxnews.com/opinion/2015/07/06/state-silences-bakers-who-refused-to-bake-cake-for-lesbians.html> accessed 4/4/16

42   <http://nypost.com/2015/04/26/christian-bakers-face-135k-fine-for-refusing-to-make-cake-for-gay-wedding/> accessed 4/4/16

43   <http://dailysignal.com/2015/08/16/fund-aims-to-help-christian-baker-offset-wedding-cake-losses/> accessed 4/4/16

44   <http://www.adflegal.org/issues/marriage/marriage-is-our-future> click on the personal stories of individual adults, especially Katy Faust. accessed 4/4/16

45   Ibid., see previous stories from endnote

46   <https://www.facebook.com/Ex-Homosexual-Through-Jesus-Christ/227709067265250/><https://www.youtube.com/watch?v=A1SAkpEyUrk> accessed 4/4/16 <JanetBoynesMinistries.com><www.awmi.net> The first site may change quickly, so you may have to Google it. The third website is a former lesbian who was interviewed on the last website. You can judge for yourself whether the threats these people have received are "normal" workings within our Constitution.

47   <http://www.adflegal.org/detailspages/client-stories-details/barronelle-stutzman> accessed 4/4/16

48   <http://www1.cbn.com/news/us/2016/april/christian-pharmacy-forced-to-stock-plan-b-appeals-to-high-court> <https://www.lifesitenews.com/news/washington-state-pharmacists-defy-radical-pro-abortion-governor-with-legal><http://www.dailycaller.com/2016/01/04/planned-parenthood-is-about-to-shut-down-a-christian-pharmacy-for-refusing-to-sell-abortion-drugs/> accessed 4/11/16

49   <http://www.csmonitor.com/USA/Justice/2011/0614/Prop.-8-ruling-gay-judge-didn-t-need-to-recuse-himself><http://www.nytimes.com/2011/06/15/us/politics/15prop8.html?_r=1> accessed 4/4/16

50   <http://www.supremecourt.ohio.gov/Boards/BOC/Advisory_Opinions/2015/Op_15-001.pdf><http://dailysignal.com/2015/08/14/can-you-oppose-gay-marriage-and-be-a-good-judge-the-chilling-opinion-of-an-ohio-courts-board/> accessed 4/4/16

51   <http://dailysignal.com/2015/06/11/n-c-legislature-overrides-veto-allows-government-employees-to-not-do-gay-marriages/> accessed 4/4/16

52   <http://www.telegraph.co.uk/news/worldnews/northamerica/usa/9766840/US-newspaper-publishes-names-and-addresses-of-gun-owners.html> accessed 4/4/16

53   <http://www.foxnews.com/us/2015/09/01/gun-control-groups-accused-swatting-open-carry-permit-holders-putting-lives-at/?intcmp=hplnws> accessed 4/4/16

54   <http://www.abc2news.com/homepage-showcase/conceal-and-carry-permits-difficult-to-obtain-in-maryland><http://www.washingtontimes.com/news/2015/feb/23/maryland-joins-gun-rights-trend-after-election-of-/?page=all> accessed 4/4/16

55   <http://law.ubalt.edu/downloads/law_downloads/Williams%20v%20State.pdf><http://
      www.washingtonpost.com/politics/cases-lining-up-to-ask-supreme-court-to-clarify-
      second-amendment-rights/2011/08/11/gIQAioihFJ_story.html> accessed 4/4/16

56   <http://www.supremecourt.gov/opinions/09pdf/08-1521.pdf> accessed 4/4/16

57   Federalist No.37 can be seen at many sites. Here is one <http://avalon.law.yale.edu/18th_
      century/fed37.asp> © 2008 Lillian Goldman Law Library, accessed 4/4/16

58   Thomas Jefferson, "Query XVII, Notes on the State of Virginia" In "The Works of Thomas
      Jefferson" Edited by H.A. Washington. Volume 8; 399-402. (New York: Townsend Mac
      Coun. 1884)

59   Ibid.

60   Ibid.

61   <https://www.monticello.org/site/jefferson/quotations-jefferson-memorial> These are
      words from two separate sources of his writings. See site's explanation. accessed 4/4/16

62   This is a YouTube clip titled "Number One with a Bullet" <https://www.youtube.com/
      watch?v=pELwCqz2JfE> accessed 3/2/16

63   <http://crimeresearch.org/2016/01/new-cprc-research-do-background-checks-on-
      private-gun-transfers-help-stop-mass-public-shootings/> accessed 3/15/16

64   Ibid. When I visited this site, they had various links to other research on gun violence and
      rate reduction of violence among those places where gun ownership is high. Please click
      on those links for further educational purposes.

65   <http://www.nytimes.com/2013/08/13/nyregion/stop-and-frisk-practice-violated-
      rights-judge-rules.html?_r=0> accessed 3/15/16. Some might question since I am such
      an advocate for our inalienable rights, that the policy of New York City violated those rights
      for those targeted for "Stop and Frisk." Maybe; and only if they were not so successful in
      confiscating an overwhelming number of illegal guns and lowering the crime rate as they
      did. Certainly there were some shenanigans going on with this court opinion, as noted
      by Mayor Bloomberg in the cited New York Times article. I would concur that some law
      abiding citizen's rights were violated, but there had to be a balance here, especially in light
      of the overwhelming success of the program in targeting criminals. I am of the opinion
      that a criminal loses benefits in covenant (proportionally) when committing a crime. What
      that balance is, as far as I am concerned, should be up to the citizens of New York and their
      law enforcement; not up to judges, elected or unelected.

66   Cass Sunstein, "Second Amendment Minimalism: Heller as Griswold," 122 Harv. L. Rev.
      246 (2008)<http://nrs.harvard.edu/urn-3:HUL.InstRepos:10875734><https://dash.
      harvard.edu/bitstream/handle/1/10875734/sunstein(2).pdf?sequence=1> accessed
      4/4/16; you can read the various ideas in interpretation.

67   Joseph Blocher, "Categoricalism and Balancing In First and Second Amendment Analysis," NYU Law Review, Number 2, Vol. 84 (2009)<http://scholarship.law.duke.edu/cgi/view-content.cgi?article=2727&context=faculty_scholarship> accessed 4/4/16, see various in interpretation.

68   "A Real Live Violation of the Third Amendment," Ilya Somin <http://volokh.com/2011/10/18/a-historical-violation-of-the-third-amendment/> © 2015 The Volokh Conspiracy, accessed 4/4/16.

69   You can look at the endnotes or the Further Reading Section to find noted several places where you can get a copy of our Bill of Rights or the First Ten Amendments. This site will also give you a copy of all 27 Amendments <http://www.heritage.org/constitution> The site was last accessed 4/4/16 and it is somewhat interactive. All endnotes are used for educational purposes. This one more so than most, since many Americans are not aware of our governing documents.

Chapter Two

THOSE ALREADY TAKEN CAPTIVE

Keep in mind what you have read of the wording of our first ten amendments as you read these true stories. Then ask yourself this question: Do you think we need to engage colleges, politicians, a majority of the press and the average citizen in a lesson concerning what it means to maintain a covenant and our inalienable rights?

Thirty plus years ago, during the 1980s, there were between 2,000 and 3,000 no-knock warrants issued a year. By 2010 that number had risen to around 80,000.[1] A no-knock warrant is as it sounds. Police don't have to knock at the door to let you know they are coming in. The premise for this rise is as crime has risen, so has the need to quietly and surreptitiously arrest the violent as well as the drug-selling deviant. Yet as violent crime stats have fallen, the use of this device has increased, almost exponentially.[2] I'm all for law enforcement having the best equipment. I'm also for giving local communities the left-over equipment from the military. It's the best way to make use of equipment which otherwise cannot be sold. I also understand the feeling and reality in many violent criminal cases, police have targets on their backs and need to be kept safe from harm.

It is a sad reality police officers are killed in the line of duty. It must never happen. All of us need to protect them. There is a sinking feeling as good men and women in uniform are targeted, all of us are targeted. They are there to protect us. If the "protectors" aren't safe from the deviant, is anyone? It is not easy juxtaposing the absolute need for safety and the equal need for commonsense law which cherishes our inalienable rights. My premise is the modern-day church— Spirit-filled and blood bought— is the best hope to go into difficult communities to create an atmosphere of hope and betterment. Having said that, it is also true the legal premise for the aforementioned invasive warrants is sketchy at best. If you have justified evidence a criminal is at a location, getting a warrant from a judge and doing due diligence along with appropriate due process does not take that much longer and can avoid the mistakes thousands have experienced from being the wrong recipient of this misguided policy.

Right on the heels of this policy is the warrantless entry. This says in the presence of exigent circumstances a police officer may enter a premise. These include the need to prevent physical harm, the destruction of relevant evidence, the escape of a suspect (in hot pursuit) or some other consequence which would improperly frustrate legitimate law enforcement efforts.[3] There have been major problems in executing both these procedures which, in my opinion proves the lack of understanding civil covenant and which also proves that mantra of hell: Desensitize and escalate propaganda in an effort to marginalize our humanity. Once done, this makes it much easier to strangulate inalienable rights. By calling people of different beliefs "haters" or "racist," you do so to marginalize their humanity. It should not surprise us this subtle tactic is sapping other inalienable rights, other than our First and Second Amendment rights.

The acronym most used for our present police force raid is a SWAT team. It stands for Special Weapons and Tactics (team). The first thing these military-styled teams of SWAT do in executing a no-knock warrant is to shoot the dogs upon entry if they encounter them. Why? Well, most folks who have pets, especially dogs, will tell you they will try to protect their owners. This simply will not do since these officers are coming in, assault rifles blazing, after they have knocked down the door, probably thrown in a flash grenade for good measure. If the dog hasn't run to hide before it gets shot, then a bullet is in its future. Unfortunately, this is not just limited to the no-knock phenomenon; it happens with warrantless entry as well.

In August 2013, as a couple slept, Escambia County, Florida, deputies were chasing down a lead from a disturbance earlier that day in which a man brandished a weapon. Unfortunately for this couple, that man had the same first name, but not last name, as one of our sleeping householders. Knocking at the door on a Sunday night at 10:30 P.M., and receiving no answer, the cops climbed in through an open window. The facts from here on get a bit murkier as police tell one story and the sleeping couple tell another. What is not in dispute is police dragged the couple from bed and shot both their dogs; one in the bed, the other curled up on the floor on blankets. One had to be euthanized and the other eventually recovered from its injuries. Of course, it was later discovered this sleeping couple had nothing to do with the man police were looking for.[4] If the dogs aren't safe, then you can easily imagine the children are in trouble.

No one wants to see a child in a drug-cultured domicile. Unfortunately, that has become all too common. It is this break-down in society which makes the role of the church even more necessary. It is also the reason why warrantless as well as no-knock warrants should go through the same channels and extensive checks and balances as other warrants to make sure mistakes are kept to a minimum and the rights of the innocent are protected. Even when an officer is in pursuit of a dangerous felon, he or she should have hours of training— and most do— concerning whether or not their pursuit will irreparably harm innocents.

Thirty-five years ago I lived in an urban, densely populated environment, and we had a dog. "Benny" was an admirable mutt, always trying to "help" when he could. The day he saw one of our local boys in blue chasing a suspect, he decided he should *help*. Larger than a muscled Black Lab, but smaller than a Saint Bernard, Benny was a force to be reckoned with. It was a sight: My husband chasing our dog, our dog chasing the cop and the cop chasing the criminal! Thank God for our local law enforcement. Their training was admirable. As the officer calmly cuffed the "perp" he turned to my husband and said, "Could you please get your dog off of me?" No shouting, shooting or drama; just calm, respectful, well trained and effective police work. We all pray for those days.

Unfortunately, things have gotten more complicated; namely, in the form of regulation and tort claims— overheated language which call police names and people "haters" or racist— along with criminalizing the unsuspecting innocent. This has led to a nervous energy, which has caused a deterioration in our corporate, civic and personal relationships. It has led to an environment where forgiveness and attempting to work through our secular, non-sectarian covenant is not even safe inside the homes and businesses of the religious, let alone their houses of worship. I will prove to you socialism is at the heart of this outrage. Unfortunately, there are facile events which do not help the climate.

I don't have any hard figures on how many of our returning war veterans are entering the ranks of our police forces, Federal agencies and other bureaucratic policing apparatus. We desperately need them and I thank God for them. But coming home from places controlled by religions which do not respect life like the God of the Bible commands, or even religions like Buddhism and some Hindu practices demand, they can become reactive to the devaluation of life those war-time theaters portray. De-stressing and re-training them back into a culture of covenant and secular compact might go a long way in helping them re-enter a new and civil workforce which does involve violence and, at the very least, conflict. I have no intention of "blaming the cops" here. Their jobs are hard enough. The vast majority of police forces are well trained. It is very unfortunate as we have seen a drop in violent crime, what is portrayed by the media seems to escalate the perception the violence is somehow worse than it is. This only adds to an already heated atmosphere. The movies and other media which depict the "thug" and "gangsta" lifestyles and other forms of violence as "normal" and valid, only makes life more difficult in societies where it is necessary for peace and tranquility to reign supreme.

An environment of stability is necessary for children— for all of us— to thrive and contribute to our communities. In my opinion, today's press and Hollywood, as well as other media are just as guilty of encouraging the volatility we experience, as we, the people, are guilty in accepting this unfit environment. When the press tries to create an environment for protests which turn so ugly as to ruin a community, the press is to blame. We don't need day and night coverage of honest mistakes made by good cops as well as ignoring the obvious criminality of suspects. It is done, not to further harmony and covenant— the need to be transparent— this type of coverage is done to cause instability as well as "sell" their media brand. The citizens as well as the police are forced to remain in a community, picking up the shattered pieces which could have been made whole if they had been allowed to work through the issue together, privately and quietly. Instead, we have "certain" Federal bureaucracies criminalizing local law enforcement while the media pumps up the adrenaline and rabble rousers from outside the community burn buildings! And we wonder why some officers are on a razor's edge?

Of course, the effects of all of this is academic until it happens to you. What happens to the parents, grandparents and the children who are innocent when a no-knock or warrantless "visit" is coming? If I went through all fifty states and every incident, your eyes would tire from reading before you were done, and that's before we even talk about what's going on at the Federal level. Let me relate three instances from the state of Georgia. In September 2014, a 59 year-old grandfather was gunned down in a late night drug raid, with no drugs being found. In November 2006, a 92 year-old woman was killed in a drug raid on her home with no drugs being found.[5] But one of the worst in recent memory happened on May 28, 2014, when a no-knock raid was conducted on the home of nineteen month-old Bounkham Phonesavanh. His relative, who lived down the road, surrendered easily to police with a knock at his door, after they had already blown the face off the nineteen month-old with a flash grenade. Habersham County, GA, police got a tip a meth dealer was at the home. So as everyone slept, they threw in the flash grenade which landed in the baby's playpen, destroying his nose, collapsing his lung and tearing up his face and little body down to the bone. Of course they found no drugs at the house, since they got the wrong house; the relative was down the road. This family has accrued a million dollars in medical bills, with more surgeries planned, while the county refuses to pay the medical bills and no grand jury has handed down indictments to anyone for this act of culpable incompetence.

Currently (until pending legislation is passed) no requirements for training in procedures and deployment of these grenades is necessary; nor is there a law demanding a true emergency be in place before such a raid is conducted. There are no policies in place to find out if there are pets, children or elderly or other innocent victims in the residence, nor is there any oversight in place as to whether they even have the *correct* home.[6] A June 2014 ACLU report shows some troubling circumstances for American citizens. While initially SWAT raids were done in extreme cases where active shooter and hostage-taking events occurred, drug raids now comprise some 60 percent of SWAT team usage, with half of those incidents retrieving no drugs.[7] So we have escalated and incorporated the use of paramilitary style tactics in domestic criminal cases where innocent people become victims in their own homes. Again, as with our First and Second Amendment rights where we criminalize religious and civic behavior, we are escalating abuses and destroying what was a superior non-sectarian covenant-compact. So these stories alone, with the resultant governmental abuses they have allowed, have thrown our Fourth through Ninth Amendments under the bus.

The use of warrantless or no-knock warrant arrests can have their place. There is no doubt of that. The problem is we have desensitized our emotions and have no knowledge of covenant among our citizens. We have allowed foreign ideologies to creep into our American framework. At that point, it is easy to view one another with a militarized, war-zone mentality. Instituting a scorched-earth policy to put the God-fearing business owner out of business and on the street is a very real threat to the inalienable rights of all. What starts with denying school children the right to learn how much the Bible, Christianity and the Jewish religions played in the history-making of this country, ends with a hedonistic populace having few qualms when it comes to denigrating life and health and inalienable rights.

Why is that? Well, the Bible teaches us when you accept Jesus as Lord, it is His blood which binds us. The "flesh" is not as strong as the Holy

Spirit in relating us to one another. Christians are truly brothers and sisters, regardless of race. Since we know George Washington was a Christian, that means all American, Bible-believing children have George Washington as their forebear. That means a great man like him is as much their forebear as great men like Frederick Douglas and George Washington Carver. It was those ideals which birthed the principles of a Martin Luther King for racial equality and a Ronald Reagan in freedom from socialism in government. All American children— the White child and the Asian, Hispanic, Black, Brown or any other color, then learn at what great sacrifice the Puritans came here and why. They learn there is a reason why you do unto others as you would have them do to you. They learn the various differences between the different religious beliefs on our shores now, and how they differ from the religious beliefs of the people which formed our covenant-compact.

They also learn why atheists become a part of the non-sectarian compact. It is not taught in some vacuum. You say, "You are trying to teach religion." Actually, I am not espousing that at all. I am espousing the teaching of truth in our schools instead of socialism and the sterilizing effect of bureaucracy. I was taught truth in a public school environment without being taught religion, yet I was still taught the truth of our founding nation. If we keep this nonsense up, we will become China or Russia. Much like we see in many Asian and African nations, this atmosphere escalates death at the hands of government— not to mention the violation of the rest of our inalienable rights. The spiral downward at that point makes a mockery of the ink the Bill of Rights is written with.

The New Testament states clearly in Christ, the genders are equal; the Jew and the non-Jew, the rich and the poor are all on the same terrain. The Bible does make a distinction between the criminal and the saint. In our topsy-turvy world we are attempting to criminalize *thought*.[8] This is exactly what the founders fought against. Is there a blurring of the lines between criminal and civil violations? Are we being labeled criminals for simple civil infractions, or no infractions at all? Are the religious being hauled away for their religious beliefs, being labeled haters and criminal violators of some targeted grudge by an elected official— or bureaucrat or appointed judge— because of a lack in understanding our first inalienable right and where it actually came from? As we see by the example of Lyndon Johnson, the bureaucratic "human rights" commissions and the no-knock/warrantless entries, the answer is obviously yes. But it has gotten worse.

The saying, "It's a free country" is not really true anymore. With foreign and environmental laws criminalizing what are minor mistakes— even violations of a civil, not criminal nature— we are all easy prey to be arrested, indicted and bankrupted because of eating a French fry, running a business, or working on the job.[9] These are not hypothetical "stories." The 12 year-old was actually arrested for eating one French fry. The businessmen were sentenced to two and eight years, respectively, in Federal prison for breaking no law. A doctor and his wife, working hard in a poor community clinic, were pretty much bankrupted because of a few paperwork mistakes.[10] American soldiers going to war to fight for freedom probably would not agree to spill a drop of their blood if they were told they were doing so in order to allow an American city (Palo Alto, CA) free access to arrest a grandmother battling cancer because her hedges were over two feet high.[11] Unfortunately, she lost her battle with cancer fifteen months after her arrest, spending ten of those months negotiating with the city in an attempt to avoid jail time.[12]

You say, "These stories just cannot be true!" Oh, my fellow citizen, they are. I could go on for pages and pages. We all wonder why our economy is not as free as it was. Contrary to popular myth, socialism/progressivism does not extend economic freedom to all, just to a select few. We wonder why our stress levels are through the roof and why people just seem more immoral and less friendly. Wonder no more. Allow a government, a bureaucrat or some other "institution" or political party to infringe upon any of our inalienable rights and life does not go well for the rest of the citizens. In other words, whether we like one another or even agree with one another, just like the Puritans of old, we are all in this together: The wolves are already at the door. In fact, they have made a phony "warrantless entry."

A study done by the Small Business Administration in 2005 says that 1.1 trillion of American business dollars go for the cost of Federal government regulation. The cost *per employee* for firms with fewer than 20 employees is $7,647. Those numbers have climbed, and according to some estimates, possibly doubled.[13] It is said from 2009 to 2012 that 106 new major Federal regulations were added, costing all Americans an added $46 billion per year.[14] These numbers really don't tell the whole story. In one single instance, under ObamaCare, the FDA is tasked with new restaurant labeling guides. Those guides for restaurants were *400 pages long.* This means places like pizzerias with over 20 locations have to post all the different iterations of flavors in their establishments. Most of these chains post them online because most of the customers order online and because there are potentially over one billion different types of combinations of pizzas available.[15] Hopefully a pending compromise will become law. I have a better idea, let's just get rid of the initial mandate demanding we buy "their" healthcare and ask restaurants to label under commonsense language!

In 2015 alone 2,178 new regulations were added.[16] One report cited 21,000 new regulations under a current socialist/progressive regime, (almost seven years worth) and that administration still has time left to endanger us further.[17] These are on the civil end. In other words, they cover everyday citizens and businesses. They are *in addition* to what is already on the books. Nobody really knows what that number is on either the criminal or civil side. There are approximately 5,000 Federal crimes which cover anywhere from 10,000 to 300,000 rules and regulations. The Congressional Research Service and the American Bar Association do not have enough staff to adequately categorize every law, hence the uncertainty in numbers.[18] I have gleaned some thoughts from others who indicate those numbers could be higher than 400,000.

That means Americans will probably break laws they know nothing about, have no intention of breaking, yet can be charged for them anyway, and they are. In more cases than we realize, when someone breaks one of these regulations they get arrested. More people have been arrested by the Federal government for breaking these regulations than those who lived under Stalin. In 2010, 80,000 people were in federal prisons for *minor offenses.* 788,157 people have been sentenced to federal prisons for crimes from 2000 to 2010. The last time I checked there were a total of 207,111 people in Federal prisons.[19]

I have actually had acquaintances who were socialists (progressives), or their relatives tell me, "You know why we are okay with changing things? We'll be on top. We won't have to work and *our* people will be in power." Ignoring the obvious problems with this attitude, my response is, "So you think *your people* won't be affected? You think because you're a *good Democrat/socialist/progressive supporter* you won't be touched by this?" Here are a few stories which should change that point of view. We should understand the psychology of these kinds of regimes. The lie starts off with "We are good for *abc country*." They then spin the next lie socialism is more equal or it is about *equality*. That lie is especially easy to unmask and I will do so shortly. But people do get fooled and sign up. They become part of the police apparatus: the KGBs and Stasi (German socialist units of police) and other monikers of various bureaucrat. Before they know it they are *"good socialists"* or comrades and then they are killing, injuring and denying basic inalienable rights to their fellow citizens. These folks become trapped themselves, unable to stop their own actions, in some cases.

There is a joke told among many Christian parents: "Send your sweet, Christian, God-fearing child off to a secular college for four years, and you will get back a communist." Okay, I admit, not the most PC and funniest of jokes.[20] So college professors and artists, as a whole, are not well known for their conservative points of view. Arguably, Steven Kurtz, a professor of visual studies at the University of Buffalo, had no idea his unorthodox work would land him in a four-year ordeal with the Federal government.[21]

It started when he found his wife unresponsive and needing emergency medical attention. Because his artwork involved visual performances depicting bioweapon warfare, he had a little lab area in his home with Petri dishes of harmless bacteria growing in them which he used in his performances. Because of his wife's emergency, police came to the home. Suspicious of the equipment, the authorities called in the Federal government. Preparing for his wife's funeral, the FBI picked him up as he was walking across the funeral home parking lot. He was held for 22 *hours* on suspicion of bioterrorism. Eventually it was found the bacteria in the dishes were harmless and neither Mr. Kurtz nor his Petri dishes had anything to do with his wife's death.

In a bizarre reasoning which only today's bureaucrats seem capable of, they indicted the man on fraud charges because the lab he got the bacteria from did not include "artwork" in its contracts for sale. Really, who uses harmless bacteria as artwork? Obviously those who used their free will to attend one of his protest-artwork performances agreed to the use of the harmless bacteria. It was also Mr. Kurtz's right of free speech to display his protest in the manner he did. I don't think any company could have thought of that one though, and included it in their contracts for purchase. Because he and a colleague got the bacteria from mail order and discussed getting it in an email, they were charged with breaking federal wire and mail fraud statutes. Because they worked at a university, the Feds, in what the judge later found was quite a convoluted way of thinking, charged them with defrauding the university as well.[22] The colleague, being of frail health, cut a deal to avoid jail time. But Mr. Kurtz fought on. He was eventually acquitted. Unfortunately, the incident has had a chilling effect on researchers at universities all over the world, as well as in the United States.[23] So this one case alone affects us in a way to prevent possible research which could help all of us.

Krister Evertson, a poster boy for conservation and environmental technology, was using his talents by making a new kind of fuel cell using pure sodium and borax.[24] Unfortunately for him, one small slip-up in shipping the sodium eventually landed him in a Federal penitentiary for thirteen months, a halfway house for eleven, and robbed him of over $100,000. This story has enough twists and turns to do a soap opera proud. He was actually acquitted the first time around, but the Feds decided there had to be something to convict him of. They scoured police reports and found he had legally purchased and safely stored $100,000 worth of pure sodium. He was then arrested and his legally obtained and stored material was confiscated and destroyed. So he was theoretically charged twice for the same crime and his personal goods, which were legally obtained, owned and stored were confiscated and destroyed. The sad reality is if he had been allowed to get his fuel cells to work, the progressive environ-mentalists who demonize petroleum might actually be driving in experimental sodium-fueled cars by now! Heck, all of us might be driving in them. If you think this is an isolated incident, think again.

Did you know if you are traveling down the road and get pulled over in a traffic stop, the cash in your vehicle can be seized? It can be seized even if you are not charged with a crime. Hawaii resident Straughn Gorman was taking a cross-country trip in a motor home. A Nevada state trooper pulled him over for going too slow on I-80.[25] The trooper let him go, but suspected he was hiding cash. So the trooper called the county sheriff's office to have him stopped again, along with a canine unit. If the canine hit on a drug scent, it would have given them probable cause to search the camper. Fifty minutes later, the county sheriff, along with a canine unit did as the state police requested and pulled Mr. Gorman over for two alleged traffic violations. They never found any drugs but seized his vehicle, computer, cellphone and cash— $167,000 worth, hidden throughout the camper.

He was never arrested or charged with a crime. Guess what? The Feds refused to turn the cash over to Gorman. He spent $153,000 taking the Feds to court. You see, federal agencies can take assets seized by state and local law enforcement agencies. The judge— the only sane one in this whole episode— said the second stop would never have happened without the trooper calling for it and specifically mentioning the need for a canine, without which they would have no probable cause. The whole episode was legal poison from the beginning. One would think the Feds would have let this one go instead of spending more of our taxpayer dollars. Well, they took it for appeal— citing no reason for what grounds the appeal is based— to the most liberal (socialistic) appellate court in the country: the 9th Circuit Court in San Francisco. Time will only tell if the law will eventually win out, allowing Mr. Gorman to keep his cash, the little bit left by the time he is done.

Supposedly the Justice Department is changing its seizure practices. That's because more people complain about their money being seized from what's called "structuring." Banks are required to notify the Feds when $10,000 or more is deposited. I didn't know the government had a need to know when you decided to move your own large sums of money. That's probably because I don't know anybody with that problem! In any event, I guess people deposit less than the targeted amount to avoid the reporting. Now, arguably, this might be done to avoid being caught for some criminal activity or to avoid paying taxes. In which case the activity is illegal. But the point of our laws is to prove criminal activity first, not the other way around. You know, "Innocent until *proven* Guilty." From 2005 to 2012, the IRS has seized more than $242 million, totaling roughly 2,500 *alleged* structuring violations. Yet NO criminal activity was reported in roughly 33 percent of those cases, other than the alleged structuring.[26] But, you guessed it, the Feds still want to seize the funds! No wonder people have been complaining.

The story of Lawrence Lewis would normally be a harbinger of trouble for all of us, if it weren't for the fact there are so many people like Lawrence Lewis. Yet his story, like others, should have all of us in the streets, demanding politicians stop the madness.[27] Lawrence Lewis should have wound up a statistic. Raised in the projects of Washington, D.C., life was not something he hoped for. Instead of succumbing to the statistics, he took night classes while working as a janitor. As he tells it, he worked hard to show his children how to lead a life they could be proud of.[28] Life was progressing as it should for a hardworking and enterprising man: children, a home and a good job. He worked as a facilities manager at a military retirement center.

Quite frequently the sewage disposal system would back up, clogging the pump. In March 2007, Mr. Lewis and his team pumped sewage into the storm drain, which they believed flowed into the city's sewage treatment plant. This was the accepted practice and had been done before to prevent the flood of sewage from moving into an area of the home where the sickest people lived. In fact, it was later found only 30 percent of the storm-drain waste fed into the city's facility.[29] Unfortunately, that day the waste flowed into Rock Creek, a small tributary flowing from Maryland, through D.C., and into the Potomac. A jogger in a park nearby noticed the water was murky and called the Park Police, which traced the source back to the retirement home. Lewis was charged with violating the Clean

Water Act. Even though he was innocent of knowingly polluting the environment— he did nothing to cause the overflowing toilets— it was useless for him to try and fight the Federal charges since it was a liability case, making it unnecessary for the government to prove he *intended* to break the law. So Mr. Lewis was guilty before he could prove he was innocent— in fact, with no need to prove his innocence— thus he was charged criminally.

Initially, the Federal government only had jurisdiction over water navigable by boat. In 1972, Congress expanded this definition to include tributaries like Rock Creek. Fast forward to 2015, and the EPA is trying to potentially include land which is dry most of the time, but puddles when it rains.[30]

Mr. Lewis' lawyer advised him to take a deal, since legally, it was unnecessary to try to prove his innocence. He pleaded guilty, afraid he would lose his house, custody of his children and put his elderly mother on the street. He got probation and a $2,500 fine. The sad reality about this story is this man did everything his entire life to prove to himself, his children, and in fact, the world, that just because you were raised in the projects with darker colored skin, you don't have to wind up in jail and with a criminal record. He told the story about the humiliation of regular visits by probation officers.[31] He could no longer keep his legal firearm. He got pulled over for a traffic stop with no ticket or violation being issued. Yet shortly thereafter, probation officers made a surprise 6 a.m. visit at his home, going through everything in the house. He had to fill out monthly financial statements proving he wasn't involved in any criminal activities. Now off probation, he still has a criminal record for backed up toilets. Yes, folks, backed up toilets!

This is the insane world of Federal and state bureaucracies, with their crazy morass of regulations and political malevolence. I neither know, nor care what the political persuasions are of these individuals. My question is, do you see a familiar pattern with those who are being violated for their religious beliefs? As we see from these stories, our Fourth through Ninth Amendment rights have been targeted and violated. We may as well throw in our Tenth Amendment rights. Why? Well, do you honestly feel as if we, the people, have any rights left which have not been grabbed by the Federal government? Rights we never agreed to give them, they have fundamentally robbed. When you allow your First Amendment rights to be diminished, the rest can be made into by-gone history.

ENDNOTES

1   <http://usatoday30.usatoday.com/news/nation/2011-02-14-noknock14_ST_N. htm><http://www.policemag.com/blog/swat/story/2011/03/no-knock-searches-reasonable-or-deadly.aspx><https://en.wikipedia.org/wiki/No-knock_warrant> accessed 4/4/16

2   <https://en.wikipedia.org/wiki/Crime_in_the_United_States><https://www.brennancenter.org/publication/what-caused-crime-decline><http://www.ons.gov.uk/ons/dcp171776_394470.pdf> accessed 4/4/16

3   <http://www.le.alcoda.org/publications/point_of_view/files/EXIGENT_CIRCUMSTANCES.pdf> Alameda County District Attorney's Office, Winter 2010, Point of View "Exigent Circumstances" accessed 5/26/16.

4   <http://www.theblaze.com/stories/2013/08/09/horrific-allegation-couple-says-cops-climbed-through-window-without-warrant-and-shot-their-dogs/><http://archive.wtsp.com/news/article/328987/19/escambia-county-deputies-shoot-two-dogs> accessed 4/4/16

5   <https://news.vice.com/article/toddler-maimed-by-swat-flash-grenade-sparks-georgia-bills-on-no-knock-warrants> accessed 4/4/16

6   Ibid., <http://www.cbn.com/cbnnews/us/2015/February/Police-State-Orwells-Nightmare-Becoming-Reality/> accessed 4/4/16

7   <https://www.aclu.org/sites/default/files/assets/jus14-warcomeshome-report-web-rel1. pdf>accessed 4/4/16. The use of this report is for statistics only, not recommendation/conclusion support.

8   <http://www.nationalreview.com/article/426979/safe-spaces-colleges-campus-incompatible><http://www.nationalreview.com/article/426853/yale-student-protest-safe-space-political-correctness> accessed 4/4/16

9   Paul Rosenzweig, editor. "One Nation Under Arrest," Second Edition. Introduction by Edwin Meese III, Washington, DC : © 2013 by The Heritage Foundation, 214 Massachusetts Avenue, NE, Washington, DC 20002. In order of arrest: (the French fry) 50-52, (the businessmen) 3-11, and (a doctor and his wife working on the job) 53-60

10 Ibid.

11 Ibid., 23-30

12 Ibid., "One Nation...." 27, 30

13 <https://www.sba.gov/sites/default/files/files/rs264tot.pdf> accessed 4/4/16

14 James L. Gattuso and Diane Katz, "Red Tape Rising: Obama-Era Regulation at the Three-Year Mark" <http://www.heritage.org/research/reports/2012/03/red-tape-rising-obama-era-regulation-at-the-three-year-mark> © 2015 The Heritage Foundation, accessed 4/4/16

15 <http://www.foxnews.com/politics/2015/08/27/big-pizza-bucks-burdensome-obamacare-label-mandate/?intcmp=hpbt4> accessed 3/27/16

16 8/29/15 news report by an ABC affiliate news station, WEAR, in Pensacola, Florida. <http://www.weartv.com>

17 <http://www.washingtonexaminer.com/report-21000-regulations-so-far-under-obama-2375-set-for-2015/article/2558050> accessed 4/4/16. These two endnotes come from two separate research groups. The first, from a TV show, was a conservative institute while the Internet used a more liberal group, the Competitive Enterprise Institute.

18 <http://townhall.com/tipsheet/mattvespa/2015/06/06/how-many-federal-laws-are-there-again-n2009184> accessed 4/4/16

19 <http://www.bop.gov/about/statistics><http://www.bop.gov/about/statistics/population_statistics.jsp> Clicking on the various links at this site will give you the various statistics quoted. The administration in 2015 started releasing Federal inmates at unprecedented levels so there should be substantial differences in numbers, see for details <http://www.breitbart.com/big-government/2015/10/31/obama-releasing-nearly-6600-federal-inmates-starting-weekend> accessed 4/4/16

20 <http://www.foxnews.com/opinion/2015/09/01/universities-are-becoming-gender-neutral-zones-where-free-thought-is-outlawed.html?intcmp-trending><http://www.nationalreview.com/article/426853/yale-student-protest-safe-space-political-correctness> accessed 4/4/16

21 Paul Rosenzweig, editor. "One Nation Under Arrest," Second Edition. Introduction by Edwin Meese III, Washington, DC : © 2013 by The Heritage Foundation, 214 Massachusetts Avenue, NE, Washington, DC 20002. 97-106

22 Ibid., 102-103

23 Ibid., 104-106

24 Ibid., "One Nation...." 107-114

25 <http://www.foxnews.com/politics/2015/08/29/feds-fighting-to-keep-cash-seized-from-person-never-charged-with-crime/?intcmp=trending> accessed 4/2/16

26 Ibid.

27   Article by The Wall Street Journal, "A Sewage Blunder Earns Engineer a Criminal Record" <http://www.wsj.com/articles/SB100014240529702049038045770827701353394 42> accessed 4/2/16

28   Ibid.

29   Ibid.

30   <http://amac.us/epas-new-power-grab-includes-rain-water-says-amac/><http://www.thecitywire.com/node/37690#.VdjNsihK620> or <http://www.talkbusiness.net/2015/05/farm-bureau-sens-boozman-and-cotton-critical-of-new-epa-water-rules-updated/#.VdjNsihK620> accessed 4/2/16

31   Ibid.

Chapter Three

LEGAL HISTORY TO HELP
OUR UNDERSTANDING

We don't have the space to talk about the robbery— I mean "loan"— of our Social Security funds OR the treachery of ignoring Simpson Boles, which was a bipartisan effort to fix the spending problem, which has caused our Social Security funds to be *"borrowed;"* OR the Affordable Care Act (a.k.a "ObamaCare"), which robbed Medicare, strong-armed our economic and health choices, and has already bankrupted the very sickest.[1] Books could be written proving criminality in Fast & Furious[2] and the cover up of the Benghazi nightmare.[3] Then there is the rape of our military readiness, as well as the blatant invasion of our privacy, as so many of our personal records and data are stored for "future" need. The Feds even have local police in on the captivity, as they advise them not to disclose the details concerning the surveillance technology they use to snatch basic cellphone data from whole neighborhoods. These Feds have intervened in routine state public records cases concerning criminal trials, denying access by citing "security" reasons.[4] Before socialism took over the Feds rarely intervened in policing matters such as this. By doing so, it is proof of broken covenant.

Speaking of our military, the Feds do one thing right: the military. But even they are being crushed under the weight of Federal largesse. In fact, the only true job our Federal government does have is security: individual, group-to-group, governments-to-groups/individuals, nationally and internationally within economic, social and religious domains. In other words, the safety of its covenant citizens. When it can't even identify a security problem because its political correctness refuses to address the source, that in and of itself is an example of broken covenant. In a future book in this series we will look at the attitude and difference in training our military and security forces today— under a regime which denies them their own religious beliefs— and the military/security forces of yesteryear.

I have lived in hurricane, tropical storm, tornado occurrences and blizzard environments for many years. While experiencing damage from some of these events, God kept us and helped us recover. But I can tell you what it is like for many in catastrophic situations when the National Guard, the Marines, the Coast Guard, the Red Cross, Operation Blessing— and countless other rescue groups come into an area to help. For many people, it is like being rescued from death, because if the military or these groups did not show up, it would have meant death. Many people who do not have a safety net are saved. Without our military—as well as private Christian institutions—many more thousands would not be alive today. During Hurricane Katrina alone, the Coast Guard rescued 33,500 people.[5] So I am not espousing the demise of our Federal government, just a drastic "weight-loss" program, losing thousands of pounds of regulations, several bureaucratic and Cabinet departments which we really don't need. We could potentially apply funds to projects we really need like EMP-proofing, upgrading our electric grid and other infra-structure. Such things as replacing aged military equipment, building walls on our borders, getting cyber-crime protection without the Feds trying to control the Internet, and new roads and bridges. The limited government of our original documentation is our best example and should be our goal.

Nowhere is this more evident than with the illegal immigration problem. This issue is also evidence of broken covenant. There are, obviously, millions of people who have put skin in the game and immigrated into this country legally. It has taken them years, but they did it right. Unless your ancestors were native American Indians or settlers who came here from the 1600s to the very early 1800s, you come from an immigrant; in other words, they were not settlers. They were likely to be legal immigrants, as all were before 1914. We now have millions who want to stay here their way, by receiving all sorts of government incentives. We Americans pay for their health care, their children and now a current socialist administration wants to pay them medicare, social security, as well as giving them tax refunds, even while they don't pay enough into the tax system.[6] This causes many problems for both legal citizens and those trying to become citizens legally who are working. The practice of the God of the Bible is to put His people smack in the middle of the world and then bless them and their land and show the rest of the world— firsthand, up close and personal— what it is like to serve the God of the Bible. As a result of the blessings surrounding the keeping of covenant, a land and a people become blessed. Everyone sees this and they want to live there. This country is a clear example of that practice and so is Israel.

Unfortunately, the attitude now is to either steal the country or its resources! That attitude was not what God instituted nor intended. The outcome God intended was for people to see the benefits of this covenant to bring back to their land and then covenant with God on their land. In this way the blessing of Godly covenant is spread throughout the globe. Each country is given land by God, and they and they alone are responsible to make sure the resources in their land go to their people first. No other country in the world allows illegal immigration. Countries all over the world refuse immigration and screen all who want entry.

There is a hard reality connected to our illegal immigration problem: **Someone has to pay for it.** That means you must raise taxes. But the political elite who espouse this system have a problem: *Why would you want to vote for a group who raises taxes to all time highs, while giving your money to someone else?* Well, the answer to the question is obvious. Sooner or later the majority of voters will become wise to this nonsense and the party promoting this system will begin losing voters. So lies must be told to subterfuge this process. Something else must happen: **You must get new voters.** One quick fix is to bring them in by the thousands. Let's see, where could you get thousands of new voters who have never voted before and would vote for you because you gave them some goodie? This is what makes illegal immigration dangerous and this is what was changed by a current socialist administration when they relaxed enforcement of immigration laws.[7]

Now Americans are battling the effects of international drug cartels, potential terrorists and social policies which take trillions of our tax-dollar usage and loss of life of our own citizens to violent immigrant behavior. This is not due to only one nation of illegals. There are many nations who send us their illegals. Many different multi-nationals come here illegally with the same baggage which has made their own countries impossible to live in. In fact, by leaving their own troubled countries, those countries are losing the impetus to change the behavior which caused their citizens to flee. They should remain in them, and band together and change their own countries first.

Of course, it has been logically argued immigration, whether legal or illegal is not the question, but it is the free market access to work which makes people want to migrate.[8] What is needed at that point are rules to prevent a drain on our systems of capital and resources. Up until 2008 we had those rules in place. I realize many immigrants are hardworking families. That still does not excuse coming here illegally or without a job. Politicians who are weak on this issue should be voted out immediately. It really is that simple. It is not a democrat problem or a republican problem. This problem requires the politicians to love their country first, solving the citizens' problems first. Making it easy for illegal behavior by giving them incentives to come here and get "goodies" has to stop. Strengthening the border, repealing the "anchor-baby" problem, and revoking the regulations which give money and subsidies to immigrants (legal or illegal) would go a long way to stopping many of the devastating effects of illegal immigration. It will not stop immigration, but it certainly will not drain the resources of a nation.

Immigrants must pay taxes and must not be criminals. In fact, it is the duty of a country's leaders to decide *when or even if* we need immigration. In other words, what *kind* of immigrant is needed. If an immigrant's ideology, manners, education or other practices are harmful or not needed, they must be refused entry. These changes will encourage hard work and help our free-market economy. Then the citizenry can decide if more legal citizens are necessary. Many Americans would be shocked to know Congress has tried to stop the illegal immigration problem by enacting a law forcing Federal agencies to report an illegal when they find them. But mid-level bureaucrats have "rewritten" the law to suit their own agenda, thereby nullifying their need to obey (more on that later).

Like the welfare problem, where there are exceptions for the infirm, elderly, orphans and temporarily indigent, there should be exceptions for immigrants, i.e., those who must seek asylum quickly. That already falls under two categories: religious persecution and political persecution. Just because they must seek asylum does not mean they can do so without a job or the possibility of jobs. It matters little whether you are legal, illegal or an asylum-seeking immigrant from an economic point of view.

On the social side of the argument, I think most folks know the two top persecuted religions are Christianity and Judaism. We all know they are killed, jailed and enslaved in Muslim countries. You would think when the 44th President made a dictate that he was bringing in Syrians from a war-torn area in which atrocities were committed against Christians and another minority religion, Yazidi— that the majority of the thousands brought in would be of the persecuted group— not from the group which persecutes them. Well, folks, hold on to your hats, because this proves without a shadow of a doubt we have lost the Democrats to this foreign ideology. I will continue to prove that unfortunate truth in the next chapters. When the 44th President said there should be no religious test for what refugee to bring in, many, including myself thought he was genuine. What he didn't tell anyone is that the religious test already existed and he used a very bad situation to ignore the plight of the Christians as well as other minority groups.

Only ten percent of Syrians were Christians, but they experienced the greatest danger from their Muslim captors. Of the 358 refugees granted asylum from Syria since January 2011 to December 2014, only 31 were Christian. From January 2015 to November 2015, there were 1,829 Syrian refugees let in. Of those only 30 were Christians.[9] A whopping

96 percent were Muslims with 25 refugees being atheist, no religion, Bahai, Yazidi, Zorastrian or "other."[10] The second tidy little obfuscation by the then sitting president is the fact America got its refugees from UN refugee camps. Many of these camps are infiltrated by ISIS and jihadist groups which form gangs, making the Christian men vulnerable to forced conversions or murder and the women (of all ages) vulnerable to rape and sex trafficking.[11] The Christians, knowing what awaits them, avoid the camps. But if you can't get "refugee status" you can't get into the system. The way to do that is to get into the camps. The UN needs to empty these camps at all cost, so they do not seek those outside of them.

The UN has finally (February 4, 2016) termed the beheadings and other atrocities committed against the Christians as well as other minority religions by ISIS "genocide." This will at least give an impetus for action in attempting to stop the genocide.[12] Whether a present US administration will follow UN mandates to act on behalf of the Christians, is far less clear. Many do not know we let in the persecuted religious when they are Muslim, but since 2009 more and more Christians are routinely denied asylum.[13] When ISIS set off attacks against France in 2015, it was discovered early on at least two of the attackers used the Syrian refugee hordes to infiltrate France.[14] Our lawmakers know of the limited ability in the UN vetting process and the difficulty in our own vetting abilities. It doesn't matter how long they stay in the process—that is quite lengthy— it is our inability to trace their roots and associations. So the House of Representatives overrode the threat of a presidential veto and passed a refugee bill which could put the pause button on taking in 10,000 Syrian refugees until the screening to make sure they are not terrorists is better. Only 47 Democrats joined with 242 Republicans.[15] It stalled in the Senate.

The loss of the Democrat Party to socialism is proof of broken covenant. As this has happened more and more patterns are beginning to emerge of what the implications are for Christians. The real prejudice against Christians by socialism is easily seen in voter fraud. The more fraudulent the voter, the easier the tendency in that voter to vote for a party who will give a reward for a vote. Many honest voters put their vote behind a party wanting to see a strong country. Socialism/progressivism weakens a country on every level imaginable. I will prove that statement shortly. True Christians, and/or true and principled voters will not give their vote to the highest bidder. Usually, they will not vote for those who wish to give their hardworking dollars to sluggards who refuse to work. So when a political party or politician says we shouldn't protect Americans from voter fraud by demanding people show identification when they vote, you know something is screwy.

The proof voter fraud exists is overwhelming.[16] So if an attorney general and vice president from a socialist/progressive regime said asking for voter identification meant you were motivated by hatred, or voter fraud didn't exist, you would think they were scamming you, right?[17] Well, when states like Alabama, North Carolina, Texas, Georgia and Tennessee enacted laws requiring voters to have ID, the socialists went nuts. They claimed minorities were adversely affected by these ID laws. Well, minority voter turnout either stayed the same or increased after the ID laws were enacted in those states.[18] Chances are your own state will offer a free ID, if it also requires you to present identification at the ballot box. So what is the real reason? The real reason is to allow voter fraud, since all other reasons are proven bogus. Socialists/progressives overwhelmingly benefit from this fraud because anyone voting fraudulently is more inclined to allow their vote to be bought by some incentive. Socialism provides incentives, though, as I will prove, the benefits turn out to be a Ponzi scheme.

People of principle and faith are adversely affected by voter fraud. American citizens and our American system of elections and the rule of law takes a huge hit as well. Only criminals as well as an ideology foreign to our shores benefits from voter fraud. So it stands to reason the desire for voter fraud persecutes all American citizens, but specifically the faithful voter (of any belief) who will not participate in such fraud. Why should socialism want to do this? To take over, of course. Our country of natural resources and wealth is a great prize for any foreign ideology able to muster it.

Not all religions are persecuted equally, though. We all know how our school children are not allowed to celebrate Christmas in school unless it is about Santa Claus or a snowman, like Frosty. So you would be shocked if a teacher taught our young children a song about how great Islam is and sent them home with exercises promoting Islam. Well, folks, there was no screaming from the freedom of religion crowd for this atrocity. Here's the song: "Like a sandstorm/on the desert/sending camels/into motion; Like how a single faith/can make a heart open/They might only have one God/But they can make an explosion."[19] The teacher got the melody from the song "This is My Fight." After being taught this song, Nicole Negron's son brought home a notebook which included a stick-figure saying, "Believe in Allah! There is no other god." It is odd the freedom from religion groups never sue the schools when they promote Islam. Many have observed it might be the threat from the *"explosions"* (see preceding endnote).

Once you start marginalizing the founding religions of the country (Christianity and Judaism), you must marginalize the founders as well. Only socialism does this, and it does it for a reason. That reason is to make sure the rule of law which makes the country strong is aborted. We are already seeing this happen. A memo was sent out to workers in San Diego, CA, that they are barred from using the expression "Founding Fathers" during 2016's President's Day celebrations.[20] The supposed reason for this obvious breach of these workers' First Amendment rights is because the city finds it is biased to term the early generations who founded the nation as *founding fathers.* This is the nonsense which takes place when you start down the road of abrogating our inalienable rights to foreign ideologies. Foreign ideologies like progressivism/socialism need to obliterate the ideology it is replacing. While this takes time, those opposing socialism will be targeted and persecuted.

Given what I have already shared about the prejudice the IRS revealed when it targeted political non-profits; you can imagine the outcry when the IRS thought it could foist its new agenda on charities. In November 2015, the IRS posted a notice on the Federal Registrar that it would *like* non-profits (read: all churches, ministries as well as other Christian and Jewish groups) to hand over their donors' social security numbers when they make a contribution of over $250.[21] This problem is fraught with real dangers because the IRS has already been hacked and even admitted to the problems with charities keeping someone's social security number. The real question is why need them? The answers are not what the IRS would like you to believe. Charities already send statements to those claiming charity deductions. The recipient must keep and, if used as a deduction, file them.

Thankfully, the IRS decided not to go forward with the idea. Recently the IRS settled a case with the National Organization for Marriage when it was revealed the IRS leaked their donor list to the pro-gay rights Human Rights Campaign. The donor list contained the name of the then presidential candidate, Mitt Romney (who was running in opposition to the then sitting socialist president). Predictably, the judge said there was not enough evidence the IRS did it willfully.[22] Very few know how frequently Christians and Jews are persecuted in socialistic countries. If you believe in home schooling and you live in Sweden, Germany and parts of the United Kingdom, you are in danger of having your family ripped apart and/or fined into oblivion.[23] Most of these families are religious, realizing the dangers in sending their children to public school systems who are antagonistic of their religious views, while indoctrinating them into socialistic thinking. Socialists do this by design. I will prove to you it is tyranny personified. I pray the few state Democrats who are still conservative will be able to wrestle their national party back from socialism/progressivism's ideology.

After reviewing the previous experiences of private citizens and businesses suffering bureaucratic legal abuse, and the obvious disregard by politicians concerning the law, I had to ask, "When was it that our legal system was co-opted by a system whose legal tenets are dubious, at best?" At this point it would suit us all to review the cultural understanding surrounding "law." While I have gone into some detail concerning our initial covenant-based legal system— and its metamorphosis to what was a just and fair covenant-compact legal system— I have not gone into any depth concerning the ubiquitous politicized-bureaucratic polity we all suffer under presently.

I have, to some extent, shared a small snippet of that history— that which encompasses American Compact history— and an even smaller microcosm of America in its covenant understanding. In its basic legal form— pre-Bible, as well as other ancient legal texts— early man always delineated good and evil. Quite often, but not always, that included a connection to an understanding of a deity. Each community, bound by a specific understanding of law, based right and wrong around criminal behavior it considered evil with the understanding the criminal behavior needed to be stopped. The method employed to stop the behavior a community decided was damaging to the community, was punishment. Punishment took on many forms. Early on, the adage, "an eye for an eye" (Exodus 21:24) was employed.

The most basic and broad understanding of criminal behavior was murder, rape, intent to bodily harm— or whatever the method, the outcome was bodily harm— stealing, theft or fraud. These actions would fall under what we now call criminal law. At some point societies enacted what we now call civil law. In their basic form they entail the monetary harm people cause to other people through various actions which do not include criminal behavior. Quite frequently, this entailed the loss of livestock or food and clothing due to another's non-criminal actions. Fast-forward, for a moment, to our present age, and we have what we call tort law. That is the law surrounding the compensation due from a violation of civil law, or better said, the liability involved in damages.

So what most of us understand as right and wrong would fall into three aspects of the modern, western legal system: criminal law, civil law and tort law. They come to us through pre-historic legal understandings—I use the term loosely—ancient codes of law, which would include Oriental, Egyptian and Biblical law: and pre-modern codes of law, which would include Greek and Roman law. Mayan as well as other South American dynasties would be included in this legal timeframe, but never made an impact or continuation through to a broader understanding of modern law. Some would argue Sharia Law should be included in the time which includes South American history. Like Mayan and other South American communities, Sharia, for obvious reasons, never finds wide-scale popularity, unless it is enacted by force. Such force is considered tyranny, in our modern legal sense. I realize those who espouse and practice Sharia do not consider it so, but I write here concerning the practice of modern western law. Such is based upon consent and in some areas, covenant. It can easily be argued subjugation of half the population through duress cannot be considered true consent, but indeed is coercion, or at the very least, brainwashing. Many South American sacrificial rites would also fall under this veil, since people— especially children— would be drugged or somehow incapacitated to be ritually killed (rightfully considered in our time as murder).

Monarchial forms of government have ruled all throughout history. They are of many different flavors, depending upon the monarch. Yet they all have the common experience of loss of liberties based upon the monarch's governance. After the timeframe of Greek and Roman influence in law we see the French-Norman and finally English codes of law. These are heavily influenced by Greek, Roman and to some extent, Biblical legal codes. After this time period American Compact-Covenant history is seen and the legal codes enacted therefrom; namely, our Constitutional Republic. Lastly, in our modern times we have laws belonging to Socialism, Communism, Fascism and Progressivism. These last set of laws would fall under laws made through duress and coercion, either by force of violence or force of will through punitive taxes and other punitive regulations made from the force of law. They are quite similar in effect to forms of monarchial government. While these last set of laws masquerade as modern and western, they are anything but. They belong to the ash-heap of history, as does Mayan-like or other religious laws like Sharia, because their ultimate end is coercion by the removal of individual freedom and choice— even choice to do what might be considered wrong.

Even the Bible gives mankind the right to choose what the God of the Bible considers wrong (Deuteronomy 6). The consequences for choosing wrong are ingrained into the very fabric of the creation. Wrong acts are always segregated into criminal and civil types. Civil types are acts committed by accident, even if bodily harm is done. Biblically speaking, commission of a wrong act, and punishment for it, can be immediate or take years to become evident. For instance, one can, by some form of incompetence, cause a neighbor's livestock to become injured (Exodus 22:10-15). This will be made evident rather quickly and the neighbor will come seeking restitution (Exodus 22:1-5). Likewise, most murders, rapes, assaults and thefts are usually discovered in a timely manner, while the persons and their families harmed by those acts quickly desire to be vindicated for those events (Genesis 4:8).

When bodily harm takes place by accident, the Scriptures provided a place where the offender could escape punishment from the victim's family members, simply by invoking lack of intent (Numbers 35:14-15). On the other hand, one can spend time in the biblically wrong acts of drinking and carousing (Proverbs 20:1; 1 Corinthians 5:11), but the effects on the human body of these wrong acts may not be evident for ten, twenty or more years (Galatians 6:7-8; Ephesians 5:15-18). Although, anyone who ever suffered a hangover would testify they felt the effects the next morning. But eventually the long term harm of this behavior (as a lifestyle choice) on the human body will be made known, and the loss of extra years on the earth or some other disease is the result: in other words, the punishment. My point is that we all have a very defined understanding of right and wrong and that understanding— whether religious or not— comes from a higher power. For much of the western world, that understanding comes from the Bible. This is ingrained into the very fabric of our being.

Our modern law calls intent *mens rea* (Latin meaning guilty mind) and acting wrongly with serious public threat *actus reus* (Latin meaning guilty act). In other words, if you did not intend for your neighbor's property to be harmed by whatever action you did, you could pay the price for the damages done to your neighbor's property. (See the book of Deuteronomy, as well as some aspects of Exodus, Leviticus and Numbers.) This was your liability or your responsibility to make your neighbor whole. This is considered the crux of civil law. Its basic foundation is seen in the Bible as well as other ancient and Oriental texts. Within the Scriptures it is the outcome of a covenant between humans. Although, one could say other cultures exhibiting these elements had to agree among themselves to the tenets or they would not have obeyed their laws.

When humans enter into a covenant understanding they do so to benefit the community as well as protecting individual inalienable rights. No state, nor human entity can remove an inalienable right. I cannot even consent to remove my own inalienable right. When you can prove scientifically certain behavior damages the community, or that one's fundamental and inalienable right has been damaged because of some manmade right, then covenant has been broken. Why? Because you cannot covenant to remove your inalienable right. You cannot covenant to cause yourself bodily or economic harm. This is the crux of the Fifth Amendment, and it is seen as *one* outcome of the Tenth Amendment. Only punitive and tyrannical forms of government demand the loss of inalienable rights, when no crime has been committed.

The first inalienable right is the right to life. This is connected or one with the right to bodily wholeness. The next is the freedom to choose your religion or the God you will serve and the method in which you will worship. It is not unthinkable to place this as the first of our inalienable rights since, in the most common form of understanding concerning a just religion, it cannot demand arbitrary murder or self-mutilation. It cannot demand arbitrary imprisonment or confinement. It cannot demand arbitrary economic fines. In a careful study of the Bible, the book never does this, unlike Mayan-type or Sharia legal avenues. I realize there are folks who will try to argue this point with me. Usually their arguments are based on a biblical misconception or attributing a manmade church or religious teaching and crediting its source as the Bible. So much of today's liberal and secular teachings make this mistake. The New Testament never demands the murder of innocents or the bodily harm or mutilation of anyone. The New Testament never demands involuntary loss of economic freedom.[24]

In our American context, our first right or Amendment (freedom for religion), along with others (represented within the first Ten) are considered rights that we, as a people refuse to negotiate (read the Tenth Amendment). Former legal bodies not only understood that but honored it in almost every venue. The reason becomes obvious when we all understand the source of freedom does not originate with mankind but with the God of the Bible. If it originates from any other god or any other source, like mankind, then that freedom and those rights may be taken away by any old arbitrary god or however many men make a decision to do so.

This is why when religion is abrogated by something manmade, like let's say an addiction or something which is not built into the core of the creation, then our liberties are in peril and the covenant is broken and we, who have agreed to the covenant or compact no longer agree to abide by it. The reason why none of our inalienable rights suffered harm when those who are afflicted with disabilities were added to the covenant, or women, or those of other skin colors (in our case as a country, slaves) were added, is because in the case of disabilities, these are either caused by a mutated disease or trauma; or in the case of women and those of differing color, we are built into the core of creation. But when you begin to add practices then you run afoul of the compact. For by adding practices, you now add manmade and artificial liberties that while, as human beings who practice such, deserve the liberty of life and dignity, enshrining a practice which conflicts with life will eventually take place.

Let's look at an example. The practice of abortion is now enshrined. Who is to say over time the practice of euthanasia or the practice of three people or ten people in a marriage will not be enshrined? The psychology enshrining abortion is the same as that for other manmade practices. This is why judges are supposed to judge based on law, not "feelings." Now try to force people to allow these practices in their religious events or force them to be silent when they either refuse such practices or speak out against them because of good science or religious belief, and you have broken the covenant.

Some have tried to say religion is a practice. But remember that traditionally and historically religion— specifically the God of the Bible— involves life, free speech, the right to freedom from violence or freedom from removal or infringement upon one's property (criminal and civil laws). So when you now make a law to remove one's property and free speech rights because of a manmade practice, you destroy the compact or covenant agreement. *I am not espousing the desire to stop manmade rights as a part of the amendment process.* My point is you cannot make them inalienable, or non-negotiable when a conflict arises by denying religious (or atheistic) waivers. I will explain this shortly.

We have another aspect of broken covenant easily traced to breaking religious covenant, but atheists and agnostics alike can become entangled by it. Let me explain. We have always understood you had to *intend* to hurt someone when you broke a law, or you had to intend to specifically want to commit an unlawful act. As we saw from the last chapter, we can be charged committing a criminal act because we broke a civil law, even though we *intended* to do neither. As we saw previously, there was an unspoken understanding the officials who made the laws or those who had to otherwise officiate in some capacity would be honorable in the execution of the law. That was one step in the process which became broken. Those who had to officiate (the bureaucrats), refused to stop and say, "Wait a minute, is this grandmother worthy of jail time?"

The question was never asked because no one in the bureaucracy ever wondered whether they had broken a covenant. They never knew they were there to protect and serve. At least the police have had that drilled into them for years. The military used to be trained in such matters as well. Police have the right— no, the duty— to say, we are not charging so and so with a criminal act because their hedges have become a little higher than two feet. But civilian or federal bureaucrats are not trained to protect and serve. They are not trained to understand there ever was a covenant in place when our compact was agreed to. The reason for that is because the Constitution gives *elected officials* the job of making laws. The fact bureaucrats are making laws is proof of a broken covenant.

Since bureaucrats are not elected, they carry no special training in making law. So they never stop to ask whether a law is just or even needed. In fact, they are trained to make sure they do charge someone, all in an effort to show the necessity of their jobs. After all, it is the mindless maze of these regulations which keep them busy. Mid-level bureaucrats at the IRS have proven this all too well. Remember when we discussed how Congress has tried to stop the illegal immigration crises? Congress passed the Illegal Immigration Reform and Illegal Immigration Responsibility Act. It basically mandates Federal agencies must cooperate in reporting illegal immigrants, and they can't enact rules or other mandates to stop the reporting, one agency to another. Eventually, this would reveal the illegals and eventually they would be deported. Well, bureaucrats at the IRS decided that the legally passed Act by the people's representatives didn't apply to the IRS![25] Nobody has stopped them and it has been roughly eight years since they have refused to follow the law. Lawlessness starts at the top. When a sitting president gets away with it, his (or her) minions (think bureaucrats that they hire to stay in the job for decades) will eventually believe it is their right to do the same.

Connected to the former aspect of broken covenant, we are now following a predictable pattern: **Religious tests**. As we have just seen, there are religious tests going on all over this country. The Constitution states clearly under Article VI: ". . . no religious Test shall ever be required as a Qualification to any Office or public Trust under the United States." States continued to use various religious tests for office holders until the Supreme Court struck down the need for religious tests in public office in Torcaso v. Watkins (1961). Following which, most state laws were amended. This decision used the First Amendment as its foundation. So here is the kicker: States are now requiring everyone follow the mantra of the atheist religion.

All Christian ministers will exhort youth to be responsible and celibate in their sexuality. There is a biblical reason why. There is also a scientific reason why. To not tell someone different, is to refuse to minister. So, unless you adhere to the state's idea of religious testing, you cannot volunteer or run for office or get hired by the state (and in some states run a business). The point in ministering is not to make the individual feel disrespected, but to show them God's way of doing things— in contradiction to man's way— it is to show them the awesome truth of their total being and why they were created the way they were, and the possible ways spiritual as well as soul-based issues can collude to thwart their health. This also runs into problems for those of true science. Pediatricians are being muzzled when they see certain practices being foisted upon our children to "normalize" certain gender identity issues.[26]

Here is one case in point. David Well, a volunteer chaplain (ordained minister) served for thirteen years at a juvenile detention center in Kentucky. The state revoked his credentials because they had enacted a new regulation which said he had to promise or covenant (otherwise agree) not to tell the youths homosexuality or any of the other sex-u-practices were "abnormal, deviant, sinful or that they can or should change their sexual orientation or gender identity."[27] Obviously, the minister could not make such an oath or make such a promise. Folks, we are losing our First Amendment freedoms in all sorts of ways socialism's main-stream media have not told you about. There is a stifling going on here of not only free religious practice, but free speech and free thought. The truth is when you teach bureaucrats to honor and respect our Bill of Rights, and then give them the religious freedom— their own First Amendment rights, and tell them those rights are protected— more and more of society relaxes and just follows laws protecting all.

Another case in point is North Carolina. Once the legislature allowed elected and non-elected officials the rights of conviction to opt out of performing genderless unions, triple the amount signed up to receive the exemption.[28] Predictably, North Carolina is now being sued so freedom of religion can be abrogated.[29] If the courts do not stand up for freedom of religion in this lawsuit, the effect would be to allow only atheists to function in governmental authority. Part of the problem is the fact those who claim Christianity do not stand up for the Scriptures. Others believe "opting out" of religion is the solution. But that is a lie because atheism is also a form of religion. All religions leave an atmosphere or pervading tone in place. This leaves a cold, bureaucratic monopoly unhindered access to deny, arrest and thwart ALL citizens of their inalienable rights.

I am not saying anyone should be denied access or rights of association. What I am saying is it is high time to dump these various "endorsement" tests as well as others that have been implemented and understand our non-sectarian structure. A non-sectarian approach would not target the institution but be based on various access for the individual. In other words, allow various chaplains access to teach all the effects of the "sex-u-practices." If a state can only afford one chaplain, then make sure they understand how to teach all the various problems and/or benefits. In the case of the baker, make sure individuals can have access to various bakers who will bake everyone cakes. To force secularization and atheism on our institutions and businesses is insanity. Can you imagine if we forced Islam on atheists or atheism on Muslims?

States can surely have employees available with no qualms to provide all necessary state licensing needs. If a state feels the need to get involved, it should only be to make sure there are enough bakers in their state to supply the need for everyone! The only exceptions should be safety. Obviously, large hotels are placed in many cities and at many exits of highway ramps to provide the weary traveler rest. As long as hotels understand their policies would be co-opted as a result of safety issues, there should be no problems. Some of these issues have affected the small bed-and-breakfast market. There are so many of them in this country that it is unfathomable all of them are religious. This way everyone is treated equally and with dignity. We make compromises and we understand the need why. The bakery owner, photographer, homosexual, Christian, atheist, all work to compromise in a non-sectarian fashion. We respect the religious, and the homosexual can easily find a facility meeting their needs. In fact, certain states can make emblems or some other marking for businesses stating they serve all. The free market loves those kinds of ads.

What we see evidenced in all these examples is that not everyone is treated equally. Presidents break the law. Attorneys general selectively apply the law and mid-level bureaucrats ignore it. Judges rule based on the snake den of "precedence" instead of how the law was originally written. Criminals become honored through slogans ("hands up, don't shoot") and groups use it to carve out an idea that somehow one racial, sexual or religious group of lives matter, but other lives matter less. This enables a black man to "tweet" the idea of "kill all the white people in town."[30] Hopefully, medical tests will show this man mentally incompetent. I say that because if he is not, and these attitudes are allowed to become pervasive in our society, all colors of citizens of all religions are doomed. If the attitude exists that only one group of citizens matter, then we will begin to see more and more racial and religious attacks.[31]

These incidents (see the last endnote) are not done to promote racial harmony, but chaos. The law becomes parsed out through the lens of social media and mob protestation. The frightening reality is if the God-fearing— all colors of black, brown, red, white, pink and yellow alike— don't load up in buses to protest as the Holy Spirit directs, their inalienable rights and our very country will be lost. You ask, "Why is that?" Because words and images do have an impact. The religious can make a difference. Unfortunately, the violent type of protestation activity also has an impact in leading a society downward. It is rarely fair and more often dangerous. Special interests let a popular, monied quarterback go free (think deflate-gate) while a lowly and unpopular clerk (according to the media) is jailed for her religious beliefs. I make no comment on guilt or innocence here, just the unequal application of laws.

Rabble-rousing and violent protests is a mistaken belief that two wrongs can become a supposed right. In other words, they "hurt" us so we can hurt them. To think, scientifically, *good* can come out of that is to deny reality. Only more *wrong* can take place. This harms all kinds and colors of people. What was a covenantal idea that law applies equally is now trashed because we can see the law is not equal nor is it equally applied. This undermines the very fabric of our American society. Of course, it is the goal of socialism to do just that. One method of socialists for takeover is protestation. In fact, it must do that in order to take over. The takeover *begins* with the regulations and the bureaucracies which enable them. But why have we gone down the road of bureaucrats to begin with?

ENDNOTES

1   <http://www.reviewjournal.com/news/obamacare-leaves-las-vegas-man-owing-407000-doctor-bills> accessed 4/5/16

2   Katie Pavlich. "Fast and Furious: Barack Obama's Bloodiest Scandal and Its Shameless Cover-Up." © 2012 Katie Pavlich. Washington, DC: Regnery Publishing, Inc.

3   <http://www.foxnews.com/politics/2014/09/15/damage-control-ex-official-claims-clinton-allies-scrubbed-benghazi-documents-in/> accessed 4/5/16

4   <http://www.foxnews.com/politics/2014/06/12/us-pushing-local-cops-to-stay-mum-on-surveillance/?intcmp=obinsite> accessed 4/5/16

5   "Paratus" 14:50 <video.aptv.org/video/2365552604/> accessed 4/5/16

6   <http://www.thenewamerican.com/usnews/immigration/item/19674-obama-immi-gration-plan-would-give-cash-benefits-to-illegals><http://www.judicialwatch.org/press-room/press-releases/judicial-watch-uncovers-usda-records-sponsoring-u-s-food-stamp-program-for-illegal-aliens> accessed 4/5/16

7   <http://www.fairus.org/publications/president-obama-s-record-of-dismantling-immigra-tion-enforcement> <http://www.fairus.org/DocServer/Omama_Enforcement_Report.pdf><http://www.cairco.org/highlights/obamas-royal-decree-executive-amnesty-illegal-aliens><http://www.washingtonexaminer.com/expert-obamas-amnesty-profoundly-unfair-to-4-million-legal-immigrants-a-new-high/article/2563279> accessed 4/4/16

8   Milton Friedman accurately argues why the question of whether an immigrant is legal or illegal is irrelevant. Maybe if we framed the issue in that light and made the necessary need for work and non-criminal activity the litmus test, the issue of how many new citizens to allow would be resolved by free market needs, and not the socialist necessity for new voters and dependents. If you cannot find the video under this url, look for Milton Friedman, "Illegal Immigration, Part One and Two" These are short clips, and "Who Protects the Worker?" It runs a little over 52 minutes. Since the urls are constantly changing from month to month, you will have to Google, and/or log into YouTube and search these video clips if these do not work.<https://www.youtube.com/watch?v=VE5YBnX8juY> <https://www.youtube.com/watch?v=3eyJlbSgdSE><https://www.youtube.com/watch?v=NfU9Fqah-f4>

9   <http://www.foxnews.com/world/2015/11/17/refugee-resettlement-process-leaves-syrian-christians-in-cold/?intcmp=hpbt2> accessed 4/5/16

10 Ibid.

11 Ibid.

12 <http://www.newsweek.com/european-parliament-recongizes-isis-killing-religious-minorities-genocide-423008> accessed 4/5/16.

13 <http://www.foxnews.com/us/2015/11/21/while-dc-debates-religion-refugees-iraqi-christians-feel-uncle-sam-boot/?intcmp=hpbt1> accessed 4/5/16

14 <http://www.foxnews.com/world/2015/11/20/france-pm-says-paris-attacks-ringleader-used-migrant-crisis-to-get-into-country/?intcmp=trending> accessed 4/5/16

15 <https://www.govtrack.us/congress/votes/114-2015/h643> accessed 4/5/16

16 <http://www.discoverthenetworks.org/viewSubCategory.asp?id=1666> click on "See Also: Part 2; Part 3." This is a three-part documented history of voter fraud starting with

October 28, 1986 and continuing until September 2, 2015. Unfortunately, I am sure they will be updating the site after the 2016 elections. Accessed 2/10/16 and © 2015 by DiscoverTheNeworks.org. If the url is inactive go to <http://www.discoverthenetworks. org> and click on "Voter Fraud" button.

17   <http://www.wsj.com/articles/SB1000142405270230338000457952160312022557 2> Site accessed 2/10/16 and © by The Wall Street Journal; article by Robert D. Popper, "Political Fraud About Voter Fraud, updated 4/5/16.

18   Ibid., see also <http://www.wsj.com/articles/the-voter-suppression-myth-takes-another-hit-1419811042> Site © by The Wall Street Journal; article by Robert D. Popper, 12/28/14; accessed 4/5/16.

19   <http://www.foxnews.com/opinion/2015/11/20/schools-sing-praise-to-allah-create-propaganda-posters-for-isis.html?intcmp=hplnws> accessed 4/5/16

20   <http://www.foxnews.com/politics/2016/2/10/city-workers-in-san-diego-barred-from-uttering-biased-term-founding-fathers.html> accessed 4/5/16

21   <http://www.foxnews.com/politics/2015/11/20/charities-chafe-at-irs-proposal-to-collect-donors-social-security-numbers.html?intcmp=hplnws> 4/5/16

22   Ibid.

23   <http://www.hslda.org/hs/international/Germany/><http://www.hslda.org/hs/international/Sweden/><http://www.hslda.org/hs/international/UnitedKingdom/default. asp> accessed 4/5/16

24   Some quote Jesus' words in Matthew 5:29-30; (see also 18:9): "If your right eye causes you to sin, tear it out and throw it away! It is better to lose one of your members, than to have your whole body thrown into hell." (NET Bible ®) Here as elsewhere, the understanding is the fact Jesus has come to fulfill the Mosaic Law— exempting us from the need to, when we accept Him as Lord and Savior. In this context, He now lays down His life so we can live by and through the Holy Spirit. The Puritans, as a whole group had a hard time understanding the difference between the Old and New Testaments when it came to laws they enacted. That same problem permeates the culture of the American church when it comes to life in Christ. We have mixed, on almost a visceral level the two. The Apostle Paul, most notably in Romans and elsewhere, went to great lengths to try to help his fellow Jews who believed in Christ, separate the two Covenants— Old from New. Yet in our modern church age, many have confused them. No wonder the media and others today do so. It is no different within this passage. There have been those in our pre-modern church age who have taken this passage literally. Jesus did not intend that. When you keep in context every passage in which He mentions this type of action, you come away with an understanding of a trap. That certain behavior can trap us in a sin in which the

effects become life altering and potentially permanent— thus the exacerbated example of cutting one's limb off or plucking out one's eye. The question could be asked, "If Jesus were speaking literally, why did He only mention the right eye and not the left?" Well, the answer reveals the absurdity of the supposition. It simply cannot be that only one eye is sinful or offensive. If you do not deal with the sin issue, plucking out one eye will still give you the ability to see with the other one.

Obviously, the whole passage, taken in context is Jesus trying to help His hearers (and us centuries later) understand the difference between the Old Covenant and the New Covenant He was instituting. This included the major difference in how the sin issue is dealt with between the two. In like manner, those places in the Old Testament in which death is required for certain crimes, would have to do with the Mosaic Law. God does not demand death for every crime, nor is He a God of death, contrary to some modern portrayals. It isn't until the Mosaic Law is instituted that requirements and substitutions pertaining to sin are made. When Cain slew Abel, God is the family member that steps in to require restitution. But instead of demanding Cain's death (an eye for an eye), God puts a seal or some other designation on Cain to identify that Cain is given protection from civilizations' eye for an eye requirement. (Genesis 4:13-16, see the NET Bible® for an excellent translation of the passage. Within the Jewish culture, this gives ancient understanding to imprisonment.) God protects Cain, giving us one of the first documented cases of grace in light of sin. It is as a result of sin and its ever-increasing negative effects on the creation that God institutes the Mosaic Law. It has been said that the world was so lawless, if God had not enacted it, there may never have been a virgin Jew left for Messiah to be born from— nor a Jew to welcome Him into the world. There were many codes of laws from an ancient point of view. Yet, over time within the western world's context, the Bible won out for many reasons and we have reviewed many in this book. But civil rights embedded in what constitutes a government based on a covenant or agreement among mankind and a higher power is one of the overriding reasons. Along with the message from that Divinity that He has bought and paid the price for freedom— and so mankind is free— makes it a superior and enduring example of what good citizens and good government has the potential to look like. This is what made it so popular compared with former rules of law.

25   Jay Sekulow, © 2015. "Undemocratic,." New York, NY: Howard Books, an imprint of Simon & Schuster, Inc. 86-89

26   <http://www.familywatchinternational.org/fwi/policy_brief_ss_parenting.pdf> Family Watch International article highlighting scientists' research: "Same-Sex Parenting and Junk Science" For scientists that successfully work in Sexual Orientation Change Therapy

<http://www.familywatchinternational.org/fwi/documents/fwipolicybriefSOCE.pdf> accessed 4/5/16

27   "National Review," September 7. 2015. 6-10, Section "The Week," © 2015 National Review, 215 Lexington Avenue, New York, NY 10016

28   <http://www.foxnews.com/politics/2015/09/03/more-north-carolina-officials-refuse-to-perform-marriages/?intcmp=ob_article_footer_text&intcmp=obnetwork> accessed 4/5/16

29   <http://www1.cbn.com/cbnnews/us/2015/December/Religious-Rights-of-NC-Magistrates-Under-Fire> accessed 4/5/16

30   <http://www.foxnews.com/us/2015/09/03/man-faces-charges-after-tweeting-kill-all-white-people-in-town-bail-set-at/?intcmp=ob_article_sidebar_video&intcmp=obinsite> accessed 4/4/16

31   <http://www.campusreform.org/?ID-6990> accessed 4/4/16. If the ID number is not successful, you will have to Google their articles from February to April 2016. There seemed to be an inordinate amount of racial hate exhibited by students from various colors during that period of time with a real lack in understanding our Bill of Rights.

Chapter Four

SOCIALISM: A BOOGEYMAN OR THE ACTUAL MOTHER OF COMMUNISM?

For brevity's sake, it is the next microcosm of history I will make broad strokes to describe how we arrived at our upside-down descent into legal captivity. The Constitution itself talks about the limitations and functions of institutions but never specifically manages them on a day-to-day basis. The framers provided for the development of regulations for the institutions needed to run the Federal government. It was those earliest citizens who had a "governor" within them. There was even a connection between the parties because there was a belief, not just in the God of the Bible, but in the practice of covenant. Those early generations were taught their Bibles. They read them. In fact, many early school lessons were derived from the Scriptures.[1] They may have politically disagreed (think Story and Jefferson) on a great many things, but there was a common understanding as to morality and decency and covenant. There was a common knowledge that one had to have intent to commit a crime. Laws had to be published or known. A speedy trial by jury was also mandatory. It was common knowledge there was a difference between civil violations, criminal actions and simple mistakes. You truly were innocent until you were proven guilty. As you have read from my short list of real-life examples, none of what we understand from our Constitutional

Republic based on covenant concerning how we must be treated within the law *must* come to pass. Covenant says do unto others as you would have done to yourself. But there is another history which does not adhere to these tenets. It is based on a totally different psychology and/or ideology— even a different "religion."

The framing generation of the 1700s incorporated the governing religious covenant-compacts of the puritan generation and made them their own by working within secular compacts which incorporated many principles, including biblical ones. In a very similar attempt at mimicry, another ideology has crept in and attempted to engulf the compact. That parasitic amoeba-like approach will destroy the covenant, thereby destroying the compact. But like any good virus, it needs to leave the host alive long enough so it can keep infecting others, gaining ground and attempting to become so big as to make the uninfected think it is impossible to remove. We should realize this is not a democrat issue or a republican issue. This is a human issue. While one political party may very well be infected to the point of total captivity, it is our responsibility as citizens to purge the infection. Personally, I was rather ignorant of this history and the ideology associated with it until I started this research. So if I appear to be a little passionate concerning the danger, realize I did not always believe we were in danger of losing the republic. I now know differently.

You can watch any TV "murder-crime-mystery" and hear one of the investigators say when trying to find the culprit or culprits, "Follow the money." In our case here, that saying is not some imaginary TV show. It is the sad reality and motive behind so much history when it comes to governments and modern-day bureaucracies. The Bible is not silent when it comes to money either. There are approximately 750 to 850 Scriptures which deal with money. Except for the kingdom of God, Jesus talked more about money than heaven, hell or even love. In fact, it is the love of money which is the root of all evil, not as some misquote it, money itself (1 Timothy 6:10). According to the Scriptures, money is a tool, and nothing more. It is not inherently evil, but the love of it is. Jesus said it plainly, "For where your treasure is, there will your heart be also" (Matthew 6:21; Luke 12:34). The consistent mishandling of money is just a symptom of deeper issues.

The monarchal money system was simple: The crown is given its land and wealth by "God." I place God in quotes simply because that was the premise. I don't feel comfortable declaring it was God. Quite frequently monarchies just took what they wanted. We do have biblical instances where God clearly makes a point of the fact nations were given their land by Him. (Think Israel and other tribes in the book of Genesis.) The crown then, in turn gives portions of lands to be worked by individuals. Those individuals pay the crown a portion of their benefits from working the land. The minutia of those deals varied according to different monarchies. You were not free in the sense Americans espouse freedom of land, rights, and money. In each different monarchy, there were those who were connected by biology or birthright to nobility and those who were not. Wealth, land and rights were also connected to status or birthright connection to the monarchy. Our founders, for obvious reasons, revolted against more than European-based religious practices. They revolted (by a majority) against the ideology of the monarchy in which only those "connected" could have the status, land, rights and wealth bestowed by monarchal largesse. In other words, they revolted against an economy based on political ideas which were, quite often purported to be based on the Bible; but quite frequently were based only on some religious or manmade idea of what the Scripture actually said.

Much like the history we reviewed of Enlightenment growing up on the same planet with Reformation and Renaissance, another system, quite similar to the monarchal system began to become popular. It was called socialism. Socialism, by definition is the philosophical, social and economic system whereby society, its money, ventures of enterprise and industry— its people and even their religion— is owned and controlled by the state government rather than by individual people or companies or religious institutions. The socialistic doctrine demands state owner-ship and control of the fundamental means of production and distribu-tion of wealth. That is to be achieved by reconstructing the existing capitalist or other political system of a country through democratic and parliamentary means. It advocates nationalization of natural resources, basic industries, banking and credit facilities and public utilities, along with the education systems in a country. Those educational systems must now teach the nationalistic mantra of the socialists' religion or ideologies. Socialism places a special emphasis on the nationalization of monopolized branches of industry and trade. Socialism advocates state ownership of corporations in which the ownership function has passed from stockholders to managerial personnel. Smaller and less vital enterprises and institutions can be left under private ownership, thereby allowing private ownership of smaller corporations, though they are heavily regulated.

In America, the ideas and political systems now entrenched under the names of progressivism or socialism have come through three different avenues, based on an original concept developed by Karl Marx and his "prophet," Friedrich Engels. Originally Marxism developed into two groups: the Social Democrats and the Communist Party Marxists. Multiplied millions (estimates run from 120 million to over 170 million) have died under the banner of these two groups. Noting death as an unpopular political vehicle, socialists began to lose supporters. So the outreach had to change.

In our modern world, socialism emerged out of the countries of Britain, France and Germany from the 1830s on. As with Enlightenment history, I am not following a linear timeline. I have painted broad strokes. The United States has a long history of the socialists' movements and groups within it. But on a worldwide scale, socialism has three basic branches. There are the voluntary socialists who want to set up communities (think community organizers), where socialism can be set up among the people and thereby branch out. Historically a figure like Robert Owen would fit that bill. Then there are the revolutionary socialists who want to impose a nationwide seizure of political and economic vehicles within a country (Marxists, Leninists, Stalinists, the former USSR, etc.).

Finally, there are the parliamentary socialists, also known as "Fabian" Socialists. They started as a socialist society in 1883 in England, naming themselves after the Roman general Fabius Cunctator. Because his tactics in battle were patient and elusive— in other words, hard to find out and thereby stop— they believe the best way to infiltrate a society and change it to socialism is through legislation where socialist agenda legislation can be passed, thereby seizing whole institutions and vital enterprises within a country by more "peaceful" means (Read: less death). Historically, this is seen through the labor parties of the three European countries just mentioned (Britain, France and Germany) or the push from men like Sidney Webb and George Bernard Shaw (who wrote "Fabian Essays in Socialism").[2]

You can now see why we have gone down the road of the bureaucrat/politician and why they have been working overtime instituting "their" regulations. It is the way of socialism. Any government in the process of converting from the freedom of capitalism must become entrenched by political bureaucrats and regulations in order to bring the people, their institutions and their businesses under the control of the government. It is a process which takes time, but now you can see why we are on our way into captivity.

There are quite a few misconceptions out there about socialism. One is the ownership is in common, or in the community. NOTHING COULD BE FURTHER FROM THE TRUTH. I know there have been those in the presidency and those running for president who will say their brand of socialism (progressivism) is softer and not Marxist or the Leninist brand of socialism. I'm old enough to remember the lie used to be, "Oh, we're not communists, we're socialists and that is totally different." Let me ask you, does it matter whether they get your property, money, land or rights at the point of a gun or at the point of a regulation or "law"?

Remember the biblical principle of the depravity of man? It will serve us well here. Socialism came first from the ideas of both Marx and Engels, and then through Lenin communism was birthed. This makes socialism communism's Mama. Trust me when I tell you the apple does not fall far from that tree. Both Marx and Lenin saw what became communism as the final road of socialism. Once it became obvious shouting "revolution" and "Change" were nothing more than "Give Us Your Money, Wealth, Land and Rights So WE can distribute them MORE Equitably—" and that the distribution process will always be broken, distributing common poverty— large people groups moved away from socialism.

Modern progressives can tell you all day long communism can't work and socialism/progressivism is purer and better. But mankind will never be happy with only *one* power grab. Mankind will always want more, and more until only the well connected are in power and everyone else is a worker in some form of poverty, with absolutely no way out. All socialism does is exchange the government or the state for the monarchy. This is why it is so easy for those in Europe and England to adopt socialism. It works well as an attempt at replacement for the monarchal system. Our original form of government— not what it has become— is far superior to either socialism/progressivism or a monarchal system.

Neither Marx or Lenin regarded equality as an element to implement EXCEPT as it was needed when moving a society from freedom (read: capitalist or non-Marxist societies) through socialism and then into communism. "Equality" was to be used only as a means of protestation or as a battle cry to arouse the public to campaign for. Both found equality impossible to carry out in a society in which socialism was in control and not needed when communism was in charge.[3] Why is that? Well, in societies who have bought into the socialistic state, they are already on their way to communism, whether they realize it or not. Remember the battle strategy of the Roman general the Fabian society named itself after? The hope from all progressives is folks will not realize the lie of "equality." Equality is not needed in communistic states because people own nothing. They are already trapped and in captivity. But in places of capitalism, people are free to engage the system as their skill and success enable.

Equality also needs to be defined. Equal does not mean the same. Everyone knows we are not equal; namely, because some will work harder, others have different talents and others receive different opportunities. Greed and depravity want what they cannot generate on their own. So the temptation for "equality" (read: give me what somebody else has so we are "equal") is just part of using greedy human nature to trap. It is the hunter who quietly traps its prey by using a lure. The lure is "equality." The lie is that we are equal or the same. We are only equal in the eyes of our Maker and that is in order to access His love, provision and salvation— He created us equal in that sense— all mankind equal before Him in dignity and self-worth. That does not equate to us being the same. The Bible supports equality as mankind equal in value and dignity. So the lie is, give us your successful and they must give us their money so we can make everyone equal. But remember we are already equal.

In progressive or socialistic systems, no matter what brand you use, no one will work their hardest when they know someone else will own it or otherwise take it. The progressives always have winners and losers. They hand pick them. All systems have winners and losers. I just prefer the government not do the picking. Give me a free market any day of the week. That market will choose who makes a better product and who does not. At that point you are only limited by your own hard work and talent and not by what government decides to take from you because of your success.

The religious ideas— excuse me— philosophical ideas of Marx follow a very similar path we saw with Enlightenment: anger over the Catholic Church. This time the history included anger over Protestant understanding, with biblical undertones, aimed at how Marx thought the feudal system was connected to "God." I have found in every century somebody always tries to blame the real God for the wrongs in the world, based on ideas or systems which have very little to do with the Bible. Since the Bible clearly moves from philosophy to money and government, all movements wanting to annul the Scriptures feel the need to replace biblical worldview. Since worldview can produce economies and societies, they must also be reformed into the "NEW image and Likeness" of their purveyors. Marx and his followers are no different in their predictable path. Remember the re-education "training"?

Since it was proven long ago socialism is quite unscientific and cannot produce a healthy economy, Marx set out to "conquer" the science by, among other things, attempting to prove logic was unable to be applied universally to all mankind for all time. That the "thought" needed to disprove socialism was applied by a class of thinkers who basically can't be trusted because of their class interests. So if you buy into that nonsense, i.e., 2+2 does not equal 4, let's go one better. *Experiment + Observation = Resultant science* is NOT TRUE— according to Marx— no matter what your eyeballs and experience tells you. According to Marx, this is because you are from a class which won't accept what you cannot see in socialism, or whatever brand of "correct" thinking the progressives or social engineering class want YOU, the common worker, to think. Next— and this one is priceless— the discussion over whether to be socialist or not to be socialist— the need for socialization of production and the desire not to socialize production— is unnecessary because all history will bring all societies to socialized production because it is the necessary end of all societies! Finally, socialists are basically not to engage anyone in talking about what a socialistic state will or will not look like— because their faith says it is inevitable— that any discussion along those lines will open them up to logical thinking and that would be to renounce socialism![4]

Now you know why the socialistic (liberal) media refuse to allow discussion or actual science and research concerning social issues or the need to bring on true conservatives to have a legitimate debate. Now you know why the news has become so tainted. It is not just because they don't like what conservatives say or think, they are actually indoctrinated NOT to allow any other speech or thought which does not go along with the progressive agenda. No need for freedom of speech HERE! So out goes the First Amendment. Remember the Roman general? They will just placate you into thinking the First Amendment is still in effect, but they will keep whittling away at it until it is no longer viable. This is why they must go after freedom of religion FIRST. Since historically in this country they could not, they just started slow and quiet until, VOILA! Now they want you to be silent about your scientific as well as religious proofs and beliefs!

The Second Amendment must go, because once the people realize progressivism leads to communism, and their money has been stolen, they will not be happy. They will do something about it, and they have guns to do it. I am not suggesting violence, just revealing the progressive's thought patterns. It has also been proven to be far easier to silence free speech rights in socialist countries than in those with capitalist and free speech liberties.[5] In fact, socialism is a religion because you must believe with faith. The God of the Bible fosters choice, as well as the ability to question (even test Him), and the ability to disobey Him, if that is what you choose. The consequences or results of your choice are within your wheelhouse. Many times that reveals the science of the Bible. The God of the Bible also does not shrink away from science, and neither do His people. It has been much harder to get out the real science and research concerning many social issues. I hope to bring many more in the coming texts to you. Once you see the research you will be astounded, as I was, at the sheer volume of lies we are being told, and how many researchers and scientists are being silenced.

Socialism's religious outreach is atheism, though many atheists are not socialists, recognizing the cult-like demand to ignore science which disproves socialism.[6] Nevertheless, the real unraveling of socialism does not always come from simple science or logical argument, though those easily decimate its tenets. The real exposure comes from the Scriptures. I can hear many, "Oh, I believed socialism WAS biblical." The two are diametrically opposed to one another and cannot exist in the same land. Now, if you are an atheist and want to make sure you get rid of Christians, then socialism, progressivism or communism might seem a good avenue. I would take heed, though, if that is your thought. It has been proven in China, Russia and Cuba, when free societies were once again allowed to look inside those bastion walls Marx and Engels plastered, Christians not only thrived, but being sent underground, grew in tenacity and miraculous working power of the Holy Spirit.[7] Socialism is a true religion all on its own. It only uses atheism as well as the Bible. The "true" god of socialism is itself and the faith it demands from its believers is unwavering. It demands your inalienable rights, civil rights and your money. In fact, anyone not of the *faith* is also not allowed to question the *religion*. No matter how scientific and intelligent the argument, those who do not believe are to be silenced.[8]

ENDNOTES

1   <http://www.angelfire.com/la2/prophet1/educationamerica.html><http://www.freere-public.com/focus/news/2201818/posts> accessed 4/7/16. I used those sites so you can have a quick glance at the history.

2   <http://www.britannica.com/topic/Fabian-Society> accessed 4/4/16. See also the Future Reading Section.

3   H.B. Acton. "The Illusion of the Epoch: Marxism-Leninism as a Philosophical Creed." © 1962 H.B. Acton. (Indianapolis: Liberty Fund, 2003).[Online] available from <http://oll.libertyfund.org/titles/877> see the Preface, vii and viii. Site © Liberty Fund, Inc., 2004-2016; accessed 3/13/16

4   Von Mises does not actually say what I have written. He more accurately translates Marx's thinking better than I could. I view what I have written as a pretty good interpretation of Marx's ideas after viewing several different aspects of them from many sources. To read: Ludwig Von Mises, "Socialism: An Economic and Sociological Analysis," translated by J. Kahane, foreword by F.A. Hayek; (Indianapolis: Liberty Fund, 1981) March 13, 2016 <http://oll.libertyfund.org/titles/1060> see 8.

5   <http://www.economist.com/blogs/erasmus/2015/08/free-speech-and-europe> accessed 4/4/16

6   Ludwig Von Mises, "Socialism: An Economic and Sociological Analysis," translated by J. Kahane, foreword by F.A. Hayek; (Indianapolis: Liberty Fund, 1981) March 13, 2016 <http://oll.libertyfund.org/titles/1060> see 9

7   <http://www.cbn.com/cbnnews/world/2015/September/Miraculous-How-Suffering-Made-Cubas-Church-Grow/> <http://www.academia.edu/11044970/Christianity_during_the_Chinese_and_Russian_Communism> <http://www.economist.com/blogs/erasmus/2015/07/religion-russia> accessed 4/4/16

8   Ludwig Von Mises, "Socialism: An Economic and Sociological Analysis," translated by J. Kahane, foreword by F.A. Hayek; (Indianapolis: Liberty Fund, 1981) March 13, 2016 <http://oll.libertyfund.org/titles/1060> see 18-19.

Chapter Five

EXPERIMENT + OBSERVATION = RESULTANT SCIENCE

In order for any commonality of study to take place we all should agree on the formula. I have never heard an atheist or anyone else suggest the observation of an experiment never produces a result. That result is then what can make the basis for science. What I term as pseudo-science or fake science are those folks who decide to start the formula with only the observation or somehow change the experiment to suit a desired outcome or result. Our world, which claims pride in its sciences has a blind spot: It changes the experiment so the result is usually tainted. Quite often the observation can be the same and some aspect of the experiment is the same, but the totality of the result and the totality of the resultant science is going to be different. That can, in some instances produce pseudo or fake science. The Bible is a book describing the God who made the universe. There is more than enough evidence out there to prove that statement. It is not the purpose of this text to do that. I mention that only to say the faithful never shy away from good science. I mean that to say, science which does not "add" data to change outcomes and science which does not ignore data, which will have the same effect. The scientists who decimated socialism's (progressivism) claims, did so early in the 1900s. The research has existed for decades and continues to be made.

Unfortunately for the faithful, many scientists in this field ignore key elements in the beginning of the experiment data. They also then ignore observation elements simply because they ignore experiment data. What do I mean by that? The Bible is a book which discusses many things, other than its main topic. One of those items is government. It describes what I will call for our discussion here, an "experiment" made by God in the beginning, even though He knew what the outcome was going to be. Let's say for example's sake, without trying to be sacrilegious, He was being a good scientist and trying to prove without a shadow of a doubt what results take place when you ignore the laws of nature and nature's God.[1] He does so in two realms of "nature:" The physical we see and the spiritual which we can no longer see.

In the spiritual realm through the laws applied there, He speaks and creates what becomes the physical realm. Our Earth is created somewhere in the process and man is created therein. God bestows upon man a governing position on Earth. Because man is in his infancy of learning how to govern at that point, he is given occupation and then law. It is revealed in "baby" steps: "I Give To You". . . . Is basically how God starts out with blessing man. He instructs (law) what not to eat. It is a law based on blessing. But man disobeys, and in "the experiment" we observe forces put in motion from both the spiritual realm and the physical which change the result God originally intended.

The result now looks very different from "the beginning." A whole new set of laws emerge because a new avenue or offshoot of the first experiment is taking place. It is in this experiment, "the second phase," if you will, that all secular scientists start from. Therefore, in some cases, but not all cases, the observations will be different and the results will also be tainted. You might ask, "Why not in all cases?" Well, it depends on which aspect of the "experiment" you are looking at. If you want to start with what medicine works for what ailment, it is quite possible to start with a human body ravished by the planet's new environment and perform experiments there giving you medicines based on some form of herb or other material endemic to our planet to provide the alleviation of symptoms or the eradication of some type of disease-causing element. If you want to know why man suffers disease at all or why he dies, and if you only start with the second phase and never review the first, or even realize there are remnants which can be found to help you view the first phase of the "experiment," I dare say you will not arrive at conclusions to help you ameliorate death; not in the spiritual realm, and certainly not in the physical realm.

When we talk about socialism and the science of economics which obliterates its tenets, this has some application, but does not change the outcome of the result. Like the example I used concerning medicine to heal a sick body, going back to the first phase of our "human experiment" will not horribly change the outcome or resultant science needed to fix the problem. It is when we look at socialism's pseudo-psychological science we need to go back to the beginning to decimate its tenets. Like in the second example I reviewed concerning why the human body dies or suffers disease at all, this review of the experiment does need to go back to the first phase of our "human experiment" to understand why outcomes or results will be different.

What do I mean by that? Socialism purports to work on a psychological plane which produces social "superiority." It also claims the same on an economic plane or sphere. Within the psychological sphere, one must go back to the first phase of our "human experiment" to understand the science why socialism cannot even work in that realm. It is in the economic sphere that is not entirely necessary. For our purposes of covenant, I also do not need to go into the economic scientist's whole documentation, proofs and various results arrived at for our discussion here. In fact, I will only be looking at the most basic and rudimentary arguments of the science for this proof of broken covenant. You can look at the endnotes to read excellent sources of science to get a more complete picture of why socialism is literally bankrupted economically.

Economic scientists from the turn of the century bulldozed much of Marx's economic theories. One in particular was an atheist. Ludwig von Mises starts his thesis with economics from ownership. He negates and tries to refute any and all need for ownership to have originated from a divine hand to be effective in the science needed to prove Marx's theories as defunct. My point is ownership is still ownership, regardless of who you say owns something. Because he starts from the second phase of our "human experiment" he makes the observation that ownership always comes from either occupation and/or violence.[2] Because he starts from the second phase, he would not be incorrect, just not reveal a totality and a whole. That totality and whole is not needed to arrive at a truthful result in the end because both the Bible and Von Mises agree on the same "middle." Let me explain. The Bible is a book retelling the course of history in several dimensions. One of these elements or dimensions is economics. God as Creator, Sovereign, Owner, *gives*. What He gives is then stolen through deceit, ignorance and disobedience. Had Adam trusted the Lord, and then *obeyed*, the deceit and ignorance would have been marginalized and the planet not taken from him.

The Bible then goes on to describe what *became* of what God created and the generations of the people He gave different portions of the earth to.[3] That description leads us to review ownership through occupation or possession, violent taking or various other appropriation of the land God had given. It describes one specific man (Abraham) God covenants (law) with, to occupy (own) a portion of land for one nation of people. These people are mentioned as specifically gifted with a covenant by God (as original owner) to bless the earth in order to "buy back" the earth (economics)— and mankind himself— from the thief who stole the planet. It wasn't just a title deed to a planet which was stolen. He "stole" or otherwise attempted to circumvent the spiritual essence of the governing power of mankind. The book records many stories and aspects concerning this over-riding theme. Until finally, in the end we have the last chapter (Revelation) which lets us know a battle ensues with a system that will not let anyone buy or sell (economics) unless they take the mark (or governing and descriptive seal) of this original thief.[4]

I am paraphrasing here in grand leaps and bounds, and ignoring most of the other aspects of the book. I don't do this just for brevity's sake, but to remain as non-sectarian as possible. Twelve times in Genesis we read the phrase "This is the account of. . ." or "These are the generations of. . ."

and family groups are listed with land locations where they lived. Twelve tribes make up the nation of Israel. We later see planted trees producing fruit twelve times a year (see the Greek in Revelation 22:2) that have a healing balm specifically designed to heal the nations. Jesus endows twelve disciples as representatives of the spiritual healing Jesus' sacrifice purchased for the earth, the individual and the nations.[5] The Bible has been called a book of redemption and that is not incorrect. But it is the economics of how that redemption is made which is its telling feature. It describes how God purchased the planet back from a thief, even though He gave it to a being (man) who was given free will and governance rights to lose it. In other words, in a real sense the thief has legal ownership rights because they were taken from a legal owner. The book describes the law, in both the physical and spiritual environments in which this redemption takes place and the final dispensation of the planet by its original and rightful owner.

It does this in a way and a form which takes a no-holds barred approach by letting us know 'God tells the end from the beginning' (Isaiah 46:10). This is the science of God. He does this over and over again all throughout all spheres of nature: physical, spiritual, cosmic, microcosmic, et cetera. I could go on, but that is not the purpose of this text. Almost all economists start with the second phase, making the correct observations of ownership, appropriation through either violence or in some other way, and then keep the observation fluent through economics (and law), which the Bible does as well. On the physical side of the law of nature, our results, will, more or less, agree. I say that because the Bible's original economics is based totally on mutual blessing; but the second phase of the "human experiment" changed how we view God's total desire for economics. The moment Adam fell, mankind would be changed on many levels, but how he operated in economics would change dramatically.

Secondly, many atheistic economists never see a covenant, but a social contract. Quite often they deny its basis in natural law. This may be a point of agreement. It is easy to see God's law given to one man as a covenant, but a social contract is never given to that one man. There are those that use the two terms interchangeably. The older economists lived in a timeframe in which European governments and history were not the type of covenants we see on our side of the world. From our point of view today, the two terms are different (as they were for our founding generation). A contract is not a covenant and it is not a covenant from the biblical sense. I have already gone to great lengths explaining the two. The discussion also has no bearing on our subject matter here in order to arrive at a knowledge of socialism. Another difference with many secular economists will be their total rejection for any divine revelation or inspiration within their thesis of law. Although the most honest of them will admit that law can't birth itself.[6] It is not my purpose here to discuss true biblical economies and how they can override the laws put in place when sin or the second phase of the "experiment" entered the world.

I do need to discuss another misconception made concerning biblical economies, especially as seen after sin entered into our "human experiment." Many have the mistaken belief somehow capitalism and the biblical economy are at odds with one another. Nothing could be farther from the truth. God's economy, pre-fall of man is totally different from what we see reflected after Adam broke covenant. God's law is totally different within those same parameters. Quite often when we speak of biblical law, every mind goes to the Mosaic covenant. I now refer to law and economics before Moses and before the fall. The Bible did not invent capitalism any more than the Puritans invented covenant. The Bible describes societies with various money systems as well as various covenants. We have already reviewed the seven or eight covenants seen as biblical covenants. The Puritans just stepped into both economics and law and brought their understanding of covenant as well as economics with them. What we define as capitalism developed over centuries and is reflected in its development by many different societies. Quite often capitalism gets a bad reputation as a greedy, steal-from-your-neighbor system. Capitalism is defined as an economic as well as political system in which a country's trade and industry are owned by private owners for profit as opposed to the state. The Bible describes God's original system as one of mutual blessings or mutual beneficence. It is not limited to money at all— in fact it can include money but it does not start with money— though it does start with ownership or occupation. I will explain this later.

While in the timeline of this second phase of the "experiment," Jesus talks about a system which can include money, but his discussion involves so much more (Matthew 25). One of the attitudes in that system is seen when he uses a parable concerning a man going on a journey and giving money to his servants (Matthew 25:14-29). He gives five talents to one, two talents to another and one talent to a third. When he comes back the first put the money to work and gained five totaling ten, the second gained two, doubling the funds to four. But the last one who received one talent made this statement: "Sir, I knew you were a hard man, harvesting where you did not sow, and gathering where you did not scatter seed, so I was afraid, and I went and hid your talent in the ground. See, you have what is yours" (Matthew 25:24, 25; NET Bible®).

This last individual is chastised for much more than this, but his unbelief and lack of work ethic get him in hot water. Some have used this, as well as other passages to define socialism. We will look at this later, but for now, this shows the opposite. The "master" who gives the talents is seen as God, going away and not coming back for a while. It is not the "state." This passage, in fact this whole chapter is talking about much more than money. But that economics is seen is undeniable. God's original economics is seen as reproducing more and doubling your yield as a common occurrence. In fact, the "master" in chastising the servant says: "Then you should have deposited my money with the bankers, and on my return I would have received my money back with interest" (Matthew 25:27; NET Bible®)! This is not a system which ignores profit and private ownership.

In point of fact, it is the idea that when people in a nation covenant with God, He blesses that nation with much. One of those areas is money. The nation is blessed so much, especially in its economy, that others passing through are supposed to want to know about the God who has blessed, so they can covenant with Him as well. Unfortunately, because of being in our second phase of the "human experiment," the others passing through desire to steal the land for themselves. This would be the point where our secular conservative economists and the Bible concur. This is what is being done now in our very own country. It can be seen scientifically in Israel. When the majority of land owners in Israel were not Israeli, the land was not seen to "blossom as a rose" (Isaiah 35:1). When Israel returned in large numbers during the 1940s and was given her rightful ownership, thereby increasing the number of Jews on her land, the previously referenced Scripture verse came to pass. Today Israeli farmers feed other nations.[7] So instead of desiring to covenant with the God who blesses, people groups passing through the land want to take what they have not worked for. This is stealing or a system based on violence. This is what our system looks like now without the Holy Spirit's indwelling.

There is also another point of fact which needs review. When people talk about capitalism, they make reference of one word, that in their minds can describe many different things: system, economics, attitude, money, et cetera. Yet money is an underlying thought. From the second side of the "human experiment" needing profit within the system of capitalism would be an overriding theme. This does not produce the best character traits in people. Many argue it produces greed. All systems on our side of the fall of man easily produce greed, including those with a form of righteousness, or religion. Capitalism is no exception. Socialism/progressivism produces systemic greed. If I haven't already proved this result by the examples I have used, in a future chapter, I will prove how socialism aligns with the voice of the deceiver.

Like money, capitalism has, as well, a foundational example in a Scriptural analogy. The Bible says the *love* of money is the root of all evil (1 Timothy 6:10). As mentioned, it is not money which is inherently sinful. So it is with capitalism. It can very easily be said of it that the love of capitalism can produce an unhealthy result. Remove sinful humans from the equation and all capitalism is, is a tool; nothing more. This cannot be said of the system of progressivism/socialism. I will prove why shortly. Of course, the argument is easily made within our second phase of the "human experiment" that you cannot divorce humans from capitalism. Therefore, you will always experience the greedy nature of mankind reflected within it. That is totally true.

Whatever system you employ, if humans function within it, you will always see sinful human nature. The only exception is when blood-bought, Spirit-filled humans make a decision to override whatever system they are in and function according to God's original design. This is not easy and it can become close to impossible to break out of a social-istic system, simply because of its inherent features of unnatural behavior and results. It is much easier for people who decide to connect to God's spiritual laws, to function within capitalistic venture systems simply because these reflect natural laws more thoroughly. Within capitalism all can access the free market with whatever talents or gifts are available to them. So the Bible is not capitalism, but it works easily within capitalistic structures because it works with, or "covenants" within natural systems quite closely. It is mankind who must choose how to behave as capitalists. It is mankind who can define covenants and choose whether or not to accept the one described within the pages of the New Testament.

Theologians are probably not going to be happy with my analysis and many church leaders are going to start screaming that I have jumped over so much and ignored so much. My purpose here is not in exploring theol-ogy and capitalism, per se. My purpose here is not in exploring eschatol-ogy. (The study of the church and/or mankind, especially as these relate to "end times.") I have known and/or been friends with atheists in the past who thoroughly acknowledge the historical founding of this nation when it comes to the reference of a majority Christian tradition. Some have even agreed with the history of Christianity within the common law. They also agree a covenant of sorts (in our country) was enacted. They usually called it a contract, which in times past, I would not neces-sarily totally disagree with them, but as I have explained, our nation was founded on much more than a contract. That would be where we would come to an end of our areas of agreement.

My atheist friends made the observation from "our experiment" that to be truly free, there should be no stick at the end of the lure. In other words, to do what God says is beneficial to our lives, and observe the fact that He IS, there should be no consequence to get us there. In other words, (as this group of folks told it) you can't really enjoy your freedom if you think there is a hell at the end of it all. In times past people have used "freedom" to define drinking, carousing and other practices. I'm not saying all atheists or agnostics feel that way. Very few of the ones I knew did. But I always felt that kind of thinking odd and told them so. The analogy of the parent and child would suit my example. People who want to raise their children in total freedom and define that by NO rules come upon an inconvenient rule of thumb themselves. Every child says NO. The next untidy reality is the world into which a child is born. Sooner or later, in most families, one is going to have to cook a meal. Whatever your parenting methods, at some point you will have to teach the child the stove is hot and they must stay away from it until they have the skills to manage its dangers and benefits. Some parents just tell a child. Some parents try to teach them how to cook, and other parents try to make sure their world is so sterile this issue never arises. It is the environment or the laws of nature already ingrained into the fabric of the world into which we are born which give the dynamics for the lesson.

If the parent in our analogy was somehow legally removed from the environment by let's say a tyrannical government, but left the child with its environment as well as a book to explain how to overthrow the tyranny, one would say that parent did an excellent job ahead of time to fix a bad situation. But let's say the child, while growing up refused to read the book, or somehow tinkered with its message in a way to delay or even deny how to overthrow the tyranny; then whose fault is that? Some would say the tyranny and that would not be wrong. But if this child, now turned adult had a real source of true freedom inherent in its very existence— or could tap into a hidden environment through the book to eradicate the tyranny— but refused to use the sourced help, wouldn't the child, now turned adult assume some fault as well? Without the choice or knowledge of the real consequences, one can argue that the freedom is not genuine freedom. Much like a parent who attempts to create a sterile environment where the child never has to make a decision, good or bad. That kind of environment is not true freedom.

In the next chapter I will talk about the spiritual environment and why God made declarations for Adam to follow. But for now, we can at least agree to the basic observations of ownership (occupation), the appropriation of ownership (mainly through violence) and the fluid line of economics in between.[8] Let's accept the basic science of most economists for the definition (within the second phase of our "human experiment") of ownership as *having or occupying*. Occupation is synonymous with ownership simply because when you occupy, you *have*. There is a difference between ownership in consumption goods and durable goods. A consumption good is used up and gone; so its ownership is in the hands of the one using it. Thus there can be only the one consuming a good that is used up who is the owner. If you eat an apple, you are the owner. Even if you give your apple away, or let it rot, or cut it up to share with others, in each case it is disposed of, the ownership is not divided, nor can it be. In the case of a consumption good used by a number of people, it can still only be used by the person who consumes it at that time— or in their possession, regardless of legal constructs. So even in this case the ownership is in the *having*, but it is still in a moment in private ownership. Scientifically it can be nothing else, no matter what anyone calls it. Ownership/occupation are in the *Having*.[9]

For us to go further in economics one would have to separate and define production goods and other aspects of economics like land ownership (and renting), the differences in ownership, not only between durable goods, goods that are used up and production goods of both varieties, as well as ownership in sociological and legal concepts.[10] It is not my purpose to review an economics class, since I am certainly not qualified to do so. Besides which, I have probably offended economists already with my broad and simplistic descriptions, right behind the theologian and church leader. Suffice it to say within production goods the ownership is already in common by the nature of production, with the understanding of whether it is a durable good or a good to be used up.

For example, if I am a producer of TVs, or a farmer with a large production company growing and selling avocados nationwide, I might have a legal piece of paper telling me my company is in the shares of a corporation, but the reality of the *having* is that it is multi-faceted. On the one hand you have the one who physically *has* and you have the one who indirectly *has*. In both of these cases, the "owner" does not control the production as someone who grows food for their family does. The family farmer using their home-grown consumption goods are private owners. Production good "owners" are controlled by end *"have"* consumers— both the durable product TV owner and the consumption good single avocado owner. Even those who need trucking companies, stores and electronic parts in order to produce and sell these goods have a division of labor involved in the production of them. So the natural, scientific ownership of production goods is different from the natural ownership of consumption goods. In other words, you don't need to own an electronics store to own a TV and you don't need to own a farm with avocado trees in order to own an avocado. So in a society in which production goods labor is divided, no one is an exclusive owner of the means of production. It's really the consumers who are the true owners in this environment.[11] They would be the reason why the producer enters into an economic endeavor. So they would be owners in a natural sense and the producer the administrator in a legal sense of other people's property. This is why the *"having,"* or the ownership is multi-faceted in a production-good economy and is different from the consumption-good private owner. Scientifically, ownership can only fall into these two categories.

So if I haven't made the economist angry because of my oversimplification, let me go a step further. If you, no matter what anyone can define you as, own what you consume (use) as the end user as a private owner, and you own what you purchase from others as an owner in common within a system of production, then what is socialism/progressivism really offering you? What it is doing is stealing what you already own and lying to you that you can own everything else in common but, in a very real sense, based on natural laws of science, you already do. So it is stealing into the hands of an "entity" (the state) you do not have any ownership rights in (remember ownership is in the *having*), what you already owned in common in a production setting and what you already owned privately in a consumption setting. Although if you ate an avocado, or other consumption good, no matter what state or government says about that avocado, you owned it! Socialism is violently appropriating what it never had to begin with, now making itself the legal owner of what it would never, according to natural laws of science, own anyway. It's worse than a shell game. It's a con game on the gullible leaving them penniless.

One of our economists from the previous century, Ludwig Von Mises, made a calculation that was interesting.[12] In fact, it was quite famous at the time it was introduced. It leveled an explosion inside the camp of the socialist machine. So calculations already exist which prove mathematically that socialism/progressivism cannot work. Forgive my oversimplification again, but let me try to explain it on a national level. If you have an economic system which does not utilize or value money in specific ways according to natural laws of science, financial calculation and market pricing will not be able to value capital goods and coordinate production. So progressivism lacks what is needed to perform economic calculations in the first place. This is basically a scientific calculation in algorithm format (or at least that's how I see it). Maybe this is why we are constantly being told how great the numbers are in our economy while we all are experiencing less than optimal growth in GDP. You must remember all progressives/socialists are commanded to lie in order to attain their goals of total implementation of their policies.[13]

So being "told" what to think and actually experiencing the results are going to be worlds apart, unless you are part of the progressive machine. Then you will be on the gravy train of another's property. By way of example and a sad reality, the administration of George W. Bush (an opponent of socialism) grew the government in a very socialistic way. Even though aspects of capitalism remained in tact, it easily set the stage for the next administration, which was wholeheartedly socialistic/progressive in every avenue of its function. Of course, this historical experience alone is proof capitalism and socialism cannot be "blended" as progressives try to claim. There had been an economic crisis in between, which many economists prove socialistic policies to blame (see Milton Friedman).[14] This gave cover to the Democrat (progressive), to blame the poor numbers on the crises. The reality is that it happens to be the repeated rape of our economic and civil wellbeing from socialism which makes a sick victim of all Americans.

This takes us back to Von Mises and 70 years of economists after him.[15] If you are in a system which cannot calculate the elements needed to coordinate all sorts of complex productivity systems, and you force, by central planning everyone into that system, deficits will emerge quickly in all sorts of areas. The modern-day central planners (progressives) try to blend the two systems. Unfortunately, that is like mixing oil and water. You must whip the two in chaotic fashion in order to make it look like a blend. But leave it for 20 seconds, and the breakdown will begin to manifest. A capitalistic system from the start is more like milk. It is natural, so no need to force fat and water together. Even with a finished product that you want to change, you only change the one product. While my rudimentary example is not perfect, it serves a purpose.

Capitalism works within natural laws of science. Socialism does not and cannot. Every natural system must, because of the present condition of our planet in the second phase of the "human experiment," go through a cycle of violence and/or deterioration. This was not God's desire, but it happened simply because He gave the choice and ownership to man. Yet even within this phase's cycle of decay and rebirth, a normal must emerge and a balance is maintained. Whenever this takes place in a system based more closely on natural laws, as in the case of true capitalism, normal always emerges. I will look at this with a past administration. For now, when you play with a system in a very scientifically unnatural setting, normal takes a long, long time to reveal itself. In fact, you must try to replicate this die/rebirth system. Because what you are doing is unnatural, you really cannot function normally. Eventually it deteriorates, instead of ever returning to true normal.

When the tinkering you are doing removes energy from the system, it removes energy from its healing cycle. Socialism does this in various ways. Economically it ignores what specific products to produce, then it does so inefficiently. Next it cannot know the quantities needed and the various needs of the labor involved. In our present time frame, this has some application for those on unemployment. When the real numbers would be known, the "central planners" (federal government's bureaucrats under executive direction) opened the doors for more to be placed on welfare and disability. In this way the true numbers for unemployment are never revealed and you gain your other goal in creating dependence on a central government. The proof is in the explosive numbers for those on welfare as well as other government assistance.[16]

We really need to go no further than the recent socialistic/progressive mandate for healthcare, commonly termed ObamaCare, to see how inefficient central planning can be. If you threw yourself into the system, without fully realizing the five, ten and twenty year rules and regulations for eventually denying you service and forcing you to pay it back when you became ill, you will receive a surprise in 20 years time.[17] For those who refused or "didn't quite fit" into the inefficiency of government largesse, you are paying a lot more for healthcare insurance.[18] This system took over an industry which needs to work on efficiencies. We need to look no further than Canada or Great Britain for the result, over time. They wait days, weeks, months and even years on "waiting" lists to see doctors and specialists. People die "waiting" in the process. This is because inefficiencies in social planning take time to accrue.[19] Many make the observation this is because more people are now in the system. Those people, who are basically healthy with minor ailments, would probably get herbal care or mom's chicken soup to fix what ails them. They would be better for it because chemical drugs of any kind (except the lowly aspirin) cause harm to the body over repeated use. That is the human equation for the reason of the long waiting lines.

There is another reason why socialistic healthcare systems hurt. Because the markets deny the "plant producers;" namely, the *doctors* the needed incentives through pricing of ownership rights they would normally have in a natural system, they remove themselves from the system. Now you have a shortage of doctors, as well as innovative cures and specialized new technology entering the system. It won't be too long before other shortages accrue. This backs the lines up for those waiting for the product. Now, you must give the product to what the central planners think is logical. That would be the young. This is already sown into the laws of ObamaCare (Affordable Care Act) by the IPAB Boards. These are fifteen unelected officials appointed by the progressives in charge to carry out the social policies of socialists, which work with their economic policies.[20] Because those are illogical and inefficient, you must make up for it somewhere else. Well, the old and very sick and disabled are really not needed, so we will make them wait and wait, until, eventually they die; OR the boards will deny them the funds needed to survive. We will review how their corrupt thinking in the first phase of our "human experiment" really produces results which make the economic side look easy by comparison to expose. Because ObamaCare is a "blended" progressive system, the inequalities and inefficiencies will take longer to accrue. Sort of like bleeding a patient one cut at a time, instead of straight to the throat.

I mention the inefficiency of the system and make an analogy with removing energy from that system. What I mean by that is what happens to people, as well as the system, when you remove reward incentives. If someone else is paying for your healthcare, why worry about overeating, smoking, drinking, drug abuse/overuse, or aberrant sexual behavior? All of these produce a sicker society in general. If you can never really prosper from the limited skills you have, let's say in growing corn, because someone else owns the field and you are only given a limited amount of reimbursement for your time and effort; you will never branch out into maybe grinding corn and making a product. This is because the central planners will eventually make so many regulations for your product you will not be able to produce it at a profit. Does anyone remember what George Washington Carver did with the lowly peanut? Socialism/progressivism would not have produced that man.

That brings me to technology. In each various generation what is innovative is so for that generation. There is a moment in time when a need arises. When natural value incentives or rewards are in place (capitalism), many innovative entrepreneurs rush to fill the need. We have patents for a reason. We produce technological advances in the military which have been used to keep our country safer in a very violent world. There is a reason why China and Russia must hack our companies to steal our technology secrets. Socialism is a virus, draining health and vitality to all it touches. Those countries can't produce the initial technology on their own because they can't create a healthy environment for this innovation to arise. If we lose our edge through theft and removal of innovation, we will lose our freedoms at a more alarming rate than we already are presently. All progressivism is, is communism at a slower rate. I will prove to you progressivism is socialism (if I haven't already) and that there is no difference. It is in a natural system, where you find mankind free and able to access the Creator and your own natural talents, and the rewards they produce which create and feed liberty and civil rights. Whether it is in economics or civil rights, these freedoms and healthy liberties have given us an edge to stay ahead of the "wolves" who are walking through our doors.

ENDNOTES

1   Obviously God was not toying with mankind and making an experiment when He created in the beginning. I realize Christian and Jewish leaders can take exception with my terminology. I use it by way of example because those involved in science would find it easy to understand and more importantly, it really does no particular violence to the fact that God "created in the beginning." If your persuasion is atheistic and you disagree with the premise that God created, you must still agree that the planet exists. While not everyone will be pleased with my "experiment" metaphor, it helps to easily convey what it is I am trying to explain.

2   Ludwig Von Mises, "Socialism: An Economic and Sociological Analysis," translated by J. Kahane, foreword by F.A. Hayek; (Indianapolis: Liberty Fund, 1981) March 13, 2016 <http://oll.libertyfund.org/titles/1060> see 25. You can purchase a copy of this book at this <https://mises.org/library/socialism-economic-and-sociological-analysis>

3   When the Bible uses the term "This is what became of...." or the KJV translates as "These are the generations of...." it then describes all the various people and descendants which occupy the earth. While it is covenantal in its origin to mankind in general, it may not be ceremonial as we see with Adam, Noah, Abraham and Jacob, or even specifically mentioned as promissory as we see in cases like Ishmael or Esau. We then see a specific covenant made to the descendants of Israel with the formalization of the Mosaic Covenant in the other four books of Torah.

4   To be clear I am not discussing creation theory here nor eschatology, or any exegesis of the book of Revelation, literally titled "The Revelation of Jesus Christ." I am speaking in the most basics of linguistics here to discuss the true motives and captivity of systems aligning themselves in tyranny.

5   I don't mean to imply individuals or the nations will be redeemed without specifically asking Christ for His atonement in their lives.

6   Ludwig Von Mises, "Socialism: An Economic and Sociological Analysis," translated by J. Kahane, foreword by F.A. Hayek; (Indianapolis: Liberty Fund, 1981) March 13, 2016 <http://oll.libertyfund.org/titles/1060> see 28.

7   For a look at some of the economic structure and the more immediate reference to agriculture, see the © documentary, "Made In Israel" at this © site <http://www.cbn.com/special/made-in-israel>

8   I have placed this source here for those of you who have not studied this topic from your favorite economic site or source. Also see Note 15 below for other economists. Ludwig Von Mises, "Socialism: An Economic and Sociological Analysis," translated by J. Kahane, foreword by F.A. Hayek; (Indianapolis: Liberty Fund, 1981) March 13, 2016 <http://oll.libertyfund.org/titles/1060> see 20-24.

9   Ibid., Chapter 1

10   Ibid.

11   Ibid., "Socialism: An Economic and Sociological Analysis" 25

12   Ibid., 119

13   <http://www.foxnews.com/us/2015/01/06/econ-book-acclaimed-by-left-based-on-faulty-premise-factual-errors-study-finds?intcmp=trending> accessed 4/4/16

14   MIlton Friedman was probably the most famous of economists to prove socialism must create ups and downs, but he was not the only one. I place a quick clip here in which Friedman had one of his famous question and answer sessions after one of his lectures. This quick clip answers in a very short time frame the problem with mixing a system based on free enterprise with a system in which government controls. <https://www.youtube.com/watch?v=rQLBitV69Cc&feature=related> If this moves, look for "Free To Choose Network" "Milton Friedman Crushes Man's 3 Questions Like Dixie Cups."

15   Wilhelm Roepke, F.A. Hayek, Murray N. Rothbard, Ronald Harry Coase, Milton Friedman; There are so many that I could not possibly list them all. There are many sites out there for you <http://www.policyofliberty.net/famous.php><https://mises.org><http://www.theimaginativeconservative.org> sites accessed 4/4/16

16   <http://usatoday30.usatoday.com/news/opinion/editorials/story/2012-02-02/disability-Social-Security-recession/52940278/1><http://www.heritage.org/Research/Reports/2010/06/Federal-Spending-by-the-Numbers-2010><http://economyincrisis.org/content/percentage-of-americans-now-on-welfare-paints-a-disturbing-picture-of-the-state-of-our-economy><http://www.heritage.org/research/reports/2014/12/federal-spending-by-the-numbers-2014> accessed 4/4/16

17   <http://www.washingtontimes.com/news/2015/apr/27/66-pct-obamacare-customers-paid-back-subsidies-irs/?page=all><http://hotair.com/archives/2013/12/16/fine-print-state-can-seize-your-assets-to-pay-for-care-after-youre-forced-into-medicaid-by-obamacare/> accessed 4/4/16

18   <http://www.factcheck.org/2014.04/skyrocketing-premiums><https://www.washing-tonpost.com/news/wonk/wp/2014/09/10/yes-you-are-paying-a-lot-more-for-your-employer-health-plan-than-you-used-to/> The first site looks at ObamaCare recipients but says there is no way to know what the effect is on the individual market. I can tell them. I have not used my healthcare insurance and my premium has gone up 10% per year since ACA was enacted. In their eyes that is subjective, but there are enough people like me to make it a pattern. See the possible reasons why <http://www.dailycaller.com/2015/11/01/obamacare-premiums-to-soar-3-times-faster-than-feds-claim/> accessed 4/4/16

19   <http://www.city-journal.org/html/17_3_canadian_healthcare.html><https://secure.cihi.ca/free_products/HCIC2012-FullReport-ENweb.pdf> see page 2; here is an email from 2007, it has only gotten worse <http://www.snopes.com/politics/medical/canada.asp> accessed 4/4/16

20   <https://en.wikipedia.org/wiki/Independent_Payment_Advisory_Board><http://spectator.org/articles/37727/ipab-acronym-death-panel> accessed 4/4/16

Chapter Six

DETROIT IS THE OLD EXPERIMENT

It is the amount of time it takes to fully implement progressivism/social-ism that is proportional to the amount of time you see that poverty emerge in large numbers. In Russia and China they saw the poverty in a much quicker fashion because they implemented the system more quickly. The winners— and there are winners in their systems— are far fewer in number than the masses who live in systemized poverty. In the late 1980s and through the 1990s both systems relaxed restrictions and attempted to implement more capitalistic nuances into their business structures. They became progressives! This created more of the "haves" but they are still systems with oppressive economic lifestyles. Here in America, because our system contained the energy of federated repub-licanism with a capitalistic economic environment, it has been slower in revealing itself. But the statistics are still there.[1]

The administration in charge from 2009 to January of 2017 implemented unprecedented "progressive" changes to the capitalistic system. It has taken time, but we are beginning to see larger segments of the popula-tion crumble. Many don't realize the changes started aggressively in 2006 with an election which swelled the ranks of the political elite with progressives. I don't make this statement lightly, but there is no longer a Democrat Party. It is now a socialist/progressive party with communism as its endgame. The changes those 2006 progressives made were not removed by the next Democrat Party administration, only encouraged. In fact, they doubled down on them. We will review history shortly to look at exactly when progressivism started to become entrenched in aspects of our American system. This is what makes a system sick. We don't have to go to France or Spain or Greece to see how it happened or what it looks like. We don't have to travel to Russia or China to view its end result. Detroit, the "Motor City" is our best example here.

Centralized city planning came with that old pirate-turned president, Lyndon Johnson. He instituted the "Models Cities Program."[2] The last of the conservative mayors served Detroit in 1961 when he lost his position to a Democrat by the name of Jerome Cavanagh. That would be the last time a republican government served Detroit. Tellingly, Cavanagh would come to serve ten years in prison for tax evasion. But I'm getting ahead of myself. Cavanagh used the racial issue for political benefit, marching with Martin Luther King and pandering to black minority voters, at that time. He did not do this for altruistic reasons. He was the only elected official who was on Johnson's task force for the program. In Detroit, it attempted to turn a nine-mile section of the city, with 134,000 occupants into a "model city."[3] This program soon became the impetus to tell people where to live, what to build and what businesses to open or close. In return the poor received cash, training, education and healthcare. As a whole, the best the program did for the city was give them higher taxes. Since the Democrats had increased their voting ranks with poor, predominantly black voters, who weren't paying the high tax rates anyway, the Democrats kept winning. Needing cash, because these systems cannot support their needy, Cavanagh pushed through a new income tax from the state legislature and a new commuter tax on city workers. The hemorrhage of predominantly white voters came quickly. By 1966, over 22,000 middle and upper class folks moved out of the city.[4]

In July of 1967, a late-night party in the middle of the "Model City" complex needed to be broken up by police (coupled with other arrest activities— history reports are less than clear about that). It started the worst race riot of the 1960s. Over forty people were killed and roughly 5,000 became homeless.[5] Who was hurt the most? Black businesses.

Among the first stores to be looted was a black-owned pharmacy. The largest black-owned clothing store in the city was burned down.[6] As we see today with allowing protests, riots and illegal occupation movements, Democrats do very little to stop lawlessness; in fact, almost escalating the problem. Remember progressives (socialists) need chaos to implement their ideology. Cavanagh did very little to stop the riots, fearing a large police presence would make matters worse. Within five days, Lyndon Johnson sent in two divisions of paratroopers to stop the lawlessness. Within eighteen months another 140,000 residents fled the city, most of them white.[7] You would think after the observant result of a failed experiment, socialism would be jettisoned from Detroit. Seeing its failure, the voters kept voting in Democrats. Loving the votes as well as the now captive proletariat, these politicians just kept doubling down on the dependency.

In 1974, they expanded the program by using a Community Development Block Grant. As before, the politicians would decide who exactly would receive the state funds (even individually). As time went on, they reached out to captains of industries to "include" them by giving them big concessions. By the 1990s, the Big Three automakers "gave" $488 million to Detroit to use in the schemes.[8] Did more money work? No; by the 1990s nearly all of the upper middle class left Detroit. The poor have also done their best to leave. The "model city" area lost 63% of its population and 45% of the housing units from the inception of the program to the 1990s.[9] In July of 2013 Detroit, as a city, declared bankruptcy.

The question is, have they recognized their mistakes? Not socialists; as we shall see from our next chapter, under their ideology it is impossible for them to acknowledge errors. To do so would mean they were not "thinking correctly." They have poured more money into the city. In the heyday of the American dream, Detroit started with close to 2 million residents. Now the population is below 700,000 residents, yet the city still employs a staff with one of the highest resident to city-worker ratios in the nation.[10] The problem is in the firing. The unions (those bastions of socialism's worker endeavors) control much of the city's policies.[11] In 1960, Detroit had one of the highest per-capita income rates in the nation. By 2013, the median household income in the city was less than half that of the rest of the nation and the poverty rate is triple the national average. Half of Detroit's population is illiterate and 57 percent of its children live in poverty.[12]

This is what the progressives have brought to Detroit. They were able to implement socialism at a much faster rate than the rest of the nation would tolerate at that time. In less than fifty years they are bankrupt. This is what is awaiting America. It is estimated our real national debt, since a progressive has been elected is at $65 trillion. The *official* number is over $19 trillion at the time of this writing.[13] But remember under progressivism the press is either targeted by them, or in bed with them. So there is little incentive to report the accurate news of a nation. It's only those brave souls who dare. Like unemployment, the numbers are fudged to deny any criticism. What this nation was built on was the covenant model of a healthy press who told the truth. It was another thing: It reported the truth fairly. Now the only truth you hear is what the socialists want you to know.

They don't want you to know about the health of a religious society. They don't want you to know about the health that intact families bring to a nation. They don't want you to know about economic, political and technological science; the true science the Bible confirms and agrees with. They don't want you to know that constantly stealing the funds of the hardworking and giving a free lunch to those that won't work, make the human psyche sick, thus weakening a nation. If you knew the truth, you would vote the progressives out. If you knew the truth, you would understand why our young republic, under a covenant agreement was the jewel of the world. To understand the underlying philosophical and psychological reasons why socialism does not work, we need to look at a different realm entirely.

ENDNOTES

1   Two helpful sites are <http://www.statista.com/statistics/188165/anual-gdp-growth-of-the-united-states-since-1990/> And the intellectual property for this data is owned by Decision Analyst and may be viewed in pdf format <https://www.decisionanalyst.

com/Downloads/DecisionAnalystEconomicTrends.pdf> © 2011 Decision Analyst, Inc., accessed 4/5/16

2 <http://www.encyclopedia.chicagohistory.org/pages/832.html> accessed 4/4/16

3 <http://dailyreckoning.com/detroits-socialist-nightmare-is-americas-future> accessed 4/4/16

4 Ibid.

5 <https://en.wikipedia.org/wiki/1967_Detroit_riot> accessed 4/4/16

6 <http://www.frontpagemag.com/fpm/197658/detroits-present-americas-future-arnold-ahlert><http://dailyreckoning.com/detroits-socialist-nightmare-is-americas-future><http://www.foxnews.com/opinion/2013/07/24/detroit-mess-why-future-stalled-in-motor-city.html> accessed 4/4/16

7 Ibid.

8 Ibid.

9 <http://dailyreckoning.com/detroits-socialist-nightmare-is-americas-future> accessed 4/4/16

10 <http://news.nationalpost.com/full-comment/pradheep-j-shanker-why-detroit-collapsed> accessed 4/4/16

11 Ibid.

12 <http://spectator.org/articles/55101/killing-city> Article by Ralph R. Reiland, associate professor of economics at Robert Morris University in Pittsburgh; accessed 4/4/16

13 <http://www.usdebtclock.org/><http://www.thenewamerican.com/usnews/constitution/item/21922-former-us-comptroller-national-debt-is-65-trillion-not-18-trillion><http://thehill.com/blogs/blog-briefing-room/news/259476-ex-gao-head-us-debt-is-three-times-more-than-you-think> accessed 4/4/16

Chapter Seven

THE BIBLICAL EQUATION AND REASON FROM THE NATURAL MIND

When discussing the foundational arguments of socialism and capitalism, it is the religious aspects of the arguments most people, including many Catholics and mainline Protestants miss. The purpose of this book is not to debate capitalism versus socialism. I have already noted excellent resources with the expertise to debate the science as well as benefits of capitalism versus socialism, for the atheist as well as the faithful. My purpose here is to prove covenant. That our American covenant, reflecting some foundations of biblical covenant, are superior to all other forms of government currently practiced. The purpose of this section proves our Federal government has broken covenant. Socialism is at the heart of that betrayal. We reviewed a tiny portion of the science economists use to obliterate socialism's economic claims.

To explain many truths by way of examples, Jesus tells parables. In one He tells of a nobleman who leaves on a journey. He leaves instructions for his servants. One of them is, "Occupy till I come." (Luke 19:13) The Greek word means to carry on a business or be a banker or someone involved in trade; in other words, economics. I have already shared how I feel economics was just as important as the religious (bill of rights) issue in ratification. Economics was a major reason why the Revolution took place. Both liberty and freedom (the religious issue is within the liberty and freedom side) and the economics were, in my opinion two sides of one coin. Or, as relevant as our souls are to our bodies. The religious quite often ignore the economics and the atheist often ignores the religious aspects. Neither can, nor should be ignored.

Decades ago you could find economists from both liberal and conservative beliefs. Liberalism has a long European history, but it found an easy home in America. The Democrats were formerly liberals. The reason why they worked well with the Republicans is because liberalism argued for government to be as small as possible and allow the exercise of individual freedom. Its economics was conservative. Both parties were formerly two sides to a coin. Because they had many similarities, they worked on behalf of the country. Once socialism swallowed up the Democrats, that unity (on the secular side) ended. There are no true liberal Democrats any longer in our government. They can argue all day long and call themselves what they would like, but unless they decide to vote that way, they are gone. Unless the minority religious Democrats are able to extrapolate themselves from the trap of progressivism and unite with the Republicans, our government is lost.

The Bible espouses economics, which can relate to capitalism in many respects. It encourages freedom of choice. Many Republicans and Democrats were religious and related to free markets, freedom of choice and conservative values. Even those who were atheists or agnostics agreed with free markets and freedom of choice. This unity and agreement ended as soon as socialism began to overtake the Democrats and capitalism was "mingled" with socialism, basically throwing capitalism under the bus. God has come very close to receiving the same treatment.[1] It is my opinion the reason why capitalism and biblical environments work easily together is because both can work within natural scientific laws. As we have seen, it is impossible for socialism or progressivism to do that. Once you tinker, you must keep interfering with nature. The "Genie" cannot be put back in the bottle.

It can be easily argued capitalism produces greed. The reality is progressivism produces organized systemic greed on a level never seen by capitalists. Quite often capitalists are religious people, or people who understand the need to give back. Sometimes it's just good business to do so. Because it works more closely with the laws of nature, that nature can produce greed (or violence). Humans can make choices in overriding those actions, when necessary. Even within the natural cycle of despots, nature can handle those actions violently. The obituary of every dictator usually has death at the hands of those who opposed him. Very few die of old age. In fact, the church is supposed to be at the forefront acknowledging as well as exposing the problem by applying real life biblical applications for solutions. The religious were negligent in that, getting on the gravy train of the greed. Instead of making choices overriding the natural flow of events, they just succumbed. It is not fair to say all the religious did that. But when the numbers of those speaking out dwindle, and when they are not allowed equal access to mainstream media; in fact, becoming repeatedly marginalized by that media, their effects are minimal. I am not trying to blame the victims here, either the religious or otherwise.

Socialism (progressivism) tries to tell you it is more in harmony with the Bible. It is more benevolent somehow for you to give up what is yours. They can sing love songs all day, but the reality is they still take your money. I have shown you scientifically how that is a lie. You already own what you use and you are already an owner in common within a production setting. You own nothing within the artificial entity called "the state." Many believe giving to their church is the same as giving to the state. That is also a lie. An institution closest to the people knows the people and knows exactly what they need. That institution must work within natural laws of thrift and incentive to meet needs or else it will not survive. The state is an artificial entity, taking by deceit what is rightfully yours. It never needs to work within laws of nature because it has an endless supply of people it owns, taking from them to sustain itself. We will look at this reality shortly. Atheists also believe a lie. That lie is once you believe in God you have no choice. That somehow believers have their freedom of will and choice removed from them and they become slaves to do whatever God says. Well, it's obvious that is not how things work. If that were the case, then the world would be filled with these loving and giving people that do everything right. We are never sick, and when we are, miracles happen constantly, and we are all living in Shangri-La. Total nonsense; obviously our choice and free will remains. The very fact we do "wrong" things and even believe lies proves the fallacy of utopia.

The Bible is clear that the lie is from the devil. He is called the deceiver and all evil emanates from him. Socialism uses the voice of the deceiver exclusively to get you to give up what is yours, all in an effort to control and marginalize what and who you are. It is a shell game, playing with a sleight of the hand and removing the little item you are looking for so it is never under any cup. Just because you think it's under one cup, doesn't make it so. Capitalism allows all voices, including the deceiver access. The choice is yours as to whether you give up ownership, act greedily or work for a profit and give back (if that is your choice). The Bible encourages the giving and it encourages something else: ownership. We will look at these issues more closely later. But for now, ownership carries responsibilities. Those responsibilities and/or incentives are what make economics work with the natural environment. The Bible reinforces that point in a number of real world ways. The book explains why there should be a "for the moment" help made to the poor, elderly, disabled or orphaned. The book explains how that is to be done and why that is to be done, and when it must not be done. We will look at other aspects of its ability to minimize "the greed" factor of a capitalistic environment. What it cannot do is work with progressivism/socialism.

In point of fact, socialism is totally incapable of following any biblical equations, especially those relating to money. Remember socialism has another side to its own coin. One side is economic the other is "social" or philosophical. The ideas of socialism started long ago and attempted to form in the womb of Enlightenment, but having a surrogate birth, it jumped hosts and grew up in another generation. For those with in-depth biblical knowledge, this should awaken you to the reality this is a spiritual battle, and the paternity is not from the hand of God. So let's look at the arguments from the "natural" mind.

Reason and logic were seen as scientific observations and experiments from the Reformation, flowing into many branches of Enlightenment thought. Removed from their biblical moorings, they floated like coconut seed on the shores of unregenerate man's mind. Once planted, the seed's DNA struggled, eventually implanting in progressively eviscerating environments. This produced two fundamental ideas based on the evolution of the human mind. One said because man needed to function on a day-to-day basis, he needed to create constructs in his mind to connect the dots. These constructs are, broadly speaking, reason and logic. This gives us matter and substance, cause and effect, positive and negative, experiment and observation, etc., all in an effort to pave a path through history, which helps us to understand our world. I am using broad strokes here.

Initially this is the argument as framed by the early reformers of the Reformation as reason— along with the folks from the Renaissance— and it commits no grave injustice toward the Scriptures. Though it certainly does not "hit the mark" of complete biblical thought. Out of the ashes of the historical arguments, that view became known as the materialistic view. But here is the first degradation of the seed of both logic and reason. This materialistic view holds that the world exists independently from mankind and that human consciousness is a reflection of the world we see. While true enough, it is not entirely biblical. It has an ever so slight omission, which we will discuss shortly.

The second or different branch from the tree of corrupting logic and reason says that it is mankind's thought and/or consciousness that is primary here or "creating" and that it is the *thought* that is the cause of the world we see. That view became known as the idealistic view. While there are glaring theological corruptions in this view, from a biblical standpoint, it is a view that *begins*— I say, *possibly* begins, in a very rudimentary form— to understand biblical spirituality. But this is where true biblical thinking stops on both fronts. Functioning with the glaring and corrupting omissions, it is easy to see any complete understanding of science or of the actual world or of the world of the spirit realm would never take place— almost like a matrix movie in reverse— with hideous eternal consequences!

Any minister who has taken hermeneutics courses (especially from the German school of thought) can easily see the problem. Thinking ourselves wise, we become like fools (Romans 1:18-25; 1 Corinthians

3:16-23; 1 John 1). After reading these verses, you can see why the social-ist apparatus will use any excuse to stop ministers from preaching Romans 1, which, by the way, they now do in certain countries. The Germans (among others) brought some of this into their theology classes, which were taught to minsters. Hermeneutics is one of those classes. It deals with Bible interpretation. Being filled with the Holy Spirit, and engag-ing these German hermeneutics classes, it was easy for me to see Jesus' teaching to the Pharisees of His day come alive: "But woe to you experts in the law and you Pharisees, hypocrites! You keep locking people out of the kingdom of heaven! For you neither enter nor permit those trying to enter to go in" (Matthew 23:13, 23; Luke 11:46, 52 NET Bible®). It is one thing to have a method to interpret the Scriptures (hermeneutics). It is another thing entirely if aspects of that method turn you into an automa-ton thinking yourself straight out of what the Bible clearly says. In fact, it was so universally insidious in its doctrine, in order for me to get a good grade I had to basically write their prose word for word. Our instructor, seeing the dilemma, listened patiently to our objections; but alas, we still had to recite the dogma. This was back in the 1980s. It does not surprise me that college students today who are conservative are experiencing the same kind of problems within the halls of socialist education— I mean, today's modern universities. Their battle is not concerning the existence of God, but the existence of reality!

Two key players in this exercise (before Marx entered the thought process) were Immanuel Kant (1774-1804) and Georg Whilhelm Friedrich Hegel (1770-1831). Hegel built upon Kant's logic. Though they were not the first. Actually, the Greeks were quite fluent in this thought centuries before either Kant or Hegel. We do have an early record of the Apostle Paul addressing their fallacies when it came to theology (Acts 17:16-33). While the totality of Paul's argument is not recorded, he does expose the holes in their doctrine by telling them God did not originate with their skill in imagination, craftsmanship or with mankind's thought. In other words, instead of worshipping idol gods made of wood, they worshipped idols made by the imagination of man's mind. They even made man's mind an idol.

Both Kant and Hegel meant their reasoning to be applied to all aspects of life. But it is in the theological realm I will briefly analyze, because this is where socialism's Achilles heel is most obvious, at least to me. Kant's philosophy on all things is a long and arduous path to a basic consensus of transcendental idealism. The idea everything nonphysical or spiritual originates in the mind. You can imagine theologians picking that one apart. Hegel's method starts off with his proof that *"a thing"* is not unknowable, but is an ever progressing reality passing into its opposite in order to return to a richer form of itself. Hegel's method of philosophy consisted in breaking "a thing" into three stages, which he says must always progress from "itself," *out* of "itself," and then *in* and *for* "itself."

Again, the Greeks, most notably Aristotle argued these matters all day (as we see from Paul's comments to them in Acts). For Aristotle the importance of "a thing" was itself— its *being*. For Hegel it was its *becoming*. For example, Aristotle saw a table and said "it is, what it is"— it is a table. Hegel did not deny this, but added the reality the table was a tree, which became a table, that will become ash. In this train of thought *becoming* is the highest form of the expression of reality as well as thought because it is the way we have the fullest knowledge of a thing. Hegel then divided this philosophy into three divisions: (spirit) "God" (the idea) reveals the truth that the idea must be studied (in itself: logic or metaphysics) and then it must progress out of itself and become the study of nature or the philosophy of nature and then progress in and for itself again, or become the philosophy of the study of the mind.

As you can imagine, something which attempts to conclude only the rational is real and even "God" is progressing to "becoming," can't hold up against the biblical record. Gnosticism (long before Hegel) rationalized everything into a progression of knowledge which eventually had knowledge and decay as the ultimate expression of all reality. Hegel's philosophy followed a similar path. It broke into the "right" branch and the "left" branch. The rightists developed his teaching in accordance with what they considered Christian and the leftists went down the road of atheism, developing into political societies, of which socialism is one of them. As mentioned before, both Kant and Hegel's philosophical arguments contain portions of biblical reality—Primarily because of their view within the "second phase" of our human experiment. Hegel comes the closest, but then his philosophy comes apart, especially as it travels down the road toward socialism, though that is not necessarily a scientific outcome of his teaching.

Marx grabbed hold of Hegel's as well as Kant's ideas toward his idealistic inevitabilities. In Marx's world— and the worldview of all progressives— you will always have class strata or distinctions in a society. They call it a continuing class struggle, which has to be overcome to work toward a "classless" society. In other words, it is *a thing* which must evolve and come to its end. In their minds man will always be classed, and those not of the "right" class will not think properly to see how wonderful socialism is. So they must not be listened to, they must be silenced. In order to go from a classed society, socialism must rule, then perfection will bring mankind into communism— or the greater good of a "classless" society. In their world *the thing* is class strata and it is evil and must be overcome. In order to do so, socialism creates the proper medium because we are all working toward that end anyway (in their minds).

Yet from the dialog of all Marxists, it is a smokescreen, since their reality— even their constitution— highlights various different classes which must pay into their government. After the 2008-2009 crash, a recent 2009-2017 progressive/socialist Administration gave our money to Wall Street as well as other socialist agenda programs, sending the country into an even greater spin and "recovery" cycle, only without the impetus of a true recovery. Oddly enough, the socialists argue that agenda was not socialism but capitalism. Well, anyone who has studied what capitalism is, knows that marketplace rules govern and if a business (Wall Street and bankers are businesses) acts irresponsibly, they cannot stay in business. Capitalism's tenets stress the fact they must fail and NOT get bailed out. Yet socialism stresses the government's eventual ownership of these "too big to fail" commercial and industrial businesses. So socialism decides when and how much money they receive, NOT capitalism.

This is the pattern of many of their arguments: They are not what you think— because YOU are the problem— and *your* thinking will always be the problem. It is "a thing" that will be overcome anyway, working itself out to the obvious communistic end. So we cannot do what has worked for the first 140 years of this country, because it was just an image working toward a progression of downward trend— and the outcome will be communism anyway— our *true* American selves![2] You can see why Marx said the discussion over whether to be socialist or not to be socialist, especially the discussion concerning the need to abscond with the property of others is unnecessary, because all history will bring all societies to socialized property/production because it is the necessary end of all societies! This is the normal progression of this kind of philosophy/reasoning or logic. Those espousing all aspects of Hegelian philosophy could well argue Marx is not a good representation of Hegel. In that we would have no disagreement.[3]

The inconvenient truth of Marxian philosophy is that it matters very little what portion of history you want to look at, all society was either in private ownership or, as we saw with production goods, ownership in common anyway. On the philosophical side he has another problem. He confuses "class" structure with talents and various creative abilities. In a free society these are what satisfy and these are what produce rewards and results. All humans break up into geographic and nationalistic tribes or societies—from early man to the present. It is the gifts and abilities of each member of their tribe which produce skills to keep them alive or cause them to die off. If you try to eliminate this, you kill humans. We are created to feel fulfilled by our relationship to God, our families and our talents which enable our work and benefit our families. It blesses God to see us blessed. This is the beginning of understanding biblical economies. These talents can also fulfill God's mission in that they benefit the planet and its occupants as well.

To eliminate this structure by calling it evil class structure is to deny what makes a human alive. What is socialism/progressivism's end game? It is totalitarian manipulation of human beings. It is not some altruistic endeavor to help lift the common class worker out of his doldrums. It is selfishness personified because it demands to control all of what a society has in order to accomplish goals which are a lie to begin with. Politicians which are progressive/socialist or "democrat socialists" are only interested in keeping themselves on top and fluid with your cash. Whether or not they have been duped by socialism is irrelevant. They still take your goods and services, providing little or nothing in return. Socialistic societies are not more peaceful. That is another lie. It takes hard work and innovation to protect ourselves when the wolves are at the door. Progressivism saps this energy, as I have already explained.

The other philosophical difficulty for socialists is that man is not "a thing." He is not a tree or a chair, or becoming either. Although his body can become ash, this is not his total and highest calling. In fact, he is a complex tripartite being with a spirit, a soul and a body. We will look at this dynamic from its origins next. This dynamic is always going to throw Marxist ideology into what I call its "gobbledegook" theories. If you want to know if a theory is truth, break it down to its lowest common denominator— or its axis— into the most simplistic of understanding. When you do that with progressivism, its theories look and sound like nonsense. As already mentioned, Marxism (progressivism), Hegel and Kant all pull truth from the realm of the Bible, but unfortunately either leave it dangling there, or more frequently corrupt it into something else entirely. Once that is done all you have left is falsehood.

ENDNOTES

1   I refer to the experience I had of watching the 2012 DNC convention on PBS. They were voting on their platform as a party. To vote a measure in required a verbal aye, or some audio affirmation (I can't remember which now). When they voted whether to acknowledge God in their platform, to my hearing the nays had it. The leader over that aspect of the ceremony overrode the attendees vote, at least to my hearing. So the DNC is very close to kicking God out of their party.

2   You can see all pro-Marxist writings as well as a 2009 constitution at this site <http:// www.marxistoutlook.com> Click on "Dialectical Materialism as a Practical Method. Part III: Practice- Building the Party." You can see when reading this next article, that the 2009 Fabian socialist administration in the White House did exactly as the socialist agenda demanded, but then the socialists say the cure to fix the problem it created was ... wait for it ... COMMUNISM! Click on "Proposal: A Fight for a New Democracy." accessed 4/4/16

3   There is so much research and books and websites out there concerning Kant, Hegel, Marx, progressivism, socialism and communism. If you decide more research is necessary, you can easily find it out there. I will leave you with a few works that were my favorites. You decide whether I have accurately represented the position of the aforementioned. The previous endnote of research is quite pro-Marx. Others here decimate his tenets. These various resources can have you tied up in philosophy for years! This is why I have painted broad strokes in my attempt to explain the history. Cutting to the chase with Marx's arguments is more like science to me than the "artwork" others espouse. But you can judge for yourself: Turner, William. "Philosophy of Immanuel Kant." The Catholic Encyclopedia. Vol. 8. New York: Robert Appleton Company, 1910. Accessed 4/4/16 © site <http://www.newadvent.org/cathen/08603a.htm>. Turner, William. "Hegelianism." The Catholic Encyclopedia. Vol. 7. New York: Robert Appleton Company, 1910. © site <http://www.newadvent.org/cathen/07192a.htm>. Toke, Leslie, and William Edward Campbell. "Socialism." The Catholic Encyclopedia. Vol. 14. New York: Robert Appleton Company, 1912. © site <http://www.newadvent.org/cathen/14062a.htm>. "Progressivism: A Primer on the Idea Destroying America," by James Ostrowski, © 2014, James Ostrowski, Buffalo, NY: Cazenovia Books. Biography.com Editors, "Karl Marx," The Biography.com website, A&E Television Networks, accessed 4/4/16 and can be seen at this © site <http://www.biography.com/people/karl-marx-9401219>. Ludwig von Mises, "Socialism: An Economic and Sociological Analysis," trans. J. Kahane, Foreword by F. A. Hayek (Indianapolis: Liberty Fund, 1981. Accessed at this © site <http://oll.libertyfund.org/titles/1060>. H. B. Acton, "The Illusion of the Epoch: Marxism-Leninism as a Philosophical Creed," (Indianapolis: Liberty Fund, 2003) Accessed 4/4/16 at this © site <http://oll.libertyfund.org/titles/877>

Chapter Eight

THE BIBLICAL EQUATION FROM
THE SPIRITUAL REALM

Let's start from the beginning, since it is a good place to start. I will give a heads up to those of the atheistic and agnostic persuasions that I will be talking about God. It is possible you may read things here you may never have read before. Since you have made it this far, it can't hurt to go a little further. What I relate here is not all-inclusive, or all-encompassing. It will be similar to the method I took in reviewing American history by looking at religious dynamics as opposed to secular history. These few realities from Genesis will only relate to our present subject matter, not to an exposition on the book of Genesis.

I will also give you another heads up. The biblical economy encouraged in both Testaments fosters the tithe, which is giving ten percent of your income. The promise is that you will see abundance and an ability for the ninety percent left over to do more than 100 percent could have done before. Obviously, this, like miracles is illogical to human minds. The Bible makes no excuses for this. When you say to Christians what they believe defies logic and so does their God, you are having a "duh" moment with them. We know it makes no sense. We also know, by experience, that it works. It freaks us out too. In God's economy this is by design. It is so you see the audacity of this, walk through the door and experience

Him up close and personal. Now, you don't have to do that in a society which allows the covenant people to pray and function in the totality of their inalienable rights. That is because blessing will extend to all secular covenant citizens when biblically covenant citizens actively engage their covenant. Of course, you can make personal choices within that system to hamper your own personal experience of betterment, but that is your choice. So let's get started.

"In the beginning God created the heaven and the earth" (Genesis 1:1). If you do not have an awareness of Genesis 1-3, now might be a good point to read it from your favorite Bible translation. The Bible makes it abundantly clear both heaven and earth are not some construct of the mind or from the mind of man. They are actual, real and created, much like everything else God created. Man did not create the world. In fact, man did not create his own mind either. Everything in the Bible is really best understood by its Hebrew language concepts as well as the similarly translated concepts from the Greek, as well as Aramaic languages Jesus spoke and the New Testament apostles wrote with.

In Genesis, as we see God creating, there are several concepts sometimes lost in English. One of the concepts from Genesis we see are patterns. In the Hebrew language there are consonants and vowels, but consonants can be numbers as well as giving an understanding of punctuation marks. For example, some of the words which become patterns within the concept of the creation process are: "Let There Be . . . and So There Was . . . and It was Good." These are word phrases but they are like little exclamation points as well. One pattern explicitly seen and taught within this scene of creation is the fact God creates by His word. In the New Testament we are then told the Word is a person, The Lord Jesus Christ. The Hebrew for "word" is *Davar* and it means *word* but can carry a concept of a driving force who creates something out of nothing. Certainly this is spiritual which brings reality into our understanding. In fact, it can be said, "All things were made by him; and without him was not any thing made that was made" (John 1:3). So whatever branch of a competing theory of existence one adheres to, if you do not start with the right source, you easily go off into oblivion.

Secondly, as God creates He makes what I will call a mutual exclusivity of separation. Instead of the idea of divide and conquer mankind has when separating, God does this to bless. For example, we see light separated from darkness, the waters above from the waters below, earth (land) separated from the waters. Ten times within Genesis 1 & 2, we see the Hebrew word play of "Let There Be" and "So There Was," and it appears like a ta-da-ta-da! Not only does it *APPEAR* and there is a little celebration, but we have the Hebrew "It Was Good." With sort of like an exhale, carried along as an idea of being a blessing to God.

In fact, it is so much of a pattern that with each act of creation, what is created blesses the next created thing. All of this is like a cascading waterfall, flowing from the fact that it Blessed God So Much that it flows into a celebration! You might say, what's the big deal of separating becoming a blessing? Well, I don't know what it was like for God, but as humans, I am certainly blessed to be able to sleep at night in darkness and walk on dry land instead of travel by boat all the time. I certainly like working in the daylight. This pattern of mutual exclusivity continues after the fall of mankind as well. We see it through the Mosaic covenant. In fact, God has to tell Peter in the New Testament, "What God hath cleansed, that call not thou common" (Acts 10:15). He says this because Peter wants to maintain the separation and the Lord doesn't want that.

Just like the pattern of mutual exclusivity, the pattern of mutual beneficence continues throughout the creating process and then throughout the whole of the Bible through both Testaments. We see an understanding of plants blessing the earth, and vice versa. The sea creatures would be blessed and be a blessing to the water. Animals would be blessed by the plants and earth; and the earth blessed by the animals as they ate. This follows down the line of creation, with each being celebrated as they are created. Inherent in this pattern of God creating and blessing something or calling it "good" is the fact that whatever God names, He has sovereignty over. Because of His sovereignty there is peace and blessing; or said another way, there is no conflict with what He blesses. "Let There Be" and "So There Was" is found ten times in the language and this final understanding of "It Was Good" is seen seven times in the language. This numbering of 7 x 10 is a basic understanding of spiritual completion, with the number ten having symbolic meaning in earthly government. So *being* is not just ultimate, but it has a celebration because GOD did the creating. In fact, when asked by Moses what His name is God says, I AM That I AM. YAH or Yahveh, Yahweh, what we spell in English as Jehovah. We also see the Jewish understanding in The Name, or Ha Shem.[1]

The Triune God in an eternal context of functioning within an interdependent and mutually beneficial relationship of Father, Son and Holy Spirit creates as well as depending upon what He created to give Him enjoyment. John 1:1 in Greek says, "In the beginning was the Word and the Word was with (toward) God." The Greek words, *pros ton theos* are usually translated as toward God, describing movement. Scholars have debated this language for centuries. I am not about to solve its dynamics here. Socialists have tried to use it to explain their idea of progression. Yet their idea of progression has a root cause of misunderstanding. Simply put, John is attempting to describe an environment where a whirlwind or driving force (the Word) is creating out of nothing. This Word, whom John tells us is Jesus, eternally with the Father before time, in time, creates within a mutually beneficial relationship of Father, Son and Holy Spirit. This blesses. I get the impression of a worship party in the heavens. We have to remember the prophets were trying to describe what God was showing them through the Spirit, and attempting to place it in words we can understand.

The last created being would be man. God says some very interesting things about humans and what their gifts from Him would entail. We also have a word phrase in Hebrew which says, "This is what became of. . ." The English translates this phrase as "These are the generations of. . ." The reason for this is the Hebrew comes from a verb meaning *To Beget*. So the Bible gives us little bullet marks in the story *("this is what became of")* to let us know what happened to what God created because "something" changed the creation from its original purpose. So Genesis not only describes the *"being"* argument long before the Greeks, Kant or Hegel show up, but solves its beginning and carries with it the story of what became of it to the end of the last book of the New Testament. The Bible says God tells us the end from the beginning. "Declaring the end from the beginning, and from ancient times *the things* that are not yet done, saying, 'My counsel shall stand, and I will do all my pleasure'" (Isaiah 46:10).

Before some of this is finalized in the story, Genesis discusses the creation of mankind. First of all, God breathes into man and man becomes a living soul. This is different from the other creatures He created. The first difference is seen because mankind is created in the image and likeness of God. This can best be described as eternality and something else: Mankind received a responsibility inherent in being a blessing. Remember ownership carries responsibility. He is supposed to represent God to the earth and the earth to God. It is part of the command to subdue given him in Genesis 1:28. This idea of subduing is not in destroying or subjugation, as we humans think from the "second phase" of our human experiment. The original idea from the "first phase" was in blessing and imparting life, just as was described previously about God.

It is very hard for us humans in this "second phase" of the human experiment to understand subduing, pre-fall of man. It was meant to be a blessing. We are to use and harness creation's potential and resources for our benefit and to benefit others, *including* the creation. The guideline is not just inherent in the benefit, but in understanding the greater good of the whole creation. Because our subduing (after the fall of man) only involves blessing ourselves, all natural systems will do so. Economic systems that follow a natural course will involve greed. While they easily entail violence or theft as the economists from the 1900s observed,[2] they can easily allow for the greater good when man follows and trusts what the God who created all of this tells mankind to do with that ownership/responsibility of authority in ruling the earth. It does not *have* to be full of greed.

Socialism can never do this because the greed of the state (the entity you must give everything to) becomes God and decides who must get what. In natural systems "nature" works that out. So choice, benefit, ownership are all free-flowing tools which can bless all involved, or unfortunately hurt all involved. It is natural and the system will work better that way. The "state" (or progressivism's way) can never work it out. The state picks the winners and losers. The state can never allow the humans the tools of choice because those choices will not benefit the ownership of the state's microcosm or macrocosm decisions within the system.

When you use a product outside of its originally intended purpose, you void the warranty. Well, mankind was originally made to be that "governor" or *owner*, having responsibility in decision-making on a small, private scale and on a larger scale in order to bless. The state, an unnatural entity which is a system, is not meant to govern in small decisions on a wide scale. The creation of the state was made by humans to oversee what and how we decide to bless those unable to fend for themselves. It is meant to oversee and minimize the violent aspects in our world to remain safe (warfare). Many say, "Well, that's what socialism does." No, that is not. What socialism does is remove mankind's private decision making process, interjecting itself into families, business and large scale economies. The state can never— nor should it ever— make those decisions. When it does, we violate both warranties; mankind's, because he was not created to be without authority, and the state's, because it was not created to usurp mankind's authority concerning his inalienable God-given rights. Progressives attempt to blend the systems on both sides of the economic and social aspects. As you can see from the economic side, that is impossible. On the social side that is impossible as well for many of the same reasons. I don't have the space to discuss all of them (please refer to the endnotes).

Once humans are given the power of a bureaucracy, selfishness, greed and violence (from the second aspect of our "human experiment") will ensue because this is the natural progression. No matter what anyone says, unless the Holy Spirit is the "governor" all humans will function naturally: the religious, the atheist and everyone in between. Once thrown into an unnatural system (progressivism), humans will always try to grab more from those with the purse strings or the power in order to tinker with the system because it is an unnatural system. (Remember the concept of the depravity of man?) This is why our government keeps getting bigger with progressives or socialists in charge. Because they believe the state can control and own or possess these decisions, the social problems will continue to manifest in the same manner we see the economic problems continuing to manifest.

On a private basis mankind can only control his/her own decision-making process for the same reasons private ownership carries responsibilities. In a natural setting, the responsibilities are what incentivize. When you remove them, you work outside of a natural system and must now tinker with it. The reason why you can help people temporarily or on some other defined as-needed basis when they are in trouble is because the first phase of our "human experiment" does so. It is to be a blessing. Mankind was originally given authority to bless the creation, using the resources to do so when necessary, on an as-needed basis. We will look at this in the next chapter. Socialism cannot do this. It only blesses what blesses itself. This is why the "haves" consolidate more power, decreasing their numbers and exploding the numbers of the "have-nots." Capitalism takes on all comers. It leaves the doors wide open, allowing everyone the access to make of themselves as they are able. A biblical economy does the same, while minimizing the deleterious effects of greed (sin) by allowing for "as-needed" moments for help and giving.

One other issue concerning Genesis and progressivism should be noted. Socialism is jealousy. In doing this research, I have come to believe it was conceived by Marx because of jealousy. In modern times we can see socialism is instituted in nations which are or have the potential to be prosperous. This is to take their prosperity because of jealousy and covetousness. Look at this statement from Hamilton:

> "But what merits still more serious attention is this. There seems to be, already, a jealousy of our dawning splendour. It is looked upon as portentous of approaching independence. This we have reason to believe is one of the principal incitements to the present rigorous and unconstitutional proceedings against us. And though it may have chiefly originated in the calumnies of designing men, yet it does not entirely depend upon adventitious or partial causes; but is also founded in the circumstances of our country and situation. The boundless extent of territory we possess, the wholesome temperament of our climate, the luxuriance and fertility of our soil, the variety of our products, the rapidity of our population, the industry of our country men and the

commodiousness of our ports, naturally lead to a suspicion of independence, and would always have an influence pernicious to us. Jealousy is a predominant passion of human nature, and is a source of the greatest evils. Whenever it takes place between rulers and their subjects, it proves the bane of civil society."[3]

When men covet someone else's goods they do so because of jealousy. While Hamilton's example is referring to the King of England (and Parliament), it is easy to see jealousy from one nation to another or one system for another. When nations or systems do this, they then figure out how to take what would normally not be theirs, thus stealing from another. Socialism does this by trickery and using human emotion as well as innocent ignorance or the greedy nature within those hearing progressivism's claims. In the next few paragraphs we will review the place in Genesis where we see the first time these traits and situation arise in biblical history.

Let's go back to the line of creation from Genesis. Mankind is made from the soil. Adam (Hebrew) means soil or ground. The Hebrew word used to fashion the man out of the soil is *yatsar*, which is similar to the word *yotser*, which carries the image of an artist's work. So reflecting the image of God endowed mankind to represent God's heavenly court in both spiritual and physical matters. This is extremely important to remember in our discussion. I will get back to this later. I cannot leave Eve out of this because without her mankind cannot function properly. This fact is extremely important in our understanding as well. It is diametrically opposed to the understanding those who do not know their Bibles (or the Hebrew) believe. Eve was not created as a door mat, or as a being incapable of leadership. In the Hebrew we see an idea that God creates everything in the woman the man needs and God created everything in the man the woman needs. They would each supply whatever was lacking in the other's design. This has to do with more than the physical realm. They would not be able to bless the earth or fulfill their destinies without the other. They would not be able to govern, procreate, function in blessing the planet, and so much more. These words used here to describe this relationship are not used for anyone else other than the male-female relationship in the whole of the Bible; EXCEPT in describing what God does for mankind.

This is true intimacy, from a biblical perspective. As humans, we must understand the intimacy of this dynamic. It is not necessarily based on love, although love surrounds it. It is based on government fulfilling the sovereign call of God to bless, not harm. Adam and Eve were to govern in the same symbolism of interdependent unity they saw God function in. Is the Father less than Jesus? Is Jesus less than the Holy Spirit? The answer is "no" to both questions. So for those who feel the New Testament or the fall of man means Eve is something other than perfect after salvation, I would say you don't understand the new creation God has made us to be (2 Corinthians 5:17).

There is one other gift God gives mankind. Man has the ability to speak God's word and see similar effects on the earth as God made when He created in the beginning. So Adam and Eve were to speak to a situation, naming it and have dominion in a healthy setting to bring a fullness to the earth. In order to learn how to function with this gift, their first lesson was trust, showing that trust through obedience: "Do Not Eat. . ." In the New Testament when God tells us to confess our sins, in effect, naming them, it is not to beat us up. It is to show us our dominion over them. This is why blood-bought, Spirit-filled believers are so crucial to holding covenant together. They are not some after-thought, like those who view Eve as such. They are a critical part to fulfill the destiny this nation has in blessing the nations of the world, as well as the non-believing members of our Constitutional covenant. We are to be a blessing in authority, not be door mats.

The real devil— not some make-believe evil or bad tempered serpent— the real deceiver could not allow this newly created being to have dominion over him. The devil was quite jealous concerning God's devotion to this new being. He was covetous over this being's gifts as well. Having the image of God conveyed the authority of God through the use of sovereign activity for the planet. Coveting what was not his, the devil had to trick or otherwise steal what was given to Adam and Eve. So seduction, disobedience and rebellion ensued. We all know the story. If you do not, you can read it in Genesis 3:1-19. I can hear some asking the question, "Is all this necessary to maintaining our constitutional republic?" Our covenant is non-sectarian and religious extending to those of the covenant. The religious will maintain the spiritual side of it with earthly results; but no, neither atheists, agnostics or those who do not adhere to this telling of the creation story have to believe what I am saying.

I can hear those who may believe some of socialism's tenets say, "This sounds like what Hegel was talking about." I would say, it certainly does, but as I have just explained, you can see the glaring omissions in Hegel's theories as relates to theology. My point here is to show they then follow suit to aspects of political science and economics. Following an example of biblical patterns in both produce different results than Hegel envisioned. As I mentioned before, mankind was created with a spiritual gift no other created being had. He could speak God's word into the spiritual realm and see the change here on earth. This is not some thought-causing idealist noumena as Kant theorized. It is not the fatalistic ideology of Marx. If you do not understand the difference one might assume Marxism (or Hegel and Kant) could hold some validity within the Scriptures, but that is not the case. God wanted to teach Adam and Eve about their gift. He wanted to show them the appropriate way, within the special relationship each had to Father, God. In this way the planet could be blessed by mankind's care.

When Eve took of the fruit, it caused a cascading of events recorded in the Hebrew like this: God was clear, in the day they eat of the fruit from the tree of the knowledge of good and evil, *"dying, you shall surely die."* This is an odd statement, for they did not physically die. You might ask, "What's so bad about the knowledge of good and evil?" The words of the serpent might be telling here. He makes God out to be holding back on them; that they will be a "god" when they eat. The scary reality is they were already immortal. They were already a "god." All they needed was to learn God's total way of doing things in speaking and sovereignly governing the earth. They could also communicate with the creation in a way we cannot do now. Imagine swimming with a dolphin and asking, "So how's the ocean doing today? What's going on out there? How do you feel?" When we disobeyed we lost all those abilities. By partaking of the fruit they were telling God, "Your way is the wrong way and we know what we are doing better than you do." While God allowed them this choice, the consequences were real, not just in the mind. It affected the creation as well. The animals could no longer speak to us. We could no longer hear their voice. Weeds grew and a real life-giving quality in water was lost because the headwaters flowed through the area around the tree of life. The rivers flowed from these headwaters. Water is life-giving for us, but it had regenerative properties we don't quite see now.

Before the fall, there was no need to kill an animal. It is only in our fallen state we do such. If Adam and Eve had taken part in the tree of life, they would have lived forever in a corrupt state. Why? Within the Hebrew of the phrase "dying, you shall surely die," we see an odd play on words. While they did not physically die that day, something spiritual in them did die, just as things connected to mankind's spirituality died. First, they were no longer immortal and secondly, their ability to speak and see change in the spiritual realm, affecting the physical world, would be forever polluted and unclean—actually impossible to access. Their spirit became dormant. They were no longer able to connect to it. Thus there was no need for that element to be left whole in the creation. God allowed this to cause the necessary separation. They would no longer be able to connect to Him in the same manner in which they had before. Their reproduction would be limited to physically bearing children only and their spiritual reproduction would be stopped. Similarly, water's capability to sustain pre-fall life stopped and now it just sustains our lives as our bodies' limit allow.

Another result of the fall is seen in knowing the true source of evil and the true source of understanding (knowledge). While we have some knowledge, the understanding of its true source would be stopped. Having knowledge of good and evil is not enough. Having 'God knowledge' would have accessed miracle working power, with servant-like effect for the planet. Adam and Eve would have learned how to be servants with the title of humble kings and priests. Now, that would all be lost, *and the serpent knew it.* I believe this sounds a bit like the goods the socialists are peddling. We already had a superior compact-covenant. We already had an economy unrivaled in the world. Why would we want something somebody was trying to sell us that we had already? Especially when that "something" will leave us all equally poor, *except for the ruling class.* They will get better digs.

Many question why God would stop our immortality. They theorize eventually man would learn, over time. After all, an immortal learns and morphs into their understanding of things, so the theory goes. If we go back to the original creating ideas of blessing and separating as a blessing, we then understand why God cut off access to the tree of life. Imagine a Hitler, Genghis Khan, Stalin or Lenin or some other evil from millennia ago none of us have ever heard of, living forever. If you think they would change somehow over time and be softer, with their desire to control the world somehow subdued, think again. Immortality would have left them bolder, not softer. Millions more would have been killed. I doubt the planet could sustain that much evil never dying but just growing. If we think we have a problem with extinction events in the animal kingdom now, think of what an Alexander the Great or Nero living forever and desiring to be covered in animal skin would do. No, I firmly believe God had to cut off our immortality. He did it to bless the creation and mankind as well. Seeing our evil, and knowing what's in the mind of man, He did us a favor, in the long run.

God did not leave us comfortless though. He sent His Son to redeem mankind. Virgins do not conceive— but this one did (Mary)— and it was not through in vitro! Miracles are just a normal place when one functions with the God of the Bible. They do not originate in the mind of man. God makes no excuses for miracles; does not apologize for them; just gives them to us when we ask. So when we humble ourselves and ask Jesus to come and be our Lord and Savior, He does. Something outrageous takes place. Those of us who have experienced this know it is not something we made up in our minds. We are suddenly connected to the spiritual realm again. It truly is a born-again experience. I can hear the argument from many unbelievers, "Then why don't we see you do hocus-pocus and get us all out of this mess?" This question is very similar to the one the observers said of Jesus when He was hanging on the cross: "He saved others; himself he cannot save. If he be the King of Israel, let him now come down from the cross, and we will believe him" (Matthew

27:42, see also Luke 23:35; Mark 15:31). It is a good question. The reality is the question is from the same fruit our parents ate. It is a natural question to ask. There is nothing wrong in asking it. The mind of man was designed to ask questions. To arrive at the answer one needs to access the Holy Spirit, the real third person of the Trinity.

The reality is no one can speak and see results except God release them. Now, that does not mean we do not see the results when we speak according to His will. Humans are still in the learning phase of this. I will look at some of these questions shortly. The short answer is if God commands us to speak or promises us a result from belief and confession, then we do see results. They may be spiritual which takes time to be seen in the natural realm and results may be seen immediately. Quite often that is governed by laws within the spiritual realm, and sometimes it is within the purview of the Creator. But maintaining a confession in accordance with God's order in the spiritual realm is important. If I ask a human judge to do something for me in accordance with an order or ordinance, he will do it. If I go before him and curse or speak some other evil words to that judge, or curse the order or the ordinance— or in some other way my actions do the same thing— that judge may not be able to do what I ask simply because my actions have broken the order or ordinance or impeded the path for him to act.

Many folks simply cannot access the spiritual realm because their minds, will and emotions make them unable to do so. When we are born from above, born-again or otherwise ask Jesus to be our Lord and Savior and start walking with Him, our dormant spirits are made alive by the Word and Holy Spirit. I can now access something I could not before. Yet we are still in our human bodies which house a soul, and now awakened spirit. We have become accustomed to feeling our bodies ache, and our emotions rise or fall. But we now experience this "new" understanding of our spirits. Unless we connect to the Bible— in other words, obey the Holy Spirit and start reading— we are like new babes with no parents. Most new believers do quickly pick up the Word and do listen to the Holy Spirit and start walking in a newness of life. But— and this is unfortunate— sometimes they do not, and sometimes churches do not tell them the need to do so. These churches keep them in a stunted and malnourished system of law and striving and punishment and ever-obeying their creeds, but never arriving at the spiritual food so necessary for life in Christ. The Puritans did this, to some extent, to their own children. Sometimes they connected spiritually, but more frequently, as with other denominations of Christianity, it was a dry rationale of rules and regulations. This is not life in, by and through the Holy Spirit.

Jesus said in John 3:3-6: " 'Verily, verily, I say unto thee, Except a man be born again, he cannot see the kingdom of God.' Nicodemus saith unto him, 'How can a man be born when he is old? Can he enter the second time into his mother's womb, and be born?' Jesus answered, 'Verily, verily, I say unto thee, Except a man be born of water and of the Spirit, he cannot enter into the kingdom of God. That which is born of the flesh, is flesh; and that which is born of the Spirit is spirit'. " In John 6:63 Jesus said this: "The Spirit is the one who gives life; human nature is of no help! The words that I have spoken to you are spirit and are life" (NET Bible®). (See the Greek, and also within the NET Bible® the understanding 'the words are spirit-giving and life-producing.')

What men like Kant, Hegel and, to an even greater insult Marx, Engels and Lenin did was try to produce life from the flesh. No wonder the first two missed the mark, but nevertheless, had some success. Yet the last three did not just miss the mark, they jumped ship, only to float on a sea of nothing! No wonder scientists can easily decimate socialism's tenets. As a side note, all witches and spiritualists try to access the spiritual realm, using their biblically unregenerate word gift to change a reality. What all of them have done though, is attempt to understand a spiritual realm from the tree of the knowledge of good and evil. Not only is that fruit going to be tainted, it will never quite have you seeing a perfect reflection or image of what you are looking at.

The early church dealt with these issues because, as has been said before, the Greeks sat around debating them. One early church father, James, the brother of our Lord said this: ". . . for if someone merely listens to the message and does not live it out, he is like someone who gazes at his own face in a mirror (this word phrase is 'the face of his own beginning or origin'). For he gazes at himself and then goes out and immediately forgets what sort of person he was. But the one who peers into the perfect law of liberty and fixes his attention there, and does not become a forgetful listener but one who lives it out— he will be blessed in what he does" (James 1:23-25; NET Bible®). None of us can see ourselves as we truly are. None of us have ever seen ourselves without the assistance of a mirror or camera or some other reflective image. Without what the Bible calls itself, "the perfect law of liberty" we cannot rightly discern even ourselves, let alone spiritual matter around us. I am not surprised Marx, Engels, Lenin and other socialists find it impossible to understand the success of capitalism or the success of other economies based on natural cycles. Socialism makes it clear you cannot challenge socialism's teachings. Furthermore, you can't even go into detail concerning what a society based on socialism will look like.

Hegel's logic came closer, but ignored repentance and the need for the washing of the mind by the Word and the Spirit. The thinking of mankind is corrupt when he refuses to connect to the true Holy Spirit. Some might say, "Oh, you are just like the socialists telling us we can't challenge or disagree with you because our minds won't think right." Again, you can challenge and disagree all you would like or refuse Christianity totally. Unlike socialism, God gives you choices. Unlike socialism, the Bible gives detailed descriptions of heaven, hell as well as other created beings, including God's past creation events. What the Bible says is that you also have the ability— if you so choose— to believe, and then connect to the Holy Spirit yourself. In this way you can actually experience whether or not I am telling the truth. Let me ask, have you humbled yourself and at least gone to God and said, "If you are real, show me?" Jesus said: "…and him that cometh to me I will in no wise cast out" (John 6:37b).

ENDNOTES

1 I am again painting with broad strokes here. Genesis 1 uses the name Elohim. YAH does not appear until Genesis 2:4 (in English Bibles). The difference can be important to note, especially as it would relate to YAH carrying an idea of covenantal relationship. I am also not wading into the waters of various scholarly debates concerning Genesis. One of the

prominent debates asking whether Genesis 1 describes God creating matter. Many scholars do not believe so. They then refer to John 1:3, which describes the creation of matter as God created everything out of nothing. There are many other debates scholars dive into concerning the Hebrew. In fact, there are some scholars who view Genesis as just another creation myth. They link it to the Babylonian texts describing creation events, purporting Moses copied those texts. Yet Genesis truly is in a league of its own. While all other creation myths discuss the water, sun and moon as deities, Genesis makes no connection to such things. In point of fact, all earthly myths of creation include deities and relate them to the various created entities Genesis describes. There are many other scientific facts surrounding Genesis we never see in competing creation stories. In theory, if one takes socialism to its zenith, man becomes the creator because all things originate in his mind. Since socialism controls man, then in the line of succession socialism becomes the creating god. My point is to let you, the reader know I am generalizing in my recounting of the creation story, without looking at the various, as well as important matters of translation and how the various hypotheses in translating the Hebrew relate to the science as well as the story itself.

2   Ludwig Von Mises, "Socialism: An Economic and Sociological Analysis," translated by J. Kahane, foreword by F.A. Hayek; (Indianapolis: Liberty Fund, 1981) March 13, 2016 <http://oll.libertyfund.org/titles/1060> see Chapter 1.

3   "The Farmer Refuted, &c., [23 February] 1775" In Alexander Hamilton, "The Works of Alexander Hamilton." Edited by John C. Hamilton. Volume II (New York: John F. Trow, 1850) 49, 50.

Chapter Nine

THE UNEXPLAINED WITHIN
THE BIBLICAL EQUATION

Hegel and Kant's theories also stemmed from other unexplained concepts seen in the Scriptures. These have tried to be explained. The reality is that doing so is like explaining a miracle. I can tell you what happened, but I cannot explain miracles. God does them. They are an outcome of His very nature and being. Marx ignores them, Hegel tries to explain them as only his rationale limits him to, and Kant, well, frankly, can't. To make them a little easier to understand, let's look at time. When I related aspects of the creation story I did not discuss the creation of time. What we see in Genesis is really the Jewish time scale, "evening and the morning were the first day" (Genesis 1:5b). In America most folks start their day at sunrise. Biblical Judaism starts its day from the evening. Certainly time is in the constructs of the mind of man. Yet we see here that time is a created entity. We know the sun is a real, created entity. If you don't think so, sit out on a clear, sunny day in July from about noon to three PM, somewhere in North America. Then tell me what your skin, exposed to direct sunlight will look and feel like the next day. It is well known we measure a revolution of the earth on its axis as a day and the revolution of the earth around the sun as a year.

So time is a measured and actual experience on our planet. But time is not the same off our planet, is it? God is both outside of time and inside of time, at the same time! All throughout the Scriptures we see what many people call paradoxes. I will share in a moment why this is not an accurate word to use. Have you ever had anyone tell you the Bible is full of contradictions because of these 'paradoxes'? How about the word anomaly? Have you ever heard scientists describe some act of God as an anomaly? All of these words are attempts from human wisdom to describe the God of the Bible, who is not easily described. Since they are attempts from the mindset of human wisdom, as valiant as those attempts might be, they eventually lead us on a road lower than the road God would have us take to understand Him (see Proverbs 8).

How has He made Himself known? Throughout all the Scriptures, it has been through the Word, His Son, Jesus Christ (see Psalm 2; and 40:6,7; Hebrews 9; and 10:6,7; Colossians 2:8, 9). Through our study of the Bible we see God is One and He is also Three in One: Father, Son and Holy Spirit. We see Jesus Christ is 100 percent God and 100 percent man. We see God is totally sovereign in all that He is and does, and we, as humans are totally responsible for all that we do. We see the Bible as the written Word of God and it is written by man. The Word is a person, Jesus Christ. We see God is outside of time and space, since He created it and yet He works within time and space as He so chooses. God is transcendent, yet immanent. Our perspective of truth on earth is seen as positional truth and experiential truth— both true at the same time— as it relates ourselves to God. Our resurrected bodies will be both ethereal, yet physical. . . "BUT Wait a minute," you say. "Aren't you describing the contradictions and paradoxes and anomalies everybody talks about when they talk about God and the Bible?" I realize many genuine Christians were raised in an environment which described these things as 'paradoxes.' But let's define those words and then let's define what would describe some of the concepts I just listed. Once we do that, I believe we can all see why it's important not to use words like paradox or contradiction and anomaly. Because of the nature of many who tried to corrupt these truths, it is important to be as accurate as possible in the terms we use to describe them.

A contradiction is to assert the opposite. To deny the statement of (a person); to declare to be false or incorrect. Let me ask a question. Is God opposed to Himself? Has He denied His Word or ever declared Himself false? You can see the word contradiction is not the right word to use about God and the Bible. How about a paradox? A paradox is defined as something contradictory or unbelievable or absurd but that may actually be true. It is defined as something inconsistent with common experiences. From its definition we may like to use this word to describe some of the concepts I listed. Many times a paradox is one-sided and it is used to imply only apparent contradictions. It is often used for verbal contradictions. In a paradox if you change the situation or wording you can eliminate the problem. If you say, "I have nothing in the natural, but I have everything in Christ," all you have to do to solve the issue is say, "The less I have the more I rely on Jesus." But the concept that God is Three and yet One is not solved by rewording it. Nor is it solved by lifting one side of the concept up over the other. It is not one-sided. If you lift up His Oneness over the fact that He is Father, Son and Holy Spirit, (Three, yet One) you deny who He is. If you say these things are anomalies then you would be saying these concepts are abnormal and they deviate from the regular or general rule. Well, that also does not apply to God since God is not abnormal. He lives in a realm which is quite normal to Him. He is the one who makes the rules (gravity, space, physics, sowing and reaping, etc.). He can't possibly deviate from His 'regular or normal' rule, since He made it.

So what are we looking at here? Obviously we are looking at two equally true concepts which must be taken together as a whole. One may not be lifted up against the other or be 'one-sided,' but when we take them together as equals or as a whole, it goes against the law of our human reasoning.[1] What do I mean? Jesus is 100 percent God, right? Yet He is also 100 percent man. According to my human reasoning something cannot be 100 and 100 of anything. It has to be 50/50 in order to make 100. But 50/50 is not how Jesus purchased our redemption. Because He was God incarnate in human flesh, He suffered and died as a man and yet as the perfect divine sacrifice who was totally able to purchase redemption for all mankind because of His total divinity and total humanity. No other human could do so for no other human is God. From before the foundation of the world the Scriptures point to this (See John 1:1 and 1 Peter 1:18-20). If you try to lift His divinity up over His humanity you run into trouble because eventually the thinking will be, "Well, of course Jesus was perfect. He was God. I could never be that perfect because I'm human." When, in fact, it was Christ's total obedience as a human, even to the point of the cross which purchased our redemption. All of us as humans can be obedient in whatever way God calls us to. Jesus did not function in the supernatural through acts of divinity but through the Holy Spirit. The Bible tells us that He had the Spirit without measure (John 3:34). We also know we have been given the exact same Holy Spirit.

So we can see from these simple exercises we cannot compromise either side of these concepts in order to force them to be taken together as a whole. The early Gnostics tried to solve them and it led to such error within the church Paul spent almost as much time addressing their thinking in the New Testament as he did about law and grace. The other apostles addressed similar issues in order to birth the church in doctrinal purity. How about the concept of Father, Son and Holy Spirit? How can God be One through all eternity and yet be Three (the Trinity)?

Here is where many of the Jewish faith as well as Muslims have a hard time with the Christian faith. It really is in our effort to "solve" these concepts that we lift one side up over the other and fall into controversy (this is what defining them as a paradox will eventually do). These concepts are not made to be *solved* by the reasoning of human beings. So what are we to do? The reality is more promising than many realize. We can accept them. It is precisely because the God we serve is so awesome that we cannot always fathom Him or reason Him out. If we served a God who was always easy to explain and never went against our human reasoning, would you believe He was truly God? Remember this is the God who made the universe and flung the stars and planets out into space.

The Bible makes it clear the Scriptures were written by men as the Holy Spirit spoke to them (see 2 Peter 1:21). Isaiah 55:8-9 says that God's ways are higher than our ways and His thoughts are higher than our thoughts. Many other philosophies and ideas just try to solve the God of the Bible by creating a system that's easier to follow than the one laid out for us by Him in the Scriptures. Even professing Christians can fall prey to this trap. Kant tried to make 'religious' empirical formulas in an effort to classify these truths. Hegel's work looks and sounds better, but leads to similar theological error. Even in our own efforts today of sharing the Gospel and explaining God to people who have never gone to a church or experienced Him, we forget to let folks know God Almighty is the one who reveals Himself. It is by revelation we begin to understand Him, not because we can 'reason' who He is. He doesn't send anomalies or contradictions. He may challenge us with who He is. Actually it is because of how awesome He is we are challenged by these concepts. It is not the purpose of this book to work through all the dynamics of these biblical facts. You can review the Future Reading Section to find books on these topics.

Science does not know why human bodies die.[2] God originally did not intend for us to die or suffer decay, but distrust and disobedience are the hallmarks of decay. There has also been some exciting discoveries at absolute zero. At those temperatures two particles can become one and instead of being in one location, the atoms are everywhere at once.[3] The Bible, written thousands of years ago, has let us know mankind was created to live forever. It was a physical act of spiritual disobedience which changed things in a spiritual realm. This change affected the physical realm so our present human bodies no longer live forever. The Bible, written thousands of years ago, lets us know the God of the Bible is three distinct personalities, but One True God. He is omnipresent, omniscient, omnipotent, yet can be in YOUR one place. Let me think, are there any other religions which explain that? I can't think of one. I am not saying God resides in absolute zero, or any other action. These naturally occurring events only give example to the One who created them. What I am saying is God blows our scientific minds right out of the water. We have yet to understand all the scientific information He could give us. Hegel tried to explain what Kant could not. At every stage of our scientific discoveries, we need understanding and a connection from the same Word which created all of this.

ENDNOTES

1   You can also read many books that look at this issue from a theological perspective. An excellent one is "God, I don't Understand," by Kenneth Boa and published by David C. Cook

2   <http://www.washingtonpost.com/wp-srv/national/horizon/june98/microbes. htm>accessed 4/7/16

3   <http://www.pbs.org/wgbh/nova/transcripts/3501_zero.html> You can read the whole transcript but it is at Hour 2 this endnote references. Accessed 4/7/16.

Chapter Ten

THE BIBLICAL EQUATION
PRODUCES CONNECTIONS

Socialism demands we stop that connection. It does this on more than a conceptual ladder. It also does this on a level in which we relate to one another. When you take what someone else has worked for and give it to someone who will not work— not that they cannot work— this is called stealing. No one wants to give their hardworking dollars to people who continue to have more children so the government pays them for more, with no father responsible for these children. There are so many engineered money-grabs out there. These breed mistrust and actually encourage selfishness. Instead of going through all of them and how these affect cultural attitudes, we will look at Scriptures socialists try to commandeer for their cause. These will prove the lie that you are some how unkind or mean or awful for not giving your money away because progressives want you to feel bad. Instead, you will realize they are not being altruistic in the use of their bullying. Furthermore, you will know when we do need to help those who are less fortunate. And more importantly for how long. In other words, when does the "giving" stop?

The Bible is clear: Those who do not work, should not eat (2 Thessalonians 3:10). It matters little whether they are legal, illegal, persecuted immigrants, the poor or the disabled. I know disabled who perform tasks to enrich their communities. The infirm and elderly or totally incapacitated disabled cannot physically work. So there are biblical exceptions as to why their need will last longer than someone who is out of work for reasons beyond their control. The New Testament is clear benevolence is to be given to widows and orphans and those widows were not to be young women who could work. These had to be those who were not gossips, sitting around idle and "talking." They had to serve the saints and take care of many in the congregations who could not take care of themselves (1 Timothy 5:3-16). The Catholic church developed the nunnery for this purpose. Other denominations solve this through volunteers or by other institutional programs.

We have a younger generation who has grown up accustomed to welfare, unemployment compensations, gossip, and an attitude of everyone else working for them. Those in many churches have no concept of helping the poor and disabled in their own congregations. Yet there are congregations out there who teach these truths. It warms my heart to see young people helping those too sick to work. I've seen them travel miles across our country in order to fix the damaged homes of the elderly and indigent. This is just one aspect of what the body of Christ does for their communities. By helping the poor, these young folks learn many skills. They also learn covenant up close and personal by doing for others what they would like someone to do for them.

In point of fact, the Bible teaches and supports free enterprise as well as private property. If that were not the case, why the commandment prohibiting stealing and covetousness? Socialism uses mankind's fallen nature, which desires what someone else has, without working for it. To yearn to possess what someone else has is to covet it. This is strictly forbidden (Exodus 20:17; Deuteronomy 5:21) and its root causes are to be exposed and repented of (Philippians 2:12,13). In the biblical economy we are to care for the sick, the old and the otherwise indigent. We are also to work and expect blessing and riches to follow. That God will give us enough to give to others and He will provide all our needs according to His riches and glory in Christ Jesus (Philippians 4:19). The biblical economy is to work hard and prosper. All throughout the Old and New Testaments this is the foundation. The New Testament unlocks charity through the institution closest to the people. That institution is the church (or other religious organizations). God gives mankind talents to bless people and God with.

Socialism teaches man is talented in order to give it to the government or the state. The socialist manifesto endorses the abolition of private property. It endorses a progressive income tax and the abolition of inheritance. It endorses the confiscation of dissidents property. Eminent domain laws are supposed to pay market value for property which must be taken for the common good. A recent administration has figured a way around that.[1] Progressivism/socialism endorses a national bank and state-run communications and transportation systems. It endorses state-run factories, land management, farms and corporations as well as 100 percent employment. No unemployment benefits here! People simply do not know what the end result of the progressive democrat campaign is all about. Socialism/progressivism endorses forced relocation and forced free education programs, or public schools. One recent administration has figured out regulations to make it possible to "free" neighborhoods from people they didn't want living there. This is to "redistribute" folks according to government dictates (buzzword: diversity).[2] It matters little that hard work and enterprise will allow people to put themselves in the places they want to live and work in. According to progressives/socialists this will take too long. IT MUST HAPPEN NOW. Folks, beware because that truly is the communist way.

Not all governments elected or formed are put in power because God wanted them to be there: "They have set up kings, but not by me; they have made princes and I knew it not" (Hosea 8:4). The phrases used here in the Hebrew are not that God didn't know about the situation, but it wasn't in His mind people elect or place these individuals in these offices. Remember, the God of the Bible gives us free will and choice. Our choices are not always His idea. Also remember the founders/framers purposely chose the slower form of government in order that people get the time and opportunity to debate a matter (republics, not democracies). This fosters peaceful discussion instead of mob-rule protests. The rush-through process we saw with the ACA Act, a.k.a ObamaCare, was done on purpose. The architect said so himself because they needed to push it down the American people's throats in order to hide the true nature of the laws secreted within its massive overreach. In fact, he called Americans stupid for tolerating that approach.[3]

Many progressives/socialists use Romans 13:5-7 to say we are commanded to obey even ungodly rulers because God institutes them. This is a total mischaracterization of the truth. First, the book of Romans was written to the "beloved of God, called to be saints." Those saints who lived in Rome; Romans 1:7. When interpreting Scripture one must never divorce the verse from the chapter and the chapter from the book or epistle it was written in, OR the writer the Lord used. Biblical interpretation appropriately reviews the audience as well as the timeframe a book was written. Paul is not just talking about the saints. He is talking about the internal workings of the church. Furthermore, if Paul was talking about obeying Rome— the ruling government and empire at the time— then why did Caesar want to kill him? Caesar never would have had him killed if Paul was promoting unquestionable obedience to Rome. Rome had the same problem with Paul as Rome had with Jesus. Jesus preached about the Kingdom of God, which in Rome's mind was another government. Rome interpreted this portion of Scripture correctly. I don't understand why some try to misinterpret it today.

Secondly, socialists try to use Acts 2-5 as a support for taking people's money and redistributing it. There are several reasons why the Bible does not support that interpretation. One is seen in Acts 2:44, 47, and it is the tense of the verbs used in the Greek. Most of the time you would expect a "once-for-all-action" in a historical narrative like this, but that is not what is seen here. It's more like a "from time to time," or when the occasion arose. In fact, this is clearly seen in Acts 4:34, 35, with some translations stating clearly, "From time to time" or as the need arose, the believers would sell or give money. We see something similar in relation to Acts 5 with Ananias and Sapphira. It wasn't the fact they didn't give all the money, but they lied to the Holy Spirit and judgment fell on them. The early church had to be built in doctrinal purity and integrity of action. This is necessary on so many levels. The believers had to know the Holy Spirit was not just some thought or feeling, but God.

In studying Marx, you can understand lying is no big deal for him. The focus of the New Testament is not money. It is Jesus Christ and how we humans can be changed into the image and likeness of Christ (purity, love, truth, etc.). Initially this was done through economics: God purchased us back. After this, we can only be changed by the infilling of the Holy Spirit and our trust and obedience to His word. When reading the English of this passage in Acts, one might assume it was about keeping some of the money back. Yet Peter goes on to say, "Whiles it remained, was it not thine own? And after it was sold, was it not in thine own power? Why hast thou conceived this thing in thine heart? Thou has not lied unto men, but unto God" (Acts 5:4). The early church was filled with such love and caring that from time to time they would sell their goods and give it to the elders and apostles to distribute for the needs of the congregations. No one was compelled to give. It is obvious from the verbs used it was clearly their own to hold back some and give what they chose to give. Ananias and Sapphira professed to give all in an effort to look like big shots. In order to look good, they had to lie. It is the lie which is condemned.

If you read Marx, lying is just a necessary part of implementing a progressive/socialist agenda. So naturally progressives don't pick up on the sin of lying condemned in this passage. Furthermore, if socialism is what the text is supporting here then there would be a state or secular government getting the money, not the apostles and elders of the church. If the progressives/socialists really want to follow the Scriptures, are they supporting giving the money to the church and letting the leaders of the church distribute it as the Lord directs? I don't think so.

Only capitalism allows charitable institutions to do that. Socialist/progressives never support that. They have to put up with it if it is a part of a society they are infiltrating. But give them time, they will make it illegal— through one excuse or another— all in an effort to control charitable contributions. In fact, they already do. Peruse the IRS code on 501c-3 Organizations sometime and tell me they are not regulated up to their ear lobes! These organizations were loosely regulated until the 2006 mid-term elections which swept in progressives (a.k.a Democrats) by a landslide. The administration in office at the time no longer controlled much of anything, becoming "lame duck" quickly. New regulations were instituted for 501c-3s at that point, before the 2008 elections.

The Scriptures are clear throughout that it is the congregation or institution closest to the people who should take care of the benevolent needs of the people. Why is that? Well, if you are a sluggard, criminal or enable criminal and addictive behavior, your neighbors know more about you than some nameless, faceless bureaucracy. They may not know everything— especially in this day and age, and especially if they are not on Facebook— but they know more than the welfare boards do. The Bible also gives advice to the churches in giving funds. Trust me when I say we would save billions if we really did it the way the Bible exhorts us to. More people would be working and taking care of their own families.

Progressives control money from the top down. If you don't think from the top down governance is a problem, let me give you some evidence. Whether people will admit it or not, they do what they see. If they see Hollywood promote a certain lifestyle, they will mimic that behavior. People will behave the way they see their leaders in a company or corporation behave. "After all, if so and so can do it, so can I," goes the thinking.[4] The biblical perspective alters that phenomena in positive ways. Progressives (a.k.a socialists) only give to those who support them. The Bible commands us to bless those in need. The only restraint on us is as the Bible as well as the Holy Spirit directs.

As soon as progressives get into power, they create an environment which makes it clear if you open your mouth, you will be fired and/or hunted down. Isn't that what is going on with all the various protests? Many think they are supporting a cause. When that cause denies inalienable rights, it is not a cause. The protesters are being used and duped by socialism. If you do not support them, they will find a way to thwart you. We have seen this with every recent scandal from the IRS to the Pentagon.[5] The Secret Service is supposed to protect and serve; namely, the president. It has been the practice of a 2009 progressive administration to silence their "foes." Those would be the American citizens who disagree with their illegal behavior. It has been recently discovered dozens of Secret Service employees were encouraged by their leaders to target an elected congressman from the "other" party who exposed and criticized illegal and incompetent practices within that agency.[6] One of the leaders within the Secret Service said the congressman needed to be targeted in order to be "fair." Let's see, haven't we had a president as well as democrat politicians talk about making everyone "equal" and that will some how be more "fair"?

If you don't think this is a problem, then keep voting for the same people, while expecting a different result. There are actions which are immoral and actions which are full of integrity. What we have seen from the Federal government recently are immoral actions, targeting those of faith as well as those who disagree with progressive/democrat political policies. This is the way of socialism. Socialism/progressivism is not patriotic or American. The policies and practices are very unAmerican. But we have a press that is not telling the American people the truth. That is immoral. The press, just like the church, is fostered in its inalienable First Amendment right for a reason: We are to root out corruption; preaching against it and printing it out for others to know the problems.

Having said that, I do want to make something clear. If you are a Christian Democrat or some other and vote Democrat, I am writing to you to show you the sham going on with them. We pray for the Democrats to have their eyes opened to see the danger they are putting their country as well as themselves in. I am not attempting to disrespect you. What I am attempting to do is expose the scam being perpetrated against you and against your vote as an American citizen. If I have been able to prove this to you, and you want to pray; pray for the Democrats as well as the Republicans to stop their own actions which foster this problem. If prayer is something you do not believe in, then at least consider your vote as a citizen far more closely in light of what I have written.

Let me share a very pervasive attitude our framing generation learned from their ancestors. It comes from James, the brother of our Lord:

> "If any man among you seem to be religious, and bridleth not his tongue, but deceiveth his own heart, this man's religion is vain. Pure religion and undefiled before God, the Father is this, To visit the fatherless and widows in their

affliction, and keep himself unspotted from the world. My brethren, have not the faith of our Lord Jesus Christ, the Lord of glory, with respect of persons. For if there come unto your assembly a man with a gold ring, in goodly apparel and there come in also a poor man in vile raiment, and ye have respect to him that weareth the gay clothing, and say unto him, Sit thou here in a good place; and say to the poor, Stand thou there, or sit here under my footstool: Are ye not then partial in yourselves, and are become judges of evil thoughts? Hearken, my beloved brethren, Hath not God chosen the poor of this world rich in faith, and heirs of the kingdom which he hath promised to them that love him? But ye have despised the poor. Do not rich men oppress you, and draw you before the judgment seats? Do not they blaspheme that worthy name by the which ye are called? If ye fulfill the royal law (Mosaic Law) according to the scripture, Thou shalt love thy neighbor as thyself, ye do well. But if ye have respect to persons, ye commit sin, and are convinced of the law as transgressors" (James 1:26-2:9).

Here is an attitude saving us more than just tax dollars: It is the attitude of servanthood. The Bible is the one book inculcating servanthood to public "workers." In fact, they are called public servants here in America for a reason. It is not to act like bigwigs, but to serve one another. Progressives (a.k.a socialists) cannot function that way. When you control from the top down you are going to have bigwigs. Our original design is to break up the power so as to limit the control. It is called checks and balances for a reason. Progressivism's hallmarks are revenge, stealing through regulation, greed, jealousy and lying. Don't believe the hype. You can clearly see from researching modern news feeds this is all a part of the Marxist agenda. There is no way to make a sow's ear into anything other than pigskin. When the foundation is crooked, the whole organization is crooked. Progressivism (a.k.a socialism) is not biblical in any real world, and not according to the Bible.

The biblical economy is based on sowing and reaping. It is to be done as a blessing. We are expected to be blessed financially when we do as God

invites us to. Being an agrarian society, our early founders/framers understood this concept, even as they looked forward to other frameworks of
future enterprise. We will review some Old Testament promises first.

Deuteronomy 28 makes some very plain statements: "If you
indeed obey the Lord your God and are careful to observe
all his commandments I am giving you today, the Lord
your God will elevate you above all the nations of the
earth. All these blessings will come to you in abundance
if you obey the Lord your God: You will be blessed in the
city and blessed in the field. Your children will be blessed,
as well as the produce of your soil, the offspring of your
livestock, the calves of your herds, and the lambs of your
flocks. Your basket and your mixing bowl will be blessed.
You will be blessed when you come in and blessed when
you go out. The Lord will cause your enemies who attack
you to be struck down before you; they will attack you from
one direction but flee from you in seven different directions. The Lord will decree blessing for you with respect
to your barns and in everything you do— yes, he will bless
you in the land he is giving you" (Deuteronomy 28:1-8,
NET Bible®).

" 'Bring the entire tithe into the storehouse so that there
may be food in my temple. Test me in this matter,' says the
Lord who rules over all, 'to see if I will not open for you
the windows of heaven and pour out for you a blessing until
there is not roof for it all' " (Malachi 3:10, NET Bible®).

One last passage from Proverbs: "Trust in the Lord with all
your heart, and do not rely on your own understanding.
Acknowledge him in all your ways, and he will make your
paths straight. Do not be wise in your own estimation; fear
the Lord and turn away from evil. This will bring healing to
your body, and refreshment to your inner self. Honor the
Lord from your wealth and from the first fruits of all your
crops; then your barns will be filled completely, and your

vats will overflow with new wine. My child, do not despise discipline from the Lord, and do not loathe his rebuke. For the Lord disciplines those he loves, just as a father disciplines the son in whom he delights" (Proverbs 3:5-12; NET Bible®).

Now from the New Testament: "So then, don't worry saying, 'What will we eat?' or 'What will we drink?' or 'What will we wear?' For the unconverted pursue these things, and your heavenly Father knows that you need them. But above all pursue his kingdom and righteousness, and all these things will be given to you as well." This is Jesus speaking in Matthew 6:31-33; NET Bible®.

Here is Luke sharing one of Paul's sermons: "By all these things, I have shown you by working in this way we must help the weak, and remember the words of the Lord Jesus that he himself said, 'It is more blessed to give than to receive' " (Acts 20:35; NET Bible®).

Paul to the Corinthians: "My point is this: The person who sows sparingly will also reap sparingly, and the person who sows generously will also reap generously. Each one of you should give just as he has decided in his heart, not reluctantly or under compulsion, because God loves a cheerful giver. And God is able to make all grace overflow to you so that because you have enough of everything in every way at all times, you will overflow in every good work. Just as it is written, 'He has scattered widely, he has given to the poor; his righteousness remains forever.' " (Paul is quoting Psalm 112:9.) "Now God who provides seed for the sower and bread for food will provide and multiply your supply of seed and will cause the harvest of your righteousness to grow. You will be enriched in every way so that you may be generous on every occasion, which is producing through us thanksgiving to God, because the service of this ministry is not only providing for the needs of the saints but is also overflowing with many things to God. Through the evidence of this service they will glorify God because of your obedience to your confession in the gospel of Christ and the generosity of your sharing with them and with everyone. And in their prayers on your behalf they long for you because of the extraordinary grace God has shown to you. Thanks be to God for his indescribable gift" (2 Corinthians 9:6-15; NET Bible®)!

These verses are a tiny group of the whole. What we are seeing is a miraculous promise. First we are to give ten percent of our income (tithe) and God makes a promise He will bless the ninety percent left over in such a way it would become more than the hundred we originally had. Unfortunately, the IRS despises this so much computer programs will trigger you for audit when your returns show this. I am told by many Christians they no longer allow their returns to reflect this. But, that does not mean all the charitable contributions made need to be claimed. In God's economy saints will still be blessed even if some of the legal deductions are left on the table. Right from the start God makes statements about finances which will defy the progressive agenda.

Paul also lets us know when we give, the saints will pray for us and those prayers are priceless. In fact, Paul lets us know God loves when we give cheerfully and not under compulsion. Corruption costs time and money. *The forced surrender of our money through regulation is corrupting.* Selfishness, jealousy and laziness go hand in hand with poverty. God clearly tells us to flee these practices and to behave and function honestly. We are to function in everything we do with excellence. This also frees up capital to be spent elsewhere. We know our Federal government does not spend wisely nor efficiently. This is a spiritual issue first and can only be solved spiritually. Sure, practices will have to change; but the initial impetus must come from spiritual forces and energy. Only God's covenant people can do this. WE MUST DO THIS. Like Mordecai told Esther of old: "And who knoweth whether thou art come to the kingdom for such a time as this" (Esther 4: 14b)? Prayer, fasting and the spiritual efforts of putting our actions to work, will do more than our meager efforts could do alone. Why? Because we know God is fighting on our behalf.

So how did we get conned into believing the progressive lie? It is sort of like a slow drip from a leaky faucet. You don't see the damage to the plumbing immediately. It takes time. Usually leaky faucets are a symptom of bad water. In our case here, one generation was not taught the blessings the previous generations had and why they experienced them. This makes it difficult to understand the problem. Let's look at a short history of the American descent into equalized poverty (a.k.a progressivism).

ENDNOTES

1   <http://www.foxnews.com/politics/2015/09/15/family-says-feds-resorting-to-criminality-in-low-offer-for-nevada-land-near-top/?intcmp=ob_article-sidebar-video&intcmp=obinsite> accessed 4/7/16

2   <http://www.foxnews.com/politics/2013/08/08/obama-administration-using-housing-department-to-compel-diversity-in/><http://www.foxnews.com/politics/2015/06/15/feds-accused-trying-to-push-utopia-on-wealthy-neighborhoods-with-diversity-regs/> accessed 4/7/16

3   <http://townhall.com/tipsheet/katiepavlich/2014/11/10/obamacare-architect-yeah-we-lied-to-the-stupid-american-people-n1916605><http://www.forbes.com/sites/theapothecary/2014/11/10/aca-architect-the-stupidity-of-the-american-voter-led-us-to-hide-obamacares-tax-hikes-and-subsidies-from-the-public/> accessed 4/7/16

4   <http://www.businessinsider.com/obama-administration-and-isis-intelligence-2015-9> accessed 4/7/16

5   <http://www.thedailybeast.com/articles/2015/09/09/exclusive-50-spies-say-isis-intelligence-was-cooked.html> accessed 4/7/16

6   <http://www.foxnews.com/politics/2015/09/30/secret-service-tried-to-discredit-gop-rep-chaffetz.html> accessed 4/7/16 As an update, <http://www.cnn.com/2016/05/26/politics/secret-service-jason-chaffetz/index.html> I do wonder though, how it is no one is ever reprimanded when they deceive the American people. Since this was a sitting Congressman and it made headlines, then something was done. See next for an example of what I mean <http://www.foxnews.com/opinion/2016/05/26/any-american-who-believes-in-rule-law-and-fair-play-should-be-afraid-very-afraid-our-government-right-now.html?intcmp=trending>

Chapter Eleven

PROGRESSIVE-SOCIALISTS
INFILTRATE AMERICA

It can be said the socialist desire to infiltrate the American system came early. Being a nation filled with natural wealth, the Marxists (progressives) desired that wealth quickly. But the road to America was marred by LIBERTY! We had no pope or monarchy to rail against. Since the common worker in America was far better off than any other in the entire world, the shout of injustice concerning labor and management was falling on deaf ears. Here in America, the common workers were able to purchase property and other goods. In other words, they personally owned stuff. The progressive buzzwords of inequality, injustice and revolution just sounded hollow. It took time, but eventually politicians bought into it. Why? Well, they needed to buy votes. Some would suggest the industrial revolution produced mass workers who were not well paid and they needed to unionize. We had industrialization, and workers did need to unionize in order to get a fair wage and safer working conditions. Unions in that sense are more like our modern "Right-to-Work" states. These are laws which say just because a union exists at your work place, does not mean you must join it. In other words, you can't be bullied, fired or targeted because you will not pay union dues and join the union. It has been successfully argued it is the free market which protects workers.[1] Good workers are always in high demand.

What socialist and government-connected unions do now is bully workers into joining, forcing them to pay dues. These unions then financially support the campaigns of candidates through their union member's dues. Well, that may be fine if the union member supports said candidates, but this is becoming less of the case as people realize the dangers this relationship imposes (see previous footnote). Oddly enough, it is the years of repeated assault by socialistic regulations which have created the environment in which the message of socialistic "equality/inequality" has become popular. For example, remembering the small list of cases I have cited of the malevolence of socialistic bureaucracies, you can sense how unequal and helpless the captives must feel. Yet this is the very result of the socialistic policies which have been instituted. The political elite, made up of the bureaucrats, many within the justice systems, as well as many career politicians, most of the media, Hollywood and tenured professors shout how awful this "inequality" is. Their tired responses go something like this: "YOU must rise up in protest and demand new laws to stop the injustice." Yet they never reveal how the injustices were produced by passage of new laws!

This duplicity is reflected in the upheaval we see in protestation from racial, gendered and economic "causes." As we saw with just one experiment in Detroit, it is the ideologic and economic practices of progressivism which causes poverty and inflicts more oppressive outcomes on those closest to the poverty levels. This means all folks become poorer and injustices become more widespread. By making this a racial issue, you lie to said ethnic groups, telling them to revolt. You then give them reward incentives to cause mayhem by caving to their demands or by allowing their "peaceful" protests to become violent. In this way the real cause (progressive policy) is never revealed. By enabling violent protests you enable progressives' takeover of more institutions.

I always found it amazing how the protesters within the "Occupy" movement protested unethical practices in corporations but never the unequal as well as unjust rule of government by the socialists. They are the same practices. Both practices use tyranny, intimidation and bullying to create a culture in which honesty, fairness and excellence are silenced in an effort to produce a goal. In the case of some business adventures, that is to make a profit. In the case of socialistic practices, that is to promote socialism. Socialism promotes a profit to an "entity" for more control and power. Whether the practice is done by a dictator, a state entity or a small business group, the practices are the same to produce similar results. While a state entity is more likely to do this by laws and regulations instead of by fiat demand, the power grab is still the same. The demand, the law, and in some cases, even the protests are the tools used to continue the power grab.

One of the first progressives to gain real power was, believe it or not, a Republican. But tinkering with our Constitution began early. The most notable drum roll toward "tinkering" started with the Jacksonian democrats. It was the Jackson Administration that was crucial in the growth of democracy as opposed to republicanism. Republics are important in that change is slower and through representative votes from their geographic constituents, thus government is more stable and its citizens have more opportunities to thrive within the stability. Citizenry have more opportunity within true republics to make their desires known. Democracies just need majority protestation or mob rule. It is not only messy and dangerous, but it attempts to crush all opposition the "mob" doesn't like. No freedom for religion in the public square or freedom of speech. And if the "mob" doesn't like the Second Amendment, well, then, just cause chaos through the very real threat of mob protests which endanger far greater numbers in life as well as property. Let a few criminals bring a few guns, just to get *"your point"* across.

From the Sixties on we have seen nothing but an encouragement from one party for violent protests. Many of us can remember the hatred and lies levied at the peaceful as well as grassroots protests of the Tea Party in 2010. Now think of how many Democrats in cities all across the country encouraged the "Occupy" movement as they camped out and caused nothing but filth and crime in their wake. Communities had to scream at officials within the Democrat Party to get them to do something to stop the madness of that thing. The crime and connections to the Democrat

Party went widely under-reported, as well as the stipends paid to homeless and others to camp out. This made it look as if it was grass roots. This is what scam protests are all about.[2] Socialists need the chaos.

Jackson's understanding for democracy may have been different from what we see now, but over time the effects are still the same. Jackson increased the power of the presidency through his extensive use of the veto and of political patronage through the "spoils system." Unfortunately, if you are not in a political history class, most of us will just call this system *business as usual*. Frankly, I did not know this history until I did this research. What it entails is a system whereby appointments made to public office, as well as employment in the public service are given based on political affiliation or personal relationships rather than on the fitness or merit of the appointees. It entails an extensive form of political patronage. Many also include in its definition favoritism in the awarding of contracts for public works or other public needs as well as the expenditure of public funds to favored individuals, citing one purported need or other to cover up the favoritism. This second part of the definition is outlawed. But think of a recent governor from the state of Illinois (Rod Blagojevich), who tried to sell a senate seat after the departing of its occupant to the office of the Presidency of the United States, and we all understand why this is a problem.[3]

Spoils systems were practiced among the states since colonial times. Yet the Federal government's model was based on Washington's demand that those of the greatest fitness for an office be placed. He had men like Jefferson and Hamilton in his administration, though they were from different parties. Successive presidents were not as tolerant of the practice. It wasn't until Andrew Jackson's administration that the spoils system comes to the Federal government on a wide scale. Jackson had some reasons which were noble enough for this shift. One of which had to do with changing out the bureaucracy every so often so as to avoid entrenchment. As has already been mentioned, his guise of "religious liberty" debate concerning mail delivery on Sunday, as well as his refusal to issue days of proclamation of thanksgiving, fasts, etc., would also remain easier to enforce with his spoils system. So the downsides became obvious to many. In point of fact, we see this has also made it easier for the recent scandals to take place. The system was named after the saying *to the victor belong the spoils of the enemy.*

As covenant citizens, there is not supposed to be an enemy, except those fighting to destroy the covenant. Making enemies of those of different American parties originating on our shores is also Marxist strategy and is foreign to our Federal system as originally implemented. I am not saying there were no political dog fights, just the idea of mortal enemies was understood for those of British or other foreign background when trying to influence our American system. It got so bad that the Pendleton Act of 1883, which started the civil-service system was passed. Other local community reforms instituting council-manager systems of governance were also enacted. Unfortunately, the spoils system goes hand in hand with a Marxist strategy of control because it works well for all political parties wishing the same outcome of control and discrimination. It has been used recently by one progressive-socialist administration to grow the federal payroll.[4]

There is another way to grow government when using hiring based on ideological basis. In other words, how to get around being accused of a spoils system approach. Data released from the Bureau of Economic Analysis shows when you combine benefits and wages, Federal civilian workers, on average, have a 78 percent higher overall compensation rate than those who work in the private sector.[5] In 2015 the wages and benefits for executive branch civilian workers cost more than $260 billion dollars (excluding postal workers).[6] Since the 1990s this trend has gotten worse. From 2011 to 2013 a partial freeze was imposed on federal wages which saved billions of dollars. Once that freeze expired, those figures skyrocketed. While several administrations have existed since the 1990s, only one has been shown to abuse this system to the maximum amount we have seen, thus causing a real problem for average Americans and the insanity of our national debt.[7]

By reading the previous reference, it is easy to see the problem as a top heavy bureaucracy stacked with Federal workers used as a special interest group fueled by politics. At that point you turn them into lobbyists, without having actual lobbyists. Thus progressives try to claim they don't hire lobbyists! Taxes must be imposed at higher rates to compensate for this staff of in-house soldiers for a political cause. We are among the top countries in corporate tax rates in the world![8] This trend will only get worse if more progressives/socialists are placed in government. We have American companies merging with foreign corporations in order to save millions and billions in U.S. taxes.[9]

Not only did the spoils system empower the office of the presidency, Jackson extended the electoral franchise by the use of the convention system for presidential candidates. He did something else which truly harmed the republic, and by extension, covenant: He extended Federal authority over states' rights. In a tariff dispute with South Carolina, Jackson opposed the issue of nullification, which held that a state couldn't reject federal authority. Jackson's position led to the resignation of Vice-President John Caldwell Calhoun, who supported states' rights. Now that's something you never hear of today: A man in the second highest office of the nation declaring the theft of rights and liberties must stop, and willing to sacrifice his job to do it! Even if you don't agree with his position historically, it is still something we rarely see from someone in that office today.

While I am on states' rights, I may as well sacrifice one of my own sacred cows: Abraham Lincoln. Without a doubt, the freedom of covenant citizens from slavery was absolutely a necessary endeavor. Until I did this research Lincoln was my second favorite president behind Washington. I no longer believe he deserves that listing. By the time Lincoln suspended the writ of habeas corpus, thereby suspending First and Second Amendment rights, as well as so many other inalienable rights, a civil war was a foregone conclusion. As a result, historians have, for the most part sided with his legal positions.[10] Personally, I think they are probably right *if* we use the legal case of a president to stop rebellions. I am divided as to whether it initially was true rebellion or freedom of speech. Unfortunately, I am in the minority when it comes to what I believe were the underlying causes of the Civil War. It is the environment and the decades leading up to the Civil War which forged the inevitability of the war, thus making my case for the ability to avoid the war.

The way to avoid what became the Civil War is called covenant, and the avenue which would have bought the time for a solution is called MONEY! Before anyone misquotes me, let me make it clear from the start I do not believe the Constitution, nor any part of our federal compacting documents gave any state, government or other human being the right to make a slave out of any human being. Yet I also do not believe it gave Lincoln the right to waste 1,100,000 American souls.[11] It split our nation in a way we still suffer from today. It is also my opinion this war had economic stress issues which dealt more with mid-western expansion and southern-state resource waste, than northern and southern antagonisms.[12] There were economic solutions which could have been given to the South, long before Lincoln was elected. Those economic solutions should have been employed by him. Sure, it would have cost lots of money. The northern churches also should have waged a huge campaign within the southern churches to extend the hand of brotherhood. This could expose the lies concerning slavery; especially any attempting to use the Bible to support the practice.

This approach would have taken longer, with pockets of slaves made free over time. It also would have entrenched an outreach in economic, governmental, legal, psychological and spiritual forms of covenant. In other words, the understanding that no one wants slavery. No one wants to be treated as property. How can we "grow" people into an understanding which covenants the idea of freedom with the outreaches already named in a society? For those arguing against the slower approach which would have avoided war, the "faster" way still showed the racial divide in the 1960s, clearly 100 years later! By not approaching this solution in a covenantal way, we have allowed those so marginalized to ignore covenant responsibility. The same is true for those causing marginalization. In our present society, this has almost nothing to do with skin color any longer. Social, criminal corporate and governmental bullies come in all stripes. This war also set up the writing of the 14th Amendment. Poorly written, it has been used to deny covenant citizens, born and unborn their inalienable rights. It is now being used to bludgeon religious and scientific conscientious objectors. It was used long before that to deny states' rights.

Waging an economic, spiritual and social plan based on the covenant of mankind probably would have taken 30 to 50 years (my guesstimate). In the long run, it would have saved lives and established American brotherhood for all colors of people in half the time than what Lincoln didn't really do before his own assassination! Lincoln could have easily set up the system legally: emancipation, money payments, jobs programs (initially, only), and the role of the churches, the teachers and others to address the social, educational and psychological issues. He would have had to hand it off to another administration to continue the programs. Yet that is the right way to fix both a scientific and social wrong. Today we claim wrongs which have no science or sociological basis, but attempt to remove inalienable rights anyway! This issue reminds me of married couples who come in for counseling and blame money problems for their marital grievances. Giving them money will not solve their issues. The money might buy some time for them to dig deep into what their real issues are, and then solve them.

Concerning the Civil War, that is surely the case. The pat solutions of throwing money at, or bludgeoning an issue with the law is not a solution. It can buy some time for the real solutions of covenant, science and cultural formulas to be implemented. Employing the legal card with the money card will not solve the deep-seated issues of slavery or race. Of course, hind-sight is always 20/20. For those who may disagree with me concerning the Civil War, I would like you to know I would have disagreed with me as well, before I did this research. You can read the Future Reading Section for books from many sides of this argument.

These clashes over our American civil rights, were American. It wasn't until the election of the Republican, Teddy Roosevelt, that party agenda turned truly foreign with ever increasing and devastating effects. Roosevelt was not the worst. The administrations of Woodrow Wilson, and Teddy's cousin, Franklin Delano Roosevelt would prove, with history, to be highlights of delayed captivity or impending imprisonment. These three are not the only administrations encouraging the loss of freedoms. Unfortunately, not all these influences on the erosions of our freedoms are noticed or felt by the generations in charge at the time. Looking at a more recent experience, we have an administration like William Clinton, who worked well economically with the minority party (at the time Republicans) by balancing the budget. That action alone gave us a robust economy. Both democrats and republicans worked FOR the people. But his decision to fire 93 Federal U.S. (district) Attorneys proved disastrous for the rule of law.[13] It ushered in an ideological framework into the courts which subsequently set the platform for the 44th president to unravel Constitutional moorings. Politics has not just become murderous, but filled with those from foreign shores with foreign ideologies (socialism) corrupting what could be a fair and balanced system.

One might ask, "How could this start with a Republican?" Initially that was my question as well. The question morphed into the reality it is those designated with First Amendment rights who are to blame. When they are weakened (the church preaching to political leaders concerning corruption) or they choose to weakly report the truth (socialism monopolizing a good portion of the press), all Americans are in serious danger of losing our cherished inalienable rights. From my point of view, that reality was mitigated by the fact socialism is the economic tool used by wealthy financiers who hide, not only their intentions, but their influence, by either paying off political parties to keep quiet or, more recently, paying off the parties, the court system, as well as the press. So there is a hidden force which is the real engine of the resultant assault of progressivism on our covenant rights. This has to be viewed separately, but symbiotically with the obvious end results which come from policies political parties enact when they control the reins of government.

ENDNOTES

1   Milton Friedman, the Nobel Prize winner in economics discusses in this clip what actually protects workers. <https://www.youtube.com/watch?v=EJEP7G7C0As> accessed 4/7/16

2   <http://www.breitbart.com/big-journalism/2011/10/28/updated-occupywallstreet-the-rap-sheet-so-far/><http://www.foxnews.com/us/2011/10/26/exclusive-acorn-playing-behind-scenes-role-in-occupy-movement><https://www.youtube.com/watch?v=DLlkyPtTuAU<http://www.theblaze.com/stories/2011/10/07/

video-exposing-occupy-wall-street-was-organized-from-day-one-by-seiu-acorn-front-the-working-family-party-and-how-they-all-tie-to-the-obama-administraion-dnc-democratic-socialists-of-america/><http://www.freerepublic.com/focus/bloggers/3058975/posts> accessed 4/7/16

3   <https://en.wikipedia.org/wiki/Rod-Blagojevich_corruption_charges> accessed 4/7/16

4   These arguments have a back and forth statistic. If one looks at the growth of only the Federal payroll from January 2009, there has been a significant uptick in every year, whether or not one includes the census-gathering years where temporary Federal workers increase. But if one looks at all government employees from state, local as well as federal, then the numbers go down. Again, this is because of recession and a loss of municipal tax revenue at the local/state level, which is based in large part on local economies. Review the first article and then the second for a note on the danger ahead based on spending policies. The third source sites many facts, including the January 2015 numbers. I include it here so you may review those subsequent numbers every January, no matter what year you read this book in. <http://www.aei.org/publication/has-government-employment-really-increased-under-obama/><http://www.forbes.com/sites/mikepatton/2013/01/24/the-growth-of-the-federal-government-1980-to-2012/><http://www.factcheck.org>accessed 4/7/16

5   <http://www.cato.org/blog/federal-government-pay-exceeds-most-industries>accessed 4/7/16

6   <http://www.downsizinggovernment.org/federal-worker-pay#_edn1> accessed 4/7/16

7   Ibid.

8   <http://taxfoundation.org/article/corporate-income-tax-rates-around-world-2014> accessed 4/7/16

9   <http://www.usatoday.com/story/money/2015/11/23/pfizer-allergan-merger/76248478/> accessed 4/7/16

10 <http://www.heritage.org/research/lecture/abraham-lincoln-and-civil-liberties-in-wartime?> site accessed 4/7/16. "Abraham Lincoln and Civil Liberties in Wartime," by Hon. Frank J. Williams. This article does not specifically address the Civil War, but the legality of Lincoln's actions in light of Bush's actions in 2004. I felt it was an excellent article to give us a more modern perspective instead of viewing Lincoln in a sanitized history lesson on civil liberties.

11 <https://www.phil.muni.cz/~vndrzl/amstudies/civilwar_stats.htm> accessed 4/1/16

12 "Clash of Extremes: The Economic Origins of the Civil War," by Marc Egnal, published by Hill and Wang, 2009, NY. Instead of one page, please google this or pick up a copy. I've often felt there was a brewing going on over this issue for centuries. In reading this

work, I have to agree that Egnal makes a forceful argument for westward expansion with a weakening of southern soil production bringing it to a head.

13   <http://www.freerepublic.com/focus/f-news/1817411/posts><https://www.mrc. org/biasalerts/nets-ignored-clinton-firing-93-us-attorneys-fret-over-bushs-8-3142007> accessed 4/7/16

Chapter Twelve

THE VIRUS (PROGRESSIVISM)
KEEPS A SYMBIOTIC HOST

I saw a bumper sticker recently which read, "Capitalism pays for Socialism." This reality is so widely known, frankly the only people lying about it are the politicians and state-run media news stations. I say state-run, because this is what you have when they repeatedly tout a socialistic government's cause. One could easily argue monetary interests connected to financial exposure was the real reason why all 93 Federal district attorneys were fired, but political reasons were involved as well.[1] I am not sure we will ever have all the evidence to prove the tangled web from that instance surrounding the administration Clinton built. It will surely take a brave journalist, willing to risk life and limb to bring us that story. The sad reality is with today's media news cycle you will probably not hear it on "60 Minutes," or any other network television. There are many reasons for this which look plausible on the financial books of the networks. The truth is the "new financiers" now control the news we hear through intermediary outlets supplying news stations with the sound bites of a 24/7 news cycle. These sound bites dumb down the populace with constant stories of what Hollywood star did what, sprinkled with a hodgepodge of selected local, national and international news, basically telling us nothing of what is really going on in the world. The reason for this is because these intermediary outlets feed many news stations through organizations which are partially or wholly funded and paid for by today's socialistic financiers.[2]

Think back just ten or fifteen years ago to the in-house investigative journalism we watched. In today's media, instead of investigating both political parties, the "Big Three" media outlets only investigate conservatives. They substitute the investigation they should be doing with these intermediary outlets. Because of the money they are saving, it looks great on their financial books. Little of what you hear on TV news stations have conservative or non-socialistic news input. I have always found it odd the late night "comics" spend far less time making fun of socialist/progressive leaders/issues; but those espousing conservatism or Godly values are constantly ridiculed under the guise of comedy.[3]

This has gone from ridicule to attempted bankruptcy. Never was this more obvious than when a cable network host began uncovering the sinister connection a mogul-financier like George Soros and his network of minions had between the media networks and progressive politician/bureaucrats.[4] We are all in trouble when one insanely rich socialist and his buddy moguls can attempt to take down the prosperity and freedoms of an entire nation through political and financial influence. They haven't done this for honorable reasons, but because it makes them money, and they don't like our traditional and conservative foundations. Equally frightening is the continuity with which they function: Finding new progressive/democrat/socialist politicians, lawyers and foundations to keep up the "good work" of corrupting elections as well as our court systems.[5]

Unfortunately there was a template for them to follow in history. The "Soros era" has used the J.P. Morgan era's design of monetary influence in politics like a gambler addicted to sports betting. The sad reality is that today's progressive/socialist financiers make yesteryear's moguls look like infants crying for bottles.[6] Around the turn of the twentieth century you had two financial houses who joined in a war against each other. Called the J.P. Morgan era, it involved Morgan on one side and an alliance of Rockefeller, Harriman, Kuhn and Loeb on the other. The Morgan side started in investment banking and branched out into railroads, commercial banking and eventually manufacturing. The Rockefeller side was more diversified from the beginning with assets in oil, the railroad, investment banking as well as other investments.

These two sides began accruing politicians like children in another generation would collect marbles and baseball cards. Theodore Roosevelt was aligned to the Morgans and was used by them to attempt to break up the financial interests of Rockefeller, et al., through antitrust regulation.[7] Later President Taft was positioned by the Rockefeller side to break up Morgan-held trusts. It was when both sides joined to pass what we know as the Federal Reserve, supported by the progressive socialists, that the game became deadly. In November 1910 the groups held a secret meeting of top bankers at the Jekyll Island club in New York to frame the prototype of what eventually became the Federal Reserve Act.[8]

While this hidden agenda with the nation's money is playing out in quiet corners of the world, the surface game of politics is attempting to make heroes for the masses: Teddy Roosevelt, Woodrow Wilson, Howard Taft, down the lines of history to Franklin Delano Roosevelt, including White Houses of today. On history's surface, Theodore Roosevelt assumed office because of the assassination of President William McKinley. He represented what was at that time a little known faction of socialists called progressives. Their definition and connection to Fabian socialists has already been mentioned. What Theodore did initially was break up what he believed to be the offenders of what was then the industrial age. Known as "trust-busting," he went after the industrial engines of the country: railroads, coal, manufacturing industries who employed thousands. These held on to great accumulations of wealth and power. They had previously functioned with little regulatory restraints. Under Theodore, that would no longer be the case. Initially, many welcomed his moderate reforms. But it was becoming increasingly clear progressives wanted more. He wanted monetary policy as well as the tariff system changed, regulation of railroad rates, workmen's compensation, an income tax, the regulation of the stock market and the abolition of child labor. He supported what was then known as the Pure Food and Drugs Act (what we know as the FDA). Some of these ideas are common sense (stopping abusive child labor), but others would have disastrous results (income tax).

He won re-election, served his term and left office without implementing his plans. He supported the next Republican candidate, William Howard Taft (1908), but found him too conservative as president, and decided to run in 1912. The party did not support him and he won the nomination of the newly minted Progressive Party. As a third-party candidate, this split the republicans and gave the White House to the Democrat, Woodrow Wilson. While Theodore railed against Wilson as president, "oddly enough," it was Wilson who implemented many of Theodore's, as well as the progressive agenda. I put the previous in quotes because it's hard to know how much of what presidents enact is due to their belief system and how much is influenced by the "era of the moguls." It is not the purpose of this book to debate these historical issues, except as they affect covenant. Obviously today's socialist financiers are "going in for the kill." Their success will obliterate the covenant and destroy our republic.[9]

In reviewing Woodrow Wilson as our next pawn for progressives, we see an odd character indeed. He was what we would consider today a racist. Yet he supported women's suffrage and advocated child-labor law. It was his desire to remain neutral in foreign affairs which actually got America into World War I. Because of this, he increased the power of the presidency and sold that agenda by the power he used as a college professor: his oratory skills. It wasn't only his handling of problems abroad which caused America trouble. We can look back at some of his other domestic creations and now realize the dangers central banking causes: the Federal Reserve System and the Federal Trade Commission. To understand the problem with the Federal Reserve System one must understand, on a very basic level what it is. It is a central bank to the United States Government and it acts like a central bank to its commercial bank members (their numbers have been dramatically lowered since regulation from 2009 on). Much like the jerk-knee response we see concerning gun control when the mentally ill, terrorist or criminal deviant kill people, the Federal Reserve was used to hype up banking crises and institute a jerk-knee response in an all-out poker play for the nation's money.

Our founding fathers were very much opposed to a central bank like we see today in the Federal Reserve. On its face, it looks like a smart decision. It isn't until we realize it is a private organization— with public entity and quasi-Federal institutional largesse— which has never been audited, creating monetary policy for the nation. To realize the resistance our founding fathers had to a central bank, one has to look at the Federal Reserve. Many think Alexander Hamilton created a central bank.[10] Hamilton's bank was forbidden to buy government bonds. It had to have a mandatory rotation of directors and it could not issue notes nor incur debts beyond its actual capitalization. Hamilton did not envision a central authority who could easily print the money it desired, thus devaluing the dollar and playing with the supply of money and credit. Not only is that a problem, the Federal Reserve is run by unelected and unaccountable bureaucrats. In fact, my whole young life was spent with one chairman at the helm of the Federal Reserve. No "mandatory" rotation there!

As I noted, on its face it looks like an open market solution to keep the nation's money flowing and economy healthy. One chairman and vice-chairman as part of a seven-member board of governors, an advisory council, an open-market committee, twelve Federal Reserve banks and their 24 branches with, as of August 27, 2014, 6,638 institutional member banks; dividing the country into twelve districts serving a fixed region of the country. This is supposed to break up the power, thus avoiding centralization.[11] It is unusual in its makeup simply because our nation is unusual in its inception and its traditional hatred against central power, whether that be in government and/or banking (or a monarchy). While the quasi-federal, quasi-private institutional system sounds great, the numbers can be much less so, once one finally gets to see the real numbers—Which, by the way, has never been done! In 1970 the population of America was 205.1 million, and 5,869 commercial banks were members. That is one bank for every 34,946.3 individuals. The population in 2014 was 318.9 million. When we factor in today's bank numbers, that means one bank now services 48,041.6 individuals. The numbers are going in the wrong direction. We have less banks servicing the population, not more, thus moving power centrally (not branching it out). That's just in the last 45 years. Some might argue that is not a bad thing. Okay then; let's look at the health of our currency.

Since the Federal Reserve's inception in 1913 the dollar has lost over 95% of its value![12] As in many things, centralized governments can be quite inefficient in handling money. That wasn't always the case in our young republic, but more on that later. Who does this hurt the most? The poor and middle class. That's because they consume life-sustaining goods quicker, being the closest to their dollars due to lower disposable incomes than the rich. By controlling what is known as fiat money, the Federal Reserve can play with money values, credit, foreign exchange rates, etc. Fiat money is printed money. It is not based on a commodity like gold or another value like production or earnings. Like progressivism, it's pie in the sky. This kind of money system asks its citizens to trust it based on governmental decree. In other words, if the government has all the ability in the world to spend itself out of existence, it can do so. Many would say, "Well, that would never happen." If you read the previous paragraphs and endnotes, you have already seen the proof of financiers who would love to see America do just that. They are financing progressive candidates and socialist policy-making institutions who desire our demise rather than those whose politics do not espouse that doctrine. In fact, you have already read the proof (within endnotes) the media protects these moguls, so you will not be seeing that bit of fact on any network newscast. The analogy of a teenager with a limitless credit card has been applied to a government which prints its own money. The analogy is not wrong, but a teenager only ruins himself or her family paying the bill. In the case of a government, its citizens are on the hook.

Hard currency systems force governments to spend only what comes in from their citizens on a limited basis relative to the revenue raised from that country's economic health. This is why our credit rating as a nation has been downgraded in recent years. Since this system of credit and money control was implemented, we have seen far more boom-and-bust cycles than before it was created. That's because of the tinkering of the economy done by the Federal Reserve. For example, the Federal Reserve decides, for whatever reason, to artificially lower interest rates below the market rate. This increases the supply of money. This then sends the message to economic producers to borrow more or increase their production rates. But these investments usually lead to wasted capital and economic losses because they are based on false value. You cannot continually expand the credit because the longer you do so, the worse the bust will be. Now, a false boom needs to take place.

As previously mentioned, the Federal Reserve has never been subjected to Congressional oversight. It has never been audited. No one knows what's going on over there. We do have an idea though: The policies always hurt the poor and middle class, eroding the standard of living, while Hollywood, media moguls and financiers get richer. If you think I am railing against the rich, that simply is not so. I am not against anyone making a profit, including Hollywood. What I object to is when they collude with socialism, knowing full well the science that it is impossible for the poor or middle class to ever escape the captivity a progressive state will relegate them to. A true capitalist system, or a system based on biblical values has rules applying to all, not a secreted-away few or a group of well-connected political special interests.

While I am not a Constitutional expert, many feel the Federal Reserve is unconstitutional. Whether that is the case or not, a minuscule audit was done by the Government Accountability Office in 2011. The GAO was not allowed to view a good portion of the Fed's monetary policy or its transactions with foreign governments and banks. This minor audit revealed *$16 trillion* in secret bailouts to corporations and banks around the world in less than three years! I wonder how much of this corporate majority have progressive-socialistic politics/policies in their DNA.[13] This is true socialism, NOT capitalism at work. No one in the peoples' House (Congress) was ever given a chance to vote on these funds. Remember it is the House of Representatives who is given Constitutional authority to control the purse strings of the nation. But— and here is the kicker— when the government gets to print money when it deems fit, it gets to spend that money. Who is in charge of the spending? The buck stops with Congress.

So the policies of the Federal Reserve encourage a runaway Federal government to continue spending, even though it doesn't have the money to do so. This "secret" $16 trillion (in 2009-2011 funds, remember it was only a three-year audit) could have paid off the national debt at that time. Remember what I said before about the socialists blaming capitalism and requiring more rules to regulate the citizenry in an effort to "stop" the thieving? Actually, they cry out (using pawns) to "stop" the "injustice" of the well-connected "One Percenters" and those horrible religious people standing on principles of conscious and those standing on principles of science. What a joke! Remember when you stand on science or religion for the next generation, you are taking away the economic masses social-ism needs to control in order to remain in power.

It is socialism, not capitalism which hides money and bails out the selected few or chosen few. Capitalism says if you overspent or are inept in your business, you suffer, not the citizenry. Socialism bails out the "too big to fail." It is socialism not capitalism which ruins the monetary health of nations. Capitalism supports a full employment ratio and encourages thrift, work and something far more important: The ability for the system to help the truly less fortunate. Capitalism does not support the lazy nor the criminal. It is unequal in its application simply because many will work hard, others will receive opportunities because of that work and others will receive it because of the connections they make. Laws can be enacted to discourage true criminality, not sham bureaucratic regulations. It has been said socialism is the equal distribution of poverty. From our "science" experiment as a nation with socialism since 1913, the numbers prove that case.

It has also been said capitalism is the unequal distribution of wealth. There is truth in that as well. But socialism does not distribute wealth at all. Nations all across the world are becoming more and more socialis-tic. We can now see why economies worldwide are struggling. It is not because they are poor, but because socialism refuses to allow the people a leg up out of poverty. Electing those who understand the difference between a socialistic law and a law based on the fairness of freedom, liberty and a free market, will go a long way toward the health of our nation. Unfortunately, it is not always easy to figure out what a politi-cian's monetary policy is before they get elected. There are good political economists warning us this is a house of cards. There are even a few in the House of Representatives right now who want to help our country out of this mess. Auditing the Federal Reserve and stopping it from this sea-saw policy of runaway spending and exposing its slush funds will go a long way in bringing our nation back from the brink, economically. To be fair, it is not just Democrats who have encouraged this system, but Republicans as well.

When we have the benefit of history, we can see how progressive policies deeply harm our nation. Woodrow Wilson is viewed by many in the progressive/socialist camp as helping our nation. It was due to his influence that the League of Nations was born, precursor to the United Nations. The socialistic policies of the present United Nations and those same policies enacted here in the United States are being weaponized, removing the effects of our inalienable rights. By allowing a demand for the annihilation of Israel— a whole country of one religious minority— and by ignoring the rights of the religious the free exercise of religious beliefs, these "laws" become weapons. Wilson also enacted the Underwood Tariff Act, the Clayton Act (labor unions), the direct election of senators, instead of representation by the states (17th Amendment). This put the nail in the coffin of states' rights. By removing the decision of states to choose the senators, you consolidate power centrally in the Federal government and you remove the decision-making potential states have at the federal table. This amendment alone is proof of broken covenant. Wilson enacted prohibition (alcohol), women's suffrage, the income tax, (16th Amendment) along with the IRS.

Effects of socialism become even harder for many from a certain generation to realize when a president like Franklin Delano Roosevelt is involved. He came to power depicting his rival (President Herbert Hoover) as uncaring and insensitive to the economic crisis at the time (depression of 1929). He won by a landslide. Of course, few believed and even fewer understood how socialistic policies influenced that depression. FDR promised a New Deal for the "common" man, who by then was on soup kitchen lines. He began by instituting massive governmental programs. The first was the Works Progress Administration which became the Works Projects Administration and then the Civilian Conservation Corps. He also suspended antitrust legislation, encouraging labor unions and eliminating price competition through the National Industrial Recovery Act. He encouraged the process of farm subsidies by enacting the Agricultural Adjustment Act, Social Security and Unemployment Compensation.

By expanding the Federal government to unprecedented as well as dangerous levels, he was taken to court. The Supreme Court at that time invalidated many of his key measures. Roosevelt took a lesson from the history of emperors: He tried to stack the Supreme Court by appointing his own supportive new justices (thus expanding the number over nine justices). Thankfully, Congress voted that down. He enacted 3,723 executive orders, instituting many policies which hurt us economically. One such order made the ownership of gold bullion or gold certificates illegal.[14] This is the best protection the "common" man has to avoid the vagary of inflationary governmental monetary policy. Remember his early campaign promise? There are some still alive from that generation who cannot fathom how FDR's policies are harmful to our nation. It took time for Jackson's effects, Theodore Roosevelt's actions and Wilson's debacles to influence America. Many historians have proven Franklin Delano Roosevelt's socialistic policies actually prolonged the recessions which plagued America at that time.[15]

ENDNOTES

1   \<http://www.freerepublic.com/focus/f-news/1817411/posts>\<http://www.mrc.org/biasalerts/nets-ignored-clinton-firing-93-us-attorneys-fret-over-bushs-8-3142007> accessed 4/7/16 see the comments sections and see the next footnote, reading it through to the Clinton time line.

2   \<https://en.wikipedia.org/wiki/Media_Matters_for_America>\<http://www.infowars.com/media-matters-boss-admit-soros-funded-group-works-to-destroy-alternative-media/>\<http://eaglerising.com/20073/george-soros-media-matters-admits-breaking-law-and-consistently-violating-tax-exempt-status/> accessed 4/7/16

3   See video clips from 10/15/15 parody on a "Jimmy Kimmel Live" show as they clip together heavily edited words of an elderly TV minister, Pat Robertson. In stark contrast, the next day 10/16/15, this elderly minister interviewed Ron Lauder, chairman of the

World Jewish Congress concerning a possible new intifada and the under-reported genocide of Christians in the Middle East.

4   <http://www.discoverthenetworks.org/individualProfile.asp?indid=977><http://www.
zerohedge.com/news/2015-06-01/hacked-emails-expose-george-soros-ukraine-puppet-
master> The first site has traceable footnotes with a far more scholarly approach, while the
second purports to show a hacked email, but the provability question is hard to know. I
include it in this endnote section simply because they allege a very frightening connection
to our U.S. Treasury. After reading the first endnote, that is provable, you should judge for
yourself whether or not the second is possible, if not provable; accessed 4/7/16.

5   <http://thehill.com/policy/national-security/264542-liberal-billionaire-soros-regrets-
backing-obama><http://virginiahouse.gop/2015/06/11/speaker-howell-on-dpv-photo-
id-lawsuit/><http://www.nytimes.com/politics/first-draft/2015/06/05/bankroller-of-
democratic-voting-rights-cases-george-soros/> The second site, from Virginia's elected
republicans has a Quinnipiac survey showing overwhelming support from all voters for
their state's voter ID laws, so it can be easily argued the lawsuits are not being done to
"help" the voters; accessed 4/7/16.

6   See endnote #4 first reference; <http://www.foxnews.com/politics/2014/05/02/taking-
look-inside-secret-leftist-billionaires-club/> accessed 4/4/16. Compare endnote #4 with
the history sited on endnote #7.

7   Murray N. Rothbard. "A History of Money and Banking in the United States, The Colonial
Era to World War II" © 2002 by the Ludwig von Mises Institute, 518 West Magnolia
Avenue, Auburn, AL, 36849-5301; can also be heard at <https://www.youtube.com/
watch?v=Q8e-e9xtFWA&list=PL6D09BB9900764D5F> If this site changes, use
YouTube's search engine and several links will pop up. Can also be viewed in pdf form at
<https://mises.org> Click on the title and refer to the chapter beginning "From Hoover
to Roosevelt: The Federal Reserve and the Financial Elites," see 263-271; If this moves
as well, you can use their search engine and retrieve the noted source; accessed 4/7/16.

8   Ibid., 264

9   Here are 45 goals uncovered by a Mrs. Patricia Nordman of DeLand, FL, in 1963, and read
into the Congressional Record, Appendix, pp. A-34, A-35 from January 10, 1963, the 88th
Congress, 1st Session. It may be seen at this © site <http://www.uhuh.com/nwo/com-
munism/comgoals.htm> accessed 4/7/16 © 1996 by Forest Glen Durland. After reading
the goals and remembering or viewing our history, it is truly frightening how close we are
to the edge of total capitulation to communism, though very few understand how or why.

10   Carson Holoway. March 18, 2016. "The National Bank: An Early Lesson in Constitutional Fidelity" Accessed through "Public Discourse." The Witherspoon Institute. <http://www.thepublicdiscourse.com/2016/03/16467/> accessed 4/9/16

11   <https://en.wikipedia.org/wiki/Federal_Deposit_Insurance_Corporation> accessed 4/7/16

12   <http://blogs.wsj.com/wallet/2009/01/28/the-buying-power-of-a-dollar-on-a-down-swing/> accessed 4/7/16; this address moves frequently, but you can use their search engine if it has done so again.

13   <http://blogs.wsj.com/economics/2009/08/31/what-would-a-federal-reserve-audit-show> this address moves frequently, but you can use their search engine if it has done so again.<http://www.businessinsider.com/feds-16-trillion-dollar-secret-slush-fund-props-up-our-way-of-life-2011-7#ixzz1hgHQxuwi> accessed 4/7/16

14   <http://www.forbes.com/sites/jimpowell/2014/01/30/how-president-obama-could-be-swept-away-with-his-executive-orders-that-defy-congress-and-the-courts/> accessed 4/7/16

15   <https://mises.org/library/how-fdr-made-depression-worse><http://newsroom.ucla.edu/releases/FDR-s-Policies-Prolonged-Depression-5409> accessed 4/7/16. The following reference is unabashedly political. There are several excellent links to research material that will help anyone who does not believe socialism is a problem, come to some kind of an educated decision, without taking an economics course. <https://startthinkingright.wordpress.com/2011/08/11/fdrs-economic-policies-failed-but-dont-take-my-word-for-it-listen-to-obamas-top-economic-adviser/> accessed 4/7/16. Some of the links in the article by that time were out of date. See also Note 8 from this section to view how close we are to going over the cliff of progressivism into communism.

Chapter Thirteen

ARE THERE SOLUTIONS?
(ECONOMIC)

Once folks look at the history, many come away with a question. How are we going to pay for our government and military if we do not raise taxes? Since I was not around before taxes and before a great many of these socialistic programs, I had no idea how our government could operate without them. Therein lies the problem as well as the lie: None of us know a time before the income tax, levies, regulations and a federal bureaucratic police state. The lie is in the fact we all believe we *need* these to pay for everything. In doing this research I discovered there is another way: Look at the practices before all these situations, laws and regulations took place.

Between the Civil War and before the socialistic policies of 1913 were enacted, America experienced an even greater explosion of economic wealth than she had before the Civil War.[1] That wealth was unequally distributed wealth (through capitalism). The difference between that and distributed poverty (through socialism) is revealed in the numbers. All economies have what I call panic periods. But they recover far quicker under a system functioning with natural science, like a capitalistic model rather than with a system like progressive socialism, which does not. After the panic of 1873, a quick recovery was made as a result of "hard" monetary policies and industrialization. In other words, we made stuff and only spent what we made.

From 1869 to 1879, the economy grew at a 6.8% rate of real GDP and 4.5% for real GDP per capita and that's even with the panic of 1873. The economy repeated this same period of growth during the 1880s. The nation saw its wealth grow at an annual rate of 3.8%. Here's the kicker: the GDP doubled![2] Then the income tax was enacted in 1913. By now we pay almost 30% of our incomes to the Federal government, not including all the other taxes we pay. Americans work from January 1st, to April 24th to pay the government.[3] In 1900, just before mandatory income tax was implemented, the date was January 22nd and some folks fell under various thresholds and paid no tax before mandatory income tax. Just think about your wealth. Since 2009 has it grown 4.5% or even 3.8%? Imagine keeping the money you give to the government or imagine keeping the money the government wastes in giving your money to someone else. From 22 days to pay your taxes, it now takes you almost four months.

So the question becomes how did the government fund itself prior to the 16th Amendment (the income tax amendment)? First, the government was not bloated and only maintained those duties the Constitution called for. In fact, the job of our elected officials originally was part-time, not live in Washington 24/7. Outside of war time needs, the federal system was financed by import taxes, also known as tariffs. This is the income the progressives blocked. There were no Welfare, Social Security, Medicare or agricultural subsidies. Taxes were excised on alcohol, tobacco and inheritances— yes, the rich paid for their wealth. When additional revenue was needed, as in a time of war, a direct tax method was temporarily instituted. These methods produced budget surpluses on a consistent level and to such an extent as to almost entirely paying off the national debt on a regular basis during that time period.[4]

In point of fact, the federal government rarely needed our money. When debating the 16th Amendment, this is what Massachusetts Rep. Samuel McCall said:

"The character of the argument which has been made, ...leads me to believe that the chief purpose of the tax is not the financial, but social. It is not primarily to raise money for the state, but to regulate the citizen and regenerate the moral nature of man. The individual citizen will be called on to lay bare the inner-most recesses of his soul in affidavits, and with the aid of the Federal inspector, who will supervise his books and papers and business secrets, he may be made to be good, according the notions of virtue at the moment prevailing in Washington."[5]

Think of what all the paper work does to our lives or hiring of professionals costs us to get our taxes done, and what Washington now considers *good* and it is obvious the congressman was right. Direct taxation is imposed on people and property, but indirect tax is imposed on things or events like retail sales, import and exports. The promise back then was that income tax would remain low. Remember when progressives/socialists are voted in, taxes will never remain low. In 1913, the tax was 1% on incomes above $3,000 and between 2% and 7% on incomes from $20,000 to $500,000.[6] Since our dollar has been devalued 95% since this period of time, just by doing the math, it means in real valued pre-1913 dollars today, if we assume a 2% tax rate, those making $50,000 should pay $50 in taxes! Imagine that as a reality. . . AND you wouldn't have to hire an accountant!

We already pay indirect taxes on top of our already bloated income tax. Remember what the definition of indirect tax is, and then look at this list. Granted, a portion or possibly all of these funds may go to your local and state governments. You will find if you are an adult, living/owning a residence, with a vehicle, a phone and a job, you will have paid some or all of these taxes:

Vehicle Registration tax, utility taxes, worker's compensation taxes, tolls, traffic fines, tire taxes and other repair tax additions for oil recycling, etc. Telephone state and local taxes, telephone minimum usage surcharges, telephone Federal Universal Service fees, telephone Federal Excise tax. New A.C.A. (a.k.a ObamaCare) tanning tax, A.C.A. Individual Mandate

Excise Tax, A.C.A. Surtax on Investment Income (this is a new 3.8% surtax on investment income, if you have investments) and A.C.A. Medicare Tax surcharges on high earners. State unemployment tax, Social Security taxes. The following five items apply if you own your own property: Septic permit taxes, property taxes, school taxes, fire department surcharge rates, building permit taxes and various service charge taxes. If you own your own business: Self-employment taxes, as well as other Federal government taxes because businesses pay part of their workers' social security, etc. Various and many sales taxes, recreational vehicle taxes (if you own one). Medicare taxes, marriage license taxes (if you are married). Luxury taxes (if you bought an item considered so), liquor taxes (if you drink the stuff) and inventory taxes. The next three items apply if you participated in such: Inheritance taxes, gift taxes, hunting license taxes; gasoline taxes, food license taxes, fishing license taxes (if you fish), drivers license fees, Federal Unemployment taxes. IRS interest charges and IRS penalties, if you don't pay your taxes, or God forbid, you make a mistake on your taxes. These last taxes are if you participate in them: Court fines, cigarette taxes and capital gains taxes.[7] I know I have missed some.

The reality is the Federal, as well as many state governments, are in desperate need of gastric by-pass surgery. We, the American people, must be the surgeons! We can easily remove the Department of Education because since its inception our children are scored worse, not better. Look at this number: Canada ranks in the top third of countries in the world for science and fourth for math and that country has absolutely no centralized or federalized department for education.[8] All of its education is as ours formerly was, local (see endnote for possible changes). Allow the states to do the job they did before, and allow the private schools to do the job of excellence they have always done. For students unable to afford private schools, have a lottery program based on rewards or a vouchers program, starting with kindergarten! Parents too busy or lazy to get their kids a voucher or enter them in some kind of merit system can still go to localized education. I grew up in public schools before the Feds roughshod over them. I remember that system was moral and based on excellence. It can be that again. In today's system, the local schools must conduct learning according to Federal regulations. We know now that the system is broken. We can thank a Democrat/progressive/socialist (Jimmy Carter) for it by creating the Department of Education. Get rid of the monster and kids will be free from fear as they learn. You can pretty much unload several other departments freeing up our money.

My point is there has to be a massive de-centralization program put in place which cuts out whole departments and views federal jobs with an axe, not a scalpel. Once several departments/agencies are nixed (commerce, energy, education, environmental protection, to name a few), the scalpel can be implemented to root out regulations that need to go. The multitude of various regulations, and a corporate environment involving more federal socialistic policies has changed corporate profits in a myriad of ways, and not always for the better.[9] The first problem is with our tax code, as it taxes regular corporations twice; once for their profits and then again as profits are passed to its shareholders. In today's climate we also have many corporations leaving our shores. This is because they find a much more favorable tax model overseas.

If we implemented a tax similar to when we first started this mess, and made a period of time of amnesty for corporations to bring money back to the U.S., you would see job creation. Next, get rid of the IRS, and implement a drastically reduced line item tax deduction. This opens the spigot for money to flow again. The IRS spends $2.45 for every $100 it collects in taxes.[10] By substantially reducing the tax rate and reducing deductions, you eliminate much of any department you might create to run returns through it. You increase revenue and bring money back to our country, and generate more money. I am no genius. Others have proposed these ideas and Ronald Reagan implemented some of them. Even if we went back to the laws for welfare and disability Bill Clinton allowed, millions who should not be on welfare or disability would become productive by going to work.

Next go after the big regulatory problems: A.C.A. (a.k.a ObamaCare), replacing it with the system we had before, only one that regulates the insurance companies, not the citizens. Most folks do not realize that A.C.A. does not benefit them or their doctors, but benefits the insurance companies. That is how they got them to go along with it. Any new system should allow insurance companies the ability to compete all across the country, thereby keeping their numbers of customers up by making it cheaper and friendlier for people to want insurance. As it stands now, the system is so regulated that insureds really do not get the best care. Instead, we are paying *more* for our insurance— substantially more— and there are even more and varied regulatory nightmares awaiting citizens in the future.

The president that signed the cruel pit called ObamaCare into law postponed much of its more egregious rules until *after* he left office. In a system making insurance companies compete for customers, the best insurance companies will have more insureds. This is true capitalism. The new system would also remove the horrendous penalties for pre-existing diseases and allow children to remain on their parents policies for the already determined ages we have in place. It should be understood if you engage in dangerous practices like smoking or sky diving, your policy would cost more than those who do not. This also reflects personal responsibility which does not give a free ride to the reckless. ObamaCare robbed Medicare of $700 billion. It should be paid back. Work can begin with the best ideas among the states for Medicaid systems.

Social Security has been gutted by our politicians for years. The Federal government has to pay back its "loan" taken out on the backs of the elderly. The bleed has to stop and the system has to be changed to reflect those who can afford to forego the ride. Warren Buffet and Bill Gates do not need their Social Security benefits. Even though someone has paid in, we should have a cut-off rule in place. If someone has retirement income over $100,000 and/or property and financial trusts totaling more than, let's say $750,000, they do not need Social Security. Likewise, the age limit should be raised to reflect the fact Americans are living longer and healthier lives and can afford to work longer. Not all can, but disability safety nets would still be in place to help them.

Dodd-Frank and Sarbanes-Oxley are also regulatory nightmares we should remove and replace. A compromise could be reached repealing the estimated 400 regulations incurred by Dodd-Frank which kill jobs, while keeping some of the 2002 regulations for Sarbanes-Oxley in place which protected whistleblowers. If you think Dodd-Frank would have stopped the 2008 economic nightmare, think again. It has done nothing but kill jobs and make banks much bigger than they were before.[11] There are economists out there that have proposals to help.[12]

If we keep some aspect of the Federal Reserve, it has to start working FOR America, not for itself. The first reform should be in an audit. There are other reforms needing to take place with that behemoth as well. All of this can be done without foregoing military readiness, cyber security for our infrastructure (which, by the way we do not have), as well as other protections many approve of, even though their effectiveness is questionable (I think of the CDC, FAA, FDA, etc). This would also free up money and revenue to create an electric grid which can stand up to cyber as well as EMP attacks.

After taking the scalpel through these systems, Homeland Security should be modified and substantially changed to be made efficient. It is worse than a behemoth. It employs over 240,000 federal workers and contains 16 departments which were originally 22 federal departments in 2002 at its inception.[13] If you looked at a chart of the bureaucracy, you would understand why it is a department with the lowest morale among its workers.[14] Like the A.C.A., socialists have made it a maze of inefficiency. We cannot allow socialists to make any of these changes because they will only corrupt the system again. It was a republican (George W. Bush) who created it after 9/11/01, in an attempt to get these departments talking to one another so another attack of that magnitude could be averted. That desire can still take place by having many of the critical departments report to one clearing house like DOJ while others can work within the Pentagon and still others within another cabinet department. Then keep a truly non-partisan clearing house along the lines of a GAO which looks at the data and gives the reporting to an office inside the Administration. I'm not sure that would allow for a harmonious working environment or maintain the efficiency necessary, but I'm sure there are other solid proposals to make this work.

All these proposals are not new ideas. They are just ideas which meet with the buzz saw of democrat/progressives who get elected and decide to sap more and more from our economic, political and social freedoms. We also need to reform how lawyers are taught. Just because foreign law sounds nice, does not mean we should implement it or allow its inception here. In fact, throughout this book I have shown the difference between our initial laws and the laws we see lawyers who are taught socialistic legal thought make. The root problem is that socialists needed to change Constitutional legal thought, removing its moorings from moral boundaries like the Bible. So what did they do? They said the Constitution was a "living" document, like the Bible. That idea is alien to the document. What thought was formerly in place? The idea was that the Constitution was to be updated by its slower amendment process so as to be brought in line with the ideas of freedom it was originally written with. That would mean most of what has passed as regulatory law today would be thrown out. Next, the idea of compact/covenant and the true history of the three documents we hold as dear would be followed. This helps us understand inalienable rights as rights we never give up. That means man-made rights may not trump religious rights. That also means we get back our Tenth Amendment rights, because as of now, we have lost them.

Getting our government off its addictive behavior by repealing the 16th Amendment, instituting a balanced budget Amendment and retrieving our money from the Federal Reserve will all help. Since we are in a terrorist age, we need to maintain some kind of wartime direct tax, unfortunately. Until we are ready to have a real, and truthful discussion concerning the ideology of a religion/foreign government with foreign law (sharia), which purports peace but follows war and subjugation, we will always need a wartime tax. This is an expense we could easily avoid, but not until we are ready to work with the actual reformers who wish to abolish all violence from their own ranks. That means getting rid of CAIR and the Muslim Brotherhood.

We need to root out the professors in our colleges who teach and promote socialism and/or foreign ideologies. It is beneficial to learn about such things, but unproductive to bully young minds into submissive adherence to their tenets. This does not need to be a witch hunt, just a re-education program: Teaching the teachers how hideous social-ism really is. My fellow covenant citizens, we cannot continue to elect this foreign ideology. Socialism, along with sharia law, as well as other foreign laws are foreign. When newly naturalized citizens take the oath to become Americans they make a covenant to defend our Constitution against enemies foreign and domestic. Well, the foreign laws associated with socialistic thought have most certainly become domestic. They must be exposed for what they are and removed. It must start on a local level. It can transfer to state and national levels once the progressives realize they cannot win. Both Republicans as well as Democrats like to be elected. Once they realize that the populace will vote them out if they continue to create a socialistic state, they will change their tune.

We should uncover financier-moguls who are implementing and buying socialistic reforms. Socialism needs to be exposed as treasonous. A major campaign needs to be enacted letting the public know how dangerous socialism is. We, as a people have to stop buying into Hollywood and the lies the media spouts. Hollywood must be made to realize that filth is not good food for healthy minds. I hope in future texts to bring the science to you concerning many of these truths. For now, we must all realize the need to turn off the nightly news, or at least get our news from a news source which proves to bring us all sides of a story.

The majority of Christians, who claim such in this country, must vote the Bible and stop voting for foreign ideologies which have proven disastrous for all. Helping people for a moment of time in which life has gone very bad is a Christian model to follow. That does not mean they get help for a lifetime. We know the Bible supports benevolence on an as-needed basis, not on an as-I-want basis. The elderly indigent and infirm, either mentally or physically do need help. Those temporarily and suddenly unemployed need temporary help; not two years worth! Those truly disabled through mental deficits or physical inability should be helped as long as their dis-abilities handicap them. The science proves why children need gendered male and female adoptive parents. Although, I have mentioned those exceptions where only one family member is left to care for them. In many cases, they are best left with family. They should not be placed in a system which has a great potential to wound them. It actually costs us more when we neglect the important care of our needy children. If government regulations will get out of the way of harming charitable organizations with a proven track record of sustaining the lives of these children, that alone will save this nation billions. Savings in prison expenses, medical expenses and lost productivity due to damaged adults who were children growing up in systems of sterilized socialist bureaucracy can be realized when we allow honorable charities to work.

Education is a privilege and all of us should create an environment for learning. The church was formerly one of the great engines for education. It can be again. Credit can be a blessing, but no nation should be allowed to spend more than it makes or allowed to borrow more than the growth of its GDP. State governments must balance their budgets. Households must balance their budgets. It is time the Federal government enacts legislation to balance its budget. We, the people must force them to do so. Citizens also need to come off their credit addictions and start learning how to save again. Do you really think the media shows you how movie stars live for *your* benefit? No folks, it's so you want the newest and flashiest car, clothes, trinket and gadgetry. It's to make you feel bad about yourself, and "Oh, gee, buying this *whatever*, will make you feel better."

If the press will not shout out the real truth, then I suggest those covenant citizens from religious as well as atheistic backgrounds begin to organize and protest, peacefully. We should form on local and statewide levels to do just that— and do it regularly— all in an effort to specifically root out all the tendrils a monster like socialism has birthed. I understand many in the Tea Party have done this. They are a political movement which began as grassroots. That is not my goal here. If others wish to organize that way, I applaud them as well as the Libertarian and Tea Party groups. What I believe we need is organization on an economic level with political effect as a social outreach. The black churches can organize this because they have experience in this method. It is time as the religious, atheists and the agnostics we got together to save our country. If we cannot work together to do this, then when will we be able to work together? Boycotts of socialistic companies, especially those who preach the message should be used. When these corporations threaten states for maintaining their citizens' religious freedoms, then class action lawsuits by the citizens of that state against the threats might be the only way to stop being bullied. Lawyers will have to be enlisted to work through the necessary steps in legal action. It's amazing how the "Occupy" groups don't scream when these big corporations are actually bullying the citizens of a state with the loss of their safety and religious liberties. The media conglomerates who own and have a hand in everyday commercial enterprises which make products we all use should be listed and their products and other company outreaches shunned when they attempt to bully us. Obviously, this section is not all encompassing, nor can it be. One person, one author, one idea cannot be an island. We need the ideas and solutions from all covenant citizens with the same goals of restoring our governing compact.

ENDNOTES

1   <http://www.zerohedge.com/news/2013-04-15/100-years-old-still-killing-us-america-was-much-better-income-tax> I do not include the comments section; it is up to you whether you view that as well as those links as helpful; accessed 4/9/16.

2   <https://en.wikipedia.org/wiki/Economic_history_of_the_United_States> See under "Late 19th century" see also "Gilded Age," accessed 4/9/16.

3   <http://taxfoundation.org/article/tax-freedom-day-2015-april-24> accessed 4/9/16

4   <http://www.thenewamerican.com/culture/history/item/14268-before-the-income-tax> accessed 4/9/16

5   Evans, Lawrence, B., 1916, *Samuel W. McCall, Governor of Massachusetts*, Boston and New York: Houghton Mifflin Company, 97 & 98

6   <http://www.zerohedge.com/news/2013-04-15/100-years-old-still-killing-us-america-was-much-better-income-tax> I do not include the comments section; it is up to you whether you view that as well as the links as helpful; accessed 4/9/16.

7   Ibid. I do not include the comments section; it is up to you whether you view that as well as those links as helpful.

8   <http://www.pewresearch.org/fact-tank/2015/02/02/u-s-students-improving-slowly-in-math-and-science-but-still-lagging-internationally/> accessed 4/9/16. There was a recent election in Canada in which they elected a socialist, so it won't be long before Canadian education will probably change.

9   <http://www.factcheck.org/2016/02/sanders-corporate-tax-comparison/> accessed 4/9/16. They use a comment the socialistic candidate for president in 2016 made. Not specifically said, but in a roundabout way, are all the various socialistic programs enacted and taken in direct taxes to corporations, which have played a role in the loss of profits.

10   <http://archive.9news.com/money/taxes/29093/301/Random-facts-about-taxes-to-ease-what-may-be-a-painful-day> accessed 4/9/16

11   <http://www.breitbart.com/video/2015/07/18/hensarling-repeal-dodd-frank/> accessed 4/9/16

12   Ibid.

13   <http://www.dhs.gov/about-dhs>and<http://www.dhs.gov/components-directorates-and-offices> accessed 4/9/16

14   <https://www.dhs.gov/sites/default/files/publications/Department%20Org%20Chart.pdf>and<http://www.downsizinggovernment.org/dhs/spending-cuts> accessed 4/9/16

Chapter Fourteen

SPIRITUAL SOLUTIONS

This leads me to the next category in our solutions' section. The church has great weapons during times like these. The first is prayer. Targeted prayer geared at the socialistic engines of the society as outlined in this work, and as the Lord leads is crucial. Targeting the spiritual forces behind them for capture by the angelic forces will go a long way in removing this demonic force from our midst. The next weapon is forgiveness. Many make forgiveness out to be weakness. Like grace, many have ignored the biblical definition of both. Grace is Divine enablement to do all the Lord commands us to do. If you think grace is some sloppy gift to absolve repeated sin, then your definition has to change. Grace is a strong and targeted weapon in the hands of a believer. Think about forgiving someone who has done horrible things to you. It is not easy, not easy at all. It is impossible as humans to do. Yet I have seen folks exercise this choice under conditions which defy human logic. I am not espousing lack of self defense here, or an attempt to negate the death penalty. As a society we must have consequences for criminal activity.

The choice to forgive entails much from the throne of God by way of grace. The gift of grace gives Christians the ability to forgive when human nature would surely rather kill. Forgiveness releases the accusatory spiritual forces holding this nation hostage. Prayer targets those spiritual forces for capture, to angelic authority in the heavens. Prayer releases humans and human entities involved in socialism, opening blinded eyes and deafened ears to the freedom this nation once espoused. Along with the fact those freedoms are based on rights our Creator gives us (inalienable rights). We are born with those rights. Prayer also looses the eyes and ears of fellow covenant citizens to see and hear the solutions necessary to bring our nation back from the abyss.

There is another weapon all humans have the potential to enact: Repentance. Like prayer and forgiveness, repentance releases ungodly spiritual forces off from us, opening the flow of God's blessings to us. Again, this third weapon is a choice. It is a spiritual choice with earthly consequences. As Christians, once we realize our pride or stubbornness in espousing all forms of socialism, we can repent and be renewed by the power of the Holy Spirit. These are three spiritual choices for the Christian, but others can surely participate, if they choose. Implementation on a wider scale can make our nation great again. They can also enact social change which does no harm to the religious or the atheist (and all folks in between).

The next solution is action (2 Corinthians 10:5). I place it in this section of spiritual solutions because it has two fronts. One is spiritual. The other is not. Consistently throughout my time in writing and receiving this word I keep thinking of Esther. We all know the story found in the book of the Bible by her name. God's people were getting ready to be slaughtered in their homes when word came to the Jewess, queen in a foreign land, that she was placed in her position for "such a time as this." If you are in a position in government or other place of authority and you can preach or give access to those who can, or you can encourage God's people or give access to those who can, YOU HAVE BEEN PLACED THERE FOR A REASON. Your country needs you.

If you are a Christian, it is time to act. I don't understand how it is we can be silent to those around us concerning what God has done in our lives. The Bible makes it clear: Go into all the world and preach, make disciples, pray for the sick and cast out demons (Matthew 28). Your pastor cannot do this alone. Each one of us who claims Christ must do this. If each believer would see only one other person saved every year, we could see this country saved in less than ten years or as quick as five. The time scale depends upon what study you believe accurately relates how many true Bible-believing Christians there are in America. If you do not have the capability to disciple that individual, then send them to a congregation who does, and get them a Bible. We should be witnessing to many, many people in a year and sowing much seed. This way one can sow and another can water and another can reap (1 Corinthians 3:5-9).

Here is a hard truth many Christians find difficult to believe. You can have revival after revival and great moves of God. Thankfully, many thousands of people can be saved at that point. Each one of us must live in the presence of God each day. I did not go into all the historical moves of God this nation has been blessed with. But those moves tend to lose their effects after a number of years. What is the only thing which can keep them going (on the human side)? Discipleship; and it cannot be any easy-going, whenever-you-want discipleship. We must not only disciple based on biblical teaching, we must also disciple based on government. The pastors in the pulpits before the Revolutionary War taught the people biblical worldview, law and politics and how it affected economies and governments within nations. I didn't include the thousands of those sermons which have survived. This idea that we are not allowed to preach political theory is a lie. We must preach biblical political, economic and social theory. We (if you are a leader in a church) must make our people understand how these ideas relate to everyday lives and how they relate to science. As a pastor if you are not able to do that, then call in people who can or get the teaching material to help you do that. You cannot sit this one out in the hopes it will go away, or someone else will do the work. If you are not a pastor or church leader, but you have a gift in relating this information, then do so. Start a Bible study on these matters where you live or work or in some other venue the Lord opens to you.

I referenced 2 Corinthians 10:5. We have national strongholds in this nation. They are ideas and knowledge which *seem* so perfect, but are total lies. We, in the church, have stronghold ideas and beliefs which have nothing to do with the truth of the Bible. We have to repent of these things. We need to go to the Lord and find out where we have missed the mark in not functioning as He would have us do. I realize I mentioned repentance, but sometimes our actions are not "smoking and chewing and going with those who are doing." Sometimes our actions are as simple as refusing to talk about Jesus or share the true biblical foundations of our nation. We don't all have to be great heroes of the faith to faithfully share Jesus with someone.

We have other ideas which are inaccurate as well. Sometimes we want to make every person from yesteryear out to be an "on-fire Holy Ghost" revivalist. That simply was not so. I have shared where economics was front and center in an underlying action for American Revolution. Sometimes we want to ignore the spiritual climate and actions of the foundations of America and review only politics and economics. We have all sorts of ideas not connected to reality which try to make the religious look ignorant of our foundational traditions. By totally ignoring the spiritual ideas and actions of our early republic, we miss the true flavor and nuances as to why we are not Europe. We can fail to see how unique America really is. Her uniqueness is directly related to her religious heritage.

By refusing to reach out (on a secular) level with fellow religious Americans, the non-believing are literally refusing America. Let's make the most obvious observation that can be made: Neither the religious or the atheist are going anywhere. There will always be the faithful and there will always be the atheist and there will be people in between for as long as any of us will live. If we think America should go forward without the religious, you will miss the aspects of why America moves in excellence. You will miss why she has been blessed. Even if you renounce belief in a God, just by being the people who reach out in reason and forgiveness to your fellow citizen, makes America easier to live in.

I have proof for those of you who disagree. Remember when a very confused young man with racist and criminal action walked into a church in South Carolina and murdered many lovely Christians? The media descended. Being a predominantly black church, the race baiters showed up as well. The victims' family members reached out in forgiveness, and the leadership refused to allow the race baiters their pulpit. They did not allow their community to become a Ferguson, MO, or a Detroit.[1] While not denying the horrific and hideous nature of what this church experienced, regardless of the race of those who attend is, their one act and choice to forgive helped the entire nation overcome what could have been a community with gutted and burned out buildings. These acts of forgiveness helped the rest of the nation to experience a spiritual environment of peace, regardless of what human emotions felt. Regardless of one's religious beliefs, we can all be thankful to these Christians for their actions of forgiveness. It is a lesson to all Americans of the potential for healing and deliverance that a nation can see.

I have heard the criticisms what I am suggesting is what got our nation into trouble to begin with: Collaboration with sinners or some multiple faith gathering, where nothing gets done. I am not suggesting that at all. What got our nation into trouble in the first place was a spiritual environment which refused the full counsel of God. When Jesus came to earth, to His very own, the religious believers could not stomach His refusal to ignore sinners. They condemned His actions of healing on the Sabbath and His refusal of what they had done with the Temple money exchange system. I am suggesting that we, as Christians, accept the full counsel of God. If you never speak to atheists, agnostics or those of other faiths, how will you share the gospel of Jesus Christ? It is because the churches have refused the full counsel of God in evangelism, preaching and practicing the fullness of the gospel and all that entails that we have gotten into the mess we have.

I will never agree to a covenant which refuses my ability to share the gospel of Jesus Christ in every situation the Lord sends me to. Our forefathers did not either. We need to hold services outside of the four walls of our churches. In recent years I have not been able to spend the time I formerly did in street ministry. So as a church, we make sure funds get into the hands of those who do. Radio, television, Internet and social media are all tools enhancing and promoting the street ministry aspect of sharing the gospel. All of these reach people where they live. But unless you actually take it to the streets, those avenues alone are not going to see the solutions we need to see for this nation to be made whole. The presence of God is not limited to the four walls of a church, nor can He be.

Every time you try, He decides to break the bonds humans put Him in, thankfully. We desperately need revival— even a great spiritual awakening— and I believe we will see them. *As we do, we must stress discipleship along with its teaching (like Wesley did) or we will lose the gains made through revival.*

ENDNOTES

1   <https://www.washingtonpost.com/news/post-nation/wp/2015/06/19/i-forgive-you-relatives-of-charleston-church-victims-address-dylann-roof/> accessed 4/9/16

Chapter Fifteen

SOCIAL SOLUTIONS

This brings me to the last solution in this "sandwich" of solution choices. It may be the most difficult for atheists and other forms of faith to agree to. It is the understanding that the right to religious freedom is the first right because it is the most important right. If rights which are given by man are the most important, or if government and others mouth an acquiescence religious inalienable rights are okay to believe in, but better kept in a house of worship, or personally held, never to be mentioned, then you are one step away from communism. This is because communists, socialists and progressives all have a commonly held belief that *'belief'* is not something you are born with and it is not that important. I hope I have, to some extent proven the lie and problems with that thinking. The first problem is somehow inalienable rights are debatable and can be rearranged to suit government's purposes. Governments which do that are tyrannical and no different whether they use the barrel of a gun or the pointed dagger of a regulation.

The second problem with that kind of thinking is it purposely, or more particularly has a purpose in denying the existence of the United States of America. The inalienable right to freedom of religion undergirds the very origin and existence of America.[1] The third problem with an ideology which tries to assume religious belief is equal to or not as important as other rights is that once you divorce the right to serve the Creator as He mandates, you convey that right to government. Government then becomes god. This is exactly what Christians for centuries fought against in the monarchy, and one of the reasons why America was founded. The fourth problem with this thinking is it makes government the master. Our system is foundational to the ideology the people are **sovereign** and government is to serve the people.

In point of fact, the Bible does mention such a system in which a government makes itself out to be god. It is found in the book of Revelation. This system does not allow anyone to buy or sell if they refuse to take the "mark" of what the book calls "the beast." If you do decide to read it, or you have read it, you know what goes on in the earth because of the effects of that government is not pretty. The problems described on the earth at that time are the direct result of this kind or form of government gaining worldwide dominion. This is why adhering to progressivism/socialism or communism is so hideous for Christians. Nevertheless, atheists should be forewarned: The book lets us know it doesn't matter you don't believe in a god, you also will be forced to worship the leader this future government demands you worship.

Even if you don't believe the book I have sourced here (the Bible), the idea of government forcing its citizens to "worship" at its feet with its money, work and families is not something we are that far away from. We already work until April 24th to support this monstrosity we call government. It now demands you send your kids to be brainwashed— unless you fight for your right to homeschool— but there are few degrees for those home-schooled through college. Try and get a job based on your "home school" degree. Just try to decide not to pay a fee or tax of some kind and let's just see what jail you get thrown into. Even if you own your own home free and clear with no mortgage, try NOT paying your property taxes, and see how long it will take for them to put a lien against the property, eventually selling it right out from under you. Let's say you own your own car outright with no lease or car payment. What would happen if you drive on the road with no title, tag or license? You will be thrown in jail. If for some reason you get a sympathetic cop and he just rights you tickets worth, probably thousands of dollars in fees, try not paying them. A warrant will be issued for your arrest.

I realize many of the economic reforms I examined cut the weeds of socialism, but leave many roots in tact. That is the nature of the social discussion. To go further in rooting this cancer from among our Constitutional compact, we need to have a discussion as a nation. Furthermore, the mainstream press has proven incapable as a healthy platform for this discussion. They will not only present the debate in the most deceptive manner socialism fosters, but they will continue to make caricature fun of anyone espousing capitalism, conservatism or the original principles laid down by our inalienable rights, especially for religious conscientious practice. This is done in an attempt to win the debate before it even takes place.

Socialism is truly racist. It promotes a homogeneity. It does this almost by default. Its first goal is to create chaos. It does this by dividing and conquering. If religious divisions make up a country it works to cause dissension in those areas. Other forms of tyranny do this as well. These forms of government must separate the population in order to control them. If a diverse racial mix makes up a group, it must use those differences to create the needed effect. Christianity, Judaism and other peaceful religions will most often resist this effort. Unfortunately, not every Christian or other religious group can see the sneak attack. When voices of reason and logic expose what is going on, the endeavor to control becomes unsuccessful. Even if cooler heads prevail, socialists will call *them* racist, uncaring, archaic, even homophobic. All of these monikers are an effort to hide the true nature of what is going on.

In those countries where there are no major differences within populations, (old Europe) dissimilarity must be attained in order to create the necessary chaos. A look inside the recent refugee crises is a clear example. Many wondered why the American president (2009-2017) did nothing to stop the destruction of the neighborhoods where these refugees came from (Syria, Iraq and other areas). His reasons were touted in many news feeds, although not quite clearly, since it made no sense why he wouldn't help. As millions and millions fled the war-torn areas, the resultant refugee crisis could not be overlooked. After all, such a "wise" man should have known better. Many disregarded his progressive/socialist reasoning as a cause.[2]

Progressivism/socialism bases its outcome on situational ethics. This affects us in how we spend our money and how we choose a mate. It affects what we put into our bodies as well as how to make our families stronger. Children taught situational ethics instead of morality-based responsibility will usually think any standard works. When their standards are raised, most of them will not need to be disciplined through law enforcement, the court system or the school systems. Their discipline is first generated through their families. The school system, based at a local level, only reinforces what family deems important. When children are raised in healthy morality, it gives them self-esteem and helps them self-govern. Isn't that ultimately what our documents of social-compact/covenant reveal?

Social responsibility through self-government has to be taught in order to make people realize socialism's real goal is to have the citizen give up their rights and responsibilities in order to be replaced with socialism's sham demands. This hits folks at almost every level of their lives. Effects of situational ethics are easily found when the public comes in contact with law enforcement. During intense encounters, individuals will be asked by police to remain silent instead of mouthing off. Police do this initially to put folks and themselves in "safe zones." The majority of officers are then taught how to help citizens communicate without becoming violent. In today's situational ethics, mouthing off and becoming violent go hand in hand. Is it because we have lost the personal responsibility of being human? Maybe it's because socialists need to keep adults with childlike needs and demands. When they don't get what they want, a temper-tantrum is thrown. Churches of all stripes and colors can teach their members, parents and children what it means to "use your words." We then learn the skills of de-escalation. These instructions can go a long way in making sure citizens will not have to learn the lesson by a police officer.

When we self-govern we do not need democrat/progressives (socialists) to tell us how or what to think. We must give our children the TRUE history of how this nation was formed. Churches must teach this and schools must teach this. The press must stop lying about it. So they can claim truth in their reporting, they just omit the religious history of the nation. The proof of this happened recently when a senator from Utah took to the floor of the senate and shared snippets of the enduring religious history of this nation in three speeches. The national press totally ignored him.[3] That's when you know the press is hiding the truth. As children get older, true education based on the real science of economic, philosophical and even theological facts can be revealed about socialism and capitalism. These facts decimate socialism, proving it a lie. Then the true history of its murderous past must be taught.

We need to start quoting all of the founders. Children and adults need to learn what they really said about morality, the God of the Bible, providence and economics. We need to quote those who did not appreciate organized religion, but surely did believe in morality based on a "God." Children raised in atheist homes will not be wounded by this. That's because their parents must and should answer those questions concerning why they believe as they do. Teachers can and should reinforce the need for all of the children to ask their parents questions concerning religion when the true history of the nation is revealed. When this is done, it becomes obvious real solutions which do not violate our inalienable rights can be enacted. We have secular solutions being worked out right now regarding some of the most divisive social issues the nation has seen.[4] These are under-reported in the national media as well. Worse than that, you have media and corporate conglomerates targeting those states enacting religious freedom directives and safety within hygiene spaces. As citizens of a state so targeted, we need to strike back with class-action lawsuits against these conglomerates. I realize that is not covenantal, but it appears to be the only way to get the attention of both the corporate bullies and the media who frame the issue in the most deceptive of manners possible.

It is high time we promoted the inalienable right of the child, along with parental rights establishing a child has an absolute right to both mom and dad. The New Testament addresses such issues (Ephesians 6:1-4). Even the United Nations (not the most conservative of bodies) has agreed to this inalienable right. We have given everyone else a right. I'm waiting for the rights of mosquitos. They deserve to be able to bite us and pass on diseases! That was my attempt at humor because the sad truth is our country treats the rights of its children no better than the mosquito. We kill mosquitos all the time. We murder children regularly. Children have an inalienable right to life and an inalienable right to their mothers and fathers. Once that is done, it is high time we closed the "rights" book.

Am I encouraging some kind of unequal or racist pattern? Absolutely not! It just seems to me we have given out all the rights there needs to be given in a just society. What is needed is education as to why the first ten are listed in the order they are. Once we cheapen our inalienable rights with all sorts of issues, not inalienable, then we have played right into the hands of those who desire America's demise. Don't let them do it. When our citizens and children get a chance to study the real and full history of America, socialism will never be able to lie to them. Politicians and the media alike will be forced to tell the whole truth or be made a laughingstock.

The last condition I want to talk about is really the first problem a socialistic/progressive based government functions in. A socialistic government ultimately believes it is better than the people, much like the monarchal government our forebears experienced. Both forms of government believe the people need to be controlled by them. Hence, all the material the people produce really belongs to the government (whether socialistic or monarchal). They believe the government is better at distributing it than the people who made the produce or the ones purchasing it. As a result, because the government (or monarchy) is supposedly better, then there is and must be a separation— a wall— between it and the people. In open and free governments a transparent barrier exists only to prove to the people it will not show favoritism. Whether that is in distributing the help of a military, the benefits of funds to the old and sick or in favoritism to one political party of people in a state. This is the most basic understanding of why transparency exits.

There is a far more fundamental reason in free societies. The Puritans and founding Christians made the government transparent so the people could participate and give input and make suggestions and changes to the law. They were not viewed as a smelly inconvenience.[5] They *are* THE GOVERNMENT. Liberty means transparency in government. In progressive/socialist thinking, governments are separated by a wall, becoming a "high" wall to protect the secrets and true desires of the government, thus protecting the government from the people. Why? Because the people are separate. It is not a government of the people, by the people and for the people. It is government by the elite. I have already shown that puritan ministers of yesteryear preached against favoritism in government as well as government by the aristocracy or the elite (see the chapter on Plymouth Colony).

Why have I left this idea or quality, which is emblematic of a government truly of the people, by the people and for the people in this last chapter? Because it has a solution all its own. Each one of us have a story that is sovereign. Remember the legal thinking initially embedded into our governing documents was that the people are THE Sovereign. That means your life story and experience will have either a negative effect on those around you or a positive one. You are the one with the responsibility to make sure it brings life, health and an ability to recognize when freedom is licentiousness which will destroy. You are the one with the sovereign ability to recognize patterns which will lift folks out of captivity and complacency or lead them into depression and ignorance.

When we view our governing documents as covenantal, we are able to put ourselves in another's shoes. That concept does not depend on religion. It can be fostered by religion, but it can be secular. To view another's story and understand it is not our job to gobble them up and spit them out so we get our own rights— to heck with everyone else— is covenantal. When we see clear-cut science proving a faith and practice like socialism (progressivism) destroys nations and bankrupts people, it is our responsibility to understand our sovereign duty to change that pattern and help others to do the same. It is easy to see our responsibility as sovereigns means to embody the lessons learned from our founding generations. It is our responsibility to uphold those lessons and that tradition, restoring them when necessary. It is our responsibility as sovereigns to remove and quickly discard those policies which make a mockery of the blood, toil and tears of all generations who fought long and hard for the freedoms we take for granted. The lessons the framing generation left us are crucial to our governance today. Those lessons are easily read in the quotes they made. I leave you with a few here as you ponder your own responsibility and decision to either covenant or to assign yourself and others to captivity. The choice, at least for now, is yours.

"Can the liberties of a nation be thought secure when we have removed their only firm basis, a conviction in the minds of the people that these liberties are the gift of God? That they are not to be violated but with his wrath? Indeed I tremble for my country when I reflect that God is just: that his justice cannot sleep forever. . ."[6] (excerpt). Thomas Jefferson

". . . The sacred rights of mankind are not to be rummaged for, among old parchments, or musty records. They are written, as with a sunbeam, in the whole *volume* of human nature, by the hand of the divinity itself; and can never be erased or obscured by mortal power"[7] Alexander Hamilton (Italics NOT mine, excerpt).

"We have it in our power to begin the world over again. A situation, similar to the present, hath not happened since the days of Noah until now. The birthday of a new world is at hand, and a race of men, perhaps as numerous as all Europe contains, are to receive their portion of freedom from the events of a few months. The reflection is awful, and in this point of view, how trifling, how ridiculous, do the little paltry cavilings of a few weak or interested men appear, when weighed against the business of a world."[8] Thomas Paine

"But some people try to make you believe we are disputing about the foolish trifle of three pence duty upon tea. They may as well tell you that black is white. Surely you can judge for yourselves. Is a dispute, whether the Parliament of Great Britain shall make what laws and impose what taxes they please upon us, or not; I say, is this a dispute about three pence duty upon tea? The man that affirms it deserves to be laughed at. It is true, we are denying to pay the duty upon tea; but it is not for the value of the thing itself. It is because we cannot submit to that without acknowledging the principle upon which it is founded; and that principle is, *a right to tax us in all cases whatsoever"*[9] Alexander Hamilton (italics, NOT mine).

"But is the spirit of the people an infallible, a permanent reliance? Is it government? Is this the kind of protection we receive in return for the rights we give up? Besides, the spirit of the times may alter, will alter. Our rulers will become corrupt, our people careless. A single zealot may commence persecutor, and better men be his victims. It can never be too often repeated, that the time for fixing every essential right on a legal basis is while our rulers are honest, and ourselves united."[10] Thomas Jefferson

"The experience of past ages may inform us, that when the circumstances of a people render them distressed, their rulers generally recur to severe, cruel, and oppressive measures. Instead of endeavoring to establish their authority in the *affection* of their subjects, they think they have no security but in their *fear*. They do not aim at gaining their fidelity and obedience, by making them flourishing, prosperous and happy; but by rendering them abject and dispirited. They think it necessary to intimidate and awe them, to make every accession to their own power, and to impair the people's as much as possible. One great engine, to effect this in America, would be a large standing army, maintained out of our own pockets to be at the devotion of our oppressors. This would be introduced under pretext of defending us; but in fact to make our bondage and misery complete"[11] Alexander Hamilton (italics, NOT mine).

Is life so dear, or peace so sweet, as to be purchased at the price of chains and slavery? Forbid it, Almighty God! I know not what course others may take; but as for me, give me liberty or give me death!"[12] Patrick Henry

"Hence, also, the origin of all civil government, justly established, must be a voluntary compact, between the rulers and the ruled; and must be liable to such limitations, as are necessary for the security of the *absolute rights* of the latter; for what original title can any man or set of men have, to govern others, except their own consent? To usurp dominion over a people, in their own despite, or to grasp at a more extensive power than they are willing to entrust, is to violate that law of nature, which gives every man a right to his personal liberty; and can, therefore, confer no obligation to obedience"[13] Alexander Hamilton (Italics NOT mine).

"The Religion then of every man must be left to the conviction and conscience of every man; and it is the right of every man to exercise it as these may dictate. This right is in its nature an unalienable right. It is unalienable, because the opinions of men, depending only on the evidence contemplated by their own minds cannot follow the dictates of other men: It is unalienable also, because what is here a right towards men, is a duty towards the Creator. It is the duty of every man to render to the Creator such homage and such only as he believes to be acceptable to him. This duty is precedent, both in order of time and in degree of obligation, to the claims of Civil Society."[14] James Madison

"But being ruined by taxes is not the worst you have to fear. What security would you have for your lives? How can any of you be sure you would have the free enjoyment of your religion long? Would you put your religion in the power of any set of men living? Remember civil and religious liberty always go together: if the foundation of the one be sapped, the other will fail of course."[15] Alexander Hamilton.

ENDNOTES

1   <http://www.hatch.senate.gov/public/index.cfm/releases?ID=0d5defac-3af3-4795-be3c-40888c1b45fa> see also the Senator's two other speeches, which gives a good amount of history and legal theory as to why religious freedom is so important and why it is to be observed above all other freedoms. <https://www.youtube.com/watch?v=q8d7cRrapwM&feature=youtu.be&t=1s><https://www.youtube.com/watch?v=Icguz3yMGBQ> accessed 4/9/16

2   <http://www1.cbn.com/hurdontheweb/archive/2015/03/16/warnings-sweden-is-headed-toward-a-cliff><http://www1.cbn.com/cbnnews/world/2015/August/The-Immigration-Flood-Will-Europe-Still-Be-Europe> accessed 4/9/16

3   <http://www.hatch.senate.gov/public/index.cfm/releases?ID=0d5defac-3af3-4795-be3c-40888c1b45fa><https://www.youtube.com/watch?v=q8d7cRrapwM&feature=youtu.be&t=1s><https://www.youtube.com/watch?v=Icguz3yMGBQ>accessed 4/9/16

4   <http://le.utah.gov/~2015/bills/static/SB0296.html> <http://www.sltrib.com/home/2363586-155/why-utahs-nondiscrimination-law-differs-from> accessed 4/9/16

5   <http://cnsnews.com/news/article/reid-grateful-he-won-t-smell-tourists-capitol-thanks-621-million-visitors-center> accessed 4/9/16

6   This quote is on the Jefferson Memorial. See various in Thomas Jefferson, "The Works of Thomas Jefferson," Edited by Paul Leicester Ford, Federal Edition. (New York and London, G.P. Putnam's Sons, 1904-05). Vol. 4. See the etiology of this quote as excerpted <http://www.monticello.org/site/jefferson/quotations-jefferson-memorial>Site ©Thomas Jefferson Foundation, accessed 3/17/16.

7   *"The Farmer Refuted, &c., [23 February] 1775" In "The Works of Alexander Hamilton" Edited by Henry Cabot Lodge. Vol. 2 (New York and London: G.P. Putnam's Sons, 1904)*

8   Thomas Paine, "Common Sense," Appendix in "The Writings of Thomas Paine." Collected and Edited by Moncure Daniel Conway (New York: G.P. Putnam's Sons, 1894). Vol 1. <https://www.gutenberg.org/files/3755/3755-h/3755-h.htm> accessed 3/17/16

9   Alexander Hamilton (December 15, 1774) "A Full Vindication" in "The Works of Alexander Hamilton" Edited by John C. Hamilton. Volume 2 (New York: John F. Trow, 1850) 24. I use this quote to show example of the attitude of taxation without representation as opposed to the literal event Hamilton was referring to. The attitude today among the progressives is that there is no tax they do not agree with. When you bring up the assault made by them on our compacting documents, they roll their eyes or heave a sigh of frustration, to exhibit the thought you are bothering them, similar to the attitude of three pence for tea.

10   Thomas Jefferson. "Query XVII. Notes on Virginia" in "The Writings of Thomas Jefferson." Edited by H.A. Washington. Volume 8 (New York: H.W. Derby, 1861) 402

11   Alexander Hamilton, "The Farmer Refuted" in "The Works of Alexander Hamilton." Edited by John C. Hamilton. volume 2 (New York: John f. Trow, 1850) 50. Our National Archives has a different word. The word "pretext" here, but the Archives has "pretence." I stayed with the older work. If I am wrong, then reader beware. The National Archives: Hamilton, Alexander. (1775) "The Farmer Refuted, &c., [23 February] 1775" Founders Online, National Archives <http://founders.archives.gov/documents/Hamilton/01-01-02-0057> Accessed 3/17/16. I do not use this quote as a literal example of the incident Hamilton was referring to, but as an example of the various police apparatus within the Federal government, from the EPA to IRS. I also use it to show the attitude of today's bureaucratic socialists they are the rulers and the people must be ruled. This obviously is contrary to our federated republic.

12   <http://avalon.law.yale.edu/18th_century/patrick.asp> © 2008 Lillian Goldman Law Library, New Haven, CT. All copies of this speech are not from the pen of Henry himself. They are garnered from the memory of those in attendance and reconstructed in a biography by William Wirt of Patrick Henry published in 1817.

13   Alexander Hamilton, "The Farmer Refuted" in "The Works of Alexander Hamilton." Edited by John C. Hamilton. Volume 2 (New York: John f. Trow, 1850) 44. Public domain. I use this quote to show the understanding that inalienable rights are not to be negotiated and when men or government try to do so, we are not obligated to comply.

14   James Madison, "Memorial and Remonstrance" June 20, 1785, (Boston: Lincoln & Edmands, 1819) This was a tract printed of the famous remonstrance. See 5 & 6. Public domain.

15   Alexander Hamilton (December 15, 1774) "A Full Vindication" in "The Works of Alexander Hamilton" Edited by John C. Hamilton. Volume 2 (New York: John F. Trow, 1850) 25, 26. Public domain.

Future Reading

Within this list are also documentary video sites. Sometimes it is easier to see it put on the screen, or Internet than it is to read. I also make no claim to the accuracy concerning all of these sources for future reading. I mention them to you as sources if you desire more history. I do not agree with many of these sources; nevertheless, they can give you opinions from all sides.

The Bible (I love all versions, but I typically read from the King James Version; the New King James Version; the New International Version (the older ones which do not remove verses); the Amplified Version; the New American Standard Version and the NET Bible®

All encyclopedias are useful. Picking those with the least bias is a talent and an education more than anything else. I used the online ones as well as one in my own library. The same would hold true for dictionaries. My favorite is the Oxford English Dictionary.

DOCUMENTARIES:

These three are by the same company. The first, "Made In Israel" can be seen at this © site <http://www.cbn.com/special/made-in-israel> It records some of the technological breakthroughs from the nation of Israel. The second is a modern history of the modern State of Israel. "The Hope: The Rebirth of Israel." And the third, "Whose Land is It?" All three are © by the Christian Broadcasting Network, Inc.

Westminster Theological Seminary has produced a documentary by Capstone Films. This is a history of the Reformation, as well as others. It can be seen for free at this site <http://the protestantrevolt.com> There are eleven of them and there are also books that can be purchased as well.

A DVD enactment of the meeting of the House of Burgesses where Patrick Henry gave his famous speech can be had by logging on to St. John's Church Foundation's website <http://historicstjohnschurch.org>

BOOKS/RESEARCH PAPERS:

"The Origins of American Constitutionalism," by Donald S. Lutz, © 1988, Louisiana State University Press, Baton Rouge, LA

Covenant and Civil Society: The Constitutional Matrix of Modern Democracy by Daniel J. Elazar

Covenant and Constitutionalism: The Great Frontier and the Matrix of Federal Democracy, The Covenant Tradition in Politics, Volume 3 (1998), by Daniel J. Elazar,

Covenant in the Nineteenth Century (ed.) (1994) by Daniel J. Elazar

Recovenanting the American Polity, by Daniel J. Elazar: All previous titles by Daniel J. Elazar can be seen at this © site <http://www.jcpa.org/dje/index.cov.htm> The Jerusalem Center for Public Affairs houses Daniel Elazar's titles. You can visit their © 2015 site <http://jcpa.org/publica-tion/daniel-elazar-library/> for The Daniel Elazar On-line Library

"God, I Don't Understand," Kenneth Boa © 1975, 2007 Kenneth Boa, and published by Victor, an imprint of Cook Communications

"The Godless Constitution," Isaac Kramnick and R. Laurence Moore © 1997 & 2005, W.W. Norton & Company, NY, NY & London

"Christianity Through The Centuries," by Earle E. Cairns, © 1981 The Zondervan Corporation, Grand Rapids, MI

"A Covenanted People: the Religious Tradition and the Origins of American Constitutionalism," by Donald S. Lutz and Jack D. Warren, ©

1987, The John Carter Brown Library at Brown University, Providence, RI and sponsored by The Lily Endowment, Inc; The Rhode Island Committee for the Humanities

"Colonial Origins of the American Constitution: A Documentary History," Donald S. Lutz, ed. Donald S. Lutz, Indianapolis: Liberty Fund, 1998, © Liberty Fund, Inc.

"The Pastor of the Pilgrims, A Biography of John Robinson," by Walter H. Burgess, New York: Harcourt, Brace & Howe, 1920. A reprint has been done and can be found on Amazon.

"The Life of Major-General Peter Muhlenburg of the Revolutionary Army," by Henry A. Muhlenburg. Philadelphia: Carey and Hart, 1849. Now in the public domain.

"Common Sense," by Thomas Paine, Philadelphia 1776. Now in the public domain.

"The American Crisis," by Thomas Paine, London: R. Carlisle, Fleet Street, 1819. Now in the public domain.

"Defining America's Exceptionalism," by Roger Anghis, © 2011, 2012 by R. Peter Anghis, Jr., published by WestBow Press, a Division of Thomas Nelson, Bloomington, IN

"Jesus The Jewish Theologian," by Brad H. Young, © 1995 and published by Hendrickson Publishers, Inc., Peabody, MA

"Handel's Messiah, Comfort for God's People," by Calvin R. Stapert, © 2010 by the author and published by Wm. B. Eerdman's Publishing Co.

"Spiritual Lives of the Great Composers," by Patrick Kavanaugh © 1996, published by Zondervan, Grand Rapids, MI (Now under HarperCollins Publishers.)

"Floods Upon the Dry Ground," by Charles P. Schmitt, © 1998 by Destiny Image Publishers, Shippensburg, PA

William Jackson Johnstone, "George Washington, the Christian," (New York: The Abingdon Press, New York & Cincinnati, 1919) At this site <http://www.constitution.org/primarysources/george.html>

"The Life of George Washington," Authored by David Ramsay and published in 1807. It is now part of the Keigwin & Mathews Collection and can be seen as an ebook at this site <http://www.earlyamerica.com/lives-early-america/ramsays-life-washington/life-george-washington-david-ramsay-chapter-one/> © 1995-2015 Archiving Early America®

"Benjamin Franklin," Volume 1, by Carl Van Doren © 1966 by Anne Van Dore Ross, Margaret Van Doren Bevans and Barbara Van Doren Klaw. One reprint is by Penguin Books in 1991 and one by Simon Publications in 2002.

"Christian Life and Character of the Civil Institutions of the United States, Developed in the Official and Historical Annals of the Republic." By Benjamin Franklin Morris: Philadelphia: George W. Childs, 628 & 630 Chestnut St., Cincinnati: Rickey & Carroll, 1864

"7 Men and the Secret of Their Greatness," by Eric Metaxas, published by Thomas Nelson, Inc., Nashville, TN, © 2013

"March To Victory, Washington, Rochambeau and the Yorktown Campaign of 1781" by Dr. Robert Selig. It can be seen at <http://www.history.army.mil/html/books/rochanbeau/CMH_70-104-1.pdf> By the U.S. Army Center of Military History.

"Our Presidents and Their Prayers: Proclamations of Faith by America's Leaders," Senator Rand Paul, © 2015 Rand Paul, Center Street, Hachette Book Group, NY, NY, 10104

See in its entirety: Thomas Jefferson, "The Works of Thomas Jefferson," Federal Edition (New York and London, G.P. Putnam's Sons, 1904-5), in 12 vols. Now in the public domain.

See in its entirety: James Madison, "The Writings of James Madison, comprising his Public Papers and his Private Correspondence, including his numerous letters and documents now for the first time printed," ed.

Gaillard Hunt (New York: G.P. Putnam's Sons, 1900). 9 vols. Now in the public domain.

Alexander Hamilton, "The Revolutionary Writings of Alexander Hamilton," edited and with an Introduction by Richard B. Vernier, with a Foreword by Joyce O. Appleby (Indianapolis: Liberty Fund, 2008)

Mary V. Thompson, Research Historian, Mount Vernon Ladies' Association, 2003-2010, titled, "George Washington's References to God and Religion, Together with Selected References to Death, Eternity, Charity, and Morality."

Ellis Sandoz, "Political Sermons of the American Founding Era: 1730-1805, in 2 Vols., Foreword by Ellis Sandoz (2nd. ed. Indianapolis:Liberty Fund, 1998).

"The Wall and the Garden, Selected Massachusetts Election Sermons, 1670-1775," edited by A.W. Plumstead, published 1968, 400 pages, new edition published by University of Minnesota Press.

"Religion and Politics in the Early Republic: Jasper Adams and the Church-State debate," edited by Daniel L. Dreisbach, © 1996 by The University Press of Kentucky

"Mutual Contempt: Lyndon Johnson, Robert Kennedy and the Feud that Defined a Decade," © 1997 Jeff Shesol, published by W.W. Norton & company, 500 Fifth Avenue, NY, NY

"New Fabian Essays" by R.H.S. Crossman, C.A.R. Crosland, Roy Jenkins, Margaret Cole, Austen Albu, Ian Mikardo, Denis Healey, John Strachey, © 1952 Turnstile Press, Ltd., 10 Great Turnstile, London. A second impression was printed in June 1952 by The Camelot Press, Ltd., Southampton, both in Great Britain.

"The Socialist Tradition: Moses to Lenin" by Alexander Gray, © 1963 Spottiswoode, Ballantyne & Co, London, England.

"The Illusion of the Epoch: Marxism-Leninism as a Philosophical Creed" by H.B. Acton, © 2003 Liberty Fund, Indianapolis, Indiana.

"Socialism: An Economic and Sociological Analysis" by Ludwig von Mises. From the German translation, which was © in 1922 to English and © in 1951 by Yale University Press, New Haven, CT, and © in 1981 by Liberty Fund, Indianapolis, IN. It can be purchased at this © site <https://mises.org/library/socialism-economic-and-sociological-analysis>

"Omnipotent Government, The Rise of the Total State and Total War;" and "Bureaucracy;" and "Human Action, a Treatise on Economics." All by Ludwig von Mises; they are all published by Yale University Press, though I believe only the first and third have been translated into English.

"Reviving America," by Steve Forbes and Elizabeth Ames, published by McGraw-Hill

C.L. Gray, "The Battle of America's Soul," <www.physiciansforreform.org>

"Rethinking Life & Death," Peter Singer; Fair warning alert: this author contends that to keep the old and sick alive is inefficient and it is more efficient to let them die.

"The Life and Times of William Samuel Johnson," by Eben Edwards Beardsley. This work was originally written in 1876. It has now been reproduced © 2008 BiblioBazaar, LLC.

Kirtland, Robert Bevier. *George Wythe: lawyer, revolutionary, judge.* Garland, 1986.

"Progressivism: A Primer on the Idea Destroying America," by James Ostrowski, © 2014, James Ostrowski, Published by Cazenovia Books, Buffalo, NY.

"Clash of Extremes: The Economic Origins of the Civil War," by Marc Egnal, published by Hill and Wang, 2010

"Company Aytch, First Tennessee Regiment," by Sam R. Watkins, published by Providence House Publishers, 2007

"The Killer Angels," by Michael Shaara, published by Ballantine Books, 1987

"The Civil War: A Narrative," by Shelby Foote (see The Civil War Trilogy Box Set) Modern Library, 2011

"Look Away! A History of the Confederate States of America," by William C. Davis, © 2003

JOURNALS AND RESEARCH PAPERS:

"Morality and the Rule of Law in American Jurisprudence," James Lanshe, 2009, Rutgers Journal of Law & Religion, Volume 11, Part 1

Donald S. Lutz, "The Relative Influence of European Writers on Late Eighteenth-Century American Political Thought," American Political Science Review, Vol. 78, No. 1 (March 1984), pp. 189-197

"Natural Rights, Natural Law, and American Constitutions," Philip A. Hamburger, The Yale Law Journal, Vol. 102: 907; 1993; see 916 & 917

Huebner, Timothy S. "The Consolidation of State Judicial Power: Spencer Roane, Virginia Legal Culture, and the Southern Judicial Tradition." *The Virginia Magazine of History and Biography* (1994): 47-72.

Frisch, Morton J. "John Marshall's Philosophy of Constitutional Republicanism." *The Review of Politics* 20.01 (1958): 34-45.

Anderson, Leanna M., 2002: "Executive Orders, The Very Definition of Tyranny and the Congressional Solution, and the Separation of Powers Restoration Act." Hastings Constitutional Law Quarterly 29 (spring): 589-611 <http://law.jrank.org/pages/6656/Executive-Order-FURTHER-READINGS.html>

Ostrow, Steven; 1987, "Enforcing Executive Orders: Judicial Review of Agency Action under the Administrative Procedure Act." George Washington Law Review 55 <http://law.jrank.org/pages/6656/Executive-Order-FURTHER-READINGS.html>

Raven-Hansen, Peter; 1983, "Making Agencies Follow Orders: Judicial Review of Agency Violations of Executive Order 12,291" Duke

Law   Journal   <http://law.jrank.org/pages/6656/Executive-Order-FURTHER-READINGS.html>

Sterling, John A.; 2000, "Above the Law: Evolution of Executive Orders." University of West Los Angeles Law Review 31 (annual) <http://law.jrank.org/pages/6656/Executive-Order-FURTHER-READINGS.html>

Turner, William. "Philosophy of Immanuel Kant." The Catholic Encyclopedia. Vol. 8. New York: Robert Appleton Company, 1910. Can be seen at this © site <http://www.newadvent.org/cathen/08603a.htm>

Turner, William. "Hegelianism." The Catholic Encyclopedia. Vol. 7. New York: Robert Appleton Company, 1910. Can be seen at this © site <http://www.newadvent.org/cathen/07192a.htm>

Toke, Leslie, and William Edward Campbell. "Socialism." The Catholic Encyclopedia. Vol. 14. New York: Robert Appleton Company, 1912. Can be seen at this © site <http://www.newadvent.org/cathen/14062a.htm>

CPSIA information can be obtained
at www.ICGtesting.com
Printed in the USA
BVOW06s1155270417
482500BV00005B/14/P